Letters of H. P. Lovecraft

VOLUME 8

LETTERS TO J. VERNON SHEA, CARL F. STRAUCH, AND LEE MCBRIDE WHITE

J. Vernon Shea in 1975
at the First World Fantasy Convention in Providence, Rhode Island

(Courtesy William Hart)

H. P. LOVECRAFT

LETTERS TO J. VERNON SHEA, CARL F. STRAUCH, AND LEE McBRIDE WHITE

EDITED BY
S. T. JOSHI AND DAVID E. SCHULTZ

Hippocampus Press

New York

Published by Hippocampus Press
P.O. Box 641, New York, NY 10156.
http://www.hippocampuspress.com

Cover design and Hippocampus Press logo by Anastasia Damianakos.
Cover production by Barbara Briggs Silbert.

First Edition
1 3 5 7 9 8 6 4 2

ISBN 978-1-61498-156-5

Contents

Introduction

This volume differs from those that have previously been published in the Collected Letters series in that it contains letters to three individuals who do not fit into the several broad categories in which Lovecraft's correspondents generally fall. J. Vernon Shea, Carl Ferdinand Strauch, and Lee McBride White were neither amateur journalists whom Lovecraft encountered at an early stage of his career (such as James F. Morton or Maurice W. Moe), nor are they professionals or even full-fledged fans of weird fiction (such as August Derleth, Robert E. Howard, or Robert Bloch), nor are they young—in many cases teenage—devotees of weird and science fiction (such as Donald A. Wollheim or Wilson Shepherd). Shea, although certainly fond of Lovecraft's and others' stories in *Weird Tales,* had many other interests at this time, and his six-year correspondence with Lovecraft largely covers subjects relating to general literature, politics, world affairs, and other issues. Strauch was a librarian and academic, while White was a college student much more interested in mainstream literature than the weird. Accordingly, Lovecraft's letters to these individuals cover a much broader spectrum of topics than those for many of his other correspondents.

Joseph Vernon Shea (1912–1981) was nineteen when he first wrote Lovecraft in 1931. One assumes that he sent a letter to *Weird Tales,* since he had evidently been reading that magazine for several years. Indeed, in an amusingly callow letter published in the magazine's letter column, "The Eyrie," for October 1926, Shea wrote:

> It might be interesting to you to know that you have young readers as well as old. I am just a boy of thirteen, but I am in the opinion that *Weird Tales* is the best magazine ever published. Such writers as Eli Colter, Seabury Quinn, H. P. Lovecraft, Robert S. Carr and Edmond Hamilton deserve special mention for their excellent work. I can never forget 'The Outsider', by Lovecraft. It was the weirdest, most thrilling and most eery tale I have ever had the good fortune to read.[1]

A subsequent letter, published in the September 1931 issue, speaks again of "The Outsider" (which had been reprinted in the June–July 1931 issue), referring to it as "the greatest weird story ever written."[2]

And yet, it is clear that Shea had much broader literary tastes. It would seem that Shea had entered the University of Pittsburgh around the time of

---

1. Cited in S. T. Joshi, ed., *A Weird Writer in Our Midst: Early Criticism of H. P. Lovecraft* (New York: Hippocampus Press, 2010), 66–67.
2. Ibid., 73–74.

his earliest letters to Lovecraft, but he had to drop out after a year because of financial considerations. Whether from his brief college stint or from other reasons, Shea found himself discussing with Lovecraft a wide range of mainstream writers, especially such leading contemporary figures as Thornton Wilder and James Joyce.

Shea was also attempting to write fiction and poetry, both weird and mainstream. As he wrote in a letter to August Derleth, just a month after he had gotten in touch with Lovecraft:

> I have long been stricken with the writing craze. At fourteen I had the audacity to send to Farnsworth Wright a frightful concoction entitled "The Werewolf's Victim". Thank God, it is no longer around the house to humiliate me. At fifteen I sent to the Forum a 250-line poem in blank verse entitled "What is the Soul?" Around fifteen and sixteen I wrote dozens of poems—all terrible. The other day I sent a few to Lovecraft, and he took them seriously! Also at fifteen I began, and almost completed, a detective novel, "The Stabbing From Above"—it was even worse than that melodramatic title—with the heroine as the murderess. . . . At sixteen I continued to turn out junk, as I did also at seventeen, when I wrote a long dramatic poem based on the Aeneid. At seventeen, however, I suddenly got wise to myself, and began to study books on the subject of writing technique. My year's silence after that was unfortunately broken by a 33,000-word pseudo-scientific novelette, which I wrote this summer. . . . I have no longer any illusions about my writing—it's terrible. Some day, though[,] I do intend to write something far better than "The Earth Taint"—my novelette—, this time a novel. However, I won't attempt it until I greatly improve—if I ever do.[3]

Lovecraft read a number of these works in the first year or so of their correspondence and expressed polite approval of them with some suggestions for improvement; but in October 1932 Shea sent Lovecraft a story called "The Tin Roof," which Lovecraft felt "marks a *radical, meteoric advance* on your part." He urged Shea to submit it to significant literary magazines in which their mutual colleague August Derleth had appeared—*Pagany,* the *Midland,* and so forth. Whether Shea actually submitted this story, or any others, at this time is unclear; in any event, none of these tales were published and they all appear to have been lost or destroyed.

Shea was also interested in film, and he perhaps encouraged Lovecraft to see more films than he might otherwise have done. It was to Shea that Lovecraft waxed eloquent about *Berkeley Square* (1933), a film he saw four times and which clearly influenced "The Shadow out of Time" (1934–35). Shea and

---

3. J. Vernon Shea to August Derleth, 20 August 1931; ms., Wisconsin Historical Society.

Lovecraft also shared a fascination with language and dialect, and many passages in the letters discuss peculiar regional usages and pronunciations.

The correspondence is an unusually intimate one chiefly because Shea himself expressed a frank and somewhat nosy interest in the details of Lovecraft's life and his beliefs. His first letter to Lovecraft appears to have been a series of rapid-fire questions about personal matters (he did the same thing in his first letter to Derleth), and Lovecraft's surprisingly candid responses—even on such delicate issues as his ill-starred marriage to Sonia Greene—show how willing he was to accommodate the interests and queries of a virtual stranger. Shea probably reciprocated in kind, telling Lovecraft of his troubled family life and his financial difficulties in the early years of the Depression.

The most controversial aspect of the correspondence relates to Lovecraft's discussion of the rise of Adolf Hitler, who in 1933 was appointed chancellor of the German government by President von Hindenburg and in 1934 unlawfully seized power following Hindenburg's death. Lovecraft's muted and conflicted praise of Hitler has not done Lovecraft's reputation any favors, but it was an inevitable consequence of the worldview that Lovecraft had evolved up to that time. For him, a nation's culture was sacrosanct; and although by this time he had given up any belief in the *biological* superiority or inferiority of individual races (aside from blacks, whom he always believed to be biologically inferior to Caucasians), he sided with Hitler in opposing what he believed to be excessive Jewish control over the literary and artistic culture of Germany—a control that Lovecraft felt also extended to Jewish control over American publishing. This narrow-minded and exaggerated view led to a belief in the extreme incompatibility of given culture-streams, so that the best thing to do was to keep them as separate as possible: "a real friend of civilisation wishes merely to make the Germans *more German*, the French *more French*, the Spaniards *more Spanish*, & so on." This sounds benign, but it is merely a mask for a kind of "culture-line" that would replace (or augment) the "color-line" (i.e., a belief that individual races should not intermingle) that Lovecraft always maintained.

But it is interesting that the discussions of Hitler fade away by 1934 and rarely recur thereafter. There is some evidence that, late in life, Lovecraft heard from a neighbor of the atrocities that the Nazi regime was already perpetrating in Germany in the mid-1930s, so there is some reason to hope that Lovecraft came to regret his early praise (which, it cannot be emphasized too strongly, was always mixed with a liberal dose of disapproval over many of the methods Hitler was then using to enforce his policies) of the German dictator. And we should always remember that Lovecraft did not live through World War II and the revelations of the atrocities of the Holocaust. Had he done so, there is little doubt that his views on race would have been significantly revised.

Shea went on to do some literary work in both mainstream and weird fiction. He compiled two anthologies, *Strange Desires* (1954) and *Strange Barriers* (1955), which, in spite of their titles, are in fact concerned with interracial romance and race relations, respectively. Derleth accepted an original Lovecraftian story by Shea, "The Haunter of the Graveyard," for *Tales of the Cthulhu Mythos* (1969), and Shea went on to write several other weird or Lovecraftian tales, the most notable of which is probably "Dead Giveaway."

By the 1970s, when Shea had become a kind of celebrity because of his correspondence with Lovecraft, he began participating in the Lovecraftian fan community. As early as 1966, he had published an interesting essay, "H. P. Lovecraft: The House and the Shadows" (*Fantasy and Science Fiction*, May 1966), and in 1977 he began issuing a quarterly magazine, *Outré*, for the Esoteric Order of Dagon amateur press association. This copious journal contained a great deal of interesting matter, including stories, poems, and essays by Shea and others. Some of this material was gathered in a small-press booklet, *In Search of Lovecraft* (Necronomicon Press, 1991).

By this time, Shea was living alone in an apartment in Cleveland. In the 1960s he donated over what he believed to be all his letters from Lovecraft to the John Hay Library of Brown University; but upon his unexpected death in early 1981, ten more letters were found among his effects. These were sold to a rare book dealer, the Boston Book Annex, and subsequently purchased as a lot by an unidentified collector. This collector has not made these letters available for consultation, and all we have of them are brief excerpts made by Shea himself and passed on to August Derleth for inclusion in the *Selected Letters* project. Even without these ten letters, the correspondence with Shea is one of the most revealing of any in Lovecraft's corpus of letters.

Carl Ferdinand Strauch was born on September 25, 1908 in Lehighton, Pennsylvania, the son of Henry and Anna Margaret (Foesch) Strauch. He attended Allentown High School (1922–26), then attended Muhlenberg College in Allentown, receiving his B.A. in English in 1930. He did graduate work at the University of Pennsylvania (1930–31), Lehigh University (1933–34; M.A. in German), and Yale University (1937–39), receiving his Ph.D. in English in 1946. His Ph.D. dissertation was "A Critical and Variorum Edition of Emerson's Poetry" (1946). Ralph O. Orth, an authority on Emerson, writes in the preface to *The Poetry Notebooks of Ralph Waldo Emerson* (Columbia: University of Missouri Press, 1986): "Carl F. Strauch . . . forty years ago undertook the first significant modern research into the tangled skein of [Emerson's] poetry notebooks and showed the way to the present volume."

Strauch was assistant librarian at Muhlenberg College from September 1930 to June 1933. Shortly after this time he wrote an article, "A College Library Goes Regionalist," for the *Wilson Library Bulletin* (December 1933). In September 1934 he became an instructor in the English department at

Lehigh, where he remained for the rest of his career. In 1941 he became an assistant professor, in 1946 an associate professor, and in 1953 a full professor. In 1962 he received the Lindback Award for distinguished teaching. In 1968 Emma Richards, one of his graduate students, endowed the Carl F. Strauch Fund to support the purchase of books in American literature for the Lehigh University Library. Strauch retired in 1974 as Distinguished Professor Emeritus of English. The previous year he received an honorary Doctor of Humane Letters from Muhlenberg College.

Strauch's first published book was *Twenty-nine Poems* (Boston: Bruce Humphries, 1932). He was the editor of *Style in the American Renaissance: A Symposium* (Hartford: Transcendental Books, 1970) and *Characteristics of Emerson, Transcendental Poet* (Hartford: Transcendental Books, 1975) and served on the editorial board for the *Collected Works of Ralph Waldo Emerson* (Harvard University Press, 1971f.) and of *ESQ* [*Emerson Society Quarterly*]. He published poems in the *American Poetry Journal, L'Alouette, Wings,* and the *Galleon,* and articles in the *English Journal, PMLA, Philological Quarterly, Modern Language Notes, New England Quarterly, Harvard Library Bulletin,* the *Personalist,* and other scholarly journals.

Strauch was married to Helen Dery, who predeceased him. He had one daughter, Helen. He died on November 13, 1989.

Carl Ferdinand Strauch is not a familiar name in Lovecraft studies. He escaped the attention of the editors of Lovecraft's *Selected Letters,* and indeed he is mentioned only very briefly in Lovecraft's published letters. We are fortunate indeed that Strauch's letters were deposited among the Lovecraft papers at the John Hay Library in Providence.

Lovecraft's and Strauch's mutual friend Harry K. Brobst, like Strauch a native of Allentown, PA, had suggested that Strauch write Lovecraft. The two maintained a prolific correspondence for nearly two years, and Strauch visited Lovecraft in Providence in September 1932, staying at a vacant room in Lovecraft's residence at 10 Barnes Street. Lovecraft clearly enjoyed Strauch both as a correspondent and a visitor. He wrote to August Derleth:

> I reached home just in time to welcome young Strauch, who had come from Allentown to visit Brobst & me. He is a delightful youth—slim, dark, handsome, & extremely brilliant—& I believe he will go far in the poetic field. I shewed him the historic & antiquarian high spots of the town, & took him through the famous Harris Collection of Poetry in the Brown Univ. library. He is now in Boston visiting friends. I was extremely sorry he could not spend a longer time here.[4]

---

4. Letter to August Derleth, 12 September [1932]; *Essential Solitude: The Letters of H. P. Lovecraft and August Derleth,* ed. David E. Schultz and S. T. Joshi (New York: Hippocampus Press, 2008), 2.500.

And when Robert Bloch asked Lovecraft in the summer of 1933 who might be "promising correspondents in the weird," Lovecraft suggested Strauch:

> *Strauch, Carl F., 812 Washington St., Allentown, Pa.* Age 24. Poet with one published book to his credit. Bosom home-town friend of Harry Brobst. . . . Graduate of Muhlenberg College & has acted as assistant librarian there. Authority on Pennsylvania folklore with weird *Hexerei* beliefs. Working on a realistic novel. Delightful & affable—he visited Providence last summer & will probably come again this September. Enthusiast in Germanic literature. Rather anti-scientific by temperament—affording material for heated & interesting arguments with Brobst.[5]

Although Lovecraft never addressed Strauch less informally than "My dear Strauch," his letters were not merely polite replies. The early exchange of letters focused primarily on their common interest in weird fiction, but expanded into many other subjects including general literature, Lovecraft's travels and antiquarianism, Providence architecture, folklore, and others. Yet their correspondence ended abruptly around August 1933 and Strauch did not visit Lovecraft again. The exact reason for the dissolution of their friendship is unknown, for Lovecraft does not seem to have mentioned the matter in his letters to others, but three conjectures may be postulated: (1) the critical comments made by Lovecraft and others on a story written by Strauch may have severely discouraged the would-be writer, (2) his interest in weird fiction may have waned, as evidenced by the literary interests of his later years, and (3) his post-graduate work beginning in late 1933 may initially have hampered continued correspondence.

The twenty-nine surviving letters and postcards from H. P. Lovecraft to Strauch are not abundant with new facts about or insights, but they strengthen our grasp of Lovecraft's psychological make-up and numerous interests and augment the vast knowledge already gained from the tantalizing yet fragmentary *Selected Letters*.

Lee McBride White, Jr., was born on June 24, 1915, in Monroe, North Carolina, the son of a Baptist minister. In his early years his family lived in Jacksonville, Florida, but it moved to Birmingham, Alabama, in the summer of 1932, where White attended his final year of high school at John Herbert Phillips High School. It is likely that he contacted Lovecraft in the autumn of 1932 through *Weird Tales*.

In 1933, after his graduation from high school, White went to Howard College (now Samford University) in Birmingham, graduating with a B.A. in English in 1937. He worked on a number of college publications at Howard,

---

5. Letter to Robert Bloch, [c. late June 1933]; *Letters to Robert Bloch and Others*, ed. David E. Schultz and S. T. Joshi (New York: Hippocampus Press, 2015), 55.

including *The Howard Quill* (at least one issue of which he sent to Lovecraft), *Campus* (also sent to Lovecraft), *The Crimson,* the college's weekly newspaper, and the 1937 edition of the college yearbook, *The Howard Crimson.* White also acted in a number of college stage productions, as did his younger brother Harvey.

White then did graduate work at Harvard (working with Howard Mumford Jones) and Columbia, then returned to Birmingham, where he worked on the *Birmingham Age-Herald.* He enlisted in the armed forces on June 27, 1941, and during World War II he was in the Air Force, staying in North Africa until 1945. He then moved to Montgomery, Alabama, where he worked as the editor of a paper, *Folsom's Forum,* for Alabama's Governor Jim Folsom. He married Anne Mary Trebing on May 31, 1947, and eventually had four children, two sons and two daughters. The couple moved to Atlanta, where in 1950 White began working at the regional headquarters of the Communications Workers of America; in 1957 he moved to the central office in Washington, where he lived until his retirement in 1980. For the Bicentennial he edited a book, *The American Revolution in Notes, Quotes, and Anecdotes* (Fairfax, VA: L. B. Prince, 1975). He died on February 5, 1989, and is buried in Arlington National Cemetery. White had one of the greatest private collections of 78-rpm jazz records of his day, and was also a voluminous book collector.

Lovecraft's correspondence with White probably did not consist of many more than the nine surviving letters we have. The first extant letter dates to September 1932. After an early hiatus of two and a half years, they reestablished contact in May 1935. Although Lovecraft's letters to White are short, infrequent, and somewhat impersonal, they reflect his literary tastes and reading, even his general awareness of modern literary works and modern sentiments about writers from other periods of history. We find that in 1932—six years after he wrote "Cool Air"—Lovecraft could still say that Poe "probably continues to [influence me] more than any other one author." And it is amusing to know that the blue-nosed Lovecraft could recommend bookstores where one could purchase what was euphemistically termed "curiosa" (i.e., erotica).

A Note on the Text

All manuscript letters consulted are held at the John Hay Library with one exception. The Shea letter of 8 November 1933 held by the library is partial. Sheets VII–XXI were among Lovecraft's letters to Robert Bloch when Bloch sold them; these sheets were presumably lent to him by Shea but not returned, and we obtained copies from the individual who bought them. Other fragmentary letters derive from the Arkham House transcripts, a set of which is held at John Hay Library. Unlike most letters in that set, Shea's letters consist only of very brief extracts that he himself prepared. (Most others were prepared by Arkham House staff and are far more robust, even though edited, in content.)

Acknowledgments
The editors wish to thank Dr. Harry K. Brobst, Professor Edward J. Gallagher of Lehigh University, and Ruth L. Seither, Office Coordinator of Alumni Relations at Muhlenberg College, for information concerning Carl F. Strauch. For information on Lee McBride White, the editors are grateful to White's widow, Anne (Trebing) White, and his brother, Harvey O. White. We would also like to acknowledge the assistance of John H. Stanley and Christopher Geissler of the John Hay Library, Kenneth W. Faig, Jr., Donovan K. Loucks, Eileen McNamara, and Christopher O'Brien.

Abbreviations

AHT	Arkham House transcripts of Lovecraft's letters
ALS	autograph letter, signed
ANS	autograph note, signed
AT	Lovecraft, *The Ancient Track* (2001)
CE	Lovecraft, *Collected Essays* (2004–06; 5 vols.)
CF	Lovecraft, *Collected Fiction* (2015–16; 4 vols.)
JHL	John Hay Library, Brown University
JVS	J. Vernon Shea
LL	S. T. Joshi, comp., *Lovecraft's Library: A Catalogue* (rev. ed. 2012; numbers refer to entries)
NAPA	National Amateur Press Association
OFF	*O Fortunate Floridian: H. P. Lovecraft's Letters to R. H. Barlow* (2007)
SL	Lovecraft, *Selected Letters* (1965–76; 5 vols.)
WT	*Weird Tales*

Letters to J. Vernon Shea

1931

[1]   [ALS]

Home Address
10 Barnes St.,
Providence, R.I.,
June 19, 1931.

My dear Mr. Shea:—

Your interesting letter of June 5 lately reached me after considerable forwarding, for I have been visiting various places in Florida since the first of May. Cold weather prostrates me utterly, so that after a winter of close hibernation I generally break out into a round of travel as southerly as my alarmingly limited finances will permit. This time I actually made Key West—going just as far as the U.S. goes—& was bitterly disappointed because I couldn't get across to Havana. I am by nature an antiquarian as well as a tropical bird, & love to prowl about old cities where narrow streets & venerable architecture greet one on every hand. That is why I am lingering in ancient St. Augustine right now—the oldest city in the country, founded 366 years ago & still containing many edifices built in the late 1500's. For over a fortnight I was in Dunedin—on the gulf coast—visiting our weird-tale friend Henry S. Whitehead, who is an altogether delightful character. I also saw Miami—with its Seminole Indian village on the edge of the Everglades & its neighbouring coral reef whose surface (as seen from a glass-bottomed boat) is a veritable submarine garden of tropical fauna & flora. Cash is now running low, however, so that next Monday I shall have to embark on the long trek north—pausing in such favourite antiquarian haunts as Savannah, Charleston, & Richmond, (Poe's home town, & full of memories of his boyhood) & finally stopping a week or so with our young weird friend Frank B. Long Jr. in New York City. I had hoped to get up to the weird Catskill region to visit my friend Bernard Dwyer in West Shokan, (do you recall his verses "Old Black Sarah" in W.T.?)[1] but fear that a dwindling purse will prevent. I surely wish that I had the type of talent which enables many people to get cash as well as aesthetic satisfaction out of the writing process!

Naturally it pleases me very greatly to hear of your favourable opinion of my stuff, & I hope that future efforts of mine will not cause you to alter your opinion. But you are really much too gracious in comparing my attempts with the work of Poe—who has probably influenced me more than any other one person. If I have ever been able to approximate his kind of thrill, it is only because he himself paved the way by creating a whole atmosphere & method which lesser men can follow with relative ease. I make no claim to membership in the first rank of weird writers—a rank represented by Poe among the dead, & by Arthur Machen, Algernon Blackwood, Walter de la Mare, Lord Dunsany, & Montague Rhodes James among the living. It is enough for me if I can make a good shewing amongst the smaller fry represented in the cheap magazines.

Others—including Editor Wright—agree with you in liking "The Outsider", but I can't say that I share this opinion. To my mind this tale—written a decade ago—is too glibly *mechanical* in its climactic effect, & almost comic in the bombastic pomposity of its language. As I re-read it, I can hardly understand how I could have let myself be tangled up in such baroque & windy rhetoric as recently as ten years ago. It represents my literal though unconscious imitation of Poe at its very height. In those days I couldn't help aping the mannerisms as well as reflecting the spirit. However—I'll concede that the tale has the single merit of an original point of view. It is my constant complaint that allegedly weird writers fell into commonplaceness through reflecting wholly conventional & ordinary perspectives, sympathies, & value-systems; & in this instance (as in others) I sought to escape from this pitfall as widely as I could. It pleases me that you grasp this matter so spontaneously—for some persons seem unable to understand what I mean when I bring it up. For example—I once said that a werewolf story *from the wolf's point of view* ought to be written. H. Warner Munn, taking me up, thereupon produced his "Ponkert" series;[2] in which, however, he made the werewolf an unwilling one, filled with nothing but conventionally human regrets over his condition!

In my opinion, my best tale is "The Colour Out of Space" (1927). Second comes "The Music of Erich Zann" (1921), & after that my own preferences are very vague. I don't care much for the ultra-fantastic tales I wrote under extreme Dunsanian influence—"White Ship" &c.—although one more ("The Strange High House in the Mist") is still due to appear in W.T. Yes—I had a very short tale called "The Terrible Old Man", but I don't think much of it. The best thing I ever did in that brief, quasi-folklore line was "The Cats of Ulthar" (1920). I've written an endless number of stories, but have saved only 40 so far for permanent preservation. After I get home, if you like, I'll send you a list of all my stuff; & later lend you copies (either MSS. or printed sheets) of any you haven't seen but might care to wade through. Glad you liked "The Dunwich Horror". I used considerable realism in developing the locale of that thing—the prototype being the decaying agricultural region N.E. of Springfield, Mass.—especially the township of Wilbraham, which I visited for a fortnight in 1928. My "Whisperer in Darkness" will reflect a Vermont visit made in the same year. I am very fond of giving weird tales a minutely realistic setting as a sort of foil for the unreal extravagances of the central theme.

As for your questionnaire—I don't know that I'm any more "mysterious" than any other minor scribbler too unimportant to receive the very doubtful boon of personal exploitation. My address is 10 Barnes St., Providence, R.I.—which is an old-fashioned house in a quiet, village-like part of the city—on the crest of a virtual precipice which checks the spread of commerce & modernism. I have only one large ground-floor room & alcove—filled with what I have saved of my family furniture & belongings—but the place is so quiet that it seems like a real home; especially since my elder aunt (whose age & health do not permit of housekeeping) has a room on the floor above in which is still more furniture & material from my birthplace. The history of my family for the last few years, alas, is one of continual financial decline. My age will be 41 on the 20th of next August—so that I am really very much of a fossil who can remember when there were no automobiles or cinemas or wireless telegraphs, & when even telephones & phonographs were relatively rare curiosities. I can even recall the last of the horse & cable cars! I have written stories of one sort or other since the age of 7—back in 1897, before the Spanish War—but none of the juvenile stuff was any good. When I was 18 I destroyed all this early material except two specimens—the earlier of which was written at the age of 14. I also tried my hand at verse & other types of writing, & for a time repudiated literature altogether in favour of the natural sciences—astronomy, chemistry, physics, geography, anthropology, &c. I have a very keen curiosity about ultimate things, my constant question—addressed to the universe in general—being "what is anything?" Ill health pursued me till the age of 30, so that my education was very fragmentary & never reached as far as the university. Between 1908 and 1917 I wrote no stories, deeming myself poorly qualified for such work. In 1917, however, a man who saw one of my two surviving specimens advised me to start again—which I did, beginning with "The Tomb" & "Dagon".[3] Since then I have had no long hiatus. I have so far had no occupation other than literature, though much of my writing is mere revision & "ghost" production. It is an excess of this which prevents me from doing more stuff of my own. The reason I wrote nothing in 1929 was that my programme had too much revision. I wrote the "Whisperer" in 1930, & this present spring have written a long antarctic novelette called "At the Mountains of Madness". This has been sent to W.T., but Wright has so far given me no report on it. If he finally does accept it, it will have to be a serial, since its length amounts to 38,000 words—115 pages. As I get older, I find myself writing longer & longer stories. This makes them harder to place, but they bring bigger cheques when they do land. I have not had stories in any magazines other than those named; for my style is not a popular one, & the field for such materials is very limited. W.T. is my one standby. I had never had anything in any full-fledged magazine before W.T. published "Dagon" in 1923, although I belonged to an amateur writers' association which opened some non-professional columns to me. I don't recall how much I was paid for "The Outsider"—but the rate was

1¢ per word.[4] I get nothing, of course, for the reprint—although I receive a small cheque whenever an anthology reprints anything of mine.

Frank B. Long, Jr., Donald Wandrei, Wilfred B. Talman, H. Warner Munn, August W. Derleth, & Clark Ashton Smith are indeed all friends of mind, but it would hardly be fair to their own talents & initiative to call any of them my "proteges". I have tried to encourage the younger ones & help them with their style whenever such help seemed in order, but they all succeed on their own merits. I am proud, though, to have been the first to persuade Long & Talman & Munn to send stuff to W.T.[5] Long is 29, Talman 26, Wandrei 23, Munn 25, Derleth 22, & Smith 38. Since writing for W.T. I have also come to know Robert E. Howard (a splendidly interesting old-time Texan) & Henry S. Whitehead—a brilliant Episcopal clergyman of 49, who has done about everything & lived about everywhere under the sun. I don't know Farnsworth Wright personally, but my friends Wandrei & Talman have met him. He is about 42 years old, a war veteran, & in very bad health. Whitehead knows E. Hoffmann Price, who is a West Point graduate, ex-cavalry officer, & expert orientalist with a knowledge of Arabic. Talman recently met Seabury Quinn & likes him very much. It is possible that I shall meet Quinn—if he is in town—when I re-pass through N Y on my way home. He is about 40, & is an ex-lawyer & editor of an undertakers' trade journal called "The Casket." Clark Ashton Smith is a Californian whom I have known through correspondence for years though I have never met him in person. He has published 4 volumes of weird poetry, & is also a fantastic pictorial artist of very uncanny power. He is a profound French scholar, & has translated Baudelaire.[6] In case any of these writers interest you, I'll give you their addresses so far as I remember them:

> Long—230 W. 97th St., N.Y. City.
> Quinn—352 Jefferson Ave., Brooklyn, N.Y.
> Talman—2215 Newkirk Ave., "   "
> Whitehead—1159 Broadway, Dunedin, Fla.
> Smith—Box 385, Auburn, Calif.
> Dwyer—Box 43, West Shokan, N.Y.
> Francis Flagg—Box 40, Oracle, Arizona.
> Munn—168 Bliss St., Athol, Mass.
> Wandrei—1152 Portland Ave., St. Paul, Minn.
> Derleth—Sauk City, Wisconsin.
> Howard—Lock Box 313, Cross Plains, Texas.

I also know Arthur Leeds, who wrote "The Return of the Undead",[7] but can't find his latest address. Adolphe de Castro & Zealia Brown Reed are revision clients of mine, as was the late Houdini. All their work has appeared in W.T. The verse writers Harvey W. Flink & Thelma Johnson are clients of my friend Long.[8]

As for my favourite W.T. authors—it would be hard to make a list. The very best tales have been written by persons not at all well known. In my opinion, the really high spots run something like this:

Beyond the Door———————————	Paul Suter
The Floor Above———————————	M. Humphreys
The Night Wire———————————	H. F. Arnold
In Amundsen's Tent—————————	John Martin Leahy
The Canal————————————————	Everil Worrill [*sic*]
Bells of Oceana———————————	Arthur J. Burks
Passing of a God——————————	Henry S. Whitehead[9]

The authors who turn out the best steady output are Whitehead, Smith, Long, Price, Burks, Howard, & perhaps one or two others. Quinn could be a first-rater if he chose, but popularity & easy money have cause him to write in a tame, conventional, flashy, & superficial way. Hamilton was originally clever, but repeats the same plot endlessly. Dyalhis is sheer cheap hokum. Owen is fair but affected & mediocre. Price is excellent—though more Oriental than weird. Howard is very good, but hampered by adherence to a popular "action" style. Carr is very fair. Smith is first-rate, but writes too much, so that he produces both good & bad. Whitehead is splendid at his best, & has a fine gift for handling West Indian atmosphere. Worrill is good in the main, but has produced some fearsome trash. La Spina is trite & mediocre—except for one vampire tale a few years ago.[10] Arnold's one story was splendid. Colter never seems to register with me. Burks is splendid except when he tries to copy the popular "scientifiction" formula. Munn is a youth of vast promise, but stronger on romantic adventure than on weirdness. Wandrei has real genius, & deserves watching. Long has a magnificent style & fancy, but is hampered by a conventional point of view & an unfortunate desire to introduce cute & whimsical little snickers amidst his horrors. I wouldn't begin to list the 50 best things in W.T.; but such a list would include the 7 I just listed, plus a good many of Long's, ("Space Eaters", "Black Druid", &c) Whitehead's, ("The Tree-Man" &c) Smith's, Howard's, ("Skull Face") Wandrei's ("Red Brain" &c),[11] &c. &c.—& perhaps young Derleth's best 2 or 3 efforts. Yes—& a lot of Burks' Haytian tales—plus some by W. J. Stamper—&c. &c. &c.

Why haven't I written any "scientifiction" since the "Colour"? Damned if I know, except that my imagination doesn't tend to move that way often. Possibly my newest thing comes within the category, being full of geology, & geography. Do I rewrite & criticise stories? Hell, I'll say I do! And hateful drudgery it is! But it brings more dependable returns, in my case, than original writing. Why did I happen to hit on weird fiction? Haven't the least idea—was merely built that way. Since I could talk & walk nothing has ever interested me so much as the imaginative liberation of fantastic fiction—the casting off, in fancy, of all the chafing limitations of time, space, & natural law, & the achievement (on paper) of an unbounded sense of opened vistas fraught with adventurous expectancy. I ate up all the fairy tales in Grimm, revelled in stories from Greek & Roman mythology, & began scribbling weird things as soon as I could scribble anything at all. Struck Poe when I was 8, & have been devoted to him ever since. Have always sought out spectral landscape & architectural effects, & am fascinated (as indeed you have noted) by the idea of subterranean mysteries. Never, however, saw a real cave till I explored the Endless Caverns (near New Market, Va.) in 1928. Am I married? No, not now, though I was once. Financial difficulties, plus increasing divergences in aspirations & environmental needs, brought about a divorce many years ago—though wholly without blame or even bitterness on either side.[12] Have I travelled extensively? No, damn it! Hadn't the health in youth, & haven't the money now! Farthest east, tip of Cape Cod. Farthest north, Quebec. Farthest west, Cleveland & environs. Farthest south, Key West. What do I look like? Like the very devil! 5 ft 11 inches tall, weight 145, stoop-shouldered, chalk-white complexion just now covered by an almost Cuban coat of tan, long, horse-like chin, a proboscis like an elephant's, dark brown eyes, dark-brown hair getting thin on top & grey on the sides—well, anyhow, I don't have to look in the mirror except when dressing & shaving! I'll send you a snap shot of the pathetic spectacle after I get home. What do I think of the leading novelists of the day? Quite a crop, but many hampered by being caught in a period of radical transition. In the old manner, Galsworthy, Wells, Bennett, Wharton, &c. &c. merit their reputations. Dreiser, Lawrence, Anderson, Floyd Dell, Ben Hecht, Hemingway, & others well interpret transition. Joyce & Proust most considerable & significant figures of all—especially the latter, since Joyce is too deep in the principle of transition to be a really coherent & integrated artist himself. However, I don't take my own valuations of the present very seriously, since my interest in current literature is more scientific & historical than aesthetic. Literarily, I am too deeply plunged in the past to have much in common with the present. I am greatly attached to the 18th century, though not at all to the 19th. For me, the Victorian age has virtually never existed. Does writing come easily to me? Yes, very—though I take time with my stuff because I don't want to produce anything which isn't solid & well-developed. I had rather write a very little good stuff than a bushel a day of junk. Output per day? Usually zero, sometimes a whole story. No stable quantity whatever. Possibly, though, my hack work—revision &c—tends to average 10 longhand pages a day. I *hate* typewriting, & never touch the cursed machine except when I have to. I work mostly at night—midnight to dawn. In summer I do a good deal in the open air, taking my work out to the woods & fields in a black enamel-cloth bag. I can't use the muscles of my hand for writing in a room under about 74°, & can't exist at all in an outdoor temperature under +20°. The cold gets successively at my respiratory, digestive, & cardiac systems; & finally at my muscular-nervous coördination & seat of consciousness. At temperatures of 14 above I have gone dizzy & uncon-scious. I ought to live in the tropics, but love of ancestral scenes has so far kept me in the north—though I stay in the house all winter. I don't know what it is to suffer from the heat—the hotter a summer day, the better I like it. The climate of Key West last week suited me exactly. Do I think up plots easily? Well, that depends on what you mean by "plots". If you mean com-plex artificial systems of forcedly interdependent incidents culminating in a neat, thread-connecting climax, I may reply that I almost never use or try to use such a device; since I deem its principle (so universal a desideratum among popular editors) a cheap mechanical trick alien to life & unworthy of a genuine artist. If, however, you mean basic story-ideas & theme for simple atmospheric development, I may say that they do occur to me in vast abun-dance & with complete ease & spontaneity. In fact, I have far more ideas than I can ever hope to develop. One lifetime is too short. When something espe-cially good occurs to me I jot it down in a commonplace-book—& the book is so full of unused stuff that I often donate ideas to other writers who claim to have more difficulty in thinking up original notions.[13] Is my coming "Whisperer" interplanetary? Well—yes & no. There are Entities which come from *Outside*—from the ultimate unimaginable abysses, & with the new planet Pluto ("Yuggoth") as a stepping-stone—but all the action is in Vermont & neighbouring regions. Anything new coming in W.T.? Yes—"The Strange High House" and the long novelette **if** Wright accepts it. Stories liked best? "Colour Out of Space", "Erich Zann", "Dagon", "Cats of Ulthar", "Dun-wich", "Randolph Carter"—&c. Why don't I publish my things in book form? Because no publisher wants to buy them for that purpose! Just now Putnam's is looking over a lot of my junk—at their own request—but I ex-pect to hear of its polite & respectful rejection any day. Stories of mine in an-thologies, aside from "Red Hook" & "Cthulhu", are "Pickman's Model" (Not at Night, London 1929) & "The Rats in the Walls" (″ ″ 1930). What do I think of Poe? The greatest weird writer of them all. Nobody else has ever woven an atmosphere of menace as he could weave it. He suffered only from the faults of his time—pompous, occasionally naive & sentimental style—& from tendency to exalt the merely physically gruesome at the expense of the imaginatively terrifying cosmic element. Villiers de l'Isle Adam? Splendid in the *conte cruel,* but nothing extra for cosmic weirdness. Ambrose Bierce? Splendid within limits, but somewhat stiff, un-cosmic, preoccupied by a sort of sadistic physical gruesomeness. F. Marion Crawford? Splendid in "The Upper Berth" & "The Blood is the Life". Of modern weird writers, Algernon Blackwood is best in content, but crude in style. Arthur Machen is admirable. Dunsany is the king of all fantaisistes, but doesn't go in very often for stark terror. M. R. James is fine & unique. Walter de la Mare can closely approach perfection when he chooses—infinite subtlety of atmosphere. My favourite magazine? *Harper's* by a wide margin. *Am. Mercury* is also magnificently alive.

Atlantic has good stuff, but is a bit atrophied. *Forum* getting pretty good. Why am I unknown to critics, who praise my 'inferiors'? Well—I'm not sure that they *do* praise my inferiors! I have an idea that I still belong down in the literarily inferior group myself. I don't think the standard reviewers would have any hesitancy in giving me the usual amount of notice if I ever produced anything as good as Blackwood's "Willows", Machen's "Hill of Dreams", or de la Mare's "Seaton's Aunt." I am not much of a believer in mute inglorious Miltons. What caused me to write "The Outsider"? Well—a sort of wish to carry Poe's stock type of 'dark, obscurely [born] tragic hero' to a greater extreme than [he] ever carried the type himself, plus a desire to experiment in my special hobby of the *unconventional angle.* I certainly wish I had broken away from Poe-esque rhetoric more fully when I perpetrated the thing. Indeed, when I published it 5 years after writing I ought to have revised it. It never satisfied me, & when I sent it to Wright it was only for his personal perusal & not for publication. But his enthusiasm for it caused me to let him print it as it was.

I am interested to hear that you are interested in writing, & would like to see specimens of your work some day. Do you incline toward the weird, or are your creative tastes more general? I fancy you might be interested in hearing from some of the writers whose addresses I have given. Many of them might give you useful suggestions—& young Derleth would probably be especially prompt about replying. Since you are so much of a student of weird writing, I will send you a kind of historical sketch of this field when I get home—a sketch I wrote four years ago, & which was printed in a sort of amateur magazine.[14] You may find parts of it dull, but it might give you one or two suggestions for reading.

Well—by this time you know a good deal more about me than you did before—whether or not information about a nonentity have any value! Hope you aren't too badly disappointed in discovering a very prosaic old cuss—but not every word-slinger can be a romantic figure like Poe, a roving character like Blackwood, or an eminent scholar like M. R. James.

Best wishes—& send me some of your work some time.

Yrs most cordially & sincerely,

H P Lovecraft

Notes

1. Bernard Austin Dwyer, "Ol' Black Sarah" (*WT,* October 1928).
2. H. Warner Munn, "The Werewolf of Ponkert" (*WT,* July 1925); "The Return of the Master" (*WT,* July 1927); "The Werewolf's Daughter" (*WT,* October–December 1928); "The Master Strikes" (*WT,* November 1930); "The Master Fights" (*WT,* December 1930); "The Master Has a Narrow Escape" (*WT,* January 1931);
3. W. Paul Cook (1880–1948) published HPL's juvenile tale "The Beast in the Cave" (1905) in the *Vagrant* in 1918. HPL wrote "The Tomb" and "Dagon" in the summer

of 1917. Cook published the other story HPL saved, "The Alchemist" (1908), in 1916, as well as "Dagon" in 1919 and "The Tomb" in 1922.

4. About $26.00 (more than *Amazing* paid for the much longer "The Colour out of Space").

5. Long's first appearance in *WT* was "The Desert Lich" (December 1924); Talman's was "Haunted Island" (verse, January 1928); and Munn's was "The Werewolf of Ponkert" (July 1925).

6. *The Star-Treader and Other Poems* (1912), *Odes and Sonnets* (1918), *Ebony and Crystal: Poems in Verse and Prose* (1922), and *Sandalwood* (1925). Many of CAS's translations of Baudelaire remained unpublished in his lifetime; they have now been published in CAS's *Complete Poetry and Translations* (New York: Hippocampus Press, 2007–08), Vol. 3.

7. *WT*, November 1925.

8. Both had a few poems in *WT*.

9. Paul Suter, "Beyond the Door" (April 1923; rpt. September 1930); M. L. Humphries, "The Floor Above" (May 1923; rpt. June 1933); H. F. Arnold, "The Night Wire" (September 1926; rpt. January 1933); John Martin Leahy, "In Amundsen's Tent" (January 1928; rpt. August 1935); Everil Worrell, "The Canal" (December 1927; rpt. April 1935); Arthur J. Burks, "Bells of Oceana" (December 1927; rpt. April 1934); Henry S. Whitehead, "Passing of a God" (January 1931). In the paragraph that follows, HPL refers to the *WT* authors Seabury Quinn, Edmond Hamilton, Nictzin Dyalhis, Frank Owen, Robert Spencer Carr, Greye La Spina, and Eli Colter.

10. HPL probably refers to La Spina's novella "Fettered" (*WT*, July–October 1926).

11. "The Space Eaters" (*WT*, July 1928); "The Black Druid" (*WT*, July 1930); "The Tree-Man (*WT*, February/March 1931); "Skull-Face" (*WT*, October–December 1929); "The Red Brain" (*WT*, October 1927).

12. HPL and his wife separated, but he never signed the divorce papers.

13. HPL lent his commonplace book to Frank Belknap Long and Henry S. Whitehead. Whitehead's "Cassius" derives from an entry in HPL's book.

14. "Supernatural Horror in Literature" (written 1925–27).

[2]   [ALS]

Home Address—
          10 Barnes St.   Brooklyn, N.Y.,
                    Providence, R.I.,   July 19, 1931

Dear Mr. Shea:—

          Yrs of 22nd ult. found me still abroad—& various kindly hosts have kept my time so full since my arrival in the N Y region that I have had no previous opportunity to reply. I shall be home again on Tuesday, after nearly three months of pleasant wandering. This trip shatters all my previous records.

          No—I don't think I'm unduly modest in my estimate of my own stuff. Two recent incidents confirm my estimate. (a) W.T. has rejected my new 115-

page antarctic novelette,* & (b) G. P. Putnam's Sons has practically rejected the collection of short stories which the book editor asked me to send in last March. My junk isn't as bad as some, but it just fails to make the grade as first-class work.

You surely have some important & interesting reading ahead of you. The ghost stories of Montague Rhodes James have just been issued in collected form, (one volume, thin paper) & certainly ought to be on every weird writer's shelves. Of Dunsany you ought to read at least the following:

> The Gods of Pegana
> Time & the Gods
> A Dreamer's Tales
> The Sword of Welleran
> The Book of Wonder
> The Last Book of Wonder
> Tales of Three Hemispheres
> Chronicles of Rodriguez
> The King of Elfland's Daughter

The Modern Library has four of these—under two titles, "A Dreamer's Tales" with "The Sword of Welleran" included, & "The Book of Wonder" with "Time & the Gods" included. Arthur Machen's "Bowmen" does not even begin to suggest his best stuff. Read the following—which will introduce you to some of the best weird literature ever written:

> The House of Souls†
> The Hill of Dreams
> The Three Impostors†
> The Terror

Blackwood is in some respects the greatest of all weird writers—despite a persistent mediocrity of style. Read at least the following:

> Incredible Adventures
> John Silence—Physician Extraordinary

I have just been reading de la Mare, & some of his tales don't grip me as they did a few years ago. "Seaton's Aunt", though, still holds me. Read it again & see if it hasn't a subtle, malign spell which eluded you the first time.

Your selection of W.T. items with a real suggestion of the cosmic coincides in some respects with my own choices—though it includes things which

---

*I have not seen the title "At the Mts. of Madness" used before, but it wouldn't matter if it had been.
†obtainable in Knopf's dollar series of reprints.

didn't ring convincingly with me—"The Malignant Entity", for example.[1] "The Last Test" is virtually a story of mine—for I revised it & introduced all the Atlantean background. Munn's best story so far, I think, is either "The Chain" or "The City of Spiders".[2] Those other torture tales were well done, though this genre does not particularly appeal to me.

If you can stand reading all those old tales of mine, I can certainly stand lending them. I'll shoot along the titles you mention as soon as I get home. Hope the "Whisperer" (which you have by this time seen) has not bored you to death. No—of my 40 tales, only 25 or 30 have appeared in W.T. You'll see how they stand when you receive my list. As for my early stuff—the first story I can recall writing was called "The Noble Eavesdropper", & concerned a boy who overheard some horrible conclave of subterranean beings in a cave. I no longer have it. I do, though, have copies of some 8-year-old junk which my mother saved—"The Mysterious Ship" & "The Secret of the Grave."[3]

Providence, July 30

This is the first chance I have had to continue the letter begun in Brooklyn—whence I returned home over a week ago. I found so many accumulated tasks awaiting me that correspondence was virtually out of the question. As soon as I get out from under the present mountain of mail I'll send you a list of my stories—from which you may pick any you haven't read. I think I can find "Ulthar", "Randolph Carter", & "Dagon" amongst the junk which Putnam's has just fired back at me.

I'd like to see some of your tales some time—they sound exceedingly interesting, even though they may have the usual limitations of the beginner. You have no need to be ashamed of crude early work, for everyone has to go through a period of experiment & pioneering. We all tend to overwork the dictionary & thesaurus at a certain stage, but this soon passes. Your general reading, as you outline it, sounds gratifyingly vital & well chosen. The more you read of good literature, the better equipped you will be for any sort of writing—even though your especial field may be restricted to the fantastic as mine is. Conversely, the less you read of popular magazine trash the better will be your chances of achieving genuine artistic expression. It is the machine-made, insincere trash that brings in the money—but that is another story which has nothing to do with literature. I am assuming that your wish to write is a profound & spontaneous one, such as only the production of real literature can satisfy—a wish that takes the form of imaginative glimpses & conceptions so poignant that you cannot feel easy till they are in some measure captured on paper. Practice & reading are the best aids to the fulfilment of the urge. *Simplicity* in style ought always to be cultivated—for it leads to the best results in the end, even though it may prolong one's period of apparent crudeness. It is better to be simple, sincere, & a little crude, than to achieve a glib facade of unctuous fluency through the use of cheap & popular artificialities of rhetoric. The best style is the one with the least complexity & the fewest mannerisms. Delicate shadings & subtleties can be depicted with care & accuracy, yet without any of the flamboyant extravagances common to immaturely pompous writing. The specimen of your prose impresses me very favourably indeed, although it is of a somewhat more florid sort than I usually aim at nowadays. It really shews a splendid sense of colour & imagery, & to my mind is very distinctly the utterance of one who has something to say artistically. Certainly, it is better than I could have written at your age. With time you may feel inclined to write rather more objectively & restrainedly—with less of what might be taken for mannerism & sentimentality—but for the present I believe you have vast reason to congratulate yourself. I must read "The Earth Taint" as a whole some day—in print, I hope! Glad to see you are departing from hackneyed convention enough to make your earth-folk the villains. One step farther from convention, & you won't find it necessary to divide your characters into heroes & villains at all. In real life, everyone is a compound of hero & villain—though some individuals naturally incline toward certain disproportions of character which roughly correspond to the stereotyped categories.

Long received your letter while I was at his house. Hope he has answered it by this time—though he & his parents are now away on a motor trip of several weeks' extent. Smith, Derleth, Munn, Whitehead, Talman, Wandrei, &c. would certainly appreciate hearing from you. "The City of the Singing Flame" is indeed magnificent—I read it in MS. several months ago, & understand that *Wonder Stories* has given it a cover design.[4] What you say of Smith's style versus his ideas seems to me highly sensible. He writes too many stories as pot-boilers, & consequently runs dry of ideas very frequently. Primarily he is a poet & pictorial artist. He has had 4 books of poems published, & his bizarre pictures are truly haunting—even though somewhat weak in technique. Whitehead has a very profound & convincing charm, even though he prefers to deal with less extravagant horrors than some. He specialises in actual folklore—mainly of the West Indies, which he knows intimately through long residence there. His style is somewhat affected by the popular magazine tradition, though I would hardly call it poor. He has hitherto lacked a certain atmospheric tensity—but I think he is slowly developing this quality. Have you seen his striking tale, "The Black Beast", in the July 15 issue of *Adventure?*

Stories in W.T. in which I have had a hand include—among others—the following:

The Last Test	} Adolphe de Castro
The Electric Executioner	
The Curse of Yig—	Zealia B. Reed
Two Black Bottles—	W. B. Talman
The Loved Dead	} C M Eddy, Jr.
Deaf, Dumb, & Blind	

It is amusing that you should at one time have thought me a clergyman, since I have not entertained any belief in the supernatural since the age of 8. About "In Amundsen's Tent"—you may be right, but just the same this story aroused in me certain sensations of vague apprehension which other tales of "too-horrible-to-mention" objects have utterly failed to arouse. It may be very subjective & unintelligent to measure fiction by its effect on oneself— but that's my vote, anyway.

I met Quinn twice during my stay in N Y, & find him exceedingly intelligent & likeable. He is 44 years old, but looks rather less than that. Increasingly stocky, dark, & with a closely clipped moustache. He is first of all a shrewd business man, & freely affirms that he manufactures hokum to order for market demands—in contrast to the artist, who seeks sincere expression as the result of an obscure inward necessity.

I haven't seen any recent work by Robert S. Carr, but hope he is living up to his spectacular early promise.

For H. L. Mencken I entertain the greatest admiration, even though he sometimes becomes needlessly vociferous & extravagant in his tirades. His general philosophy of the universe is a sound one, & he has been of inestimable service to American letters in helping to explode the mawkish & insincere "genteel tradition" which formerly stultified all our aesthetic expression. His principal weakness (recognised by himself) is an inability to enter sympathetically into the spirit of poetry.

Joyce is hardly worth reading unless one be a specialist in the history of literary form. Proust is not at all like him, but inherits many qualities from the main tradition of the French novel. Gertrude Stein is an erratic extremist whose work is a total loss so far as real art is concerned. Extravagance of that sort is merely a curiosity—though sometimes a fairly significant curiosity—in the museum of aesthetic development.

As for *weird* reading—my recommendation stands as before:

Algernon Blackwood
Arthur Machen
Lord Dunsany
Montague Rhodes James
Walter de la Mare

If you want further tips, I'll send you an article which I wrote 5 years ago, & which appeared in a privately printed magazine.

Your travels may add up to more than mine in mileage & variety, even though not drawn out into a straight north & south line as mine have been. It is my antiquarian taste which keeps me close to the historic Atlantic coast. The colonies so far entered by me are the following:

Rhode Island (1890)	Delaware (1925)
Massachusetts (1890)	Maryland (1925)
Connecticut (1903)	Dist of Columbia (1925)
New Hampshire (1921)	Virginia (1925)
New York (1922)	Vermont (1927)
New Jersey (1922)	North Carolina (1930)
Pennsylvania (1922)	South Carolina (1930)
Ohio (1922)	Quebec (1930)
Maine (1923)	Georgia (1931)
	Florida (1931)

I was interested in your description of yourself. Here's a snap shot which Talman took of me a couple of weeks ago—I'm far enough from the camera not to break the lens.

Please pardon the damnable penmanship (& probably vacuous content) of this hurried scrawl. When I have more leisure I'll write more intelligibly— on the typewriter, much as I hate the cursed thing.

> Best wishes—Yrs most sincerely
> H P Lovecraft

Notes

1. Otis Adelbert Kline, "The Malignant Entity" (*WT,* May–June–July 1924).
2. H. Warner Munn, "The Chain" (*WT,* April 1928); "The City of Spiders" (*WT,* November 1926).
3. By "The Secret of the Grave" HPL probably meant "The Mystery of the Grave-yard."
4. CAS, "The City of the Singing Flame" (*Wonder Stories,* July 1931). The cover illustration was by Frank R. Paul.

[3]   [ALS]

> 10 Barnes St.,
> Providence, R.I.,
> August 7, 1931

My dear Mr. Shea:—

Let's see how this letter is for chirography—I'm trying to decide on a new fountain pen, which for me is the most exacting of all tasks. It seems almost impossible to suit my hand except after about a dozen trials. A brief test in the shop is no good at all—I have to get a pen home & write a couple of pages before I can form a really good idea of the way it fits my degree of pressure & muscular patterns. This is the 7th or 8th pen I have had since I began looking for one last May—& I have half an idea I shall keep it. I shall have to have two pens, so that one will be ready to fall back upon whenever I begin the long series of trials & exchanges culminating in the purchase of a new one. This is a Waterman—the good old fashioned make to which I always return after experiments with more modern makes. But it sure is the bunk to call any pen a *lifetime* affair. A spell of 3 or 4 years at my rate of usage will wear down any point ever made—iridium'd or not. I never employ a typewriter except when absolutely forced to do so—hence the amount of text my pen has to handle is virtually infinite. Nothing rasps my nerves more than a spell at the machine—it gives me a headache in half an hour, & after another half-hour sends a shooting pain through my shoulder-blades. Possibly the posture has something to do with it—I don't know; but I do know that honest, old fashioned script is the only medium of expression in which I feel absolutely at home.

Keep the snapshot—Talman gave me an excellent supply of prints, generous soul that he is. Here's another one shewing young Long which you can keep if you wish—pardon the repetition of yours truly on it, but I haven't any separate one of Belknap. I also enclose two snaps of Clark Ashton Smith—which I will assume (though I've never seen him) look more like him than like Laurence Tibbett.[1] I'll have to ask you to return these, since I have no duplicates. You can get considerable of Smith's facial expression by using a magnifying glass. As for your interpretation of my portrait—I fancy you overrate the intellect, though the cynicism exists in connexion with my interpretation of the cosmos. Whatever "suffering" I have undergone is largely in the form of a dull falling short of aspirations, a general sense of futility in the universe, & a steady decline in worldly fortunes. I am not of the over-emotional type which takes its troubles seriously & enjoys acute misery. As for humour—I certainly don't think it belongs in weird fiction, & am not sure how complete my general lack of it is. I am not without a perception of ironic incongruities, but on the other hand do not consider these incongruities very significant. A person who is continually snickering because of something allegedly funny in everything seems to me essentially superficial—in that he is postulating some arbitrary standard of consistency & sanity in a cosmos essentially purposeless & irrational. However—a good deal of the comic attitude is sheer physiological exuberance—a matter of glands—& I dare say my glands are not the sort to produce a perpetual smirk or giggle. Yet I doubt whether I am actually as unqualifiedly sour as I look. I can be almost civil on occasions.

Yes—Wright "explained" his rejection of the "Mountains of Madness" in almost the same language as that with which he "explained" other recent rejections to Long & Derleth. It was "too long", "not easily divisible into parts," "not convincing"—& so on. Just what he has said of other things of mine (except for length)—some of which he has ultimately accepted after many hesitations. Those once-rejected & later-accepted things include "Cthulhu", "The Tomb", & many others. It is very possible that I am growing stale—that is for readers of the "Whisperer" & "Mountains of Madness" to judge—but if so it merely signifies the end of my fictional attempts. There is no field other than the weird in which I have any aptitude or inclination for fictional composition. Life has never interested me so much as the escape from life. However—there is a region on the border betwixt weirdness & "scientifiction" in which I might conceivably experiment. Indeed—the "Mountains of Madness" belongs largely to this type.

Yes—all the tales you mention were in the batch shot back by Putnam's. The grounds for rejection were twofold—first, that some of the tales are not subtle enough . . . . too obvious & well-explained—[admitted! That ass Wright got me into the habit of obvious writing with his never-ending complaints against the indefiniteness of my early stuff] & secondly, that all the tales are too uniformly macabre in mood to stand collected publication. This second reason is sheer bull—for as a matter of fact unity of mood is a positive asset in a fictional collection. But I suppose the herd must have their comic relief! The book editor—Winfield Shiras—added some slices of bologna about later discussions concerning a volume in which the heavier tales might be sandwiched in betwixt lighter ones . . . . but I'm not expecting to hear much from him. It satisfies me amply to let the incident remain a closed one. I don't think the John Day Co. would care greatly for anything of mine—they have not communicated with me concerning anything for their Hammett anthology.[2]

Neither do I think that Harpers would be any market for my stuff. The standard magazines take weird material only from the most famous & established writers—to say nothing of demanding a technical skill far in advance of mine. After all, the unreal is such a confoundedly *minor* phase of general human experience! Its place in the life of the majority is so slight, & the number of those to whom it is important is so small! Editors, having such an ingrained distrust of the whole genre, naturally confine their few acceptances to specimens in which the workmanship is of the highest possible level—& in which the weirdness is as mild & innocuous as possible. All of which lets me out. I never heard of "Jungle Stories" before, though I knew that Clayton contemplated a new magazine of the weird to be entitled *Strange Stories*. I have had a couple of things turned down by that outfit[3]—though the editor, Harry Bates, lately wrote me that the ban on atmospheric, non-plot fiction (my sort) is about to be lifted. I shall probably try Clayton again, though with no expectation of having anything accepted. This is the bunch that turned down tales by Smith & Derleth with the identical explanation that the respective heroes were not in danger often enough. Angkor wouldn't be a bad locale for a weird tale—in fact, Edmond Hamilton has used it in one of the rehashings of his single plot. I may yet have something to say about it.

No—I've never been either in or through Pittsburgh; my single journey to Cleveland having been via Albany & Buffalo. I'd like to see it some time, though; for I am of course aware of its historic antecedents as Ft. Duquesne—& later Ft. Pitt—in the French & Indian wars. I shall surely notify you if I ever do get around that way. It would be interesting to make a trip down the inner frontier of the colonies—Pittsburgh, Winchester, Kentucky, Tennessee, &c. So far I am acquainted only with the approximately coastal region of the first few generations of settlement—except, of course, for that one Cleveland trip of 1922.

About the tales mentioned by B K H[4] which you haven't seen—here is the dope so far as I can recall. Items marked with a star are owned by me & can be lent you if they aren't accessible in your local library: (those marked † are in the batch of books already sent)

> The Willows—Blackwood—in "The Listener & Other Stories."
> *White People—Machen—in "The House of Souls"
> †*Black Seal—Machen—in "The Three Impostors"
> *Halpin Fraser—Bierce—in "Can Such Things Be?"
> House of Sounds—Shiel—"The Pale Ape & Other Stories'.
> *Yellow Sign—Chambers—"The King in Yellow"
> *Suitable Surroundings—Bierce—in "In the Midst of Life"
> Wendigo—Blackwood—in "The Lost Valley & Other Stories"
> *Skule Skerry—Buchan—in "The Runagates Club"
> †*Bethmoora—Dunsany—in "A Dreamer's Tales"
> *Ep. Cath. Hist—James—in "A Thin Ghost & Others"
> *He Cometh & He Passeth By—Wakefield—in "They Return at Evening".
> *17th Hole at Duncaster
> Dream of Armageddon—Wells—"30 Strange Stories"

What is "The Furnished Room"—that pallid & artificial thing by O. Henry? Lytton's "House & Brain" is good, but lacks some obscure element of naturalness. Haven't yet found "Triumph of Night"—don't think it's in the local libraries.[5]

I've sent Klarkash-Ton the original "Moon Pool" & instalments I & III of the expanded A.S. version. Also, have started "The People of the Pit" on its indirect way to him. Later he will send the whole outfit to you for ultimate return to me.

I note what you say regarding both pedagogical & photographic professions. Surely, remunerative avenues are hard to find these days! As for photography catering to vanity—I'd hardly say that this is entirely so. It seems to me that elements of really aesthetic portrayal are very largely present—though of course most subjects like to have their egos adorned & inflated.

You must be having strenuous times getting acclimated to college, though the spice of adventurous expectancy doubtless redeems & enlivens the ordeal. In the end you will find it is worth your while. Glad you have a brilliant pedagogical staff to deal with—& hope the "Mts. of Madness" didn't scare you off from geology!

You've read more of Bromfield[6] than I have—but I want to read all of him ultimately. Hemingway probably is overrated, but there's something there just the same . . . which his many imitators don't usually catch very well! I hope to see "Five-Star Final"—which reminds me that various persons say

I missed something good by not seeing "The Front Page".[7]

Whitehead's brief & indirect acknowledgment is probably due to his health—for he is waging a terrific fight against ulcers of the stomach & duodenum, & may yet have to resort to surgery. He is now much thinner than the snapshot he probably sent you. (Is it the one with his father?)

After a period of chill, the autumnal equinox has brought some warmer weather; hence my outdoor sessions have a new lease of life. Next Saturday & Sunday I shall have as a visitor W. Paul Cook—editor of the defunct Recluse. Best wishes—H P L

Notes

1. Laurence Tibbett (1896–1960) was a celebrated American opera singer (baritone), film actor, and radio personality.

2. Dashiell Hammett's *Creeps by Night* (1931) included HPL's "The Music of Erich Zann."

3. In April and May 1931, HPL had submitted at least five stories to Harry Bates, the editor of the newly formed *Strange Tales* (not *Strange Stories*): "The Doom That Came to Sarnath," "The Nameless City," "Beyond the Wall of Sleep," "Polaris," and "In the Vault." All were rejected. Clayton published a magazine called *Jungle Stories*, but it lasted for only 3 issues (August, October, and December 1931).

4. B. K. Hart, literary editor of the *Providence Journal*, had discussed weird fiction in several columns in late 1929; several mentioned HPL or quoted letters or lists of weird tales by him and his colleagues. See "The Sideshow," *Providence Journal* (23 and 25 November 1929): 2; (30 November): 10.

5. HPL refers to O. Henry, "The Furnished Room" (*New York Sunday World Magazine*, 14 August 1904; rpt. *WT*, September 1925); Edward Bulwer-Lytton, "The Haunted and the Haunters; or, The House and the Brain"; Edith Wharton, "The Triumph of Night" (*Scribner's Magazine*, August 1914; collected in *Xingu and Other Stories* [1916] and *Ghosts* [1937]).

6. Louis Bromfield (1896–1956), American author and conservationist who won the Pulitzer Prize and pioneered innovative scientific farming concepts.

7. *Five Star Final* (Warner Brothers, 1931), directed by Mervyn LeRoy; starring Edward G. Robinson, Marian Marsh, and H. B. Warner. *The Front Page* (United Artists, 1931), directed by Lewis Milestone; starring Adolphe Menjou, Pat O'Brien, and Mary Brian.

[4]   [ALS]

10 Barnes St.

Providence, R.I.,

August 14, 1931

Dear Mr. Shea:—

Glad to see further specimens of your versification, & think that most of them shew a vivid visual sense & appreciation of dramatic values which promise well for future development. Naturally they have their juvenile side—an exaggerated sententiousness now & then, a use of sonorous rhetorical cliches, (which sometimes appear to motivate the theme instead of the desirable reverse) & a more or less uncertain command of metrical media—but for all that they are certainly not discreditable for a young bard whose technical training is still at an early stage. If I were you I'd read some standard work on versification—especially that by Brander Matthews. Gummere's "Handbook of Poetics" is another good one. If you want to give your instinctive poetic taste a thorough test, I can lend you the extremely clever Abbott-Trabue test devised by Columbia College—which consists of making you pick the correct passage of poetry from a group of four; the three wrong passages being intentional distortions of the original, each representing a different type of cheapness & banality. In a year or so there will be a handbook of poetic appreciation which I shall recommend to you with the utmost enthusiasm as the nearest approach to a royal road to poesy—but unfortunately it is still in the manuscript stage. This is—or will be—"Doorways to Poetry"—by my old friend Maurice Winter Moe, of the English Dept. of West Division High School, Milwaukee, Wis. I have had a hand in knocking this into final shape, but the merit (& a very extraordinary & unprecedented merit, at that) is all Moe's.[1] I don't think anyone has ever analysed the essence of *false* taste as well as Moe has. By shewing what is cheap & trivial in every species of tawdry verse, he guides one to the essence of real merit through elimination—buttressed, of course, by plenty of positive demonstrations of what real merit is. Meanwhile, of course, one ought to read plenty of the best poetry—especially the newer specimens, since the older classics are full of rhetorical devices which time has rendered stale & unsuitable for serious use.

Curious how deceptive snapshots are! Of all our gang, Long is probably the one who looks *most* like an author—for he goes in for wavy locks & a thin, undernourished line of downy filaments on his upper lip. He's quite a kid—which much of the small boy remaining in him despite 29 years of terrestrial existence. A weak heart has prevented him from leading an active & independent life, so that he is still very much of a home child, close to papa & mamma. He is slowly growing stronger, however, so that he will probably be able to increase his range of activities as time goes on. But it will take quite an interval for the original psychology of vegetative coddling to wear off. As for my 'woebegone expression' in that snap—boy, yo' ain't seen nothin' yet! A portrait-lens close-up which Talman took of me at the same time looks as if I were just on the point of loading up the old gat & ending it all! And yet I was in excellent spirits. Evidently I am one of those who take their pleasures sadly. Only a Poe could hint how I must look when actually sunk in despondency by the return of some hard-typed manuscript!

The daemon high-priest of Tsathoggua, Klarkash-Ton (otherwise Clark Ashton Smith) has told me about "The Blue Barbarians",[2] & I look forward to its perusal with considerable pleasure. I have read enough "scientifiction" to be able to appreciate its point. Klarkash-Ton plans to send me the quarterly shortly—which reminds me, that he also intends to slip me a copy of Wonder Stories with his "Singing Flame" cover design, so that I shan't have to impose on your charity.

No wonder you still ascribe merit to my work, since you've read only 14 specimens! Probably you formed the idea that these were the excusably weak by-products of one whose major efforts really do amount to something. I shall gradually begin the process of disillusion—slipping the checked titles on the list as I come across them in the chaos of my storage dump. Never mind about the C.O.D. After you've read some of them you'll think it's bad enough to have to pay the return postage yourself. As a starter, I am putting you on the private circulation list of the carbon of my final senile maundering—"At the Mountains of Madness." This MS. will come—I can't say just when—from one Bernard Dwyer of West Shokan, N.Y. I'll tell you later whether to return it ultimately to me or to inflict it upon another candidate for ennui & drowsiness. You'll find some of my early truck full of the very kind of stilted rhetoric I now condemn in others, so don't use it as a model. "Dagon", for example, ends something like this—"God, that hand! The window! The window!" I wrote that 14 years ago, it is true; but when I reflect that I was going on 27 at the time, I temper my natural amusement with a becoming humiliation. In sending "The Lurking Fear" I must apologise particularly for its blatantly cheap construction. I wrote that to order as a 4-part serial for an indescribably wretched rag—the editor's instructions being as follows: (a) you can't make it too morbid. Go the limit! (b) each section must have exactly 2000 words. (c) each section must end with a gruesome sub-climax. That was the last tale I ever wrote to order. The process began to disgust me so that I swore off for all time. Klarkash-Ton's illustrations aren't his best work, so that I may send you a less misprinted version than the *Home Brew* sheets. I must, though, let you see some of his grotesque heads some day. His chief pictorial specialties are the rugose, many-snouted heads of nameless Things & the tentacular convolutions of equally malign, nameless, & extra-mundane vegetation. One of Klarkash-Ton's forests is a place that any honest, god-fearing Rotarian would hate to be lost in!

As for Derleth—I don't wonder you find his W.T. stuff mediocre! He holds all records for leading a literary double life—for his serious work is no more like this commercial junk than Marcel Proust is like Nictzin Dyalhis! He despises his pot-boilers utterly & eloquently—but continues to write them because they bring in highly welcome cheques. His real work is of a minor-keyed, delicate quality—brooding memories & impressions woven together as they impinge on a single life-stream, & brief tragic vignettes of hidden lives & strange, lonely people. Some day he will probably go farther in literature than anyone else in the whole W.T. crowd. His first novel, still unpublished, will be called "Evening in Spring."[3] Derleth is only 22, & graduated from the U. of Wis. a year ago. He is an associate editor of a very intelligent intercollegiate magazine called *The Mid-*

western. He is a small-towner, living at his birthplace, Sauk City, Wis., & having his literary roots deep in the soil. Vast promise there—mark an old man's words!

I haven't seen De la Mare's "On the Edge", but have probably read considerable of the contents elsewhere. I have certainly read "A Recluse", & recall the indefinite climax. For a moment I thought Walter had got ahead of me with the idea I use in "The Whisperer"—i.e., that the recluse was not human, & that his human mask or something like that would be found around the house—but, much to my relief, such was not so. I distinctly like these tales whose endings leave so much to the imagination, but fancy you prefer more concrete & obvious things—judging from your indifference to Blackwood's "The Willows". I am free to say that I consider "The Willows" the greatest piece of weird fiction ever penned by human hand. "Don Rodriguez" isn't Dunsany's best work, but it's eminently worth reading. Don't miss Machen's "House of Souls" & "Three Impostors"—or Blackwood's "John Silence" & "Incredible Adventures." I wish I still had a *first* reading of some of these ahead of me!

Jungle Stories sounds interesting, though I don't know just where I'd fit in there. I have, by the way, just heard of a new "scientifiction" magazine published by Harold Hersey.[4]

As for your new story-title—"Its Shuddery Embrace" seems to me much too obvious & melodramatic. "It" would be infinitely better if it hadn't been used dozens of times before in just the same way. Can't you think of a third—as laconic, yet as fraught with shadowy, compressed menace, as "It"?

I'd like to see that "Easter Island" book. It has long been in my mind to utilise that remote brooding-place of nameless colossi as a theme for fictional palpitations. About the Necronomicon—I like to have other authors in the gang allude to it, for it helps work up a background of evil verisimilitude. I have worked it into certain things done for clients, & Klarkash-Ton, Long, Robert E. Howard, & Wandrei have also given it free advertising. In return, I am occasionally referring to Howard's "Bran", Smith's "Tsathoggua", Long's "Tindalos" & "Chaugnar", &c. Team-work, as it were.

Of the Chaney cinemas which you list, I have seen "The Miracle Man", "The Hunchback of Notre Dame", & "The Unholy Three." I believe he would have appeared in "Dracula" had he lived.[5] I saw that film in Miami on Whitehead's recommendation, but didn't get much of a kick except for the castle scenes at the very beginning.

I suppose any civilised point of view would be puzzling to the readers of *Astounding Stories*—since the majority of them probably have no point of view at all. But if the editors objected to such a thing it would probably be because it lacked "punch" & "action" rather than because of any affront to the Santa-Claus credulities of our amiable forefathers. But of course, the chances of any beginner's acceptance by a Clayton publication are slender. This bunch demand a certain assured glibness & superficial polish which one doesn't ordinarily get except through long apprenticeship in the ignominious trade of rabble-catering. As for your specimen scene—whatever its limitations, it is certainly much less inane than most of the "heart interest" stuff laboriously pumped into most W.T. junk to give Senf an excuse for a still largely irrelevant cover design containing the commercially sure-fire element of pulchritudinous muliebrity! With time, practice, & the gradual crystallisation of an individual slant, you will come to judge for yourself just what does & what doesn't belong in an effective tale of the sort you're aiming at. At first there's nothing to do but try your hand at all the prevailing models & see what fits you best.

And now I must get to work on some accursed revision. Still all at sea about a fountain pen—this thing rasps like a saw. Don't know why my daemoniac claw is so hard to suit with writing materials!

Best wishes—& stories soon.

Yr most ob^t h^ble Servt

H P Lovecraft

Notes

1. Moe's *Doorways to Poetry,* which HPL revised in 1929, was never published.
2. A science fiction novel by Stanton A. Coblentz.
3. Actually this was AWD's twelfth published novel.
4. Hersey founded and edited two issues of *Miracle Science and Fantasy Stories* (April/May and June/July 1931).
5. *The Miracle Man* (Famous Players–Lasky Corp., 1919; silent), directed by George Loane Tucker; starring Lon Chaney, Betty Compson, and Joseph J. Dowling. *The Hunchback of Notre Dame* (Universal, 1923; silent), directed by Wallace Worsley; starring Lon Chaney, Patsy Ruth Miller, and Norman Kerry. *The Unholy Three* (MGM, 1930), directed by Jack Conway; starring Lon Chaney, Lila Lee, and Elliott Nugent (or the MGM original [1925] directed by Tod Browning , which also starred Lon Chaney, and Mae Busch, Matt Moore). Chaney died on 26 August 1930. *Dracula* (Universal, 1931), directed by Tod Browning; staring Bela Lugosi, Helen Chandler, and David Manners.

[5]   [ALS]

August 21, 1931

My dear J V S:—

Still changing & re-changing fountain pens—it's a great life! Just now I've dug up some of the old steel pens that my mother used to use, & am writing this in the traditional dipping style. Next thing I'll be back to the quill—which, by the way, Lord Dunsany actually *does* use in all his original MSS. & correspondence.

Yes—Erich Zann was one of my unobtainables. I have only the copy in the W.T. file, & wouldn't let that out of the house for any amount. Under separate cover yesterday I shipped you a whole raft of old junk for leisurely perusal & ultimate return. Please be fanatically careful about the MSS., because most of them are almost torn & rotted to pieces, yet are in some cases my only lending copies. Putnam's manhandled my stuff frightfully—I ought to sue the cursed vandals for damages. A spoilt MS. is no joke with me, for I loathe typing so violently that I'd let a story be lost rather than copy it again. I'd like to soak those butter-fingered editors or readers $50.00 or $75.00 for stenographic expenses! The freshness of my indignation is due to the fact that I did not open the rejected bundle till yesterday, when getting some MSS. for you. When I saw the crumpled mass those divinely condemned sons of beech-nuts had left, I azured up the atmosphere with remarks that would have brought a blush to the leathern cheeks of the marine corps!

The Hammett anthology, I learn, is also to include Long's "Visitor from Egypt"—an excellent choice, though I wish they'd taken his "Black Druid" instead . . . . or as well.[1] If the book does well commercially, I suppose the John Day Co. would be a fairly logical place to send a collection of MSS.—though I'm so damn disgusted by the Putnam episode that I doubt if I'll send anything more out for a hell of a long while.

I didn't know you were so closely in touch with professional photographic standards. Surely, random snaps must look pretty crude to you! Talman, of course, is the most casual of amateurs with the kodak—though, oddly enough, he is an artist of sorts with pen & ink; having studied in his day at the R.I. School of Design. A couple of years ago—in exchange for revisory services on his MSS.—he did me a bookplate which I still think is a delightful specimen of its kind. I enclose one (needn't return) for your edification. It expresses my personality about as well as any design could—for (as I may or may not have mentioned to you) I am a natural-born *antiquarian* to an even greater extent than I am a weirdist. The ancient doorway represented is highly typical of the Old Providence whose colonial hill streets, Georgian steeples & fanlights, railed flights of steps, & cobbled lanes & courtyards formed the source of my earliest & most poignant impressions.[2] From earliest infancy I have been devoted to these dream-evoking reliques of yesterday—old houses, old wharves, old warehouses, old belfries, old vistas of sagging & weather-worn gambrel roofs—& it was only appropriate that my bookplate be symbolic of such things. Talman captured the spirit splendidly—& I think I'll have a new set of the plates on better paper when these are used up. Nowadays, also, many of my beloved pre-revolutionary scenes are succumbing to the destructive march of Babbittesque "progress"—it is appalling to reflect how many colourful old colonial neighbourhoods have been wiped out in the last five years. In other towns it is much the same, though a few old backwaters keep faithful to the traditional past. My chief delight is to visit old towns which preserve much of their quaint 18th century appearance—Quebec, Portsmouth N.H., Newburyport, Gloucester, Salem, Marblehead, Concord, Plymouth, New Bedford, Providence, Newport, Bristol, Wickford, New London, Deerfield, Kingston N.Y., Philadelphia (& Germantown), Annapolis, Alexandria, Fredericksburg, Williamsburg, Charleston, Savannah, St. Augustine, Key West, & so on. I'm hoping to get to Plymouth next Sunday. Quebec still gravely in doubt for 1931.

By the way—send one of your pictures along, if you have one to spare. How do you suppose the shock could injure me when I've looked at shots of myself & still live? My last formal photograph was taken 16 years ago . . . . in those days I looked merely vacuous instead of savage & melancholy.

I've never read Blackwood's "Education of Uncle Paul"—& think I've also missed some of the contents of "On the Edge". Sorry my glimpses of Chaney were so predominantly unrepresentative. I bought "Strange Tales" last Tuesday, but have not yet had a chance to read it through. Doesn't look over-promising to me, though the Smith tale (which I saw in MS. in a somewhat different form) is excellent. The original title of that was "The Return of Helman Carnby."[3] I think certain crudenesses toward the end are not of Smith's volition—but inserted (as diagrams for the dumb) at the command of Editor Bates. The reason Derleth doesn't contribute serious work to W.T. is that his serious work isn't at all in the weird vein. He places some of it in such select "intelligentsia" sheets as "This Quarter"—published by American expatriates in Paris. When I say that Derleth will soon lead all the rest of the "gang" I speak seriously & advisedly. He has a profundity, seriousness, simplicity, & human insight that none of the rest of us can even begin to duplicate. In comparison with his promise-laden sketches my own tales are the superficial tinsel of a played-out never-was. My stuff represents the last thin output of a small-timer who has nothing fresh in reserve—but Derleth is a mine of ideas & crystallised experiences just beginning to yield abundantly. His only peril is that his incessant pot-boiling may subtly & unperceivedly pollute his genuine aesthetic work—just as Wright's goddam insistence on obvious plots has insidiously given some of my work a naive & rather cheap twist without my knowing it. But so far he has kept the work of his right & left hands astonishingly separate & dissimilar.

Your "Shuddering Embrace" sounds decidedly interesting, though some critics would suggest that you lay the macabre pigments on a little less thickly. When horror is rubbed in so violently, it sometimes loses the fresh emotional effect which it has when more sparingly & scientifically employed. It is, in a word, sometimes better to hint at a terrible thing in a glancing objective way—using relatively commonplace language—than to comb Roget's Thesaurus for striking & mouth-filling daemoniac adjectives. It is one of my own faults to pile on the gloom & terror so thickly that the reader tends to react against such resonant verbiage, & to lose the sense of pseudo-reality as connected with the tale in question. You'll do more poetry yet. I'll send along an Abbott-Trabue test when I dig one up from my files. Moe's book will be great when it appears. Glad you've seen Klarkash-Ton's "Ebony & Crystal" & Lurking Fear sketches. I'll shew you some of his grotesque heads quite shortly.

     As regards isolation & worldly inexperience—I am almost in the class with you & Long myself, & was quite so till well along in my twenties. I was virtually an invalid—a nervous wreck with a thousand subsidiary weaknesses—in childhood, & never really got on my feet physically till I was thirty. Nor was my emergence from hermitage ever very complete. I did, surely enough, break away from belated juvenility enough to travel around independently so far as waning finances allowed; & to meet different people in person where previously I had conversed only through correspondence—but this long-deferred semi-introduction to the world did not "take" as thoroughly as it might have done had I been chronologically younger. The era of expansion & late-dawn was a relatively brief one, & was followed by a sort of slow drift back to the hermit patterns of my early days. Vistas faded & contracted, & the glitter of adventurous expectancy receded farther & farther—till at length I saw the wider horizons fall off one by one. Before I knew it, I was virtually back in my shell. Came to hate New York, whither I had moved, like poison; & was back in Old Providence in 2 years & 3 months from the time I started out. Old age tells—you can't be flexible & expansive when the chill of the thirties gets into your bones. That's why I hope Sonny Belknap will break away from mamma's apron-strings before it's too late for him to enjoy a sense of freedom. To think the little rascal will be *thirty* next April

. . . . . & he seems like a kid of about 17 emotionally! However—I can't say that my own return to a final senile hermitage has been altogether complete. Enough remains of the faded expansion period to make me keep up my occasional antiquarian journeys, & to visit congenially with such members of "the gang", new & old, as may reside along my routes. That much is surely net gain from the total stagnation of my early twenties! I fancy you'll achieve a reasonable independence soon enough to avoid a static & devitalised old age—heaven knows you have time enough! Incidentally—your self-portrait looks very interesting, & is far better than anything I could ever draw. I haven't a fundamental grain of pictorial talent, though I wish like hades I had. A drawing of myself by myself would have to be something like the accompanying enormity—which succeeds

I really look worse than this.

H. P. Lovecraft —
On his 41st Birthday
— Aug. 20, 1931
(recognisable, if at all, by the nose.)

marvellously in looking like nobody I ever saw in or out of the
mirror. I might get a job drawing portraits for Wonder Stories. Your "Lurking Fear" scene
is very vivid—better than I
could do, as witness the following. I dodge the job of drawing
any of the *Things*, but concentrate on what was revealed inside the hut—how the narrator
learned what had occurred. On
the whole, I doubt if Mr. Senf,
with all his faults, has a serious
rival in me. Not every would-be
lit'ry guy can hope to become
his own illustrator as William

" ... there was no longer a face "

Blake was, & as Klarkash-Ton may some day become. But you still have
youth—so who shall set a boundary to your iconographical evolution?

I have seen miscellaneous things—reviews &c—by Stanton A. Coblen[t]z,
but don't think I've read any of his "Scientifiction", ironic or otherwise. Klarkash-
Ton has sent me the W.S. with "City of the Singing Flame", & I think the pictorial work is not at all bad. I have just finished reading the unpublished sequel, "Beyond the Singing Flame",[4] & hope it will gain acceptance from Herr
Gernsback. It is very good as sequels go—& has a cataclysmic climax of highly remarkable character. "At the Mountains of Madness" will reach you before long. Keep it as long as you like, & then send it on to

R. H. Barlow, Fort Benning, Georgia

It's getting quite a circulation in spite of Bre'r Farnsworth. Hope it won't
bore you. To think I typed all those *115* pages! Well, at any rate, Wright didn't
mangle the MS. the way Putnam's did my other effusions. The boy has his
good points! About "The Strange High House"—you are right. Farny turned
it down soon after its completion, & did not experience a change of heart till
years & years later. He is cursedly fickle—Derleth sometimes sends stuff in
repeatedly & gets it accepted the 3d or 4th time. I've only tried that game
once—& unsuccessfully—with "The Nameless City." My policy is to wait till
he asks himself.

"The Stranger with Blue Spectacles" seems to start out very promising-
ly—though of course the setting is of a type frequently used. Be careful about
your linguistic details. For instance—you oughtn't to say "a task *to quail* the
bravest heart", for *quail* is not a transitive verb, but an intransitive verb mean-

ing *to sink under fear.* You'd better say "a task to make the bravest heart quail." And beware of trite phrases—& of words chosen for sound or visual impressiveness rather than for necessary meaning. The best style is the plainest style. Very few can get away with the bizarre vocabulary of Clark Ashton Smith .... he doesn't always get away with it himself! "Strange Things Lie in Caves" is a splendid story title—& so is "That Which Crossed the Gulf." Keep it up! and live up to the title in the text!

Well—now to make another try for a fountain pen!

Hoping that the miscellaneous loaned junk sent yesterday may not totally asphyxiate you before you're through with it,

I remain

Yrs most cordially & sincerely,
H P Lovecraft

[P.S. on envelope] Thanks for the birthday reminder which just arrived! The years do fly!!

Notes

1. Frank Belknap Long, "A Visitor from Egypt" (*WT,* September 1930); "The Black Druid" (*WT,* July 1930).

2. Whereas Talman's view is of a closed doorway from the outside, HPL's original conception was of a view looking out through an open door (with fanlight) at a "tangle of ancient roofs & belfries on the hillside"—an actual view of a Providence scene—so similar to the scenes about which HPL rhapsodized in his letters and captured in his fiction.

3. CAS, "The Return of the Sorcerer" (orig. "Halman Carnby"), *Strange Tales* (September 1931).

4. "Beyond the Singing Flame" (orig. "The Secret of the Flame"), *Wonder Stories* (November 1931).

[6]   [AHT]

August 28, 1931

[. . .]

It is the fantaisiste's business to give latitude to the single emotion of cosmic rebellion, & other emotions must be introduced only in an ancillary capacity. Naturally, these things must be handled accurately so far as they legitimately figure in the tale—but none of them must usurp the supremacy which belongs to the major emotion chosen.

[. . .]

Our experiences and tastes are very largely dictated by forces beyond our control, and . . . it is the part of good sense to improve the narrow gifts one has, rather than flounder after greater gifts which are not natural to one. Of course, no one without wide experience & sympathies should ever try to write *general* literature. But the minor special field of the fantastic is somewhat more modest in its requirements, so that those with curtailed outlooks can occasionally 'get by' fairly adequately. It is their best bet to stick to the one thing they *can* do, rather than waste time reaching out for wider laurels—for such belated reachings generally end in vain tragedy or absurdity. Of course, it is not self-flattering to admit that one is skilled only in a minor field—but the wise man accepts reality as it is and makes the best of it. He finds he can do better by intensively cultivating his small garden-plot & pushing its qualitative development to the limit, than by trying to branch out & annex a bigger plot than he can properly cultivate. Better a fair-sized frog in a small puddle, than an invisible frog in a big puddle. . . . I know damn well that I have not the equipment for general or realistic writing, and I have never been fool enough to attempt such.

[. . .]

I deny likewise that "The Colour Out of Space" represents even approximately the limit to which my literary mood can be pushed. It may indeed represent the best that I, personally, will ever do; since I am now on the declining side of forty and without the incentives and adventurous expectancy of a younger man. But it is absurd to think of this trifle as representing the ultimate development of the mood which gave it birth. Given greater skill & energy, one with the selfsame mood of revolt against terrestrial limitations could weave a phantasy a thousand times more potent in its symbolism, more graphically opulent in its illustrative details, more movingly intense in its suspense, and more ingeniously extensive and profound in its conception and depiction of bizarre, non-terrestrial, unhackneyed, and imaginatively liberating cosmic vistas and conditions. . . . I could have done far better myself if I had steadily stuck to the weird genre from boyhood, and not allowed myself to be sidetracked to science in my teens and to poetry in my twenties.

[. . .]

In a way, a love of the past is not a bad thing; for when a man gets on in years and no longer has the possibility of fresh vistas and novel experiences, the past is about all he has left. Then, if he already have a taste for it, he will not have so bad a wrench as the chap who has lived excitingly in the present and feels lost when crowded out of stimulating contact with youth and its typical perspectives.

[. . .]

The essence of basic masculinity, I think, is a certain stark truthfulness & uncompromisingness of perspective—a superiority to the trivial aspects of things which makes one scorn surface frills & enables one to survey the purposeless chaos of life with a genuine (though not necessarily obtrusive or aggressive) 'don't-give-a-damn' attitude. This is a long way from cheaply external 'hard-boiledness'—for it includes the quiet dignity and sense of proportion of the *gentleman* as well as the stamina and inflexibility of the 'rough guy'—and I think it is as much a matter of mental philosophy as of daily demeanour. . . . I think I've always been reasonably masculine, but I never had any burning ambition to be a sport or prize-fighter. I don't smoke, because I don't like tobacco; and I don't drink, because I feel a disgust at the pollution of mental development inherent in intoxication. There isn't any mincing sissification in such lines of procedure, however. I do as I do because that is my preference; and if anybody doesn't like it he can to go hell. . . . I lack the competitive or sporting instinct altogether, and am bored by all games, athletic or sedentary. Football or backgammon—it's all the same to me. Just one long yawn. Neither can I dance, swim or drive a car; though I may conceivably remedy the two latter defects in my old age's later stages. In fact, I would certainly learn to drive if I had the cash for a car. Talking is a thing I seem to practice in cycles. In youth I was garrulous, then came a reserved, laconic period, and in middle age—with the improved health of my thirties—I became garrulous again. Now, with the forties, I am tending to lapse into a decorous reserve once more—except on paper.

[. . .]

Your longing to see New York would probably abate after a year there. The tall towers are very delightful on the skyline at a good distance—and that's about all there is to it. The rest is a tawdry mess of mixed garishness and squalor—confused, foreign, backgroundless, and without any of the beauty and repose of smaller places. One becomes starved for the sight of green vegetation and gentle, quiet, natural things. It's all right to visit briefly—its museums, libraries, &c. are undeniable advantages—but as a residence it's no place for a white man. In general, I think you'll find that's true of all large cities and their noise. They have a great attraction when one *isn't* there, but on attainment soon pall. That is true, indeed, of most things in life. What we really enjoy is always the adventurous expectancy—seldom the realisation. The light, music, & glamour of a great town certainly have a definite and genuine place in life, but are best taken in small doses. And as one grows older, on wants the doses smaller and smaller. What is really enchanting about such glamour is not any quality intrinsic to it, but merely the sense of expansion and liberation surrounding it. When we get too used to it, the aura of expansion and liberation disappears—and then we have to look for something new. My choice of a residential site would be a quaint small town with natural beauty and historic continuity at their maximum. Then I would visit a city perhaps twice a year or less. . . . that is, apart from frequent scenic and antiquarian travels which would naturally take me briefly through various cities now and then.

[. . .]

Glad you find my epistles readable. They are another phase of my antiquarianism; for as you know, the art of letter-writing was assiduously cultivated in my favourite 18th century. . . . I do, undoubtedly, spend a reprehensible amount of time on correspondence—so much that I really haven't time to do the serious writing and revising I ought to be attending to. It would, however, take an unprofitable amount of effort to break a habit so strongly ingrained. I can hardly count the number of correspondents I have—including the long-interval ones as well as the rapid-fire ones. They must, in all, run between 50 & 75. Ten or fifteen are voluminous debaters on various themes—and in general, I dare say this interchange of ideas does considerable to abate the narrowness I might otherwise acquire from my sequestered existence.

[. . .]

Now for that 25 pp. of typing. Farewell, O circumambient world of sunlight of flowers . . . into the depths.

[. . .]

[7]   [AHT]

September 3, 1931

[. . .]

As for the autobiographical type of novel—that is probably the one exception to the foregoing rule. Probably every reasonably intelligent and artistic person could write an aesthetically tolerable (though not necessarily commercially acceptable) tale based on his own personal history; for in this case knowledge is adequate, while egotism supplies the driving urge. However, this one book would ordinarily mean nothing in the writer's future—except as an exercise in style. He would remain an *homo unius libri*,[1] without the slightest added capacity to project himself into other personalities and reflect types of temperament and experience alien to himself. What is more, even his one book would be likely to suffer from grotesque disproportions, and absurd misinterpretations of human nature in characters differing from the writer. The one thing this kind of writer sometimes manages to do is to write himself up over and over again under slightly varied exteriors—creating a stock character based on himself. But all this is very tedious and cheap; and I feel so little inclination to do it, that I am certain the result would be tame and commercially unacceptable.

[. . .]

I like "Dagon" because I believe there is something fundamentally and intensely terrifying in the notion of a great land area upheaved from the nighted and immemorial deep. The unnaturalness of such a land, with its aeon-old sea-secrets upthrust to the sun of a virtually alien world, is to me about as poignant as anything within imaginative experience. That's why I value the *theme* of Dagon, though of course I didn't even begin to do it justice. "God—that hand—the window! The window!"

[. . .]

The 18th century is a favourite age of mine through sheer circumstance—largely because it represented a period different from the 19th century in which I was born and which I always bitterly hated for its hypocrisy & affectation. Then, too, I am sensitive to architectural values—& the architecture of the 18th century represents an infinitely high level as opposed to the monstrosities and puerilities of Victorianism. Also—its literature is classical and rational in tone, as opposed to the hollow and florid sentimentality of 19th century literature. To me the ancient hill with its Georgian spires and doorways joined with the ancient long-f'd books in the family library to represent an ideal world of escape from the intolerable ugliness of the 1890's. Costume in the 18th century—which could be as simple as one might choose—excelled the grotesque scarecrowism of the 19th century as day excels night. I wish right now that I could have on a good suit of dark velvet with smallclothes, silver buttons, & plain powdered periwig. There was a degree of taste around 1770 or 1780 which has never been parallelled since.

[. . .]

The only way to know the past is to read of it from many angles—including its own records and literature—and to become familiar at first hand with the tangible objects connected with it—houses, books, furniture, landscape, utensils, &c. &c. &c. To me, who have lived a lifetime amidst the accumulated deposits of an old and settled civilisation, the past is even more real than the dazzling, mutable, & evanescent present. I am most at home in the Newport or Philadelphia or Charleston of 1760.

[. . .]

I used to be damnably noisy myself—humming & whistling—but quieted down a decade or so ago.

[. . .]

Heyward's "Half Pint Flask"[2] is very fine—about the only weird tale about another race that ever fascinated me. Ordinarily voodoo & Yogi stuff leaves me cold, for I can't feel enough closeness to savage or other non-Caucasian magic.

[. . .]

Hugh Walpole is a little thin for my taste.

[. . .]

An isolated or otherwise unique character probably encounters a bit of friction in college at the start; but before long he tends to expand & mellow unconsciously—so that the experience is worth the trouble in the end. There's nothing like getting oriented to the surrounding scene, fully and easily. That's something, however, which I could never quite accomplish. It's a good thing that you have an antithesis for a close friend. I used to have some very dissimilar intimates, who gave me second-hand linkages with the actual outside world, but with the years most of these friendships have gradually atrophied for lack of any enduring raison d'etre. Most of my friends, therefore, date from my middle period—say 15 years ago—when I gave up trying to be 'broad' and began to limit my contacts to people with whom I really had something tangible and interesting to discuss.

[. . .]

No—I'd never take to bridge, because I haven't the energy to puzzle my poor old head over irrelevant & unmotivated problems. I have tried chess—but couldn't summon enough interest to make real efforts to win. The fact is, I'm not an 'intellectual' in any sense. *I don't like to think*—the process of mental concentration is uninviting & fatiguing to me unless that process tends toward the satisfaction of curiosity—toward extending my perception out into the black, unknown void. Thus all diversions based on the pleasure of abstract thought's sake are futile and wearisome to me. I want to save my thinking for serious, coördinated realities which have some significance in the problem of entity, and which therefore hold for me a real interest & dramatic value. It is impossible for me to experience the sensation of interest in connexion with any arbitrary and artificial set of conditions—trivial, unmotivated arrangements without any natural origin or meaning—such as constitute the basis of games and puzzles. But of course if I had more energy—physical, and the mental that goes with the physical—I might have a wholly different attitude. It is really unfortunate to be of such limited energy—though I really have more now than when I was younger. Racking headaches are much less frequent than in youth, and my powers of pedestrian endurance have become so marked as to cast my boyhood bicycling achievements quite into the shade.

[. . .]

As for *music*—I'm not sure but that your parents are right in discouraging lessons on your part, for the nervous strain really is tremendous. I speak as one who has been through the mill—for I began the violin at 7. By the time I was 9 the close application had played hell with my nerves, and the doctor told my mother that the now hateful lessons would have to stop. A psychologist might draw highly interesting conclusions from the rapidity with which I forgot all my musical acquirements. Today I can't [read] music, and couldn't play three premeditated notes on a fiddle! What is more—the incident permanently destroyed any real taste for good music, so that in later youth I had (&—gawd 'elp me—still have!) an utterly Babbitt-like set of harmonic predilections. In 1897 I was trying for Beethoven—but by 1900 I was whistling the popular coon songs & musical comedies of the day. A whole phase of aesthetic experience had become closed to me.

[. . .]

The Eyrie fans[3] are for the most part a sorry lot—their caprices being beyond all explanation. It always makes me crawl and wonder what's the matter with me when they give a thing of mine the popularity vote . . . thus grouping it with the work of their precious Quinn, Dyalhis, Kline, &c.

[. . .]

I don't think I like the patchwork cinema technique at all. It was evolved through the unlimited opportunities for change of visual setting afforded by the camera, and worked well as long as the films were silent and trivial. But I can't stomach it for serious spoken plays. Impressions shift too quickly to sink in, and the lifelikeness of a snatch of speech is curtailed by the lack of content or continuity. The Elizabethan drama had fragmentary scenes like that—but you can see how posterity has had to eliminate them from effective acting versions. This snatchiness was the only fault I had to find with "Cimarron" last winter.[4]

[. . .]

I doubt if I'll try any MSS. on any book publisher for some time now—indeed, I'm about convinced that the early junk isn't fit to print without a more thorough revision than I have time to give at present. I wouldn't want any introduction. The tales are what they are, and it's up to the reader to make his own comments. This modern preface mania makes me tired.

Notes

1. "A man of one book."
2. A ghost story by Dubose Heyward.
3. Contributors to the letters column of *WT*.
4. *Cimarron* (RKO, 1931), directed by Wesley Ruggles (uncredited); starring Richard Dix, Irene Dunne, and Estelle Taylor. Based on the novel by Edna Ferber.

[8]   [ANS]

[no date; c. early September 1931]

Another chap just returned the enclosed. And yesterday I sent you the privately printed magazine containing my long article on Supernatural Horror in Literature. You can keep that magazine if it is of any really permanent interest to you—but if it is destined for the waste basket, I'll be glad to serve as such. I have about 6 duplicates.

May have to go to Brattleboro, Vermont, later this month to do a job of revision for the Stephen Daye Press there—a book of about 500 pages. If it were July I'd welcome the jaunt; but in September it is quite another matter. I'm trying to persuade them to have it done by mail—which is really possible, if they only knew it.

Of the enclosed yarns, Polaris was written in 1918 & The Picture in 1920. The odd thing about Polaris is that despite the apparently Dunsanian style I had never read a line of Dunsany when I wrote it.

Find that my "House of Souls" is lent to somebody else, but will send it eventually. I'll try to let you see "Three Impostors", "John Silence", & some Dunsany before long. Regards—

H P L

[9]   [ALS]

Septr. 8, 1931

Dear J V:—

Thanks for the safe return of material—& for the pleasing photograph, which goes at once into my choicest gallery. You surely have no legitimate complaint to make against old Ma Nature for the set of features
handed you—& one may add that the photography forms an excellent testimonial to the artistic accomplishments of your revered parent.

The juvenilia—which I return herewith—proved highly interesting, &
displays an enviable degree of thoughtfulness & scholarship. You surely have
a good panoramic grasp of history, & the amount of erudition in the "soul"
poem is quite appalling! The estimate of Book 6 of the Æneid shews great
penetration, analysis, & general taste—though you err in assuming the doctrine of metempsychosis to be essentially modern. It had extremely ancient
eastern—Hindoo—sources, & was adopted by Pythagoras & so introduced
to the western world. There are plenty of places where the Mantuan swain
could have picked it up.[1]

The "soul" poem[2] reveals a cosmic imagination which justifies the adoption of a poetic medium, but you doubtless realise that your scheme of verse
has not the rhythm & regularity essential to successful form. Also—that your
language (occasionally careless & inaccurate) is essentially the statement-
language of prose rather than the picture-&-symbol-language of real poetry. It
is hard to make good poetry of didactic verse—the secret seems to have died
with Lucretius & Virgil. The short poems also reveal an imagination worth
cultivating—though they likewise indicate the need of technical improvement. I feel free in calling attention to defects because of the early date of the
specimens. They are certainly remarkable enough when the author's age is
considered—a highly promising augury for the future.

Still turned out of house & home by the steamfitters, but the woods &
fields are always there. When it is too cold or rainy to work outdoors, I take
my work to the vacant flat of my younger aunt, who is still away (brrr . . .) at
Ogunquit, Maine. Speaking of the arctic—I've arranged to do that Vermont
job[3] by mail at home, thank Gawd!

Took a walk to Attleboro, Mass. yesterday—about 12 to 15 miles. Countryside very attractive, with no visual signs of autumn as yet. But I could use
about 20° more heat!

Best wishes—
          H P L

Notes

1. HPL refers to Virgil (P. Vergilius Maro, 70–19 B.C.E.), author of the *Aeneid*, who
was said to have been born near the Italian city of Mantua.

2. "What Is the Soul?" (nonextant; see Introduction).

3. HPL presumably refers to his light revision of Leon Burr Richardson's *History of Dartmouth College* (1932), a job given to HPL by Vrest Orton of the Stephen Daye Press (Brattleboro, VT).

[10]   [ALS]

Septr 13, 1931

Dear J V S:—

Glad you survived the three additional tales. That just about finishes the list of sendable yarns—though I'll try to dig up a copy of the rhymed "Psychopompos" some day. As for the dreamlike Dunsanian style—I don't think I do very well in it myself, but believe it can be exceedingly powerful when handled by the right workman—such as Dunsany himself. I have heard of the new Dunsany volume,[1] & shall read it if possible—though I've seen some of the tales in separate magazine form. I don't think Dunsany's new work can compare with what he did about 20 years ago—you'll see what I mean when I lend you "A Dreamer's Tales." By the way—was the "Book of Wonder" you saw the Modern Library edition or the standard edition with the Sime illustrations? If the latter, I shall lend you mine—which is the former—since that edition includes "Time & the Gods" which the other does not. Just as soon as those damned steamfitters clear out of here I shall set my disordered room to rights & begin the 1931–32 lending season! As for the "Strange High House"—I hardly thought you would like it, though Derleth rates it as the 3d best thing I have ever done. For my part, I rate it the best of my Dunsanian attempts, but think that all of these attempts belong quite a way down the scale. You don't appear to value atmospheric subtlety greatly— as witness your indifference to "The Willows" & "Seaton's Aunt", & to the Dunsanian style generally—hence would naturally prefer the other & more quasi-realistic phase of my efforts.

Glad you liked the article—which you can keep if it's of any permanent use to you. Whether I'll ever expand it is a question. It would take loads of time & energy—& I surely shan't attempt it if any other good work of the kind exists. I must somehow get hold of a copy of Scarborough's "Supernatural in English Fiction" & see what it's like.

Good luck with "The Earth Taint"—but don't hope too highly regarding Bates. Beginners have far more chance with the Shylock Gernsback outfit— chance to "land", that is, not chance of getting prompt or adequate remuneration. Good luck, too, with "Brother & Sister"—though you naturally realise how little chance anything has with a "quality" magazine unless the style is extremely mature & polished. I have never submitted any piece of mine to a first-rate magazine, since my sense of proportion tells me how inadequate my style is.

Yes—that sundial phrase "It is later than you think" certainly seems to form a fine idea for a horror tale. Why not go to it & see what you can develop? Also—go ahead & give Klarkash-Ton a writeup for "Fantasy". I could never get around to it.

I haven't read "The Openers of the Gate", but will keep it in mind.[2] As for an anthology—I don't believe I could ever place one if I did try to assemble it. Some day I may compile a list of favourite weird stories for the benefit of anybody else who wants to edit an anthology—& heading it will be M. P. Shiel's "House of Sounds". It's a crime that that tale is not in available form. Harré almost put it in "Beware After Dark", but the publishers said it was too long.

I have never been in the Dismal Swamp region[3]—my farthest south in tidewater Virginia being historic Jamestown. Coaches bound southward cut inland to Danville & Winston-Salem N.C. Some day, though, I hope to do Virginia more thoroughly—going to Norfolk, & seeing old St. Luke's church in Isle of Wight Co.—built in 1632 & the oldest building of English workmanship on this continent. I can well understand the weird spell of a great swamp region, & wish I knew one well enough to write about it. A man I met in Dunedin last spring came from Georgia, & told me that in his opinion the vast Okefanokee Swamp there is the most spectral region in America. There are brick ruins on islands quite well within the swamp, about which almost anything might be imagined. The Florida Everglades also offer distinct possibilities, & I was sorry not to be able to penetrate them to any extent during my recent travels.

As for your novel—the longer you wait about it, the better it will be. It is astonishing how a few added years of life—with their accretions in point of education & experience—change one's estimates of the things one has *apparently* understood before. Characters, motivations, values, &c., all alter in the light of enlarged perspective. What is more, I doubt if you can fully reflect the present till you shed some of your contempt for the past. No person, place, or set of institutions is anything except the product of antecedent influences; nor is there any drama or interest in any thing or event except in relation to the continuous & unending time-stream. The best novels are those which possess the quality of pageantry—tracing the experiences & reactions of a group or line through several generations, as in Galsworthy's saga of the Forsytes. Early writing, to be effective, ought to deal with relatively simple events & emotions within the experience of the author. Its main value is in perfecting style—& you of course realise how vast an amount of care & practice is needed to transform the average beginner's ponderous, verbally uncertain prose into the accurate, assured, flexible, & emotionally vivid medium of the mature & accomplished author. As the writer lives longer, observes & reads more widely, & undergoes a wider & wider range of experiences, the area of material which he is competent to treat increases rapidly. But of course each individual will always have his special aptitudes, so that some one direction will be better suited to his progress than any other. It is his business during the formative & experimental years to find out what this direction is—then, afterward, to follow it assiduously; though with a broad recognition of general life which may serve to prevent specialisation from degenerating into narrowness or disproportion. Some writers need to specialise more closely than others, while a fortunate few stand at the opposite extreme & find themselves able to do justice to an unusual variety of moods & phases of life. I, unhappily, belong in the former class—& only time can tell you which class is yours. At the present stage, your best policy will be to try everything you feel like trying—meanwhile working constantly to make your style fluent, musical, graphic, & precise. When you find your rightful promise, be content with it; & don't regret your inability to write like somebody else whose province is different. Especially, don't regret your inability to write a "Bridge of San Luis Rey."[4] That book is clever & striking, but undeniably artificial & in places even mawkish. It was absurdly overrated upon its appearance, & now seems to be receding into something more like its proper niche. Derleth swears by it—but I don't admire his general critical opinions quite so much as I admire his own serious work. I hope you can manage to get to college this fall—though of course no harm will be done if you have to wait another half-year or year. I feel sure, from the experience of most of my friends, that you will find it a great broadener of perspective—& believe I would have been much less narrow in abilities & limited in interests had health permitted me to go in 1908. You ought to be thankful for your health—fancy anyone who has never had a headache! Your walking probably helps to keep you in trim—I am sure that mine does much to prevent me from lapsing into the semi-invalidism of my 1908–1920 period. In boyhood I was a constant bicycle rider—which both exercised me & helped me to see more of the countryside than most people saw in those pre-motor-touring days. I couldn't do much long-distance walking till about the year 1924, but by that time built up an ability to cover surprising distances without fatigue. Last Monday I took a walk—purely for pleasure—to the neighbouring town of Attleboro, Mass., a matter of about 12 or 13 miles; riding home on the 'bus for chronological reasons rather than because of weariness. Walking is really the only way in which to see the countryside at its best; for automobiles are much too swift—& too narrowly confined to recognised highways. And as for exploring a *city*—I'll go so far as to say that *nothing* but pedestrianism is of any value whatever. But I'd surely have a car for long-distance runs if I could afford one. Too bad your initial bad luck has stalled your motor education! Sooner or later, though, I'm sure you'll get a chance to learn driving. Many nervous people, though, refuse to drive. Frank B. Long won't learn, & another friend of mine says he'll never get a car till he can afford a chauffeur. I imagine, though, that even these timid souls would get along all right if they would stick largely to country roads & avoid driving on congestion-breeding Sundays & holidays. Music is another thing which you can probably take up later as well as now. If the urge to do so continues, it would probably pay you to follow it. I don't think I was ever deeply or basically musical. If I had been, the early violin practice would never have worn so badly on my nerves. Writing practice didn't annoy me in the least—in fact, the more crude things I wrote & tore up the more I wanted to write. Prose was obviously my natural medium for expressing whatever I had to express—& it is worth remarking that James Branch Cabell says that a natural prose writer cannot be musical, & vice versa.

In the matter of vocations, it's pretty hard to give really intelligent & effective advice. During your four years of college you'll probably acquire many new vistas which will aid you in deciding maturely. Journalism isn't much of an asset for the careful, artistic writer; though it does enhance one's chances for quick popular success by inculcating a direct, incisive style & giving a wide array of glimpses into highly diverse aspects of human nature. It is essentially a field for the naturally worldly & gregarious person, & would be unthinkable for myself—& probably for you as well. All told, I'd be inclined to favour education as a career for one of your obvious tastes—& you might find a college instructorship devoid of many of the drawbacks attending high-school teaching. That is what young Wandrei has—at his alma mater, the U. of Minn. When a student specialises in educational subjects, his university generally aids him in securing a position. No—I never worked in a bookshop, although a surprisingly large percentage of my friends do. It is a good business for a literarily inclined person; for the day's routine often brings pleasant bookish conversations, & sometimes new acquaintances of permanence & value. I'd like to land a job of that sort—though it would have to be a minor one, since I don't know books from the bibliophile's standpoint—first editions, commercial values, rare items, & all that. The fact is, I'm distinctly bored by such formal, artificial, & essentially non-literary bibliophily. But when a man does have this specialised knowledge—as my friends Kirk, Leeds, Loveman, & Orton do—there is no limit to the extent they can progress in the field of bookselling. Kirk has his own business, & Loveman gets $60.00 per week as an expert cataloguer for the well-known N.Y. firm of Dauber & Pine.

As for bridge—I doubt I could become any more interested in it than in any other game. It may not be difficult—but I mentioned at the outset that the easy games bore me just as much as the exacting ones, even if they don't tax my energy. They consume time—& at my age one begins to count the moments! I lack some psychological twist which gives the majority their interest in the uncertain or competitive element of sports. It's all the same to me whether I or the other guy wins. What of it? The very artificiality of a game makes the empty act of winning devoid of all significance for me. I can't make an authentic motivation of it . . . . can't see where the fun comes in. And because of this inescapable sense of emptiness, I always resent the expenditure of time & energy on games. Whenever I used to be dragged into them, I always fretted because I wasn't free to be doing something else that I really wanted to do—& nowadays, heaven knows, I need every second I can spare from revision for the profusion of things awaiting performance! I'll get interested in bridge about the time you get interested in colonial architecture & archaeology . . . . . de gustibus non disputandum est.

Your idea of a subterranean land upheaved to the day in a crowded community is very good—so good that I think you ought to develop it yourself. Don't get your expectations up about the "Mountains of Madness", for you'll almost certainly dislike it. You tend to call a story "verbose" when the author uses subtle precision in building up the necessary nuances. The words required to convey the exact mood—being more numerous than those which a more action plot would demand—tend to seem superfluous to you; hence your impatient verdict. My antarctic tale is largely a series of atmospheric pictures, so that it will almost undoubtedly impress you as a flood of needless language. Still—you'll probably want to see it for yourself. A card from you might accelerate Dwyer a bit—though perhaps the 22¢ postage embarrasses him . . . . . his finances being in a desperate state just now.

You & Klarkash-Ton shall both see the original "Moon Pool" in due course of time. I wrote him about it the other day. I have never read "Through the Dragon Glass".[5] If you want to ask J. O. Bailey about his scientifictional history,[6] you can probably reach him with the address *Chapel Hill, N.C.* There is a box number, but I can't recall or find any record of it. Yes—I think Prof. Scarborough once edited a weird anthology including "The Willows", but I never saw it.[7] About Derleth's new tales—I like both "The Thing that Walked on the Wind" & "They Shall Rise in Great Numbers['] very much.[8] The latter has defects—especially in details of the way the student-narrator recognises the old mad physician from book & portrait—but as a whole it has the requisite shudder.

Thanks for the A.S. letter, which interested me greatly. The scientifiction magazines do keep on a discouragingly low & hackneyed level, as an article in the Writers' Digest pointed out last spring. I have never sent anything to *Amazing* since the "Colour", for the simple reason that none of my later things have been scientifictional. I may eventually try the "Mountains" on them—surely your letter keeps me in their minds in a most favourable light!

Thanks, too, for the reading recommendations—which I'll keep in mind & follow as opportunities present themselves. As for Charles Dexter Ward— no, he doesn't exactly take the old wizard's place in the grave, but nevertheless he is not among the survivors at the end of the story. That tale is due for a rewriting some day—a rewriting which may condense it to about the length of "Mountains".

I am surprised to hear of so many meritorious cinema films now current. "Street Scene" is here now, & I meant to see it on the strength of the play's reputation; but I let "An American Tragedy" go by (though it will return to dozens of small houses) because Dreiser himself is reported to have disavowed the film as cheap & untrue to the spirit of the original novel.[9] As for the fragmentary quality of the cinema—I will admit, in agreement with you, that it does have the one advantage of overcoming the stage's defect of overcrowded & unnaturally grouped action; but must still complain that in many cinemas the isolated glimpses are too brief to allow conversation to get under way & produce a coherent emotional impression. It was all right when the glimpses were merely visual, but oral speech has a certain unconscious form & rhythm which robs very short snatches of their full emotional value. However, let me concede that a good share of my reaction is sheer prejudice—due to the fact that I was brought up on the legitimate theatre before there was any such thing as a cinema—except for travel reels used to chase out the audiences between performances of Keith's continuous vaudeville.[10] I suppose some compromise in methods of arrangement can ultimately be worked out by the producers of films—allowing for a reasonable flexibility of scene while avoiding too brief & disjointed snatches of dialogue. One film I found excellent was "Anna Christie"—a year & a half ago—but of course that had a good deal of the continuous text of the original play. But the fragmentary quality did grate on me in both "All Quiet" & "Cimarron".[11]

I'll have to try a Shea-ffer pen some time—but now that I'm loaded up with two Watermans I guess I'll make my next move a wholesale point-exchanging orgy when I can get around to the Boston home office of that company. Best wishes—

Yr obt h[ble] Servt H P L

Notes

1. Lord Dunsany, *The Travel Tales of Mr. Joseph Jorkens*.

2. Elizabeth Louisa Moresby, who wrote under the name L[ily] Adams Beck (1862–1931), *The Openers of the Gate: Stories of the Occult* (New York: Cosmopolitan Book Co., 1930).

3. The Great Dismal Swamp lies along the coast between Norfolk, VA, and Elizabeth City, NC.

4. A novel by Thornton Wilder. It won the Pulitzer Prize.

5. A. Merritt, "Through the Dragon Glass" (*All-Story Weekly*, 24 November 1917).

6. J. O. Bailey of the University of North Carolina wrote to HPL on 16 June 1930 concerning a history of science fiction that he was writing. Bailey's *Pilgrims through Time and Space* (1947) was the first academic study of science fiction.

7. Dorothy Scarborough, ed., *Famous Modern Ghost Stories* (New York: Putnam, 1931).

8. "The Thing That Walked on the Wind" (*Strange Tales,* January 1933), and with Marc Schorer, "They Shall Rise" (*WT,* April 1936).

9. *Street Scene* (United Artists, 1931), directed by King Vidor; starring Sylvia Sidney, William Collier, Jr., and Estelle Taylor. Based on a play by Elmer Rice. *An American Tragedy* (Paramount, 1931), directed by Josef von Sternberg; starring Phillips Holmes, Sylvia Sidney, and Frances Dee. Based on the novel by Theodore Dreiser.

10. Benjamin Franklin Keith (1846–1914), theatrical impresario generally credited with the creation of vaudeville in America.

11. *Anna Christie* (MGM, 1930), directed by Clarence Brown; starring Greta Garbo, Charles Bickford, and George F. Marion. Based on the play by Eugene O'Neill. *All Quiet on the Western Front* (Universal, 1930), directed by Lewis Milestone; starring Louis Wolheim, Lew Ayres, and John Wray. Based on the novel by Erich Maria Remarque.

[11]   [AHT]

September 18, 1931

[. . .]

To make a fictional marvel wear the momentary aspect of exciting fact, we must give it the most elaborate possible approach—building it up insidiously and gradually out of apparently realistic material, realistically handled. The time is past when adults can accept marvellous conditions for granted. Every energy must be bent toward the weaving of a frame of mind which shall make the story's single departure from nature seem credible—and in the weaving of this mood the utmost subtlety and verisimilitude are required. In every detail *except* the chosen marvel, the story should be accurately true to nature. The keynote should be that of scientific exposition—since that is the normal way of presenting a 'fact' new to existing knowledge—and should not change as the story gradually slides off from the possible into the impossible. Emotions should be handled very subtly—the dominant note being one of *gathering tensity*. Little incidents or allusions strown here and there—each in itself apparently prosaic—should slowly weave a subconscious air of growing strangeness or menace. When the marvel actually appears, it should have its magnitude registered in the emotions and behaviour of the characters concerned—and these emotions and acts should be described with the greatest regard for genuine psychological accuracy. All the methods of popular fiction in this problem are simply too infantile and laughable for sober consideration. The best tone for weird fiction is that of scientific exposition—let the characters, rather than the author, do the 'Oh-ing' and 'Ah-ing'. My own early junk is absurd because of lack of faithfulness to this principle. It is possible, though, to enhance certain kinds of narratives by giving the whole prose structure a darkly menacing cast—*if* this can be done with enough subtlety to avoid the impression of hokum and theatricalism. So far, I don't think I have ever seen a magazine story which succeeds in employing this sort of menacing style successfully. Poe was the only one to master it fully—and it is safer for the minor living author to stick to purely scientific objectivity except in the case of Dunsanian poetic fantasy, which is something else again.

[. . .]

If any object is worth trying for, it is not the doubtful honour of success with that outfit of complacent ten-raters;* but the genuine achievement of some small niche in actual literature beside Blackwood and Machen and James and Dunsany. I doubt if I can ever make the grade, but it is at least more becoming to fail in a worthy struggle than to enjoy a cheap prestige in a vulgar and thoroughly contemptible field of popular charlatanry. My abilities are not great, but I am not so constituted that I can dicker with shoddy and insincere things. If I could easily do it with my left hand while my right hand worked seriously—as Derleth does—I certainly would; but I can't, so that's all there is to it. I don't think I'll do any original writing at all for quite a period—and when I begin again, (if I do) it will probably be in such a vein that Wright wouldn't even consider the results. There's no use in sending in work only to meet with rejections—and such rebuffs gradually build up an unfavourable and discouraging psychology adverse to future efforts. If I write again, it will be strictly for myself—with results shewn only to the few who like that kind of thing.

[. . .]

My family kept me away from gymnasiums after I had a fainting fit in one at the age of 9.

[. . .]

I agree with you in preferring Bromfield to the rather *precieuse* Wilder. . . . I like Cather and Hemingway. . . . Hemingway is the sort of guy I intensely admire without any great impulse to imitate him. His prosaic objectivity is a very high form of art—which I wish I could parallel—but I can't get used to the rhythm of his short, harsh sentences.

[. . .]

[12]　　[AHT]

September 24, 1931

[. . .]

About collaboration—I really think it has more drawbacks than advantages. The writers get in each other's way oftener than they help each other out. For instance—I never saw a Derleth–Schorer tale that even approached the merit of the average thing which Derleth writes alone. I don't think I'll ever waste time and energy on collaboration, for I have a notebook stuffed with more original ideas than I can ever develop in a lifetime. Anyhow, there really ought to be perfect homogeneity betwixt idea and style. No "Willows" ever came out of anything but one man's inward vision. There is more to real art than any mechanical coöperation can achieve—it is the

---

Shea's note: the W.T. readers.

unique outpouring, through necessity, of a single individual's unique mood; and any alien intrusion is fatal. As for correspondence with established writers like Blackwood and Dunsany—Good God, child, but where do you suppose my sense of proportion is? Only an immature upstart forces his feeble attempts on the attentions of real authors, and I am proud to say that I have never written a line, or thought of writing a line, to any celebrity whatsoever. When a man really achieves artistic heights on his own account, contact with the great comes casually and naturally enough—but until then he keeps quiet if he has any dignity or good sense.

[. . .]

[13]   [ALS]

#10—

Septr 28, 1931

Dear J V:—

Why the wincing? You don't call us clumsy W.T. hacks 'real authors' do you? I'm sure it would never occur to me to classify Long, Quinn, Howard, Smith, myself, & so on, with the sort of writer substantial enough to make communications from novices absurd. Hell, no! I'd write any of these mediocrities any day if I happened to have anything to say to him. The difference between the veriest novice & this grade of scribbler is infinitely less than that between such scribblers & the Blackwood–Dunsany–Machen–James type. As I've been trying to make clear, the popular magazine world is essentially an *underworld* or caricature-imitation-world so far as serious writing is concerned. Absolutely nothing about it is worthy of mature consideration or permanent preservation. That is why I am so absolutely unwilling to make any 'concessions' to its standards, & so much disposed to repudiate it entirely in an effort to achieve real aesthetic expression even on the humblest plane.

Nor is my opinion of your material at all low. Naturally one can't expect a relative beginner to be mature & assured all at once, but I have tried to make it clear that I consider your output much better than my own at a corresponding stage of inexperience. "Brother & Sister", for example, is really excellent, & shews a surprising advance over the other specimens you have submitted. It took Derleth a much longer while to hammer out a good style from his original juvenile jauntiness.

As for the plot—the chains did not tell as much as you intended, since the date of their application was not made clear. And some signs of self-punishment on Obadiah's part are really imperative. You could easily subtilise Obadiah's unattractiveness, & the coincidence about the discovery of the infant could be remedied by the use of a little reflection. You could have the cottage a little less remote, so that passers-by would not be so rare, & could have the discovery come more gradually. Some one could see a strange light

& tell about it at the village. No need to have Obadiah identified at the time—but have the villagers talk about it & whip up curiosity until somebody gets to the point of scouting around & digging. The sentimentality can easily be eliminated. As for precision of style—if I can find an extra copy of Parker's Aid to Composition (which my grandfather studied back in the '40's) I'll send it along for you to keep as long as you like. That sterling old-timer has all the precepts for accurate writing which modern textbooks neglect. You can pass over the occasionally pompous rhetorical devices of the period—for they will be self-evident—& fasten to the solid substratum of intelligent & effective construction-advice on which the work as a whole is based.

Young Belknap's "Brain Eaters"[1] is about a ship which sailed accidentally into an alien dimension & encountered the monstrous marine denizens thereof. I suppose he is trying it on Wright now—but have not yet heard of results.

Yes—you'll find college a vast help & stimulus. Trust you've by this time selected & developed a suitable theme, & that the results may meet with pedagogical approbation.

"Halpin Frayser" was about a man who walked through a haunted woodland & met with a soulless lich that had at one time been his own mother. A great story—even though clumsily told, & somewhat obscure in inner point. Read it again—if you can't find "Can Such Things Be" around Pittsburgh, I'll lend it to you. I never liked O. Henry, for his stuff always seemed to me impossibly mechanical & artificial, & overcast with an atmosphere of false sentiment & wholly conventional values. He almost broke into literature shortly after his death, when much was made of his work; but for the last decade he has obviously been receding. His stuff was clever, & flashily well constructed, but never got very close to actual life. What buoyed it up was its contemporaneousness—its really deft delineation of the external surfaces of things. Now that the types & conditions portrayed have largely passed away, the thin, insincere quality of the art is revealed in a merciless objective light.

I suppose that real art in photography is about as hard to sell commercially as real art in literature. Indeed, painting affords a still closer parallel. Fond parents doubtless insist on having their offspring cheapened by "cute" poses inspired by a Boug[u]ereau-like sentimentality,[2] while older folk demand ego-exalting effects which give the artist but little chance to exercise a purely aesthetic judgment. It's a tough world—in fact, I always say that the only real salvation of the artist is an ability to pick up money in some other way & thus remain free to express himself in his own fashion for the sake of expression alone.

No—I haven't seen any snapshot of Whitehead alone. Unless it was taken less than a year ago, it shews a much stouter man than the H S of today. At present (or at least last May & June) his physique is almost a precise duplicate of my own—so that I wore some of his white drill tropical suits while visiting him. He had just had them taken in by a local tailor.

I've never read anything of Charles Willard Diffin[3]—in fact, I can't get a kick out of any "scientifiction" except the early work of H. G. Wells. All this stuff in the magazines is thin-blooded, artificial, & unconvincing—so that the descriptions of strange devices & adventures do not produce any feeling of reality or plausibility. Just words strung together—moods & stock phrases & situations—with nothing behind them.

Sorry to hear of your parents' motor accident, & trust the ill effects will not be long in wearing off. Highways are getting so congested these days that traffic is increasingly hazardous. Eventually the automobile may defeat itself by crowding everything to a standstill!

Best wishes—

Yr most h^{ble} & o^{bt} Servt

H P L

P.S. I am asking Dwyer (to whom it has been lent since last spring) to send you Machen's "House of Souls" as soon as he is through with it.

Notes

1. Frank Belknap Long, Jr., "The Brain-Eaters," *WT,* June 1932.
2. HPL refers to the French painter William-Adolphe Bouguereau (1825–1905), known for his realistic paintings, especially of women.
3. Charles Willard Diffin (1884–1966), American science fiction writer who published extensively in *Astounding Stories.*

[14]   [ALS]

Technology Chambers,
Boston, Mass.,

Octr 4, 1931

Dear J V:—

Received your interesting letter just before hopping off for Boston for three days. Have been changing pens at the Waterman home office, & *think* I have one which is satisfactory. But it is not this one—& I'm going to try another changing siege tomorrow. Now let us make a transition to the pen I *think* I like.

Better—oh, hell yes—distinctly better! If this one is really right, it will give me an incentive to try for better things in connexion with the other. Can it be that I have actually found a half-decent pen at last? Let me not be too optimistic.

Turning to your letter—I don't agree with your classification of my stuff in relation to Blackwood, Machen, James, &c. The more I reflect upon it, the more I see its weak points. James excels me in almost every way—& suffers only from a choice of manner. The rest are so far ahead that comparison is useless. Dunsany & de la Mare are of course primarily poets, but as such they create certain incomparable weird effects. Judge de la Mare by "Seaton's Aunt", "Mr. Kempe," & "All Hallows."

Take your time with the loaned stuff. No hurry. I can imagine how full your days must be now you are in college. Glad so many varied activities are opening up. I think military drill is a good thing in the end. It teaches coördination, & forms an accomplishment of great value to every well-rounded character. I vastly regret the absence of traditional accomplishments— fencing, horsemanship, military science, &c. &c.—caused by an early ill health & lack of appreciation of the quality of well-roundedness.

Later (Monday)

Trying still another pen-point—admirably easy, but rather coarse for handwriting the size of mine. No use talking—it's only by accident that one ever gets a decent pen! The present situation surely involves a difficult decision. This point is obviously clumsy in results—but dare I change it for anything less easy? Let's see how the other one which I *did* decide on works. . . . . This, without question, is the best yet; & I fancy it would pay to go back & continue the campaign till I can get another more like it. It writes just as easily as the other, yet has a much less clumsy stroke.

Getting back to business—I don't think "The Earth Taint" need discourage you so much. Derleth's advice, in the main, is apparently very sound; & ought to prove a helpful influence. It indicates that the tale is about what I imagined—but this is not anything alarming in a beginner. I'd be glad to read it a little later on, when I emerge from the accumulated work I'll probably find when I get home—& I can assure you I shan't be shocked. I don't know whether I can add anything to what Derleth has said, but I might furnish at least a fresh point of view. The points about his criticism which I would tend to object to at present are mere minor details. For example—he heatedly says that 'men are *not* machines', whereas of course they are; albeit machines of natural origin, & of vast complexity & still inexplicable variability. I assume that you used the term "machine" in its broadly correct sense of a structure with interdependent parts which serves to transform & utilise energy for specific functions. There is nothing in the term which precludes the idea of natural origin. But of course Derleth is handicapped by a residual belief in the supernatural. Another point I'd challenge is Derleth's objection to the cleft chin—which you noted. The only thing which could justify that objection is the possibility that all the rest of your description indicated your intention to convey an idea of beauty—in which case the detail would be self-contradictory. Otherwise, it is of course absurd (except from the despicable popular magazine point of view) to have a heroine especially good looking. In fact, it is rather absurd to have any particular heroine at all. Also—if your characterisation is detailed enough to make ethnic elements count, the objection to "Irish wife" is unnecessary. However, are you sure that you used the effect of Celtic heritage accurately rather than conventionally? It is needless to say that the superficial conception of the nature of various racial & national heritages is often amusingly at variance with the actual facts. As for "Erotian"—Derleth probably fancies that the reader might take the term in an erroneous sense—connecting it involuntarily with "Erotic." Thus you will see scientifictioneers using the clumsy word "Venusians" instead of the more Latinically correct "Venerians", for obvious reasons. I doubt if I'd use any single term at all. I'd say "inhabitants of Eros", "outsiders", or something like that—not for the reasons above indicated, but because of a certain naivete in the use of a glib, settled word to describe something having no part in human experience. As for pimply faces—I suppose Derleth is simply giving advice from the sales point of view. Of course, genuine art describes whatever really exists—whether anybody likes it or not. 24 hours is really too soon to call an international convention. Nations could get in touch telegraphically, but there would not be time to make & coördinate appointments.

But don't fancy the tale is necessarily too crude to revise. On the contrary, its revision would probably form the best possible way of promoting your progress. The criticisms can't do you the maximum amount of good until you get at their underlying essence by *applying* them. And why do you doubt whether you'll be a writer? How do you expect to acquire the necessary experience—by magic? Authors are not evolved over night. It's a matter of slow, painful hammering into shape. You've only begun. It would be inconceivable for anybody but a freak genius to write really mature material without at least 5 years of gradual practice, criticism, & intelligent disillusionment. 2½ years to get rid of youthful egotism, & 2½ more to build up a secure proficiency on a modest basis. "Brother & Sister" represents a substantial advance on your part—but of course is not what you will be writing later on. Have you let Derleth see it? It is as erroneous to underestimate it as to overestimate it. I'll send you the first spare copy of Parker's old fashioned manual that I come across. By all means get a good dictionary—preferably Webster's International—& Roget's Thesaurus.

If I recall O. Henry's "Gift of the Magi", it involves a coincidence so puerile that mature taste must needs balk at calling it good. I can't abide such stuff—it doesn't even begin to interest me. I haven't read "The Revolt of the Pedestrians"[1]—but I probably sympathise. Glad your mother is better. Glad your theme obtained a good rating, & hope later ones will fare as well. Let me see a few of them some time.

Thanks for the picture of H S—which is really admirable in the way it conveys his present appearance. I'm very grateful for permission to keep it. Thanks, too, for the Parry column. I let "Waterloo Bridge"[2] slide by, but may pick it up on its return trip.

As for your contrast between the writing conditions of my time & your own—I fear you make the common mistake of harbouring a badly proportioned picture of former times. You can never understand the stream of civilisation until you pay more attention to the past—for the real past & its relationship to the present are not what the casual modern imagines. You make the mistake of juxtaposing eras—like the theatrical costumers who invariably dress the civilians of the Civil War period in the costumes of 1830–40.

When I was young—1900–1910, let us say—there was just as much amateur striving for authorship as there is now. The same old correspondence schools & journalistic courses were flourishing, & the same old writers' magazines were purveying their mixed wisdom & hokum. There was not such a vast array of cheap magazines, but everybody was trying to make the bunch (vast enough, hell knows!) that did exist. And the number of persons wishing to write *well*—not professionally, but as a gentleman's accomplishment—was even greater than at present. That is, there was more emphasis on excellence for its own sake, & less on "practical" results. Style, in general, was far better than it is now—that is, in prose. Verse was still encumbered by Victorian artificiality & 1890-period jauntiness. There was *less* excuse for writing badly then than there is now, since flashy & imperfect models were less distractingly common. It was the age of Dreiser's best work, & the strongest novels of Mrs. Wharton. Kipling's influence, however, still lingered; & all too many fell for O. Henry. Stevenson was overrated—but the current praise of Lafcadio Hearn was well merited. The popular trash of the day—George Barr McCutcheon,[3] &c—was not taken very seriously. Only the elders clung to memories of the Dickens age. The general tempo was that of a reaction against the 1890's. It was considered bad form to mention the fact that Oscar Wilde ever existed—& college dramatic societies used to perform "The Importance of Being Earnest" without giving the author's name. The great fault of the age, in literature, was *not* poor style, but naive emotion & limited intellectualism. Good writing was more common than now—but it was largely wasted on artificial & conventional conceptions of life. It was, dominantly, the age of polite & correct insipidity—the last, inane petering out of the "genteel tradition", with the illusion of moral values clinging in people's emotions even when their scientific intellects had discarded it. No—the writer of 1900–10 most distinctly did *not* have to blaze a trail for himself.

Paradoxically, the reason I was slow in escaping from my pompous (though correct) Johnsonese style was because I did **not** belong to my age. As I told you once, I disavowed everything around me, & went back to the models of the 18th century. I veritably swam in an ocean of ancient models & textbooks from the age of six onward—but they were the models & textbooks of 1750–1800—**not** of 1896–1914. A writer of 1896–1914, really belonging to that age, had a better chance of successful maturing than one of today. The "brilliant" models & methods of the present, in prose, are generally the *wrong* ones—& the percentage of bad writing in proportion to good is much higher than of yore. The one *real* advance (aside from psychological & intellectual advance) is in *poetry*. As for the style of "B & S"—it may not be the ideal one, but it has the quality of directness & simplicity which the ideal one ought to have.

This outing of mine is turning out delightfully. Weather is sunny & blazing hot, & all the open country is exquisite. Am visiting with W. Paul Cook—the Recluse chap—in Boston, & making side trips to ancient spots with him. Saturday we explored the South Shore—Hingham, with its 1681 church, &c—& yesterday invaded the Merrimack Valley—Haverhill & Newburyport. The latter is probably the best preserved example of a city built up between 1700 & 1820 that the U.S. can afford—I really grow inclined to place it higher than before on my scale of admiration. Home tomorrow—but I may try another trip next week.

Best wishes—& don't get discouraged. Simply realise that mature authorship requires years of development.

Yr obt grandsire—

H P L

Notes

1. David H. Keller, "The Revolt of the Pedestrians" (*Amazing Stories,* February 1928), portraying an automobile-dominated society in which pedestrianism is illegal.
2. *Waterloo Bridge* (Universal, 1931), directed by James Whale; starring Mae Clarke, Douglass Montgomery, and Doris Lloyd. Based on the play by Robert E. Sherwood.
3. McCutcheon (1866–1928) was an American popular novelist and playwright, best known for a series of novels set in Graustark, a fictional East European country, and the novel *Brewster's Millions.*

[15]   [ALS]

Tuesday [13 October 1931]

Dear J V:—

Well—I've done some travelling & labouring since I sat on Boston Common writing you a week & a day ago! Got home at 1:30 a.m. & found a telegram summoning me to Hartford, Conn. the next afternoon to discuss a book job with representatives of the Stephen Daye Press of Brattleboro, Vermont—who would come down to that convenient half-way point to meet me. I had never been in central Connecticut before; & since the weather was warm & fine, I welcomed the chance to get a free trip through unknown realms of probable scenic beauty. Nor was I disappointed. The landscape between here & Hartford proved magnificent, & the early autumnal colouring put it at its best. Hartford itself isn't so distinctive, although it has fine old public building (a former state house) designed by Bulfinch. On the return trip the next day I chose an indirect route through Norwich &

Plainfield for variety's sake, & was at most knocked flat by the utter splendour of the scenery. To think this region has lain unsampled at my very doorstep throughout a long life! Hills, valleys, lakes, breath-taking vistas—a
veritable Vermont on a slightly reduced scale. Norwich—where I paused for
several hours of antiquarian exploration—is ineffably quaint & attractive;
built up the steep terraces that rise above a bend in the river Thames. I must
surely revisit this region—indeed, the next time I go south I think I will cover
the Prov–N Y lap by zig-zagging through the interior of Connecticut.

The job which I discussed at Hartford is now tying my nose down to the
grindstone in the most emphatic way—though it is by no means as repulsive
as the revisory work I have been doing for miscellaneous dumbbells here &
there. It consists of editing & proofreading the text of a long quasi-official
history of Dartmouth College by one of the professors therein[1]—a really
scholarly work, though in a damnably slipshod style. The pay is not great, but
I am making concessions in the hope of getting a steady stream of work from
the Stephen Daye. If I could handle all their important MSS. & proofs I
would be in great luck—& could afford to tell magazine editors to go to hell!
The Stephen Daye handles (at present, at least) all the printing for the Dartmouth College Press. I may have to go up to Brattleboro for a brief consultation when this job is finished—though the Vermont temperature at this time
of year will minimise the recreative potentialities of the jaunt. The book itself
is really interesting—giving many sidelights on that colonial period which is
the seat of my keenest absorption. The later chapters, though, will probably
be duller than those I've so far tackled.

I see now what Derleth was driving at in the matter of human machines.
Yes—of course different individuals have differences of reaction to external
stimuli; especially sensitive or high-grade individuals with a reasonable
amount of mental background. The ignorant herd, however, certainly do tend
to fall into general types with approximate similarities of response.

As for "Brother & Sister"—there is a good deal of sense in Derleth's
suggestions, for it certainly does subtilise the tale vastly to have the child already born—to eliminate all overt happenings & have the narrative purely
one of mental implications. I agree, however, with your own counter-
suggestion that the *death* of the child would be unmotivated & therefore inar-
tistic. I might add that its *sickliness* would also be rather artificial unless both
brother & sister be notably sickly—for science long ago exploded the myth
that there is necessarily anything unhealthy about the offspring of close kin.
In ancient Egypt the marriage of brothers & sisters was very common, & no
harm ever came of it. All that a consanguinous union really does, is to intensi-
fy in the offspring whatever latent hereditary weakness or strength the parties
may possess. If you rewrite the story, I'd advise following Derleth's suggestions except as to the extreme sickliness & death of the child. Let him survive
as a strange, potentially tragic figure. Indeed—it occurs to me that a finely

tragic novel might be written about the life of a boy who grows up with such a possible shadow over him. Written from the boy's point of view, it would be an equally powerful tale, albeit of a rather different type. Derleth's advice about erotic experience seems to me rather more debatable. While the traditional system of sex ethics is probably rather clumsy, it still has certain advantages over that which seems to be replacing it; & is certainly the most sensible one to follow unless one's temperament makes it wholly impracticable. At present, the following of an alternative course involves so much commonness & ignominious furtiveness that it can hardly be recommended for a person of delicate sensibilities except in extreme cases. It remains to be seen what sort of middle course the future will work out. No conceivable system can be really perfect, for there are opposite emotions which make for ceaseless conflict under any sort of arrangement; but it is possible that some improvement may be made on the existing state of things—a state in which the actual situation tends to depart farther & farther from the nominal one. In these transitional days the luckiest persons are those of sluggish eroticism who can cast aside the whole muddled business & watch the squirming of the primitive majority from the side-lines with ironic detachment. Sex experience is certainly not necessary to good authorship or other aesthetic endeavour, although of course in dealing seriously with real life one ought to have all the experience & perspective one can possibly command. I'd reverse the general tenor of Derleth's advice by merely suggesting that the bulk of one's work dealing with the details of erotic relationships be postponed till after one is domestically established in the accepted way. Not that experience be hurried, but that certain types of heavier writing be deferred. I never thought premarital experience worth the attendant ignominiousness, & doubt very much if I was the loser thereby. Indeed, I can't see any difference in the work I did before marriage & that I did during a matrimonial period of some years— none of my stylistic transitions corresponding in the least to any change in biological status. Weird work, without a doubt, is to an enormous degree independent of objective circumstances.

Yes—"People" is great stuff, & I hope Derleth can get it published as a whole—separate from "Evening in Spring." Did he tell you that the tale of "Michael Dervais" is founded on his own grandfather?[2] I find it hard to pick favourites in this work, but think your own choices are all good ones. I am aware that A. W.'s preferences in the matter of weird tales differ from mine, & am hardly disposed to be dogmatic about such things. All standards are more or less subjective & variable. Any idea of the essence of a weird tale is that it successfully present a picture of some impressive violation of the established order of things—some defeat of time, space, or natural law, or some subtle intrusion of influences from another imagined order of being upon the familiar order of being. It is hard to achieve this effect with the hackneyed stage properties of the old-time ghost story, (with which Derleth is all too often content) hence I find greatest merit in those tales which I call *cosmic*—tales which bring in sharp reminders of the vast unplumbed recesses of space that loom perpetually around our insignificant dust-grain. That is the only way one can be weird & quasi-realistic at the same time—*supplementing* reality rather than actually *contradicting* known reality. But every man to his taste. I agree with you that horror is not necessary to be a good weird tale—as proved by the bulk of Dunsany's work. I have experimented in this direction, though without success. It takes a greater amount of subtlety & adroitness than I possess.

Glad you saw "American Tragedy." I missed the second run by being away, but may catch it on the third if I think it worth bothering with. From your description I judge that Dreiser's rage at the cinema was not altogether unjustified. Dreiser's style is certainly very trying, & I find little actual enjoyment in his works—despite my profound appreciation of their scope & power. I have not, unfortunately, read "The Hand."[3] Nor have I read Maurois's "Weigher of Souls" or Casey's "Easter Island"—although I have seen the latter advertised & have been meaning to get hold of it if possible. The mystery of Easter Island has always fascinated me, & I have paused with awe before the great effigy in the National Museum in Washington.

You are right in believing that no one can really grasp the inmost life of an era without having lived through it, though I might add that sound historic study often greatly improves our comprehension of bygone ages. We do not know the exact feelings of a Greek or Roman in every department of life, yet we know a great deal more about them now than we did 150 years ago. Our ignorance of all things is relative. I have often tried to test the authenticity of my conception of certain former periods, but doubt if I could fully enter into the moods of any of them. Every now & then I get an unexpected side-light which forces me to revise a previously settled view. Only this week I have received impressions from the book-revision job which slightly alter my picture of 18th century life in the Connecticut Valley—where the people were evidently cruder & more fanatically pious, even down to the Revolutionary period, than I had suspected before. The motivating springs of any age are complex & largely concealed; & to recapture them from history & documentary remains is a well-nigh impossible job. This reminds me that a new book is just out—"All Ye People"[4]—which is said to go far toward capturing the daily life & spirit of the 1810 period. All this is important because we can never understand the present or speculate intelligently about the future until we have formed some conception of the general time-stream of which the past is so important a part.

About "The Metal Emperor"[5]—thanks for the offer, but I don't believe I'll take advantage of it unless the *entire* tale is involved. I believe you said that, as in the case of the Moon Pool, it was available only in part. I never got much satisfaction from fragmentary reading. By the way—I think I said that I have sent Klarkash-Ton the first & last M P instalments, as well as the original Moon-Pool in the All-Story, & "The People of the Pit." These will come to you, for retention as long as you wish, but for eventual return to me.

I didn't say that "Satampra Zeiros" was categorically Smith's best, though I did say it seemed to me one of his best. It is an out & out phantasy—not a realistic story at all—hence is to be judged in relation to Dunsany rather than to Machen or Blackwood. I did not pay much attention to the plot—which is of course elementary—but enjoyed the atmosphere & colour. Somehow I could very vividly see that immemorial Hyperborean city of Commoriom amidst its jumble of age-long desertion. As stories go, I don't like this as well as the more recently written (though previously published) "City of the Singing Flame" in Wonder Stories. Have you, by the way, seen the sequel in the current issue?

By the way—Wright has at last accepted "In the Vault", which he rejected six years ago on the ground that it was 'too horrible'. Derleth lately asked to see it again, & surprised me by preparing a fine new typed copy—which he insisted that I send in for a second trial. I was rather reluctant, but since the child had gone to all the labour of typing I couldn't courteously do otherwise than humour him—& lo! the thing actually hit the capricious Farnsworth right this time, so that I shall be $55.00 the gainer at some undetermined future date! I'll have to hand it to Little Augie for once!

Haven't seen "Creeps by Night" yet—nor have I received the 25 fish supposedly due me. Congratulations on your 10-spot. Derleth thought $50.00 was due him, but anticipations on the part of others probably whittled the sum down. I didn't know of the suggesting contest until a date I regarded as too late. I skip rather hastily over the "Books & Authors" column of the Times, where I believe the proposition was set forth. Had I been making nominations, I'd have voted for Shiel's "House of Sounds"—though, come to think of it, that might have been ineligible because of non-magazine origin. I tried to get it into Harré's anthology—but the publishers considered it too long.

I think you'll find Dwyer a fascinating correspondent. His sense of the fantastic, & his response to delicate suggestions of the unreal in landscape & atmospheric effects, are the most highly developed I have ever encountered in any human being. Of all my correspondents he is the most perfect *Machen*. He has always lived in the picturesque countryside of Ulster County, or in the ancient & sleepy town of Kingston, (full of stone houses dating from 1668 to 1720 &c) & has become permeated with the brooding mystery of such an environment. I have met him twice—spending a week with him in 1929 & again in 1930. But why can't you picture me eating bologna sandwiches? It is true that I don't eat as *many* as our 240-lb friend does, but I can't think of any objection to them up to the normal amount. As a matter of fact, I was fat myself for several years—the result of an overfeeding originally established by my mother, who sought to counteract my lack of an active appetite. In 1925, when I was first free from all family obligations, I experimented in diet-readjustment, & knocked off 50 lbs. in 5 months; nor have I had any tendency to pile up adipose tissue again. If Dwyer would follow my regimen, he would soon lose that growing convexity! By the way—if you want a good laugh, get an eyeful of the enclosed picture of Belknap & me a decade ago. Some contrast with the 1931 view of the same subjects! (please return)

        Best wishes—H P L

P.S. Whitehead is worse—lower aperture of stomach closing. He'll have to have an operation in a fortnight, poor chap!

Notes

1. See JVS 9 n3.
2. "People" is a short story that AWD later wished to incorporate into the novel *Evening in Spring*. It is not clear whether the published novel actually includes this story, as the novel underwent extensive revisions prior to its publication in 1941. "Michael Dervais" is an unidentified short story by AWD.
3. Theodore Dreiser, "The Hand" (*Munsey's*, May 1919), a ghost story.
4. By Merle Colby.
5. *The Metal Emperor* (*Science and Invention*, October 1927–August 1928) was A. Merritt's extensive rewriting of *The Metal Monster* (1920).

[16]   [ALS]

                             Friday [23 October 1931]

Dear Jehvish-Êi:—

        Glad to hear from you, & to receive the interesting art matter—which I will forward to Klarkash-Ton in the very near future. It is a testimonial to the arresting power of "Suicide in Costume" that I singled it out for semi-fascinated notice among a page full of art reproductions in the N Y Times Rotogravure Section *before* receiving your letter![1] There was no accompanying comment—for New York takes modern art more as a matter of course than either Pittsburgh or Providence—but the thing itself forcibly struck me as a case of odd grotesque power. I would not call it 'badly executed', for the artist had no intention of achieving realistic perspective. Modern art does not emulate photography, but tries to incorporate some essence of the subjective—some hint of the inward & unreal perspective through which the artist individually & uniquely views his subject. No two persons see exactly the same thing when they look at the same object—for each one unconsciously selects a certain number of details (out of the ungraspably infinite total) for emphasis & conscious registration. Modern art tries to shew what an artist sees when he looks at a thing. It is not, except nominally, a portrait of the object. Essentially it is a diagram of the artist's mood. It began with the French impressionists in the mid-19th century, gained a climax in Gauguin &

Cezanne, & has been carried to absurd extremes by many inferior theorists today. But I would hardly call "Suicide" an absurd extreme. It has, in my opinion, a very legitimate power; so that I am not at all surprised by its selection as a prize-winner. It excelled the pretty canvases because it represented a sincere & strongly individual creative impulse instead of a mere bland imitativeness. Watkins had something he had to get off his chest—& that is what real art is. He didn't merely say, 'now I'm going to paint a picture,' look around for a conventional subject, & then do his best to imitate a camera. The colour—which of course I haven't seen—must play a part almost as important as the lines. However—I am free to say that modern art is not my favourite form. I recognise its power & appreciate many manifestations of it, but as an antiquarian am far more attracted by the classical themes of yesterday. In paintings my favourite subject is the landscape—of the wide architectural vista—& I find most of my favourites extending from the 17th to the middle 19th century. Salvator Rosa, Hobbema, Claude Lorrain, Constable—a very mediocre taste, according to any art authority, but at least not a tenth as bad as my utter taste-vacuum in the domain of music. Now & then I like a touch of the fantastic in pictorial art, hence am fond of the engravings of John Martin, (fl. circa 1820) Doré, & Sime. And in a slightly more popular field I can thoroughly endorse the admiration which our 240-lb friend B'na-Dwi-Y'hah bears for the drawings of Howard Pyle. However—I make no pretensions to the role of art critic. It is surely interesting that you should happen to have been interrogated & photographed in connexion with this art exhibition, & I trust you'll send me any newspaper article in which your likeness & opinion may appear.

As for "Brother & Sister"—why try to bring it to a conventional "conclusion"? No episode in life is ever definitely "concluded"—all things are merely snatches of a continuous stream. The logical ending point would simply be where the narrator becomes vaguely (though perhaps only subconsciously) convinced of what the boy's real parentage is. This could be hinted at in a number of ways. The child's close resemblance to his "uncle & aunt"—the absence of any feature or expression that is not Westcott. The odd way the "uncle & aunt" regard him—an ambiguous way in which fear & repulsion play a small part. Reports vaguely floating from places where the couple have previously lived—rumours that they had no other brother or sister—rumours that there was something secret or unwholesome about them—nothing definite, but enough to make the narrator feel that something is vaguely & deeply amiss, & to give the alert reader enough of a hint to form an artistic ending. Artistic literature is essentially undramatic—as well stated in a cutting (reviewing a new play by the author of "Street Scene") which I am sending under separate cover. You might return this cutting some time, for transmission to one or two others.

And speaking of "Street Scene"—I thought you'd like it. I had missed "Five-Star Final" through being confined to the house with the book job (now finished) & with the sick-headache & digestive upset which accompanied the unusual concentration, but expect to catch it on its second appearance hereabouts.

Easter Island is a great latent theme for the weird fictionist. It has been cheaply used in at least one W.T. serial, but no first-rate story has as yet been woven around it. There was a fine illustrated article on the place & its images in the National Geographic Magazine for April 1921.[2] I have it packed away somewhere, & will try to hunt it up & send it along if you'd care to see it. Easter Island was probably a sacred shrine of some sort in an early archipelagic civilisation developed by the Polynesian race—the same culture which produced the Cyclopean masonry at Ponape. Probably many of the islands holding this culture have sunk through volcanic action, though it is not likely that (as popularly supposed by many) there was ever a great Pacific continent. Also—the date of the archipelagic civilisation was probably not very picturesquely remote; not anterior, at any rate, to the middle or later period of classical antiquity in Europe. But of course the novelist is at liberty to indulge in whatever fancy he chooses regarding these things. I wish I could get hold of what is reputedly best of all books on this theme—"The Riddle of the Pacific", by Prof. J. Macmillan Brown. (a New Zealander) It is not in the public libraries of New York, Providence, or Boston, but I have seen it tantalysingly quoted. Why not try your luck in Pittsburgh? I wish I had thought to try in various other cities I have passed through—Phila—Baltimore—Washington—Richmond—Charleston—Savannah. Possibly I will on my next trip.

Glad the Macheniana has come from B'na-Dwi-Y'hah. Don't be in any hurry to read it—there's plenty of time. Derleth changed one or two words of "In the Vault", but made no perceptible revision. Wright's change of mind was only his perennial caprice. I doubt if it would pay to try any others on him. Derleth persuaded me to re-submit "The Nameless City" a couple of years ago, but it was again rejected.

"Creeps" & the XXV have both duly come—though I have had no chance to read the former. It is certainly a sizeable enough tome! According to young Derleth, there is a vast amount of good material in it.

Yes—"Solomon Kane" surely is a husky bozo! I think—recalling his early letters—that he has fought in the ring, though I don't know how professionally. I judge he has also participated in shooting & stabbing affrays in connexion with cattle & boundary warfare—still a live reality in western Texas. He is a living compendium of the sanguinary annals of the southwest—which he re-tells with all the fresh gusto of a primitive epic poet. In truth, his milieu quite exactly reproduces that early & untrammelled Aryan world which evolved such bardic productions as the Iliad, Beowulf, & the Norse Sagas. I thought the old picture of Sonny Belknap & Grandpa would amuse you.

Even then the child was trying to nurse that semi-visible moustachelet, but the cruel camera wouldn't shew it. It depends largely on lighting conditions. I don't wonder I looked stiff & secretarial. Carrying all that weight was a responsibility calling for a very trying & orderly coördination of forces! By the way—since these views have been of interest, I am enclosing a few others illustrating sundry members of the gang. You will note the genial & gigantic B'na-Dwi-Y'hah against the exquisite background of the circum-Kingston countryside. New York State, as you may observe, has rambling stone walls of the kind traditionally associated with New England. (Please return all pictures)

Fra Bernardus' description of me is so excessively favourable that I shall have to lie low in order not to belie it! Not often can I carry off the bluff of a "colossal" intellect or "encyclopaedic" information. As for speaking "Bostonese"—if B'na-Dwi-Y'hah were himself a Bostonian (or Novanglian of any sort) he would not fall into that error. My speech is simply the ordinary literate medium of Southern & Central (not Northern) New England *outside* Boston—the daily speech of Providence, Hartford, New Haven, Springfield, Worcester, Salem, & so on. If you ever heard real Bostonese (which my younger aunt has picked up through a 20-year residence in Cambridge amid Harvard circles in middle life) you would know the difference in a second. While we ordinary Yankees don't use the flat Midwestern *haff, caff, gräss*, &c, we certainly do not *linger* & *gloat* over the broad *a* as the Bostonians & Cantabrigians do. We don't sound any final *r* in words like *car, far*, &c. (phonetically, our common pronunciation is indistinguishable from *caa, faa*, &c.), but this is not a Bostonism or Briticism at all; but merely the ordinary usage along the Atlantic seaboard (with the single exception of the Philadelphia zone) from Maine to Florida. It is curious that inhabitants of New York City do not notice any difference in our accent from theirs, although we find theirs irritatingly different from hours [*sic*]. They do not sound final *r*'s, & are by no means as flat in their *a*'s as the midwesterners; but have certain unmistakable tendencies in sound & inflection which grate on many. They tend, for example, (though the younger generations are breaking themselves of the habit) to interchange *oi* & *er* sounds; so that they pronounce the name "Ernest Boyd" as if it were "Oinest Bird"! They would say, for example, "The Oil of Joisey bought erl stocks" if they were describing a purchase of Mr. Rockefeller's securities by Lord Dunsany's father-in-law. They also say "mom*ent*" when they mean "mom*e*nt", & so on. Likewise—in compound words they tend to accent the *first* word where we tend to accent the second. They eat *lamb′* chops & *ice′*-cream, while we prefer lamb *chops′* & ice-*cream′*. In *northern* New England & *upper* New York State the rolled *r* is heard; (hence Dwyer's notice of my lack of it) though by no means so violently as in the west. In Philadelphia it reappears mildly, together with a peculiar kind of inflection of possibly Germanic influence. This is also (except for backwoods Northern New England) the present northerly limit of the primitive -*aow* sound (*daown, raound*, *abaout*) formerly prevalent throughout the United States except in academic circles. Beginning in southern Maryland we find the deep-vowelled speech made familiar in literature & the drama as the dialect of the south, & due to the effect of negro pronunciation upon a population largely rural & thus out of touch with urban corrective influences. This dialect seems thickest in Georgia, & is probably even thicker in the inland states—Mississippi, &c— which I have never visited. In urban Charleston, S.C., however, it is & always has been entirely absent, for purely local reasons. Charleston was from the start a city of great independence & cultivation, & preserved European contacts to an unusual degree. It was separated from all other colonial centres by a wide zone of almost impassable terrain, & the population of its agricultural hinterland were forced by lowland fever-&-malaria conditions to live within its compact area for a large part of the year. Thus it was the scene of a more extensive urban social life than was found anywhere else in the south—all the neighbouring planters having town-houses there & participating in cultural activities impossible to a purely rural people. They customarily sent their sons to Oxford & Cambridge, & in general had more to do with Europe than with the rest of the colonies. Under these conditions, their speech was too fixed by frequent social use to suffer any modification from the nigger talk around them—hence has remained to this day distinct from the speech heard in places as close as Columbia & Savannah. It is, oddly enough, almost identical with that of the greater part of New England—so that I was once mistaken for a native Charlestonian. Probably this plain type of speech is not dissimilar to the speech of the majority of small towns in central & southern England— the basic form of the language, from which this north-country burr, the Oxford & London drawl, & the various colonial variants have diverged. There have, though, been many changes in this base—even since the late 18th century—so that it is remarkable that places as far apart as Charleston & New England should have kept so closely parallel. Of the dialects of the west I know relatively little—though the exaggeratedly rolled rrr . . . (as in *carrrr, farrrrm, arrrdirrr, Mistirrrr Carrrtirrr* [Mr. Carter] &c) is the principal earmark as judged by the standard of the Atlantic coast. Westerners flatten the short *a* (*haff, laff, păss, glăss*), & seem also to handle their vocal cords slightly differently in ways almost too subtle for exact definition. This stridency seems at a maximum among people from Ohio & Michigan—at least, I have not noticed it so much among Illinoisans & Wisconsinians. Californians & Northwesterners roll their *rrr*'s, but do not share the other qualities of midwesterners. In the southwest—Texas, Arizona, & New Mexico,—the Southern influence has softened the Western burr & produced a wholly distinct dialect—or rather, a congeries of dialects subsisting side by side. The rolled rrr . . . . & the wholly suppressed final *r* seem to exist in close juxtaposition, while Hispanic words are frequent—notwithstanding the fact that the Spaniards have not left any influence on the pronunciation or vocal quality of the local English. Robert

E. Howard has made many interesting observations on the dialects of the southwest—one of which he probably speaks himself. As for the rolled *rrr* . . . .—while it probably once existed among all English-speakers, it seems to have had a tendency to drop out of all English dialects except those strongly affected by Gaelic speech—as in Scotland, Ireland, & the north English counties near Scotland. The other Celtic branch—Cymric—does not seem to have had this effect; since there is no tendency toward rrr . . . rolling in the neighbourhood of Wales & Cornwall. In America, the *rrr* . . . is found (so far as regions of original colonial settlement are concerned) only where the founding stock was predominantly Scotch-Irish (as in New Hampshire—thence Vermont & northern N.Y. State—& Pennsylvania) rather than purely English. The cause of its prevalence in the West is still a matter of debate, though it is possible that a predominance of Scotch-Irish may be traced in the first pioneering wave which fixed the dialectic forms. Also, the large-scale German infusion subsequent to 1848 may possibly have had something to do with it. A still greater puzzle is afforded by the *oi–er* interchanging peculiar to New York City. It is hard to trace it to Dutch speech, since it does not occur anywhere in the equally Dutch rural Hudson Valley. Even its date of origin is subject to dispute, though it certainly reaches well back into the first half of the last century.

It interests me to learn that you share my distaste for marine fauna as a source of nourishment. Ugh! It is odd, but all forms of fish, mollusca, crustaceans, & the like have been violently & nauseously abhorrent to me ever since I graduated from the lacteal bottle & Mellin's Food in the very early part of the Mauve Decade. The sight of them is pretty bad, but I can stand it in a pinch. The smell & taste, however, are beyond me. Even urbanity cannot stand the test of reality in this respect, & I had to ask Whitehead once last spring to move a platter of some ichthyic delicacy away from my section of the dining-table. It was a case of it or me . . . . or the contents of my interior! I have no grudge against meat, though, & am quite fond of well-cooked & highly seasoned beef, lamb, pork, & veal dishes. I don't care so much for steaks & chops, & can't bear liver, tripe, or rare meat at all. I am extremely fond of the white meat of chicken & turkey, but hate the dark meat almost beyond endurance. I like good bologna, frankforts, & ordinary fried sausage. But my favourite dinner has meat only as an ingredient of its sauce—to wit, spaghetti in the full Italian manner, with clouds of flaky Parmesan cheese. *Cheese,* by the way, is my favourite among all comestibles—being, together with chocolate (in nearly any form) & ice cream (preferably vanilla or coffee) a member of a triad of especial likes. But my cheese tastes are very common & plebeian. I like the most ordinary bulk cheeses, & merely tolerate Camembert. Roquefort & all *rotten* cheeses are anathema to me.

As for the 18th century—as you read more of it, I fancy you'll see how the "brawls & piracy" form only a very minor part of an extremely rational &

tasteful age. They did not amount to any more than the holdups & racketeering of today. And *cats*—well, you're welcome to your own opinions, but I can tell you that if I had a regular home the first thing I'd get would be a pair of coal-black, silky kittens with large yellow eyes! I still mourn my old Nigger-Man, who vanished into his native night in 1904. Yes—letters are very revealing, & I think you have Little Augie to a T. A great kid—but fond of A. W., & given to certain harmless affectations (monocle, dressing-gown, long, wasp-waisted overcoats) which he'll get over as he gains maturity.

Don't know yet whether I'll have to go to Brattleboro. And now to another of the other 19 letters that have accumulated!

Best wishes—

E'ch-Pi-El.

P.S. Under separate cover I'm forwarding two stories of Derleth's that he asked me to pass along. I suppose you're to return them to him.

Notes

1. "Suicide in Costume" is a grim painting by American painter Franklin Chenault Watkins (1894–1972), now in the Philadelphia Museum of Art. It won first prize in the Carnegie International Exhibition. It was featured in the rotogravure section of the *New York Times* (16 October 1931).
2. Edmond Hamilton, "Across Space," (*WT*, October, November, and December, 1926); Mrs. Scoresby Routledge, "The Mystery of Easter Island," *National Geographic Magazine*, 40, No. 6 (December 1921): 628–46.

[17]   [ALS]

Friday before
the Witches' Sabbath.
[30 October 1931]

Dear Jehvish-ÊI:—

Hope the alleged dog victim hasn't raised any trouble. Some fakers will go to any length to collect dishonest damages

Haven't had word from H S since writing you, but this must be about the time of the operation. I shall drop a brief inquiry soon, which his secretary can answer even if he can't.

Thanks for the cinema tips. I've probably let most of the good things slip by during my recent spell of hard labour, but they'll doubtless come again.

Glad the pictures interested you. Derleth is no blot on the landscape, & if he'd get a regular haircut would be handsomer still. Talman is the handsomest member of our gang—& the most intelligent as measured by ability to make a living. Aesthetically, though, he runs to Philistinism; & his prose is halting, clumsy, & inexact as compared with Belknap's or Wandrei's. Wandrei is better-looking than the snapshot (an old one [of] 1927) indicates. His normal expression is not so sullen, & he dresses more neatly (or did in 1929 when I saw him last in person) than he once did.

I can see that you easily beat me in number of table-aversions! How can anybody dislike *cheese?* And yet Little Belknap hates it as badly as you do! I don't suppose you would like spaghetti if you don't like cheese, for the two rather go together. I share your liking for sweets, & take an inordinate amount of sugar in my coffee. I, too, am an enthusiastic potato-ite—& guess I like the fried form best of all. Shake! Of other vegetables I like peas & onions, can tolerate cabbage & turnips, am neutral toward cauliflower, have no deep enmity toward carrots, prefer to dodge parsnips & asparagus, shun string beans & brussels sprouts, & abominate spinach. I like rhubarb—& am also really fond of baked beans prepared in the ancient New England way.

I have never perused anything by Walter Winchell, & (from hearsay) hardly fancy that I have thereby denied myself any acute enjoyment.

I sent the Pittsburgh art material (Shipment I) to Klarkash-Ton, & have now done likewise by Shipment II, recently received from the youthful Augustus. It interested me to see your portrait (for whose deficiencies I am making due allowance) & interview. I think "Suicide in Costume" will grow on you in retrospect. Yes "Of Human Bondage" is great stuff—as is all of Maugham's best.

I'll shoot you that Easter Island *Geographic* as soon as I can dig it up—remind me again if I am unduly tardy. If you can find "The Riddle of the Pacific" anywhere, I'll be the most grateful loan recipient on record. I think it must have been lost or stolen from the N.Y. library. It was catalogued, but always failed to appear when asked for.

Take your time about the book loans. I'm in no hurry. "Bethmoora" certainly is great—as are virtually all the "Dreamer's Tales." As for Machen's "White People"—I still maintain that this is *incomparably the finest* of all his weird tales; being, like Blackwood's "Willows", almost a model of what a weird tale ought to be. The 'lack of anything concrete' is the *great asset* of the story. A weird tale is not an account of *things & happenings,* but a skilful *transcript of a certain sort of human mood.* Tangible aspects & events can never be more than incidental properties. The real thing is the *dark current of half-formulated feelings* that sweep relentlessly along. The 'childish rambling' in this tale is potently effective as a foil to the hellish background. Nothing is more ghoulishly hideous than the delineation of monstrous elder evil in the guileless language of childhood. Nothing in the child's discourse is really irrelevant. It taps fount after fount of dim, dark folklore as it babbles along, marshalling a terrible array of evidence to lead up to the last ineffably subtle denouement. Make no mistake—& Derleth & Dwyer & the whole gang will back me up when I say so—this is the greatest weird thing Machen ever wrote. It is just about *perfect* for its *genre.* Later on I'll lend you his "Hill of

Dreams", which really falls outside the strictly weird fold. "The White Pow-der"[1] is cheap & mechanical as compared with "The White People."

I received & read "Creeps" at last, & am rather disappointed in it. Too many merely gruesome *contes cruels*, & not enough really weird things in the Machen–Blackwood vein. But I think you'd like it. My favourite tale is Ewers' "The Spider."

As for dialects—here are a couple of cuttings which may interest you, & which you might send back eventually. I was greatly interested in your re-marks on Pittsburgh local usage, & did not realise it was so distinctive. It probably partakes of both Pennsylvanian & Middle Western characteristics— I recall that the use of *leave* for *let* is common in Cleveland & Milwaukee, & probably in other western towns. *Crick* is a rusticism heard in the backwoods everywhere from Newfoundland to Key West & Maine to California, but I never heard of *food* rhyming with *hood*. The rising inflection at the end of sen-tences is encountered in Ireland, but rarely elsewhere to my knowledge. It may be part of Western Pa's Scotch-Irish heritage. The so-called "Dutch" of Pennsylvania, by the way, are not really from Holland, but are *Germans*. In the 18th century the common Anglo-Saxon name for Germans [Deutsch] was "High-Dutch" as opposed to the "Low Dutch" of the Netherlands. Thus a man in 1731 would say that the people of Penna. are High-Dutch whilst those of New-York are Low-Dutch. Thus arose the common term "Pennsyl-vania Dutch", which misleads many today.

I appreciated very keenly the landscapes you sent, & would appreciate any others you may send. Surely you have some exquisite vistas, & I hope some day to get around to that part of the country. I have been told the Lehigh Valley is also very picturesque. Correspondents in Allentown (the very heart of the "Pennsylvania Dutch" region) have told me much of the local landscapes & folklore.

I read the Derlet[h]ian extract with interest. I distinctly think he said something about the effect of parentage in his suggested sickliness for the B & S child, but if he didn't, so much the better for him. Yes—of course the later history of the boy would mean expert work, but I think I said so when writing. As for an unmotivated death—all I meant was that the death must not come at some precise time to aid an action otherwise based, unless some-thing inherent in the action makes it a probable happening at the given time. My idea was to get rid of the implication of undue coincidence. Of course I wrote in haste—when the hell don't I?

I haven't seen B'na-Dwi-Y'hah's "Night Call" unless it's an African tale he wrote years ago, or a new title for a new poem of his. "The Castle of Golden Dreams"[2] is good—as Long & I agree. **Of course** many of the pas-sages are 'sheer slush', for isn't the whole damn thing the pathetic mental maundering of an illiterate, cheaply sentimental, frustrated old maid? This isn't a weird tale—it's a study of a pathetic & simple type in the spirit of Derleth's "People" though in a widely different manner. Still, I dare say it hasn't the professional finish some could give it. It is a study from life—from an actual old maid in the Shokan hills, who (unlike the heroine at the end) is still living & in good health. Dwyer has a sensitiveness to atmospheric nuances beyond that I have seen in any other person, & if he only buckled down to the art of technical form he could knock the rest of the W.T. gang off the map.

By the way—I meant to say last time that if you don't know who *Maturin* was, you haven't read that history of weird fiction which I sent you. Look again on page __!³ ¶ After being cooped up with work for nearly a month, I'm making a break for the open. Thank heaven the warm weather continues.

Best wishes—

Yr obt grandsire

E'ch-Pi-El

P.S. Am going to Boston tomorrow for another week-end with W. Paul Cook. We'll probably do ancient Salem (Arkham) & Marblehead (Kingsport).

Notes

1. "Novel of the White Powder" is an episode of *The Three Impostors*.
2. "Night Call" and "The Castle of Golden Dreams" are presumably stories by Bernard Austin Dwyer (unpublished, so far as is known).
3. HPL neglected to fill in page number (chiefly p. 31 but also 30 and 32).

[18]   [ANS]¹

[Postmarked Boston, MA,
1 November 1931]

You don't care much for antiquity, but if you love beauty you couldn't help liking the archaic backwaters of old New England. We've been doing Portsmouth N.H. & Newburyport Mass—marvelous places! Regards—E'ch-Pi-El

Greetings!
W. Paul Cook

Notes

1. *Front:* Pleasant Street, Showing Jacob Wendell House, Built 1789, Portsmouth, N. H.

[19]   [ANS][1]

[Postmarked Salem, MA,
2 November 1931]

Just a bit of that past which holds no interest for you!
    Your ob[t] grandsire,
        E'ch-Pi-El.

Notes

1. *Front:* Old Witch House, After 1780, Salem, Mass.

[20]   [ANS]

Wooded Banks of the Seekonk
—Novr. 10, 1931

Dear Jehvish-Êi:—

Well, well, well, well! The elements do favour the old gentleman once in a while, for here it is almost 70° in the shade, & Grandpa outdoors in his cherished rustic haunts watching a golden sun give witchery to
bare boughs & withered leaves while a mystical haze rises up from the blue
river that laps the road at the bottom of the bluff. Indian summer! And thank
Pegāna for the circumstances which have kept this neighbouring bit of primal
nature intact since my earliest infancy . . . . always the same, & a perennial
gate to yesteryear.

Now that I rack my brain about "The Night Call" I seem to recall it—
but hades! With the number of MSS. I see, it's a wonder I can keep track of
any of them! About "The Castle of Golden Dreams"—it seems to me that
you get *wearied* too easily with any work of literature that isn't disproportionately crowded with Wild West action! Take stock of yourself & see whether
the fault is always with the author in such cases! What interests one in a work
of art always depends on the associative equipment & imaginative sensitiveness of the reader, & one ought to be sure that one's receiving apparatus is
working at maximum capacity before formulating quick critical judgments. As
I've said, life is made up largely of subtle static impressions; & when one feels
this acutely, he does not get bored with a slow-moving, reflective piece of
writing which is faithful to the atmosphere & moods of reality.

I think you'd like "Melmoth" in places, despite what you would consider
its excessive length. Try to get it at the Pittsburgh library—it's rather hard to
find, & is not in the public libraries of Providence or New York.

About *oo*—the sound in *root* is much more variable everywhere than in
food. It is this latter case which marks Pittsburgh as so highly unusual. I don't
believe there's any variant from the dominant pronunciation of this word in
any other part of the globe. Yes—I imagine that one of the Abbey Theatre

group would have an excellent pronunciation. I was interested in the sidelight on Edward John Moreton Drax Plunkett. Hope you make the Pitt Players—a very appropriate organisation for you in view of your interest in drama.

I saw the Easter Island review in the Times, & was tantalised by the reference to Brown's book.[1] If you ever get to Washington D.C. you must not fail to see the Easter Island images in the National Museum. About "The White People"—again I advise you to suspend judgment & see what your verdict will be after a year of good reading & relative abstinence from pulp thrillers. I consider this the second-greatest weird tale ever written, Blackwood's "Willows" coming first.

Thanks exceedingly for the "hex" cuttings. Someone ought to use this local folklore in literature—as someone probably will in the course of time. One of my Allentown correspondents—a bright young poet named Carl Strauch—is getting more & more interested in his native milieu, & may yet give the world something with an inside angle. I vastly appreciated the landscape cuttings, by the way. No—I never heard of either "Eagle's Nest" or "Narrows"—that's how ignorant I am! But some day, I must see all of this region for myself.

I see that the Parry column[2] is not incapable of dropping into the "just folks" attitude now & then. Our local B K H gave Peter Arno quite a writeup when he was here.[3] I'll see if I can find it for you. B K doesn't slop over very often. I note with interest your changing attitude toward "Suicide in Costume." It's a good thing to be able to appreciate types of aesthetic expression that aren't exactly in one's own personal line. I'd like to see your thesis on that subject—send it along when you get it done if you have a spare copy.

As for diet—I thought I was bad enough, (& so do my hosts sometimes when I have to strain tact to its limits about fish, liver, &c!) but I fear you're even a more horrible example! I'm not enamoured of deep layers of butter, but I like a little on bread if I have to eat bread at all . . . . . . which is seldom from choice. But as for jam or jelly—I am your utter opposite, for I like it so well that I pile on amounts thicker than the bread which sustains them! I'm not fond of milk or any milky drinks. If I take fluid at a fountain it's some thin fruit beverage with orange, grape, cherry, lemon, or lime as a base. But I more often take ice cream, of which my favourite flavours are vanilla & coffee (the latter hard to get outside New England) & my least relished common flavour is strawberry. I don't care for tea at all, but don't dislike it with lemon. I like coffee exceedingly, but relish its imitation Postum just as much. I am nauseated by even the distant stink of any alcoholic liquor. As for vegetables—I don't mind cauliflower, & don't think you would either if you tried it. It is rather neutral & politely unobtrusive. But I doubt if you'd like Brussels sprouts. I never heard of "kale" except as a slang term for what is academically known as jack, berries, dough, mazuma, & long green—although I dimly realised that the frozen metaphor had some sort of obscure vegetable basis.

Black-eyed peas are a new one on me—but in New England we are very fond of baked yellow-eye beans.

B K H commented on "They Walk Again" in this morning's Sideshow, incidentally giving me a glancing mention.[4] I haven't seen the anthology, but feel sure it must have some great stuff. Haven't seen O'Brien's 1931 book, but think he ought to have mentioned Whitehead's "Passing of a God" & perhaps a few other W.T. items.[5] Whitehead, by the way, has had a turn for the better, & thinks he may be able to escape the threatened operation. I surely hope he can. Of Derleth's two new ones, "The Telephone in the Library" is much the better despite the basis of coincidence. But much could be made of "The Satin Mask" through revision. "The House in the Magnolias" struck me as pretty good, despite the fact that more could have been made of the old lady.[6] Of course the zombi theme is not new, but any fresh handling of it is worth consideration.

I'll keep those cinemas in mind, though I have had very little time to view the outside world of late. Last night I heard the eminent astronomer & mathematician de Sitter[7] lecture on the size of the universe, & enjoyed his exposition very much. He is a little old man with bald head & snowy beard, & speaks excellent English. His theory of an expanding but finite universe could probably be worked into "scientifiction" somehow or other. Tonight—to prolong the scientifictional atmosphere—I am invited to attend a demonstration of *television,* which will be utterly new to me. I suppose the process will be rather crude, since it is still very new; but in any case it will give a strikingly unique impression.

Thanks for the coloured views of exhibition items. Your galleries surely have a healthy variety of material. Providence has an excellent art museum, & some time I'll send you cards of some of its contents. Incidentally, Cook & I went all through the Boston Museum of Fine Arts last week—a great institution, containing among other things the finest collection of Japanese prints outside Tokio. I also—as you know—made a round of the ancient towns north of Boston—Portsmouth, Newburyport, Salem, & Marblehead—but young folks aren't interested in such things! This, I fancy, will form my last real trip of 1931; for Indian summer weather like this can hardly be expected to last.

Best wishes—

Yr obt grandsire

E'ch-Pi-El

Notes

1. Uffington Valentine, "Easter Island and the Teasing Mystery of Its Monuments" (a review of Robert J. Casey's *Easter Island: Home of the Scornful Gods*), *New York Times Book Review* (1 November 1931): 11.

2. Apparently a reference to Florence Fisher Parry, columnist for the *Pittsburgh Press.*

3. Peter Arno (1904–1968) was a celebrated American cartoonist who contributed extensively to the *New Yorker* and other magazines and newspapers. B. K. Hart wrote about him in his "Sideshow" column of 12 November 1931 (p. 14). Arno was in town for the opening (and swift closing) of his musical comedy, *Here Goes the Bride.*

4. In discussing *They Walk Again: An Anthology of Ghost Stories* (1931), ed. Colin de la Mare (son of Walter), Hart concluded, "What has become of my mentor in these matters, up in Barnes street? I want his verdict on the wisdom and probity of this selection." "The Sideshow," *Providence Journal* (10 November 1931): 14.

5. HPL alludes to the list of best stories of the year found in Edward J. O'Brien's *Best Short Stories of 1931* (New York: Dodd, Mead, 1931).

6. AWD, "The Telephone in the Library" (*WT,* June 1936); AWD, "The Satin Mask" (*WT,* January 1936); AWD and Mark Schorer, "The House in the Magnolias" (*Strange Tales,* June 1932). Both HPL and JVS must have read these stories in ms.

7. Willem de Sitter (1872–1934), Dutch mathematician and astronomer who devised a variant of the theory of relativity.

[21]   [ALS]

16 November 1931

[Text unavailable.]

[22]   [AHT]

19 November 1931

Dear Jehvish-Êi:—

[. . .]

To have lived to my age without producing more than two really good stories (Colour—Zann) or more than ten even fair ones, is to have demonstrated rather lamentably that fiction isn't in one's line. I was probably right in 1908 when I decided that systematic good production was beyond me, and destroyed all but two of the tales written up to then.

[. . .]

The population [of New York City] is a mongrel herd with repulsive Mongoloid Jews in the visible majority, and the coarse faces and bad manners eventually come to wear on one so unbearably that one feels like punching every god damn bastard in sight.

[. . .]

The real New Yorker today is the most tragic figure in America—a man who has seen the submergence and destruction of the world which bred him and of which he is inextricably a part. The more I saw of the place the more acutely I realised its ghastly vampirism. It has killed a civilisation, and its obscene fungi are sprouting from the corpse. There are those who think it gay, but to me it is the most melancholy spot on earth. There is nothing left there for a man of any family or cultivation to live for.

[. . .]

[23]   [ALS]

Decr. 9, 1931

Dear Jehvish-Êi:—

Glad the atmosphere of "The White People" is beginning
to manifest itself to you. As for the essentials of the plot—you haven't quite
got 'em yet, though you probably would have if I had sufficiently stressed the
relationship between this tale & "The Great God Pan." This, then, is the
dope: I. The image found in the woods was that of two entities locked in a
monstrous & obscene embrace—from which, had they been living things,
would have been born a Thing of non-human horror . . . . . like Helen
Vaughan in "The Great God Pan", or the boy in "The Black Seal." II. On
account of a sympathetic action like that described in the prologue, the now-
adolescent child—though without contact with any creative element—
becomes pregnant with a Horror to whose birth (knowing what she did of
dark tradition) she could not look forward without a stark frenzy far beyond
the fear of mere disgrace. Thus she killed herself. If she had not, a nameless
hybrid abnormality of daemoniac paternity would have been loosed upon the
world. There seems to be very little question about the correctness of this interpretation, since several small allusions toward the end—especially regarding the girl's age & the nature of the image—join with earlier allusions to
sketch the implications. Most analytical readers get this idea without much
difficulty, & others see it unmistakably after being tipped off. This kind of
plot was what the 1890's regarded as about the acme of horror—& it certainly does pack a pretty sombre shiver. But as I said before, that isn't the real
crux of the tale. The big thing is the tense, insidious atmosphere—landscape,
half-hinted legendry, & all that. Whether it's mathematically the second-best
weird tale ever written, is a matter of no transcendent significance. I'd hardly
take young Derleth's verdict as final in matters of weirdness, & I'd have valued Klarkash-Ton's verdict more before his popular-magazine success than I
would now. But all I'll say is that, in my opinion, it's the second-best weird
tale which I myself have read. I don't see any of your objections against Machen's style, which is certainly one of the most fluent & harmonious imaginable. If you had brought the same objections against Algernon Blackwood, I
could have agreed with you; for his ragged journalese sometimes develops the
most unreadable cacophonies & prosaicisms. But Machen is glibness itself—
though in a far from formal way. If I have any semi-objection against his style
it is that it's too unctuously literary—too self-consciously artistic & precieuse.
Possibly a little of the meaningless jauntiness of the Stevenson tradition still
clings around him—but as for downright poor style, one simply must look
elsewhere! "The Red Hand" was especially shivery to me because of what it
implied concerning Those Who Dwell Beneath. Possibly the atmosphere impressed me more than anything directly stated. When you get all through with
your present Macheniana, I'll send you "The Hill of Dreams"—the one book

in which Machen makes contact with the main stream of major literature. It is not supernaturalism, though one long day-dreaming episode partakes very much of the atmosphere of the marvellous.

Sorry to hear that your "Suicide in Costume" theme was not well received, & can't bring myself to agree with the instructor who so ruthlessly condemned it. He certainly must be a martinet—though perhaps he forms a useful corrective for young minds disposed to overlook reality in favour of fairy-tale extravagance. There is no question but that realism must form the groundwork for any first-rate piece of writing, no matter how far from reality the author may push any one line of development. Unless the writer knows how to describe & vivify the every-day scene around him, he will never know how to describe & vivify anything. But although he must begin at home, there is of course no obligation for him to stay there. Your "Ten-Cent Matinee" is really very good, even if you don't care for it yourself. Details of that kind make a scene real, & such reality is necessary even when the given story is to end in unreality. What I object to in your instructor's attitude is his illogical prejudice against the unusual. He ought to realise that the exceptional as well as the commonplace has a legitimate status in the general pattern of things. All one can justly censure in a pupil is an excessive devotion to the unusual—a devotion so great as to bias his perspective & cause him to overlook or misinterpret the usual. Your "Shoe Repairer" theme is excellent—though for once I can see what your instructor means by monotony of sentences. Read the thing aloud, & see if there isn't a preponderance of short, similar sentences rather trying to the rhythmic ear. Good prose must be simple, but it must have a certain musical flow & variety if it is to represent the highest art. Dunsany exhibits one phase of perfect prose about as well as any writer I know, & Wilde was another titan in that line. Prose style was better 30 or 40 years ago than it is now—a lower technical level being one of the prices we are paying for the higher intelligence & deeper insight of our contemporary literature.

Winter has indeed struck these plantations, & I am in hibernation at last. There's a lecture at the college tonight on a new philosophic system of Prof. Whitehead;[1] (not our friend H. S.) but although I'd like to go, I fear I can't unless the thermometer abates. It's of no use for me to try to go out under +20°—I always get close to collapse if I do, & a couple of years ago was nearly knocked out for the entire winter by a mile walk at +17°. I'm naturally a tropic bird, & must lie low till spring comes, or until I can get the fare to Havana or kindred places. I'm still letting the teeth go—it's only a dull sensitiveness as yet—though I'll probably have to begin the dental siege before long. And so the Pittsburghian *food* accent is not purely local! I wonder what the geographical scope of the variant is? It certainly doesn't exist anywhere in the Atlantic Coast region, north or south, unless I've overlooked it during my admittedly infrequent peregrinations.

And speaking of food—what causes me to shiver at the drinking of milk is not its origin but its remembered taste. I simply don't like it. That is, I don't like it clear; although I relish a bowl of crackers & milk with cheese if the proportion of crackers is sufficiently high. My mother used to camouflage it with *both* chocolate & vanilla, & it wasn't bad in that form; but I fancy I get enough to eat without taking so much bother. I can't understand your considering the maple flavour as "sickeningly sweet"—in fact, that term itself is subjectively meaningless to me. My 'sweet tooth' has no limit—I like my cake to be all frosting, & take five (domino-shaped) lumps of sugar in an average-sized cup of coffee. Hershey's sweet chocolate is one of my favourite nibbles. Nothing pleases me more than maple sugar or syrup.

I hope your Thanksgiving guests had a true Gallic appreciation for the art institute in general, even though they did not care for "Suicide in Costume." I celebrated Thanksgiving by persuading my semi-invalid aunt to go out to a good turkey dinner for the first time since last Christmas. Now that she sees it didn't produce any ill-effect, it will probably take less persuasion to get her out Christmas.

Glad you are contemplating fraternity affiliations; for although they undoubtedly involve much meaningless frivolity & Babbittesque tradition, they are also infinitely valuable aids to environmental adjustment & wholesome gregariousness—especially for one predisposed toward hermitage. As I believe I've said before, I know I'd have been immeasurably better off—less awkward, retiring, & ill-adjusted—had my early health permitted me to follow a standard educational course with accompanying social activities.

I fear my random metropolitan observations will only bore Mrs. Parry, since columnists are usually inundated with all sorts of mail from admiring or dissenting readers. Glad you found my remarks of interest, & that you thought their phrasing acceptable. Close examination, I fear, would reveal many a solecism & inept passage—for all my first draughts (& letters are no more than that) generally do. When I intend a thing for publication I revise it endlessly.

Hope you can arrange to take music lessons some time, for you probably know what you want better than I did at seven. Not everyone can be musical, though, & was consoled recently by reading an interview in which James Branch Cabell confesses himself equally ignorant of the art—not merely ignorant, but positively unashamed & defiant! He says:

> "No—music means nothing to me. The arts of literature & music are very different, in that music, I am told, is based upon harmony, whereas prose, I know, is based on variety. It follows that nobody who takes prose seriously can enjoy music, though of course he retains the invaluable privilege of lying about it."[2]

As for my fiction—whether or not there's anything potentially in it, I know that it needs a damn thorough overhauling. It is excessively extravagant & melodramatic, & lacks depth & subtlety. After more than thirty years of intermittent effort, the last fourteen years of which are continuous, I have produced nothing within even gunshot distance of Algernon Blackwood. My style is bad, too—full of obvious rhetorical devices & hackneyed word & rhythm patterns. It comes a long way from the stark, objective simplicity which is my goal—yet I find myself tongue-tied when I attempt to use a vocabulary & syntactical pattern other than my own. All my recent experimenting came to naught. I tore up all the tentative versions & wrote the god damn thing the way I would have written it in the first place—producing 68 pages which I shall probably never bother to type.[3] Whether I'll try any more experiments remains to be seen. I'm too cursedly busy just now to do so even if I wished. Yes—I find the novel technique better suited to me than that of the short story. Of late, I fail to get much pleasure from short stories—either reading or writing them. No—I don't think lack of acquaintance (direct or indirect) with publishers has anything to do with the non-book-publication of my attempts. Whitehead has all sorts of friends close to prominent publishers, but it has never helped him get a collection published. Robert H. Davis is no influence in the field of real literature, although he can make or unmake a popular magazine writer who has the goods. He once rejected my "Rats in the Walls" on the ground that it was 'too horrible'. At bottom, the real reason why my stuff has no standing is that it isn't good enough to have.

Thanks for the cuttings. So Maude Adams is getting fat? Critics here praised her "Portia" to the skies.[4] I didn't see the performance myself. The cadets look impressive, & your art galleries always seem to have interesting material. I haven't been able to get around to any cinemas except "Frankenstein"[5]—which vastly disappointed me. The book has been altered beyond recognition, & everything is toned down to an insufferable cheapness & relative tameness. I fear the cinema is no place to get horror-thrills!

Best wishes—

Yr obt Grandsire

E'ch-Pi-El

Notes

1. Alfred North Whitehead (1861–1947), British mathematician and philosopher who collaborated with Bertrand Russell on *Principia Mathematica* (1912–13) and later attempted to reconcile science with religious belief.

2. From an unidentified interview by Julian R. Meade. The interview was reprinted in Meade's *I Live in Virginia* (New York: Longmans, Green, 1935), 192.

3. HPL refers to "The Shadow over Innsmouth" (begun in November 1931 and completed on 3 December)

4. American actress Maude Adams (1872–1953) played the role of Portia in Shakespeare's *The Merchant of Venice* with various regional companies in 1931.

5. *Frankenstein* (Universal, 1931), directed by James Whale; starring Colin Clive, Mae Clarke, John Boles, and Boris Karloff.

[24]   [AHT]

December 24, 1931

Dear Jehvish-Êi:—

[. . .]

There is a very substantial art in the assimilation and expression of significant detail, and Evans knows just what to pick in order to give the reader a
full sense—visual, auditory, olfactory, tactile, and even gustatory—of the scene
he is depicting. I have very little of this power myself, and regret it tremendously. The lack would handicap me if I ever tried writing about actual life.
My tendency is to envisage the world as in a dream, with attention concentrated on certain high spots. That will do for weird fiction, but wears thin in
the more solid sorts of literature. I'd give a good deal if I could write an essay
as rich in concrete content as this Evans specimen.*

[. . .]

It is true that the highest art is not that which touches the singular, but that
which presents the typical and universal in such a way as to make it suggest or
symbolise the vast general laws of cosmic cause and effect, and the vast general
emotions which lie beyond all the diversities of human action and sensation.
Balzac is greater than Baudelaire, & Synge is greater than Dunsany.

[. . .]

I've read Remarque and Cather, but couldn't hit that tempo if I tried till
my 150th birthday. It would mean nothing less than a linguistic reëduca-
tion—the acquisition of a whole new set of natural symbols for ideas and objects—and the process would be even harder than the acquisition of a totally
foreign language, since the greater resemblance to my mother-tongue would
set up the worst kind of confusion. *Of course* my written style is the same as
my conversational style, else how could it be a real style at all? What makes a
style except the exact reproduction of a man's most deep-seated and spontaneous mode of saying what he has to say?

[. . .]

The only way to write effectively is to ramble along exactly as one talks,
without any conscious thought of form. Technique—except when subconsciously operating—is only a barrier between writer and reader. The time to
use conscious rhetorical precepts is after the first draught is in some sort of
shape. *Then* one can safely go back and apply all the little niceties which were
overlooked in the original rapid outpouring. That is the way I do—except
that in letters I don't stop to go back and revise, being hopeful that the charity of my correspondents will condone all defects and refrain from judging my
literary prose standards by such random outbursts. The reason for the non-
colloquial quality of my prose is that in youth and early manhood I read a

---

Shea's note: referring to a college theme by Maurice Evans, a friend of mine.

great deal more than I talked—and that my reading centred largely in the 18th century.

[. . .]

If I had the money, I'd never be north of Charleston from November to June.

[. . .]

There is only one Anglo-Saxon civilisation, and Britain is its maternal focal point. Distant branches may well have variations in *manner* and *subject-matter*, but variations in *details of mechanical usage* are simply pointless and unmotivated.

[. . .]

[25]   [ALS]

Last of 1931
[31 December 1931]

Dear Jehvish-Êi:—

If the weather is not cold tomorrow, I shall take a chance & go to Boston for a three-day museum & antiquarian session with W. Paul Cook. There is a possibility that H. Warner Munn may get down from Athol, in which case the reunion would surely be festive enough! But if it's really cold, that's all off. Grandpa's had too much experience with low temperatures to take any chances!

Derleth's "Those Who Seek" is a good story, whether he likes it or not. "The Malignant Invader" is one of Belknap's poorest—spoiled by the stilted conversation he puts into the mouths of his characters, as well as the absurd element of coincidence in the monster's appearance. I see your point about the "Nameless Offspring"—the folly of not removing *it* before—& noticed it when I read the thing. However, the massed effect of the story is very powerful. I can hear that *scratching*. . . . .[1]

I guess you're right about O'Neill—in fact, I've held him at the top of the contemporary dramatist list ever since I saw "The Emperor Jones" back in 1922. I must get hold of "Mourning becomes Electra" sooner or later. Everyone seems to unite in according it tremendous honours.

In time I think you'll gradually work into a perspective which will cause you to see new & subtle poignancies in things like "All-Hallows", "The Willows", & "Seaton's Aunt." Popular reading is enough to cripple one's taste for a while, but with a change of dominant diet a change of appreciative faculties is sure to come. Faulkner is generally regarded as one of the most important young writers in America. He likes an involved & indirect approach now & then, but this often contributes to the ultimate effect of his story.

Your graphological experience was certainly amusing enough. Handwriting doesn't reveal much except the general degree of cultivation of the writer, (as judged by evidences of assured, rapid, unlaboured strokes) & even this indication is breaking down now that all the younger generation are using typewriters & leaving their handwriting relatively stuff, unexercised, & immature-looking.

Your estimate of the year from a cinematic standpoint is certainly analytical & impressive, & sounds professional enough for a newspaper review. Of all the items you list, the only ones I have seen are "Street Scene", "The Front Page", "City Lights", "Cimarron", "Trader Horn", & "Svengali".[2] You go into the thing profoundly. I never notice the names of the actors—except old standbys like Chaplin & Barrymore—& never even think of noticing who *directs* the picture.

The second Evans theme is certainly good stuff, although I don't think it comes up to that first one. He has the true eye for significant detail—which I wish to hell I had. Your theme is also vivid & moving, & there is evidence that your command of observation & detail is increasing. I note with great interest your remarks on your style. Your letters are very fluent & pleasing, & I am sure that a literary style based on their mode of expression cannot fail to be a graceful one. We all copy unconsciously now & then. I suppose my natural style is built up of memories of Poe & the 18th century essayists; while as you know, I have been through a period of rather pale Dunsanian imitation. In isolated cases—or over short intervals—I have doubtless had other imitative spells; but in the end one approximately homogeneous diction (such as it is) seems to have emerged out of the earlier vacillation. But it isn't good for much, I fear.

Well—I must get some sleep if I am to have any expectation of taking that trip tomorrow. The temperature gives me doubts. . . . . .

Trust you had a pleasant holiday season, & hope you'll enjoy a 1932 marked by consistent pleasure & progress.

Best grandpaternal wishes—
    Yr obt hble Servt
      E'ch-Pi-El

Notes

1. AWD, "Those Who Seek," and Frank Belknap Long, Jr., "The Malignant Invader" (both in *WT*, January 1932); CAS, "The Nameless Offspring" (*Strange Tales*, June 1932).
2. *City Lights* (United Artists, 1931), directed by Charles Chaplin; starring Charles Chaplin, Florence Lee, and Harry Myers. *Trader Horn* (MGM, 1931), directed by W. S. Van Dyke II; starring Harry Carey, Edwina Booth, and Duncan Renaldo. *Svengali* (Warner Bros., 1931), directed by Archie Mayo; starring John Barrymore, Marian Marsh, and Donald Crisp.

1932

[26]   [ALS]

Dear Jehvish-Êi:—

Yes—I did get to Boston, but Munn didn't! However, Cook & I had a sufficiently good time alone. We did all the museums of the Harvard group in Cambridge—Germanic, Semitic, Peabody, (anthropology) Agassiz, (nat. hist.), & Fogg (art)—& would have done more had not a touch of malaria confined Cook to the house on the final day. Rainy weather, however, prevented us from indulging in any antiquarian exploration. Last Sunday I attended a poetry reading by Prof. S. Foster Damon,[1] but was nearly knocked out by the cold. The weather has since moderated, though today is snowy to an ethereally picturesque degree. If the cold isn't below my danger-limit, (+20° F) I'm going down town to take advantage of a bargain advertised for today only—a cheap unpainted pier cabinet or set of shelves to fit in a narrow space & accomodate some of the hopelessly stacked & scattered papers that clutter up my quarters. Only $2.98—& if it looks really substantial I'm tempted to get two, for gawd knows I need all the odd shelfage I can possibly tuck into any remaining space hereabouts!

Your recent reading is certainly solid & well chosen enough—I wish I had the time to keep up such a pace. I have not read "Ulysses," because such extracts as I have seen convince me that it would hardly be worth the time & energy. Without doubt it forms an important landmark in the history of prose expression, but so far as I can see it is of theoretical significance rather than actual aesthetic value. It represents the intensive development—the concentration or exaggeration—of a literary principle which will greatly affect future writing, but which defeats its own ends of normally-proportioned portrayal when isolated & intensified to this extreme degree. The same is true of Joyce's later "Anna Livia Plurabella," extracts from which I have seen. And yet there is no more powerful or penetrant writer living than Joyce when he is not pursuing his theory to these ultimate extremes. I don't underestimate Faulkner. "A Rose for Emily" is a great story, & all I said[2] about it was that it is not *weird*. It belongs to a different genre, & brings a shudder of repulsion & physical horror rather than one of cosmic wonder. It is essentially a *conte cruel* of the Level type. If you are a Cather fan, don't miss "Shadows on the Rock", which I read last month. It is full of the spirit of old Quebec, & makes me long to behold that ancient fortress town again. I read French's "Ghosts, Grim & Gentle", & have twice seen the anthologist. He is an old man—must be high in the 70's—but very vigorous mentally. About M. R. James—I think

I can see what you mean, but can't classify him quite as low as you do. And if you can't see his utter, prodigious, & literally incalculable superiority to the W.T. plodders I must again urge you to give your sense of appreciation a radical analysis & overhauling. James has a sense of dramatic values & an eye for hideous intrusions upon the commonplace that none of the pulp groundlings could even approach if they tried all their pitiful lives. But I'll concede he isn't really in the Machen, Blackwood, & Dunsany class. He is the earthiest member of the "big four." Cram's "Dead Valley" is great stuff, & makes me wish desperately I could get hold of his other weird stuff. Whitehead knows Cram personally, & says that the latter himself has no copy of his own book of spectral phantasies, now rare & unobtainable.

Hope "The House of Unrest" turns out well. It doesn't matter at what speed you write, & different moods often dictate different speeds. I've written tales at a single setting—yet have also dragged single specimens out over a month. Dunsany is probably the most rapid of modern fantaisistes.

Have you heard of the new weird magazine about to be published by Carl Swanson, Washburn, North Dakota? It will not pay high rates, but is very easy to break into. Swanson has recently accepted my old "Nameless City" & "Beyond the Wall of Sleep", & is taking considerable material from Klarkash-Ton. He aims to use reprints as well as new material.[3] I'm not trying to follow Merritt's new yarn. The trouble with him as a writer is that he is a good business man. He knows what the public wants, & gives it to them— which explains why we don't get any more "Moon Pools." I shall be interested to see what comprises the second Omnibus of Crime. I now have the first one, & have read "Green Tea."[4] The latter isn't at all bad, & I would probably have spoken less lightly about Le Fanu had I previously read it. As for cinemas—"Jekyll-Hyde" has been & gone, but I didn't have the energy to attend it. I fancy "Frankenstein" somewhat discouraged the cinematic interest which "Street Scene" almost awakened. "Arrowsmith" has not been here.[5] I may try to see it when it comes. No—I haven't yet read either M. B. Electra or The Lady Who Came to Stay.[6] The former seems to evoke an unanimous chorus of approval from all my correspondents, hence I shall expect great things of it. I can hardly imagine "Strange Interlude" in the cinema.[7] As a play, it was barred by the pure-minded censors here & in Boston, but was presented in the more civilised city of Quincy, Mass.—8 miles south of Boston, & the seat of the celebrated Adams family. You certainly manage to keep track of all the celluloid flickers—ah, me, it must be pleasant to be young & interested in things!

As for a Japanese war—I can conceive of many conditions which would make such a thing highly necessary for the future safety of the Anglo-Saxon areas in & around the Pacific. We can't tell from present externals just what Japan's ultimate aims are, & of course under many conditions an early war would be a bad mistake; but none the less one ought not to take a dogmatic position in the matter. It would certainly be unsafe to allow a strong & potentially rival nation like Japan to gain full control of China, for in that case all the prodigious (though now unmanageable) resources of that vast & populous area would be a weapon in Japanese hands. Japan would be absolute mistress of the Pacific, & in a position to enforce her will high-handedly on Australia, New Zealand, California, & British Columbia, just as she is now enforcing it on China. That cannot be permitted, for the first requisite of a great civilisation is complete control of its own territories & inhabitants. Pacifistic talk is merely evasion & idealistic hot air—although of course it is well for as many nations as possible (those able to share a certain amount of common natural interest & perspective) to form treaty agreements calculated to eliminate minor causes of dissension. The plain fact is, that when any group wants a certain thing with a certain degree of intensity, it will forget all about agreements & paper restrictions, & will go after it with all the physical force it can command. And it is plain that in many cases one group could manage to muster enough force to defeat all the united strength which any international action could bring against it. There will always be wars, & the victors in them will always be those with the greatest wealth, man-power, stamina, & intelligent preparation. When a hostile tiger jumps at you, the only thing to do is shoot at it—& it's just the same with a hostile nation. I endeavoured to enlist in the late war, but my health caused my rejection. I fancy I'd do the same in a future case—for although I fear I'd make a rotten soldier, I think it well for the members of a group to signify their willingness to uphold its interests. However—I doubt if the time is ripe yet for drastic action toward Japan. She may moderate her course until her strength is greater.

Best wishes—

Yr obt Grandsire

H P L

Notes

1. Samuel Foster Damon (1893–1971) of Brown University was a poet, critic, and specialist in William Blake. It was he whom R. H. Barlow consulted about the deposition of HPL's papers at the John Hay Library.

2. In correspondence with August Derleth.

3. Swanson attempted to start a magazine, *Galaxy,* consisting largely of reprints from *WT;* but when *WT* refused to license such reprints, Swanson's venture collapsed.

4. HPL refers to two anthologies by Dorothy L. Sayers, the first of which included J. Sheridan Le Fanu's "Green Tea."

5. *Dr. Jekyll and Mr. Hyde* (Paramount, 1931), directed by Rouben Mamoulian; starring Fredric March, Miriam Hopkins, and Rose Hobart. Based on the novella by Robert Louis Stevenson. *Arrowsmith* (United Artists, 1931), directed by John Ford; starring Ronald Coleman, Helen Hays, and Richard Bennett. Based on the novel by Sinclair Lewis.

6. A weird novel by R. E. Spencer.

7. *Strange Interlude* (MGM, 1932), directed by Robert Z. Leonard; starring Norma Shearer, Clark Gable, and Alexander Kirkland. Based on the play by Eugene O'Neill.

[27]   [ALS]

March 22, 1932

Dear Jehvish-Êi:—

Glad to hear from you! Here's hoping your weird tale thesis meets with a favourable reception. I want to see it when you have a spare copy conveniently handy, for I may get some fruitful reading suggestions from it. I'd also be *infinitely* obliged if you could shoot along the Scarborough book for a brief perusal & faithful return. I've wanted to see that for ages, since it would seem—from all accounts reaching me—to parallel my own sketch about as closely as anything in print. Do you know Railo's "The Gothic Castle" & Birkhead's "The Tale of Terror"? Both are excellent expositions of the earlier phases of horror-fiction in English—the Walpole–Radcliffe–Lewis–Maturin type. I could lend you the Birkhead book.

Congratulations on the collegiate A's! Both themes impress me as vivid & excellent, though I agree that the fishing one is the better. You are steadily gaining in command of detail & sense-impressions, & will undoubtedly score A's right along now if you keep up your present pace. Incidentally, I fancy I agree with you regarding the subject-matter of both essays; although I have never witnessed the service in a Catholic church. Protestant services—except in the most high-church Episcopal joints—lack most of the colour & tradition which fascinate you, though they are just as strong on stupidity. What appeals to me in churches is their architecture, plus the historical glamour surrounding their former place in the life of the community. I can still get a kick out of the sight of a white New England steeple embowered in the verdure of a distant valley, or from hearing the music of chimes borne on the wind from the tower of some far-off Gothic pile reminiscent of Old England's parish fanes.

Congratulations on your dramatic debut! I'm glad the performance turned out so well, & fancy you will participate quite frequently in such pursuits in future. I imagine, from your general interest in the theatre & cinema, that you ought to possess considerable natural talent in the direction of histrionics.

I haven't read any of the new books you mention, though I've owned the original edition of "City Block"[1] for years—it having been given to me in 1925. Possibly it's a rare-book item by this time! What deterred me from it was Frank's rather whiny style in other fields—though I did vastly appreciate his "Chalk-Face." I hadn't heard of the new scientifiction magazine—but then, my interest in this field is rather lukewarm. Derleth gave me the instalments of Merritt's new *Argosy* serial,[2] & I managed to read it through despite its concessions to the poplar magazine fetish. Merritt has a very distinctive fantastic touch which would make him excellent if he'd only leave the servitude of the cheap pulp ideal.

As for cinemas—I haven't been to one since the "Frankenstein" disappointment! I have heard "Arrowsmith" well spoken of, & hope I can catch it on one of its returns to town. A friend of mine saw "Jekyll–Hyde" & was woefully disappointed. Nevertheless, I guess the average of the best pictures isn't as low as it used to be. The changes in "The Man Who Played God" are amusing—& provoking. And those in "Freaks" must be exasperating. Rhode Island has censors—or rather, the city of Providence has a single police censor—but this oversight isn't considered as meddlesome as that in some states. I'll be warned & remain absent from the "Rue Morgue."[3]

The Swanson venture wasn't abandoned when you thought it was—but alas, it is *now!* Only yesterday morning I received a letter from S. saying that he couldn't arrange for the financing & printing of *The Galaxy,* as he had arranged to call the new magazine. He still has vague notions of trying to publish either a magazine or some booklets on the mimeograph—but that doesn't sound very impressive. Too bad such a potential market blew up. Incidentally, Wright was rather incensed at the possible rivalry offered by Swanson, & tried to persuade his authors not to sell their second rights to S. I, however, told him to go to hell on that score—for the fellow has rejected too much of my stuff to deserve any favours from me.

The other day a friend of mine—Arthur Leeds, now in the book business—told a guy in the Vanguard Press office about my stuff, & as a result I received a letter from that firm inquiring whether I had any novel needing placement. I said I hadn't, but mentioned my shorter things—whereat the corporation's interest fell very measurably. Nevertheless they asked to see some of my short tales, & I have sent them four—"Pickman", "Dunwich", "Rats", "Cthulhu"—(other good ones all lent) though it's only a matter of routine without any expectation of results.

As for the question of war—I'm sorry my attitude disappoints you, but I really don't see any other rational attitude to hold. I'm not denying the extreme ill effects of modern warfare, or even that a future world war may mean the end of civilisation; but in spite of all that I can't blind myself to the plain & simple fact that war is no more avoidable than earthquakes or cyclones. We don't want these latter—but we build earthquake-proof houses & cyclone-cellars in the affected districts just the same. And as we prepare defences against these natural inroads, just so must we prepare defences against the natural inroads of embattled enemies. War is no formal institution which legislation can abolish. It is simply the inevitable result of basic human instincts under certain recurrent & unavoidable conditions. Whenever a group has an united wish for a certain thing, it will always reach out for that thing with its maximum physical strength—& will get it unless there is some superior physical force to stop it. Sometimes one group can manage to muster up—secretly or otherwise—enough strength to whip any possible combination which can be brought against it; & if each other group be not adequately prepared all the time, this "sometimes" will be damned often. No diversity of groups can ever be depended upon to act permanently & dependably together—& despite all the current pretence & hokum there is no indications of any *real* trend in this direction. Radically different interests & heritages make such a collective policy virtually impossible for all time—& he who banks on such a thing gets woefully left. Each nation is out for what it wants in any way it can get it—& the notion that any one nation can be sure of the forbearance of any other (especially any very dissimilar) nation is sheer puerility. Look at Japan, Manchuria, & the impotent comic-opera league today! If Japan ever wants California, what but good powder & cold steel is going to prevent her from getting it? The only guarantee of any people that their descendants will live in safety under the same institutions with the same language is in being adequately armed for defence & willing to fight like men when an emergency comes. The price of not being men is being a race of cringing dispossessed skulkers like the Jews, or sly, crafty, insinuating underlings like the Hellenistic Greeks in Roman times. No Nordic could consider such a fate even for a moment. I'll agree, though, on one thing—that under present conditions it is a little too much to fight for mere foreign trade privileges. Defence of one's own land & race is the proper object of armament.

Well—best wishes. And if you send the Scarb. book I'll be quick & careful with it.

> Yr obt grandsire
> E'ch-Pi-El

P.S. One of my correspondents from the Pa. "hex" country that I told you about—Harry Brobst—has just, by a singular coincidence, moved to Providence to take a job as student nurse in a local mental hospital. A very bright & congenial youth—23 yrs old & highly appreciative of local traditions & antiquities. I've shewn him quite a bit of the historic territory hereabouts.

[P.P.S. on envelope] Young Derleth complains of not hearing from you lately!

Notes

1. A novel by Waldo Frank.

2. *The Dwellers in the Mirage* (*Argosy*, 23 January–27 February 1932). Some critics detect a Lovecraftian influence in the work.

3. *The Man Who Played God* (Warner Bros., 1932), directed by John G. Adolfi; starring George Arliss, Violet Heming, and Bette Davis. Based on the play by Jules Eckert Goodman, adapted from the short story by Gouverneur Morris. *Freaks* (MGM, 1932), directed by Tod Browning; starring Wallace Ford, Leila Hyams, and Olga Baclanova. Suggested by the story "Spurs" by Tod Robbins. *Murders in the Rue Morgue* (Universal,

1932), directed by Robert Florey; staring Sidney Fox, Bela Lugosi, and Leon Ames. Based on the story by Edgar Allan Poe.

[28]   [ALS]

March 31[, 1932]

Dear Jehvish-Êi:—

Thanks tremendously for the Scarborough book, which I read with keen interest & am going to return the first moment I can get to a post office. It was certainly kind of you to send it. The material is really of great value, & I am immensely glad I had a chance to go through it. As you say, the weakest parts are those dealing with later work. The author does not mention M. R. James, & her prim distaste for Machen's macabre suggestions is rather amusing. Likewise, her efforts to be continually jocose & flippant become a little strained as one reads on. There is no conflict with my article, because the scope & method of the work are entirely different. This book covers not only horror but all forms of the supernatural, & includes the comic & the lightly whimsical as well as the grotesque & the terrible. Also, its plan of development & system of emphases is entirely different. What I am trying to do is to give a list of especially notable works containing supernatural horror; listing them by periods & authors & allotting them notice on the basis of their strength & merit in the given field. Dr. Scarborough, on the other hand, is trying to trace certain types of subject-matter through literature in a less critical way—being interested in the mere mention of a certain superstition by an author, & listing items simply because they deal with such-&-such—not because they have a special power to influence the emotions. This system involves a radically different form of outline, as you see. Instead of going ahead chronologically & treating the most powerful books of each period, Scarborough follows first one stream of subdivided subject-matter & then another—i.e., ghosts, devil, vampire, werewolf, wandering Jew, metempsychosis, alchemy, folklore, science, &c. &c. In the course of this scheme she lists many things so pallid & inane that one can hardly think of their deserving a place except from the standpoint of academic scholarship. And yet, for all that it's a valuable book. It certainly brings out many essential facts & tendencies amazingly well, & will bear comparison with anything else on this theme ever written. The separate & perhaps encyclopaedic bibliography edited by Dr. S. must be another item of great importance.[1] Let me know any time you want to see the Birkhead book. Since Cook's financial collapse I don't know what's become of his copy of the Railo treatise, but I imagine that either he or H. Warner Munn has it. Wandrei knows about that French work, & has used it in sketching out a tentative weird bibliography.[2] No—I've never seen "The White Ghost Book."[3] Is it any good? In the course of time I hope to see your own study of weird fiction. No—I've read none of the three items you mention. I obtained several hints from Scarborough, & also copied two tributes to the weird as a genre from the introduction—Lafcadio Hearn's & the author's own.[4] Whether I'll ever get around to preparing a second & amended edition of my article, I'm sure I don't know. Let me thank you also for the loan of the theme book—which I have read through, & which certainly contains some remarkably fine material. Many of the sketches shew a singular poignancy in the analytical description of scenes, effects, & moods; & out of all this galaxy of youthful talent I am sure that more than one real author will ultimately emerge. Glad to hear, by the way, that one of your brilliant classmates likes my tales—& hope that her own stories will continue to have success. Hope your new plot idea will develop well—you ought also to handle that Siamese-twin idea, which I am sure you could work up advantageously. I have so many ideas waiting that I don't know what to start first. Since "The Shadow over Innsmouth" I've had time & energy enough for only one story—not yet typed—called "The Dreams in the Witch-House." It is laid in Arkham, & combines the ideas of ancient witchcraft & the fourth dimension.

Don't worry about the condition of "The Moon Pool"—I knew it was doomed sooner or later, for wood-pulp paper always pulverises in the end. It's the fault of time & chemistry alone. I have now torn it out & saving the crumble-edged sheets in an envelope. Naturally, I shall guard it carefully from now until it disintegrates. If I had more energy I'd make a typed copy.

I doubt if anything comes of the Vanguard Press matter—& am really not enthusiastic nowadays about the idea of a book. I don't think I have first-rate stuff enough to make one, & it doesn't do any good to parade the old mediocrities. Glad to hear that you've read "Mr. Kempe" & other de la Mare material, & that your appreciation of fantastic subtleties is increasing. I'll admit that "The Tree" is rather obscure, & wouldn't swear that I understand the final details myself quite as clearly as the author might wish; but gather that the tree vaguely symbolises *the quality of genius*—bizarre, unknown, hated by sober folk, & attracting strange winged things (= thoughts & images) from far-away regions. I don't think it's a vampire except in the sense that a man's genius saps his physical vitality & wracks his worldly prosperity & social adjustment. The scars on the tree I take to have been made not by the artist but by the villagers around—for it is the outside world that hates genius. You'll recall that P.P.'s place had a sinister reputation, as evident in the cabman's attitude. As for "Out of the Deep"—it was the basic idea which captivated me. I don't care for the light, whimsical style, & was not greatly charmed upon a second reading after five years. I rather regret the extreme praise I gave it in my article. But "The Tree" & "Seaton's Aunt"—& of course "Mr. Kempe" & "All-Hallows" continue to hold me. De la Mare is certainly a fantaisiste of the first water. About Buchan's "Skule Skerry"—the disillusioning climax was like a wet rag thrown in one's face, yet the general atmosphere is marvellous for all that.

When warmer weather gets me out more, I shall no doubt see "Arrowsmith" & perhaps others of the cinemas you mention. There are certainly many possibilities of genuine art in the motion picture. By the way—I have not read "Maurice Guest",[5] although I have heard it highly spoken of on every hand.

As for the matter of war—I don't see that there's any way to look at it except on a hard fact basis. Nor do I see why the question of fighting can be left to the individual caprice of a flighty & heterogeneous population when the safety of a whole civilisation is at stake. If whim, softness, propaganda, & idealistic theory be permitted to govern every person's decision regarding the defence of his country at a time of peril, there can never be any certainty of effective action in a crisis where promptness & unity mean survival itself. The Minoan civilisation of Crete was wiped out & forgotten because the people would not stand together against the invading Dorians & Achaians. When a nation is caught in an emergency, there is no time for argument & theory. If something isn't done right away, the enemy will be able to put something disastrous across. We can't wait for every scatterbrained theorist to make up mind as to exactly what he wants to do. It is the nation which has given its citizens the safety that enables them to enjoy life at all. Whatever they have, they owe to it. And when the nation is in peril they owe it all the support they can give. I don't say that conscription is necessary in every war. Sometimes a regular army is enough for security. But I do say (with proper shame at my own military ignorance & probable incompetence) that universal *training* ought to prevail, as indeed it did in early New England. Look at the messy & appalling unpreparedness of the U.S. when it entered the World War! Suppose that emergency had been a sudden Japanese–Mexican invasion (as we may have some day) instead of a distant conflict with allies already holding the enemy at bay? I leave the situation to your imagination. You'll undoubtedly outgrow your present attitude, for it is really inconsistent with realistic reason. As for the matter of the Nordic race & culture—there is no question but that, allowing for all blood mixture, the North-European represents a distinctive heritage with self-respecting characteristics all its own.

And so it goes. Best wishes, & thanks again for the Scarborough book & the theme brochure. // Yr obt Servt E'ch-Pi-El

P.S. Pity an old man. I begin a siege at the dentist's tomorrow!

Notes

1. It is not clear what HPL is referring to. Scarborough does not appear to have published any bibliography of weird fiction separate from her treatise, *The Supernatural in Modern English Fiction* (1917).

2. Wandrei's bibliography of weird fiction was not published.

3. By Jessie Adelaide Middleton.

4. HPL refers to Hearn's essay "The Value of the Supernatural in Fiction" (in *Interpretations of Literature*, Volume 2 [1915]) and Scarborough's introduction to her treatise.

5. A work by Henry Handel Richardson, described as "a novel of erotic obsession."

[29]   [ANS][1]

[Postmarked New Orleans, LA,
5 June 1932]

Hail, O Jehvish-Êi! At the farther end of one of my long annual travel jogs. Stopped in N.Y. a week with Frank B. Long, & then began the voyage proper. Shenandoah Valley of Va. & Cumberlands of Tenn. are magnificent. First sight of Father Mississippi at Memphis gave me quite a kick. The old river towns—Vicksburg & Natchez—are highly appealing. The latter has the most splendid subtropical scenery I have ever beheld. ¶ New Orleans is as marvellous architecturally as Charleston & Quebec, but the presence of a modern metropolis outside the old quarter detracts from its charm a bit. You wouldn't mind that, though! Am drinking it in at leisure—staying over a week. Next on the programme, Mobile, Ala.
Regards—
H P L

Notes

1. *Front:* Old Absinthe House, New Orleans.

[30]   [ALS]

10 Barnes St.,
Providence, R.I.,
Octr 13, 1932

Dear Jehvish-Êi:—
          Everything arrived safely, & no harm was caused by the delay. Amidst your intensive reading programme I don't wonder that these volumes were a bit retarded! Evidently you are out to capture young Derleth's record—at any rate you are away beyond me!

Like you, I didn't care greatly for "Creeps by Night". Hammett's definition of the weird is a long way from mine, & his admission of comic items seems to me incongruous. I thought Benet's story the worst of the lot, but "Green Thoughts" is bad enough. One of the things I did like was Aiken's "Mr. Arcularis"—which had a genuine crawling horror in it despite the psychological explanation which I knew all along was coming.[1] Oddly, this anthology seems to have succeeded better than any of its predecessors. A

British edition entitled "Modern Tales of Horror" has just come out—& the London agents have just written me that some editor wants to purchase the British periodical rights of "Erich Zann" . . . . . which means 6 or 7 guineas for me. Probably the best story is Faulkner's "Rose for Emily."

I had *not* seen that 1931 O. Henry list before, & am very grateful to you for transcribing it. I see that five of our crowd (not counting Quinn) are mentioned, & am glad that Belknap made it twice. Some of the other items I recall as rotten. Of those cited, I think that Whitehead's "Passing of a God" is probably the best.[2]

Glad you are beginning to appreciate "The Willows." Keep it up! My opinion that Blackwood leads the weird writers is unchanged, & lately received independent & unsuggested confirmation from a man of high intelligence & keen sensitiveness who has set two of my Yuggothian fungi to music—Harold Farnese of Los Angeles, Dean of the Inst. of Mus. Education thee, & a graduate of the Paris Conservatory, where he won the 1911 prize for composition. He got hold of me through W.T.—& now wishes me to collaborate on a fantastic libretto with him.[3] In discussing weird fiction, & before hearing any of my opinions, he singled out "The Willows" as the foremost thing of its kind. I've already told you that most of our gang agree in giving this tale supremacy.

Your travels sound highly interesting, even if the territory covered was not extensive. No—I've never been near Olean or Rock City—the whole of western N.Y. & Pa. being a terra incognita to me. Your description of the cyclopean tangle of monoliths sounds interesting in the extreme, & I surely hope I can get around there some day. I'd like to see Norfolk, too—to which I've never been nearer than the Williamsburg region. Glad you got a bit of N.C. & cypress growths.

My own travels this year were pretty ample, though they did not all constitute one trip. Between the two trips came a very sad event which makes 1932 a black year for this household—the death of my elder aunt at the age of 76.[4]

The prime objective of trip #1 was New Orleans, which I wished to see before the destruction of the old French Market. On the way I stopped in N.Y. a week to visit Long, & afterward proceeded south via Washington & the exquisite Shenandoah Valley. From Roanoke, Va., I proceeded westward to Knoxville, Tenn., & thence south through splendid landscapes to Chattanooga. The latter is one of the most fascinating places I have ever seen—with its surrounding mountains & the sinuous windings of the yellow Tennessee River. I went all over Lookout Mountain, & explored the magnificent network of limestone caverns inside it—culminating in the vast & newly-discovered chamber called "Solomon's Temple", where a 145-foot waterfall bursts forth from the side—near the roof—& dashes down to a pool whose outlet no man knows. From Chattanooga I proceeded west along the bluff-lined Tennessee, enjoying some of the finest landscapes I ever saw in my life.

At Memphis (modern & unpicturesque) I beheld the mighty Mississippi for the first time—witnessing a splendid sunset over it. I then headed south through the alluvial cotton lands of Mississippi—where nothing but flat vistas & nigger cabins are found—finally reaching the Yazoo country & climbing the bluffs to picturesque old Vicksburg, which I like tremendously. Just south of Vicksburg I began to strike typically Southern flora—live-oaks & Spanish moss. Natchez—dreaming on its river-bluff—captivated me completely. It is one of those splendid survivals of the past exemplified by Quebec, Portsmouth, Newburyport, Salem, Marblehead, Annapolis, Fredericksburg, & Charleston. Founded in 1716 by the French, & later passing through British & Spanish hands, it came into the U.S. in 1798, & soon afterward became a great cotton port. Between 1800 and 1860 it was built up with a splendid type of classic architecture, nearly all of which survives to this day. The financial ruin attendant upon the Civil War stopped its growth, hence it remains today a bit of crystallised history. Its landscape setting is as fascinating as its architecture—live-oaks, moss, cypresses, rolling hills, & old roads deeply sunken in the friable yellow soil. Natchez is one of the few places I'd really like to live in. From there I descended straight to New Orleans—not pausing at the largely modernised Baton Rouge. South of Natchez the landscape grows flat & unpicturesque, & palm-like growths begin to appear. Later on the vast embankments & spillways of the levee system come into view, & occasional plantation houses (both of the slant-roofed French type & of the later pillared classic American type) are seen. At last New Orleans comes in sight—a large modern city with the ancient nucleus still surviving & imbedded close to the waterfront. Probably you've read a good deal about New Orleans. I stayed there over two weeks & came to like it immensely. It was founded by the French in 1718, & taken over by the Spaniards (though without any change in language & customs) in 1763. In 1788 a vast fire nearly wiped it out, but it was very solidly rebuilt—in a fashion slightly Spanish because of the aid furnished by government engineers. The American purchase came in 1803, but the Anglo-Saxon influx established itself south of the older city, leaving the former intact. In the course of years all activity & change centred in the newer American section, so that the original Creole city as rebuilt soon after 1788 still stands unchanged—as quaint a spectacle as Charleston or Quebec. It is a rectangle along the water front some 4000 ft. long & 1500 ft. deep, & now receives the name of "Vieux Carré", or "Old French Quarter." The houses are largely of brick & stucco, & have pointed roofs not unlike those of Charleston & Quebec. Wrought-iron grilles & balconies are everywhere present, & the Spanish influence shews itself in the many picturesque patios or courtyards. I spent most of my time in this ancient section, & came to know it very well. Outside toward the south is the modern American city of broad avenues & splendid gardens, & northward is the modern Creole (though English-speaking for the last two generations) district with houses shewing the hereditary French influence. New Orleans has some fine old live-oaks, & a wealth of tall palms. It is so low that only levees & an artificial drainage system can keep it dry—& until recently no cellars could be dug. Burials have to be above ground, & the ancient cemeteries with their tall tombs & thick walls pierced with oven-like vaults are highly picturesque. The drainage canals were formerly open ditches, but in latter years they have been covered over one by one to form boulevards. People of American & French descent still predominate in New Orleans, & niggers of every hue are numerous. There is a large Italian population, centreing chiefly in the northerly half of the Vieux Carré. The southerly half of the Quarter, somewhat reclaimed from slumdom, is a sort of mild Greenwich Village with antique shops & artists' studios.

New Orleans was, at the time of my visit, the home of the brilliant weird-taler E. Hoffmann Price; but since I had never been in touch with him I thought I wouldn't butt in & introduce myself. However, it happened that during my sojourn I wrote to Robert E. Howard of Texas—who, noting the hotel address on my stationery & being in epistolary touch with Price, took it upon himself to telegraph Price of my presence & whereabouts. The result was an unexpected telephone call from Price, followed by the longest call I have ever paid—or ever expect to pay—in my life . . . . . . a call lasting *25½ hours* without a break, from the middle of a Sunday evening to close upon midnight Monday. Price had a room in the Vieux Carré, & now & then his roommate would brew tea or coffee, or prepare a meal. Once we went over to the old French Market for professionally made coffee. Nobody seemed to get sleepy, & the hours slipped away imperceptibly amidst discussions & fictional criticisms. Later calls lasted 10 hours or so each—& I was in touch with Price until I left. Shortly after my departure Price himself moved out of town—to the quiet little village of Bay St. Louis across the line in Mississippi.* Price is a remarkable chap—a West-Pointer, war veteran, Arabic student, connoisseur of Oriental rugs, amateur fencing-master, mathematician, dilettante coppersmith & iron worker, chess-champion, pianist, & what not! He is dark & trim of figure, not very tall, & with a small black moustache. He talks fluently & incessantly, & might be thought a bore by some—although I like to hear him rattling on. Up to last May he was well off—holding an important job with the Prestolite Co.—but the depression finally got him, & he is now depending on fiction for his income. The result is rather bad aesthetically, for he caters painfully to the pulp standard. I fear we shan't see anything more of the quality of "The Stranger from Kurdistan."[5] Still—he couldn't be as bad as most of the contributors to W.T. & its congeners. Just now he is trying to get me to collaborate on a sequel to my Silver Key—introducing a dimensional element suggested by his mathematical side. I did not meet the

---

* Just got a note from P.—he's moved back to N.O.

other former New Orleans weird-taler—W. Kirk Mashburn—for he had previously moved to Texas.

Well—after New Orleans I proceeded to quaint old Mobile, which I liked exceedingly. Then up to Montgomery (original Confederate capital) & across to Atlanta. There was nothing in the latter modern city to hold me, so I hastened right on along the western Carolinas to Charlotte & Winston-Salem—& thence through Danville to good old Richmond. I love Richmond despite its fairly extensive modernisation. The landmarks of Poe's boyhood are readily traceable, & the bluff at the foot of Clay St. above old Shochoe Creek (near the White House of the Confederacy) is still unaltered—standing just as it did when little Edgar went swimming at its base. The creek, however, is filled in. As always, I visited Maymont Park on the banks of the James— a former private estate exquisitely landscaped & containing the finest Japanese garden in the U.S. After Richmond I paused at Fredericksburg, Annapolis, & Philadelphia—all favourite antiquarian havens of of [*sic*] mine—& finally wound up by visiting a friend—Samuel Loveman—in Brooklyn. From this visit I was called home by a telegram announcing an acute attack on the part of my invalid aunt—an attack which terminated fatally on July 3d.

My second trip began Aug. 30 with a visit to W. Paul Cook in Boston. On the 31st we went to Newburyport to see the total solar eclipse, & had a most impressive view of that phenomenon. Two days later I started on a cheap rail excursion to Montreal & Quebec—thus entering the northern part of that New-France of which Louisiana formed the southern part. As perhaps you know, the French of Quebec Province are more retentive of their language & customs than those of Louisiana, so that they insist on an official bilingualism. All official signs are in the two languages, so that one comes on things like RAILWAY CROSSING [/] TRAVERSE DU CHEMIN DE FER or NO PARKING [/] NE STATIONNEZ PAS at every turning. Montreal (which I had never seen before) is more Anglo-Saxon than Quebec City, & does not seem at all foreign except in the French section east of St. Lawrence Blvd. It must be a great deal like the New Orleans of 75 years ago in its cultural division. Some parts are purely English, but in the French section all the store & street signs are in French. (as none are in New Orleans) There are really twice as many French as English in the city, though they have lost the real social & commercial dominance. Montreal is a highly attractive place, well set off by the towering slope of Mt. Royal, which rises in its midst. The ancient part—where I spent most of my time—is that closest to the southern waterfront, but it does not compare with the Vieux Carré of New Orleans or with the whole of old Quebec City. Montreal, taken all in all, would seem like any large high-grade American city but for the profusion of horse-drawn vehicles. I explored it thoroughly, & also visited the adjacent Lachine Rapids— beside which La Salle had his seigniory.

However—I was glad to move along to old Quebec at last, for that is utterly unique among the cities of this continent. As in 1930 I revelled in the atmosphere of massed antiquity—the towering cliff, frowning citadel, silver belfries, tiled red roofs, breath-taking panoramas, winding, precipitous alleys & flights of steps, centuried facades & doorways, venerable stone monasteries, & other picturesque reliquiae of bygone days—& I also took a ferry & 'bus excursion around the neighbouring Isle d'Orleans, where the old French countryside remains in a primitive, unspoiled state—just as when Wolfe & his men landed in 1759. There were endless brick farmhouses with curved eaves, wind & water mills, wayside shrines, & quaint white villages clustering around ancient silver-steepled parish churches. Nothing but French is spoken, & the rustic population live where their ancestors have lived for more than 200 years—seldom visiting even Quebec. I hated to go home, & when re-passing through Boston eased the transition by making a side-trip to ancient Marblehead. Since my return to Prov. I have been kept on the move by two successive guests—first the young poet Carl F. Strauch (now Asst. Librarian of Muhlenburg [*sic*] University) of Allentown, Pa., & then our brilliant W.T. colleague Donald Wandrei. As a result of this social activity on top of my travel orgy, my work & correspondence are hopelessly piled up, so that I don't know when I'll be able to see daylight again. However—I did take a day off last Sunday for a cheap excursion to Boston, which permitted me to get up to Salem & Marblehead again. There won't be many more days warm enough to let me enjoy the outdoors.

The eclipse, as I said, was a success for me—though many places in the totality zone were clouded. Cook & I picked ancient Newburyport as a post of observation; & although there were clouds in the sky, the sun & moon were entirely clear of them at the climactic moment of totality. We reached Newburyport long before the eclipse started, & chose a hilltop meadow with a wide view—near the northern part of the town—as our observatory. Naturally the clouds made us anxious, but the sun came out every little while & gave us long glimpses of all stages of the phenomenon. The landscape did not change in tone until the solar crescent was rather small, & then a kind of sunset vividness became apparent. When the crescent waned to extreme thinness, the scene grew strange & spectral—an almost deathlike quality inhering in the sickly yellowish light. Just about that time the sun went under a cloud, & Cook & I commenced cursing in seven different languages! At last, though, the thin thread of the pre-totality glitter emerged into a large patch of absolutely clear sky. The outspread valleys faded into unnatural light—Jupiter came out in the deep-violet heavens—ghoulish shadow-bands raced along the winding white roads—the last beaded strip of glitter vanished—& the pale corona flickered into aureolar radiance around the black disc of the obscuring moon. We were seeing the real show! The earth was darkened more deeply than in the eclipse of 1925[6] (which I saw, half frozen, amidst the January snows of Yonkers, N.Y.), though the corona was not so bright. We absorbed the whole spectacle with the utmost impressedness & appreciation. Finally the beaded crescent reappeared, the valleys glowed again in faint, eerie light, & the various partial phases were repeated in reverse order. The marvel was over, & accustomed things resumed their wonted sway. I may never see another—but it is not everyone who has, like me, witnessed two total solar eclipses!

Sorry your Pitt course is interrupted, & hope it can be resumed before long. Glad you'll have musical instruction to brighten the interim. It must be hard choosing betwixt piano & violin!

Congratulations on your dramatic appearance! I'll wager you did well [wi]th the role. Glad you've had some opportunities to witness various dramas. Of the cinemas you mention I have seen only "Arrowsmith"—in New Orleans. It was indeed very good as cinemas go, & I'd be less bored with such things if pictures of this quality could be depended upon right along. Incidentally—I haven't seen a picture since.

I can't comment in detail on all your reading, for I've been through only a fraction of it myself. "Shadows on the Rock" pleased me because I know every inch of the ground covered; but were I less of a Quebec-fan I imagine I'd have found it insipid. Of Proust I have read "Swann's Way" & "Within a Budding Grove"—& appreciated both profoundly. Proust is possibly Derleth's principal literary source—but Belknap professes to see nothing in him. Glad you appreciate "The Hill of Dreams"—which is of course Machen's real masterpiece.

Recently I picked up quite a few good remainders at a local sale— O'Brien's "Dance of the Machines" (exposé of the shallow artificiality of the Am. commercial short story), Huysmans' "A Rebours", Perutz's "Master of the Day of Judgment", & some excellent scientific items. I haven't yet read the Perutz book, but many correspondents have spoken very enthusiastically of it.

I was much interested in the dialect notes which you enclosed—& which I return in case you keep a file of such material. Several of the idioms are more than local, though perhaps they are used more frequently in western Pennsylvania than elsewhere. Others, so far as I know, are absolutely local— & utterly new to me. Among the latter are *bealed, rosette, footy, spreads, haps, hippens, flannel cakes*, &c. *Mind* for *remember* is a Scotticism. "My! but—" is common in New England as in Pa. So is *peaked* for thin & drawn. The pronunciation of *were* as *wāre* is absolutely correct in Old England, & is favoured by many in New. It is a spontaneous survival in northern Maine. "Graveyard" is universal throughout N.E. So is *spare room. Happen in* & *set up housekeeping* are also Novanglianisms. The Pittsburgh *inflections*, however, appear to be purely local. Of late dialect has been studied more than ever before, since radios & talking cinemas threaten to eradicate most localisms. As friend of mine is greatly interested in the speech of the Hudson Valley, & is actually trying to learn the debased South Holland patois called "Jersey Dutch" still spoken by certain decaying backwater elements.

I read your weird tale article with intense interest, & believe that it is in the main based upon sound critical principles. Its preparation must certainly have involved a lot of digging—though of a not unpleasant kind. There are—as your teacher pointed out—certain verbal infelicities—but time will iron these out of your style. I notice that in recent years young writers do not use words & phrases as aptly & accurately as in former times. There is more clumsi[ness in] the choice of terms & constructions, & less sense of architec[ural] harmony in the correlation of the parts of a sentence or parag[raph.] This is probably due to the lessened emphasis on pure gramma[r &] rhetoric in the schools of today. Most writers outgrow their early awkwardness—as Derleth & Wandrei are doing—but a generation ago they had more academic help in this polishing process. By the way—let me thank you for the favourable references to my work in your article. I perused the entire text with great pleasure, & believe it would form a valuable little manual if revised & published. I return it herewith.

As for writing on my part, I believe I am finished for good. Unfavourable estimates of my recent work have destroyed my own confidence in it, & I do not find myself able to get on paper what I really want to express. It is possible that I may attempt more stuff to please myself, but I doubt if I shall exhibit it to any one. If I attempt any hack work for magazines it will probably be under another name. Revision takes most of my time now—& amusingly enough, several tales which are virtually mine have landed with W.T. & others. By the way—I see that *Wonder Stories* has become thinner & gone down to 15¢. Someone tells me that *Oriental* is now a small monthly called *The Magic Carpet.* And a note from E. Hoffmann Price which has just arrived (since I began this epistle) reports the discontinuance of *Strange Tales.* This last news will disappoint Smith, Whitehead, & others who have been landing regularly with *Strange.*

And now—as climax—to consider your "Tin Roof." Damn it, boy, but you've found your metier at last! The sheer excellence of the thing veritably knocked me cold, for I was wholly unprepared for anything so solidly good as early in the game as this. Your year of training under the Pitt martinets has certainly done you an universe of good! It marks a *radical, meteoric advance* on your part. Keep it up & you'll be crowding Derleth for honours before you know it! Try it on the serious magazines—*Midland, Pagany,* &c. Shew it to Derleth & ask his advice about placement. Don't waste it on the trashy women's magazines. God, but you've struck your vein with a vengeance. *Realism* is the stuff for you! Not since Norris's "McTeague" have I seen the squalor of decay & of the lower-middle-class scene put across as vividly as you have done it. I can actually *smell* that Huntington Hill neighbourhood. How the deuce did you think up all the details? I couldn't concoct a thing like that if I tried five years! Keep it up! Write more along this line, & get suggestions from Derleth. If you can do this sort of thing repeatedly, you certainly have a literary future. Thanks for the glimpse of it. My only criticism would concern trivialities of linguistic construction. ¶ Well—best wishes & all that.

Your most obt Grandsire

H P L

P.S. Pardon penmanship. I *cannot* get a fountain to suit me, & have gone back to the old dipped pens of my youth. Even they are hard to get right!

Notes

1. HPL refers to the following stories in *Creeps by Night:* Stephen Vincent Benét, "The King of the Cats"; John Collier, "Green Thoughts"; Conrad Aiken, "Mr. Arcularis."

2. In *O. Henry Memorial Award: Prize Stories of 1931,* ed. Blanche Colton Williams (Garden City, NY: Doubleday, Doran, 1931), covering stories published from July 1930 to May 1931, the following stories from *WT* were listed: (a) "Stories ranking second": W. Elwyn Backus, "The Phantom Bus" (September 1930); Robert E. Howard, "The Children of the Night" (April/May 1931); Theda Kenyon, "The House of the Golden Eyes" (September 1930); Frank Belknap Long, Jr., "The Black Druid" (July 1930); Charles Henry Mackintosh, "Guardians of the Guavas" (September 1930); Katharine Metcalf Roof, "A Million Years After" (November 1930); (b) "Stories ranking third": Ben Belitt, "Tzo-Lin's Nightingales" (February/March 1931); Francis Flagg, "The Picture" (February/March 1931); Lieutenant Edgar Gardiner, "The Galley Slave" (January 1931); Edmond Hamilton, "Pigmy Island" (August 1930), "The Mind-Master" (October 1930), "The Horror City" (February/March 1931), "Ten Million Years After" (April/May 1931); Hugh Jeffries, "The Dust of Death" (April/May 1931); Ainslee Jenkins, "Men of Steel" (December 1930); Frank Belknap Long, Jr., "A Visitor from Egypt" (September 1930); N. J. O'Neail, "The Flame Fiend" (September 1930); Seabury Quinn, "The Ghost-Helper" (February/March 1931); Robert C. Sandison, "Burnt Things" (December 1930); Jane Scales, "The Thing in the Bush" (February/March 1931); Nat Schachner and Arthur L. Zagat, "The Dead-Alive" (April/May 1931); CAS, "A Rendezvous in Averoigne" (April/May 1931); Gertrude Macaulay Sutton, "Gesture" (September 1930); Marian Thornton, "The Treasure of Almeria" (April/May 1931); Henry S. Whitehead, "Passing of a God" (January 1931); (c) "Short short stories ranking highest": Paul Ernst, "The Tree of Life" (September 1930); Wallace West, "The Last Incarnation" (October 1930); (d) "Short short stories ranking second": Francis Flagg, "The Jelly-Fish" (October 1930); Dorothy Norwich, "The Game" (January 1931); CAS, "The Phantoms of the Fire" (September 1930).

3. HPL gave Farnese permission to set "Mirage" and "The Elder Pharos" (*WT,* February/March 1931) to music. Farnese sought HPL's assistance writing a libretto for a proposed musical drama in one act set on Yuggoth to be called *Fen River,* but HPL demurred, and the piece probably was never written.

4. Lillian D. Clark died on 3 July 1932.

5. E. Hoffmann Price, "The Stranger from Kurdistan" (*WT,* July 1925; rpt. December 1929).

6. There was a total eclipse of the sun on 24 January 1925. Manhattan and other areas of the New York metropolitan area were in the zone of totality. HPL had gone to Yonkers to get a better view; as he notes to his aunt, he "went up to Yonkers & had a magnificent view of the entire thing from the summit of a high hill. Corona was splendid, & planets were brilliantly visible" (HPL to Lillian D. Clark, [25 January 1925]; ANS postcard, JHL).

[31]   [ALS]

10 Barnes St.,
Providence, R.I.,
Octr 27, 1932

Dear Jehvish-Êi:—

No, I don't think I was too favourable toward "The Tin Roof". I didn't mean to imply that you had produced something literally equal to Norris's "McTeague", but simply that you had mastered the art of calling up the peculiar sort of environment handled in that novel—the deadly greyish-brown sort of decay which is peculiarly devoid of all beauty, & which has not even the nightmare picturesqueness & tragic dignity or drama of absolute gutter life. The most significant thing about it is in its complete difference from anything else of yours. The improvement is startling & radical, & argues such a felicitous finding of yourself that one may well be pardoned a somewhat demonstrative amount of enthusiasm. I spoke relatively—but see no reason to take back any statement made. Probably Derleth could parallel the job—but then, he's been doing this kind of thing for three years or more, & had a general literary training long before that. No—this piece is a landmark for you, & I believe you'll later look back on it as such. Probably your forte will be the realistic rather than the fantastic—which is all in your favour, since unreality is at best a minor, limited specialty without many opportunities for expansion. As for the relative ease of realism & phantasy—that's all in the individual. For me, it would be very difficult to think up or observe enough details of real life to fill a narrative, whereas it is easy to devise imaginative vistas & supply touches of cosmic atmosphere. With others—perhaps with you—it is just the other way around. Each to his specialty—though of course it takes a great deal of experimenting in various fields to discover what one's specialty is. Wandrei is beginning to experiment in realism, & tells me that he is at work on a reminiscent novel in something like the Derleth vein. I was greatly interested in your account of the sources of "The Tin Roof", & congratulate you on your ability to observe & store up such a wealth of significant detail. Don't mind the essentially photographic nature of your early products. Style, situation, cosmic intimations, & all that will come later one as a natural development. Derleth's style was rotten up to two or three years ago—loose, careless, unrhythmical, & even doubtful grammar—but since then he has trained it into something really fine, with precision, vividness, & a subtly musical rhythm.

As for myself—no, I couldn't turn out work like that. Whenever I assemble realistic detail it is with great effort—& more important still, I simply haven't anything to say in any field outside the unreal. I have not a keen sensitiveness for the drama of actual life. Academically I appreciate its importance, & I can admire the artistic skill which captures & utilises it; but it does not interest me enough to make me want to get it down on paper myself. There can be no real authorship without a genuine & imperative urge for expression—& I have not that urge except in connexion with the haunting conception of impinging cosmic mystery & the liberation implied in the suspension or circumvention of the tyranny of time, space, & natural law. Writing—or rather, trying to write—in some other vein would be an absurd & unmotivated procedure. I shall keep silent a while, & if I begin again shall not shew the results to anyone. Unfavourable criticism, while it does not anger me, has an adverse effect on my creative ability. I must write freely if at all—to suit myself, & with no thought of any audience.

Yes—social or settlement work, like that of your sister, would surely give you a valuable insight into the workings of human nature in the raw. Possibly you can get cases from her, like the one you mention, to work up literarily. I fancy that much matter of this sort must exist in the records of settlement workers, & the published reports of charitable institutions & sociological commissions, if you could only get access to such. In looking over the N.Y. Times's list of "100 Neediest Cases" each Christmas I have often thought what splendid material some of these brief & tragic sketches would make for an author gifted enough to use them. Derleth digs up a great deal of his information about family relationships, histories, & tragedies through systematic absorption of village gossip & actual prying into the affairs of his neighbours. He frankly admits that Sauk City people consider him an utter pest & nuisance. I fear that no one can be a genuinely great realist without doing an obnoxious amount of nosing & gossiping. That sort of thing is instinctively repulsive & abhorrent to me; though I can, objectively speaking, excuse it in a serious artist whose sole motive is an honest curiosity about life as a whole & a genuine creative desire to capture the texture of life in lasting words. Here's wishing you luck with your attempted suicide story. I wouldn't mind seeing it when it's done.

As for dialect—I have never heard either "comfort" or "comfortable" used in connexion with bedclothes, though in N.E. the word "*comforter*" (note the exact form) is applied to a very heavy quilt, thickly stuffed with cotton. In Great Britain (—& also here, despite the conflicting usage involved) the same word is used to describe a heavy outdoor muffler for the throat & chest. A great deal of the homely local slang of yesteryear is perishing everywhere in this generation, despite the attempts of antiquarians & traditionalists to keep it alive. On the other hand, there is a tendency for certain other localisms to spread alarmingly & become a part of the nation-wide *eloquium vulgare*. An example is the use of *like* for *as* or *as if*, once peculiar to the less educated classes of the South. ("It looked *lahk* he was go'n' to call awn you-all.") This form of speech first rose upward in the social & cultural scale in its native South, & then spread into the Middle West. I think it entered Ohio & such states about 30 years ago or more. Up to the time of the Great War it was still unknown in New England except in either conventional southern dialect or the speech of illiterates. Meanwhile, however, it had conquered the west, entered New York, & secured a hold on the cheaper grade of syndicate writers. This cheap use in printed matter, plus the effect of the radio & talking cinema, has now definitely introduced the solecism into the common speech of New England's lower middle class, & is beginning to affect the careless Babbitt fringe of the upper middle class. It will never conquer our most careful academic circles, however. In the west one now finds it in the casual speech & writings of even university instructors. Other cases of modern degeneration have to do with corrupt pronunciations. I have seen *add'ress* (for *address'*) rise from a frank barbarism to a sort of left-handed recognition in the Standard Dictionary. About 1912 I began to notice the lower classes saying *kew'-pon* when they meant *coupon*, & I see that in New York this is more prevalent than in New England. It is still confined to a very common element here. The latest of all popular corruptions—which I never heard till 1924 or 1925 (in N.Y.), & which did not invade New England till about 1930, is the mispronunciation of *car'-a-mel* as *cär'mel*—a dissyllable identical with *Mt. Carmel!* I have reason to suspect that it has been a Westernism for some time—for although it is still an emphatic plebeianism here, it was used in all unconsciousness last month by no less cultivated a youth than Donald Wandrei—of St. Paul, Minn. A less explicable & less excusable sort of corruption is that which arises in upper circles & proceeds from fashionable affectation. The chief case I can recall is that of the pronunciation *pro-grum* for *programme*, which sprang up about 1915. This may have been due to an attempt to ape certain phases of the extreme Oxford accent, but more probably it was a corruption of insidious *visual* origin, resulting from the silly & unjustified popularity of the corrupt spelling of *programme* as *"program"* in the less conservative American periodicals. Now, unfortunately, this corruption has spread to some quite conservative papers. I have always maintained that the arbitrary corruptions of spelling popular in the United States will ultimately have a disastrous effect even on pronunciation. In the less cultivated parts of the Middle West—say Iowa & Nebraska (where this cheap faddism reaches its maximum) one occasionally finds forms as absurd as *thot* & *brot* for *thought* and *brought;* & I'll wager that within a generation (unless counteracted by radio & sound cinema) the younger people there will be pronouncing these words to rhyme with *shot* & *blot,* which the ridiculous misspelling unmistakably suggests.

As for the current decline in prose style—it has really been going on for over half a century. Even back in my day the teaching of rhetoric was by no means as exact as it had been in the day of my parents & grandparents, & my early writings were constantly picked to pieces by my more rigidly trained uncle & grandfather. If my prose has any merit, it is due to that criticism, & to the ancient books of rhetoric (1797, 1812, 1818, 1842, 1845, &c) in the family library, which I studied assiduously as part of my ingrained antiquarianism. In reality, my writing reflects not the standards of my own chronological period, but those of a century & more ago. For real, honest training you can't beat Blair's Rhetorick (of which I have a late—1820—edition), Alden's Reader (1797), or Parker's Aid to Composition (1845). The latter—redolent of the scholarship of the Poe period—is what I really grew up on. If I had depended on the weak-kneed stuff dished out to me in the early 1900's, I would have a damned sight worse style than I do now . . . . . although even as late as that things weren't as slipshod as they are today. I first realised the ineptitude of 20th century pedagogy when a member of the United Amateur Press Assn. back in 1914 & 1915. I was appointed to the critical department, & had occasion to handle the aspiring attempts not only of high-school & college fledglings, but of many teachers & principals. (It would surprise you to see some of the creative yearnings of the genus *praeceptor!*) God, what crap! The blunders that even high-school principals, bearing (tho' gawd knows how) ostentatious A.M.'s & Ph.D.'s, managed to pull! But all teachers aren't like that. My friend M. W. Moe of Milwaukee is an admirably thorough, intelligent, conscientious, & scientific pedagogue, & succeeds in giving most of his pupils a real appreciation of literature & a real ability to write at least reasonably well. One reason why modern pedagogy lays less stress on good writing is that it wishes to concentrate on the more important subject of literary appreciation. This is a sound principle as far as it goes—but I think it would do no harm to insist on good writing as well as appreciation. By the way—I still serve on critical boards in amateur journalism, although my old United has long ago gone down to oblivion. I now belong to the still older National Assn.—recruiting matter of which I believe I sent you last year. Here's a brochure of my criticism which you needn't bother to return.[1] I handle only verse this year.

As for books—no, I haven't yet read "The Lady Who Came to Stay." Too damned rushed to read anything—last 2 W.T. & final S.T. remain on my centretable unread. Your postscript to your own reading list sounds as solid as the main section—& shews me how far I am left behind! Concerning Beardsley—bless your heart, I think I've seen every illustration he ever drew! I own the Modern Library book of his stuff. He was certainly a titan among the decadents of the 1890's, & Beerbohm has christened that whole age "The Beardsley Period."

Norfolk has at least one fine colonial church, & must have many old houses—although everyone tells me that it is not really notable in an antiquarian way. Have you noticed the progress of restoration in Williamsburg? I was last there in 1930, just after the Raleigh Tavern reproduction was finished. Now I believe the old Colony House at the end of Duke of Gloucester St., & the

Governor's Palace fronting Palace Green, are at least under way. Another place I like is Yorktown—which retains the ancient Virginia atmosphere to a surprising degree. So you never saw a large boat closely till this recent visit? That's a bit singular, since I believe you've been to N.Y. City, where the very largest are on view for all who will take the trouble to explore the waterfront. I don't know what the antiquities of Pittsburgh are—but many of them have probably perished in the intensive industrialisation of the middle XIX century. I saw a reproduction of the old blockhouse at the Philadelphia sesquicentennial in 1926. Richmond well repays exploration, for it is both intrinsically beautiful & full of historic sites. Colonial houses, however, are not as numerous as one might wish. If you're interested in spots associated with Poe, I'll make you a list—with directions for reaching each one. Have you ever seen the Poe Shrine—the old stone house (oldest edifice in Richmond, also erroneously called "Washington's Headquarters") beyond the railway station in the easterly part of Main St.? It has no original connexion with Poe, but is used to house Poe reliques. The garden in the rear is highly attractive, & in one annex is a marvellous model of the whole city as it was in Poe's boyhood. The oldest Allan home—12th St. & Tobacco Alley—is still standing. It has been a warehouse in the recent past, & for the last 3 years has stood empty. I certainly hope it will not be demolished. The later Allen mansion—"Moldavia", at Main & 5th—was demolished years ago. The Japanese Garden is in Maymont Park—contiguous to Byrd Park. You ought not to miss that—it would keep you dreaming for a week. There is a very fair Japanese Garden in Brooklyn N.Y.—near the museum—where I used to do all my reading & writing on fine summer days when I lived in Flatbush. Glad you saw Mt. Vernon—which I explored in 1928.

Yes—the gang have quite taken possession of the final S.T. Klarkash-Ton isn't exactly disparaging Blackwood & de la Mare, but is trying to shew that a less human perspective than theirs is occasionally desirable. I probably shall try that Silver Key sequel with Price sooner or later, though it will be some time before I can get around to it.

Hope you'll progress smoothly with the music. Doubtless the piano is the best all-around instrument to know if one isn't going to be a professional. There is something fundamental & universal in it—all composers use it exclusively for creation, & most virtuosi on other instruments also play it.

As for those new weird books listed by O'Brien—I've seen none of them, although Derleth has the Summers collection & says it is a vast disappointment—full of well-known stuff that everyone has read, & rather tame selections at that. There is also reason to assume that the Austin book is not so hot, since its publisher—Meador—is a recognised "vanity" firm whose sole business is the issuance of unmarketable books at the authors' expense.[2] A plodding friend of mine had a book brought out by Meador[3]—on the usual basis. I can't endorse O'Brien's approval of "The King of Cats", although I am fully with him on "Mr. Arcularis."

Incidentally—are you in the market for books? Long—whose father has cut down his allowance—is very foolishly selling off his library to raise immediate cash for such basic necessities as neckties, cigarettes, & moustachelet-wax; & has prepared the enclosed catalogue . . . . which he asks Grandpa to distribute. If you see in it anything you like, go to it. Let Little Belknap's folly be your gain. If I were in New York I'd paddle the kid in the posteriors for selling an intellectual heritage for a mess of pottage!

I note your cinematic observations, & agree that a number of very passable things must have adorned the screen during the past year. Doubtless if I had a greater interest in the drama as a whole, I'd be more assiduous in looking up worthy features on the advance bulletins of the local shrines of Thespis.

And so it goes. Again I congratulate you on "The Tin Roof", & urge you to keep it up. Blessings & the Peace of Allah—

Yr most obt Grandsire

E'ch-Pi-El

Notes

1. *Further Criticism of Poetry.*

2. HPL presumably refers to Montague Summers's anthology *The Supernatural Omnibus* (London: Gollancz, 1931; New York: Doubleday, Doran, 1932) and Lilian Edna Austin, *Shudders* (Boston: Meador Publishing Co., 1931).

3. Apparently *Props* by J. Bernard Lynch (Meador Publishing, 1932).

[32]   [ALS]

10 Barnes St.,
Providence, R.I.,
Novr. 16, 1932—
5 a.m.

Dear Jehvish-Êi:—

Well—in spite of all the advertising, the Leonid meteor shower was a fizzle—at least here. I want my money back at the box office! Beastly fog to start with, & a moon only 3 days past full, which blots faint objects from the skies. I walked nearly a quarter of a mile to the best semi-rustic oasis sans electric lights & with a good eastern horizon, but in the course of an hour (3:15 to 4:15 a.m.) saw only 5 meteors—not more than two of which were in any way brilliant. I shall look for press reports from fog-free regions—but I profoundly suspect that the whole thing was largely a disappointment, like the last expected meteor-deluge of 1899. Possibly I'll look again tomorrow before dawn if the weather is clear—but beyond that time there'll be no chance. Well—I suppose it would be too much to expect a successful total eclipse & a good meteor shower all in the same year!

Good luck with your suicide tale—you certainly have enough dark elements to contend with! As your powers grow, you will probably experiment more & more in material where not so much dependence is placed upon tragic intensity or abnormality of situation, but where the flow & colour of life are subtly suggested through more externally commonplace events. Only wide testing can shew you in the end what sort of themes you are best fitted for. As for sources—no, I don't think you'd be very good at that personal nosing which the young Comte d'Erlette seems to practice so successfully. I know I couldn't do anything even remotely like that—to begin with, a whole set of inhibitions against offensiveness, encroachment, and cheap curiosity would stand in the way; & I fear the artist in me isn't sufficient to undermine what I have been accustomed from infancy to regard as the very foundations of good breeding. Long & I have often tried to settle the question as to whether one may at the same time be a successful realist & a gentleman, & our conclusions have generally tended toward the negative side. A truly great realist must have a prodigious amount of accurate first-hand knowledge of exactly what happens among groups of people—exactly what motives operate, how they operate, & how every type of emotion expresses itself in human action . . . . also, just how the feelings & character of each type of individual develop through the years—& so on & so on. . . . . We can't see how any such body of direct information—the enormous fund of human information possessed by Dreiser & Sherwood Anderson—can possibly be accumulated without a long & persistent career of obnoxious peeping, prying, & general violation of personal reticences. How, otherwise, can these birds know exactly how all sorts of persons react to all sorts of situations? No—I don't think that first-hand settlement work would agree with you very well. Besides—it would give you data on only one side of life—the raw side. It is possible for an author to get rather warped through a perspective ample in one narrow direction but restricted in others. Reporting would afford more all-around opportunities, but as you say, is hardly the ideal career for a retiring person. I know I wouldn't last a day at such a job!

Hope you'll be able to get the Long items you wish. Yes—the kid has excellent taste, & it's a devilish shame that he is allowing his carefully collected library to be broken up. The list you saw represents only the tail-end of his original collection, for he sold all the really choice (in a bibliophilic sense) items to friends in the bookselling business.

I note the epistolary & columnar references to "Mädchen in Uniform"[1] & will guarantee to see the performance when or if it comes to Providence. I am quite sure it has not been here as yet. From other criticisms I have seen I feel sure that it must be a genuine work of art—for which reason it will probably not be popular. The bit of Americana is interesting as an exhibit. It is a beneficent thing that such an all-wise source of abstruse data exists to settle the complex difficulties of earnest seekers after learning!

Let me thank you especially for the views enclosed, which I have surveyed with the keenest interest. That panorama of your Oakland section is delightful, & I appreciate particularly the graphically annotated key. Certainly, Pittsburgh lacks nothing of beauty despite its dominant industrialism. Glad you have such vistas at your disposal—I must explore the region myself some day. Hope that "Suicide in Costume" is stimulating local art interest as it did last year!

About Richmond—notify me in advance when you're going to be there, & I'll prepare a list of Poe sites & other points of interest. It's a great old town, & I never tire of it.

As for poetry—you don't know yet whether it will form a natural medium of expression for you. Give yourself time! You don't have to like all the standard poets. Their methods & moods are very different, & it is perfectly possible to enjoy & appreciate some of them keenly while remaining indifferent to others. I share several of the dislikes you enumerate—especially Burns & Browning. The latter, to my mind, kept close to the spirit of prose—amply justifying the famous Wilde epigram—"Meredith is a prose Browning—*& so was Browning.*"[2] I don't run any temperature over Byron myself. Of Swinburne I like the earlier things, though of course he babbled himself out in repetition. Tennyson has some fine effects, but as a whole he wearies me. You are dead right in exalting Keats & Shelley. They represent the absolute zenith of the poetic art. Of moderns, Millay is an excellent minor, & Masters is powerful whether you call him poetry or prose. Robert Frost is the real stuff, & Masefield is not to be dismissed with a gesture. But W. B. Yeats is probably the greatest living poet.

Your cinema list is surely ample, & I doubt not that it forms a good guide for attendance at second or third run houses. Of the 18 performers you list, I have seen only 6 to identify them—a good index of Grandpa's complacent ignorance of a popular contemporary field! Of the plays listed I have seen exactly *one*—"Arrowsmith". Too bad "The Monkey's Paw"[3] has been spoiled.

I haven't seen "Living Alone", but read "Lolly Willowes"[4] some years ago. It disappointed me—especially since the author is Arthur Machen's niece. The witch element is so light, whimsical, & intendedly subtle that it fails to impress one very heavily—& yet it does give a sort of sense of strangeness as connected with the lonely Cotswold Hills. Sorry Merritt is so far below his best standard—but that's the way of the world. Watch E. Hoffmann Price go downhill now that he has frankly started out to be a commercial hack . . . . & reflect on the devolution of Quinn from "The Phantom Farmhouse"[5] to today's mechanical grist!

Yes—it is curious that all the elder generation are having a last literary fling this year. Barrie's new phantasy has much of the insipidity & affectation of his older stuff. I must read something by this newcomer Morgan—& must also see if "The Lady Who Came to Stay" is available at the local public library. I certainly intend to read "Peter Ashley"[6] sooner or later. Thanks, by the way, for the current magazine tips. I haven't even seen a copy of the new *American Spectator* as yet—the list of contributors certainly sounds important enough!

No—the "depression plant" is a new one on me! It surely sounds picturesque enough—possibly it is a local Pittsburgh idea. And speaking of localisms—here is something I saw in the *Literary Digest* which I never knew about before.[7] How would you like to get bashed on the bean with an *espantoon?* In recent years I have heard the term *night-stick* used—quite irrespective of the sun or clock. Another one-city localism is the New Orleans term for sidewalk—*bouquette.* This is peculiar to the town, & although of French Creole origin is not met with anywhere else or in any French dictionary. Curious that *"cär'mel"* for *cär'-a-mel* should have had so great a headway. I certainly don't recall hearing it around here till a couple of years ago, though I found it in N.Y. City in the early 1920's. Evidently it originated in the west & is spreading eastward. During the war at least three curious orthoëpic perversions attracted my notice—"en'-sïn" for *en'-sign,* *"rä'-tions"* for *rä'-tions,* & "can-tōn'-ment for can'-tŏn-ment. I haven't kept track of the fate of these forms. One word which may—through usage—be actually changing its accent is *pri'-ma-ri-ly.* More & more the careless form *"pri-mar'-i'ly"* is heard.

Many thanks for acquainting me with the O. Henry results. It rather astonishes me, in view of the usual philistine policy of this annual, to find my "Strange High House" so well mentioned.[8] By the way—did I tell you that a writer's magazine called *The American Author* had an article last July in which my "In the Vault", Klarkash-Ton's "Gorgon", & Edmond Hamilton's "Earth-Brain" were singled out for quotation & analysis?[9] Your reclassification of O'Brien's choices is interesting. By the way—Auguste-Guillaume, Comte d'Erlette has just had a letter from O'Brien stating that "Five Alone" (in *Pagany*) will be three-starred in 1933. Little Augie is surely coming on!

As for anthology-making—I'd imagine that the thing to do would be to consider the length desired, pick the stories, secure reprinting permission from the authors, periodicals, or other copyright-owners involved, copy all the material as one neat MS., select a title, write a preface, & then start the thing on the rounds of the publishers just as if it were a book of your own. Probably you wouldn't have to pay the copyright owners unless the book was accepted. As for titles—"A Vague Unease" doesn't sound quite right to me. The other discarded ones also have limitations. "Scratchings on the Rim" or something like that wouldn't be bad. Your choices seem to me largely excellent, except that my "Outsider" doesn't belong. I'll lend you "The Yellow Sign" if you like. As for other suggestions—isn't Blackwood's "Wendigo" unhackneyed enough? How about Chambers' "Harbour-Master" & George Allen England's "The Thing from Outside"? E. F. Benson's "Horror Horn"

& "The Face" are worth considering. Also Wakefield's "17th Hole at Duncaster." Buchan's "Wind in the Portico" is worth a look. But you'll have a job on your hands choosing & preparing! ¶ With best wishes—

Your most obᵗ hble Servᵗ

E'ch-Pi-El

N.B. I can lend you "The Yellow Sign" & "Night Wire"[10] if you like. "House of Sounds" might be lent by H. Warner Munn. Route 1, Athol, Mass.

Notes

1. *Mädchen in Uniform* (Bild und Ton, 1931), directed by Leontine Sagan; starring Emilia Unda, Dorothea Wieck, and Hedwig Schlichter. Based on the play *Gestern und heute* by Christa Winslow. The film concerns a young girl who is sent to an all-girls school and develops a romantic attachment to one of the teachers. It is regarded as a pioneering work in the portrayal of lesbianism.

2. The remark is found in Wilde's essay "The Critic as Artist" (1890).

3. *The Monkey's Paw* (RKO Radio Pictures, 1933), directed by Wesley Ruggles and Ernest B. Schoedsack; starring Ivan S. Simpson, Louise Carter, and C. Aubrey Smith. Based on the story by W. W. Jacobs. The film was released on 13 January 1933; JVS must have seen an advance showing.

4. Marginally weird novels by Stella Benson and Sylvia Townsend Warner.

5. Seabury Quinn, "The Phantom Farmhouse" (*WT,* October 1923; rpt. March 1929).

6. HPL refers to J. M. Barrie's *Farewell Miss Julie Logan;* Charles Morgan's *The Fountain;* and Du Bose Heyward's *Peter Ashley,* a novel about Charleston, SC.

7. See "The Lexicographer's Easy Chair," *Literary Digest* 114, No. 19 (5 November 1932): 51.

8. *O. Henry Memorial Award Prize Stories,* ed. Blanche Colton Williams (Garden City, NY: Doubleday, 1932).

9. J. Randle Luten, "What Makes a Story Click?" *American Author* 4, No. 4 (July 1932): 11–13; rpt. in *A Weird Writer in Our Midst: Early Criticism of H. P. Lovecraft,* ed. S. T. Joshi (New York: Hippocampus Press, 2011), 56–62.

10. H. F. Arnold, "The Night Wire" (*WT,* September 1926; rpt. January 1933).

[33]   [ALS]

Tenbarnes—

Decr. 22, 1932

Dear Jehvish-Êi:—

Don't mind a Harper's rejection—even Derleth hasn't landed anything there yet. Your best bet is the high-grade non-remunerative magazine such as *Pagany* or *The Midland.*

Sorry you've had influenza. There seems to be quite an epidemic in the West—now reaching the South & probably destined to progress northward.

Your freedom from illness is remarkable & enviable. I had measles at *19*, & it damn near finished me. Chicken-pox at 25. Mumps, whooping-cough, & all the rest of the juvenile maladies are evidently waiting to catch me in my second childhood. What material for an epitaph—to die of whooping-cough at 98 or so! I've heard of Pittsburgh "smog"—what a pity that the factories can't be farther from the city proper. The worst regime of grime I ever struck was in Brooklyn in 1925, when there was an anthracite coal strike & the Hylan administration sanctioned a suspension of the anti-bituminous regulation. A collar wasn't good for long under those conditions. As for weather—rain is fast disposing of last week's snow here. During the recent cold spell the mercury sank to zero one day—& I was forced to stay in three days. $+20°$ is my deadline, as repeated experiments have proved.

As for W.T.—I haven't had time to read a copy since August. I imagine it will keep along at about the same old level—with new authors appearing as the old ones drop down or out. You'll be sorry to hear that good old Whitehead died on Nov. 23—only 9 days after writing me a brisk & cheerful letter full of future plans. I don't know whether he ever had a chance to read my reply, which must have reached him the day before the end. I thought he was recovering from the long malady he had fought so bravely, but some acute gastric spasm must have got at his heart action. All the gang feel tremendously jolted—especially the usually buoyant & irrepressible Price, & Dwyer, whose correspondence with "Canevin" was unusually close. It does give one a sense of damnable cosmic waste to see a fine chap like that snuffed out—brilliant, courageous, honourable, generous, learned, dashing, & everything else admirable & attractive. Dunedin must be in collective mourning—& the blow to H S's father, aged 85, must be frightful. Here in my wardrobe is the white duck suit (made to his measure in the Virgin Islands by a mulatto tailor) which he lent me during my visit of 1931, & which he insisted on my keeping, & on my curio shelf is the long mottled snake which he caught & killed with his own hands—for he wasn't afraid of the devil himself. I hope his literary affairs will be competently administered, for he had many unpublished MSS. on hand, including two more items in the Chadbourne series (modelled on my Arkham) whose initial tale appears in W T next month.

Sorry "The Night Wire" disappointed you. It somehow gave me a very distinctive kick. I must see how it strikes me on a re-reading. I think I'll get "The Moon Pool" if the coming new edition is cheap. No—I didn't know Cabell ever wrote for the Argosy.[1] What kind of stuff? Good luck with your new Faun tale. I must get a look at that new Dunsany poem you mention.[2] I don't agree with you about Milton. How can you call his early stuff—Comus, L'Allegro, Il Penseroso—anything but vivid & sparkling? I fear that a mere difference in period idioms alienates you. I'll file the reading recommendations with care, though the utterly appalling state of my programme renders my reading time almost non-existent. Have just finished (*but not typed*—gawd help me!) a long European travel brochure.[3]

Dialect matters are always interesting. How odd that Pittsburgh should have that *I come* idiom. The mistake is of course a common one everywhere, but is—outside Pittsburgh—always associated with such kindred forms as *I seen* & *I done*. I never before heard the expression *trade* for *compliment*. Enclosed are a few dialect odds & ends. I think that convention was a bit lax in sanctioning so many solecisms. There is something to be said in favour of "Who are you looking for?", but I never heard a literate person say "It is *me*."

As for politics—a vote for Thomas[4] would have been simply thrown away . . . . . although in this case it wouldn't have caused any change in the results. When there are two main candidates in the field with any real choice between them, it is never wise to vote for a third & hopelessly minor one whom you may happen to like better than either of the big boys.. If too many do that, it may result in the election of the main guy they want *least*. Common sense tells us that the big fellows are the only possible winners. If you think one is any better than the other, vote for him—for he is the best you'll have any chance of getting. In this contest Roosevelt was undoubtedly preferable to Hoover, & Thomas was probably nearer realities than either of the others—but much in Thomas's programme was unwise. To give large powers of decision to the mass of the people is hopelessly silly & disastrous. Some way must be arranged to effect a fresh distribution of resources—now that intensive mechanisation has upset the ancient economic order—yet without removing the machinery of government from carefully trained hands. A document of tremendous importance is the recent report of the "technocracy" group which studied under the auspices of Columbia University. As you may have seen, it emphasises all that thoughtful observers have long said of the effect of the displacement of men by machines. The fact that all the work of the world can now be done by a relatively small part of the population is something which will necessitate a recasting of the whole fabric of human industry & its relation to the possession of resources. One may only hope that the transition to a more realistic order can be accomplished without a chaotic revolution & without any break in the cultural traditions of western civilisation.

Your mention of Burns, the chain-gang fugitive, was unusually timely—as recent headlines have doubtless apprised you. It's hard to get at the truth of matters like this, but even with all allowances the system of convict labour is worth looking into. Police & legal tyranny are at their absolute worst in Texas, where the intimidation of the citizenry is almost incredible. When Robert E. Howard first brought the subject to my attention I thought he was sentimentally exaggerating or falling for radical propaganda until he cited specific cases from first-hand information. Large outside oil interests control the law-enforcing machinery, & the rest of the trouble is supplied by the naturally lax standard of order in a frontier region inheriting traditions of cheap human life & ready physical violence. Howard is so used to violence that he can hardly believe it when I tell him that there are no fights on the public streets of the East except in slums & gang-ridden areas. I didn't see the Muni film, but will try to when it returns.[5] Haven't seen a cinema since last June.

As for reading—Sherwood Anderson is one of those figures whom I respect as real & important artists, but who actually (the fault being mine) bore me to somnolence. I haven't read any of his recent things. I must read more of Faulkner. What I *have* read (probably because my surviving aunt had it on a long-term loan & sub-lent it to me) is your new favourite, "The Fountain." That is the real stuff—in language & substance. It reflects a philosophy perhaps a trifle at variance with actual fact—a philosophy assigning rather too much significance to the human personality & emotions—but that does not detract from its value as a picture of the sensitive type of person who entertains such a perspective. Your information concerning the author is very timely, & adds to my interest in the book. After all, there is a vast amount to be said for the contemplative mood when it is separated from illusions involving fallacy. Sorry "Peter Ashley" proved so mediocre—I was going to get hold of it because of my fascinated admiration for Charleston.

Yes—I recall Keyhoe's piffle.[6] Your glimpse of him must have been interesting. It'll be a hard job deciding on the contents of an anthology. Of Benson you ought to have "The Horror Horn" from "Visible & Invisible" & "The Face" from "Spook Stories"—which Dwyer can lend you. Of course "Negotium Perambulans" is great—but Harré used that. I'll send you books containing "The Yellow Sign", "The Harbour-Master",* & "The Wind in the Portico." "The Yellow Sign" has a ghoulish grip that Cook, Long, & I think is pretty nearly unbeatable. Title-choosing is a job I don't envy you!

As for the linkage of realism & prying impertinence—I still think it's hard to get the real stuff about life, to any widely representative extent, without some rather painful prying. Of course, sympathetic confidences bring out many things, but the hidden factors in many types of household are things hard to get at—in their actual form—except by extorting & worming out information not likely to come to light otherwise. It is relatively easy to fathom the lives of the humbler folk who live more or less in public & possess very few reticences; but when one tries to round out the picture & tackle the more dignified sort, the problem changes. Still—compromises are possible, & it's hard to say that all realists are bounders . . . . . although Dreiser certainly is, as judged by the unsavoury revelations he has made in the public press about his own family.

Heard some good lectures recently—J. B. S. Haldane on "Biology & Politics", & the local Prof. Walter G. Everett on Spinoza. The latter lecture was

---

*not listed as a separate story in this edition of "In Search of the Unknown," but there just the same. At the beginning.

one of a monthly series like that which I attended last winter—the next one being on Schopenhauer. They are under the auspices of the R.I. Philosophical Society, which I may possibly join.

One of my correspondents[7]—embarking on a graduate course at Muhlenberg College in your state, & specialising in Latin—informs me that he is about to transfer his correspondence to that noble tongue! Obviously, I shall have to do some drilling in long-neglected fields if I hope to keep up with him! ¶ Well—I hope you have a Merry Christmas, Happy New Year, & all that.

Yr most ob^t Servt

E'ch-Pi-El

Notes

1. Cabell published the early short story "An Amateur Ghost" in *Argosy* (February 1902).

2. Probably "The Banker and the Broker," *Time and Tide* 13, No. 50 (10 December 1932): 1363–64.

3. "European Glimpses" (19 December 1932), a travelogue ghostwritten for HPL's ex-wife, Sonia H. Greene (see *CE* 4.232–52).

4. Norman Thomas, socialist candidate for president in 1932. He received 884,885 votes.

5. Probably *Scarface* (1932); possibly *I Am a Fugitive from a Chain Gang*. See JVS 35 n.6.

6. Presumably Donald Edward Keyhoe (1897–1988), a contributor to *WT*, *Dr. Yen Sin*, and *Flying Aces.*

7. Carl F. Strauch.

1933

[34]   [ALS]

10 Barnes St.,

Providence, R.I.,

Jany. 25, 1933

Dear Jehvish-Êi:—

Glad the books found more than one appreciative reader. I think "The Yellow Sign" is the most fascinating product of Chambers's pen, & altogether one of the greatest weird tales ever written. The brooding, gathering atmosphere is actually tremendous. I must read it again & see how it strikes me after many years. "The Harbour Master" gave me quite a wallop in 1926, when I read it—although I did not care for the rest of the volume. I liked "The Green Wildebeest",[1] & have it noted down for mention in any future edition of my article. By the way—my library has received some accessions lately, one of them very notable. This latter was a Christmas gift from W. Paul Cook, & formed a remnant of his shattered library—nothing less than that famous & now out-of-print Gothic novel by Charles Robert Maturin, "Melmoth, the Wanderer", in 3 volumes. I had been trying to get hold of this item for years, & you can imagine how Cook's gift virtually bowled me over! Another gift was the fairly recent scientifictional novel "The World Below", by S. Fowler Wright, wherein a man is projected into the world of 500,000 years ahead—finding furry amphibians & human giants the dominant races. A third item I picked up myself as a remainder for 79¢—that magnificent phantasy "The Worm Ouroboros", by E. R. Eddison.

Good luck with "The Tin Roof"—it certainly ought to interest *The Midland*. Yes—I knew Derleth's "Cult of Incoherence" was being reprinted. He is constantly having things in the select magazines now—the next *Frontier* will contain "A Day in March." I bought the new W.T., but haven't had a chance to read it yet. I once owned Huysmans' "La Bas", but it was lost by one to whom I lent it. I've seen mention of "Witches Still Live",[2] but have not read it. Too bad you missed the Yeats lecture. The other day I attended a reading of the poetry of James Stephens & Walter de la Mare—part of a course which is later going to bring Robert Hillyer & T. S. Eliot here in person. Am also attending a course of philosophical lectures—Schopenhauer being covered last Wednesday. *Modern Youth* must be an interesting magazine—but I'm damned if I thought Julian Huxley was under thirty![3] Sorry to hear of your Pittsburgh fire. I'll let you know if I can't get "The Lady Who Came to Stay." Good luck with both of your new ventures—"Faun" & "Cell." That chap hasn't started writing in Latin yet. I didn't hear the "Emperor Jones" broadcast (though I could have done so at my aunt's had I know in advance of it), & am very sorry to have missed it. The musical effects must have heightened the effect immeasurably. I saw the play in 1922—with Charles Gilpin—& was tremendously impressed.

Robert E. Howard certainly ought to use his Texas background in fiction, & both Derleth & I are trying to get him to do so. Yes—I fancy chain gangs, at least as now managed, are decidedly primitive institutions. Thanks enormously for the Dunsany poem, which is highly appealing. Shoreham is Dunsany's maternal region, & he spends most of his time there at Dunstall Priory, his mother's seat. Incidentally, Rhode Island has a town of New Shoreham—the only one I know of in the U.S. I don't believe you need to worry about your poetic taste—it will probably expand with the years.

I spent the holiday season in New York, whither I was invited for a week by Long's parents, to pay the kid a surprise visit. The coach fare is now down to $2.00. I arrived before Long was up, & he surely was a surprised young man when he drowsily drifted out to breakfast & found his old Grandpa nodding over the morning *Tribune!* I also surprised other members of the gang—including Wandrei, who still lingers in the East, finishing a psychological novel.[4] He has rather snug quarters despite their location near the Hudson waterfront. I saw the old year out at Samuel Loveman's new apartment in Brooklyn—where for the first time his curios & art treasures are adequately displayed. He gave me two interesting objects—a prehistoric stone idol from Mexico, & a very primitive flint implement with a curiously engraved ivory handle. Naturally I saw what there was new to see at the museums—the archaic Greek Apollo at the Metropolitan, the modernistic horrors (which make "Suicide in Costume" look quite conservative!) & blatant attic murals at the Whitney, the Dutch rooms at the Brooklyn, & the American primitives & Whistler portrait of his mother (lent by the Louvre) at the now adequately housed (11 W. 53ᵈ St.) Museum of Modern Art. Also, I saw for the first time the fine Gothic interior of the new Riverside Church, & gave the new 8ᵗʰ Ave. subway a tryout. Since my return home Long has had a severe attack of influenza, but is now comfortably convalescing.

Your recent reading, as usual, leaves me hopelessly in the shade. "Julie Logan" appeared in two parts in the *Prov. Sunday Journal,* but to my mind shares the triviality & insipidity of all Barrie's stuff. While at Belknap's I read a highly interesting book which he had out of the library—Prof. Walter B. Pitkin's "History of Human Stupidity." Parts of it are of real psychological & sociological value, & it is really an item which ought not to be missed, even if it is somewhat exaggerated & overdone in places.

Your dramatic criticisms, as usual, sound highly interesting & intelligent—I feel sure that you'll be doing such things for the press some day. My only sight of the Lunt duo was in 1924, in the over-advertised & rather insipid eschatological sketch entitled "Outward Bound"[5]—to which I was taken by the late Houdini. This Coward person surely seems to be quite a figure. I note the cinema observations—this time from a less remote distance, since the Longs dragged me to several shows as they usually do . . . . the first shows I've seen since they similarly dragged me last June. The performances were good, bad, & indifferent; & included the following items: "Strange Interlude" (excellent), "A Farewell to Arms" (about as you say), "Red Dawn" (a Russian revolutionary film which appears to ignore the Kerensky preface to the real disaster), "Goona-Goona" (acted by natives of the isle of Bali—good as geography, but nothing much as a drama), "Trouble in Paradise" (very fair comedy), "Three On a Match" (routine stuff), "The Crusader" (even worse), & "Blame the Woman" (which I largely slept through).[6] Thus ends my cinematic experience till Belknap gets hold of me again, or till something really notable hits town at a time when my lethargy is less dense than usual. I duly note the Parry & Cohen cuttings. Loveman & his roommate McGrath attended that Radio City performance & said it was rotten.

Since my return home I've been floundering in a tumult of accumulated tasks—for there were awaiting me 22 letters, 2 revision jobs, & a formidable stack of papers & periodicals. In a short time I hope to get at the job of collaborating with E. Hoffmann Price on the Silver Key sequel—though the effort may come to nothing. I changed my fountain pen at the N.Y. Waterman office, but can't be satisfied with the new one. Apparently I'm a hopeless case—but some day maybe I'll get desperate & try a Sheaf[f]er. At Christmas a misguided soul—unaware of how little time I have to waste—gave me a crystal radio set, with which I have since been tinkering. I haven't extracted many sounds from it yet—& by the time I do, I'll probably be so fed up on it that I won't feel disposed to squander many precious moments on the froth purveyed by its ear-phones. Thus do many evils carry with them their own remedies.

And so it goes. Best wishes for 1933!

Yr most obt Grandsire—

E'ch-Pi-El.

Notes

1. By John Buchan.

2. A study of black magic by Theda Kenyon.

3. Julian Huxley (1887–1975), evolutionary biologist, grandson of Thomas Henry Huxley, and brother of Aldous Huxley, was 45 at this time.

4. *Invisible Sun,* unpublished in Wandrei's lifetime. First published in *Dead Titans, Waken! and Invisible Sun* (Lakewood, CO: Centipede Press, 2011).

5. Alfred Lunt (1892–1977) and his wife, Lynn Fontaine (1887–1983), were celebrated actors. They appeared in the play *Outward Bound* (1923) by Sutton Vane (1888–1963) when it premiered on Broadway on 7 January 1924.

6. *A Farewell to Arms* (Paramount, 1932), directed by Frank Borzage; starring Helen Hayes, Gary Cooper, and Adolphe Menjou. Based on the novel by Ernest Hemingway. *Scarlet* [not *Red*] *Dawn* (Warner Bros., 1932), directed by William Dieterle; starring Douglas Fairbanks Jr., Nancy Carroll, and Lilyan Tashman. *Goona-Goona* [a.k.a. *Kriss*] (First Division Pictures, 1932), directed by Armand Denis and Andre Roosevelt. *Trouble in Paradise* (Paramount, 1932), directed by Ernst Lubitsch; starring Miriam Hopkins, Kay Francis, and Herbert Marshall. Based on the play *The Honest Finder* by Laszlo Aladar. *Three on a Match* (Warner Bros., 1932), directed by Mervyn LeRoy; starring Joan Blondell, Ann Dvorak, and Bette Davis. *The Crusader* (Majestic Pictures, 1932), directed by Frank R. Strayer; starring Evelyn Brent, H. B. Warner, and Lew Cody. Based on the play by Wilson Collison. *Blame the Woman* (Cinema House, 1932), directed by Maurice Elvey and Fred Niblo; starring Adolphe Menjou, Claud Allister, and Benita Hume. *Red Dawn* is unidentified.

[35]   [ALS]

10 Barnes St.,

Providence, R.I.,

March 24, 1933

Dear Jehvish-Êi:——

Sorry "The Tin Roof" didn't land, but one can't expect perfect luck at the outset. I'll be glad to see "The Cell", & hope it may eventually find a professional haven. The article on "Faulkner & the C.C." sounds promising, & I am sure you don't need to feel timid about your qualifications for it. Good luck with your miscellaneous shorts. I haven't seen the latest *American Spectator,* but will try to do so in view of the story you so highly rec-ommend. Glad to hear that Pittsburgh authors are so well represented in print these days. Wish Rhode Island were more to the fore. At that, though, we have a number of literary figures. The novelist Vincent McHugh is a Prov-idence boy, & the satirist Leonard Bacon (a reading by whom I attended last month) comes from southern R.I.[1] That magazine for under-age contributors must shed quite a light on the perspective of the coming generation. And the *Mercury* tale by a 16-year-old certainly is the authentic voice of the cradle! Hope the new Spencer novel[2] is good. Incidentally, Klarkash-Ton owns "The Lady Who Came to Stay", & can make me a long-term loan of it whenever I get the time to read anything. Too bad MacCormack has lost his voice—I've never hear him in person or over the radio, but used to have some exquisite phonograph records of his.[3] I saw the Coward article in *Time.*[4] As for *phrases*—I fancy the real point is that in youth one overstresses such things, while in maturity one demands the presence of something behind them. That demand by no means prevents one from still appreciating good language, & preferring it when other things are equal. As for Milton—I don't see how you & Rascoe[5] . . . or anybody else . . . . can argue away the distinctive charm of a large part of his work. He has the power of evoking unlimited images for per-sons of active imagination, & no amount of academic theory can explain that away. As for the necessary accomplishments of a young gentleman—I fancy I'm worse than you, for I don't play bridge. That, though, wasn't such a such a "necessity" when I was young . . . . but I doubt if I'd have bothered with it in any case. I'm ahead of you on one point, though—I loved firearms, & could scarcely count the endless succession of guns & pistols I owned. I wish even now that I hadn't given away my last Remington. As it is, I possess only an ancestral & unshootable flintlock musket. I've seen the Halper book re-viewed, & imagine it must be quite a performance. I shall try to read it.[6] Yes—I read of the detention of those naughty foreign pictures drawn by a dago named Mike Angelo.[7]

That Wylie Ave. restaurant sign certainly reads like fiction—it's fit to rank beside such classics as "Don't shoot the pianist", &c. I must read more of Faulkner. His style occasionally exasperates me, but he's got the goods. Yes—Comte Robert de Montesquieu certainly was the idol & model of all decadents in his day. I've never ascertained what relation he was to the fa-mous author of the "Grandeur et Decadence des Romains".[8] And so some-body expressed doubt in the reality of Tarzan! Bless my soul! First thing we know they'll be hinting that Count Dracula was a fictitious character! I never knew that Joyce was a cinema pioneer as well as a literary pioneer.[9] Provi-dence's first cinema shows (apart from the shewing of films in vaudeville per-formances) appeared in 1906, & were ramshackle affairs patronised only by childhood & the proletariat. It wasn't till well into the war period—1916 or

1917—that the cinema was frequented or taken seriously by literate adults. The introduction of the Whitehead memorial page in W.T. was at the suggestion of E. Hoffmann Price. Glad you liked it—since I wrote it myself.[10] My original text was longer, giving H S more of a personal description & tribute, but Wright cut it down for space reasons. I've seen the flood of jigsaw puzzles here & there, but haven't wasted my time on any. This is the second furore over them that I remember. Incidentally—did you see the syndicated Wortman cartoon of the "Metropolitan Movies" series touching on the jigsaw puzzle? It was drawn from life, & shewed my friend George Kirk & his Chelsea Bookshop—a genuine though sketchy likeness.[11] Galsworthy, I think, will survive. His style at times halts one, but the substance is there. I don't mind the "coldness" & "impersonality"—in fact, I think that these may be marks of the detachment & objectivity which every great novelist must have. Did 7½ pages of the Silver Key sequel when a flood of revision swamped me & stalled the job. I'm having to override Price altogether in style—it will be my prose throughout unless he proposes later changes. His mathematical ideas, however, will be retained. But gawd knows when I'll ever be able to continue the damn thing!

Yes—I fancy that my brief cinema-going career of last December–January comprised just about 3 tolerable performances & a residue of junk. I won't dispute your appraisal of "Strange Interlude", because I'm no judge whatever of acting. The literary value of the text is this one thing I seem to be exacting about in a play. Some of the films you announce for the future seem important indeed, & I shall make an effort to see a few. I wonder if "Porgy" will be taken in old Charleston?[12] "Madchen in Uniform" has not been here. I surely mean to see "Cavalcade."[13]

Your list of books makes me dizzy, as usual. I wish I had the energy & lightning absorptive power of some of you boys—or else that I could chuck everything except reading for a year or so. As it is, I've acquired—mostly by gift—more books than I've read so far in 1933. I've picked up Eddison's fantastic "Worm Ouroboros" (which I read in 1927) as a remainder for 79¢, & shortly afterward was quite knocked flat by a present from W. Paul Cook—nothing less than "Melmoth, the Wanderer" complete in 3 volumes. Shortly after that Derleth unloaded a ton of library discards on me, including some anthologies (one containing Blackwood's "Willows") which I'm superlatively glad to own. Another friend in Chicago gave me two books—S. Fowler Wright's "World Below" (not bad) & Michael Maurice's "Not in Our Stars"[14]—which I've had no time to read. And only day before yesterday there arrived from still another friend a copy of Disraeli's "Alroy"—which I had never seen before, but which I recall from an allusion in Birkhead, which compared it to "Vathek."

Harry Bates, the ex-editor of the defunct S.T. & Ast. S., is now in Clearwater, Fla. writing a play, & has heard all the details of Whitehead's death. It seems that H S W really was recovering quite well, but that he spoke of a "general malaise" on Sunday, Nov. 20. That night he suffered a fall in his room, partly losing the power of speech & shewing signs of concussion of the brain. He was kept under opiates most of the time, & died 3 days later. His father—aged 85, partly deaf, & with cataracts developing on both eyes, feels the shock heavily, but is bearing up bravely. Tragically enough, H S W had just completed a sun-porch on his new home, & had just sent for his books & furniture—stored for years in the north.

W.T. is about to indulge in a slowing-up process—bringing the date back to the real date of issuance—which amounts to the omission of one number. The May number will not be on the stands till April 15, & the June issue will appear June 1st. In the July number will appear my last story, "The Dreams in the Witch House." I didn't intend to offer it, but it was lent to Derleth for copying purposes & he shewed it to Wright. The latter offered $140 for it—& being loath to sacrifice any revenue, I let him have it. Some time within the next few months "The Festival" will be reprinted. I've just corrected a fresh MS. which Wright had typed.

I enclose a cutting illustrating one of the honours which have recently come to our young friend Auguste-Guillaume, Comte D'Erlette. (please return it) The kid is certainly getting along!

Last month I attended a reading by the enigmatical & celebrated T. S. Eliot—interesting if not quite explicable. It reminded me of the discussions of "The Waste Land" which our gang used to conduct a decade ago. I wrote a parody which was printed in the newspaper—but which sounds sadly flat today, now that the heat of combat has subsided.[15] Eliot reads well—& has picked up quite a British accent in latter years. He is now 45, & looks every inch of it . . . . unlike the pictures commonly in circulation.

A fortnight ago one of my jobs took me to Hartford to help a client conduct some research at the Athenaeum there.[16] It was my second visit to the town—which is, as I probably mentioned, not very interesting or distinctive except for the old Bulfinch state house & the Centre Church burying ground. This time, however, I had an opportunity to see the ancient suburbs of Farmington & Wethersfield—& I certainly was not disappointed. Farmington is one of the most beautiful villages in the U.S.—situate in a rolling countryside full of picturesque vistas, & shaded by a magnificent plenitude of ancient elms. The houses are predominantly of the 18th century, with occasional earlier specimens—one is of about 1650, with overhanging second story. The inn where I stopped is a rambling, composite structure, with no wing newer than 1790, & with a central nucleus dating back to 1638, the year of Farmington's settlement. The church, a white steepled affair of typical Novanglian pattern, was built in 1771. Wethersfield is also full of interest, though of vastly different aspect. It lies in a flat region, & has an immensely wide village common shaded by the largest elms east of the Rocky Mountains. There are many fine old colonial mansions, bearing the distinctive marks of Connecticut-Valley architecture. In one of them Gens. Washington & Rochambeau planned the battle of Yorktown in 1781. The steepled brick church dates from 1763, it being then considered the finest church in New England outside Boston. It was in Wethersfield that the Pequot War started in 1637.

And so it goes. I doubt if I can take any long trip this spring. My financial state is appalling, & I may have to move to cheaper quarters. Work continues to paralyse me. An 80,000-word novel-revision job seems to be headed my way—& yet I can't get more than $100. for it.[17] A tough world. Best wishes—& good luck with the new tales.

Your obt Grandsire—
E'ch-Pi-El

Notes

1. Vincent McHugh (1904–1983), American poet, novelist, and editor, author of *Touch Me Not* (1930). Leonard Bacon (1887–1954), poet, translator, and critic, was born in Solvay, NY, but apparently relocated to Rhode Island at some point. He died in Peace Dale, RI.

2. R. E. Spencer, *The Incompetents* (New York: Alfred A. Knopf, 1933).

3. John McCormack (1884–1945), celebrated Irish tenor, made his operatic debut in 1906 and retired in 1938.

4. In *Time* 21, No. 5 (30 January 1933), there was an unsigned cover article on the British playwright Nöel Coward, entitled "First Englishman" (21–22).

5. Burton Rascoe (1892–1957), American journalist and critic, wrote harshly of John Milton in the chapter "Milton: The Conscience" in *Titans of Literature* (New York: Putnam's, 1932): "Milton is lacking . . . in common sense, in true loftiness of feeling, in kindness and generosity and give-and-take, and most of all, he is thoroughly lacking in *style,* grand or common" (276–77).

6. Possibly a reference to the novel *Union Square* (1933) by Albert Halper (1904–1984).

7. In February 1933, customs agents in New York declared that photos of Michelangelo's frescos in the Sistine Chapel were obscene, but after four days the photos were released.

8. Robert de Montesquieu (1855–1921), was a French aesthete and dandy and the reputed source for the character of des Esseintes in Huysmans's *A Rebours* and of Baron de Charious in Proust's *A Remembrance of Things Past*. He was no relation to Charles-Louis de Secondat, Baron de La Brède et de Montesquieu (1689–1755), Enlightenment philosopher and author of *Considérations sur les causes de la grandeur des Romains et de leur décadence* (1734; *Considerations on the Causes of the Greatness and the Decadence of the Romans*).

9. Possibly a reference to James Joyce's founding of a cinema in Dublin in 1909, although it soon failed.

10. "In Memoriam: Henry St. Clair Whitehead."

11. Denys Wortman (1887–1958) was an American cartoonist who worked for the *New York World* from 1924 to 1954, during which time he contributed a weekly cartoon in the series "Metropolitan Movies."

12. George Gershwin had to Charleston, SC, to meet with DuBose Heyward concerning his plan to turn Heward's novel *Porgy* (1925) into an opera.

13. *Cavalcade* (Fox Film Corp., 1933), directed by Frank Lloyd; starring Diana Wynyard, Clive Brook, and Una O'Connor.

14. See Bibliography under Conrad Arthur Skinner.

15. The newspaper appearance of "Waste Paper" has not been located.

16. HPL had in fact gone to Connecticut to see his ex-wife, Sonia H. Greene. It was the last time they met in person.

17. The work in question is unidentified. It may never have been published.

[36]   [ALS]

⟍⟍ ∘∘⌐

66 COLLEGE ST,

Providence, R.I.,

May 29, 1933.

Dear Jêhvish-Êi:—

As you may note above, the parallelism in our recent fortunes is indeed an actuality! Gawd, what a siege I've been through . . . . . . among other things, rearranging some 2000 books! I feel as though I'd been through a wringer—& more is yet to come, in the way of helping my aunt move. But the coincidence is even closer than appears on the surface. You say that your new & cheaper house is appreciably better—well, so is mine, & then some! Once in a while Fate gives the poor man a break. In the first place, I'm doubling up with my surviving aunt & am therefore in a regular home once more after 8 years of rooming. Secondly—& climactically as you will readily appreciate from a knowledge of my lifelong antiquarian tastes—*the house is a genuine colonial one* (or to be technically strict, *early-republican*) *built about 1800 & having all the earmarks of a fascinating Georgian antiquity!*[1] For 40-odd years these ancient houses on the hill have held me spellbound, & yet I've never before had a chance to *live* in one. Now—& ironically enough, through an *economy* move—that thing has come to pass! Only a rare chance put us next to this phenomenal bargain—a bargain out of all proportion with normal local real estate values. We are getting a five-room upper flat, amply large enough to give each of us absolutely separate quarters, with stream heat & hot water furnished (& newly papered & painted according to my aunt's taste.), for only $40.00 per month—just what I've been paying at 10 Barnes for one room & alcove alone! And to cap the climax, there is no sacrifice in the quality of the neighbourhood. The one difference in the nature of the locality from Barnes St. is that this section is definitely *collegiate* rather than purely residential. It is right under the nose of Brown University, with the college library on one side & fraternity houses on the other side & across the street. In quality, this involves no step down; though some might prefer a less institutional district . . . . hence, I suppose, the low rent. There are, however, two other private residences (both in old & exclusive hands) close by. I certainly don't feel any falling off—& am not at all ashamed to quote my new address. I had feared I might have to enter a seedy zone, hence my relief at the present outcome. And of course, the antiquity of the place gives me a tremendous kick . . . . it is so much like a museum that I keep fearing a guard will turn up to boot me out at 5 o'clock closing time. This Georgian charm keeps me from getting homesick for 10 Barnes—aided, of course, by my familiar furniture. After all, my accustomed bookshelves & pictures & rugs & furniture take up so much space in any room I occupy, that no move can plunge me into complete alienage. The new house, yellow & wooden, lies on the crest of the ancient hill in a quaint grassy court just off College St.—behind & next to the marble John Hay Library of Brown University, about half a mile south of 10 Barnes. The fine colonial doorway is like my bookplate come to life, though of a slightly later period, (circa 1800) with side lights & fan carving

instead of a fanlight. In the rear & on the west is a picturesque, village-like garden at a higher level than the front of the house. The upper flat we have taken contains 5 rooms besides bath & kitchenette nook on the main (2nd) floor, plus two attic storerooms—one of which is so attractive that I wish I could have it for an extra den! My quarters—a large study & a small bedroom—are on the south side, with my working table under a west window affording a splendid view of the lower town's outspread roofs & of the mystical sunsets that flame behind them. The interior is as fascinating as the exterior—with colonial fireplaces, mantels, & chimney-cupboards, curving Georgian staircase, wide floor-boards, old-fashioned latches, small-paned windows, six-panel doors, rear wing (possibly surviving from a still older house on the same site) with floor at a different level (3 steps down), quaint attic stairs, &c. &c. After admiring such houses all my life I find something magical & dreamlike in the experience of *actually dwelling in one*. My furniture fits the place admirably, & makes it look as though the family had inhabited it for over a century. I have tried to live up to the Georgian architecture—being very sparing with ornaments. Of course, having 2 rooms all my own, I don't have to crowd my things as I did at #10; hence the present layout is much more tasteful. The focal point of my study is the colonial man-

tel—on which I have old brass candlesticks, old vases, & a clock that has been in the family since 1820; & above which is hung a marine view painted by my mother & now re-framed to accord with the Georgian decorative scheme. It certainly gives me a wallop to come *home* through a carved colonial doorway, & to sit beside a white colonial mantelpiece gazing o[ut] through small-paned windows over a sea of ancient roofs & foliage! Every hour a musical flood of chimes comes from the many belfries in the vicinity—the great Brown clock tower, (visible from my aunt's bedroom) the old Unitarian steeple (1816—visible from my bedroom), & the fine colonial belfry of the neo-Georgian court house (visible from my study & my aunt's living-room[)]. The house, by the way is owned by Brown University—heat & hot water being piped in from the adjacent college library. Moving was a hideous ordeal—especially the arranging of my books. I had to get 4 new cases (small, cheap ones) to make up for the built-in alcove shelves at 10 Barnes. My weird section now takes up more than 17 feet of shelfage. I also got a cabinet to file some of my pamphlets in—others being housed in the quaint chimney cupboards. Another purchase was a cheap camp cot, so that (in view of the space now at my disposal) I can house an occasional guest & save him hotel bills. Hope you can get around this way & use it—it will probably be broken in by E. Hoffmann Price, who has pulled up stakes at New Orleans & is northward bound. At present only my two rooms are furnished, but on June 1st my aunt will start moving in & complete the process. I certainly hope I can hang on here for a good long while! During the moving many old things turned up—among them a box of stuff which I hadn't opened for a quarter of a century . . . . . old writings & amateur papers of mine. In it were some blank sheets—which, for old time's sake, I am now using. Thus you are receiving a letter written on paper which I bought long before your were born!
¶ Don't worry about your literary quiescence—everyone works by fits & starts except human dynamos like Derleth & Price. And don't worry about slow progress, either. It isn't always the quick developer who is the best writer in the end. Incubation periods vary widely. I never even thought of sending any story for professional acceptance till I was *33*. As for your alleged lack of experience in life—I don't think that need bother you. There are plenty of subjects to choose from outside the specific local areas you haven't sampled . . . . . indeed, I think the greater part of literature deals with things other than corpses, morgues, hospitals, gaols, asylums, prize fights, ball games, brothels, riots, horse-races, & speakeasies. By the way—of these listed items many (i.e., morgue, gaol, prize-fight, ball game, brothel, riot, horse-race) are as unknown to me—at 42—as to you. I have, moreover, seen only one corpse (an accident victim) except at peaceful funerals, & have visited a speakeasy (as a non-imbibing spectator) only once—with George Kirk & some others in 1926. My only exploration of a madhouse was last year, when my friend Brobst (a nurse in one) took me over an ideal institution of its kind. I was never in an

hospital till 1924—but in that year & in 1929 I had occasion to call on patients in typical institutions of the sort. I have several times been in a police station—usually to inquire about stolen property, & once to see the Chief of Police about the banning of a client's magazine from the stands—but never in the part devoted to cells. But I hardly let my worldly inexperience prey on my nerves. True I wouldn't try to write a realistic novel about the underworld—but then, there are lots of things to write about besides the underworld. Moreover—when some unfamiliar phase of life pops up as a necessary *incidental* in a tale, it is often possible to treat it adequately from reliable second-hand information. Thus if I wanted realistic war colouring I'd ask Price or some other veteran for the dope. For prizefight stuff I'd apply to Bob Howard. For police dope, Joe Lynch . . . . & so on. Of course, it wouldn't do to take a *main theme* at second hand—but then, *nobody ought to choose a main theme from subjects which interest him so little as to preclude his sampling them.* I, for my part, haven't the slightest desire to write about fights or gaols or speakeasies or the like as main themes.

I read "The Cell" with great interest, & believe it has an abundance of points of promise. The chief flaw seems to be a touch of sentimentality—& a certain unreality in treating of the Valdés family. While pride often goes with humble callings in Spain, I doubt if the combination exclusive of old traditions, cobbling, & stevedoring which you depict is a very typical one. Something seems strained—it is not usual for the daughter of a stevedore & granddaughter of a cobbler to receive a sudden appointment as instructor in a far-off American college. Beware of romanticising. Look, too, to linguistic details. Are you aware that the dominant language of Barcelona—& all that part of Spain—is the Catalan dialect & not ordinary Castilian? And how about the name of that brother? In ordinary Spanish, at least, the name corresponding to *Vincent* is spelled *Vicente*—the first *n* being omitted. In writing the oath *caramba* I think you were right the first time—when you had only one *r*. And check up on that Lord's Prayer. What is it? Catalan? You have something like the French *notre* where real Spanish would be *nuestro*. If it's Catalan, I retract all criticism—for I haven't an idea of what that dialect is like. Another thing to debate is the ending of the story. Some might consider it melodramatic—yet on the other hand many cases of cell-suicide through sensitive pride are actually on record. It might be possible to record this suicide in a way from which all theatricality & sentimentality would be absent—though I couldn't say offhand how it could be done. Indeed, it is by no means obtrusively melodramatic as it is. There is really great stuff in this story—detail, atmosphere, & a realistic sense of futility—& I hope you will not make the mistake of underestimating it. Don't get discouraged—authorship isn't anything that sprouts over night! I hope you'll have good luck with your "Faun". What if it does reach novel length? Some allege that novels have a better chance for placement than novelettes. By the way—any time you want some minute, ruthless criticism from a modern angle, why don't you send specimens to Derleth? If you shewed him "The Tin Roof" & "The Cell" he might have some very useful suggestions to offer—together, of course, with some not so useful.

I note with interest your citation of Providence & Pittsburgh pen-pushers. Your town certainly has a goodly number of contacts with the lettered Pantheon, even though some—like Jeffers—are popularly associated with other regions.

Thanks exceedingly for the enclosed material. Let me know if any of it was to be returned—it's still safe. The U. of Pittsburgh views are delightful—especially the steps leading up to Alumni Hall. Scenically, the college would seem to have marked advantages over most competitors—advantages no doubt due to its deliberate choice of a site with an eye to aesthetic possibilities. Few others are so favoured by topography. *The American Spectator* seems always interesting—& I was exceedingly glad to see "Souvenir" at last. It certainly is a grimly powerful tale, & its easy naturalness of narration makes it tremendously convincing.[2]

As for the Nazis—of their crudeness there can be no dispute, yet in many ways the impartial analyst cannot help having a certain sympathy for some phases of their position. They are fighting, in their naive & narrow way, a certain widespread & insidious *mood* of recent years which certainly spells potential decadence for the western world—& one can't help respecting that *intention*, however ugly & even dangerous some of their *methods* may appear to be. Hitler is no Mussolini—but I'm damned if the poor chap isn't profoundly sincere & patriotic. It is to his credit rather than otherwise that he doesn't subscribe to the windy flatulence of the idealistic "liberals" whose policies lead only to chaos & collapse. As for his much-advertised & hysterically condemned Jew policy—there is something to be said for one phase of it. Of course it is silly to ban Jewish books, to impose disabilities on Germanically cultured Jews, or to assume that—biologically speaking—a dash of Semitic blood unfits one for Aryan citizenship. That is generally conceded. But after all, there is a very real & very grave problem in the presence of an intellectually powerful minority springing from a profoundly alien & emotionally repulsive culture-stream, defying assimilation as a whole, & using its keen mentality & ruthless enterprise to secure a disproportionate hold on the mental & aesthetic life of a nation. In such a case it is foolish to quibble about "rights" & "principles." The question is whether an enormous Aryan nation, with all the innate feelings & perspectives of Aryan culture, is going to allow its formulated expression (literary models, art, music, &c) to bely & embarrass it by reflecting an altogether different & sometimes hostile set of feelings & perspectives through the gradual & imperceptible Semitic control of all the avenues of utterance. It is needless to point out that a nation's literary & artistic utterance depends very largely on those who control the periodicals, schools, colleges, publishing houses, galleries, theatres, & so forth—this control largely determining what works & types of art shall receive preference in presentation to the public & in treatment by critics, & what attitudes shall receive official recommendation. If such control be gradually seized by a culture-group profoundly foreign to the natural culture-stream of the nation, the result is bound to be tense, awkward, & finally intolerable. In Germany I rather think such a state of things had almost come about. The loudest cultural voices were those of persons whose basic ideals & sense of values were not German. In books, education, drama, art, philosophy, &c., the voice of real Germany was almost drowned out by a voice which pretended to be German but was not. To say nothing ought to be done about this is rash. If a minority-overridden culture has any vitality at all, it will revolt in the end—& of course crudely at first. In my opinion, all nations ought to take quiet & moderate steps to get such pivotal forces as education, large-scale publishing, legal interpretation, criticism, dramatic management, artistic control, &c. into the hands of those who inherit the respective main streams of thought & feeling of those nations. Chinamen ought not to let American missionaries dictate & interpret their policies—& by the same token Aryans ought not to leave their guidance & interpretation to persons of an irreconcilable Semitic culture. Of course this does not mean that the crudities of Hitlerism are to be copied. It is absurd to think that a man of complete Aryan culture ought to be squelched because he has a quarter-share of Semitic blood, or anything like that. But it is not absurd to feel that something ought to be done to keep expression true to the real psychology of the nation involved. We really face the same problem in America—where the city of New York is virtually lost to the national fabric through its tragic & all-pervasive Semitisation. Our literature & drama, selected by Jewish producers & great Jewish publishing houses like Knopf, & feeling the pressure of Jewish finance & mercantile advertising, are daily getting farther & farther from the real feelings of the plain American in New England or Virginia or Kansas; whilst the profound Semitism of New York is affecting the "intellectuals" who flock there & creating a flimsy & synthetic body of culture & ideology radically hostile to the virile American attitude. Some day I hope that a reasonably civilised way of getting America's voice uppermost again can be devised. Not that I would advocate violence—but certainly, I can't regard the Nazis with that complete lack of sympathy shewn by those who take popular newspaper sentiment at face value. By the way—it's hardly accurate to compare the Jewish with the negro problem. The trouble with the Jew is not his *blood*—which can mix with ours without disastrous results—but his persistent & antagonistic *culture-tradition*. On the other hand, the negro represents a vastly inferior biological variant which must under no circumstances taint our Aryan stock. The absolute colour-line as applied to negroes is both necessary & sensible, whereas a similar deadline against Jews (though attempted by Hitler) is ridiculous. The Nathan parallel is rather amusing—although not all of the features included merit condemnation. For example—drastic steps against communism are certainly thoroughly justifiable & commendable whenever any real danger of radical revolution exists. Some parts of the parallel, of course, are purely whimsical in substance & intention.

Your literary notes, as usual, are of keen interest—as good as anything in the N Y Times or Prov. Sunday Journal! I'd like to get hold of "All Souls' Night".[3] I've heard about *Story*—Derleth has managed to land one or two pieces in it—& must try to see a copy for myself before long.[4]

As for the Scottsboro case[5]—it seems to me that the idealists & negrophiles are a little hasty in getting excited about it. Naturally nobody wants to kill the poor niggers unless they were guilty—that is, nobody who needs to be taken into account—but it doesn't seem to me that their innocence is at all likely. This is no low-grade lynching incident. A very fair court has passed on the case—& if the culprits were mere white bums, who hadn't happened to excite the sympathy of the radical element, there would be no stir at all about the matter. The fact that the victims were low wenches is wholly immaterial except so far as their credibility is concerned. And so far as their now clashing stories go, it seems to me that their first account is more likely to be true than is the second & changed story of the one whom the radicals of the defence very clearly bought over to their side. However, in view of the lack of testimony corroborating that of the woman, it might be just as well not to execute the blacks. I think their conviction ought to be sustained, but that the sentence ought to be commuted to life imprisonment—preferably in some remote prison where mob violence need not be feared. Then if any new evidence comes up in their favour, it will not be too late to rectify any mistake which may have been made.

As for the cinema—I have seen (a) Chain Gang, (b) Scarface, & (c) Cavalcade.[6] The first two almost cause me to endorse your opinion of Paul Muni (whom I never saw before) as the chief of cinematic performers. Both of these films impressed me as tremendously powerful, realistic, & relatively free from hokum. Cavalcade was certainly tremendous. It was an actual section of life—overbrimming with the spirit of our race. I don't know when any other film has affected me so profoundly. A few more like that would make me a cinema fan! Oh, yes—& I also saw "The Sign of the Cross"[7] for the sake of the Roman colouring. Quite a mechanical spectacle, though of course a perfect blank literarily. I was disappointed because so little of actual, normal Roman life was shewn. Yes—Nero certainly made quite a figure! I haven't yet seen any of the political films, though I guess I'll take in "Gabriel" on one of its later visits. I may do likewise with "King Kong" if its prehistoric life scenes are as good as those in "The Lost World"—which I saw in 1925.[8]

Unless you possess a superhuman fund of analytical acumen, you won't make much of The Waste Land. It is such a jumble of obscure allusions, subjective impressions, & intentional chaos that only a genius could elucidate it without a key. If it's hard to get in Pittsburgh, I'll lend you my old tattered copy of *The Dial* (Nov. 1922) containing it. In those days I kept up with the times more than I do now.

Yes—I finished the Silver Key sequel last month, & have persuaded Price to let it be as I wrote it. We haven't yet submitted to Wright, but my hopes of acceptance are not high. I had to postpone the novel-revision job on account of moving—whether I've lost it or not I don't yet know.

As for the voluminous reading programme of you & young Auguste-Guillaume—I was entirely sincere in saying that I envy you. I read altogether too little—being busy with other tasks & easily fatigued. Of course, one does not absorb such immense quantities all through life—but it is well to do it in youth if one can, in order to lay the foundations of a good literary background. I soaked up vast numbers of books in my youth; though they were seldom new ones, & were more often works on science & history than volumes of belles-lettres. I never cared for new books—which in my day, of course, was a very sensible attitude, insomuch as a great part of the current output (especially in America) was completely inane junk. I had a period of brushing up on new material in the early 1920's, & fancy I had better repeat the process soon in order to get an idea of the dominant trend.

That novel about the Florida crackers must be interesting.[9] I saw quite a number of crackers while visiting Whitehead in 1931, but had no chance to study their vocabulary extensively. Compulsory education seems likely to change the new generation vastly. Among Whitehead's many proteges were two little cracker boys whose parents could not read or write, but who were themselves bright & well-informed, & with hardly any perceptible dialect.

About V. F. Calverton—what I've seen of his hasn't greatly impressed me. Though undeniably scholarly, & effective as a populariser of anthropology, he is a confirmed & hopeless faddist—a long-haired bolshevik so full of erratic social theories that his judgments can scarcely be considered important. I'll endeavour to read his remarks on American literature in due course of time, though I differ basically & diametrically from him in virtually all criteria of values & underlying assumptions.[10] To begin with, I believe it is a childish & absurd fallacy to fancy that American literature & aesthetics either ought to be or conceivably could be other than a normal prolongation of the original English stream, with such local modifications as geography, social conditions, & historic experience may naturally introduce. The whole idea that a section of the Anglo-Saxon world ought to (or could) have a separate, autochthonous culture of its own is sheer flimsy nonsense—the product of a febrile, irresponsible radicalism of thought conjoined to a naive disregard of actual (as distinguished from theoretical) history. A culture or civilisation is a profound, pervasive thing—producible only through long centuries of continuous & homogeneous life, & having nothing whatever to do with political

nationality. We recognise, very properly, only one Greek world & Greek culture—though this world was divided into a great number of absolutely separate & often hostile political states, whose interests & modes of life in many
cases differed far more than do the interests & modes of life of the old & of
the new English nations. There were local variants, corresponding to local
differences in social & political conditions; yet no one was ass enough to fancy that Athens & Pergamus, Syracuse & Tarentum, ought to have separate
cultures in the sense that the cultures of Persia & Egypt & Phoenicia & Rome
were separate from that of Greece. And even today there are few fools bla-
tant enough to claim that Austria & Germany have different civilisations. If
North America has *any* civilisation at all, it is certainly that of the mother land
whence came all its institutions, perspectives, language, & determinant pioneering stock. *That culture, & that alone, was carried over bodily by the men who made
the wild continent a settled abode for the white race.* For 300 years it has carried on as
before, adapting itself to local conditions & crystallising into a definite local
variant. It is a natural, organic growth—as profound, ingrained, & inevitable
as our typical physiognomies & mental processes. We could not shed it if we
wanted to—& no American of sense *would* want to. It is pitiful to see a fad-
ridden American try to disavow what is deeply & naturally his, & transparent-
ly & unconvincingly pretend to be a synthetic Frenchman or Russian or general conglomerate or god knows what . . . . . theatrically labelling his new
character "New American". The new pose is shaky, false, & meaningless because it has no possible foundation. It postulates conditions which are necessarily lacking—a new culture-basis which does not & cannot exist, plus the
absence of a real culture-basis which does & must exist, & cannot be argued
away. No culture but our own English one extends behind us or behind our
native soil—if we want to find another we must go north to French Quebec
or south to Spanish Cuba & Mexico.

Altogether too much is made by radical theorists of the foreign immigrant influence. It is true that hordes of persons of non-English heritage have
entered the country—but that has nothing to do with the seated culture of
the region. These foreigners did not make the nation. They merely flocked in
later to enjoy what others had made. Our own civilisation was irrevocably
seated here long before they came, & it would be silly to suppose that we
shall allow these crumb-snatchers to disturb the foundations which we laid
for our descendants. They can either conform to the native culture which
they find, or get the hell out of here. We *made* this nation, & if any of the
skulking Jews & Dagoes who crawl after us to eat the fruit we laboriously
planted think they can dictate to us, they'll soon learn better by means of a
heavy-shod boot applied to their rear ends. Most of them are only the scum
& dregs of their own countries, anyhow—the weaklings who couldn't keep
on top among their own people. We welcome any biologically & culturally
assimilable newcomers *who are willing to abide by our institutions;* but if any crawl-

ing peasants & ghetto bastards expect to troop in here *& mould us in their own direction,* we'll shew them in short order where they get off!

It is also a vast mistake to fancy that the original foreign minorities in the colonies—the Dutch of New York, the Germans of Pennsylvania, the Huguenots of various sections, &c.—form a basis for a special non-English culture. The plain fact is that these elements were *not sufficiently numerous to affect the general fabric.* Most of their members were absorbed with absolute completeness into the English main stream, while the remaining unassimilated nuclei were not large enough to leaven the general culture. The most they did was to engraft a few new words or architectural forms or trivial customs upon the Anglo-Saxon fabric—just as the Indians did. While they gave a few faint touches of unique colour to the surface of the local culture-stream, we cannot justly say that they actually wrenched that stream from Anglo-Saxon sources. The same is true of those later waves of sturdy pioneer immigration—the Germans & Scandinavians who settled the mid-West with a constructiveness akin to our own—which must be differentiated from the modern locust-pest of Slavs & Semites & Mediterraneans. Solid & admirable as those people were, they could not alter the seated civilisation of the nation; hence came eventually within the Anglo-Saxon cultural radius. As acute a contemporary observer as André Siegfried attests the continued dominance of the native English tradition despite all the influences which seek to vitiate it.

Still less do I see any sense in the claim that the peculiar economic & social conditions of America, all apart from the derivation of the population, have successfully founded a new "civilisation" distinct from the old. That is a self-evident fallacy, because real civilisations are things of slow, natural growth, which cannot be established offhand, or in the course of a few decades. It may indeed be true that the local conditions in America—the hard scramble for material wealth & power, & the consequent worship of size, speed, & ostentation in place of quality, together with exaltation of crudeness & a contempt for refinement, sensitiveness, & traditional beauty—are *gradually undermining* our civilisation (except in certain spots of perfect preservation) & laying the foundations for a future machine-age variant; but this does not mean either that our culture is yet dead, or that the future culture is yet born. Cultures neither die nor are born in a single day. What is more—the new culture, if it ever does develop, will not in any sense be *ours.* The only one *we* can possess is the old Anglo-Saxon one which our fathers transmitted to us. When the future machine culture finally crystallises, it will be as alien to us—to our innate standards & perspectives & impulses—as the cultures of China, Nineveh, & Easter Island. It will have nothing to do with anything we now inherit or know or feel . . . . . & one may add that it will probably, because of its callously quantitative & utilitarian basis & its cheaply plebeian ideals, be vastly inferior in richness & inspiration to any of the leisurely [&] highly developed European or Asiatic cultures now dominant. I have some hope that the growth of this usurping rabble-culture may be substantially checked by intelligent effort, & by the sobering influence & possible social-economic consequences of the present depression. Our own culture is still strong in New England & the old tidewater South, & if we fight hard to preserve it we may yet defeat the machines & the mob & the Calvertons.

Meanwhile, of course, part of our upheaved generation is all at sea, & ready to swallow any cultural nostrum. Young pedants who note the moderate & legitimate contributions of foreign artistic streams to our own are ready to announce that we have abandoned our heritage & gone over altogether to one—or several—or all—of these contributing streams. Illiterate coachmen's sons who try to write & are unable to get the feel of a decent English style proceed to limp along in a graceless jargon which their ignorance & egotism proclaim as "new & superior" & purely American mode of utterance. City-bred clods with too little imagination to appreciate natural beauty devise epics of their native slums & blatantly repudiate our natural rural heritage. Myopic little Jews, insensitive to the majestic pageantry of history & tradition (for our pageantry is not theirs), repudiate the past & proclaim that the sole logical province of the poet & novelist is the pathology of neuroses & the sewer system of New York City. That is the "new Americanism". The real truth is, of course, that these radical [inn]ovators do not represent anything at all—[but] merely represent *the absence of something*. What they lack is any coördinated background & unified antecedents whatsoever. Having nothing of their own, they try to assemble a hodge-podge of cosmopolitan borrowings & call it the fabric of a new & suddenly-born culture. Actually, what they achieve is merely an unplaced & unplaceable chaos. If that is neo-Americanism, I think the powers of the cosmos I am a Rhode-Island Englishman of the old tradition! Even if my culture-stream be a thinned & effete one, it is at least *something* as distinguished from *nothing at all.* At least, I have not exchanged my one possible heritage for an expansive confusion which I could never truly possess & which would never be able to express anything worth expressing. In a time of decadence it is often better to stand by the old—which still has possibilities—than to plunge into the hapless welter of unformed barbarism which is the sole available alternative. I had rather be a Symmachus or Boëthius than an Odoacer or Theodoric.

In general, your recent reading seems admirably solid & well-chosen. Beach's "20th Century Novel"[11] must be a remarkable work, & I shall try to get a look at it sooner or later.

Belated spring is here at last—with occasional temperatures as high as 84° & 86°—but I've been too closely tied down with moving to begin my outdoor programme as yet. I did take one long walk, though, just before the deluge descended—in the ancient woods & fields & farmlands north of the city. This damned moving is ruining the whole spring—next Thursday my aunt will begin moving [&] I shall have to assist on a substantial scale—so that it'll probably be the middle of June before I can get any real freedom. I don't think my finances will let me make any real Southern trip this year, though I may attend the National Amateur Press Assn. convention in New York early in July, & perhaps try to get as far south of there (probably Washington, possibly Richmond) as the contents of my purse will allow. We shall see. But come what may, it's something to be living in a picturesque old house like this. When my aunt gets in the air of antiquity will be increased, since she has many old things, including the oldest chair (a slot-back of the early 18th century) in the family.

With every good wish—

Your most obt hble Servt

—E'ch-Pi-El

Notes

1. In fact, the Samuel B. Mumford House (66 College Street—subsequently moved to 65 Prospect Street) dates to c. 1825.

2. Vernon C. Sherwin, "Souvenir," *American Spectator* 1, No. 5 (March 1933): 1–2.

3. A short story collection by Hugh Walpole, with some weird items.

4. *Story* (1931–48, 1960–67, 1989–2000) was a highly regarded magazine for literary fiction.

5. In 1931, nine African American boys were accused of raping two white women in Scottsboro, Alabama. After several trials, the boys were found guilty, even though one of the women recanted her testimony. Charges against four of the boys were dropped; the other five were sentenced to death or long terms of imprisonment.

6. *I Am a Fugitive from a Chain Gang* (Warner Bros., 1932), directed by Mervyn LeRoy; starring Paul Muni, Glenda Farrell, and Helen Vinson. *Scarface* (United Artists, 1932), directed by Howard Hawks; starring Paul Muni, Ann Dvorak, and Karen Morley. Based on the novel by Armitage Trail.

7. *The Sign of the Cross* (Paramount, 1932), directed by Cecil B. DeMille; starring Fredric March, Elissa Landi, and Claudette Colbert.

8. *Gabriel over the White House* (MGM, 1933), directed by Gregory La Cava; starring Walter Huston, Karen Morley, and Franchot Tone. Based on an anonymous novel. *King Kong* (RKO Radio Pictures, 1933), directed by Merian C. Cooper and Ernest B. Schoedsack (both uncredited); starring Fay Wray, Robert Armstrong, and Bruce Cabot. *The Lost World* (First National Pictures, 1925; silent), directed by Harry O. Hoyt; starring Bessie Love, Lewis Stone, and Wallace Beery. Based on the novel by Sir Arthur Conan Doyle.

9. *South Moon Under* by Marjorie Kinnan Rawlings. Her first novel, and a finalist for the Pulitzer Prize.

10. HPL probably refers to Calverton's *The Liberation of American Literature* (New York: Scribner, 1932).

11. See Bibliography under Joseph Warren Beach.

[37]   [ALS]

Bench in Roger Williams Park
—July 30, 1933

Dear Jehvish-Êi:—

Glad to hear from you once more! Today is a blazer (probably 95°—yesterday was 93°) after my own heart, & I am out in the open trying to get my accumulated correspondence under control before welcoming a delightful guest—James F. Morton, who is due to blow in at 9 a.m. tomorrow. The charm of my new location continues to fascinate—& during the summer the closing of college brings a village-like quiet. But alas! a caprice of the Fates has wrecked the whole season for this household, & kept me tied down more closely than at any other period I can recall!

In brief—my aunt broke her right ankle on June 14 while descending the stairs in answer to the doorbell during my absence. Doctor—specialist—ambulance to R.I. Hospital—x-ray—setting in huge plaster cast—room in Ward K for 3 weeks—transfer home with nurse, still confined to bed—& now a bit of sitting up with half the cast removed, & an early total removal & consequent crutch period promised. No complete recovery before late autumn or winter. Assuredly, a hell of a housewarming! All this, of course, has kept me hellishly tied up—although I can't complain when I think of the plight of the main sufferer. I have to stay in each afternoon while the nurse goes out—although she sometimes very accomodatingly releases me by waiving the going-out privilege. Naturally, all trips of any magnitude have been perforce called off—though a few congenial visitors & one 2½ day jaunt have somewhat varied the monotony.

On June 30 E. Hoffmann Price arrived in his 1928 Ford Juggernaut, & for four days festivities were ample.[1] Young Harry Brobst came over twice—on one occasion staying all night for a session of literary & philosophical discussion punctuated by a trip to a hidden hillside churchyard (a ghoulish place!) at 3 a.m. On July 2 Price brought his Juggernaut into the service of antiquarian exploration—threading with me the picturesque lanes of Rhode Island's historic Narragansett Country (west of the bay), where before the Revolution there existed a patriarchal plantation life—with large estates & hundreds of niggers—much like that of the South. We saw the ancient & unspoiled colonial villages of Wickford & Kingston, & some of the finest rural landscape vistas in the world—together with such memorable sights as the old snuff mill (with machinery & huge water-wheel restored to working order) where Gilbert Stuart was born in 1755.

A later visitor was a friend of Clark Ashton Smith's from California, to whom I shewed the antiquities of Providence & Newport.[2] And last week I spent 2½ days around Cape Cod with Frank B. Long & his parents. Now comes the Morton visit, which will involve many local one-day trips. I have an invitation to New Hampshire, but fear I shall have to decline it. One further possibility is a second visit from Price (now staying in Irvington, N.Y.)—who plans to spend the winter in Florida (lucky devil!) where living is cheap.

As for Chicago & its century of Misdirected Energy—I wouldn't have visited that god-damned glorification of machine-age decadence if I had had all the cash & leisure in the solar system! Faugh! What an epitome of the rootless, traditionless, quantitative barbarism which is driving out civilisation on this continent! The loathsome oil-derrick & hencoop parody on architecture would have been enough in itself to keep me away! I can well imagine the superficial yokelry flocking to see this garish apotheosis of its ideals—but I'm damned if it's any show for a gentleman! What I mourn is that I cannot see Charleston & Havana & Quebec!

Regarding experience in life—certainly a writer can use all he can get, & a good amount of *general* experience (i.e., first-hand familiarity with the way in which average people react to average situations) is really essential to any realist. The trouble with Long is that he lacks this general experience. But I still think that all the specific *detailed* experiences you mention are more or less in the minor class. They involve what are relatively trifles in the whole human panorama—for it is only the false taste of a decadent age which gives them the prominence they have in current fiction. By the way—your morgue glimpse must have been picturesque. Hope the second & more intimate glimpse will be fruitful in literary stimuli.

As usual, I perused your literary notes with great interest. Belknap also strongly recommended that "Introduction to Eric", so I fancy I shall have to bestir myself & read it.[3] Enclosed is a circular of Klarkash-Ton's new booklet, which I can strongly recommend to you as magnificent of its kind.[4] All of the tales excel those accepted by Wright. I also enclose a circular of a new weird magazine to which Klarkash-Ton & I are contributing. The editor offers a special 18-months' subscription for a dollar—hope it lasts that long![5] There is no pay for material, but C A S & I are glad to get extra lending copies of our stuff.

Your cinema notes will form my guide to any pictures which I may voluntarily go to see. Since last writing you I have seen "King Kong" (good mechanical effects) & "Madchen in Uniform". This last was certainly an artistic piece of work—subdued & well-balanced. The physiognomy & manner of the old principal were something to remember! While at Onset—Cape Cod—I was dragged by the Longs to see a film called "Ann Carver's Profession" (mediocre routine stuff with typical hokum ending)—which completes my recent cinematic experience. Your adventures in seeing "Men Must Fight"[6] wouldn't form a bad basis for a short story! Thanks for the data on the films—"Scarface", "Cavalcade", &c—which I previously saw. Muni certainly knows how to deliver the goods! By the way—Belknap knows the fellow who wrote "Scarface"—Armitage Trail. He is a fat, boastful individual—largely philistinic, but very clever & extremely familiar with the details of the underworld.

I'd like to see the "Ghost Story Omnibus". French certainly is an active old boy—he must be in his 80's now. I've met him twice—both times in a bookshop. He spends much of his time in southern R.I. I won't blame O'Brien for leaving me out of the 1933 annual, for I can't recall anything of mine printed during the past year. Serious original writing is probably a thing of the past with me[.]

Your "To Love a Faun" certainly looks as if it would be a highly ambitious production. As for the right tone to use—it seems to me that nothing save impartial objectivity is suitable for any serious fiction. Draw the character as you conceive it—without either sympathy or repulsion, & with no departure from the confusing mixture of qualities which typifies a real person as distinguished from an artificial literary puppet. Never mind if the character doesn't seem either fish, flesh, or fowl—what real person *is* definitely any one of these things? Pay no attention to the reader. Real art has only two factors—the creator & his material. If you fear autobiographical identification, you could easily dispose of that matter in a prefatory note—which could be made to sound not too naive. What you say of your proposed method seems sound enough—though you might do some reflecting before concentrating so much attention on your central character. After all, no one person is especially important—& a section of life is really an aimless jumble with all the actors hopelessly mixed up. On the other hand, every person lives largely in a world of his own which no one else can share, & in which all the characters are coloured by the imagination of the person himself. Such a personal world, seen from the inside, is certainly appropriate material for literary treatment—so perhaps your idea is the right one after all. Your choice of a special abnormal type as protagonist (a typical beginner's choice in this decadent age) necessarily limits the work to the minor field—but after all, a first novel can hardly expect to transcend the minor class in any case. Life as a whole is something which only wide experience plus chronological maturity can grasp—& which even these can grasp damn seldom!

About the Scottsboro case—it may be as you say; but it remains a fact that the possible willingness of white whores to deal with niggers & falsely accuse them does not make niggers any the less prone to attack white women—whores or otherwise. And it is a sound principle of law that a rape is a rape, be the victim a lewd wench or not. This individual case must be judged on its own merits, & I don't know enough of the evidence to hold any real opinion. But the type of opinion which has frantically rushed to the defence side is not at all prepossessing. I don't give a damn one way or the other so far as prejudice goes. If the niggers are innocent, they ought not to be condemned—but if they are guilty, they ought not to be set free through maudlin sympathy. I'm in favor of a new trial on northern soil (if such a thing is legally possible) & life imprisonment instead of death if guilt is established without proof of the most direct sort.

As for the negro question in general—I think that intermarriage ought to be banned in view of the vast number of blacks in the country. Illicit miscegenation by the white male is bad enough, heaven knows—but at least the hybrid offspring is kept below a definite colour-line & kept from vitiating the main stock. Nothing but pain & disaster can come from the mingling of black & white, & the law ought to aid in checking this criminal folly. Granting the negro his full due, he is not the sort of material which can mix successfully into the fabric of a civilised caucasian nation. Isolated cases of high-grade hybrids prove nothing. It is easy to see the ultimate result of the wholesale pollution of highly evolved blood by definitely inferior strains. It happened in ancient Egypt—& made a race of supine fellaheen out of what was once a noble stock.

As for the Jewish problem—that is of course wholly different. It is not a blood problem at all (for despite the Nazi creed, Semitic blood wouldn't hurt us in the least), but predominantly a *cultural* problem. I don't know enough about Germany to say just how tight the Jewish grasp on its cultural life was—but the figures regarding attorneys in Berlin were certainly food for thought. Of course, the actual Hitler programme is so full of extravagances & absurdities that one can't endorse it as a whole—but I merely tried to point out that it has at least a bit of logical motivation. That Hitler is sincere & well-meaning cannot be disputed—& by the way, he is no 'foreigner' in any real sense. Only recently—since 1871—has Austria been any more separate from the other German states than they all were from one another. The whole German fabric is really one, despite arbitrary national lines. However—as I have said—Hitlerism as it stands certainly isn't anything to endorse. As for New York—there is no question but that its overwhelming Semitism has totally removed it from the American stream. Regarding its influence on literary & dramatic expression—it is not so much that the country is flooded directly with Jewish authors, as that Jewish publishers determine just which of our Aryan writers shall achieve print & position. That means that those of us who least express our own people have the preference. Taste is insidiously moulded along non-Aryan lines—so that, no matter how intrinsically good the resulting body of literature may be, it is a special, rootless literature which does not represent us. The feelings & ideals presented are not our feelings & ideals—so that today our newer authors are as exotic to us as the French symbolists or Japanese hokku-writers. This, of course, applies to literature *as a whole*. Naturally, a good deal of representative stuff manages to get published. It is not difficult to point out what is meant by this insidious exoticism. What is happening is that books are *preferred* when they reflect an emotional attitude toward life which is profoundly foreign to the race as a whole. The preferred writers are detailedly interested in things which do not interest us, & are callous to the real impulses & aspirations which move us most. Anderson & Faulkner, delving in certain restricted strata, seldom touch on any chord to which the reader personally responds. We recognise their art, but admire them at a distance—as we admire Turgeniev & Baudelaire. Whether our own representative authors do as well in their art as these foreign-influenced types is beside the question. If they do not—as is entirely possible—then the thing to do is to stimulate better & freer expression among them; not to turn away from them & encourage expression in exotic fields. This can be done without injustice to the admitted intrinsic excellence of the exotics & decadents.

As for the "colonial tradition" & others—the one really sound course is for each individual writer to forget all about "schools" & "traditions", & simply write what is in him in the best way he knows how. It is merely an incidental matter that he will probably find the methods & perspectives of his own ancestors best suited to him. Of course a geographical, social, & political setting differing from the ancestral pattern will naturally produce variations—but as soon as these variations eclipse the thread of continuity the net result is bound to suffer. A great deal of the non-English trend in American writing is simply a matter of illiteracy, slovenliness, eccentricity, affectation, & confusing foreign influence. Good books in this medium are good not because of their departures from tradition but in spite of it. There is no real difference between the language of cultivated persons in England & America. When we represent the speech of local characters, we must observe a photographic accuracy of dialect; but serious third-person writing knows no national boundaries.

As for the proper course for a young writer—I would say that it is to forget all about time & place, to assimilate all that is soundest throughout the literature of his ancestors, & to express what he has to say in that manner which his background-knowledge impels him to regard as most powerful & artistic. That is what I have tried to do. You err when you assume that I follow the style of my chronological generation. As a matter of fact, my style is largely that of many generations before my own lifetime. I cannot conceive of any really literate person *choosing* the crude, barren, & altogether inadequate manner followed by the most popular writers of today. These writers represent powerful minds handicapped by certain cultural inadequacies—& it is our business to emulate their power, not their handicaps.

Well—it's getting dark, & I must move on. Pardon the inadequacy of this screed—but I'm sure you can appreciate my limitations during this strenuous period. Good luck with your "Faun" & other ventures. Young Bloch of Milwaukee speaks of hearing interestingly from you. Quite a boy—only 16, but with a surprising variety of talents. Some of his drawings are infinitely suggestive of Klarkash-Ton, though his stories still display much youthful extravagance.

Going to be a warm evening, thank Heaven. Hope tomorrow will be pleasant for the Morton visit.

Best wishes—

        Yr obt hble Servt

           E'ch-Pi-El

Notes

1. See E. Hoffmann Price, "The Man Who Was Lovecraft," in *Lovecraft Remembered,* ed. Peter Cannon (Sauk City, WI: Arkham House, 1998), 292–93.

2. Helen V. Sully.

3. Ellis St. Joseph, "Introduction to Eric," *Harper's Magazine* (June 1933), a weird tale.

4. *The Double Shadow and Other Fantasies.*

5. The *Fantasy Fan,* edited by Charles D. Hornig; regarded as the first fanzine in the science fiction/fantasy genre. It lasted for exactly 18 issues (September 1933–February 1935).

6. *Ann Carver's Profession* (Columbia Pictures, 1933), directed by Edward Buzzell; starring Fay Wray, Gene Raymond, and Claire Dodd. *Men Must Fight* (MGM, 1933), directed by Edgar Selwyn; starring Diana Wynyard, Lewis Stone, and Phillips Holmes.

[38]   [ALS]

66 College St.,
Providence, R.I.,
Aug. 14, 1933

Dear Jehvish-Êi:—

Again I must apologise for an epistle sadly inadequate as compared with that which it answers—but my programme is still a mess, & my nerves all shot to hell as a result of my "imprisonment". My aunt's cast came off a week ago, but she is not yet able to use her crutches. Nurse still here—& I have to be on hand every afternoon while she goes out. I shall still be tied down after the nurse goes—for my aunt will not be able to get downstairs & answer the doorbell for months. A whole half-year (or really, a *whole* year, since midsummer is the only time when I am any good) has been subtracted from my existence. But at that, it's a hell of a lot worse for the patient!

I note with interest your remarks on first novels. As to abnormal themes—of course, once in a while a major book manages to get written around one, but in general they fall (like my own weird line) in the narrower domain of specialised writing. There is an especial liking for them in decadent periods, when life as a whole seems (because of the lack of general adjustment to it) remote & unreal as compared with the morbid problems of ill-adjusted individuals. Foreigners in America take to them more naturally than native-Americans—this being true also of natives influenced by immigrant perspectives. This is one reason why non-native control of drama & publishing houses tends to publicise an essentially unrepresentative type of literature. However—as to minor themes—I agree with you most emphatically that it is better for a beginner (or for that matter a more experienced writer who recognises limitations in himself) to choose a minor field & excel in it, than to attempt too big a job & achieve nothing more than mediocrity in it. That is what I did myself during my writing days—stuck to the narrow field of the weird because I knew damn well I couldn't do anything outside it.

What you say of the background of "To Love a Faun" is highly interesting—this chap Bonner must be rather a pathetic figure. Certainly, his case forms a very fruitful basis for serious fictional treatment. I guess it is true that homosexuality is a rare theme for novels—partly because public attention was seldom called to it (except briefly during the Wilde period) until a decade ago, & partly because any literary use of it always incurs the peril of legal censorship. As a matter of fact—although of course I always knew that paederasty was a disgusting custom of many ancient nations—I never heard of homosexuality as an actual instinct till I was over thirty . . . which beats your record! It is possible, I think, that this perversion occurs more frequently in some periods that in others—owing to obscure biological & psychological causes. Decadent ages—when psychology is unsettled—seem to favour it. Of course—in ancient times the extent of the practice of paederasty (as a custom which most simply accepted blindly, without any special inclination) cannot be taken as any measure of the extent of actual psychological perversion. Another thing many nowadays overlook the fact that there are always distinctly *effeminate* types which are most distinctly *not homosexual.* I don't know how psychology explains them, but we all know the sort of damned sissy who plays with girls & seems to dislike boys, & who—when he grows up—is a chronic "cake-eater", hanging around girls, doting on dances, acquiring certain feminine mannerisms, intonations, & tastes, & yet *never* having even the slightest perversion of erotic inclinations. All his romantic & sexual feelings are in the right direction—toward women—& yet he tends to reflect the personality of the women he admires. He makes a good husband & father, & seems to *dislike* other men in the long run—never being much for stag gatherings, & never seeming to understand thoroughly the *general* masculine reaction to life. It is curious how this type of sissy seems to be forgotten amidst the modern wave of interest in homosexuality. I have come across many in my time—& it would certainly be absurd (in view of their constant interest in girls & lack of any even friendly feelings toward men & boys) to assume that the basis of their peculiarities is deeply sexual. These people hardly represent a real *problem,* although they are distinctly ridiculous & repellent. In my youth they were caricatured frequently on the stage; their representation being (because of the general ignorance of homosexuality's existence) wholly free from smut, & altogether in the "good clean fun" class. Poor devils—the modern wave of sophistication must be damned hard on them, since nowadays everyone must suspect them of perversion! Your Bonner may possibly belong merely to this harmless type. There are, too, undoubtedly many masculine women whose masculine manners & outlook are equally free from actual homosexuality.

Well—I certainly wish you luck with the novel. The title you have chosen sounds as good as any to me—although "The Solitary Cell" would be far from bad. "Strange Distress" sounds melodramatic—I'd hesitate before adopting it. I guess your method—your plan of the point of view—is about the best that could be used for the given material. The extract you give is interesting—does it represent the opening of the novel? As for criticism—it seems to me that your language has a slight pomposity & involvedness (natural characteristics of youth) which greater practice will tend to eliminate. Some of your sentences are very complex, & the *rhythm* of the whole seems occasionally broken & halting. Occasionally it might be possible to effect subtle improvements in word-choice—& in at least one instance you have a word whose existence seems a bit doubtful to me—"alienity" where *alienage* ought to be. Since object-lessons are more useful than abstract precepts, I am enclosing a sheet on which I jotted down the opening parts of your selection more as I would say they ought to be. You can take or leave these suggestions—just as you choose—my chief purpose being to help you unscramble some of the ultra-extended, complex sentences. So far as the material & manner go—I think the stuff looks very promising. Keep it up! Whether or not this tale ever lands professionally, it will be infinitely fine literary practice. Don't feel discouraged at your rate of achievement. The infant prodigies you read about are the exceptions—most writers really land only toward thirty.

Your news items, as usual, interested me greatly—but the annals of our own gang can tie that Maugham cobra item.[1] Only the other day Klarkash-Ton killed a rattlesnake which had crept dangerously near him as he sat writing in the yard outside his home. However—I don't believe he used a celebrity-given cane! Yes—I think the undercurrent of comedy in O'Neill is quite perceptible.

Congratulations on attaining your majority! On August 20 I shall turn 43—but birthdays are old stuff to the aged. I trust the coming wedding will find you a suave & well-rehearsed usher. I was a sort of under-best-man—at the age of six—at the wedding of the aunt who now presides over #66. I handed the ring to the real best man (the groom's brother),[2] who passed it on to the groom. Young Bloch is quite a kid—has he shewn you any of his weird drawings? Your links with the headlined Urschel are indeed highly interesting . . . . as is likewise the history of the Slick–Urschel clan. The fate of Slick's tawny bride certainly does look fishy—no jest intended![3] Yes—I think the advisability of the death penalty for kidnapping seems extremely doubtful—especially in view of the desperate measures it might elicit.

Pray tell your father that I think his paragraphs on life & death very sensible & well-arranged. The only objections I could offer would relate to the possible air of heavy *sententiousness* about the opening paragraphs—& perhaps to such frankly *flowery* phrases as *protoplasmic pullulation*. Simplicity is a desideratum in every kind of writing. I like the concluding paragraph best of all. By the way—I assume that "collodial" is a purely stenographic mis-presentation of *colloidal*. [i.e., pertaining to colloids].

Your observations on civic affairs in Pittsburgh are interesting indeed—

Providence affords no parallel phenomena. Brobst, however, reports cases of social unrest in Allentown, Pa., (his home town, where he spent a recent fortnight's vacation) which would indicate that your state is quite fertile in agitation.

I have not seen Summers' "Supernatural Omnibus", but have been told that most of the tales are relatively dull. I'd guess that myself in view of the selection from Machen—about his worst story.[4] Most of the contents is unknown to me. Yes—Summers is a queer old duck who believes in ghosts, witches, daemons, vampires, & all the rest of the mediaeval stage-properties. He is an Anglo-Catholic clergyman of really great erudition, whose works on vampirism & witchcraft are rapidly assuming a place as classics.

Glad you survived the Witch House. I had a letter from Knopf Co. last week, asking me to send some stuff with a view to possible book publication. *Possible* is good! After the Putnam & Vanguard fiascos I realise how little such requests mean. These birds are merely scouting around to make sure they aren't missing anything. My junk will come back with a note of polite regret! Yes—I heard of the new magazine. Another weird magazine will be issued by the Jay Publishing Co., 125 W. 45th St., N.Y.C.[5]—& *Astounding Stories* will be revived by Street & Smith as a weird magazine. Also—did I send you the enclosed notice of the (non-paying) *Fantasy Fan,* on which C A S & I intend to dump our old & universally rejected tales? The editor makes a special offer of 18 mo. for $1.00. This thing will soon become predominantly weird, since the editor (one Charles D. Hornig) has just been appointed Managing Editor of *Wonder Stories,* & doesn't wish to duplicate on "scientifiction." Hope you'll eventually obtain Klarkash-Ton's new brochure. The tales are really magnificent—far better than most of the items accepted by W.T. It is about as good a quarter's value as I've seen in a damn long while!

As usual, your cinema notes offer interesting suggestions—though I've seen no shows since the Onset one to which the Longs dragged me. I shall try to see the coming Chaplin event[6]—which reminds me that I have probably seen nearly all of the immortal Charlie's efforts. "Destination Unknown"[7] ought to have some good effects, though the moral latter half sounds sappy. What you say of the quality of the different nations' films is probably true— amusingly so in contrast to the conditions when the industry was young. In those days—say '06 & '07—over half of everything came from France, so that a cinema show was almost synonymous with the Pathé coq rouge atop the warning "Marque Deposeé" [*sic*]. Italian films were also numerous—but France was in the lead . . . . so much so that cinema-devotees of that time picked up a pretty good idea of French life—houses, street scenes, urban types, &c. Some of the things weren't bad for their time—they were far less crude than the American products. I recall a splendid comedian named Max Linder, & two very fair actors named Kraus & Liabel.[8] I hope to see the cinematic "Emperor Jones".[9] I saw the original play a decade ago, with Charles Gilpin (now deceased, I believe) as the central figure. It was tremendously effective.

I also saw Paul Robeson in "All God's Chillun" in N.Y. In 1924 or 1925.

I must get in touch with *Harpers* again—you & Belknap convince me that I'm missing valuable material! Haven't yet seen a copy of *Story*—which has accepted something of Derleth's.[10] As for "Handsome Adolf"—in saying he is sincere, & that there is a certain basis behind some phases of the attitude he represents, I do not mean to imply that his actual programme is not extreme, grotesque, & occasionally barbarous. His attempt to banish arbitrarily all literature he does not like is of course essentially uncivilised—while his ethnological theories (as distinguished from any defence of a purely Aryan *culture*) are contrary to the maturest beliefs of science. I doubt if he is actually a Jew, though—for that sort of story follows a familiar folklore pattern. It would be *too aptly dramatic* if he actually did represent the group he opposes. Such a legend bears every earmark of artificial coinage. Regarding the Scottsboro matter—if all the statements in the Wilson book[11] are true—& not qualified by any still more obscure considerations—then it would certainly seem as if the prosecution's case were far from ironclad. Of course Wilson has gone over to communism—but points like these are capable of being checked up, no matter who advances them. I don't know the technique of law, but it seems to me that if as much doubt as all this exists, there will surely be some ultimate reversal of the convictions.

Your reading is certainly voluminous in the extreme—far beyond anything I could achieve! The last time I ever tried to catch up with contemporary literature was about 10 years ago. Some day I'll have to get you young fellows—yourself, Comte d'Erlette, Wandrei, &c.—to make me up a list of the 10 or 20 books most representative of the present generation's mind & mood. I recall young d'Erlette's enthusiasm for "Look Homeward, Angel."

Remarks on Andy Mellon proved interesting. Poor old duffer! Too bad some of these plutocrats can't get out of finance & politics & utilise their leisure & resources in the furtherance of the arts! Glad you ran across your old friend—the ex-high school hero. He certainly seems to be a promising specimen, & I hope he'll prove a congenial associate for you. Don't tell him—but his respected kinsman Clarence Buddington Kelland was an especial detestation of good old Whitehead's, who found his glib, conventional tales almost unreadable.[12]

No news of any importance hereabouts—except that I had an enjoyable visit from my friend James F. Morton around the beginning of August. Weather was very favourable, so that most of the time was utilised in outdoor excursions. We explored certain ancient parts of Western R.I. which I had never seen before—encountering among other things a finely-preserved well-sweep of the archaic type, & a sleepy village retaining all the atmosphere of a century ago. We also visited the colonial town of Warren down the east shore of the bay—whence we walked onward to Bristol, taking the train back to Providence. On the final day we made a boat trip to Newport—re-exploring the venerable town, & spending the afternoon on the rugged ocean cliffs where 200 years ago Dean Berkeley sat & composed his famous "Alciphron;

or, the Minute Philosopher." Morton is now in Vermont climbing mountains. I've had an invitation to New Hampshire, but fear I shall be unable to accept it on account of the needs which confine me here.

Well—good luck with your novel & all your other enterprises. I feel certain that you will ultimately succeed in authorship.

Best wishes—

Yr most ob^t h^ble Servt

E'ch-Pi-El

Notes

1. Maugham's novel, *The Magician* (1908), contains an anecdote about a man bitten by a cobra (p. 60).

2. Henry Gamwell was the brother of the groom, Edward Francis Gamwell (1869–1936).

3. On 22 July 1933, an oil magnate, Charles F. Urschel, was kidnapped from his home in Oklahoma City. He was released nine days later after his wife (formerly Mrs. Thomas B. Slick) paid $75,000 to the kidnappers.

4. The anthology included Machen's "The Inmost Light."

5. The magazine never appeared.

6. Perhaps a reference to Chaplin's beginning work on the film *Modern Times* (1936), which was announced around this time.

7. *Destination Unknown* (Universal, 1933), directed by Tay Garnett; starring Pat O'Brien, Ralph Bellamy, and Alan Hale.

8. Max Linder (1883–1925), French actor and director; Charles Kraus (1865–1931), Hungarian actor; André Liabel, French actor and director.

9. *The Emperor Jones* (United Artists, 1933), directed by Dudley Murphy; starring Paul Robeson, Dudley Digges, and Frank H. Wilson. Based on the play by Eugene O'Neill.

10. Derleth's "A Ride Home" appeared in *Story* (August 1934).

11. The reference is unclear. Edmund Wilson wrote a celebrated article on the Scottsboro case, "The Freight-Car Case," *New Republic* 68 (26 August 1931): 38–43.

12. Clarence Buddington Kelland (1881–1964), American author of popular novels and stories for adults and juveniles.

[39]   [ANS]^1

[Postmarked Providence, RI,
22 August 1933]

Well, bless my soul, son! So you remembered Grandpa's birthday! Thanks & appreciations! ¶ A less palatable birthday present was a letter from Wright turning down the joint tale which Price & I wrote. Hand of Eblis upon him! ¶ Knopf asked to see more of my stuff, & now wishes time to consider. All right—but I harbour no illusions this trip! ¶ Hope the wedding came off smoothly, & that you didn't steer everybody into the wrong pews! ¶ 43 is a heavy burden to carry. I visibly aged when the clock struck 10 a.m., Daylight Saving Time . . . . my birth-hour being 9 o'clock Eastern Standard. Regards & senile blessings—E'ch-Pi-El

[P.S. on picture side:] Wandrei has sold a story for $95.00 to the revived Astounding Stories.

Notes

1. *Front:* 67:—Statler Hotel and McKinley Monument, Buffalo, N. Y.

[40]   [ANS][1]

> [Postmarked Quebec, Canada.
> 3 September 1933]

Hail, O Jehvish-Êi! On my one vacation of 1933. Having a great time—fine hot weather so far. Dread the end of this 4-day sojourn. Positively, there is no other place quite as fascinating as La Vielle Québec! Stopped in Boston to look up a 1637 house in the suburbs, & hope to see "Arkham" & "Kingsport" on the return trip. Home Thursday. Am now sitting on the ramparts looking over a scene nowhere to be duplicated in North America.

    Regards & blessings—
      E'ch-Pi-El

Notes

1. *Front:* Chateau Frontenac, Quebec, Canada.

[41]   [ALS]

> 66 College St.,
> Providence, R.I.,
> Septr 25, 1933

Dear Jehvish-Êi:—

    My Quebec trip was certainly a thorough success—& all the more so because of its unexpectedness. On the outbound voyage I paused in the Boston zone long enough to look up the ancient Deane Winthrop house in a suburb. This edifice was built in 1637, & is one of the oldest structures in America. It is a simple farmhouse, but very solidly built. In the base of the colossal brick chimney is a secret room—of a sort very common in 17th century houses. An historical society maintains the place. I also called on W. Paul Cook—the Recluse man—while in Boston. The long train ride to Quebec was spent in reading & drowsing—& was unusually pleasant because there were no alcohol-seeking roysterers aboard as in '30 & '32. The return of King Gambrinus to the States has its compensations![1] Most of the passengers were honest, simple French peasants bent on visiting ancestral soil or on grovelling at the miracle-working shrine of La Bonne Ste. Anne de Beaupré. At last—after a post-auroral dash through the increasingly picturesque provincial landscape—came the mighty fortress of the North itself . . . . the rock-bound stronghold which defied the fleet of Phips & formed the Carthage of Cotton Mather's minatory thunderings! It gave me a tremendous hereditary kick to see our Old Flag—the time-hallowed Union Jack which greed & selfishness pulled down from the flagstaffs of the more southerly colonies—fluttering proudly from the lofty citadel & the towers of the Houses of Parliament. God Save the King!

I had four days—all delectably hot & sunny—in Quebec, & certainly made the most of them. What a town! Old grey walls, majestic citadel, dizzying cliffs, silver spires, ancient red roofs, mazes of winding ways, constant music of mellow chimes & clopping hooves over centuried cobblestones, throngs of cassocked, shovel-hatted priests, robed nuns, & tonsured barefoot friars, vistas of huddled chimney-pots, broad blue river far below, vivid, verdant countryside, & the dim, distant line of the purple Laurentians. . . . . I also took some suburban trips—a walk to Sillery, up the river (whose headland church is such an universal landmark), & a trolley ride to the upper level of the Montmorency Falls, where stands Kent House (enlarged & badly defaced as an hotel), the Georgian mansion inhabited in the 1790's by the Duke of Kent, Queen Victoria's father. I loafed, read, & wrote in all the parks & on the citadel embankment, & looked up the exact spot of Wolfe's ascent of the cliff—not an easy quest, since it is unmarked, & since the local Gauls are far from eager to point out the route of their great conqueror. One of the things about Quebec that always strikes me forcibly is the *sky*—the odd cloud formations peculiar to northerly latitudes & virtually unknown in southern New England. Mist & vapour assume fantastic & portentous aspects, & at sunset on Labour Day I saw one of the most impressive phenomena imaginable from a vantage-point on the ancient citadel overlooking the river & the Levis cliffs beyond. The evening was predominantly clear; but some strange refractive quality gave the dying solar rays an abnormal redness, whilst from the zenith to the southeastern horizon stretched an almost black funnel of churning nimbus clouds—the small end meeting the earth at some inland point beyond Levis. From a place midway in this cloud-funnel, zigzag streaks of lightning would occasionally dart toward the ground, with faint rumbles of thunder following tardily after. Finally—while the blood-red sun still bathed the river & cliffs & housetops in a supernal light—a pallid arc of rainbow sprang into sight above the distant Isle d'Orleans; its upper end lost in the great funnel of cloud. I have never seen such a phenomenon before, & doubt if it could occur as far south as Providence. Another striking thing is the almost perpetual mist which spectrally hovers about the mountains & valleys near Lake Memphramagog, at the Vermont–Quebec line. With such bizarre skies, I do not wonder that the northern races excel those of the south in fantastic imagination.

My ride back to the States was extremely pleasant—an apocalyptic sunset over a grotesquely steepled hilltop village, & a great round moon flooding strange plains with an eery radiance. Dawn came in New-Hampshire lake-&-mountain region of uncommon beauty, & I glimpsed Daniel Webster's early home from the train south of Franklin. Boston at 9 a.m.—& then good old Salem & Marblehead (Arkham & Kingsport).

In Salem I came upon some interesting new things, & got inside the fine old Richard Darby house (1762) for the first time. This structure—splendidly panelled—was rather old-fashioned even in its day. The Darbys were virtually the first of the great merchant princes of Salem—ship-captains & owners who established the thriving East-India trade. One high spot was the perfect reproduction of a gabled house of 1650 lately built on the grounds of the Pequot Mills. Every detail of the 17th century work is duplicated with scholarly fidelity, & I could hardly believe it was a modern fac-simile. But the climax was the splendid reproduction of the pioneer Salem settlement of 1626 et seq., carefully constructed & laid out in Forest Run Park. It consists of a generous plot of ground at the harbour's edge, painstakingly landscaped & covered with absolutely perfect duplicates of the very earliest huts & houses—dwellings of a sort now utterly vanished. All the early industries are also reproduced—there being such things as an ancient saw-pit, blacksmith shop, salt-works, brick-plant, fish-drying outfit, & so on. Nothing else that I have ever seen gives one so good a picture of the rough pioneer life led during the first half-decade of New England colonisation. Marblehead possessed its accustomed charm—though my inspection was broken by several showers. I finally got utterly drenched in Boston as I darted from the North Station to pay a farewell call on Cook. All told, it was a magnificent outing in spite of its brevity—& is probably the only first-rate voyage I'll get this year.

My aunt is now vastly improved—all around the house on crutches or cane. The nurse went a fortnight ago. I am not tied down quite as badly as I had feared I would be—especially since we have installed an electrical device for opening the front door from upstairs. My aunt's meals are sent in from the boarding-house across the back garden. It is possible that I may get to Boston once more this autumn—if my friend Loveman comes to these parts & wants to be shewn around. It is likewise conceivable that I may spend a week with Long in upper Manhattan.

Your epistle is, as usual, full of interest. Sorry your neighbour-periodical didn't take "The Cell"—but rejections are things to which everyone has to grow accustomed. I repeat that I don't see any reason for discouragement in your literary experiences so far. Your present intensive reading is all valuable preparation for authorship later on. Glad you found something helpful in my remarks on the beginning of your novel. Hope you'll make progress on the latter during the ensuing weeks—though of course there is no object in hurrying. As for my own experiments in further writing—they are purely tentative. Lately I have been intensively re-reading & analysing the classics of weird literature with a view to comparing the various main methods of developing certain types of supernatural ideas.[2] I'll let you see the rather mediocre "Silver Key" sequel before long—starting it on a fresh round of circulation. Which reminds me that Price, after considering the notion of hyemating in Florida, has finally gone back to New Orleans. In New York—toward the end of his northern sojourn—he got in touch with my friends Long & Morton, & the three proved exceedingly congenial. Rumours of new weird magazines continue to float around—Klarkash-Ton tells me that one William Crawford of Everett in your own state is about to launch a periodical called *Unusual Stories,* which will handle weird & scientifiction material, though without remuneration.

Thanks for the cuttings. The Pittsburgh view interested me greatly, & I can well understand the opinions of those who find the city beautiful despite its popular reputation for industrial prosaicism. The stadium has a delectably Roman aspect—& I was glad to get a concrete glimpse of the clubhouse mentioned in your novel. By the way—I think "Posturings" is an excellent title for that work. As for the Hitler cuttings—I must say, in all objective impartiality, that they impress me as being nearly as narrow & unscientific in one direction as Hitler himself is an another direction. The problem of race & culture is by no means as simple as is assumed either by the Nazis or by the rabble-catering equalitarian columnists of the Jew-York papers. Of course Hitler is an unscientific extremist in fancying that any racial strain can be reduced to theoretical purity, that the Nordic stock is intellectually & aesthetically superior to all others, & that even a trace of non-Nordic blood—or non-Aryan blood—is enough to alter the psychology & citizenly potentialities of an individual. These assumptions, most certainly, are crude & ignorant—but the anti-Hitlerites are too cocksure when they maintain that the fallacy of these points justifies a precisely opposite extremism. As a matter of fact—all apart from social & political prejudice—there indisputably is such a thing as a Nordic subdivision of the white race, as evolved by a strenuous & migratory life in Northern Asia & Europe. Of course, very little of it remains simon-pure at this date—after all the mixtures resulting from its contacts with other stocks—but anyone would be a damn fool to deny that certain modern racial or cultural units remain *predominantly & determinantly* Nordic in blood, so that their instincts & reactions generally follow the Nordic pattern, & differ basically from those of the groups which are predominantly non-Nordic. Anybody can see for himself the difference between a tall, straight-nosed, fine-haired dolichocephalic Teuton or Celt (be he blond or dark) on the one hand, & a squat, swarthy Latin, aquiline Semite, or brachycephalic Slav on the other hand. And even if a Teutonic or Celtic group happens to pick up & assimilate substantial numbers of Latins, Semites, or Slavs, it will continue to think & feel & act in a characteristic Nordic fashion as long as the old blood remains predominant, & the culture-stream remains unbroken. It is of course true that the cultural heritage is more influential than the biological, but only a freakish extremist would reduce the biological to negligibility. Separate lines of evolution have certainly developed typically differing responses to given environmental stimuli. As for the question of superiority & inferiority—when we observe the whole animal kingdom & note the vast differences in capacity betwixt different species & sub-species within various genera, we see how utterly asinine & hysterically sentimental is the blanket assumption of idealists & other fools that all the sub-species of *homo sapiens* must *necessarily* be equal. The truth is, that we cannot lay down any general rule in this matter at the outset. We must simply study each variety with the perfect detachment of the zoölogist & abide by the results of honest investigation whether we relish them or not. And what does such study tell us? Largely this—that the australoid & negro races are basically & structurally primitive—possessing definite morphological & psychological variations in the direction of lower stages of organisation—whilst all others average about the same so far as the best classes of each are concerned. The same, that is, in *total capacity*—though each has its own special aptitudes & deficiencies. The races are *equal,* but *infinitely different*—so that the cultural pattern of one is essentially unadaptable to any other. The ancient civilisation of China is not inferior to ours—yet it could not possibly suit us, any more than ours could suit a race of essentially Mongol descent. And that is where the need of realistic intelligence as opposed to idealistic & sentimental flapdoodle in matters of racial policy comes in. The fact is, that a need for a certain rational amount of racial discrimination exists *apart from all questions of superiority or inferiority.* The effective development of a civilisation depends largely upon its *stability & continuity;* & these factors cannot be ensured unless (a) the culture-stream remains relatively undiluted by alien traditions or irrelevant & traditionless innovations, & (b) the race-stock remains approximately the same as that which evolved the culture & institutions now existing. The first point is of course very obvious. The second becomes so after a moment's thought. To take a concrete instance—we live in a social group & nation whose ingrained, hereditary folkways & types of thought & feeling are emphatically an outgrowth of a Teutonic-Celtic race-stock. That is, our institutions were evolved to fit the particular biological & psychological needs of persons who are predominantly Nordic Aryans, so that they cannot fit other races except in such respects as those others may happen to resemble ours. In many cases other race-stocks have decidedly different needs & feelings—hence if they try to settle en masse in our country they create a situation of mutual discomfort. They do not feel at home among us—& when they try to bend our institutions to fit themselves they make us uncomfortable, destroy our cultural equilibrium, & permanently weaken, dilute, & set back our whole civilisation. This should not be. Therefore *just this much* of Hitler's basic racial theory is *perfectly & irrefutably sound:* namely, that no settled & homogeneous nation ought (a) to admit enough of a decidedly alien race-stock to bring about an actual alteration in the dominant ethnic composition, or (b) tolerate the dilution of the culture-stream with emotional & intellectual elements alien to the original cultural impulse. Both of these perils lead to the most undesirable results—i.e., the metamorphosis of the population away from the original institutions, & the twisting of the institutions away from the original people . . . . . . all these things being aspects of one underlying & disastrous condition—the destruction of cultural stability, & the creation of a hopeless disparity between a social group & the institutions under which it lives. *Now this has nothing to do with intrinsic superiority & inferiority.* That is what the howling sentimentalists & faddists can't get through their thick beans. It doesn't matter whether a race is our equal—or even our superior (as, in all probability, the ancient Greek race [a Nordic-Mediterranean blend] was); if it is in any way radically *different* from ours, then its blood ought not to pour by the wholesale into our nation, & its institutions (made to fit *it,* not *us*) ought not to be allowed to twist & dilute our own. Even *superior* importations can harm our culture if they break up the equilibrium existing between the people & the institutions under which the people live. Remember that a people cannot change its institutions lightly. These things, to be valid & satisfying, must be a deep-seated hereditary growth—& must above all be suited to the peculiar aptitudes of the race in question. Thus I sympathise warmly & completely with the general principle that northern nations like Germany & the United States ought to be kept *predominantly* Nordic in blood & *wholly* Nordic in institutions. This is not because Nordic blood & culture are necessarily superior to any other, but simply because the given nations happen to be essentially Nordic at the outset. I believe just as strongly that Japan ought to be kept predominantly Japanese; & would resent a wholesale influx of Aryans into Japan as keenly as I would resent a wholesale influx of Japanese into an Aryan nation. Indeed, I agree with those Japanese scholars who lament the existing dilution of Japan's art & folkways with European elements. As for this flabby talk of an "Americanism" which opposes all racial discrimination—that is simply god damned bull-shit! The ideal is so flagrantly unsound in its very essence that it would be a disgrace to any national tradition professing it. It is an ignorant, sentimental, impracticable, & potentially dangerous delusion—& any sophisticated person can realise that it belongs only to the insincere pseudo-Americanism of the spread-eagle illiterate or the charlatanic ward politician. It is what superficial Americans proclaim with their lips, while actually lynching niggers & selling select real-estate on a restrictive basis to keep Jews & Dagoes out. In other words, it is *not* a part of any "Americanism" which has any *real* existence. It is merely part of the cheap American bluff—& indeed, is not even nominally professed in that southern half of the country which was once the most important half & will probably become so again. Ever since 1924 American immigration legislation has, under the very thinnest of veils, discouraged the immigration of racial elements radically alien to the original American people; & I do not believe this sound policy will ever be rescinded. We had this much of "Hitlerism" before we had ever heard of Handsome Adolf!

But now to give the other side its due. Certainly, the Nazis are guilty of fantastic & sentimental error in assuming that *small doses* of alien blood have the same undermining effect as vast influxes, as well as in claiming that *individuals* are unfitted for participation in a given culture because of the possession of an alien blood-strain. Actually, the inherent traits of a race are those of *all* its members, taken on the *average*. This average is of course struck by the inclusion of all sorts of individual variants; & it is an obvious fact—in view of human uniqueness & variability—that many *individuals* in any culture depart vastly from the group average in the direction of the averages of other groups. Thus there are hundreds of individual aliens perfectly fitted to mingle with our civilisation *on that civilisation's own terms*—in a circumstance the more marked because, after all, a good part of the individual's personality is a matter of culture-heritage rather than biology. The absorption into our fabric of *a few* aliens can hardly produce any genuine harm. These people are not necessarily any more misfits than *some* of our own people. Their absorption merely increases *slightly* the inevitable misfit proportion; & in view of the overwhelming pressure of our culture-tradition, their descendants (with alienage constantly thinning through blood-admixture, just as the alienage of our own dark Iberic ancestors of southwestern Britain was thinned through submersion in the Nordic blood of Celtic Britons, Saxon conquerors, & Danish & Norman invaders) stand every chance of becoming completely assimilated to our national type. Thus the old Spanish families of St. Augustine are *completely* assimilated to the American type—the Sequis, Sanchezes, Garcias, &c. being absolutely indistinguishable in speech, manners, thought, & feelings from the Smiths & Joneses among whom they dwell. So also with the colonially settled Jews of various cities. Nine-tenths of their blood is indistinguishably lost in the native-American stock—as, for instance, that of the Franks family of Philadelphia, one of whose daughters married the celebrated Andrew Hamilton (designer of "Independence Hall" & advocate in the famous Zenger trial in N.Y. in 1735)[3] & became the mother of a thoroughly Anglo-American line. It would, obviously, be foolish to insist on classifying the St. Augustine Sanchezes with the jabbering Cubans of Aviles St. rather than with the general American population of the town, or to segregate the Hamilton descendants of David Franks with the loathsome scum of Philadelphia's ghetto instead of acknowledging them as genuine old Philadelphians. Hitler, in effect, *would* practice such an absurdity—hence to that extent he *is* freakishly unsound. But at the same time we must not forget that the normal & successful assimilation (*full* assimilation to *our* culture, without any compromise or concession on our part) of a *few* Spaniards & Jews has nothing to do with the totally different problems presented when *hundreds of thousands* of Cubans, Mexicans, & South Americans, or stinking mongrels from Central & Eastern European ghettoes begin pouring in & actually changing the predominant blood-composition of whole sections of our territory (today Key West is no longer in any sense a fully American city, but a place where Spanish influences dilute & alter everything; whilst the utter & repugnant Semitism of New York is a matter of common knowledge); or when certain powerful cliques of superior aliens enter our territory without relinquishing their own traditions, & commence using their influence to distort our fabric in the direction of their own. (as the Jews do in New York, & the Italians to some extent in Providence) Thus both pure Hitlerism & rabid anti-Hitlerism are almost equally absurd. On the one hand it is sheerly asinine to claim (as Hitler does) that the thoroughly German & Roman Catholic Mme. Schumann-Heink[4] is "not a German" because research reveals a Jew in her ancestry; but on the other hand it is equally puerile to pretend that the utter submersion of New York by Jews, the wholesale flooding of New England by Latins, & the subtle capture of the avenues of American expression by alien influences are not unqualified calamities tending to make us feel uncomfortable in our own country & ultimately to weaken our civilisation. I can certainly appreciate the need for racial & cultural conservation which lies behind Hitler's crude ethnic polity—& that need is not a bit less real or pressing because of the unscientific extravagance of Hitler's specific concepts & methods. What is truly to be desired is some moderate middle course which shall exclude all *large influxes* of alien blood, & curtail the political, social, literary, & financial influence of persons directly belonging to alien culture-groups; yet without depending on unsound biological theories or applying ridiculous & unnecessary ancestral tests to persons obviously belonging to the dominant culture. Of course, the question of the *inferior races* is a wholly different one—& one which does not exist in Germany. That is the peculiar burden of the American, the Cuban, the South-African, the Australian, the Anglo-Indian or Brahmin, & the West-Indian. I still seem to feel that the absolute colour-line represents the course of greatest wisdom wherever white people are in contact with vast hordes of australoids & negroes. Indeed—I would expand that view to include not only white people but other superior races like the Mongols. If Japan ever conquered Australia or the United States it would be necessary for the Japanese to draw a rigid colour-line against the blackfellows & niggers. Wherever superior races have absorbed large doses of inferior blood, the results have been tragic. Egypt is one case—& India presents a still more loathsome extreme. The Aryans in India were too late in establishing their colour-based caste system, so that today the culture of the Hindoo is probably the most thoroughly repulsive on our planet. The more one learns about India the more one wants to vomit. Aside from a few profound minds, Indian people represent such an abyss of degeneracy that extirpation & fumigation would seem to be about the only way to make Hindoostan fit for decent people to inhabit. As a final word on the Nordic—no responsible person wishes to represent him as intrinsically superior to any other white race. In pure intellection he is surpassed by the Semite, & in aesthetic delicacy & sensitiveness he ranks below the Mediterranean. His great contribution to mental life is his sense of symbolism—his mysticism & his poetry. Here he has no competitor. All the supreme poetry of the world since Graeco-Roman times is Nordic, & we know that only the dream-inspired minds of Celts & Teutons could ever have evolved the imaginative triumphs of Gothic architecture from the few hints of pointed-arch treatment picked up in the East during the Crusades. So much for that. It is not on the purely intellectual-aesthetic side that the Nordic bases his claim to prime merit. What the Nordic primarily is, is *a master in the art of orderly living & group preservation.* He is the only social & political adult since the fall of the Roman Empire. His is that peculiar strength which sweeps all before it, & makes safe from all aggression or decay the institutions he evolves. *Stamina* is the great contribution of the Nordic to the modern world. He has a natural code of ideals which places *self-respecting freedom & courage* toweringly above all other human qualities (that is why he can never reach common ground with the crafty, sensuous Latin, or cringing, ethics-worshipping Jew)—& this causes him to erect strong, permanent, & orderly fabrics which nothing can sweep away & which therefore form the places where civilisation can best achieve the unbroken continuity it needs for mellowing. Not that other races of the past & present lack kindred qualities—but simply that the Nordic is the most typical surviving example. He fosters those qualities most necessary to survival, & avoids the pitiful & contemptible masses of crawling parasitism & servile degeneracy into which other superior races tend to fall. (cf. Greeks under the Roman Empire—Jews of all ages—pseudo-Romans under the Gothic kings, &c.) It is genuinely difficult today to see how our Western civilisation can survive unless the Nordic race (i.e., the mixtures in which Nordic blood & culture remain reasonably predominant)—or ideals closely akin to those of the Nordic race—remain emphatically in the saddle; hence no excuse is needed for any attempt to preserve or strengthen the Nordicism of such groups as already possess it. But of course, the *primary* reason for such attempts is simply a sensible wish to keep *every* settled culture (Nordic or not) true *to itself* for the sake of the human values involved. No one wishes to force Nordicism on the non-Nordic—indeed, a real friend of civilisation wishes merely to make the Germans *more German,* the French *more French,* the Spaniards *more Spanish,* & so on. However—as a silent witness of the superior stamina of the Nordic in old days of fluid barbarism, just note how he forced his language & institutions on others without ever having alien speech or customs forced on him. It is now recognised that all languages & cultures known as "Aryan" are traceable to that tall, blond, dolichocephalic stock which we call "Nordic". It is this blond fighter & ruler who evolved the whole lingual-cultural pattern—& yet look at the infinite diversity of modern races which speak Aryan tongues & follow Aryan folkways! The dark, turbaned Hindoo, the swart, squinting Armenian, the hysterical brachycephalic Slav, the squat, mongrel-ised neo-Italian, the proud, explosive Iberian, & so on . . . . to say nothing of the savage races (Indians, negroes, blackfellows, Polynesians) who have had Aryanism forced on them by European conquerors in modern times. All of these diverse races have had to take their speech & traditions from the blond conqueror—*& yet to this day there is not a single Nordic group which has any language or institutions other than its ancestral Aryan.* Whenever we find a predominantly Nordic group which has suffered linguistic replacement (as the Celts of Gaul who acquired a Latin speech), we discover that the replacing language is *also* Aryan, & that the replacing people were (at least in part, as is the case of the Romans) essentially Nordic. This power, persistence, & stability *mean something,* & it is simply puerile to try to argue them away. To recognise them frankly involves no attempt to rob other races of *their* special merits. The Latin's sense of beauty & the Semite's keen mind all deserve our praise—but we must not ignore the Nordic's stamina, genius for order, & leadership in the art of unbroken survival. ¶ Now as to the non-ethnic features of Hitlerism—the attempt to guide cultural expression in certain channels by exiling authors & suppressing books antagonistic to the desired tradition—here again it is possible to sympathise with basic aims while deploring & ridiculing specific methods. No impartial friend of civilisation can help seeing, as Hitler does, that contemporary culture is in a state of vast rottenness—with weak, unhealthy concepts flourishing like weeds & constantly imperilling our survival against external foes & internal dissension. All the loudest aesthetic & philosophic voices of the hour are howling & whining doctrines & values which can lead to nothing save disintegration, chaos, & the death of all the background-factors which give life the illusion of being worth living. It is a pitiful epidemic, & requires treatment like any other disease—hence one cannot but sympathise with any man courageous enough to attempt its cure. Of course, poor Adolf has the *wrong* cure in mind. He wants to dethrone reason & substitute blind faith & mystical exaltation instead of backing up reason to the limit & forcing the pseudo-intellectuals to destroy themselves & the sound process of *thinking things through* to the conservative bitter end—hence he directly attacks civilisation by curtailing that freedom of thought & expression on which it primarily rests. All this is unfortunate & ridiculous—& yet no really sober analyst can help liking & respecting the poor devil for what he is blindly & bunglingly trying to do. He is fighting a real evil—& at worst he can't do a sixteenth of the irreparable harm that bolshevism would do. In these days we must be damn charitable toward *any* force which can save a large & important seduction of the western world from communism. This isn't to excuse his extravagances—but merely to give him the benefit of a proper perspective. As for his international policy, which alarms so many—here again we may clearly understand & sympathise with his motivations, even while deploring the possible consequences. He wants to get rid of the gross inequalities in the Versailles treaty—& there is absolutely no question but that this treaty is a rotten piece of greed & hypocrisy. That is where the decadence of our whole western civilisation comes in. The great war as a whole was one of those natural & inevitable struggles which human greed now & then makes necessary, & which can never be wholly eliminated even though they may be vastly reduced in number through the exercise of reason. In this general mess Germany was certainly among the *most* eager to start something, yet was assuredly not the *lone & unique* criminal represented for four hysterical years in our grotesque & puerile propaganda. The systematic effort of our Allied nations to reduce a normal & largely 50–50 war to the status of an unprecedented & final "moral crusade" with Germany in the role of leper & antichrist was a piece of morbid, shrill effeminacy which reeks of the stink of modern decadence. It made me sick at the time, & makes me sick today—although gawd knows I was no pro-German. I saw the struggle as a natural clash between powerful equals—Germany glad enough of a chance to swing into first place & secure a grip on the seas & on a colonial empire, & we glad enough of an excuse to give Germany a push backward in order to eliminate a potential peril & almost certain rival. The crisis having come, I had no question of allegiance. As an Anglo-Saxon, every drop of my blood is at the service of any movement designed to defend Anglo-Saxondom & keep it in first place, so that only my health prevented my serving under the Union Jack or American flag in the field. I would have been as glad as any other man to mow down a bunch of Germans or anyone else arrayed against my civilisation. *But*—I did not find it necessary to call a normal adversary a "Hun"[5] or emissary of the devil, or to assume that his position in the general alignment differed essentially from that of my side. Each for his own—fight for your blood & traditions, but realise that the other fellow is honourably doing the same for his! This was always the accepted attitude in less decadent days. In our wars with the French we never assumed that King Louis was a monster or that Quebec people ate little children alive. On the other hand, we had a genuine respect for men like Comte de Frontenac & Marquis de Montcalm—& all through the Hundred Years' War Englishmen travelled freely as civilians in France without either insulting their technical "enemiès" or being insulted by them. Contrast this with the insane treatment accorded peaceful German civilians in America & England during the late upheaval! Through the insincere swallowing of impossible humanitarian ideals, decadent nations are forced to camouflage their wars as religious crusades—& at what a loathsome cost to sound policy & common honesty! The worst tragedy of this rotten pseudo-piety came after the war was over. Then was the time to call off the bluff & get down to realities—recognising the similarity of purpose of both victor & vanquished, & having the victor seize only a *reasonable* advantage from his prostrate foe. Any fool ought to know that the utter crippling of a vast nation is a standing menace to the world's equilibrium. Suppose we had not only seized Canada in the treaty of 1763, but had bled France dry with forcibly extorted reparation? George III's ministers, with all their soon-to-be-revealed shortcomings, were better realists than George II's! To my own utter & dumbfounded surprise, the hypocrisies of 1914–18 were carried over into 1919 & dictated the major terms of the Versailles treaty. Germany was solemnly & officially declared "guilty" of something of which the other powers were "innocent", & loaded down with penalties so exacting & burdensome that no nation could meet them without a disastrous financial collapse & general cracking of morale. The rest is history. Friends of mine & my aunt's who travelled in Germany last year were shocked & depressed by the apathy, misgovernment, threats of communism, & general atmospheric menace in the air—a compound of lethal stagnation dispelled only in those rare moments when Hitler would sweep up in a motor & deliver a speech whose essential vagueness was lost amidst the revivifying electricity of his voice & gestures . . . . . not a cultivated voice or graceful gestures, but things touched with the inexplicable, paradoxical magic peculiar to ignorant & low-born leaders of men. Rather on the Jesus idea, if any one person such as Jesus actually existed—or like Mohammed . . . perhaps more so because of the essential militancy of Hitlerism. Well—the gist of Adolf's harangues was a patriotic revolt against the unjust burdens of Versailles—& when one thinks of those burdens, & of the morbid psychology behind them, one does not have to be a bad Englishman to feel that the fellow was telling the truth & urging the course demanded by the soundest patriotism. If Germany had whipped & crippled us, we would have thrilled to any voice urging us to rise up & repudiate the disproportionate disadvantages heaped upon us. And as good sports, we can't but admire "Der Schön[e] Adolf" when he does the same. However—don't for a moment fancy that I view with complacency all the possibilities of Hitler's foreign policy. His vision is of course romantic & immature, & coloured with a fact-ignoring emotionalism. Bad as the Versailles mess is, it involves a certain complex equilibrium which cannot be lightly disturbed; so that any too-forward & precipitate attempt to upset it might conceivably set off an endless chain of bellicose complications. There sure *is* an actual Hitler peril—yet that cannot blind us to the honest rightness of the man's basic urge. Brown—through hopelessly biassed by his New York & radical contests—is of course right when he points out the ridiculous features of Nazism. Assuredly, a good laugh based on a sound sense of proportion would leave very little indeed of the solemn, detailed, & extravagant programme of the bob-moustachio'd saviour. And yet I repeat that there is a great & pressing need behind every one of the major planks of Hitlerism—

racial-cultural continuity, conservative cultural ideals, & an escape from the absurdities of Versailles. The crazy thing is not what Adolf wants, but the way he sees it & starts out to get it. I know he's a clown, but by god, I *like* the boy! He has all the blind, bull-headed qualities of force & persistence which cause tribes & nations to pull out of hopeless impasses & muddle through seemingly insurmountable obstacles. Common sense ought to shew people that no utter ass could wield the power he wields. It is not merely the flighty who are with him—he is supported by thousands of intelligent, scholarly, & patriotic Germans who fully recognise his comic aspect & grotesque extravagances, yet who nevertheless see in him an amorphous force constituting the least of all available evils. It is not every nation that can evolve a real Mussolini. Incidentally—the ancient gentlewoman who lives downstairs in this house[6] (a Yankee teacher of German, & lifelong Germanophile, who—though the daughter of a Baptist minister—became an ardent Catholic a decade ago) has just returned from a three-months' tour of Germany & Austria, & finds that the morale & general condition of Germany are infinitely better than they were last year. Reports of "barbarism" are incredibly magnified—life in general going on much as usual. She was treated with uniform courtesy everywhere—though the anti-German touchiness over the Czecho-Slovakian border amused her. They spurn German & Austrian money, & refuse to guide tourists to monuments or historic sites connected with Teutonic celebrities or events. And so it goes. I am far from a Nazi, & would probably get kicked out of Germany for my opinions regarding the universe, the facts of science, & the rights of free aesthetic expression—but at the same time I refuse to join in the blind herd-prejudice against an honest clown whose *basic* objects are all essentially sound despite the occasionally disastrous extremes & absurdities in his present policy. It may be that Hitlerism's function will be to point out certain needs which wiser heads & hands will ultimately rectify in a more moderate way—not only in Germany but in other nations where similar needs or problems exist. But hell! how I am filling up space!

Yes—little Bho Blôk, the Daemon Lama of Leng, is certainly quite a boy, & his pictures display a surprising natural talent. I think the flippancy of some of his titles is due to intentional irony—one would have to see the pictures in question to judge. Klarkash-Ton recently praised a diabolic crayon sketch of his entitled "Dine & Dance." I should have thought "Suicide in Costume" would have been right in his line. On the whole, I think the kid has more talent—or at least, a better-developed talent—in drawing than in writing, though he appears to take the latter more seriously than the former. Still—his prose is away ahead of mine at his age, & all its faults are apparently those of youth—extravagance & overcolouring. Comte d'Erlette has done him great good by viciously tearing some of his things to pieces & reducing the fragments to ashes & vapour. As for taste—of course he is essentially immature as yet. To be blind to realism argues a callous spot—though it is a kind of callosity which the years dispel. I had a vilely narrow taste at 16 or 17—phantasy or nothing! Young Bloch is worth watching. A vast ability of some sort is seething inside his head, & the results will be bound to come out. But I must say that I can't discern much promise in the quoted effusion of your local football hero! It may be that the extract is below his general level—but even so, its evidence is scarcely heartening. However, time will tell. I confess with mortification that I have never read a line by either of his idols, Messrs. Smith & Thayer!

As for the casual & dismayed father-to-be—one can scarcely deny him sympathy even though his mess is strictly of his own making. But it forms a good object-lesson in the silliness & bad taste of defying group-ideals for the sake of a little cheap & immediate pleasure. The mess having been made, common-sense would certainly dictate abortion as the least of several possible evils; & one cannot help noting grimly the irony of religious scruples on the part of the wench who had so few religious scruples about the antecedent treading of the primrose path! But that, no doubt, is human nature. If the girl insists on motherhood, the youth might secure financial aid from her family & move away with her after marriage, thus allowing the child to be born free from chronological espionage—but then, if the two are unsuited, he would of course be in a mess because of the irrational Catholic prejudice against a sensible divorce. But he had it coming to him. With traditions what they are, a sensible & sensitive person of fastidious temperament is damned reluctant to get mixed up in a tawdry eroticism devoid of affection or congeniality.

Your dramatic & cinematic notes, as usual, are animated & interesting even to one who knows very little of the field covered. By the way—I presume you know that George M. Cohan is a Providence product, his maternal uncle being at this moment a police captain in our 3d precinct. It is odd that Chaplin can't shake off a Cockney accent—many make great progress in conquering undesired vocalisms. By the way, when in N.Y. I saw quite a bit of a younger half-brother of Chaplin's—Wheeler Dryden, who is also an actor in a smallish way. He was reared, however, under radically different circumstances; & has not a trace of Cockney about him—having rather the Oxford drawl against which your *Am. Mercury* article inveighs.[7] Incidentally, I'm not sure but that we in New-England pronounce *Heine* & *finer* more alike than you would. The difference would be chiefly one of the vowel—*Hy'-nah*; *fi-nah*[.] With us, the last syllables of *Carolina* form a perfect rhyme with *finer* . . . . indeed, this would probably be true all along the Atlantic seaboard from Maine to Florida with the possible exception of Pennsylvania. It would also characterise the south as far west as the Mississippi. The only exceptions in the northeast would be upper New York State, Vermont, & the inland half of New Hampshire. Dialect is an odd thing. Did I tell you that Prof. Hans Kurath, head of the exhaustive North-American dialect survey, is now at Brown University in this city? His back windows faced my aunt's at her former home in Slater Ave.

I certainly will have to acquire the habit of reading magazines at the library—though I abominate public places, & never can really do justice to a book when forced to read it amidst a promiscuous rabble. But keeping up with magazine articles isn't quite like trying to appreciate long & connected works of art, so I fancy I may in time become hardened to it. Only a financial miracle could restore the standard magazines to my humble study table . . . . . although I do keep up with the N.Y. Times (Sunday). Yes—I saw the allusion to Little Augie therein. M. le Comte is certainly putting himself across with characteristic persistence!

About those favourite quotations of your father's—they all have an undeniable felicity, & all express undoubted truth. Nos. 1, 2, 3, & 6 suffer from a certain obviousness & conscious epigrammatism, but 4, 5, & 7 have a real acuteness & profundity which fully justify the aphoristic medium. The "Art & Mrs. Bottle" conversation is quite typical of an essentially eternal debate—the clash of two basic & ineradicable types of temperament. I myself would say that artists are just as important to civilisation as their staunchest partisans claim; but that their importance in their own field certainly does *not* absolve them of the normal obligations of adult members of the community. An artist without morals or dignity or self-respect is just as absurd & ignominious & unbeautiful a figure as a stock-broker or engineer or shopkeeper without these essential social & personal qualities.

No doubt your size-up of Mellon is essentially correct. Certainly, he does not represent the type of financial prince who knows how to use his resources with the greatest amount of taste, vision, & civic patriotism. The efforts to suppress that new biography surely seem rather obvious & pusillanimous.

About circuses—it occurs to me that I have never attended one! I always associated them with noise, bustle, & ill-smelling crowds, hence never had any inclination to seek them out—yet after all, they represent an ancient & colourful tradition extending back to classical times—& perhaps to the taurine spectacles of the Minoan civilisation. Well—we all have our lacunae! As to lacunae of the literary sort—I fear that my list would become one solid abyss of vacancy so far as recent works are concerned! Concerning yours—I've never read "Piers Plowman" though, & doubt if I ever shall. In "Moby Dick" you've missed something. It is long & digressive, but has a cosmic punch that makes it well worth finishing. And if you know New Bedford & feel the romance of New England whalers you simply can't consider missing it. "Uncle Tom's Cabin" is a sentimental whine, but it does have suspense & story interest. "The Origin of Species" is of course primarily a source-book, scarcely a thing for wide popular reading. "Les Miserables" is really interesting—don't be scared off by its length. "Pride & Prejudice" appeals to all who have a keen eye for the minutiae of human manners, but it [is] hardly a favourite of mine. "The Talisman" isn't as dull as most of Scott, though I shall probably never re-read it. Meredith sometimes probed human nature pretty shrewdly despite heavy Victorian overtones. Pinero & Jones are of course dated, but they hold my affectionate & reminiscent interest as being the high spots of an age when I enjoyed the theatre more than I do now. I first saw a play in 1896, & was quite a drama-lover till boredom overtook me some 15 years ago. After all, the old boys had wit & a sense of the dramatic, even though both manner & material were hopelessly artificial. In Ben Jonson you've missed something. "Every Man in his Humour", "The Alchemist", "Volpone", "The Silent Woman", "Sejanus", "Catiline", &c. all have great stuff in them. You can't afford to slight the Elizabethans. And as for Coleridge's "Ancient Mariner"—good god! do you fail to see & feel the clutching, impalpable weirdness & hideous fatality of those stanzas? Hell! I gloated over that poem when I was six years old, & found a de luxe large paper copy with Doré's ghoulish illustrations at a friend's house. Don't tell me there's anything dull about *that!* "Moll Flanders" gives a grim though graphic slice of one side of my favourite 18th century. If you like the ugly under side of things as manifested in the "Tin Roof" & "Cell", I don't see how you can afford to pass this document up! Augustus Thomas is not so hot, though I gaped admiringly at his concoctions in my naive play going days. Bulwer-Lytton is undeniably pompous & boresome, & Newman rather gives me a pain.[8] Priestley is an author I can't seem to finish. Hall Caine impresses me as absolute slop. I never completed any work of his. Book of the Dead is hardly a thing for literary as distinguished from archaeological digestion. I've read the Bible through, & deem much of it first-rate literature; but of course there is a lot of repetition & padding. I liked "David Harum" when I read it in 1899.[9] It actually managed to reflect a New England type which then existed. I haven't read it since, but believe I will some day—for I still own it. Lyly I've never read, though my friend Morton is fond of "Euphues".[10] Mark Twain is uneven, & I confess that he is not an idol of mine. And I certainly agree about the boresomeness of the Pilgrim's Progress.

As to these trials exploited as cases of social injustice—I didn't follow any of them closely, though I did think that Sacco & Vanzetti looked pretty guilty. Providence was twice brought into that case—the first time being when a local Portuguese under a death sentence in some neighbouring Mass. town (we have no death penalty in R.I.) "confessed" to the murder of the paymaster. He also was associated with our perennial Morelli gang. Now to me there is something fishy about this post-trail discovery of *two* different & independent "slayers". It looks to me as if the radicals were using every means to frame a case proving their idols innocent whether or not the sons-of-bitches really were. But I doubt if there can ever be any real certainty. Dozens of men have been hanged on less evidence, but have remained unknown to fame because they were not associated with any plot to tear down civilisation. On the other hand, I do think that this fellow Mooney was probably unjustly convicted.[11] While I think that any underminer of government ought to be imprisoned *for that crime itself,* I certainly don't endorse any framed convictions for crimes *not* committed. This poor devil has certainly been punished enough & too much for being a radical—& if it can be reasonably shewn that he is innocent of bombing he ought to be given his freedom. As for the Scottsboro niggers—I don't know enough of the circumstances to hold a real opinion. I've seen reviews of this Hays book.[12] Hays is counsel of the Am. Civil Liberties Union, whose head—Roger Baldwin—is married to a cousin of my friend Long.

I fully agree with you concerning the importance of Proust, even though my reading of him has not gone beyond "Within a Budding Grove." I must continue at least through "The Guermante's Way"—which I see has just made the Modern Library. Assuredly, I don't believe the 20th century has so far produced anything to eclipse the Proustian cycle as a whole. As illustrated in the paragraph you quote, he captures significant nuances & details of life that everyone else has overlooked or understressed.

Your other book notes are full of interest. Machen's "Terror" is of course a minor thing, & not much esteemed by him. I own the Bohun Lynch anthology—valued chiefly, of course, because of "The Willows." Speaking of owned books—I've just picked up Blackwood's "Julius LeVallon" for 15¢. What I'm now looking for is his "Incredible Adventures."

By the way—I've just blown myself to a copy of the new dollar reprint of Roget's Thesaurus—Grosset & Dunlap—since my old one (inherited from an uncle) was literally falling to pieces. This cheap edition is really splendid—a bargain I can conscientiously recommend to anyone not adequately thesaurus'd.

I was sorry to learn a fortnight ago of the death of Bernard Dwyer's mother—which was, however, something of a merciful release, since for the last few years paralysis had deprived her wholly of the power of locomotion & partly of speech.

Autumn has now descended like a pall, & my sessions of outdoor reading & writing are perforce drawing to a close. I have, though, had some delightful rural walks north of the city—in the Lincoln Woods region so rich in vistas of ancient countryside & steepled villages.

Glad the wedding came off smoothly. That double "I will" ought to prove a favourable augury—arguing a double strength of devotion in the new enterprise!

I shall certainly be on the lookout for Dunsany's new book[13] when it appears. So far I have read everything of his to appear in book form—though I must admit that his later things can't duplicate the charm of those vivid golden tales of his naiver days.

And so it goes. With best wishes for all your enterprises, I remain
Yr most obt hble Servt

E'ch-Pi-El

P.S. Apropos of our frequent remarks on *dialect*—if you want to see a very fine & complete discussion of the rustic New England speech (now defunct as a whole, though leaving a legacy of idioms [rather than accents] in the surviving tongue) consult the introductions (one to each series) & glossary of Lowell's Bigelow [*sic*] Papers. Nowhere else is there so full a tracing of homely Yankeeisms to older English & even Norman-French sources. The Bigelow papers themselves afford a splendid & accurate exposition of the rural Massachusetts speech of the first half of the 19th century. ¶ And did I mention in a previous letter that Price noted several unique localisms in our R.I. speech? He tells me that the expression "dropped egg" [= poached or fried egg on toast or otherwise] is certainly peculiar to New England. I knew it was an *Americanism,* but never realised that its geographical extent was so limited.

Notes

1. King Gambrinus was a European culture hero and an icon of beer. HPL refers to the impeding repeal of Prohibition on 5 December 1933.

2. HPL's reading programme resulted in the composition of "Weird Story Plots" and "[Notes on Weird Fiction]."

3. In 1735, Andrew Hamilton successfully defended German-American publisher John Peter Zenger (1697–1746) against a charge of libel, arguing that truth is always a defense against libel.

4. Ernestine Schumann-Heink (1861–1936), celebrated German contralto. She lived in the US from 1906 until her death.

5. In fact, the surviving T.Ms. of "Dagon" (which must have been prepared subsequent to the first appearance—*Vagrant,* November 1919) reads: ". . . the ocean forces of the Hun . . ." (*CF* 1.52). "Hun" appears in several of HPL's poems of the period.

6. Alice R. Sheppard.

7. H. W. Seaman, "The Awful English of England, *American Mercury* (September 1933).

8. HPL presumably refers to John Henry Newman (1801–1890), British novelist and theologian who converted to Catholicism.

9. A best-selling novel by Edward Noyes Westcott.

10. A work of prose-poetry (1579) by John Lyly.

11. Thomas Mooney (1882–1942), American activist convicted of setting off a bomb in San Francisco in 1916. He served 22 years in prison before being pardoned in 1939.

12. Arthur Garfield Hays (1881–1954), *Trial by Prejudice* (New York: Covici, Friede, 1933).

13. *The Curse of the Wise Woman.*

[42]   [ANS][1]

[Postmarked Providence, R.I.,
7 October 1933]

Well, well—you are quite a migrant! Cincinnati must have its vivid points, if my recollection of pictures & descriptions be correct. It's built on terraces above the river, isn't it? Hope you'll find the new experience congenial. ¶ Am sunk with a new verse-revision job—just as I thought I had some time for fictional experimentation. The Knopf bubble burst. Just now I've heard from a chap in the state of Washington who wants to issue "The Colour Out of Space" as a booklet. [2] Hope he will—though I doubt it. ¶ Aunt improves. We were taken for a motor ride last week—to the ancient village of Wickford, down the west shore of the bay where Price & I went last July. Too cold now for much outdoor activity, though I shall try to get out to the woods & see the changing leaves.

Best wishes—

E'ch-Pi-El

Notes

1. *Front:* Faneuil Hall and Custom House Tower, Boston, Mass.
2. F. Lee Baldwin of Asotin, WA, had proposed such an edition, but it was never published.

[43]   [ALS]

66 College St.,
Providence, R.I.,
Novr. 8, 1933

Dear Jehvish-Êi:—

Yes—I decoded what I believe to be every word of your much-appreciated epistle . . . . & wonder if you can do the same with this neo-cuneiform document! My least-rotten fountain pen rolled off the table & lit on its point yesterday, with results demanding a trip to the surgeon's. It's due to be done later today, & meanwhile I'll have to piece out with one or another of my secondary, tertiary, & quaternary, &c. pens—of which this cheap stylographic, with its tasteful paint-brush effects, seems for the moment least burdensome to use.

Well—since your Cincinnatiing was so disruptive of your reading & writing schedule, & so doubtfully congenial as to locale, I'm glad it was not of longer duration—though of course any income drop is to be regretted. So you've known the town before! I hadn't realised your earlier connexion with the region—it interests me, since this locale has always held a certain glamour in my mind after my perusal of Lloyd's old weird novel "Etidorhpa" . . . . . a thing you ought to read if you don't know it already. It just missed inclusion in my article, & I'd give quite a bit for a copy of my own. Do you know any of the limestone cavern districts south of Cincinnati—which figure so extensively in the book? Kentucky must be a very attractive state, although a friend of mine in Louisville[1] says that not many reminders of old times are left. I've never been there, but intend to go some day. For one thing, I'll never feel that life is complete till I've been through the Mammoth Cave. (The locale of one of my earliest tales—which I wrote after days of boning at the library).[2] I've always understood that Cincinnati is a town of much cultivation, & I fancy it is as attractive as any place in Ohio. I hope the extensive changes you mention have not wholly destroyed its mellowness. Glad you had a good coach trip. I am very fond of coach travel, & have no patience with those who affect to despise it. Journeys to Key West & New Orleans have been none too long for me. I hate train travel, which takes one through the flattest & most desolate country available. A coach traverses the old-time highways, giving one the most traditional landscape impressions & shewing the towns along the route to the best advantage. I wish I were hopping one for St. Augustine right now! They make surprisingly good time these days. In 1926 the Boston trip from here took 2 hrs. & 15 minutes. Now the average coaches do it in an hour & a half, & one fast sedan cuts it to 1 hr. & 20 minutes. I've gone over entirely, & would hardly remember what a train looks like but for the cheap annual excursions to Quebec. Your running time of 11 hrs. for a distance somewhat over 300 m. was quite good, all things considered. About 30 m. per hour—which is much the same speed as that of the Providence coaches to both Boston & N.Y.

All told, I fancy your Cincinnati sojourn gave you quite a bit of material for realistic character-fiction. This Kopp-Davis person must be quite a study—really, his contrasts & eccentricities give him an almost Dickensian flavour . . . . at least, as described by an observant & piquant commentator. If his golden voice ever goes on the radio I may hear him some day, for my aunt's machine picks up Cincinnati with especial clearness. Well—I'd rather hear him on the radio than at a restaurant table by my side, with all eyes focussed in his direction! Oy, sol mio! [*sic*] He must be a great bird to have around the kitchen—apparently he could give points to the guy who wrote the Book of Leviticus! But if he wants to cut down the bay window he'll have to go easy on more than pork! As for his criticism of my allusion to Jewish newspaper control in New York—he missed the whole point. I didn't say that Jews *own* all the papers, but merely that they *control* their policies through economic channels. The one great lever, of course, is *advertising*. Virtually *all* the great department stores of New York (except Wanamaker's) are solidly Jewish even when they deceptively retain the names of earlier Aryan owners; & a clear majority of the large shops of other sorts are, as well. These Semitic merchants are clannish & touchy to the very limit, & will arrange to withdraw all their advertising at once whenever a newspaper displeases them. And, as Mencken has pointed out, their grounds of displeasure are limitless.[3] They even resent the frequent use of the word "Jew" in the news, so that papers speak of "East Side agitators", "Bronx merchants", "Russian immigrants" &c. Let any N.Y. paper try to refer to these people in the frank, impartial, objective way a Providence or Pittsburgh or Richmond paper would, & the whole pack of synagogue-hounds is after it—calling down the vengeance of heaven, withdrawing advertising, & cancelling subscriptions—the latter a big item in a town where ⅓ of the population is openly & recordedly Jewish, & perhaps ½ or even more is actually Semitic in origin & feelings. The result is, that not a paper in New York dares to call its soul its own in dealing with the Jews & with social & political questions affecting them. The whole press is absolutely enslaved in that direction, so that on the whole length & breadth of the city *it is impossible to secure any public American utterance—any frank expression of the typical mind & opinions of the actual American people—on a fairly wide & potentially important range of topics.* [(*in margin:*) P.S. Better not quote any of this to Bloch (who I discover is of Jewish extraction). While of course this question does not involve any aspersion on the Jewish heritage as a whole, it nevertheless makes embarrassing reading for anybody having more than an academic connexion with Semitism. One would handle it differently with a Jewish correspondent.] Only by reading the outside press & the national magazines can New Yorkers get any idea of how *Americans* feel regarding such things as Nazism, the Palestine question (in which, by every decent standard, the Arabs are dead right & both England & the Jews intolerably wrong), the American immigration policy, & so on. *This* is what I mean by Jewish control, & I'm damned if it doesn't make me see red—in a city which was once a part of the real American fabric, & which still exerts a disproportionately large influence on that fabric through its psychologically impressive size & its dominance both in finance & in various opinion-forming channels (drama, publishing, criticism &c). Gawd knows I have no wish to injure any race under the sun, but I *do* think that something ought to be done to free American expression from the control of *any* element which seeks to curtail it, distort it, or remodel it in any direction other than the natural course. As a matter of fact, I don't blame the Jews at all. Hell, what can we expect after letting them in & telling them they can do as they please? It is perfectly natural for them to make everything as favourable for themselves as they can, & to feel as they do. The Italians & French-Canadians in Rhode Island try the same thing (with less success, though the Dagoes are making alarming gains in Providence, where they must form nearly half the population despite their deceptive isolation in one vast quarter), & I blame them just as little. I criticise not Mr. Bernard Kopp-Davis—nor Sig. Giambattista Scagnamiglio nor M. Napoleon-Francois Laliberté—but merely the *condition* brought about by a reductio ad absurdum of the flabby idealism of the "melting-pot" fallacy. Within the lifetime of people now middle-aged, the general tone of our Northern cities has so changed that they no longer seem like home to their own inhabitants. Providence is something of an exception because of the continued pure-Yankeedom of the residence section atop the hill—but the downtown business section shews all the stigmata of Latin mongrelisation . . . . Italian & Portuguese faces everywhere. One has to get down to Richmond to find a town which really *feels like home*—where the average person one meets looks like one, has the same type of feelings & recollections, & reacts approximately the same to the same stimuli. The loss of a collective life—of a sharing of common traditions & memories & experiences—is the curse of the heterogeneous northeast today. There is no real solution—& all the American can do is to forget about the foreigners as much as he can, be on guard against alienation from his own tradition (apart from which he is lost & deprived of that normal adjustment to a coherent fabric & continuous historic stream which is everyone's right), & do his part toward cutting off further unassimilable immigration. I'd hardly advocate Nazi tactics, but I certainly do welcome a greater assertiveness & independence among the native stock. I think the (probable) 100,000 Yankees in Providence ought to be able to say what they choose about Italy without making apologies to Federal Hill (our local Nuova Napoli), & that the (perhaps) 1,000,000 Americans in New York ought to be able to discuss Hitler & Palestine & pork chops without glancing fearfully over their shoulders at a horde of fortune-seeking Yiddish newcomers. I have to hand it to the French-Canadians for putting up a fight for their language & institutions. While naturally I oppose their cultural encroachments outside their own Quebec province—their fights to make all Canada bi-lingual, & all that—I admire them down to the bottom line—as Gen. Murray & Sir Guy Carleton did at the very outset—for their staunch resolution to keep up the fabric of their forefathers. They were on the ground first, & by the time we licked them in 1759–60 their land was normally a French one—a spacious area with a thoroughly adjusted population, cultivated French towns, & a century & a half of local traditions. Clearly, they had every aesthetic right to demand the perpetuation of their own folkways instead of ours—yet how few have shewn any real guts in similar situations! Where is the spoken French of Louisiana, the spoken Dutch of New-Netherland, or the spoken Spanish of Texas, today? But the Canucks, by god, *did* have the guts! They kept an unbroken front, used every dignified influence in Parliament, & finally secured the passage of the Quebec Act of 1774, securing them an inviolate perpetuation of their laws, language, & religion. We respected their rights as the Romans respected the rights of the conquered Greeks—& today Quebec is still the cultivated French city it was in 1750 . . . . . just as Athens & Alexandria were still cultivated Greek cities after centuries of Roman rule. Of course, there are troublesome connotations. When the French overflow into other regions like Ontario & New England they carry their solidarity & unassimilability with them, remaining aloof & cohesive, & refusing to adopt the English speech they have so long fought on their own soil. They cannot understand why the tolerance & protection of French in Quebec Province cannot be duplicated in places only a few hours' ride from Quebec—like Vermont or Ontario or Rhode Island. In this state they have overrun certain cities & villages & made them just as French as anything in Quebec or Normandy. When I first visited Quebec in 1930 I saw nothing I had not known all my life from travels in my own state. Here, as there, one can strike towns dominated by ornate French steeples; containing statues "Erice par Societé Jacques-Cartier"; sporting shop signs such as "Elphege Caron, Epicier" or "Hormisdas Bilodeau, Cardonnier"; having "Maison a vendre", "Chambres a louer" & "Salle a louer" window cards; displaying Gallic posters of some such cinema as "Sous la Lune du Maroc; adapté de la Nouvelle par André Reuze, "Les Cincq Gentlemen Maudits" at La Theatre Laurier; & harbouring crowds of black-clad parochial-school children led by hooded nuns or shovel-hatted curés & jabbering in the French of their forefathers . . . . . . all the hereditary things of France undiluted by transplantation & expansion. These Rhode Island French fight like hell whenever any attempt is made to deracinate them or to substitute English for French in their parochial schools. In other local foreign colonies one sees a gradual Americanisation—a younger generation speaking English, & a falling off of ancestral ways—but nothing of that pervades these French centres. The French newspapers continue to flourish, & every parent strives to keep his children true to "La Tradition". It is really ironic to reflect that—despite all the *utterly* alien blood which has been dumped on New England—the *one really persistent* foreign challenge should come from none other than our *oldest* & most historic rival—the Frenchman of the North against whose menace old Cotton Mather thundered his Catonian invectives from Boston pulpits in the 1680's. Did Wolfe fall in vain? Today, just as old Cotton feared, the spires & syllables of France rise thickly from the banks of New England's rivers! But much as I hate any foreign influence, I'm damned if I don't admire those tough little frog-eaters for their unbreakable tenacity! You can't make a dent in them! . . . . . they'll probably still be French, albeit on alien soil, years after we are hopelessly Italianated or Portugesed or Yiddified or Polacked in our own back yards! If they'd only lend us a little of their guts, I wouldn't begrudge them the New England towns they've overrun! Shake, Pierre mon frére! You may be a rival, but you're nobody's football!

But this is straying a long way from Herr Kopp-Davis & Cincinnati . . . . that's the way an old man rambles. Too bad you struck so many unwholesome associations—but I presume they all form grist for your literary mill. Regarding your uncle—it really is too bad he never cared to develop his voice; & yet if he lacked a wish for such development, the process would probably have been a dreary one for him. Eventually the adverse emotional tension might have neutralised his natural talents & defeated the very object so painfully striven for. It always provokes us to see a great innate gift neglected, & yet in most cases the fact of neglect itself argues some deep-seated quality antagonistic to success. On a very modest scale I can parallel your uncle. When I was 7 years old I seemed to shew a marked talent for the violin, & took lessons for two years under the best teacher in Providence. But god, what a grind it got to be! My taste in music is not good, & (like your uncle) I wanted to have a good time with popular songs instead of laboriously absorbing the foundations of the art & working my way up through graded simplifications of the classics. By the time I was 9 the whole field of formal music & violin practice became so hateful that I was threatened with one of the nervous breakdowns so frequent in my youth. At the doctor's orders my lessons were stopped—& that was the end of H P L as Kreisler's great rival![4] Psychologists would find something significant in the speed with which I forgot everything about music & violins. Today I can't read music at sight, & scarcely know which end of a fiddle to tuck under my chin! What is more, I've since had a dislike of classical music which I never had prior to the episode. To me it is obvious that I could never have been a musician. My basic antagonism would have frustrated any further study I might have attempted. Of course your uncle has gone farther in music than I did—but at bottom the principle is probably the same. He has probably got more out of life—more that is satisfactory *to him*—by abandoning an uncongenial struggle than he could have got by keeping it up. Even had he succeeded in becoming an effective & well-paid vocalist, his success would probably have seemed ironic & unrewarding to him.

I thought the Klarkash-Ton material would give you a kick. As to the relative value of his coloured & black & white stuff—it is safer to reserve judgment till one has seen his really fine paintings. Some that he sent around (in a crate, by express) in 1926 will linger long in my memory. He really is a vivid instinctive colourist. But all the same I recognise the vast potency of the black crayon heads. One in particular *stares* with a cosmic madness that haunts me. As for C A S's tales—the "Singing Flame"[5] certainly stands well up on the list, though some of those in the "Double Shadow" brochure probably excel it in real art. And I'm not sure but that his poems surpass his prose. "The Hashish-Eater" really deserves a place in literature.

Regarding the "Silver Key" sequel—it's my last, as well as first, acknowledged collaboration. I simply can't get into a creative vein when someone else's ideas & outlines are present as constant checks. I agree with all you say about the mathematical middle part—but god! you ought to have seen it *before* I tackled it! In Price's version[6] it sounded like a treatise on conic sections & nothing else but—pure schoolmaster stuff interrupting the story, & undoubtedly dictated by his intense interest in mathematics. I went as far as I dared toward softening the thing, but now see that I didn't go far enough. This, however, is the only point where I can shift the blame. The bum ending is entirely my own. Price, in his original, had Carter switched from the dimensional Abyss straight back to Earth—to the ruined fortress of Alamut, on the Black Sea, in the time of the Crusades—but I saw anticlimax in this & invented the Yaddith episode. I also fixed up the final denouement & devised the rather unconvincing & theatrical figure of Swami Chandraputra. I don't blame Wright for turning the thing down (or wouldn't if he didn't accept so much worse crap), & shall let it remain in the oblivion which it richly deserves. By the way—Price is now in Chicago on a trip, foregathering with Wright, Hamilton, & Jack Williamson.

As for my recent fictional experimentation & its nature—it primarily concerns the type of perspective, atmosphere, & language to use in capturing & crystallising the moods forming the subject-matter. I am trying to see which of several possible types of handling best fits certain conceptions— what tales ought to begin quietly & work up through realistic detail, what tales ought to start abruptly on a note of feverish tension, when a semi-poetic style ought to be employed, how intricate explanations are best camouflaged when they are necessary to a story, what subjects demand an utterly bizarre angle of approach, what the length of a given type of tale ought to be, & how the various modulations ought to be proportioned, &c. &c &c. So far I have torn up everything that I have written, & I may decide that further writing is impossible. Meanwhile (my hatred of the typewriter being stronger every day) I have had a delinquent client type the story I wrote last August,[7] & have started the carbon on the rounds of the gang—beginning with Dwyer. If I get 2 or 3 bad reactions on it, I shall withdraw it from circulation. If not, you will receive it in the course of time—from Bloch, with a request to pass on to Barlow. I don't think much of the thing. Regarding essays—I never write well to order or except when something calls forth spontaneous comment. I haven't activities or experiences enough to evoke a series of ramblings like McIntyre's—nor have I the observation & skill to spin endless images from commonplace things.

Thanks extremely for the various cuttings. The U. of Pittsburgh certainly shews the effect of strong reactionary pressure, & I'm glad the *Press* has the courage to point out the fact. While a college naturally has a right to teach what it pleases, & while it is only a social duty for such an institution to discourage any disloyalty to the national fabric, it is certainly absurd to restrict the free discussion of political & economic principles. And even when students display actually injurious doctrines, it would be far more fitting to expose their folly through argument than to make martyrs & popular heroes of them by sending them to gaol.

Regarding pacifism, though—I really don't see how any sober adult can hold such an attitude. Of course it is foolish to *exalt* war in this age; although in the past, when less destructive, it certainly did strengthen character & national fibre. Today we admit its net adverse effect—its cataclysmic destructiveness & bad evolutionary legacy—so that all are anxious to reduce its recurrence to an absolute minimum. But this does not alter the fact that at certain times we have to fight in order to preserve an environment fit for ourselves & our descendants to live in. While we can control *our own* armaments & military policy, we have no means of controlling those of *other nations* & races, many of which have ambitions whose fulfilment demands the subordination & humiliation of ourselves. Pacifism on our part can never mean any more than the deliberate *weakening of ourselves whilst other nations remain strong;* so that sooner or later some rival group will be able to take from us whatever it wishes, leaving us in a crippled, demoralised, broken condition & finally engulfing us in its own political fabric. If there are enough madmen & cowards in this country to refuse to fight Japan when the attack comes, then those very madmen & cowards—or their sons—may some day find themselves Japanese subjects drafted into the Mikado's army & forced to fight China or Soviet Russia on Japan's behalf . . . . . with the alternative of being executed or imprisoned. It may or may not give these fanatics & swine & jellyfish pride to see the psychology of America become that of a crushed, cringing subject-nation—to see Anglo-Saxon culture debased & effeminised & tainted with Japanese elements, or perhaps confined to a huddled group of whipped dogs kicked from pillar to post around the world under alien governments. These shrinking "reformers" may enjoy the sight of a supine, lethargic, defeated America like China (a typical pacifist nation)—sprawling open to the plundering of other nations & finally suffering partitioning among them. They may like to think of themselves as the whipped Greeks of the Roman imperial age—enslaved & despised, & the butt of the normal nations which may perhaps give them a contemptuous refuge. They may like to think of themselves as herded on reservations like the defeated Indians, or crushed with unjust restrictions & demands for outrageous indemnities like the Germans of today. They may regard all these inevitable results of supine pacifism with pride & pleasure—& I can only add that such a fate is just about what they deserve. But, thank heaven, there are a few *men* in America still; so that when Japan does strike, she will meet more than a welcoming committee of college-boy sopranos with wreaths of white roses! And I fancy that a good many of those men will be chaps of basic good sense who passed through & outgrew the pacifistic phase in their adolescent period. They will probably fight all the more bravely to atone for the irresponsible sentimentalism into which a wave of decadent fashion once temporarily swept them. Not that they will be militarists, or seek any war which can be avoided through self-respecting negotiations. They will simply have too much spirit & decency to allow the race & institutions which they represent, & of which they form an inextricable part, to be whipped & enslaved & placed in a position of intolerable ignominy & ultimate disintegration. It isn't in Anglo-Saxons to accept the kicked-around squalor & brokenness of ghetto Jews, or the paralytic lethargy of the defencelsss, opium-soaked Chinese, without such a fight as the world never saw before. We belong to the Aryan culture stream which has Thermopylae & Horatius & Camillus & the Metaurus & Chalons & Tours & Lepanto & Sir Richard Grenville—not Egyptian & Babylonish captivities & Seleucid persecutions & Roman destruction & dispersal, or Tartar & Manchu conquests, foreign concessions & treaty-parts, & Japanese land-grabbings—in its traditions. When we cannot live free & unbroken, we shall not live at all. A foeman's bullet is sweeter than a master's whip. Regarding the late world war—I would certainly have regarded any Anglo-Saxon as delinquent if he had not put himself at the disposal of his nation to the fullest extent of his physical capacity. There is nothing "vindictive" in a determination not to see one's own group placed at a disadvantage & started on the road to decline & disintegration. The consequences of a German victory in the late war would have been almost fatally bad for us—just as our victory has come near being fatally bad for the Germans. If *we* rubbed it into *them,* just imagine how *they,* as victors, would have rubbed it into *us!* Anyone realising the German spirit of 1914 can understand what a fatal blow to Anglo-Saxon civilisation a German victory would have formed. It would have been the first step toward a gradual undermining, with German influences reaching in at every crack for power & advantage. France would have been a sphere of German influence, & sooner or later the spread of German colonisation in South America would have created New-World problems. History shews what the psychology of the cringing subject-nations becomes when some one virile power gains world-ascendancy. . . . & no self-respecting man of English blood would see London & Boston become an Antonine-period Athens & Alexandria while a drop of blood or an unbroken bone remained in his body. Remember that no suave pacifism of *ours* would have lessened *Germany's* zeal for conquest a single whit. If we had been supine in the past, the chances are that we'd have been gobbled up long before the recent war—by a Napoleonic France if not by a Bismarckian Prussia. Of course there was a great deal of inept diplomacy leading up to the war. Very conceivably, moderation & intelligence might have postponed or modified this particular conflict. But when moderation & intelligence lapse or fail, as they are bound to do sooner or later, there is nothing to do but defend oneself & see that one's own group does not come out disadvantageously. It is only this determination not to be crushed or enslaved that keeps any civilisation alive & healthy. That is why a defence of the unbroken, self-respecting Aryan attitude is not mere empty heroics, as our half-baked modern "intelligentsia" pretend to insist. The fact simply is, that this dogged defensive attitude happens to be the corner-stone of racial & national integrity. When a group ceases to produce a majority of men who naturally feel that way, it is on the road toward victimisation, subordination, plundering, imposition, draining, humiliation, enslavement, & final disintegration at the hands of others. Look at the races & nations of the past which have lacked the fighting spirit (& by that I mean defensive zeal, not the desire to go out & annex land & break people's heads)—where are they today? What happened to the Romans when they mixed their blood with the scum of decadent immigration & lost their racial stamina? What happened to the Vandals after they settled down in Roman North Africa & took on the effeminacy of the region? Good god—why need one catalogue the self-evident? The facts are plain. I'm no bigot. I wouldn't blame a man today if he failed to enlist—or to try to enlist—for a war aiming at the conquest of Cuba or another theft from Mexico or something like that. That kind of thing does not involve the integrity or survival of the group. Also—I'd gladly forgive anyone who stayed out of an *aggressive* war—say on Japan over the conquest of Manchuria, with economic reasons masked as idealistic crusading—*unless some turn in the fortunes of that war put America on the defensive.* Then, of course, it would be every man's duty to see that his group did not go under—the pragmatic emergency dwarfing all theoretical or moralistic aspects of the war's beginning. When a nation is in real peril, the only decent thing for any of its citizens to do is to defend it to the limit, with not a thought for anything but that dogged defence. Thus it is—one may have some excuse for opposing a needless war . . . . indeed, it is a civic duty to oppose needless wars until some ill-fortune actually precipitates them . . . . *but there is no excuse for not doing all one can when actual peril & humiliation confront the group.* Remember that refusing to do one's duty in a war *doesn't stop the war in the least.* It only stops *one's own side* of the war, so that the *other* nation can destroy & enslave more readily. This is true in an ultimate & indirect sense even when not directly obvious. If America had not entered the world war Germany would have won, & in so doing would have imposed ruinous consequences upon the greater part of that world which is closest akin to America. There would have arisen an irresistibly powerful Germany with policies basically antagonistic to any potential rival, & aggressions from this new & swollen world-empire could only have been a matter of time. Eventually, a war between America & victorious Germany would have been inevitable, & in this war there would be only cowed & defeated nations for allies. American defeat & disaster would have been very probable, & in any case the war would have been infinitely more sanguinary for the nation than it was at the time which America chose for the showdown. The war being once started, & having developed as it did, America was wise in intervening. However—remember that the question of national defence can't be decided from any one war. Even if the late world war weren't a suitable illustration of the need for defensive readiness, there are plenty of known wars in the past & plenty of likely wars in the future which *certainly are* most emphatic & irrefutable illustrations. Would you have had Aëtius offer the people of Europe to Attila, or had Charles Martel welcome an engulfment by Islam's conquering horde? Or perhaps you think that a pacifistic Aëtius could have *persuaded* the good, kind Huns to go away, or that a Quaker policy among the Franks would have stemmed the resistless Saracen tide which had left nothing behind it in North Africa & Spain! Actually, I think your attitude will change with added years & maturer reflection. It may indeed be that you will oppose many wars which others will favour, but I cannot think that you will continue in a pacifism which seems (rightly or wrongly—I may have failed to get all sides of your attitude) to be of an unthinking, purely emotional, & all-inclusive sort. Let me add that I do not minimise the destructive seriousness of warfare. It would not surprise me if some wholesale conflict with modern weapons were to play a decisive part in ending western civilisation. But what, alas, can the attacked nation do about it? Is it not better to go down into the twilight as men, unconquered still when all the familiar world dissolves to a flux, than to crawl as slaves of an alien conqueror a few years more—till in the end some other war stamps out the feebly flickering spark? To this it seems to me an Aryan can have but one answer.

Anent assorted notes—young Belknap had never heard of "Fishhead" when he wrote "Death Waters". I noted the resemblance, introduced him to "Fishhead" (which I had a devil of a time finding—I hadn't read it since 1913!), & was hailed by him as a benefactor.[8] That was in 1924 . . . . . & formed an appropriate return for his having introduced me to another great Cobb story (the one about the man with a nigger taint who shrieks out an African word through *hereditary memory* when run down by an electric train whose locomotive looks & whistles like the hippopotamus that cruelly gored a black ancestor of his in the Congo 120 years before) in the preceding year. Incidentally, I can't for the life of me recall the *title* of that hippo-locomotive tale.[9] Do you recall it? It ought to be in a collection by this time, though what Long sent me was cut from a magazine. I lent the cutting to a chap who— god damn his soul—never returned it. Long can't remember the title, either— in fact, I doubt if he recalls the tale itself as well as I do. I refer to it without a name in my article—though I tried to find the title when I wrote the thing.[10]

Later—Back from Downtown

Well, well, well, boys—what have we here? Damme if it isn't old George S. Parker all fixed up by the doctor & stuffed with blue ink! The funny thing is that it works a damn sight *better* than it did before its accident! Although it was my best pen, it spread & scratched so badly that I'd been planning a change of point. Now it's twice as good as it ever was before—still scratches a bit, but not nearly as viciously as it did. Hell—if this is what accidents do, I guess I'll lay the rest of my pens out on the car track to get run over! Thanks for the reading recommendations. I may get at those magazine items, since lately— despairing of ever restoring *Harpers* & the *Atlantic* to my hearthside—I've cultivated the periodical-room habit at the library . . . . a process which has finally given me an admiring acquaintance with the much recommended "Introduction to Eric." ¶ This case of Mellon influence regarding the O'Connors & the coal strike investigation is surely significant in one way & amusing in another. ¶ As to the very-average near-parent—it would be an excellent thing if a few others had similar setbacks to teach them lessons. Trying to pretend to follow traditional civilisation whilst at the same time practicing indiscriminate licence is a squalid business. If these young smart-alecks want to eliminate the values of the existing civilisation & substitute dog-&-bitch coupling for the genuine love based on exclusiveness, why don't they come out into the open? Why do they remain nominally in the Christian church which totally repudiates their philosophy? Who do they cover up their bastards instead of taking a bold course & demanding a repeal of the laws which make the concealment of their goatish ideals & practices necessary? I don't despise these swine so much because they are swine as because they are cowards & hypocrites. However—gawd knows there were enough of them in Victorian days! ¶ So you never heard of a "dropped egg" before! I think it will spread to New York soon; because the large Waldorf Lunch chain of New England has invaded the metropolis, & this chain has uniform printed placards for walls & windows. It isn't likely that they'll print a variant set of cards for the N Y units, hence from now on the Gothamites will daily confront the name in various connexions

CORNED BEEF HASH WITH DROPPED EGG 20¢	DROPPED EGG ON TOAST 10¢	HAM OR BACON SPECIAL WITH DROPPED EGG 15¢

.... which will soon let them know what it's all about. As for accents—I fancy the effect of the radio will be to smooth them out considerably into one uniform speech. In picking up distant stations on my aunt's machine I find that most of the local announcers keep pretty close to one standard, so that I have to listen hard to tell whether they're in Boston or Schenectady or Montreal or Cincinnati or Charlotte, N.C. As for the speech of New England—I doubt if it could be called precisely British, although the un-rolled *r's* & the occasional fairly broad *a's* make it less removed from motherland usage than the common speech of Ohio or Iowa. The differences are many. For example—Mr. McIntyre to the contrary, no Boston policeman—or Boston professor or Boston litterateur—ever said *de-pawt*. This *aw* sound of *a* does not exist at all in New England, & we notice it sharply in those British speakers who use it. There is only one way to pronounce *depart* here—a way which an Ohioan would probably represent phonetically as *de-paht'* or *depäät'*. Incidentally—that goes also for the whole Atlantic seaboard from Maine to Florida with the sole exception of Pennsylvania. Absence of the rolled rrr .... can hardly be called typically British, since it has always characterised the American Atlantic coast. Even the flattest-speaking rustics, who pronounce the *a* in *pass* like the *a* in *cat*, have not the least tendency to say *carrr* or *farrrrm*.* Incidentally, this flat *a* is used by the educated classes in the south, except in Charleston—whose speech is indistinguishable from that of New England. There is not, in New England, any tendency to follow the modern British coalescence of syllables. We do not say *sec'-re-try* & *lab'-ra-try*, but *sec"-re-ta'-ry* & *lab"-o'-ra-to-ry* .... though in careless speech the latter might condense to *lab'-ra-to-ry*. We have no tendency to sound *o* as *eo*, or to extend the *o* sound of *dog* to words like *not*. Usage is just about 50-50 in the matter of *eye'-ther* & *eye'-so-late* versus *ee'-ther* & *iss'-so-late*. In *vocal timbre* the cleavage is sharp—New England being as one

---

*Dinah & *Carolina* make an absolutely perfect rhyme in both New England and the South. In the south this usage extends westward at least to N.O. & Natchez.

with most of the U.S. (although there is a sort of Iowa & Michigan rasp which is absent in the East) & totally differentiated from Great Britain. The only place where I was ever mistaken for a British-born speaker was *Montre-al*—a focus of conflicting dialects. New York speech is a study in itself. Not only does it have inexplicable phonetic perversions, but it involves basic *rhythms* alien to ours. Despite the New-Yorker's non-sounding of the *rrr* . . ., his speech is less fundamentally akin to ours than is the Ohioan's. I think I've mentioned that *inland northern New England & upper N Y state* have a variant all their own & *do* sound the *rrr* . . . . I recall that Dwyer—as far south as Kingston—noticed the difference in my speech. Even Talman—down in Spring Valley near the N.J. line—sounds *rrr* . . . *s* in a faint, half-perceptible way.

Thanks for cinematic tips. I must see Henry VIII & Berkeley Square. Yes—& the Emperor Jones, too. What a wallop the original play gave me in 1922 or 23! Too bad "Ann Vickers"[11] is spoiled. I haven't read the book, though my aunt has. Your "Mockery" idea was certainly tremendously clever, although it's been used pretty often. Only this year I came across it in "Jones's Karma", by May Sinclair, in "The Intercessor & Other Stories". A man gets a new life, but after avoiding all his old mistakes *at the points where he made them before,* he makes them again in unexpected situations where he is not on guard against the same old set of impulses. His outcome in life #2 is precisely the same as in #1.

Nov. 9, 1933

Well—how's this for prompt tip-following? Went to see "Berkeley Square" last night, having noted its presence in town. First cinema I've attended since Long dragged me to one in Onset last July. And boy! Was it some film? Absolutely, I haven't had such a kick in years! What atmosphere! My own 18th century absolutely come to life! Not a flaw—architecture, landscape, costume, decoration—the whole thing! You can't realise the punch it gave me, since all my life I have had the oddest & most inexplicable sense of personal membership in the 18th century, & of being out of place anywhere else. When I was 3 years old I felt a strange magic & fascination (not unmixed with a vague unease & perhaps a touch of mild *fear*) in the ancient houses of Providence's venerable hill (now I live in one!), with their fanlighted doorways, railed flights of steps, & stretches of brick sidewalk, & when I began to read books widely at 6 I preferred the old half-discarded 18th century tomes (with the long ſ) in the attic to the more ornate & sumptuous Victorian volumes in the library downstairs. I learned the art of versification from a long-ſ book published in 1797, & Pope, Addison, Goldsmith, Johnson, Thomson, Swift, Gay, Tickell, &c. always seemed infinitely more *real* to me than Longfellow, Dickens, & the other Victorians shoved at me in the natural course of events. My first verse & prose were in the heroic couplets & balanced periods of Georgian days, & I have never felt quite right without a powdered periwig

& small-clothes. Nor has this feeling ever abated. From the age of three to this moment as I sit in a *real* Georgian house by a small-paned window near a white colonial mantel I have always felt, instinctively, a deep & subtle linkage with the 1700's—so that, as you know, my virtually only diversion is visiting colonial towns & merging myself into their 18th century architectural vistas. Well—with this preparation, imagine (after you see the thing yourself) the effect on me of "Berkeley Square!" Naturally my 18th century affiliations give me a decided bias, so that my judgment ought not to be taken as intrinsic or final—but allowing for everything,

grandpa Ecb-Pi-Eɭ

(as a conservative older man I stick to the writing styles of the earlier 18th century

it seems to me that the play can't be considered as other than extremely powerful & well produced & acted. Of course, the foundation is fantastic, & the emotion is woven around a romantic fallacy—cosmically permanent affection—which has no parallel in reality; but in spite of these handicaps the thing succeeds perfectly in conjuring up an atmosphere of seriousness & sincerity. It is dignified & convincing—keeping close enough to real human reactions to make one overlook the instances of departure. That leading man is a damned fine actor—even if he couldn't suppress his British accent for the American part. He understands tone, gesture, & emotional nuances—& is clearly leagues above the ordinary cinema idol. I understand, indeed, that he is a dramatic performer of some note; & that he acted this part in the original stage version of "Berkeley Square". . . . . which young Talman ecstatically recommended to me some years ago, though I never had a chance to see it. But the costumes & scenic setting—oh, boy! It was positively *uncanny*, . . . like an actual *homecoming!* The coach, the square, the house, the sedan-chairs, the carriages . . . . all the details. No dramatic production I have ever seen has been even comparable in fidelity. The cut of the coats was *exactly* right for 1784, & the hair-powdering (natural long hair for those who could grow it came in during the winter of 1775–6) was of the lighter, greyish sort popular after 1780. If I have any criticism to make, it is that the fashions were *too faithfully* followed. *Elderly* men in 1784 would still be wearing three-cornered hats & fuller coats & bushier wigs, yet I didn't see many of these in the play. But hell! what is this but a trifle? Indeed, in the ultra-fashionable circle represented in the film it is very probable that most of the old sports would be aping the new styles of the young bucks & maccaronies![12] In short, this play brought to life for a brief moment the *precise* world in which, for some unknown reason or other, (I have sometimes tried to trace my odd feeling to certain causes, environmental & accidental. Certain *pictures* at home—especially the illustrations to a certain book, over which I pored at 2½ or 3, before I could actually read—plus the ancient houses & steeples of Providence, & the fascinating isolation of the 18th century books in a black, windowless attic room—all played a part.) I have always felt myself to belong; & my involuntary exile from which has always irked me. (I always have a damnable feeling of living in some *unreal world of the future*. When I see a railway or telephone or motor-car I always have a sort of impression that it is a joke or dream; & one reason I can't take the contemporary world—or the Victorian world of my own physical youth—seriously is that I *unconsciously* assume that these worlds are nightmares *not yet born*. At times, in youth, I used candles for illumination & let the household gas-jets alone; & to this day I never use the telephone except under compulsion. I do, however, appreciate *plumbing* as a practical improvement; & as a Roman classicist—which many Georgian gentlemen were—never omit a daily bath. So complete is my absorption in the 18th century, that my performances in its prose & verse have sometimes been mistaken for the real thing by men of no inconsiderable reading. Usually it is not easy for a modern to reproduce *exactly* the tone of a former age, so that no residue of modern perspective remains. I can't imitate any *archaic* style, [the 18th century is *not archaic* to me] no matter how hard I try. My Elizabethan imitations are flat & laboured. Indeed, I can't ape the style of the present age except with difficulty. The underlying rhythms & idioms of 1780 persist.) Pardon all the tedious reminiscence—but that film awaked all the latent Georgianism in me! Remember that I now live in a sort of colonial counterpart of Berkeley Square. Of course one secret of the play's double kick was that it was not only a picture of my natural age, but also a picture of *a man of the present who felt a homesickness for that age & succeeded in getting back into it.* The details of the time-transition were *admirably* handled. A very real weirdness & sense of cosmic backgrounds inhered in both transitional episodes. That is the sort of effect I'd like to create in literature, though I know damn well I haven't the skill to do it. It occurs to me that in all the cosmos nothing so *truly* fascinates me—so *deeply & thoroughly & subconsciously* grips my emotions—as *the idea of time*. To me absolutely nothing is significant except in its relation to the time-stream; & by the same token no other factor or situation or drama in the universe can enthrall & interest me half so much as one which involves some miracle or defiance or overleaping of surprise or paradox connected with *time*. It is as if *time* were some especial enemy of mine—some barrier or frustrating agent of paramount significance. This is also Dunsany's conception—hence my overwhelming delight & interest in his work. Such an anti-time fanaticism is not merely the protest of aging humanity (both Dunsany & I had it *in youth* just as strongly as in later life), but something wholly distinct. It is not a resentment at personal aging & death (who could resent, or even conceive of, aging & death at *three*?), but one which rebels at confinement to any one epoch along the time-stream. I subconsciously resent my inability to visit Rome in the age of Scipio Africanus, & my inability to *go home* to the Providence or London or Devonshire of 1760 or 1770. Incidentally—I do not minimise the uncongenialities I would find in other ages. The bad points of the 18th century are woefully manifest to me; though very oddly, I have a tendency to excuse them as familiar evils—in a way that I cannot excuse the bad points of the Elizabethan or Commonwealth or Restoration or Victorian or 1933 eras. Here, incidentally, is a bit of my feelings anent time & change—a thing in the manner of *my own* age which I wrote while seated on a rustic hillside a couple of summers ago:

On an Unspoiled Rural Prospect

How tranquil ſpread theſe ſloping Meads
    That glow as Evening gilds the Weſt,
And verdant from the River's Reeds
    Aſcend to join the beech-crown'd Creſt!

Yon boſky Vale, where lily'd Streams
    Glide on to ſhadowy Glens unknown,
Seems drowſing with the ling'ring Dreams
    Of ages happier than our own.

For here the Breeze with ſoften'd Strain
    Salutes a Scene of changeleſs Grace,
And Spring on Spring returns again,
    As to a lov'd, remember'd Face.

Theſe Oaks and Elms ſeem echoing ſtill
    To Pipes that bygone Shepherds play'd,
As reſting on this ſelf-ſame Hill
    They grateful ſcann'd the neighb'ring Shade.

Notes that cou'd pleaſe the Naiad Band,
    And charm the Dryads of the Wood,
Sound low once more along the Land
    When Twilight looms on Solitude.

The winding Walls, that Vines enfold,
    The village Roofs beyond the Mere,
Shine antient, as the Sunſet's Gold
    Recalls each long-departed Year.

> Here the encumb'ring Weight of Age
> Its bittereſt Force a while reſigns,
> For ſylvan Spells reverſe the Page,
> And bare the long-hid earlier Lines.

> In aureate Floods o'er Grove and Field
> The vandal Æons ſink from Sight,
> Till Time and Change, diſſolving, yield
> A Breath's Eternity of Light!

By the way—before I get off this 18th century business, I must give you an eyeful of my own personal "Berkeley Square" with the aid of a marvellously opportune pamphlet (to which I was tipped off by the ancient pedagogical gentlewoman downstairs—the Germanophilic lady who has cancelled her *N Y Times* subscription because of editorials adverse to the Nazi cause!) & a set of snapshots which I took last month with a venerable Brownie #2 camera bought in 1907. I'll ask the eventual return of all these things—though there is not the least hurry about them. In the booklet you'll find a good deal of interesting Rhode Island matter well worth perusal. But to get to the pictures—the frontispiece of the pamphlet gives a surprisingly fine idea of my whole neighbourhood—the curve of College St. rising from Market Square to the college-crowned crest of the ancient hill. The only flaw is that the perspective doesn't indicate quite how *steep* the hill really is. Actually, it's a virtual precipice. Street-cars couldn't climb it without a cable counterweight system like that prevalent in San Francisco—& now they dodge it by means of a tunnel (which comes out beyond the crest) a block to the north. In this picture, if your eyes are sharp (or you could use a mild magnifier), you can see a considerable number of roofs of the Berkeley Square period. *This house* is especially clear, & I have marked it on the margin. It is, as I have told you, set back from the street in a grassy court of much quaintness. Adjoining it is the modern college library, while just a few yards east is the (also modern) college clock tower, by whose huge golden hands my aunt & the gentlewoman downstairs time the boiling of eggs & the percolating of coffee. I have marked the white belfry of the 1770 college edifice—a cane made from one of whose original rafters (during repairs in the Victorian age) I have inherited from an uncle of the class of 1869.[13] At the base of the hill you will see the splendid new courthouse, whose finishing touches were not added till last month. In the faithful Georgian architecture of this building you will see an illustration of the regard which Providence has for its own traditions. The style is not only Georgian, but specifically *Providence-Georgian*—embodying certain architectonic nuances typical of this particular town's 18th century public buildings. You will note the extreme cleverness with which the architect (F. Ellis Jackson of this city) has adapted the Georgian style to an edifice

whose enormous size would ordinar[il]y suggest a more classical or monumental medium. Instead of leaving large surfaces & awkwardly long lines, he
has broken the whole bulk up into subordinate masses; so that the effect of
the huddled gables is that of a *whole group of buildings of the size & design most typical of 18th* century Providence. This is the largest building of purely Georgian
architecture & feeling in the world—covering one entire block. In Hartford
there is a larger structure *nominally* Georgian, but its unbroken, boxlike lines
make it really a mere modern office-building with added Georgian details.
The belfry of our court house is especially fine—forming a splendid Georgian
feature on the skyline. The only thing I lament about the enterprise is the fact
that some *real* colonial buildings were sacrificed to make room for it. The
buildings barely shewn across College St. at the bottom of the picture are all
genuine colonial reliques. Some time I'll find (or take) a picture of them to
shew you. I fear they will perish before the lapse of another generation, for
they are owned by the R.I. School of Design (which adjoins them on the
north) & cover ground within the school's plan of expansion. Every night the
Court House belfry is floodlighted—which adds a weirdly picturesque element to the local landscape. But to get at the photographs—you will notice
one general close view of #66. The window above the doorway is of my bedroom, & the two at its left are the south windows of my study—which also
has two west windows. Another view shews part of the house at a greater distance, with the courtyard & high wall of the adjacent college library as a
frame. In taking this picture I was damn fool enough to leave the door (a Victorian substitution which detracts from the colonial doorway in which it is
hung) shut & visible. A third view exhibits the doorway at close range, with
my aunt in it. Note the later-Georgian fan carving where a fanlight usually is.
A fourth view shews my aunt on the steps. Shot #5 is of my aunt at the N W
corner of ancient University Hall—the edifice of 1770—in the neighbouring
college grounds. #6 is of the Old Gentleman against the same background.
This view is a bit blurred because the photographer (my aunt) didn't realise
how steady a slow-shuttered Brownie has to be held for even a nominally in-
stantaneous photograph. Or perhaps Grandpa's ugly mug & unpressed suit (I
hadn't intended to pose) were too much for the timeworn camera!

As for my childhood—I'd scarcely call it a remarkably pathetic one. At
any rate, I had a better time then than I ever have since. The early death of
my father & the death of my grandmother in 1896[14] lent an overtone of melancholy to the household, but only a limited amount of this reached me. I re-
acted against it—in fact, the deep mourning costumes worn by my mother
made me so nervous (I used to pin bits of bright cloth on her skirts) that she
greatly curtailed the period of their wear. Having certain fantastic & imaginative interests early (including my perpetual 18th centuryism) tended to give me
more new pleasures than it took away. About the only childish things I disliked were games & other *aimless* activities. Anything with a *coördinated* interest

(i.e., something like a *plot* element) gave me the keenest delight. I derived the most extreme pleasure from my toys—of which I had a profuse variety, since our really straitened circumstances date only from 1904. My favourite toys were *very small* ones, which would permit of their arrangement in widely extensive scenes. My mode of play was to devote an entire table-top to a scene, which I would proceed to develop as a broad landscape . . . . helped by occasional trays of earth or clay. I had all sorts of *toy villages* with small wooden or cardboard houses, & by combining several of them would often construct *cities* of considerable extent & intricacy. (Do they make these toy villages now? There were even steepled churches!) Toy trees—of which I had an infinite number—were used with varying effect to form parts of the landscape . . . . even *forests* (or the suggested edges of forests). Certain kinds of blocks made walls & hedges, & I also used blocks in constructing large public buildings. It must be noted that, despite a taste for realism which balked at the obvious exoticism of certain German toys, I cultivated a stoical indifference to the element of *consistent scale* in my designs. I couldn't be over-insistent that all my villages & buildings harmonise in magnitude—so that some of my private houses were undeniably larger than some of my churches & court houses, & so on. This principle applied even more conspicuously to such details as vehicles, human figures, &c. I had to accept what was commonly available, & let my childish imagination exercise a mercifully softening influence. My people were mainly of the lead-soldier type & magnitude—frankly too large for the buildings which they presumably tenanted, but as small as I could get. I accepted some as they were, but had my mother modify many in costume with the aid of knife & paint-brush. Much piquancy was added to my scenes by special toy buildings like windmills, castles, &c. I was always consistent—geographically and chronologically—in setting my landscapes as my infant store of information would allow. Naturally, the majority of scenes would be of the 18th century; although my parallel fascination with railways & streetcars led me to construct large numbers of contemporary landscapes with intricate systems of tin trackage. I had a magnificent repertoire of cars & railway accessories—signals, tunnels, stations, &c—though this system was admittedly too large in scale for my villages. My mode of play was to construct some scene as fancy—incited by some story or picture—dictated, & then to act out its life for long periods—sometimes a fortnight—making up events of a highly melodramatic cast I went. These events would sometimes cover only a brief span—a war or plague or merely a spirited pageant of travel & commerce & incident leading nowhere—but would sometimes involve long aeons, with visible changes in the landscape & buildings. Cities would fall & be forgotten, & new cities would spring up. Forests would fall or be cut down, & rivers (I had some fine *bridges*) would change their beds. History, of course, suffered in this process; but my data (culled from stories, pictures, questioning of my elders, & a marvellously graphic historic device called "Adams'

Synchronological Chart["]¹⁵—which I still have) was of a distinctly juvenile kind & extent. Sometimes I would try to depict actual historic events & scenes—Roman, 18th century, or modern—& sometimes I would make everything up. Horror-plots were frequent, though (oddly enough) I never attempted to construct fantastic or extra-terrestrial scenes. I was too much of an innate realist to care for fantasy in its purest form. Well—I got a great kick out of all this. In about a week or two I'd get fed up on a scene & substitute a new one, though now & then I'd be so attached to one that I'd retain it longer—starting a fresh scene on another table with materials not forming scene #1. There was a kind of intoxication in being lord of a visible world (albeit a miniature one) & determining the flow of its events. I kept this up till I was 11 or 12, despite the parallel growth of literary & scientific interests. I also had a toy theatre—for in those days I took an interest in the drama (I saw my first play at 6, & my first Shakespearian play at 7). Being dissatisfied with the limited array of scenery & characters furnished with it, I used my own characters & made additional cardboard scenery. Of plays, Sheridan's & Shakespeare's were my favourites. I spoke the original lines from the text, clumsily moving the characters in some rough approximation of the action. I always made programmes—

DRURY-LANE THEATRE

Novr. 1779

The Company prefents a Comedy by Mr.
Sheridan, intitul'd

THE CRITICK;

OR, A TRAGEDY REHEARS'D.

But I was by no means solitary, or confined to indoor pleasures. I had a large number of companions, & frequently joined them in outdoor diversions of great variety—generally (if I could so arrange it, for nothing else was so pleasing to me) the acting out of some vivid line of adventure (outlaws, police & criminals, Civil War or other battles, big game hunting, Indians & soldiers, firemen, &c[)]. We also had a military band, our instruments being those brass horns with membrane discs which gave a cornet-like sound to the voice. Sometimes we played *railway* with express-carts, velocipedes, & a specially-made street-car (based on a packing-box) which I had. Those were great old days. Often our playing would be transferred to the open fields & woods, since the old home was near the edge of the built-up streets & close to a wholly ancient New England countryside. Of this countryside most is gone—engulfed by the paved streets of the expanding city. One marvellous wooded ravine—whose effect on my infant imagination was tremendous—has been wholly filled & obliterated. One section, however—the wooded banks of the Seekonk River, with a tributary ravine like the filled-up one—has remained just as it was; having become a metropolitan park reservation before it had time to decay. Thither I still go nearly every pleasant afternoon in summer, taking my current reading & writing & losing myself in a timeless world at one with the past. Not a visible object is other than as it was in 1900, & sometimes I feel so wafted back that I half-expect to find the adult present a bad dream as I emerge. I half-expect to walk out of the woods into the old, leisurely streets of 1900, with the rattling waggons & smart carriages & little red & green single-truck street-cars (open, with gaily flapping awnings, in summer, but closed—with open platforms—in winter) & sputtering carbon arc-lights (supplemented by surviving gas lamp posts) & red litter-boxes (they're green now) of the period. I always go home (to my birthplace, 454 Angell St.) the same old way, & if dusk be thick, the illusion still persists. The house still stands—as a doctor's office centre—on its high terrace, though the stable perished 2 years ago. After failing fortunes banished our horses & carriages, that stable used to be my personal playhouse. I kept my carts & toy street-car & velocipede & (after 1900) bicycle in the great carriage room . . . where a buggy & a victoria still lingered desolate amidst cobwebs . . . . & used the stall-room as a stage for plays—with the carriage-room for an auditorium & the sliding door for a curtain. The harness-room was my "office"; & the deserted coachman's quarters upstairs—& the great hay-&-oat loft—were the scene of spectral adventures. After my tenth birthday—Aug. 20, 1900—I was an inveterate cyclist, becoming as the years passed almost a wheeled centaur. My bicycles (I used to wear them out so badly that I had 3 in succession) took me all over the neighbouring countryside, & gave me a daily familiarity with rustic landscapes & New England village atmosphere which has always influenced me potently. A frail constitution, however, generally limited my rides to a 15-mile radius. So after all I'd hardly call my youth a wretched one. The fact is, I was actually spoiled—having just about everything I wanted. Many thought I'd turn out to be hopelessly self-centred & recklessly extravagant—though actually I proved able to accomodate myself to greater economies & narrowings of living-scale than even the most pessimistic could have foreseen. Incidentally—I was no such paragon of classical precocity as you seem to have gathered from my early taste for the "Ancient Mariner". Remember that the Doré illustrations (God, how Doré fascinated me! We had & still have his Dante & Milton pictures.) made the edition I read a veritable picture-book. The mind of childhood is a curiously compartmented thing, so that in addition to my love of Grimm, Arabian Nights, Poe, the Greek & Roman myths, & the 18th century poets & essayists, I had a parallel set of utterly commonplace interests—street-cars, houses under construction, Alger, Nick Carter, Henty,[16] & all the customary juvenilia. After 1904 I had a long succession of 22-calibre rifles, & became a fair shot till my eyes played hell with my accuracy. Far from being a prig, I even cultivated considerable toughness when I was first able to attend school continuously. I supplemented the oaths of the 18th century with those of the present, drawing freely upon them whenever milder language would have savoured of softness. I had plenty of foes, but I don't think even the worst ever called me a sissy. I was, in fact, decidedly pugnacious—having a violent & ungovernable temper which the passage of years & a growing sense of the cosmic inevitability of all things has almost totally eradicated. Any affront—especially any reflection on my truthfulness or honour as an 18th century gentleman—roused in me a tremendous fury, & I would always start a fight if an immediate retraction were not furnished. Being of scant physical strength, I did not fare well in these encounters; though I would never ask for their termination. I thought it disgraceful, even in defeat, not to maintain a wholly "you-go-to-hell" attitude until the victor ceased pummelling of his own accord. What I would have done in a fight with lower-class boys who "fight dirty" I don't know, but I was never put to so drastic a test. Occasionally I won fights—aided by my habit of assuming a dramatically ferocious aspect frightening to the nervous . . . . the "by God, I'll kill you!" stuff. Ah, me—the spirit of youth! Now I'm an old man & scarcely ever double up my fists except on paper. A couple of years ago Long & I dramatised our incessant habit of controversy by getting photographed in the act of exchanging socks on the jaw, but it didn't look natural. As for circuses—my early hatred of crowds, plus my ultra-keen sensitiveness to the bad odours of menageries, deterred me from an experience which might have been highly enriching to the imagination. Olfactory evils played such havock with my stomach that (except for such menagerie-going as was needful to a knowledge of natural history) I always shunned any place suspected of harbouring bad odours. In later years a sinus trouble has dulled my sense of smell & removed this attitude. I was also hypersensitive to *sounds*—a pistol shot or firecracker giving me intolerable pain. This caused me to avoid places where loud reports were frequent—though at the same time I tried to acquire through slow gradations a greater hardihood. By the time I was 13 or 14 I could stand an ordinary .32 or .38 pistol shot without too much discomfort, & since then my hearing (like my sense of smell) has mercifully become less acute. Even now, though, I don't like cannonading—& I was under no illusions as to what I would have had to endure aurally had I succeeded in joining the National Guard in 1917. But I ramble. The main point is, that I really had a damn good time in childhood—a highly sensitive imaginative life giving me plenty to compensate for any such disadvantages as poor health. One favourite pursuit of mine was seeking out ancient & glamourous street scenes on the hill I now inhabit. (The old home was a mile east of the crest, in a Victorian region) I used to drag my mother all around when I was 4 or 5 & not allowed to be so far from home alone. I hardly knew what I was after, but the centuried houses with their fanlights & knockers & railed steps & small-paned windows had a strong & significant effect of some sort on me. This world, I felt, was a different one from the (Victorian) world of French roofs & plate glass & concrete sidewalks & piazzas & open lawns that

I was born into. It was a magic, secret world, & it had a *realness* beyond that of the home neighbourhood. It had, I knew, been there long before the home neighbourhood existed—& I felt it would still be there after the other had passed away. Then again, it was just like the Hogarth scenes in the big books in the parlour, & just like the pictures in the coloured books about the Revolution which were given me. It was *familiar*—I had *always* known it—I had *seen it before*—it was *part of me* in a sense that no other scene ever was . . . . . & so I dreamed about it by night & visited it by day whenever I could. I used to have (as I still do) favourite *vistas*—looking up such & such a street & wondering *what* lay around the curve at the end. Could I walk into the time of Hogarth & the Revolution if I followed one of those cryptic ways to its unknown end some evening when the twilight was purple & the yellow lamplight flickered up softly behind ancient fanlights & tiny window-panes? On rainy evenings, when the little old gas lamps (now gone) cast strange reflections on the glistening cobblestones & brick sidewalks, I could almost *see* the figures of yesterday plodding along . . . . cloaks, three-cornered hats, queues losing their powder in the rain . . . . . & I began to dream of myself in those scenes, witnessing tantalising fragments of 18th century daily life that faded too soon into wakefulness. Once I thought I saw a rider galloping madly over the cobbles, whilst all the windows were flung up by staring white-capped housewives & turbaned slaves . . . . . once I saw a troop of the King's men in red coats with muskets & beating drums . . . . were they off to join Shirley or Amherst against the French? God Save the King! . . . . But I loved the ancient fields & farmhouses & stone walls & orchards & deep woods & water-mills & village spires of the countryside, too. They linked up with all I read & dreamed & had told to me. Virgil's Georgics in Dryden's or my uncle's (unpublished) translation—the Sabine farm—Venusta Sirmio—the eternal symbolism of the plough & the reaping-hook—the fauns & satyrs & dryads of the ancient oaken groves (I *actually* thought I saw them once—for a moment—when I was 7, & I used to identify certain fragments of dead, twisted tree-roots as formless & unearthly daemons)—the meads & copses of Old England—the New England of yesterday—the scenes out of which the Farmer's Almanack (of which our family file, beginning in 1805, was & still is a fixture of the library table's [now my study's centre-table] deep drawers) grew—the background of Thomson's Seasons & Bloomfield's "Farmer's Boy" . . . . God, the spell of a great round autumn moon over a stone-walled hillside field with mystical rows of sheaves! . . . . . It drove me into 18th century couplets when I was in my teens—one of my efforts (called "Autumn") beginning:

> ARCADIAN Goddeſs! Whoſe fond pleaſing Reign
> Enchants the Foreſt, and delights the Plain;
> O'er vernal Scenes a gentle Magick pours,
> And chears the Flow'rs that bloom on summer Shoars:

To Days leſs bright thy potent Charm extend,
Nor ſcorn the ſad Vertumnus as thy Friend.

And the effect of the rural scene upon me now is just the same. Only a couple of years ago I let off steam in a near-sonnet about the way old farm buildings move me. They play on my sense of time-linkage (always my most sensitive point) as nothing else does. Here is the screed—

Continuity

There is in certain ancient things a trace
Of some dim essence—more than form or weight;
A tenuous aether, indeterminate,
Yet link'd with all the laws of time & space.
A faint, veiled sign of continuities
That outward eyes can never quite descry;
Of lock'd dimensions harbouring years gone by,
And out of reach except for hidden keys.

It moves me most when slanting sunbeams glow
On old farm buildings set against a hill,
And paint with life the shapes which linger still
From centuries less a dream than this we know.
In that strange light I feel I am not far
From the fixt mass whose sides the ages are.

After all, there is no real dividing of my commonplace & eventless existence into childhood, youth, maturity, & age. Fundamentally, I have never changed. At 3½ I was listening avidly to fairy-tales & witch-stories, feeling a strange awe & kinship with the old houses on the hill, dragging my mother around to queer street vistas, exulting in old farmhouses & ancient landscapes & spectral wooded ravines . . . . . & I'll be damned if my basic interests & major pursuits are a bit different now! 1893–1933 . . . . forty years . . . . a fair-sized lifetime . . . . . & yet there has never been any break in my continuous flow of my dominant emotional life. I can never look back, as some elders do, to a sharply contrasted boyhood & quote (or do I misquote?) "Say, could that lad be I?"[17] Today the scenes & images & thoughts & feelings of 1893 are as sharp & real as they ever were. There has been no break or reversal. Perspectives & specific single emotions have changed, details have come & gone, methods & avenues & activities have shifted, ideas & information have destroyed beliefs & built up new realisations—but beneath it all an absolutely unaltered thread of interests, feelings, wishes, preferences, & sensitivenesses has persisted. Physically a tiny fellow in a velvet Lord-Fauntleroy suit with round face, eyes just turned from an infantile (paternal line) blue to a light brown, & long yellow curls, has become a tall, gaunt old man with hatchet-face & lantern-jaws, dark-brown (maternal line) eyes, & thinning hair greyer & greyer after an increasing (finally quite dark) brownness in the middle years. *Nothing* of the 1893 exterior left. And yet almost all the recollections & moods & likes & dislikes & goals of 1893 are vivid still. It is as if my fascination with the idea of *time* had had some effect on my personality, so that *all the years I have lived or shall ever live are as a single point in my consciousness.* Curious, anyhow—whether or not linked with any lifelong phantasy-wish of being able to rove at will through the aeons. It lends a certain *irony* to the process of growing old. I see the boys of my own boyhood change & wither & grow stolid & middle-aged & forget altogether the dreams & outlooks & feelings & events of those far-off dawn-days. They would not know what I meant if I were to greet them with some bygone clan-signal of 1900, or remind them of some of the old doings & caves & huts & rendezvous of the past. Jack Hess (now sports editor of the Journal & Bulletin) wouldn't remember the hard time he had learning to walk on top of a high stone wall at 9, & Harold Munroe (a deputy sheriff at the courthouse) would stare blankly at some of the familiar orders which we passed down the line when he & I were Confederate generals in the woods leading an army against Ronald Upham's (insurance man) & Percy Sarle's (moved away—I don't know whether he's alive or dead) Union battal-ions. To them, aging has meant an actual change of emotions & spirit. They are *not,* in any *real* sense, the boys I used to play with. They have a whole new life & value-scale & personality in this altered world of the forties. Well—I look as old as they do . . . older than many of them . . . . but once in a while my age strikes me as a huge, secret *joke. For I am actually the same person that I was in 1900 & kindred years.* I still feel the feelings of 1900, & retain the essen-tial perspectives. The time-interval seems so *negligible*—so *unreal*—that the very fact of being grown up & middle aged is like an incredible marvel. Only yesterday—30 or 40 years ago—a grown-up person seemed necessarily a re-mote, alien being . . . . something that could be one's parent or grandparent, but that was hardly (despite one's own efforts to be grown up . . . . & did I fight against sailor blouses & raise hell till my mother let me wear coats & col-lars & ties?) of the same material as oneself; & today *the memory of that yesterday is so strong, & the sense of an intervening time-lapse so weak, that I often find it either grimly ironic or vaguely terrible & abnormal or completely incredible to be grown up & middle aged.* This year *1933?* What a joke! And yet . . . . It often seems to me an exquisite joke for me to be talking on terms of equality with teachers & other grown-ups. These fat or dried-up old fossils . . . . *can it be that some hidden necromancy has given me an exterior as old as theirs,* so that they talk to me as an adult instead of as a boy? Only a second (say 35 years) ago people of that age were ordering me around! Conversely, when I see a group of boys I often feel as if I might chat comfortably with them about their stamp-albums & air-rifles & chemistry sets & woodland tramps & attic-floor railway systems &

Henty books & such things—remembering only with an effort that I am probably older than the fathers of many of them, & that the things they do may be totally different from the things I did when I externally looked like them. They probably have model aëroplanes instead of railways, radio outfits instead of chemistry sets, new, unknown books in place of Henty & Edward S. Ellis & Kirk Munroe,[18] boy-scout organisations instead of haphazard groups playing Indian & outlaw . . . . & so on, & so on. So in a way my position in *time* is quite unique. I am perhaps the only living being to retain the feelings & images of the lost boys' world of 1900. The others who knew it in its physical day have become other persons with minds filled with other images & perspectives—& the modern boys who could duplicate its psychology live in a world so different that their imagination cannot bridge the gap. But I remain—one who was a boy in 1900, & to whom the long years have brought no lotos-blooms of oblivion & no prisms of altered mood & vision. Time . . . time . . . . . space-time . . . . . it doesn't take an Einstein to make it a confused chaos! Am I moving through it, or is it flowing past me . . . . or are there infinite I's, each eternally coëxisting in one simultaneous eternity? Unborn . . . boy . . . . man . . . . dead . . . . . . flash—flash—flash—Hell, but I wish I could get on paper some hint of the mystery of time & personality! There's a great field open there for some really sensitive person with a better literary sense than mine. It is amusing to see how today's narrow-visioned realists pass up the opportunity. By ignoring the tremendous significance of *the continuous time-stream* they are presenting a false & fragmentary picture which reflects only half the scope of the human spirit. Perhaps the tendency of the machine age is to forget the time-stream (owing to the effect of a constantly changing visible surface of life), but if so, it is building a low-grade civilisation in which a great part of our emotional potentialities will remain wasted & unused. And yet, curiously enough, the culture of the Greeks had a singularly weak time-sense as compared with that of western civilisation in its modern maturity.

As for New-England civilisation—just how much of it is to be regretted seems to me a rather open question. In the first place, we must remember that it has many variants—the Rhode Island & Massachusetts traditions, for example, differing enormously despite the fact that Massachusetts soil is visible from almost any East Side Providence housetop. For my part, I reject the phase which tries to overemphasise the ethical & mix it with other aspects of aesthetics. But in the general matter of emotion, I fancy there are at least two sides. The original Puritan tradition of *mere repression* is virtually dead . . . . dead from lack of *raison d'etre*. What has survived is something descended from another line of New England tradition—a respect for accurate thinking & well-proportioned perspective. This does not deny the value of emotion, but it teaches one to prefer *significant* emotion—an emotion well-proportioned to the importance of its cause, & modified by an adult comprehension of the values & circumstances involved—to that low-grade emotion which is little more than a kind of animal ebullition. Thus when I was a boy I was always getting into fearful rages, whereas now I recognise the cosmic inevitability of things & generally feel a mere weariness where I used to feel anger. In my opinion, most of the emotional manifestations discouraged by modern New England culture are vestigial & excrescences of very slight or doubtful value. On the other hand, the thoughtful, analytical attitude inculcated by the New England tradition promotes the growth of delicate sensitivenesses which the person of coarse & violent emotions can never experience; so that it seems to me more is given than taken away. The net value of the heritage, as measured in terms of receptiveness to significant human experience, certainly does not fall below that of any other regional heritage one can name. If it has certain weak points here & there, so likewise have others—& observations prove that the flaws in the others are often far more serious & devaluating than any of those in the Novanglian stream. As to the attitude toward foreigners— what if it is undemocratic? What, indeed, is democracy except a callous lack of appreciation of quality & development? Do the platitudes of politicians transform a defect to a virtue? No nation or region is called upon to modify its hereditary ways to suit strangers—indeed, it is really called upon to guard faithfully against such a modification, since only through the preservation of an unbroken continuity can any civilisation grow or remain great. Foreigners were never repulsed in N.E. as long as they came in decently assimilable quantities. Only when vast hordes of them virtually swamped us did sharp lines of cleavage arise. And even these lines are not *consciously* drawn. It is simply that people as utterly antipodal as New Englanders & the invading Latin-Slav type cannot possibly, in the normal course of events, have any thoughts or feelings or aspirations in common. There is absolutely nothing for us & them to say to each other . . . . a condition perfectly inevitable, & involving neither praise nor blame on either side. The only *fault* is our criminal folly in ever admitting these alien hordes. We did it through anthropological & sociological ignorance, plus a naive swallowing of the idealistic flapdoodle of political hypocrites. We ought to have known that these millions of antipathetic culture, exotic blood, & aberrant physical type could never form a part of our coherent civilisation—a deeply settled civilisation of (at the time immigration grew dangerous) 250 years on the soil, & 550 to 1200 years more (depending on whether we reckon it from the Norman Conquest or the earliest Saxon invasion) on the soil of the Mother Land. Now we do know it, along with the rest of the country—& the menacing hordes of yesteryear will pour in no more. Those who have come have done & will still do irreparable harm, but we can protect ourselves to some extent. A reasonable number of the foreigners can be culturally & physically absorbed in our own unbroken tradition; whilst others can be tolerated as neighbours at the same time that we refuse to let them influence us. We can take a leaf from the history of our oldest rivals, as mentioned earlier in this letter—the dogged French-Canadians who stick to "La Tradition" in the midst of exile & environmental pressure. No apologies are needed for a group that fights boldly for the integrity of its heritage—hence my admiration for a certain basic phase of the Nazi spirit.

Glad you enjoyed "Ah, Wilderness"[19]—thanks for the programme & the generous sheaf of comments. I must see or read this play sooner or later, for all recaptures of the past are delightful to me. I fancy the reminiscences in this piece are rather accurate & vivid—though if (cf. Parry review) it included the song "Bedelia" as a *new* hit, somebody made a mistake. "Bedelia" appeared in the autumn of *1903* (I first heard it played by the Orchestra between the acts of "A Message from Mars" at the old Imperial Theatre [now a shabby, 3d-rate cinema dump called the Capitol] shortly before Christmas '03.), & by the summer of 1906 was so stale that its rendition would have drawn a laugh. The song hits of 1906—which was, by the way, the first year that cinema shows existed apart from vaudeville—were "When the Whippoorwill Sings, Marguerite", "When the Mocking-Bird is Singing in the Wildwood", "I'll be Waiting in the Gloaming, Genevieve", "She Waits by the Deep Blue Sea", "Aren't You Coming Back to Old New Hampshire, Molly?", "In the Golden Autumn Time, My Sweet Elaine", "What You' Gwine to do when de Rent Comes Round?", "Bill Simmons" (by a Providence composer named George Spink), "A Picnic for Two", any old thing from "Mlle. Modiste", "Where the Morning Glories Twine Around the Same Old Door", "Colleen Brown", "Where the River Shannon Flows" (which today most of the young folk think is a century-old ballad!), &c. &c. &c. Hell, I ought to know—weren't the Blackstone Military Band's voices changing? . . . . From bad to worse, as an impartial outsider might have observed with uncharitable accuracy. But how we howled & bellowed those damned old barber-shop tunes!

"When the whippoorwill sings, Marguerite, (fancy effects by flute)
  And forget-me-nots bloom at your feet, (ditto by clarinet)
    You may know, though you yearn, (egotistical assumption!)
    That to you I'll return (that's what they all say!)
  Love's old story again to repeat; (1906 was unoriginal)

"So be true, little girl, I entreat, (a possible assumption in '06!)
  Till the time when again we shall meet; (clarinet gargling)
    Let love's star brightly shine—(high note fatal to adolescent second tenors)
    I'll return, sweetheart mine (he said so before!)
When the whippoorwill sings [fancy flute stuff], Marguerite". [touching harmony by 1st tenor]

That was the heyday of the "illustrated song"—formerly interpolated in vaudeville & sung between the acts of the cheaper legitimate plays, but then made an inseparable companion of the flickering products of Pathé Freres, S. Lubin, The Edison Co., the American Mutoscope & Biograph Co., the Selig Polyscope Co., the Essannay Film Co., George Meliés, the Kalem Co., Cie. Gaumont, the Vitagraph Co. of America, & other pioneers in your favourite industry. A wheezy tenor in a high collar would unburden himself of the melody beside the screen, whilst upon the latter would be flashed crude coloured photographic lantern-slides allegedly illustrative of the song but often embarrassingly reminiscent of slides used a year or two before in illustrating similar hits (such as "In the Shade of the Old Apple Tree", whose metre is reproduced accent for accent in the above-quoted Whippoorwill gem). Ah, me—the naivete of golden yesterdays! Well, as you & most of the reviewers seem to agree, O'Neill probably got this out of his system as a reminiscent bit—rather apart from his major creative line. Very conceivably it represents a lower level of composition than the familiar O'Neill tragedies. But one must beware of panning a thing merely because it isn't what people expect. It is a bit naive to catalogue everybody irrevocably, & fancy that each person must produce just this or that & nothing else. Every work of art ought to be judged on it own intrinsic merits, irrespective of authorship. If O'Neill happens to feel like writing in a vein which others have explored, why the hell shouldn't he? He may have some overtone to add which others have missed. Still, you know better than I whether this especial play was amateurish or not. Why don't you try a reminiscent play yourself if the technique seems congenial to you? In these quick-changing days even youngsters like you can recall closed chapters on which one must look back with wistful wonder. Psychologically, what could be remoter than the expansive 1920's? Glad the play was well acted. You may be interested in the enclosed cutting, which relates a rather exasperating experience of its famous leading man last Sunday not many rods from this door.

If you ever heard of Wheeler Dryden it was probably during your childhood—say 1924–5—when he was successively the Inspector Bucket of Margaret Anglin's "Great Lady Dedlock" (Dickens' Bleak House) & the run-down Ashley in that popular bit of hokum, "White Cargo."[20] He never seems to shake clear of mediocrity. As for his family—he, Charles, & Sydney are all half- or step brothers—none a full brother to any other. Charles & Sydney have the same father, Charles & Wheeler the same mother. At least, that's the way I recall it—I never question people about personal matters. There seems to have been a good deal of domestic trouble when the boys were infants. Wheeler's father—a rather well-known variety performer named Leo Dryden—was divorced when his son was a baby, & the latter never knew the Chaplins had any relationship to him till he was about 25. He then looked them up in California, & although very coolly received at first, was finally recognised by them. He found Charles—his blood-relative—somewhat more aloof than Sydney—his mere step-relative. Later on he & Sydney did some work together in England, & got to be extremely friendly. He intensely admires Charles but thinks that success has turned his head a trifle. Charles likes to dramatise himself as a tragic figure—to capitalise his bitterness at a squalid & neglected boyhood—which, as Dryden observes, gets to be rather an artificial pose after nearly 20 years of complete success & unlimited money! But I suppose he feels the sting of plebeian instincts & stigmata—the cockney burr which you say he can't shake off. His coolness toward Dryden may come from a subconscious resentment at the latter's greater youthful advantages & naturally cultivated speech & bearing. By the way—here's a picture of Dryden on an old blotter—which you needn't bother to return. I haven't seen him in ages now. He's a good egg, though just a bit of a sap. For one thing, he's absolutely incapable of abstract reasoning. Our gang will never forget a night in 1925 when he & I participated in a religious discussion. Poor Wheeler was apparently altogether unable to conceive of a cosmos without personal direction—although he stoutly reiterated his daring liberalism (though a devout Anglican communicant) by asserting again & again: "But I say, you kneow I deont claim that God is a nice eold gentleman with long whiskaws!"

De lacunis litterariis[21]—I'm in no position to throw stones, since (as I believe I confessed before) a list of the famous works I haven't read would be sensational ammunition for my enemies! All I can say for myself is that I don't generally let the fame of a book keep me away from it. As I argue, popular repute doesn't indicate that I *shan't* like a book any more than that I *shall.* I don't want to miss a good thing simply because other people recommend it. Hawthorne's "Seven Gables" is "prescribed reading", & all that—but God! what a poignant chronicle of shadowy borderlands! In my youth modern literature did not attract me at all. To begin with, I felt no kinship with the age I lived in—& still do not think an independent man ought to be tied to one age any more than to any other. Secondly—there was comparatively little important material then written. Style was better than it is now, but books of serious subject-matter were fewer. Of course, a keen searcher might have picked out Frank Norris, Hardy, Conrad, the early Dreiser, G. Bernard Shaw, the early Wharton, Galsworthy in embryo, the start of Conrad, &c—but I was not a keen searcher. I did see some good plays, though—Pinero, & one or two of Wilde's—the latter presented anonymously because of the author's disgrace. But the reigning idols were still Tennyson & Dickens & Browning & Stevenson & Kipling & Longfellow & Matthew Arnold & so on—all more or less pains in the neck so far as I was concerned. The only congenial stuff I could find was Poe, the Greek & Roman classics in (mostly 18th century) translation, the 18th century poets & essayists (I liked the novelists much less), & all sorts of non-literary reading—cheap boys' stuff, *anything* weird, history, science, &c. Long years later—in middle life, after the rise of a fictional literature at least attempting to portray society faithfully—I attempted to read some recent material in an effort to see how the current was moving. That was around 1920—the "Eric Dorn"[22] period. Some of the stuff impressed me as very important in its effort to depict *real* motives & events instead of the artificial motives & events common to earlier fiction. None of it, however, really interested me profoundly, since it appeared immature, one-sided, ill-written, & too unconscious of the correlation & continuity of things to form finished literature. It impressed me as useful experimental material leading to a broadening of the main literary stream to include the results of modern psychology & philosophic disillusion—but as art most of it lacked something. Really recent stuff I don't know at all. I read the earlier books of Proust in 1928, & agree that in him the 20th century has one first-rate creator. As for the right stuff to start a child on—I'd choose material, whether old or new in date, which is *universal* enough to be timeless. But surely there ought to be considerable new material in the early assignments—I guess there is now, judging from the new Macmillan readers which a friend of mine edited.[23] Regarding the Ancient Mariner—what a difference introductions make! You linked it with school work—while as for me . . . . . . imagine a tall, stately Victorian library in a house sometimes visited with my mother or aunts. Marble mantel—thick bearskin rug—endless shelves of books . . . . A house of adults, so that a 6-year-old caller's interest strays most naturally to the shelves & great centre table & mantel. Fancy then the discovery of a great atlas-sized gift-book leaning against the mantel & having on the cover gilt letters reading "With Illustrations by Gustave Doré". The title didn't matter—for didn't I know the dark, supernal magic of the Doré pictures in our Dante & Milton at home? I open the great book—& behold a hellish picture of a corpse-ship with ragged sails under a waning moon! I turn a page . . . . . God! A spectral, half-transparent ship on whose deck a corpse & a skeleton play at dice! By this time I am flat on the bearskin rug & ready to thumb through the whole book . . . of which I've never heard before. . . . . A sea full of rotting serpents, & death-fires dancing in the black air . . . . . troops of angels & daemons . . . . . crazed, dying, distorted forms . . . . . dead men rising in their putrescence & lifelessly manning the dank rigging of a fate-doomed barque . . . .

> "They groan'd, they stirr'd, they all uprose,
> Nor spake, nor mov'd their eyes;
> It had been strange, ev'n in a dream,
> To have seen those dead men rise."

Well—it doesn't argue any precocity or pedantry to state that I began lapping up the text as soon as I'd had an eyeful of the pictures! This was my kind of stuff! Actually, the poem is very easy—well within a child's comprehension owing to the mock-archaic marginal glosses appended by the bard. Did it give me a wallop? Be yourself! Boy! When I came to notice the title I saw that the poem was by Coleridge, whose gilt-backed complete works (in a Philadelphia edition of 1849 which I still have) graced our library at home. Gloria dei in excelsis! Then this thing must be somewhere in our book, & available to me whenever I might wish to read it. Later on you can bet that I found it & did read & read & reread it! And I stumbled on "Christabel" with its nameless hinted horrors . . . . . & the opiate suggestiveness of the "Kubla Khan" fragment . . . . . No academic compulsion there . . . . . I'd never seen the inside of a schoolhouse in those days. But alas—I've never owned a Doré-illustrated "Ancient Mariner." Sometimes I feel like asking the one surviving member of that bygone neighbour-family (which, fallen like ours on an evil fate, has lost its old home) whatever became of the book—but I forbear, since such a query might rouse melancholy thoughts of lost days & lost dignities.

The Joan of Arc film you describe must be quite an artistic triumph—I'll have to see it if it comes here.[24] Thanks for the page of reproductions of exhibition pictures. They certainly are an odd bunch, & would seem to indicate (unless there were a lot of conservative pictures present & ignored) that taste has gone very definitely modern in your part of the world. Providence is very conservative—barely touched by this modernism, although lectures on it are frequent. I try to maintain an open mind regarding modernism, being aware of the principles behind it—the need of expressing the artist's especial personal perspective, & the actual fact that no two persons see the same thing in exactly the same way (some minds registering one chance arrangement of lines as the dominant outline, whilst in other minds other chance arrangements seem dominant)—yet with all due allowances cannot help thinking that extremists carry the idea too far . . . . . & indeed, that the smaller fry are not original creators at all, but merely apish fashion-followers who are no more sincere than as if they used the technique of Botticelli or Guido Reni or Claude Lorrain. I note your opinions, & those of the ubiquitous Mrs. Parry. To me "St. Tropez" has a certain charm—as of some sinister, blasted land seen in a dream or delirium—though probably that is not the way M. de Segonzac would wish one to react.[25] I can't help feeling that the landscape has been intensely visualised & experienced by the artist—though I (as a conservative) certainly wish he had chosen a less nebulous medium for reproducing it. The masses are well-balanced & the selection of significant details is good—so that I can't exactly laugh at it, even though I'd choose something else to hang in the front hall. The other pictures don't get under my skin very deeply—& I must admit that "Sarah Tubb" & "Harlequin" seem to my laymanlike eyes absolutely lousy![26] My personal preferences in art are for landscapes & architectural vistas of distinctly conservative yet strongly individual cast. I love the sinister black windswept woods of Salvator Rosa, the classic harbour scenes of Claude Lorrain, the lovely English countryside of Constable, & the vistas & sunsets of J. M. W. Turner. My late elder aunt captured something of the Constable–Turner spirit in an amateur way, & I speak literal truth when I say that I display her canvases on my walls as much from intrinsic admiration as from family loyalty. My mother, too, was a very proficient amateur painter—I have a marine view of hers over my colonial study. And to think I can't draw or paint a damned thing myself! This is the limitation I regret most, for a large number of my strongest imaginative impressions & moods are of such a nature that literature could not possibly express them half so well as pictorial art. Probably I can't write literature either—but even if I could, it wouldn't be quite as effective as drawings & paintings.

November 11

Damn this pen! The residual scratch seems on the increase, so that I don't know but I'll take it down to the repair man again. I certainly do have the devil's own luck with writing materials. Hope the wait of several days won't cause them to soak me another half a dollar for massaging the point!

As for Russian recognition[27]—I don't know that it'll do any harm if care be taken to keep propaganda out of this country. Russia has a right to govern itself as it pleases so long as it doesn't interfere with matters outside its own borders. That was the objection to recognition all along—hence if it be true that external propaganda has ceased, there is no reason to hold off from any relationship which might prove advantageous. Regarding the danger of bolshevism in America—I don't say that the native masses want it. Indeed, I feel fairly certain that they don't. But masses are never their own masters. They are vast mindless reservoirs of savage physical power; which can precipitate chaos when sufficiently desperate, but which cannot map out any definite subsequent course. They are always at the mercy of leaders, & when they repudiate conservative leadership (as they may if ameliorative steps are too slow) they will be easy prey for the communist-minded foreign "intelligentsia" of New York. *They* will not want communism, but the slum-spawned Eastern European & Asiatic immigrants who lead all radical moves will steer them to it in spite of themselves unless the strictest precautions be taken. The trouble with communism is not its underlying principle of collective ownership, but the cultural overtones attached to it by flabby idealism & a literal following of Marx's least justified speculations. Conceivably, a sober, cautious nation could gradually transfer all substantial property holdings to the government, & operate industry for service rather than profit, without overturning any of the folkways & inherited mental & aesthetic perspectives which make life seem significant & interesting to us. That is what will probably have to come sooner or later, & I surely have no objection to it. Russian bolshevism, however, is not content with such an orderly transformation. Instead, it accepts the silly theory that art & folkways are direct economic outgrowths, & consequently attempts the most criminally destructive attacks upon all the settled habits & traditions which make life worth living for sensitive people. It attempts to foist upon the people a preposterously fallacious conception of society as a single organism instead of a practical compromise among individuals; &, as a corollary, to impose on the individual tyrannies & indignities which even the most arbitrary of fascist states would not think of proposing. There is, too, a ludicrous exaltation of the manual labourer & his standards; & a consequent tendency to keep the cultural level depressed to a low altitude for his benefit. All of these things are irreparably harmful to the civilisation as a whole, since they destroy all that makes life worth enduring by high-grade, sensitive persons. The bolshevik culture drags a nation down from a high-potential civilisation, in which natural human gifts & sensitivenesses are fully utilised, to a less-potential civilisation in which the race's finest qualities tend to remain dormant. Of course, as a bolshevik nation settles down, the culture will tend to rise again through natural causes; but the handicap of original destruction & of a popular psychology antagonistic to individual development (for the masses can never participate in a high culture) will prevent it from reattaining its former level. Nor can any culture without deep roots & old traditions be really emotionally satisfying. The destruction of values perpetrated by the bolsheviks is too high a price to pay for any benefits which may be achieved—especially since every substantial advantage of socialism can be attained without the aesthetically suicidal holocaust. The most savage evils of bolshevism spring from its empty idealistic side—the side which demands a social equalitarianism in addition to the financial redistribution which is *really* necessary. Russian bolshevism is a peculiarly Slavo-Semitic institution utterly unsuited to Anglo-Saxons. It is our business to keep it off until our own people can go through a gradual social-economic evolution in their own Nordic way.

As for Germany today—to call it a "madhouse" is to exaggerate in the grossest fashion. The details of Nazism are deplorable, but they do not even begin to compare in harmfulness with the extravagances of communism. You seem to forget that most of the German people are quietly going about their business as usual, with a much better morale than they had last year. If the Nazi destruction of certain books is silly—& there is no reason to deny that it is—then there is no word to express the abysmal idiocy & turpitude of the bolshevik war on normal culture & expression. Germany has not even begun to parallel Russia in the destruction of those basic values which Western Europeans live by. When I say I like Hitler I do not imply that he is a personally winning or temperately rational individual, but simply that he is an honest, ignorant man fighting bravely & blindly against the disintegrative forces which more educated & sophisticated people accept without adequate evidence as inevitable. His neurotic fanaticism, scientific addle-patedness, & crude gaucheries & extravagances are admitted & deplored—& of course it is quite possible that he actually *may* do more harm than good. One can scarcely prophesy the future. But the fact remains that he is the sole remaining rallying-point for German morale, & that virtually all of the best & most cultivated Germans accept him *temporarily* for what he is—*a lesser evil at a special & exacting crisis of history*. Objections to Hitler—that is, the violent & hysterical objections which one sees outside Germany—seem to be based largely on a soft idealism or "humanitarianism" which is out of place in an emergency. This sentimentalism may be a pleasing ornament in normal times, but it must be kept out of the way when the survival of a great nation hangs in the balance. The preservation of Germany as a coherent cultural & political fabric is of infinitely greater importance than the comfort of those who have been incommoded by Nazism—& of course the number of sufferers is negligible as compared with that of bolshevism's victims. If what you say were true—that others could save Germany better than Hitler—then I'd be in favour of giving them a chance. But unfortunately the others had their chance & didn't prove themselves equal to it. The travellers from whom I have had first-hand information were by no means casual trippers. Indeed, the old lady downstairs is a lifelong student of German history & civilisation, with hundreds of friends & correspondents throughout Germany & Austria (where she spends 2½ months every summer), & with so intimate a command of the native language & folkways that all casual acquaintances abroad think her a German. She goes about Munich or Vienna—dining, shopping, &c—just like a native, & only the passport officials & her personal friends have any idea that she is anything but a Bavarian or Austrian of good family. Your hatred of Nazism—especially in the light of your extenuation of bolshevism's vastly greater savageries—appears to me to be a matter of idealistic emotion unsupported by historic perspective or by a sense of the practical compromises necessary in tight places. Emotion runs away with you. For example—you get excited about four Americans who were mobbed because they didn't salute the Nazi flag. Well, as a matter of fact, did you ever hear of a nation that *didn't* mob foreigners who refused to salute its flag in times of political & military emergency? I'd like to have a dollar for every German who was mobbed in America for not rising at the "Star Spangled Banner" during the late war! This sort of thing is simply common herd instinct—human nature. It happens everywhere, & always will. In Russia all sorts of such incidents constantly occur—but radicals pardon them! Still—don't get me wrong. I'm not saying that Schön[e] Adolf is anything more than a lesser evil. A crude, blind force—a stop-gap. The one point is that he's the only force behind which the traditional German spirit seems to be able to get. When the Germans can get another leader, & emerge from the present period of arbitrary fanaticism, his usefulness will be over.

As to a general New England hatred of radicalism—well, it's a good thing to have a balance-wheel against destructive experiment & disintegration. Certainly radicals are the chief agents in *change*—that is their constant goal, be it good or bad, necessary or unnecessary! The point is that of all the changes they seek, only about 10% are in any way desirable—so that it is really more important to have safeguards against change than to have agencies agitating toward it. Everything really desirable in life is the result of *stability* & *continuity*—since, outside the narrow radius of crude animal sensation, virtually nothing has any interest or meaning apart from the associations twined around it through generations of racial experience. That is why the machine age tends so greatly to impoverish life—by removing us from our hereditary adjustment to the landscape, the seasons, the agricultural cycle, the acts of daily life & industry, & the familiar concepts of distance dependent upon transportational speed. Change sets us down in an alien world where experiences mean nothing to us because they form no part of any pattern we know. Thus change is intrinsically undesirable. But sometimes it forces itself on us, as when blind drift compels us to submit to the mechanisation of life—& *then* there arises a situation in which we find ourselves in real need of deliberate readjustment. That is, when an inevitable change intervenes to create a new set of conditions at variance with our existing institutions, we *must* modify the institutions to fit the new conditions. This is our present plight—mechanised industry has caused the breakdown of laissez-faire economics & *possibly* (we can't tell yet) of private property as working institutions, hence we must evolve a new system of artificially supervised economics & perhaps of collectively owned productive processes in order to restore the normal circulation of resources. Obviously, there is now a really legitimate & necessary job for the radical—though at the same time there is also a tremendously important job for the conservative. The radical, given free rein, would attempt to change enormously *more* than needs to be changed; & in so doing would accomplish more harm than good because of the vast number of traditional values destroyed. To work against him & limit change to necessary & desirable points is the normal & indispensable function of the conservative. Of course, the sheer *reactionary* can do more harm than the radical—or at least, just as much—since by insisting on the retention of unworkable elements he precipitates a breakdown or revolt & all of its resultant chaos. Don't fancy that I have any use for the old-time Hoover-Republican laissez-faire plutocracy! What I strive for is a system which will work—i.e., will restore the ability of everyone to get a living in exchange for adequate labour—& which can be evolutionally developed without any ruinous wholesale sacrifice of those hereditary values which alone give the illusion of direction & meaning to existence.

As for the morals & dignity & self-respect of artists—the fact that many top-notchers have had an under-supply is no news to me. But all I said was that there is no *more* excuse for laxity in artists than in business men & the like. One could cite just as long a list of eminent financiers & merchants & statesmen who have had very little morals, dignity, or self-respect. I merely gave it as my opinion that sloppy disintegratedness, commonness, & anti-social callousness are just as offensive in one kind of person as in another; & that if we are to tolerate these things in musicians & poets, we must also tolerate them in railway superintendents & dentists & garage proprietors. It is silly for a man to bring up his profession as an excuse for anything which he would consider less excusable in a member of another profession. That is all I meant. Of course, there is a type of person in whom defects of character are possibly associated with the disproportionate development of certain specific faculties—the "mad genius" of tradition—but relatively few belong to that type. It has become a legend—& all sorts of persons take advantage of the legend to excuse careless & irresponsible lapses into coarseness, bad manners, bad taste, & anti-social unscrupulousness. Of course, one is at liberty to have his own preferences in comparing the gentleman—who regards the process of living as an art—with those specific practitioners of various creative arts who are callous to the art-element in life. As I have said, my vote goes to the gentleman; because I believe that a well-rounded civilisation demands first of all a sound groundwork which can infuse the element of beauty (i.e., rhythm, harmony with a given pattern, consistency with major motivations, absence of excrescences, favouring of the evolved & richly rewarding sensitivenesses over the cruder instincts) into the constantly-encountered fabric of daily living as well as into the merely occasionally-encountered objects of conscious & specifically aesthetic craftsmanship. Beautiful limited creations in the midst of a squalidly disorderly set of daily human reactions are like exquisite Sevres vases set on dirty packing-boxes in a nigger hovel. As for the question of morals being involved & ambiguous—of course the details are, but there are certain basic attitudes which distinguish the evolved & artistic liver from the callous haphazard slob. By the way—despite your expressed doubts, your own fanatical insistence on *tolerance, humanity,* &c. stamps you as a most dogmatic & uncompromising moralist in certain directions! You are far surer of the evil of certain characters or policies than I am! What I would, in general, call the type of superiority manifest in artistic living, is a *sense of pattern* which calls for a certain amount of correlation with wider ranges of action & larger backgrounds of tradition, & which demands the favouring of the more evolved, complex, delicate, & permanently rewarding human sensitivenesses over the cruder, simpler, less correlated, & less strictly human ones. A superior man has so keen an imagination—so keen & sensitive a consciousness of his location in time, space, & the social fabric—that his comfortable adjustment demands the existence of certain harmonies around him, & the preservation of a certain relationship betwixt his own programme & the activities & aspirations of those whose transmitted ideas & impulses have formed his unconscious standards & reference-points. This makes for a certain natural taste & thoughtfulness in conduct, since coarse carelessness & animal irresponsibility destroy all suggestion of the pattern-arrangements on which aesthetic adjustment is based. The high-grade man is delicate, considerate, "unselfish", & non-encroaching because to him such an exercise of respect for the whole social-traditional pattern symbolises the harmony or beauty essential to his personal comfort. Thus the process is *really* no less egocentric & "selfish" than any other human course. It is simply a mature, high-grade, & enlightened selfishness instead of the dull, brutish, disruptive selfishness of the low-grade organism whose comfort does not demand any pattern-adjustment. There is nothing high-flown, mystical, or religious about it. It is simply common sense—a sensitive man's way of getting maximum comfort & pleasure. He could not have so good a time if certain basic forbearances, generosities, delicacies, & rules of non-encroachment were not generally observed in the world; while to advocate their observance by others yet to ignore them himself would involve an element of inconsistency, insincerity, hypocrisy, & falsity so disruptive of the pattern-sense as to be absolutely intolerable. So much for the general principle. As for the details—of course, these are determined largely by the particular pattern-environment into which the individual happens to be born. Harmonious living is not necessarily the same for a Frenchman, an Englishman, & a Persian, nor yet the same for a Greek of the age of Pericles & for a Greek of today. Moreover, as you suggest, there is always a certain amount of dispute regarding the validity or actuality of any given detail as part of the effective, significant tradition-pattern of a certain time & place. But in spite of these variations, it is perfectly easy to differentiate betwixt the evolved living-programme of a high-grade, sensitive man whose nature demands the following of *some* pattern, & the sloppy, reckless, uncoördinated beast-writhing of the callous clod whose dull nature feels no backgrounds & recognises no harmonic relationships.

Now as to what constitutes a *decadent age*—I would say that such an age is one in which the members of the group concerned are sinking from a civilisation in which many human potentialities are advantageously utilised, to a cultural level which utilises fewer potentialities & imposes a crippled mental-aesthetic life by leaving the finest human sensitivenesses undeveloped & wasted. Whenever the traditional patterns of a group begin to break down without the immediate substitution of equally valid patterns, the trend is certainly one which may properly be called *decadence*. A growing lack of sensitive response to accustomed values means a definite decrease in the feeling of direction & meaning in existence; & this is of course a tremendous emotional impoverishment unless the declining system is at once replaced by some alternative value-system equally practicable to the given group. Such replacement is unfortunately very rare—history tending to shew that the break-up of a race's standards is generally followed by a long period of crude, low-grade, unsatisfying existence before any fresh system of high-grade, satisfying life can be evolved. Decadence is offensively manifest in two ways—in its impoverishment of mental-aesthetic life through the destruction of traditional intangibles; & in its challenge to the material welfare & even to the physical survival of the group as a group through the destruction of clan-pride & the fostering of a supine indifference to the safety & prestige of the governmental fabric. Whether or not decadence masks itself as high-sounding "principle", "enlightenment", "sophistication", & all that, its effect is the same—to impair the harmony & zest of life, & to imperil the welfare & existence of the group. There can be no doubt but that decadence—as manifest in an indifference to traditional perspectives, a relaxation of pattern-rhythms, & a lack of pride & concern for the history, strength, courage, safety, & existence of the national-racial fabrics involved—has been steadily increasing in the western world throughout the 20th century. This decadence probably springs from various causes—largely the atmosphere of *unsettledness* resulting from our suddenly broadened conception of the universe & from the new conditions created by intensive mechanisation—but its symptoms cannot be mistaken. Careful observation can do much to distinguish its manifestations from those externally similar by-products of restlessness & change which do not not [*sic*] involve a weary softening & letting-down. Thus the Russian bolsheviki are not *decadent* but merely *alien* & *primitive*. They are a new element risen from a mass too primitive to have participated in the old civilisation, & their attitude is the very reverse of the decadent attitude of indifference & scepticism. They did not kill any older culture of their own—for the real Russian culture was never theirs in any effective sense. They were like the external barbarians who overwhelmed the weakening Roman empire & slowly founded a new & different civilisation. On the other hand, many elements in our own western world are unmistakably decadent. Certain modernistic tendencies in the art clearly embody the sort of indifference to backgrounds which means a net impoverishment of mental & aesthetic life; whilst such social trends as historic indifference, general irresponsibility & criminality, unreasoning pacifism, & cloudy internationalism in general, are obviously direct blows against the material welfare & survival of the national fabrics which make possible the continued existence & free play of the various cultural streams. It is quite possible, incidentally, to distinguish betwixt the *primitive, crude evils* of former times, & the essentially *decadent* evils of the present. Against the former the instincts of society were always ranged, so that the crudenesses of life shewed a constant if irregular trend toward abatement. There was never any doubt of the value of an orderly life based on harmonic inheritances, & never any tendency to question the importance of group-survival & group-freedom. It is the decline in these basic imponderables—belief in the value of a continuously-patterned fabric of life, & pride in the strength, integrity, unbrokenness, liberty, & honourable survival of one's own group—which form *true decadence* & establish a steadily downward instead of upward cultural trend. Unfortunately, the 19th century seems to have formed the turning-point of western culture—the period after which zest & pride & acceptance & the will to expand began to be replaced by disillusionment, indifference, scepticism, rejection, & a softening leading to contraction. (Spengler's "Decline of the West" brings this out so clearly that (despite my disagreement with many phases of the Spenglerian conception of society) I could hardly do better than quote it verbatim. Indeed, when the translation appeared in 1926 it seemed like a specific confirmation of all my long-held assumptions.) But of course, it is sometimes hard to classify any given detail of life as decadent or otherwise. It takes thoughtful correlation to decide to what general stream of feeling it belongs. However, we can safely & sadly say that decadence is manifest in one form or another over nearly all the Western World. Certain areas like Italy, Germany, the Irish Free State, & (perhaps) Spain seem to present a visible resistance to the drift, either through a certain natural youthfulness of outlook & feeling, (Ireland, Germany) or through a determined national plan to build up a positive future & pull out of the morass of a former decadence (Italy, Spain). Outside the western world we see in Japan a nation still healthy & unbroken, & in Kemalist Turkey a fabric determined to survive even at a woefully high cultural cost. Just what the declining parts of the world will do, remains to be seen. It is not too late to hope that revivals of spirit may yet take place here & there—each in accordance with the particular national temper of the group concerned. I have my eye on Sir Oswald Moseley & his element of British fascists. They may yet help in rearousing a certain vitality in our slackening stream—& corresponding developments on this especial side of the Atlantic are likewise conceivable. I'm sure I wouldn't venture to prophesy the future even five years ahead—but at least I make it a settled policy not to discourage any national tendency, however crude, which seems to operate against the prevailing drift toward softness & disintegration. Hence my opposition to active anti-Nazism—which of course must not be construed as any endorsement of the details of the Hitler programme. Before quitting the subject of decadence, one ought mention certain effects which a declining & softening society has upon the *individual* . . . . that is, effects aside from a general letting down of traditional restraints & a general indifference to social harmony & inherited pattern-elements. Foremost of all, there is a sharp decline in the hardy masculine virtues which stem from a pride in strength, competence, & independence—virtues like honour, truthfulness, courage, firmness, loyalty, & so on. These decay because their bases—strength, competence, & independence—are no longer highly valued in a fluid & sceptical society. There is also an emphatic growth of childish self-centredness, self-indulgence, & self-pity—a transference of concern from the group & pattern (no longer valued) to the ego. Physically there is a tremendous regression toward sensuousness on the one hand & inertia on the other—a tremendous lapse, that is, from any programme which links the physical energies with values & objects & purposes belonging to the imaginative, delicately emotional, or cerebral realms. Earthiness reigns, eroticism (often in grotesquely perverted forms, owing to the growing contempt for norms of any kind) usurps a disproportionate place in life, physical & mental softness (dislike of exercise or of close, difficult thinking) gains ground, & stamina falls off so spectacularly that the shrinking from all forms of pain, injury, danger, & physical combat becomes a salient feature of the popular psychology. Amusements become passive (spectacles witnessed) instead of active (things participated in). At the same time the typically feminine reactions gain force among males. Men become vain & exhibitionistic, transferring their form of ego-assertion from displays of strength, courage, & skill to flauntings of personal adornments; & the tendency to tickle the ego through the gossiping derogation of others becomes very marked. Of course these are only a few of decadence's stigmata, but they are very typical. One encounters them constantly in individuals, & can likewise trace their effects in the trend of social, political, philosophic, & aesthetic movements. It is perhaps the ego-absorption which most potently influences modern art—substituting intensive, introspective, & over-subtle analysis of simple emotional reactions for well-proportioned & dramatically balanced vistas of collective life.

As for current reading—I don't even try to keep up with the procession! You certainly do absorb material at a great rate—or at least, at what seems to be a great rate as I look at it nowadays. M. R. James certainly is a first-class figure in his field. I think I appreciated him more during my recent re-reading than when I read him first in 1925. My favourite tale is "Count Magnus", with "The Treasure of Abbot Thomas" & "An Episode of Cathedral History" as second & third choices. "A View from a Hill" is darned good, though. Yes—James fell off toward the last, as most weird authors seem to do. Dunsany, Blackwood, & Machen all traversed the same curve. As to "The Hill of Dreams"—I must read it again. Very conceivably, some of the effects impressive at first glance might ring rather hollowly a second time.

I guess that Cincinnati editor was right in saying that newspaper work is not a very good preparation for a novel-writer. There are two sides to the question—for of course reporting gives one an insight into all sorts of departments of life—but in the long run I fancy that the newspaper's devotion to speed, brevity, & surface clearness, & its inculcation of an extremely bad style, form such drawbacks that the advantages are more than offset. The press directly discourages the minute, leisurely development, careful choice of significant detail, full presentation of nuances, sharp analysis of motives & emotions, impartial treatment of values, & rhythmical grace of style, which distinguish serious novel-writing from mere capable journalism. The atmosphere of newspaperdom, so far as I can judge, is one distinctly hostile to cultivated & sensitive personalities—& it likewise requires a sort of brassy pushingness which men of artistic potentialities are not likely to possess. Incidentally—harking back to our old discussion of whether one can compose realistic fiction without becoming an obnoxious Paul Pry[28]—here is a cutting from the *Writer's Digest* which Long has just sent me, & which suggests a middle course between young Derleth's undeniably offensive nosing & Long's own gentlemanly code of never encroaching on the personal field.

Have you looked up *The Fantasy Fan*, about which I told you, as a possible amateur outlet for such of your material as verges on the weird? Here's a circular of another new medium worth investigation—*Unusual Stories*. No pay as yet, but much encouragement. They'll give you a 10-year subscription (that's optimism in view of the average mortality among pulps!) for your first accepted contribution. You can see from the circular how many of the W T group are participating in this venture. If the magazine ever becomes remunerative, we're in on the ground floor. Incidentally—a man in the state of Washington has an idea of reprinting my "Colour Out of Space" as a separate booklet.

Thanks tremendously for the two issues of *Story*, which safely arrived, & which I have read through with a vast interest—my first intensive glimpse of contemporary fiction in a long while. There is certainly some solid material in these things, even though they may represent a slight overdoing of the current tendency toward confining the short story to narrow minutiae of character analysis & mood-delineation. It would be impossible to exaggerate the gulf which separates these sincere efforts from the suavely lifeless mechanical hokum which clutters up the purely commercial magazines. Your choice of tales seems to me pretty sensible, & I don't believe we could work up a controversy about any major point. As for "Rupture"[29]—of which you say you may have missed the point—my guess is that if you did miss it, it was because the formula is *excessively simple* . . . . . a very timeworn type which one wouldn't expect to see in a magazine as modern & presumably sophisticated as *Story*. This tale—unless *I've* missed something vital, is simply a slightly dressed-up version of the old sure-fire formula of the big blustering bozo who gets a jolt & comes out at the little end of the horn while his despised, insignificant-looking butt comes out ahead of everybody else. The formula owes its undying popularity, of course, to that sense of inferiority in the average person which causes him to identify himself with the under dog & exult in the lightning reversal which gives the under-dog a surprising triumph. Here we have the fullest use of the formula. One moment—big Red-Head on the top of the heap. Tough guy, expecting to get into the CCC on a walk & lord it over the others—especially damned wizened foreign shrimps like this modest, timid, quiet little frog-eater Francois Le Grange. Then—all of a sudden—big bozo kicked out as physically unsound, & despised little French-Canuck turns out to be a nail-hard veteran of the logging camps who not only gets by physically with flying colours but even gets a Corporal's berth with authority over others! Complete turn of the tables—the mighty laid low & the humble exalted! Old stuff—but always good for a loud hand from the gallery! "Death & Transfiguration"[30] interested me in its depiction of a New England scene & speech utterly unfamiliar to me despite my close knowledge of the neighbouring town of Portsmouth, N.H. These run-down "shanty-town" nuclei correspond to the decaying backwaters of the Catskills & some of the "poor white" belts of the South, but very little is known of them. I never saw such a district, although I understand there is one called "Scalloptown" down the west shore of Narragansett Bay near East Greenwich, about 16 miles from Providence. What astonishes me in this story is the *dialect*—which resembles nothing I ever heard in my life. It sounds theatrical & literary—like some old-world picture by Hardy or Synge or Yeats—& I can't seem to make it fit into old New England.

Novr. 22, 1933

God, what a document this is getting to be! Never mind—I'll try to let this be the final sheet! Enclosed is a Holland Society paper with an article of mine which may possibly interest you.[31] Talman edits this thing, & asked for something from me. Being rather an outsider where the Dutch tradition is concerned, the best I could do was to point out a few cases where this tradition touches my own. The thing that will cause the Holland Society's patrons & burghers to prick up their ears over their long pipes & schnapps at Rem Rapelje's tavern is the reference to their ancestors' hold on the Maine coast from 1674 to 1676—an episode which I find surprisingly few laymen, either Dutch or Yankee, know anything about. The reason for the obscurity of this incident is probably the fact that the region in question was then virtually a part of French Acadia—notwithstanding a British claim & an occupation by Plymouth traders from 1629 to 1635. Its events therefore tend to fall into the stream of Canadian rather than of U.S. history. Just the same, it ought to be meat for the old Knickerbockers who make up the H.S. I'll ask the ultimate return of this article if you don't mind—though there is not the least hurry. Another thing I'll enclose, subject to return, is a folder of the latest "Seeing Providence" [s]ervice. It'll [at least con]vey some idea of the local attraction[s.]

I've done a good deal of macab[re re]ading lately, in books lent me by a new correspondent in N Y who has a marvellous library. Montague Summers' studies are tremendously erudite & interesting despite their author's amusing credulousness (he believes in witches & vampires!), & some of the mediaeval books on witchcraft contain astonishing data.

Well—the cold weather's here at last, so that my outdoor programme is at an end. I had pretty good luck all through October, though, for September's rainy season gave place to a delightfully mild period of turning leaves. When it became too cold to sit around & write, I inaugurated a series of rural explorations which took me to some very isolated places—including many I had never seen before. My general plan was to take a coach out some travelled highway, & then to alight & strike out across some utterly wild stretch of countryside till I reached another coach-traversed highway along which I could return. In this way I came upon many astonishingly unspoiled sections; with the gambrel-roofed cottages, sprawling barns & byres, gnarled hillside orchards, towering elms, rocky, rolling hills, winding rutted roads bordered by brier-twined stone walls, brook-threaded wooded ravines, vistas of meadow & river, & glimpses of distant village spires through flaming autumn foliage which make up the traditional landscape of this ancient & unbroken civilisation. On one occasion I sought out for the first time a very ancient house built by a lineal ancestor of mine—Thomas Clement—in 1654. It has a huge, pilastered stone chimney on one end, & in the yard is a venerable well-sweep in active use. The whole place is in excellent condition after nearly 280 years of existence. The house sits on the edge of a dank, mystery-filled wooded ravine, & still has an excellent landscape environment despite the increasingly close approach of a rather squalid Italian suburb. It is inhabited by an ancient gentlewoman lineally descended from the Manton family which acquired it in 1680. My final walk took place around the spectral Sabbat Tide—Octr. 31, & Nov. 1 & 2. On these occasions I dug up still another district I had never before visited, though it is located on the city's very rim—Fruit Hill. This is developing as a rather high-grade suburb, but some parts are still rustic. At one point on the hill I caught a vista of breath-taking loveliness which included a twilight-bewitched descent of stone-walled pastures, a wooded hollow with gleams of sunset-litten river, dim violet hills against an orange-gold west, a steepled village in a northward valley, & over the rocky eastward ridge a great round Hunter's moon preparing to flood the plains with spectral light. Now, however, comes the long hibernation . . . . . possibly broken by a week's visit to Long next month. We had planned on an [ear]lier get-together; but his mother was l[ai]d up with a rather bad [ca]se of food-poisoning & is rather sl[ow in recov]ering. This [seems] to be a bad year for the [mot]hers & aunts of [the ga]ng. Besides M[rs.] Long's illness & my aunt's accident, there is now the painful ca[se] of Klarkash-Ton's mother, who spilled a hot teapot on her foot & has been in bed a month unable to walk! My aunt, by the way, is making great progress. All around the residential district with a cane, & has even been down town once. The house, free from the emergency accessories of illness, is now assuming a delectably homelike tone. More old family pictures hung, more old furniture dragged out of storage—the whole thing is really marvellously suggestive of the lost old home of years ago. The latest development is a rich-looking slab of yellowish Sienna marble from the old house, which we mean to put up as a console in the front hall under the mirror if we can ever find the gilt brackets that go with it. Colonial curtains & valences at the windows, & white birch logs (which we don't ignite, but keep for decorative effect) in the Georgian living-room fireplace promote a "Berkeley Square" effect which makes me feel more at home here than I have ever felt anywhere else. I hope to gawd I can rake up the cash to carry on here indefinitely—it'll be worse than pulling a tooth to break away!

[*In margin:*] The glamorous sunset view from my west [wind]ow—where I'm now sitting—is so lovely that it takes my mind off my work! Ancient roofs & colonial belfries, [ch]urch towers, a far-off steeple on a distant hill, & barren boughs against an orange sky!

Well—I trust you're getting reabsorbed into the Pittsburgh scene after your long Ohio sojourn. Hope the novel will duly progress, & that your intensive reading programme will suffer no further interruptions. Meanwhile let me apologise for the length & tediousness of this epistle. When an old man gets reminiscent, gawd help his auditors!

> Ever yr most obᵗ hᵇˡᵉ Servt

Ech-Pi-El

P.S. Last moment news. Wright has asked to see the Silver Key sequel again. Whether this means a reversal of his former rejection, time will tell. He takes the prize for capriciousness!

[P.P.S.] Still later—he *has* taken it for 140 bucks.

Notes

1. Helm C. Spink (1909–1970), printer and fellow amateur journalist.

2. "The Beast in the Cave" (1905) was set in Mammoth Cave.

3. It is not clear what specific work by Baltimore journalist H. L. Mencken (1880–1956) HPL is referring to. During his lifetime and after his death, Mencken was accused of being anti-Semitic. See Joseph Brainin's interview, "Is H. L. Mencken an Anti-Semite?" *Jewish Criterion* (11 April 1930): 10–11, 115.

4. HPL refers to the celebrated Austrian violin virtuoso Fritz Kreisler (1875–1962).

5. CAS, "The City of the Singing Flame" (*Wonder Stories,* July 1931).

6. Price wrote a version of a sequel to "The Silver Key" that he titled "The Lord of Illusion." It is included in *Tales of the Lovecraft Mythos,* ed. Robert M. Price (Minneapolis, MN: Fedogan & Bremer, 1992).

7. Hazel Heald typed "The Thing on the Doorstep" for HPL.

8. "Fishhead" by Irvin S. Cobb (1876–1944), a story about a fish-man hybrid, was first published in the *All-Story* (11 January 1913); HPL wrote a letter of comment about it, published in the 8 February 1913 issue. It probably influenced HPL's "The Shadow over Innsmouth." Frank Belknap Long's story "Death Waters" appeared in *WT* (December 1924).

9. Cobb's "The Unbroken Chain" (*Cosmopolitan,* September 1923; rpt. in Cobb's *On an Island That Cost $24.00* [New York: George H. Doran Co., 1926]), manifestly influenced HPL's "The Rats in the Walls" (1923). HPL erroneously refers to the beast as a hippopotamus. See n.10.

10. See "Supernatural Horror in Literature": "Later work of Mr. Cobb introduces an element of possible science, as in the tale of hereditary memory where a modern man with a negroid strain utters words in African jungle speech when run down by a train under visual and aural circumstances recalling the maiming of his black ancestor by a rhinoceros a century before" (71).

11. *The Private Life of Henry VIII* (United Artists, 1933); directed by Alexander Korda; starring Charles Laughton, Robert Donat, and Franklin Dyall. *Berkeley Square* (Fox Film Corp., 1933), directed by Frank Lloyd; starring Leslie Howard, Heather Angel, and Valerie Taylor. Based on the play by John L. Balderston. *Ann Vickers* (RKO Radio Pictures, 1933), directed by John Cromwell; starring Irene Dunn, Walter Huston, and Conrad Nagel. Based on the novel by Sinclair Lewis.

12. English dandies of the 18th century who affected Continental mannerisms, clothes (as in the song "Yankee Doodle").

13. Franklin C. Clark (1847–1915).

14. Winfield Scott Lovecraft died on 19 July 1898, Rhoby Phillips on 26 January 1896.

15. "Adams Synchronological Chart or Map of History" (Cincinnati: Strobridge & Company, 1871), prepared by Presbyterian missionary Sebastian C. Adams (1825–1898). Originally published as "Chronological Chart of Ancient, Modern and Biblical History," it is a synchronological wallchart and timeline that depicts the history of mankind from 4000 BCE, the biblical beginning of man, to modern times. The timeline is twenty-three feet long.

16. Horatio Alger (1832–1899, American) wrote juvenile novels. G. A. Henty (1832–1902, British) wrote adventure novels. Nick Carter was a fictional character, first appearing as a dime novel private detective in 1886 and then in various other formats, such as the *Nick Carter Detective Magazine.*

17. Robert Louis Stevenson, "Sing Me a Song of a Lad That Is Gone," line 2 etc.

18. Edward S. Ellis (1840–1916) was the author of the popular *Deerfoot* series for boys. Kirk Munroe (1850–1930) was an American writer and conservationist, the first editor of *Harper's Young People* magazine, and author of numerous adventure novels.

19. *Ah, Wilderness!,* a play by Eugene O'Neill, taking place on the Fourth of July 1906. It premiered on 2 October 1933.

20. *Great Lady Dedlock* (1924) was a play by Paul Kester based on Dickens's *Bleak House.* Its Chicago production was produced by and starred celebrated stage actress Margaret Anglin. *White Cargo* (1923) was a play by Leon Gordon; it was filmed in 1942.

21. I.e., "on literary gaps."

22. A novel by Ben Hecht.

23. Sterling Leonard and Harold Y. Moffett, ed., *Junior Literature* (New York: Macmillan, 1930; 2 vols.). Maurice W. Moe was an assistant editor. Book Two (1930) contained an extract from HPL's "Observations on Several Parts of America" (1928), titled "Sleepy Hollow To-day" (pp. 545–46).

24. *The Passion of Joan of Arc* (Gaumont, 1928; French), directed by Carl Theodor Dreyer; starring Maria Falconetti, Eugene Silvain, and André Berley.

25. André Dunoyer de Segonzac (1884–1974), French painter. He made several paintings of various scenes in the Provençal town of St. Tropez.

26. "Sarah Tubb and the Heavenly Visitors" (1933), a painting by British painter Sir Stanley Spencer (1891–1959). "Harlequin" may refer to "Harlequin's Carnival" (1924–25) by Spanish painter Joan Miró (1893–1983).

27. On 16 November 1933, FDR officially recognized the Soviet Union, sixteen years after the US broke off diplomatic relations with the country.

28. Paul Pry was a meddlesome fellow consumed with curiosity in the play *Paul Pry* (1825), a farcical comedy by British playwright John Poole (1786–1872).

29. Seymour D. Buck, "Rupture," *Story* 3, No. 16 (November 1933): 21–27

30. Alan Marshall, "Death and Transfiguration," *Story* 3, No. 15 (October 1933): 84–96.

31. "Some Dutch Footprints in New England."

1934

[44]   [ALS]

66 College St.,
Providence, R.I.
Feby. 4, 1934.

Dear Jehvish-Êi:—

Your generous shipment duly arrived, & I greatly enjoyed
both the epistle & the *Story* material. I am returning the latter—with utmost
thanks & appreciation—under separate cover by parcel post.

The late autumn & winter have been slightly diversified by enjoyable in-
terludes. Thanksgiving Day I did something I have been wanting to do for
years—ate my Thanksgiving dinner on the soil of ancient Plymouth itself,
where the whole thing started 312 years ago. The day was phenomenally
warm—68° in the afternoon—& I explored the old town much as I would
have in summer. An enormous amount of quaint 17th & 18th century material
still remains, & some of it has been restored to its original state by careful antiquarian craftsmanship. I saw the sunset from brooding Burial Hill, & after
dark I watched the great round moon turn the harbour to a sheet of silver
flame. All told, it was a remarkable outing for the 30th of November.

Christmas marked the start of a pleasant 15-day visit to Long in N.Y. After a festive home Yule I took a midnight coach & enjoyed a duplicate Yule at
Belknap's. During the days that followed I saw all the old gang—Loveman,
Morton, Talman, Kirk, Leeds, Kleiner, Wandrei, &c—& met several new personalities, including Wandrei's younger brother Howard (this answers your
question anent relationship), a weird pictorial artist of almost startling genius
& maturity; Desmond Hall, editor of *Astounding Stories;* T. Everett Harré, anthologist of "Beware After Dark" (which included my Cthulhu); & A. Merritt,
the gifted author of "The Moon Pool" & other weird masterpieces. It gave
me quite a kick to meet Merritt & learn that he likes my tales—for I have
admired his peculiarly fancy-stirring work for 15 years. I saw the old year out
at Loveman's, & he quite overwhelmed me by presenting me with objects for
my "museum"—notably a bitumen-coated wooden ushabti from the Egypt
of 4000 years ago, & a small stone eikon from Central America—of early Mayan workmanship. Naturally, I visited my favourite museums—seeing among
other things the important new Assyrian, Etruscan, & Greek material at the
Metropolitan. I picked up two or three book bargains, chief among which
was the late Arthur Weigall's "Wanderings in Roman Britain"—which I had
wanted for years. But perhaps my greatest Manhattan achievement was the
acquisition of *a fountain pen which will actually write!* As is usual when I am in a

city with a Waterman central office (i.e., Boston or N.Y.), I pestered that institution with requests for point exchanges & feed adjustments . . . . . making three calls, & trying out an infinity of points. At last I got an almost ideal point, hence concentrated on the question of an ultra-free feed. Since the clerks gave contradictory accounts of the possibilities of feed-adjustments, I insisted on seeing the chief repair man in person—& the ultimate result is the best fountain pen I've had since 1923. It glides along smoothly & without pressure (even on this wretched bargain paper) at my speed—the feed being about as free as it can be without actually dripping ink. Indeed—so ideal is the thing, that the more or less adequate Parker of recent months seems difficult in comparison.

All that you say of Proust seems eminently just to me in the light of the two volumes I have read—"Swann's Way" & "Within a Budding Grove". Even from those two I would not hesitate to place Proust at the head of 20th century writers. It is evident, however, that I have missed the fullest merits of the author; since I have not followed the long, slow unfolding far enough to watch the real development of the characters. I envy you—& must eventually emulate—your perusal of the complete Proustian cycle.

What you say of my epistles—& of the potential essays or articles imbedded in some of them—pleases & flatters me extremely. I dare say that many of my expository or controversial harangues (as well as those of the correspondents at the other end) are equivalent to essays in length & subject matter—although they have the fatal defects of hasty thought & careless composition. They are, after all, only the random thoughts of a rank layman—not the well-considered utterances of a qualified student of the subjects involved. I used to write articles of all sorts, but in my latter years I have developed a marked distaste for inadequate & ill-informed pamphleteering. Cracker-barrel debating is all well enough for private correspondence—where all hands are laymen—but it makes me rather tired to see a half-baked ordinary guy shooting off his mouth in public on subjects which none but the special student can rightly handle. However—once in a very long while I copy certain definite arguments or expositions from letters I have just written; circulating the copy among other correspondents interested in the same thing or (though less often than 10 or 20 years ago) having it printed in one of the small papers of the 'amateur journalistic' circle. In such a case I depersonalise the text to some extent—supplying a proper opening & conclusion of the standard essay type. As a typical illustration of this I think I'll enclose an "article" on the American political situation which I copied last November from a letter to a more or less plutocratic correspondent in Chicago—a rather important official in the (ex-Insull) Commonwealth Edison Co. there.[1] This chap—Ernest A. Edkins—is a splendidly witty & civilised character with fine aesthetic appreciations; but he cannot quite escape the visionless & conventional psychology of the "business man"—hence is a bitter &

apprehensive opponent of the present administration. He & I had been desul-
torily arguing for some time, but at last I decided to undermine his position in
the most thorough way; hence wrote him an enormous letter in an effort to
get down to the very roots of the matter. When I had finished, it occurred to
me that I'd like to present the same text to many other friends & correspondents—not only reactionaries like Edkins, but wild-eyed bolsheviki like Long,
who lean just absurdly in the opposite direction. Hence I typed an imperson-
alised version of the crucial argument in my usual way, & have been letting it
go the rounds ever since. Just now it is here again, & believe I'll enclose it to
you as a sample of my latter-day "essay-writing". You may or may not agree
with the politics—I am for a fascism which includes as much socialisation as
may be found necessary for a proper spreading of resources—but at any rate
you will have a sample of the way an "article" can be made from a letter.
Please return this item.

As for the matter of childhood recollections—of course, such can be
made very interesting if one knows how; though there is always a feeling of
deficient significance unless the childhood in question be the preface to a
fruitful & important adulthood. When the high-flown imaginings of the child
peter out in a manhood of mediocrity & non-achievement like mine, there is
an ever-present sense of mocking anticlimax which makes formal exploitation
subtly ridiculous & out of place. It is all very well for a dull old man to recall
his boyhood privately & informally—in correspondence or conversation with
friends—but to publish the same material as a conscious literary attempt is
quite another matter. Of course, some literary merit might possibly be present—but the sense of anticlimax would always be a vitiating element. Regarding the extent to which recent writers have exploited or neglected the
matter of correlation with the time-stream—I was not thinking of Proust,
since I tend to group him within the main tradition rather than among the
moderns. Probably no writer has more magnificently captured the sense of
time than Proust—there are parts of "Swann's Way" which shew a marvellous identification of the adult with the child. Certainly, I must try to continue
my Proustian reading before long . . . . . what is the third book of the series—
"Cities of the Plain"? I can comprehend Proust's sensations at finding his
friends aged after a long absence from them. Only last week my best friend of
the early 1900's—Chester Pierce Munroe—turned up in Providence after
long years of residence in the South. I had not set eyes on him since 1916 or
so, & had seen very little of him since 1912 or 1913. Good god! Was this
iron-grey-headed, slightly paunchy middle-aged man (he's one year my senior)
the little Chet Monroe of 1902 & 1903? I knew, of course, that I had changed
just as much (though I *did* avoid the paunch through my 1925 reducing!)—yet
the sudden confrontation with this image, so different from the established
Chester-Munroe-image of my subconscious mind, was none the less a shock.
Only the *voice* was familiar. That, indeed, was the same as when it emerged

from the changing process around 1905 or '06. The fact is, it has probably aged far *less* than the average voice—for how many men of 44 talk *exactly* as they did in their middle 'teens? Chester's memories of boyhood are very keen, & he could name a very large number of the children in our Slater Ave. class photograph of 1903—including those (a numerical majority) whom he had never seen since then. It is probably true that the period from 7 to 14 produces more lasting impressions than any other. We can, in later life, generally return to childhood more readily than to young manhood. This is one reason why the memories of the very aged usually centre largely around the 10-year-old period—another reason being that the mental structure has in old age generally suffered a letdown to about the 10-year-old level of intellection & emotional sympathy, so that a man of 90 can often understand himself better at 10 than at 20 or 30 or 40. Differences in individual rates of aging—& differences in separate *phases* of aging (hair, face, voice, figure, gestures, intellect, emotions, &c)—are often very marked, & furnish a highly interesting study. I know men of my own age who could easily pass for sons of mine—& others who look as though they might be my father. It is all a matter of glands—of which time is only a rough measure.

Your plot—"Time Service, Inc."—offers fascinating possibilities to anyone at all skilled in the domain of "scientifiction". Why not work it up yourself some time—unless your tastes have totally moved way from the given field? I doubt if I could handle a theme like this successfully—too scientific & primarily intellectual—too large a canvas & too many human reactions—but I'll certainly offer it (with your compliments) successively to Klarkash-Ton & Melmoth the Wandrei.

I was greatly interested in your childhood memories, & hope you will some time work them into a novel of retrospective cast. It is curious how juvenile reading has changed—& ironic to reflect that of the books of my period only the very poorest (The Rover Boys' series) have survived. I suppose this series has been endlessly continued & brought down to date—so that the grandsons of the original Rover Boys are now parallelling their adventures on aëroplanes & submarines & rocket space-ships! Of the newer books you mention I have heard only of the Tom Swift series—rather poor junk according to a friend of mine who deplores his young hopeful's addiction to it.[2] Your early glasses remind me of myself—I wore them at 7, though at many later periods I tried leaving them off, so that today I wear them only for middle-distance vision (theatre, cinema, illustrated lectures, &c.) The ghost stories you heard from other children form an interesting item. I never heard *oral* weird tales except from my grandfather—who, observing my tastes in reading, used to devise all sorts of impromptu original yarns about black woods, unfathomed caves, winged horrors (like the "night-gaunts" of my dreams, about which I used to tell him), old witches with sinister cauldrons, & "deep, low, moaning sounds". He obviously drew most of his imagery from the early

Gothic romances—Radcliffe, Lewis, Maturin, &c.—which he seemed to like better than Poe or other later fantaisistes. He was the only other person I knew—young or old—who cared for macabre & horrific fiction.

My first memories are of the summer of 1892—just before my second birthday. We were then vacationing in Dudley, Mass:, & I recall the house with its frightful attic water-tank & my rocking-horses at the head of the stairs. I recall also the plank walks laid to facilitate walking in rainy weather—& a wooded ravine, & a boy with a small rifle who let me pull the trigger while my mother held me. At that period my father was alive & in business in Boston, so that our residences were around the Boston suburbs—Dorchester & Auburndale. In the latter place we stayed with my mother's friend, the rather famous poetess Louise Imogen Guiney, pending the construction of a house of our own. That house was never built—for my father was fatally stricken in April 1893, & my mother & I moved back to the old maternal Providence home where I was born. My first *clear & connected* memories centre in Auburndale—the shady streets, the bridge over the 4-tracked B.&.A.R.R. with the business section beyond, the Guiney home in Vista Ave., the poetess's great St. Bernard dogs, the verse-reciting sessions at which I was made to stand on a table & spout Mother Goose & other infantile classics, the sunsets beyond the trees—& so on. I remembered the place so well that [I] walked straight to the house from the station when I revisited it in 1908. I can just remember my father—an immaculate figure in black coat & vest & grey striped trousers. I had a childish habit of slapping him on the knees & shouting "Papa, you look just like a young man!" I don't know where I picked that phrase up; but I was vain & self-conscious, & given to repeating things which I saw tickled my elders. I was highly nervous—as restless & fidgety as you were—& distinctly liked to "shew off." This latter tendency—& the vanity & self-consciousness behind it—later succumbed to good advice & the better perspective of life imparted by reading, though its disappearance was slow & gradual. I first saw a play at the age of 6. Later, when the cinema appeared as a separate institution (it had been part of Keith vaudeville since 1898 or 1899), I attended it often with other fellows, but never took it seriously. By the time of the first cinema shows (March, 1906, in Providence) I knew too much of literature & drama not to recognise the utter & unrelieved hokum of the moving picture. Still, I attended them—in the same spirit that I had read Nick Carter, Old King Brady, & Frank Reade in nickel-novel form. Escape—relaxation. It was not till later that I got fed up & no longer enjoyed such mentally juvenile performances. The earliest "stars" I remember (their names weren't given till about '07 or '08) are Maurice Costello, Henry Walthall, Florence Turner, Hobart Bosworth, &c . . . . I recall many faces, too, without the corresponding names. I think the subsequently famous Mary Pickford didn't appear till '08 or '09. Of *stage* stars I saw most of the celebrated figures of the late '90's and early 1900's, though I most unfortunately missed Sir Henry Irving. In the matter of the justly celebrated "facts of life" I didn't wait for oral information, but exhausted the entire subject in the medical section of the family library (to which I had access, although I wasn't especially loquacious about this side of my reading) when I was 8 years old—through Quain's Anatomy (fully illustrated & diagrammed), Dunglinson's Physiology, &c. &c. This was because of curiosity & perplexity concerning the strange reticences & embarrassments of adult speech, & the oddly inexplicable allusions & situations in standard literature. The result was the very opposite of what parents generally fear—for instead of giving me an abnormal & precocious interest in sex (as *unsatisfied* curiosity might have done), it virtually killed my interest in the subject. The whole matter was reduced to prosaic mechanism—a mechanism which I rather despised or at least thought non-glamourous because of its purely animal nature & separation from such things as intellect & beauty— & all the drama was taken out of it. When the kids talked or acted dirtily I could have told them more than they tried to tell me—although (such was the state of Victorian formal medicine) my knowledge was restricted wholly to *normal* sex. I was middle-aged & married before I ever knew that there was such a thing as *instinctive* homosexuality—though I suppose there must be dozens of Haldeman-Julius booklets about the matter now. I talked as toughly as anybody else, since I didn't want to be a sissy; but my real ideals of life always inclined toward the ascetic. I didn't slop over in youthful romance, since I didn't believe—& still don't—in the existence of sentimental "love" as a definite, powerful, or persistent human emotion. I have always regarded marriage as composed of friendly regard, mental congeniality, social foresight, & practical advantage; to which *at first* the element of biological eroticism is added. Later the element of familiar affection & family loyalty develops—if the experiment happens to "take", as a few seem to do. But my idea of life has always been to depend on the animal & emotional sides—essentially capricious, mutable, & soon exhausted—as little as possible; choosing rather that abstract & contemplative side which involves the independent & permanent elements of reason & imagination. With me, the hardest emotion to bring under the control of reason was hatred—as expressed in berserk rages & general pugnacity. I had some fairly rough fights (from which I would not retreat, but in which I almost always got the worst except when I managed to frighten my foe through a dramatically murderous expression & voice) till I was 16 or 17—but as I grew up my recognition of the deterministic automatism of the whole cosmos, & the ridiculous insignificance & futility of all human actions, gave me an entirely new perspective. I could no longer see anything *personal* or *responsible* in anything that anybody did, & began to look on all mankind as impersonally as one looks on a cage full of monkeys in a zoo. This had the effect of almost deleting the emotion of anger from my personality, & of giving me a philosophic calm I had never possessed before. Today I am extremely tranquil—although of course, as a matter of aesthetics,

I take no actual encroachments from anybody. It is now much easier for me to *despise* or *laugh at* a person or thing than to *hate* him or it. When I fight (it's years since I've had any physical set-to) it is not from berserk rage, but simply from an English gentleman's instinctive need of personal inviolateness, non-encroachment, & satisfied honour. I pick quarrels with no one—but the Nordic's only possible reply to a real affront is to tell the affronter to go to hell. My first acute realisation of *time* was when I saw newspapers bearing the heavily-inked date-line TUESDAY, JANUARY 1, 1895. *1895!!* To me the symbol *1894* had represented an eternity—the eternity of *the present* as distinguished from such things as 1066 or 1492 or 1642 or 1776—& the idea of personally outliving that eternity was absorbingly impressive to me, even though I had fully realised, in an abstract way, that I would do so . . . . that I had been born in 1890 & would probably (in view of the average death-ages of near kinsfolk) live till about 1960. I shall never forget the sensation I derived from the idea of *moving through time* (if forward, why not backward?) which that '95 date-line gave me. But possibly I mentioned this in my previous letter. The one time that I seriously thought of suicide was in & after 1904, when my grandfather died in the midst of business tangles (he was president of a land & irrigation corporation exploiting the Snake River in Idaho, & the total destruction of the dam on which everything depended had caused a frightful situation) & left us all relatively poor. I was (being predominantly geographical-minded) tremendously attached to the old home at 454 Angell St. (now housing 12 physicians' offices—I walk by it still as often as I can) with the grounds & fountain, & stable, but this now had to go . . . . indeed, there had been drastic economies for 5 years before that. My mother & I moved into a 5-room-&-attic flat two squares farther east (598 Angell St., where I dwelt till 1924), & for the first time I knew what a congested, servant-less home—with another family in the same house—was. There was a vacant lot next door (although even that was later built up—during my adulthood), which I promptly exploited as a landscape garden & adorned with a village of piano-box houses, but even that failed to assuage my nostalgia. I felt that I had lost my entire adjustment to the cosmos—for what indeed was HPL without the remembered rooms & hallways & hangings & staircases & statuary & paintings (now—after 30 years of storage—my aunt & I *again* have one of the statues & several of the large paintings, since by a miracle the rooms & hallway of 66 College can accomodate them) & yard & walks & cherry-trees & fountain & ivy-grown arch & stable & gardens & all the rest? How could an old man of 14 (& I surely felt that way!) readjust his existence to a skimpy flat & new household programme & inferior outdoor setting in which almost nothing familiar remained? It seemed like a damned futile business to keep on living. No more tutors—high-school next September which would probably be a devilish bore, since one couldn't be as free & easy in high-school as one had been during brief snatches at the neighbourly Slater Ave. school . . . . . .

oh, hell! Why not slough off consciousness altogether? The whole life of man & of the planet was a mere cosmic second—so I couldn't be missing much. The *method* was the only trouble. I didn't like messy exits, & dignified ones were hard to find. Really good poisons were hard to get—those in my chemical laboratory (I reëstablished this institution in the basement of the new place) were crude & painful. Bullets were spattery & unreliable. Hanging was ignominious. Daggers were messy unless one could arrange to open a wrist-vein in a bowl of warm water—& even that had its drawbacks despite good Roman precedent. Falls from a cliff were positively vulgar in view of the probable state of the remains. Well—what tempted me most was the warm, shallow, reed-grown Barrington River down the east shore of the bay. I used to go there on my bicycle & look speculatively at it. (That summer I was always on my bicycle—wishing to be away from home as much as possible, since my abode reminded me of the home I had lost.) How easy it would be to wade out among the rushes & lie face down in the warm water till oblivion came. There would be a certain gurgling or choking unpleasantness at first—but it would soon be over. Then the long, peaceful night of non-existence . . . . what I had enjoyed from the mythical start of eternity till the 20th of August, 1890. More & more I looked at the river on drowsy, sun-golden summer afternoons. I liked to think of the beauty of sun & blue river & green shore & distant white steeple as enfolding me at the last—it would be as if the element of mystical cosmic beauty were dissolving me. And yet certain elements—notably scientific curiosity & a sense of world drama—held me back. Much in the universe baffled me, yet I knew I could pry the answers out of books if I lived & studied longer. Geology, for example. Just *how* did these ancient sediments & stratifications get crystallised & upheaved into granite peaks? Geography—just *what* would Scott & Shackleton & Borchgrevingk find in the great white antarctic or their next expeditions . . . . . which I could—if I wished—live to see described? And as to history—as I contemplated an exit without further knowledge I became un[com]fortably conscious of what I didn't know. Tantalising gaps existed everywhere. When did people stop speaking Latin & begin to talk Italian & Spanish & French? What on earth ever happened in the black Middle Ages in those parts of the world other than Britain & France (whose story I knew)? What of the vast gulfs of space outside all familiar lands—desert reaches hinted of by Sir John Mandeville & Marco Polo . . . . Tartary, Thibet . . . . . . What of unknown Africa? I knew that many things which were mysteries to me were not such to others. I had not resented my lack of a solution as long as I expected to know *some day*—but now that the idea of *never knowing* presented itself, the circumstance of frustrated curiosity became galling to me. Mathematics, too. Could a gentleman properly die without having demonstrated on paper why the square of the hypotenuse of a right triangle is equal to the sum of the squares of the other two sides? So in the end I decided to postpone my exit till the following summer. I would do a little curiosity-satisfying at first; filling certain gaps of scientific & historical knowledge, & attaining a greater sense of *completeness* before merging with the infinite blackness. Especially would I solve that always-teasing question of how & when "Romans" named *Fabius Anicius* became "Italians" named *Fabio Anizio*. Well—that fall I found high-school a delight & stimulus instead of a bore, & the next spring I resumed publication of the *R.I. Journal of Astronomy,* which I had allowed to lapse.[3] Possibly I would wait till '06 before making my exit . . . . . one could drown in '06 just as well as in '05 or '04! But *new* questions demanding answers were always springing up. First-year *physics* opened problems connected with the nature of visible phenomena & the operation of the universe which my earlier chemistry & astronomy had not even suggested; was it possible that educated men knew things about the basic structure of the cosmos which invalidated all my confidently-held concepts? And god! what a surprise *history* was proving! The whole pageantry of the *Byzantine Empire,* & its hostile connexion with that gorgeous Islam which my early Arabian Nights & my later astronomical studies (cf. terms & names like *azimuth, zenith, Aldebaran, almucantar, nadir,* Deneb, &c.) had made close to me, swept unheralded on my sight—& for the first time I heard of the lost Minoan culture which Sir Arthur Evans was even then busily digging up in Crete. Assyria & Babylonia, too, stood out with greater impressiveness than ever before—& I heard at last of the eternal query of *Easter Island.* What a world! Why, good god, a man might keep busy forever, even in an uncongenial environment, learning new things . . . . pleasantly busy, too, for each new point of satisfied curiosity gave a hell of a kick. Then there was the kick of writing out a mood on paper so that it could be recaptured . . . . I had done some experimenting in fictional structure, & achieved a new level of results with "The Beast in the Cave" (ineffably pompous and Johnsonese—I still have it), which I wrote in April '05. Could it be possible that a poor man without servants or a large house & grounds might get a greater satisfaction from remaining alive & studying & writing than from slipping back to primal nescience & molecular dispersal? The matter was worth considering—at least, the end could go over till '06 . . . . or very possibly, '07. About then I had a nervous breakdown (winter '05–'06) & had to stay out of school for months, & my lack of energy stopped my even thinking about anything. Then the *Providence Tribune* was founded, & I learned that I had a good chance of breaking into *print* at last . . . . contributing monthly astronomical articles just like Prof. Upton's in the *Journal & Bulletin.*[4] One *couldn't* miss a chance like that! Let suicide wait! And the articles landed, & I also landed others with a rural weekly[5] . . . . (this was the "Ah, Wilderness" year of '06 . . . when the Whippoorwill sang . . . .) . . . . & before long I was too busy studying & writing to make any especial plans, lethal or otherwise, for the future. So I've let matters slide for thirty years . . . . although I still intend to bump myself off when I get too broke to live on my present reduced scale. But so great is the pleasure of satisfied scientific curiosity & aesthetic experience, that I think a person of tastes like mine is better off (at least slightly) alive than dead as long as he can get his hands on ten bucks a week. That sum will decently house a frugal man & his books & more important pictures & furniture & miscellany—if he can virtually eliminate replacements (of my 5 suits 3 date from 1925, one from 1928, & the palm beach was given to me!) cut down his food bill to about $2.50 per week (I do), & do a good part of his own laundry (as I also do). But when I have to sacrifice books & family possessions I shall complete the postponed process of 1904. No use at all in dragging along under *too* inappropriate circumstances. Such, then, is the history of my own adventures toward self-destruction! As for you—I guess it's just as well that you didn't walk out on the world during the Peabody period. It isn't well to give too many damns about what people think of one. The regard & opinions of others never meant very much to me . . . . since (as I said once before) I've always a subconscious feeling that everything since the 18th century is unreal & illusory—a sort of grotesque nightmare or caricature. People seem to me more or less like ironic shadows or phantoms—as if I could make them (together with all their modern houses & inventions & perspectives) dissolve into thin aether by merely pinching myself awake & shouting at them, "Why, damn ye, you're not even born, & won't be born for a century & a half! God Save the King, & his Colony of Rhode-Island & Providence-Plantations!" Incidentally—the terrific nightmares of my infancy (peopled with black-winged "night-gaunts") probably had something to do with my feeling that I could dismiss all the modern world & its denizens by simply waking myself. In those nightmares I often knew that I was dreaming & strove in every possible way to struggle awake— hence the mental pattern of throwing off a distasteful environment by waking out of it. I still have some tremendously odd dreams—some of which I know to be such. Only last week I had a very curious one about the decay & ruin of the city. I tried to wake, but when I had come out of the dream I felt that I *was not really awake even then.* Something was wrong, even though a bright morning sun was shining on the bed from an east window. Then I realised. *There ought not to be any east window* . . . . . I was in my old room at 598 Angell St., which I haven't inhabited for ten years! But how could I wake up? After all, *was* I asleep? Was it not possible that everything since early in 1924 was a dream? That I had never left 598—never gone to Brooklyn & Barnes St. & College St. . . . ? But no! Here was the sun *where it hadn't been since 1912 or 1913* . . . . for a house had been built against my windows. I *knew* that I couldn't swear I had ever lived away from 598, but I knew that my eastern sunlight had been cut off by a new house. And yet, there it blazed! Clearly, I was asleep . . . . asleep, & on that unstable plane where anything might happen. Into what vortex of nightmare might I not be pitched without warning at any moment? But how could I escape? Pinching seemed to do no good. And even if I did have another awakening, how could I know that the *second* one would be final? At last, by a strong mental effort, I made the sunlit room dissolve around me, & emerged into a restful twilight. I stretched in relief . . . . . *& then saw that I was still at 598.* My windows were shadowed this time, but the conviction that I no longer lived at 598 was stronger. The chances were about 8 to 2, it seemed to me, that I was still asleep. I shook myself, lifted myself on my elbow, & tried in every way to push myself through another layer of dream. No use. At last a current of cold blackness swept down from somewhere, & I was caught up in a vortex which dissolved all the visible world. Everything melted to chaos, & I soared through endless night against my will. Then hazy outlines began to form—the small panes of an old-fashioned window—daylight—*I was at 66 College St.!* But was I awake? Here was the sun shining in from the south, & I was in the house I ought to be in . . . . *but I could not be sure yet.* There was an odd aura of doubt which grew & grew—& at last everything dissolved again. No vortex this time, but just a diffusive greyness. And then the outlines of the small-paned window again—this time with only the College St. arc light at the mouth of the court behind it. I shook myself once more, & speculated as to my degree of awakeness. It seemed very doubtful. Still, I might as well test my condition. I rose & turned on the light. 4 a.m. I raised the curtain & looked at the world outside. I went out into the library & to the bathroom, & returned to bed. Still devilish sleepy. Soon I was dreaming of my old home at 454 Angell St. I definitely waked around 8 a.m.—*but do not yet know whether I was really awake & up at 4 o'clock.*

What you say of the restoration of the time-sense & of the depiction of collective life in recent fiction interests me greatly, & makes me wish I might read some of the authors mentioned. I have, of course, heard of all of them—yet have been too busy with other lines to tackle any of their products. Jules Romain sounds like a figure of the highest importance—I must look him up.[6]

Too bad so much of the first "Posturings" MS. had to be destroyed—but it's all part of your literary development. Nothing is really lost. Glad you're assembling ideas in a note book, & hope the second novel will be successful when you get around to it. As for contests—of course you realise what strong competition you'll have, so that an absence of results won't disappoint you. All right to try—but with a crowded field & only one prize, each entrant's chances can hardly be very impressive. Glad you have some of the newer versions of "Posturings" written. This time I trust the style is somewhat simpler—remember what I did to the small extract you sent me to look over.

As for that alleged W.T. announcement concerning my work—just a false alarm![7] Wright thought that the Knopf deal was going through, hence issued this premature & highly embarrassing bulletin . . . . which I've been busy deflating ever since. Damn his optimism! Silver Key sequel will appear in the July W.T.—& gawd knows when I'll see the cash for it. You ought to get hold of Lloyd's "Etidorhpa"—I'd give a good deal for a copy myself. And

I'd give still more to see the Mammoth cave. If ever I go to Natchez & New Orleans again, I certainly must behold this nighted abyss—about which I have dreamed all my life, & which formed the theme of my 1905 story "The Beast in the Cave."

Have had a few more periodical-room sessions, though I can't enjoy a magazine in the library as I can at home. I must look up some of the items you mention—my surveys so far having been rather limited in scope. Yes—I agree that the poor old *Atlantic* is getting (or remaining) painfully washed-out & flabby. I haven't looked at the *Nation* or *New Republic* or *Mercury* in ages.

I perused your cinematic notes with usual interest. During my visit to Long I was dragged to the cinema several times, but the only item worth remembering was a comedy called "Three-Cornered Moon"[8]—a satire on pseudo-aesthetes. At home—& on my own initiative—I saw "Berkeley Square" again . . . incidentally beholding as a companion film the not-half-bad "Wild Boys of the Road" which you mention. Also went to see "The Invisible Man". Surprisingly good—might easily have been absurd, yet succeeded in being genuinely sinister. Since receiving your letter I have witnessed "The World Changes"[9]—a fine piece of pageantry, though incredibly naive as a drama, & not even rudimentarily comparable to "Cavalcade". I liked the pioneer period & the momentarily glimpsed horse-car. Also—the 1880-period & 1893 interiors fascinated me, since they were exactly like the houses I knew in my first conscious days. That parlour where the funeral was held might have been taken out of 454 Angell St. The 1904 scenes were good—costumes accurate, but one detail of grooming wrong. Young sports did *not* grow those little bits of side-whisker seen on the sons as early as '04. That was a fad lasting from '06 or '07 to '10 or so. In '04 the clean shave was universal among everybody under 30. I noted what you say concerning the gifted stars of "Henry VIII" & "Berkeley Square." If Leslie Howard was in that "Outward Bound" performance of 1924 I certainly must have seen him then. The years seem to have used him kindly since that period. By the way—when I spoke of his accent I did not mean that I had any trouble in *understanding* him. Indeed, no British accent ever gives me trouble, for I have heard lecturers & others from the Mother Land all my life. I merely note a certain difference from Providence speech in some cases. I noticed it especially in Howard because he was supposed to be an American. In Laughton I certainly did not seem to notice it to any such degree—but perhaps that was merely a result of my inattention. I shall probably see "Little Women"[10] sooner or later—though the book bored me to death 35 years ago, & the period is one I abominate. In all the times I've been to Concord (a marvellous repository of Colonial reliques) I've never visited the Alcott house—which is open as a public museum. Haven't yet seen "The Emperor Jones"—it was here while I was in N.Y. & hasn't returned so far. I shall go when it comes. Sorry you were disappointed. The original play gave me a great kick in 1922 or '23—with a real buck nigger named Charles Gilpin (now dead) in the leading role. Glad you've seen "Berkeley Square" at last. Talman & Long, who saw the play, say, that the cinema version is slightly inferior. As you say, there are things about the transferred identities of the two Peters which tend to arouse questions—although the first one that occurred to me was different from yours. My main objection was that *a diary apparently written by a normal 18th century Peter without consciousness of a 20th century personality or awkward position, yet covering the period of the substituted identity* was left for the modern Peter to inherit & be guided by. How could that be? If during those days in 1784 the visitor at the Pettigrew house was a 20th century invader who knew everything that was going to happen, *then why did he write in his diary as if he were a normal inhabitant of 1784?* Your point, of course, is—*what was the real 18th century Peter doing while the 20th century Peter usurped his body?* I answered that question in a sketchy sort of way by assuming that he occupied the modern Peter's body in a kind of half-stupor—drinking to drown his perplexity & being regarded by the modern housekeeper (who must have fed him) as her master in a neurotic & alcoholic state. Yet this is clearly a lame explanation. In the case of an actual exchange, the man transported into the unknown future would have had a totally differ-ent reaction—& the housekeeper would have noted a multitude of queer things. I did not gather that the subsequent remarks of the housekeeper to the modern fiancee referred to the period when the 18th century Peter was in the modern body. One of the things reported was a wild speech in which the speaker told some people (as *I* often feel!) that they wouldn't be born for over a century. Now how could the 18th century Peter, in the confusion of his plight, have known just what had happened? Or—assuming he had kept in his head & studied calendars & newspapers in the house—would he have taken the matter in just this way? Also—the master is spoken of as having tried to force his way into White's as a member. Presumably in modern dress—yet how could the 18th century Peter (catapulted into a dressing-gowned body in the 20th century) have dressed himself in the correct modern fashion unassisted? No—in my opinion all this talk of the housekeeper re-ferred to *the 20th century Peter after his return with shattered nerves & a mind filled with 18th century images & doubts of his fixed place in the time-stream.* Think this over & see if you don't agree with me. But your point is extremely just—what, in-deed, was the 18th century Peter doing during the substitution period? This is no more cleared up than the matter of the diary—a plain oversight on the au-thor's part. Also—when the real 18th century Peter got back to 1784 his diary ought to shew some trace of whatever unprecedented experience he had been through. But with all its defects this thing gave me an uncanny wallop. When I revisited it I saw it through twice—& I shall probably go again on its next return. It is the most weirdly perfect embodiment of my own moods & pseudo-memories that I have ever seen—for all my life I have felt as if I might wake up out of this dream of an idiotic Victorian age & an insane jazz age into the same reality of 1760 or 1770 or 1780 . . . . the age of the white steeples & fan-lighted doorways of the ancient hill, & of the long f'd books of the old dark attic trunk-room at 454 Angell St. God Save the King!

I must read "The Pipe-Smoker".[11] Glad you appreciated Klarkash-Ton's brochure, which certainly contains the cream of his prose. No—I haven't seen anything recent of Dunsany's. His later work—spoiled by humour—does not compare with his old tales; yet I want to read it all some day. As for Robert S. Carr—he blew in all the cash his novel gained him, repudiated writing, & started to be a business man.[12] Using certain radical connexions, he became a New York agent of the Russian Soviet trading corporation; but later transferred to Moscow, where he now is. Price knows him well—in fact, he almost got Price a job in Moscow as an acetylene machinery expert last April, although the plan didn't quite materialise. As for my idea that certain weird tales should begin with an atmosphere of feverish tension—I didn't mean anything as bald as the old "They call me madman" stuff. What I meant was far subtler—something implied rather than revealed . . . . . some faint, terrible undercurrent *barely suggested* by the prose rhythm & by certain words of whose hideous symbolism one cannot at once be quite sure. As for anticipations of later parts of a tale—there are times when a few advance glimpses serve a useful emotional end, although of course a powerful climax is best guarded till its own time of revelation.

Glad you've had some enjoyable musical opportunities. The radio certainly brings interesting stuff now & then—not only musical but general. For example—I lately heard the exercises dedicating Poe's Philadelphia home as a memorial, & also an audible voice from the *antarctic*—the Byrd expedition. I could never appreciate music as you can, for my imagination seems to be altogether *visual*. The symphony concert you heard would seem to have been quite an event—& it is certainly singular to think of a jazz artist like Gershwin as forming half the programme! I don't care much for anything with the ultra-modern element of jazz, though I like the popular syncopation of the late [']90's & early 1900's . . . . rag-time, cake-walks, &c. I note the critiques with much interest. I've heard the celebrated "Rhapsody in Blue"—though it doesn't measurably increase my blood pressure.

Glad you had a festive Christmas. So did my aunt & I. I decorated the Colonial mantelpiece of the ancient living-room while she was asleep, & arranged several other surprises around the fireplace. We had a good turkey dinner at the boarding-house across the back garden, & in the afternoon borrowed a cat to lend traditional domestic atmosphere. At dusk we strolled half way down the ancient hill to hear the carol-singing in the yard of the old brick Handicraft Club—& at midnight, as before mentioned, I took the coach for Manhattan. Your Mr. Davis certainly formed a picturesque guest . . . . . . between 5705[13] & the restaurants, I hope he got enough to eat! Regarding the gentleman's ethnic claims (It seems to be a typical Semitic gesture to claim

Jewish blood in nearly all the world's celebrities!)—he's certainly all cockeyed about Douglas Fairbanks, whose descent from Jonathan Fayerbanks of Dedham (Jonathan's house, built in 1636 & ¾ of the way from Providence to Boston, is the oldest existing structure in New England—& in all the U.S. except for St. Luke's Church in Virginia [1632] & certain Spanish houses in St. Augustine & Santa Fé.) is well known. Oddly enough, however, he's partly right about Charlie Chaplin—who, according to his half-brother Wheeler Dryden, had a Jewish father. Sydney Chaplin is also half-Jewish, though Dryden himself is altogether English.

And now let me thank you most tremendously for the loan of the *Story* anthology & of the two recent issues.[14] The whole shipment formed a highly illuminating glance into contemporary letters, & contained many items of genuine aesthetic significance. Yes—I can see the advantages which this enterprise has over the high-grade but tradition-bound magazines, as well as over the machine-made popular rags. However—it undoubtedly has amusing taboos of its own, so that many tales of the highest intrinsic merit (but not quite "human" enough to suit its especial policy) might be summarily rejected by it. Your set of opinions is intensely interesting, & I don't see much to dissent about except that "Happy Jack" seems to me a bit too mawkish & artificial to be convincing—or at any rate to deserve your extraordinarily high opinion. I would also at least mildly question the preëminence of "Missis Flanders" [*sic*] I hardly know what impressed me as most powerful . . . . though perhaps "Shepherd of the Lord" ought to get the prize. Most of them are a trifle thin & insubstantial—they lack something, though it would be hard to tell just what. Probably the authors are too keen on presenting psychological problems & situations to bother about making them seem real & vivid. They are content for the most part to be laconic & non-atmospheric; so that we say of these tales, "this might have happened" instead of "this *has* happened!" Of the tales in the Jan. & Feb. issues I agree that "Obsession" is the best. Again, many thanks for this generous quota—which is returning to you via parcel post.

What you say of "Bedelia" explains the mystery of its date & fully vindicates the reminiscent accuracy of O'Neill. For what you cite is not the original song itself, but merely an obscene or suggestive *parody* of it—the sort of thing which might easily linger on as a vulgar comic feature for years after the real song had become a joke. Such obscene parodies were very common in the old days (are they now?)—almost every supreme hit having one. I never heard this specimen before, but recall smutty versions of "In the Shade of the Old Apple Tree" (1905), "On a Sunday Afternoon" (1902), & others. Here is the *real* text of "Bedelia" as published in 1903 & popularised by the comedienne Blanche Ring:

There's a charming Irish lady with a roguish winning way,
Who has kept my heart a-thumping & a-bumping night & day;

She's the flower of Killarney, with a Tipperary smile—
She's the best that ever came from Erin's Isle
And I find myself a-singing all the while:

[CHORUS]
Bedelia, I'd like to steal you,
  Bedelia, I love you so.
I'll be your Chauncey Olcott,
  If you'll be my Molly O;
Say something sweet, Bedelia;
  Your voice I like to hear.
Oh, Bedelia-elia-elia, I've made up my mind to steal you,
  Steal you, steal you,
    Bedelia dear!

In this wholly innocuous original form "Bedelia" was a veritable knockout—a
stampede—lasting well into 1904. I remember my little cousin Phillips Gamwell (now dead—his mother is the aunt now heading my household) singing
it at the age of six. But by the fall of '04 it was played out as a serious offer-
ing. After that—like "On the Banks of the Wabash"—it became a typical
back number, for humorous or parodic use. "You're the Flower of My Heart,
Sweet Adeline" (Spring '04) was its principal immediate successor in popular
favour—& then in '05 the new riot—"In the Shade of the Old Apple Tree"
appeared. But of course the crude parodies hung on indefinitely in the underworld, so that a vulgarised pseudo-Bedelia in 1906 is no anachronism. I
note with amusement the specimen of modern song-verse you cite. Evidently
the trade of lyric-grinding is much the same, qualitatively speaking, from decade to decade! Your synthetic specimens for "Posturings" are delightfully
characteristic of the genre—you catch exactly the right note of banality!

Regarding the question of war & peace—the trouble with most pacifists
who would fight only to defend their country is that they are unwilling to
sanction such a course of rational preparedness as would make a real defence
possible. National emergencies rise suddenly; & unless a sizeable body of
trained men with proper equipment is available, there is no way of meeting
such a thing. Certainly all effort ought to be made to prevent an abuse or
over-extension of the term defensive—but at the same time universal military
training ought to prevail in order to make defence effective when it is genuinely needed. Opinions may differ regarding the last war, but it seems to me
that anyone with any sense of historic values ought to see how necessary it
was to prevent the sweeping victory of Germany. Knowing the German spirit, one may conjecture what the positions of the non-Germanic nations would
have been in a world of dominant Prussianism & vindicated militarism. There
is everything to regret in the original precipitation of the war in 1914, but

nothing to regret in America's turning the scales in 1917–18. America got off easy—her position in a Germanic world would have been utterly intolerable by comparison. As for Japan—it is possible that good diplomacy could avert a clash, though whether such diplomacy can be found is another question. Actually, Japan ought to be given a free hand in all the Far East—with the understanding that hands are to be kept off the west. A lot of mawkish sympathy is wasted on China. She has, of course, a mighty civilisation—but the capacity for self-government is lacking. Her only stable rule in recent—& even mediaeval—times has been from alien dynasties of conquerors—Tartars or Manchus. In the near future either Japan or bolshevik Russia will certainly control the bulk of the Chinese Empire—& I'd rather see Japan do it than have the Soviets extend their influence. So my idea is to let Japan alone in Asia. I suppose the great fear is that Japan could become absolutely invincible—able to subdue all the combined faces which could possibly be brought against her—if China's boundless population & resources were at her disposal. There is perhaps good sense in that fear—who can tell?

Your added list of literary lacunae interests me greatly. Some of the items—like Plotinus, Hegel, Aquinas, Erasmus, &c—are hardly necessary to a modern layman's education; being nowadays of significance only to special students of the history of thought. I've scarcely dipped into these. On the other hand, many things you list are vitally important parts of our main cultural stream; & ought to be read by all means. You certainly ought to be familiar with Homer (preferably the cadenced prose translations—Lang & Leaf's Iliad & Butcher & Lang's Odyssey . . . . I'm going to annex these pretty soon in the Modern Library), & with the King James Bible—both of these being the sources of a tremendous number of elements in our literature. As a drama student you can't afford to miss Æschylus, Sophocles, Euripides, & Aristophanes, & you surely ought to take in a representative number of Plato's dialogues—especially the Phaedo & Republic. Cicero, Horace, & Plutarch ought not to be missed—& Marcus Aurelius is worth skimming. I suppose St. Augustine is an important cultural landmark—but I've merely skimmed extracts. Volsung Saga is really important as a bit of racial background. Don't for your life miss Chaucer—the fountain-head of all our poetry, & an exquisitely fascinating old bird in his own right. Rabelais is on the famous list—though I've never read a word in him. Montaigne is worth exploring, & Cervantes ought to be included, though I'm not as wild as some about him. Oh, yes—& Dante ought to be set down . . . the Inferno anyhow. Bacon ought to be skimmed, & Hobbes, Locke, & Spinoza deserve examination—though a good history of philosophy might help more at first than a direct perusal of these sources. Swift, Fielding, Hume, Addison, Steele—& virtually all the other English classics you name—are quite imperative for any prose-writer. No man can write decent prose except through the modelling influence of the early 18th century masters. You might read Gibbon in Smith's abridgment—which I can lend you. Balzac is utterly imperative for any fiction writer. He can make characters *live* as no modern can. As a drama-expert you need Ibsen & Strindberg. And as a modern thinker don't miss Nietzsche, Marx, Freud, & Spengler. Hardy, Conrad, Shaw, Austen—all necessary. Bancroft useful, though other Am. histories will do. Brontë's important. Elizabethans imperative. Boswell desirable. Also Thoreau. Bless my soul, Son, but you have a good bit of reading ahead of you despite all your ultra-modern cramming. Why not get a better-proportioned background by reading more old & less new? Start in on Homer for a change!

Your recent reading, as usual, leaves me quite dizzy. Bless my soul, but I do believe you're actually equalling young Comte d'Erlette! I haven't read the Bradford journal, [15] but a friend of mine attacks it for reasons rather different from yours—alleging that old Gamaliel shews a sort of soft or whiny streak at times. If reading & working by the clock is a mark of Novanglian civilisation, then I'm a rank outsider—for I have no chronological regularity of any kind. I eat when I choose, sleep when I'm sleepy, work when I'm able, & let it go at that. I hadn't realised the touch of egotism in Bradford—it doesn't seem to crop out in his biographical sketches, which are excellent. I note the Calvertonian fictional precepts with interest.[16] Long dotes on V. F., but I haven't overmuch use for him—neither has my friend Morton. He's a sort of secondhand scholar. These dicta aren't so bad, on the whole. As to *opulence*—I'd say it depends on what Calverton means by that term. If he is objecting to the skeletonic barrenness of certain modern tales—something I complained of in *Story*—then I'm with him. There must be an adequate setting & an adequate representation of the significant points of the unfolding action. As for *uniqueness*—I don't know. Certainly, there is no use in repeating old stuff in a hackneyed way—but on the other hand, what is not reasonably typical of at least a fairly large human group is of very doubtful significance. I'd say rather that a certain *freshness & individuality of approach* is necessary. Regarding *inevitability*— that is an overcoloured & exaggerated expression. Nothing in human life is really inevitable except as ultimately cosmic determinism (which we can never map out) makes it so. Human behaviour is infinitely complex, varied, & unpredictable, & in a given moral situation a man of a certain type (so far as we can distinguish types) may act in any number of ways, depending on minute & imperceptible details in the situation & in his own composition. Calverton has the false notion of inevitable human reactions which goes with the crazy Marxian philosophy & the half-baked theories of behaviourism. Regarding *descriptions* & *elegance* there's nothing to object to. But I dissent from the point regarding a *philosophy of life*. That's some more of the bolshevistic bunk. Actually the only business of an artist is to express what he sees & feels, without any attempt at intellectual correlation. Usually the artist has a sort of perspective which may or may not crop out here & there—but the more he forgets about it, the better. Let the author present life itself—it is for each reader to draw philosophic conclusions, as he would from first-hand experience. Proust is right in saying that theories in a book are like a price-tag left on a pair of pants! Calverton's last conclusion—about emotional effect & the human desire for projection—seems very sound. I read some of the Eastman papers in *Harper's* a couple of years ago. There is something in what he says—for when a poet gets too subjective & individual he certainly ceases to have a message for anybody else. Poor Hart Crane (his mother, now visibly an old lady, was at Loveman's New Year's gathering) probably justified Eastman's strictures. Did you notice the analysis of "At Melville's Tomb"? One can hardly do otherwise than concur with Eastman in his estimate.[17] Regarding the so-called Scottsboro case—it would certainly seem as if the defence had quite a bit of evidence (though I don't see what the possession of syphilis & gonorrhea by one nigger had to do with it—these things don't destroy the inclination to ravish so far as I know) . . . . yet all this must have been well known to jurors who maturely brought a verdict of guilty. It doesn't seem natural to me that well-disposed men would deliberately condemn even niggers to death if they were not strongly convinced of guilt. We must not forget that these books of special pleading are compiled & coloured by professional radicals & emotional idealists—although of course prejudice & emotion exist on the other side as well. It would probably be better if all trials involving local prejudice could be conducted by Federal courts with a personnel drawn from all parts of the country—avoiding not only the sections where prejudice *against* the defendants exists, but those where prejudice *in their favour* is found. For instance—no jury of New York Jewish radicals ought to try a man accused of labour crimes against law & order . . . . for those bastards would acquit a brute who had shot up dozens of innocent people if they thought he did it "for the social revolution." Just how the present *cause celebre* will come out, I don't know—but possibly some sort of commutation of sentence will occur at the last moment. However—the damn coons are probably rather poor specimens anyhow, so that apart from the matter of precedent it really matters little whether they are bumped off or not. It is curious to analyse the system of values which, in the absence of religious belief, attaches such exaggerated importance to the sanctity of human life *as such*, & to the finely-spun abstractions of "justice" & kindred illusions or aesthetic concepts. Of course, there is an artistic side of the matter—needless cruelty being essentially vulgar—but I suspect that much of the hysterical justice-crying of radicals & idealists is simply an emotional residue from religion. My own policy would be to safeguard human life & the aesthetic ornament called "justice" *as far as is compatible with more important social & cultural necessities* such as racial & national safety, the maintenance of intellectual & artistic standards, the welfare of superior types, & so on. *Wanton* cruelty or injustice is indeed crude—but it is silly to let an exaggerated humanity interfere with the really best interests of the group & its development. There is something hollow & feminine about the position of the extreme idealist. What we need is reason, realism, moderation, & a sense of proportion. As for old Steffens—who shews an amusing inability to break away from the abstract ethical concept—what he says of Rhode Island state politics is probably correct.[18] The standard of political action in the state government (though this does *not* apply to the Providence city government) has always been very cynical & realistic, & free from aesthetic modulations or ethical pretences. However, since this is a condition well understood & allowed for, it has never caused much harm. We may say merely that the political game is played according to a different set of rules. Both parties are equally unscrupulous & the peculations from the public are no greater than what occur under virtually any system. Corrupt policies are necessary in a nominal democracy, since only through boss-ism can anything ever be accomplished. The only real remedy is a fascistic & highly centralised government administered by specially trained men—these in turn elected only by such persons as can pass a stiff intelligence test & an exacting series of examinations in political, economic, administrative, & general cultural subjects. What you say of the Coates book[19] interests me considerably, since I met the author ten years ago—when he was an unknown newspaper man. He is a red-headed, pleasant chap—perhaps slightly my junior. We were both doing some hack work for that damned cuss Henneberger, who controlled W.T. during the pre-Wright period, & I met him in Henneberger's suite at the Hotel Empire in N.Y. Another participant in that meeting was the old-time wit & columnist La Touche Hancock (once a shining light on the old N.Y. Sun), who eventually drank himself to death. Poor old devil—even then he was pretty far on the down grade . . . . doing work for a Coney Island local weekly. Coates interested me because he seemed to share my antiquarian tastes. I was then giving New York City an intensive historical & architectural exploration, & he gave me tips on several quaint byways I would otherwise have missed. At that time he was leaving for Europe, & I meant to look him up when he got back—but after the exchange of one or two letters he dropped out of sight, & I did not bother to ferret him out. However, I've followed his career with interest. One of his books—"The Outlaw Years"—reflects the antiquarianism of '24.

I note the art exhibition echoes, & can grasp the charm of the popular "Mother & Son" very readily. "Acrobats" also has undeniable grace. My aunts & I have seen quite a number of art displays at the local museum & at the Prov. Art Club—one of which ought to be of especial interest to you, since it centred around something which is coming to your own town & neighbourhood. This was an exhibit of stained glass designs, with a lecture by Joseph G. Reynolds of this state & Boston, one of the greatest living designers.[20] What touches your locality is the fact that the lecture centred around an actual specimen of modern stained glass by Reynolds—a newly-finished window which is going into the East Liberties [*sic*] Presbyterian Church of Pittsburgh. It was set up as best it could be against one of the great museum windows, though of course the situation was vastly inferior to that which it will have when in place in the church. Enclosed is a picture—with cutting—which you can keep if you like. You might drop in & see the original some time after it is installed. Other recent exhibitions I've seen are of Etruscan tomb-paintings, Chinese textiles, & Rhode Island paintings. Providence s pretty well supplied in the art line—with loan-exhibits from other museums supplementing local resources.

Thanks vastly for the name of that Cobb nigger story. As for a new edition of my article—I doubt if its commercial exploitation could be arranged. I'm keeping a list of items to include in any future version—& am indeed superficially incorporating them into the text reprinted in *The Fantasy Fan*. I don't think W.T. would be receptive toward such a feature.

No—I haven't seen that article about Comte d'Erlette which you mention.[21] God! Merely keeping track of that kid is a career in itself! Here's a recent circular of his which you can act on—or ignore—to whatever extent your inclination may dictate. The little rascal has nerve to ask so much of his friends—but that's young Augie all over! I don't doubt but that the book is excellent so far as light detective fiction goes—he has a gift for this sort of hack work.

Concerning dialect—is it merely a stenographic slip which makes you refer to the Novanglian use of 'frying-pan' for 'spider'? Actually, of course, the case is the precise reverse—the name *spider* being applied to a frying-pan. This is exceedingly common & universal—not at all confined to the lower orders. It was only in recent months that I learned that frying-pans are not everywhere called "spiders". It is probable that this name was derived from a certain old-fashioned type of frying-pan which stood on three legs over a fire, & which this had something of the aspect of an actual arachnid. The transfer of the term to legless frying-pans held in the hand was of course easy. In New York & (I think) in the Middle States—perhaps Pittsburgh—the term *skillet* is common. Perhaps you don't realise that this was originally applied not to frying pans but to shallow vessels with long handles used for heating water. The similar shape of the legless frying-pan was what caused this transfer of meaning. Phelps's article on British & American pronunciations is of especial interest to me in view of the lecture ("Is Progress a Delusion?") by Prof. C. E. M. Joad which I heard last week, & which involved as thick an Oxford accent as I've encountered in a long while.[22] At the same time it must be remembered that the British usages which Phelps cites are *by no means universal or even preferred forms in England.* The real fact is simply *that in Great Britain there exist a wider range of tolerated pronunciations than in the United States;* some being in no way different from American pronunciations, whilst others involve the peculiarities commonly known as "Oxford English". The King does not use this Oxford drawl—in fact, I couldn't tell from his radio speech that he wasn't born & bred in Providence. What is more—Stormonth's Dictionary (British—by a Cambridge man—esteemed as a conservative authority & used by my father) refuses to sanction a large number of Oxfordisms. According to the *best* British usage *doc'trinal* & *cap'italist* are pronounced precisely as in America. I've heard *la-bor'-a-try* (pretty close to Phelps's la-bah'-o-try), but this is not the preferred British form. Stormouth favours *lab'-o-ra-ter-y*—which has as may syllables as the American form, though the penultimate vowel has an *e* instead of *o* sound. Occasionally this condenses into the trisyllable *lab'-ra-try*. As for *fracas*—how the hell does Billy Phelps pronounce it? The only way I ever heard was *frah-kah'*—following the original French usage. This of course fails to make a perfect rhyme with *darker* because the accent is on the last syllable. The word *lieutenant* had the *f* sound in America till about a century ago. I don't sound the final *t* of the French word *trait*, although I hear some doing it. In Rhode Island the pronunciation of the surname Berkeley depends on how it is used. If we speak of George Berkeley, Dean of Derry & Bishop of Cloyne, who lived in this colony from 1729 to 1732, we use the form *he* used—*Bark'ly*. Also, this form in referring to Berkeley Square in London. But through local corruption we speak of *Birk'ly* Street in Boston. Also "Dirby" St. in Salem, though in speaking of the Earls of Derby (& sometimes the 'derby' hat) we say "Darby." The famous horse race is also called "Darby" in Rhode Island. We generally follow that provincial form in saying *clark* ("clirk"). Phelps is right in pointing out the vowel *o* as the chief point of Anglo-American difference. British usage makes a curious *eo* or *eow* pseudo-diphthong of this vowel. Much of the "Oxford accent" is probably of surprising recency—perhaps not going much behind the early 19th century. What I call the *real main stream* is a certain plain, straightforward mode of speech which can still be used unmodified in London, Boston, Providence, & Charleston without attracting any particular attention.

Oh, by the way—I forgot to tell you that during my late visit I saw a regular legitimate drama for the first time since gawd knows when—a distinctly high-grade melodrama with an undercurrent of macabre & sinister atmosphere, called "The Double Door."[23] It was very sketchily-based on the history of the morbid Wendel family of New York, whose dismal, shuttered brick mansion still stands in lower 5th Ave. though all the family are dead. Derleth would like it because of its powerful portrayal of a grim, dominant old maid whose fanatical will extended even to a hideous attempted murder.

And this reminds me—at last I've read "The Lady Who Came to Stay"— lent me by Klarkash-Ton. Damn good stuff! It lacks the cosmic touch, but certainly exploits the common household ghost to the very limit. The atmosphere is the real thing. Have read several more books on witchcraft lent by Koenig (whom I met in N Y—exceedingly pleasant chap), & am about to tackle the much-advertised & well-nigh interminable "Anthony Adverse",[24] lent by Bernard Dwyer.

As a final echo of my recent social season I'll enclose some pictures (please return) taken at Wandrei's with a strong electric light as the only illumination. Rembrandt stuff. I was caught with my mug slightly open, hence look almost more sappy than usual, if such be possible.

And so it goes. Thee's another non-paying fantasy magazine out now, which you might like to use as an outlet. *Fantasy,* 255 E. 188 St., N.Y. I met the editor—a nice little Jew studying at CCNY.[25] ¶ Best wishes—

   Yr obt grandsire—

E'ch-Pi-El

P.S. Glad to hear that you have some congenial study courses. When you get brushed up on stenography and German, you can go over & land a soft secretarial berth in our good friend Adolf's administration!

P.P.S. Just saw "Little Women" cinema. Extraordinarily vivid 19th century atmosphere & details, & considerable art in presentation. Sentimental in treatment, though. Even the 1860's were never *quite* like that!

Notes

1. The essay in question is probably "A Layman Looks at the Government (dated 22 November 1933; *CE* 5.96–111).

2. The Rover Boys was a series of boys' books written by Arthur M. Winfield (pseud. of Edward Stratemeyer), published in 30 volumes (1899–1926). Tom Swift was the protagonist of more than 100 volumes of boys' books written by Stratemeyer (1910–41).

3. The *Rhode Island Journal of Astronomy* was a hectographed paper that HPL had begun on 2 August 1903 and continued sporadically until February 1909. Sixty-nine issues survive at JHL, although more were probably produced.

4. HPL wrote 20 monthly astronomy columns for the Providence *Tribune* (morning, evening, and Sunday editions) from August 1906 to June 1908. Winslow Upton (1853–1914), professor of astronomy at Brown University, had a similar long-running column in the *Providence Journal.*

5. Only HPL's articles in the *Pawtuxet Valley Gleaner* (July–December 1906) have been found.

6. Jules Romains (1885–1972) was a French poet, playwright, and novelist who devised the doctrine of unamism, a doctrine that proposed a universal sympathy with life and a negation of individualism and nationalism.

7. Wright had stated that "We hope to have an important announcement to make soon about Lovecraft's stories" (*WT* 22, No. 6 [December 1933]: 776).

8. *Three-Cornered Moon* (Paramount, 1933), directed by Elliott Nugent; starring Claudette Colbert, Richard Arlen, and Mary Boland.

9. *Wild Boys of the Road* (First National Pictures, 1933), directed by William A. Wellman; starring Frankie Darro, Edwin Phillips, and Rochelle Hudson. Based on the story "Desperate Youth" by Daniel Ahern. *The Invisible Man* (Universal, 1933), directed by James Whale; starring Claude Rains, Gloria Stuart, and William Harrigan. Based on the novel by H. G. Wells. *The World Changes* (First National Pictures, 1933), directed by Mervyn LeRoy; starring Paul Muni, Aline McMahon, and Mary Astor. Based on the story "America Kneels" by Sheridan Gibney.

10. *Little Women* (RKO Radio Pictures, 1933), directed by George Cukor; starring Katharine Hepburn, Joan Bennett, and Paul Lukas. Based on the novel by Louisa May Alcott.

11. By Martin Armstrong.

12. Robert Spencer Carr (1909–1994) was an American writer of weird, fantasy, and science fiction who achieved celebrity with the best-selling society novel *The Rampant Age* (1928), adapted into a film in 1930.

13. JVS's address was 5705 Jackson Street, Pittsburgh, PA.

14. *A Story Anthology, 1931–1933*, ed. Whit Burnett and Martha Foley (New York; Vanguard Press, 1933), contains "Happy Jack" by William March (2, No. 10 [December 1932]: 26–38), "Missis Flinders" by Tess Slesinger (same, 3–17; see JVS 48, n.10), and "The Shepherd of the Lord" by Peter Neagoé (1, No. 4 [November/December 1931]: 5–26), all previously published in *Story* magazine. It is not certain which two issues of *Story* JVS had lent HPL, but the issue for February 1934 (4, No. 19) issue contains "Obsession" by Ruth Pine Furniss (pp. 63–78).

15. *The Journal of Gamaliel Bradford, 1883–1932*, ed. Van Wyck Brooks (Boston: Houghton Mifflin, 1933).

16. JVS may have mentioned to HPL Calverton's *Sex Expression in Literature* (1926).

17. Max Eastman, "Poets Talking to Themselves," *Harper's* 163, No. 5 (October 1931): 563–74. Eastman's article quotes the entirety of Hart Crane's short poem "At Melville's Tomb" and criticizes it for obscurity.

18. Lincoln Steffens (1866–1936), muckraking journalist, wrote a celebrated exposé on the corruption of Rhode Island politics, "Rhode Island: A State for Sale" (*McClure's Magazine*, February 1905).

19. HPL may be referring to Robert M. Coates's *The Eater of Darkness* (1929), an early science fiction novel.

20. Joseph G. Reynolds (1886–1972), American designer and stained glass artist. He was a native of Wickford, RI, and graduated from the Rhode Island School of Design. He was associated with Ralph Adams Cram in leading the Gothic Revival in the US.

21. It is not clear what article HPL is referring to.

22. William Lyon Phelps (1865–1943), professor of English at Yale. HPL may be referring to his article "An American in England," *Delineator* 122, No. 4 (February 1933): 4f. C. E. M. Joad (1891–1953) was a British philosopher.

23. Elizabeth McFadden (1875–1961), *Double Door: A Play in Three Acts* (New York: Samuel French, 1931). It was filmed in 1934.

24. A best-selling historical novel by Hervey Allen.

25. HPL refers to *Fantasy Magazine*, edited by Julius Schwartz.

[45]   [ANS][1]

[Postmarked St. Augustine, FL,
23 June 1934]

Back among my favourite antiquities—at the same place I stopped in 1931. Had a 7-week visit at the Barlow place—never saw a family so insistently hospitable! Nearly broke, so will have to cut out most of my intended stops on the way north.

Regards & best wishes
   —Ech-Pi-El

Notes

1. *Front:* Charlotte Street, St. Augustine, Fla.

[46]   [ANS][1]

> [Postmarked Providence, RI,
> 22 August 1934]

Hail, O Jehvish-Êi! Thanks for the birthday card, which forms my first inti-
mation of your changed address. Hope you got the various postcards I sent
during my southern sojourn. I certainly had a great time. Just now I'm stag-
gering under a weight of accumulated work. Thursday I'm going to Boston to
spend a few days with a friend (also seeing W. Paul Cook), & after that I have
hopes of getting to the ancient island of Nantucket—said to be the most utterly unspoiled survival of a colonial seaport in America. Can't stay long,
though. ¶ Your move down to the good old Eastern Shore sounds vastly interesting, & I shall be eager to hear particulars. I fancy I'd like your present
environment infinitely better than Pittsburgh.[2]
All good wishes—
E'ch-Pi-El

Notes

1. *Front:* First Baptist Church, Providence, R. I. / Founded by Roger Williams in 1638.
2. The card is addressed to Salisbury, MD.

[47]   [ANS][1]

> [Postmarked Providence, R.I.,
> 28 October 1934]

Hail, O Jehvish-Êi! Would you mind sending that typed account of my political views to
    Clark Ashton Smith,
        Box 385, Auburn, California?
He is all excited over Sinclair's candidacy,[2] & is relapsing into the archaic platitudes of the Hooverites in his fear of a disrupted social order. I'm too busy
& weary to start a fresh argument—so want him to see this inclusive summary. ¶ Hope all is well with you. Cold weather is driving me indoors, but
I've had some fine glimpses of New England autumn scenery. Regards—
Ech-Pi-El

Notes

1. *Front:* Brown University, Van Wickle Gate and University Hall, Providence, R. I.
2. HPL refers to the unsuccessful campaign of Upton Sinclair (1878–1968) for governor of California on the EPIC (End Poverty in California) ticket.

1935

[48]   [ALS]

66 College St.,
Providence, R.I.
Feby. 10, 1935.

Dear Jehvish-Êi:—

Well—the months certainly have gone by since last I had a full-length message from your direction! But I imagined you must be pretty busy, hence have not viewed the long silence uncharitably. You surely have been seeing & doing things since that other & bygone February! An arduous & grilling round, yet perhaps of value to you some day as experience. When one reflects on the number of different human types & locales & situations you have seen in your brief 22 years—as contrasted with the infinitely narrower range which I have seen in 44—one realises how much better equipped you are becoming for the task of reflecting the world with balanced perspective. In your case the good old Virgilian gag about "forsan et haec meminisse juvabit"[1] is eminently applicable!

Needless to say, I have followed your chronicle of adventure with the keenest interest. Glad you had a chance for some dramatic & near-dramatic activities before leaving Pittsburgh—& I'd indeed be grateful for a look at your play based on "The Lady Who Came to Stay."[2] Weird drama (as witness Dunsany's "Gods of the Mountain" &c) has vast possibilities, though very few in our group are likely ever to attempt such a thing. So Spencer *has* written another book! I wondered that an author so promising should lapse into total silence.

Your migrations surely form the raw materials for an epic—pretty damn raw, you will say in reflecting on the incident of the truck radiator! Well—I'm glad no greater harm was done. We all get mangled up now & then—I nearly lost a finger from a phosphorus burn in my laboratory when I was 17, & poor Crawford (editor of *Marvel Tales*) has just had his right hand frightfully crushed in his printing-press. The description of Salisbury in the page from your May letter is quite a study in Main Street—some day, no doubt, you'll immortalise the town in fiction & be burned in effigy before the court-house! Ocean City surely must be a curious place—& I'm glad you found at least one congenial soul therein. I shall be watching for Dugan's work in magazines as time passes. 15 years ago I knew many people at Penn State, the United Amateur Press Association (of which I was an active member) having a local club there—including many students & 2 or 3 instructors. Some of the freak shows you describe sound almost incredible—indeed, I can scarcely imagine the censors of any town tolerating an exhibition like that of Emmanuel J. Callahan . . . that is, if the gentleman's injuries were actually displayed. Sorry that Suffolk isn't a more interesting place. You must be within a reasonable distance of one of the most important historical objects in the United States— St. Luke's Church (1632) in Isle of Wight Co. (near Smithfield), the oldest structure of English workmanship on this continent. I've never seen it—in fact, I've never been in the Norfolk region—but I hope to do so some day. Norfolk itself, I understand, has a fine 18th Century church—St. Paul's. Too bad Suffolk isn't better connected with adjacent points—by 'bus or otherwise. When you have leisure & cash some time you might get to see the marvellous colonial restorations at Williamsburg—or the Poe memorabilia around Richmond. Richmond is one of my favourite cities—for despite the vanishment of most ancient houses, it still retains an intangible fascination & mellowness. Hope you finally connect up with the Parrott legacy—although such things are always difficult to secure. Back in 1878 my grandfather spent a bit of time & cash in London investigating a Rathbone fortune in which he thought he ought to share—but nothing ever came of it. 20 years ago I heard of a Lovecraft fortune also tied up in chancery—but never bothered to institute enquiries. But your case seems to be rather nearer home—hence the chances of some favourable development are probably much greater. Anyhow, the genealogical information is worth all the research you have put in. It's a good thing to have a chart of one's sources as far as can be conveniently compiled—although I'd never spend as much time on delving as my friends Talman & Morton have done. The old newspapers must have been fascinating. I've done considerable browsing among such things—beginning with the Providence Gazette & Country-Journal, established in 1763 . . . . whose office in Gaol-Lane (now Meeting St.) is still standing, albeit in poor condition.

Your job in the mill certainly is devastating—& discouragingly ill-paid. I surely hope that something better will turn up before long—though of course nowadays one is glad of *any* regular employment. Possibly something of the exhausting effect will diminish after you are thoroughly adjusted to the routine—but that remains to be seen. At any rate, I hope you won't get in the way of any flying blocks or otherwise incur violent injury. The hand, I imagine, will slowly regain its full flexibility, & thereafter suffer no more from the now-unaccustomed demands placed upon it. I didn't know, by the way, that you were left handed. What sounds really worst about your experience is working at a temperature of 10°. I couldn't do that—indeed, I've fallen absolutely unconscious through exposure to temperatures of 14° & above. +20° is my absolute deadline of safety—which means that I have to stay in the house most of the time during the peak of an average northern winter. Sorry all the MSS. have come back—but that's the thing most of us have to face! Don't hurry with "Posturings"—for forced writing is never effective, no matter what some people claim. It will grow gradually when the time comes—& will be all the richer when written from a background of increased experience. I can appreciate the difficulty of revision—that sense of the definitiveness of a piece of text as already written. I find it virtually impossible to change any-thing of mine once I have accepted it as final in my own mind. I'd much ra-ther write a new story than tinker with any of my old ones.

Speaking of writing—I appreciate the compliment of your suggestion that I bombard the *Atlantic* with an autobiography compiled from epistolary extracts (a damn clever way of assembling one, I'll say!), but really fear that my sense of proportion is a bit too strong to let me launch such a project. There are too damned many autobiographies as it is; & when it comes to bungling old geezers who've never done anything in particular, the line simply has to be drawn! Almost anybody could cook up a lot of childish reminis-cence & nostalgic maundering with a certain amount of "charm"—but the real importance or appropriateness of such a thing depends largely upon the calibre of the person concerned. If he never did anything of moment, an at-mosphere of ridiculousness hangs about any attempt to dramatise his sources, recollections, & environment. Montes laborant—nascitur ridiculus mus![3] One might as well write the pompously documented biography of a sandwich man or elevator boy in 8 volumes—I. Ancestry & Childhood; II. Education & Early Contacts; III. Period of Dime Novel & Western Cinema Influence; IV. Period of Tabloid, Pool Room, & Sex Cinema Influence; V. Friendships & Debates in the McSoak's Barroom Circle; VI. Industrial Evolution; VII. Opinions & Utterances of Maturity; Leadership in the Madison Square Bench-Warming Senate; VIII. Bibliography & Index. Ho, hum . . . . we great men! Which reminds me that I read Comte d'Erlette's second detective novel last autumn ("The Man On All Fours"), & guessed the solution on p. 32. I judge from your reference that you have also read his first—which is more than I've done. His third will be out some time this month. Later he hopes to arrange for the publication of his first *serious* book—"Place of Hawks." He certainly is arriving on all fours in the magazines!

Regarding political matters—I still don't see any course of action *likely to be adopted* which offers any improvement over the constant experimenting of the New Deal. The old principle of laissez-faire capitalism is absolutely dead. It has nothing but mass starvation to offer, & would—if restored—form merely the prelude to a revolution. One of the perils of the present admin-istration is that it will too seriously heed the pressure of the frantic plutocratic element & swing too far to the right—thereby playing into the hands of irre-sponsible & incompetent radicals. What is needed, quite seriously, is something considerably to the left of the New Deal—but how in hell is such a thing ever to be achieved except by slow degrees? When a "leftist" proposal is openly made, the people get frightened & defeat it—as in California last autumn. Clearly, the only practical course is to go slowly—a little at a time—& get the people used to the habit of change. Certain fixed concepts—such as the inviolability of profit & private property—must be modified & liquefied very gradually. When the first general shift toward the left is fully made, the next one will be less difficult. If the present administration cannot engineer the second step, it will naturally be replaced by one that has a better chance of doing so. The one great thing is to accomplish the needed change gradually & peacefully—avoiding the kind of violent upheaval which creates irreparable harm through the destruction of cultural values. If the Democratic party veers rightward or crystallises where it is—thus replacing the possibly defunct Republican party as a reactionary force—then the next hope is some new liberal party centreing in the La Follette element in Wisconsin. If even that fails, it will be time to see what Norman Thomas, Upton Sinclair, & even the grotesque Huey Pierce Long have to offer. But in my case one may hope that the trend will stick to genuine American movements really suited to the temper of the people, & not veer off into the insane Marxism of self-deluded European slave-populations. The imported Russian-Jewish radicalism of New York City is just as bad as the old Republican plutocracy against which it is arrayed. Both are nationally suicidal.

Regarding my use of the expression "three alternatives" in the political letter—I may only say that the interests of forcible & direct expression did not seem to justify a retention of the archaic limitations formerly governing the word *alternative*. While it is customary with some persons to observe the old restriction (I might myself in a thing designed for permanent preservation), I did not deem it advisable to do so when a sacrifice of force would be involved. You are of course aware that the wider application of *alternative* has been common in the best writing since 1880, & that all editions of Webster's International have justified it as a parallel definition since the 1890 revision. Gladstone repeatedly employed the word in its originally "incorrect" sense. The advisability of such usage depends largely on the individual case. In time, all vestiges of the original limitation will undoubtedly break down because of the strong natural pull of common sense & every-day usage in such a direction. Such a change is far more logical, & far less to be lamented, than the possible parallel change which substitutes *like* for *as*. Incidentally—I notice that in the very paragraph wherein you speak of *alternative*, you employ the word *embrasure* (which means a shallow recess containing a door or window, or else a slant-sided opening in a fortification) in its archaic & obsolete sense of *embrace* or *act of embracing* . . . . a usage definitely inadmissible since Elizabethan times. How come?

No—I did *not* suggest your name as that of a possible member of the Am. Museum. Indeed, I'm not a member myself, although I certainly enjoy going over the establishment when in N.Y. This "membership" business is simply a dodge to raise funds. I wish them well, but haven't the cash!

Regarding cinemas—my attendance during the past twelvemonth has been confined to such performances as my hosts on various visits have dragged me to. I saw "Cleopatra"—which had excellent Roman scenes, but which was spoiled by having the Alexandrian Greek court represented as *native Egyptian* in architecture & costume. As well shew the British Viceroy of India in a Hindoo turban! I saw "The Barretts of Wimpole Street"[4] & liked it—it certainly did bring up the early Victorian age with tremendous verisimilitude. I didn't see the best Catherine film, but saw a distinctly inferior piece of pageantry on the same theme with our Frau Dietrich (whom I had never before seen) in the title role.[5] I saw the Rothschild film—which was smooth, but obviously theatrical. Also saw the Esquimau film—a really fine spectacle & anthropological document despite the tacked-on hokum.[6] Saw the cinema of "Double Door"—which was more mechanical than the play. Also the somewhat insipid "What Every Woman Knows", perverted from Mr. Barrie's drama of a generation ago.[7] And I guess my sight of "Little Women" (good 19th century atmosphere in spots) post-dates my last epistle to you. The one really first-rate thing I've seen since last February is "Don Quixote"—genuine art from start to finish, without a false note.[8] Of the others you mention, I have seen none. Most of the films I've been taken to have been such unmitigated junk that I can't recall either their titles or performers. Last April both Morton & I dozed off to sleep at a show to which the Longs treated us! By the way—you'd have been interested in a lecture I heard last December (by Prof. S. Foster Damon of Brown—biographer of Thomas Holley Chivers) on the cinema as a separate & authentic art. This address was followed by a shewing of "All Quiet"—which I was glad to see again after four years, & which impressed me even more favourably than in 1930.

Interested to hear that Mr. Mellon's Fire Escape was such a comparative neighbour of yours. By this time I dare say that the window exhibited in Providence is fully in place. Various other art exhibits have shed their glow upon our city since my last report—Indo-Chinese sculpture, Sumerian clay tablets, Etruscan tomb-paintings, old French Wall Paper, &c. &c. &c. . . . to say nothing of a splendid collection of Japanese prints permanently acquired by the local museum. A series of weekly poetry readings by bards of greater or less prominence is now going on at the college, & I've attended some of them.

As for that tale of mine written in 1933—I let a few people see it, but never sent it to Wright. I have ceased to pay any attention to the magazine world, but have experimented (not very successfully, I fear) with various improved modes of saying what I'm trying to say. Pressure of other duties has prevented me from experimenting as much as I'd like to—but I'm about to finish a novelette called "The Shadow Out of Time", which I probably won't shew to anybody. Yes—young Bloch certainly is getting there. Do you see *The Fantasy Fan* regularly . . . or at all? I have a lot of duplicates of some of the issues, & could let you have them if you'd enjoy them. The Oct. issue was dedicated to me; the November to Clark Ashton Smith. An alleged biography of me (with a linoleum block cut made by young Rimel from a photograph which Barlow took last June) by F. Lee Baldwin will appear in the March issue.[9]

Your list of planned novels sounds highly alluring, & I trust you'll get around to all of them in due season. But there's no hurry—&, as suggested before, the more experience you acquire before writing them, the mellower, maturer, & better planned they'll be likely to be.

As usual I stand respectfully aghast at your reading list—even though you consider it a sadly restricted one. Bless me, but how do you manage to take in so much? Glancing over the titles, I am forced to confess that I have not read any of them—though as I said once before, I went through the two first Proust books (Swann—Budding Grove) some years ago. And so you've kept awake through "Ulysses"! That's more than I ever tried to do! This new "Musa Dagh" thing is receiving a vast amount of publicity—probably well deserved. I read the author's play "Goat Song" almost a decade ago.[10] Your mention of "Missis Flinders" in connexion with "The Unpossessed"[11] reminds me that the habit of publishing chapters of coming novels as short stories seems to be growing. I've noted several cases of late. Comte d'Erlette used to keep urging me to read "Look Homeward, Angel"—but I never got around to it. Haven't read "Seven Gothic Tales", since it appears from reviews that their kind of horror isn't the sort I'm seeking.[12] So Jules Romains *isn't* so important, after all? Then my regret at non-acquaintance is less keen. I've heard considerable about this Vardis Fisher, & guess I'll have to investigate him sooner or later—probably later. Incidentally, the Caxton Printers of Idaho, who first brought out his work, are considering the publication of a volume of verse by Samuel Loveman.[13] No—I haven't read either of the Jorkens books—for the few stories of that series which I've seen in magazines haven't impressed me.[14] Alas for the pristine Dunsany of "A Dreamer's Tales"! And yet, last year's novel, "The Curse of the Wise Woman", was great stuff from a totally different point of view. About the collection called "The Grim Thirteen"—I heard of it years ago, but never saw it. I'm tolerably sure that the editor was *not* O'Brien, but somebody named Greene.[15] I kept trying to locate it until a reader of it intimated that it didn't amount to so much after all. It must have appeared around 1920. It interests me vastly to know that your father once know John Uri Lloyd. Not long ago I learned that Lloyd is still alive & active at an advanced age. I still advise you to get hold of ETIDORHPA (*Aphrodite* backward) if you can. Yes—I did read "Anthony Adverse", though it took 4 or 5 days. I'm not sorry I did, for it surely does furnish a magnificent panoramic picture of late 18th century & early 19th century life. It has all the casual *details* which make a past age live again. However—I hardly fancy anybody without a special kinship to the 18ᵗʰ century would find it wholly worth his while, for it is full of annoying weaknesses. There is a mawkish overemotionalism—& an almost sickening religious mysticism & belief in "Fate"—while the element of *far-fetched coincidence* is stretched to such lengths as to become absolutely comic. Moreover, there is a distinct letdown in tempo during the final third. The current of interest no longer sweeps one along as formerly. Intricate dealings in international finance usurp too much space, & toward the very end there is a blurred over-acceleration of the action—as if the author were trying to compress the work within certain limits. Most of my friends who have read it like it better than I do—though each has a flaw of his own to pick. I can get along very well without owning or re-reading it. Sorry your friend the *Mercury* has fallen on evil days. I haven't seen a copy in years—for it always struck me as being somewhat artificial in its self-conscious iconoclasm.[16] The one really vital magazine in this country is *Harpers*—which on the one hand has nothing of the precieuse anility of the *Atlantic* & on the other hand nothing of the immature slipshodness of the professional "de-bunkers". I never read a copy of *Esquire*—since a cursory glance at one revealed a discouraging amount of froth & affectation.

My own record of recent reading is meagre & unsensational. I never read *new* books, since there are too many to keep track of. After a decade one can better single out the ones which really do amount to something. Much of my reading during the past year has been in mediaeval books of demonology (Montague Summers translations), lent me by the astonishingly generous bibliophile Koenig, whom I probably described to you last winter. Right now I'm half-way through the famous "Malleus Maleficarum." Koenig has also served to introduce me to a weird author of the first magnitude, of whom I had only vaguely (through Whitehead) heard before—William Hope Hodgson, who was killed in the Great War. After reading all of Hodgson's five books I decided that he ought to go into my article as reprinted by the F F, hence prepared a note for insertion.[17] Hodgson has certain grave defects, but in spite of them achieves an atmosphere of *cosmic outsideness* surpassed only by Blackwood. Other reading of mine has consisted of researches into early mediaeval architecture, some delving into geology, & the re-reading of Tacitus & parts of Virgil. Also some intensive studies in early-American architecture, precipitated by my discovery of the famous "White Pine" series of monographs.

About the pronunciation *frā'kas*—I've just found it in Webster. To what lengths is Yankee provincialism carried! But I fancy I'll continue to say *fră-kă'*, as I always have done.

Regarding my recent experiences—I presume that you've kept track of them through postcards, even though you may have missed a few through changes of address. I finally embarked on the southern trip, lingering a fortnight in N Y with Belknap & the gang. Jim Morton has got married in his old age, but seems to be bearing up very well. On my way south I had a good survey of Washington (giving Georgetown a thorough exploration), & enjoyed my first glimpse of Raleigh, N.C. I stopped a week in Charleston, & hated to move on. Savannah detained me a day—& then Florida. As I said on my card, I had a great time as young Barlow's guest in De Land. The family live 14 miles out of town, but a car keeps them in touch. Live-oaks, Spanish moss, palmettos, pines—& an ideal climate. Barlow is a tremendously brilliant kid, who will make his mark in the world if his health holds out. He has been in Washington since September, having ocular treatment & taking an art course at the Corcoran gallery. De Land is a small town on the idea of Salisbury & Suffolk—but I really like it exceedingly. What I missed there, of course, was *antiquity*. The Barlows were so amazingly cordial that I couldn't break away till late in June—rounding out a 2-month visit. I then spent a week amidst the congenial antiquities of St. Augustine—then 3 days in Charleston again—then Richmond, Fredericksburg & Washington—then old Philadelphia*—& then the pest zone of N.Y. once more. But I didn't see much of N Y this time, since I accompanied the Longs on a trip to Asbury Park, N.J.

Reaching home in July, I was busy in this way & that, & had Morton for a guest early in August—taking him on the usual rounds, including ancient Newport. Later that month W. Paul Cook came down to Boston from Vermont (he's now with his sister in Sunapee, N.H.), & I chose that time to visit Edward H. Cole in the Bostonese suburb of Wollaston. A good time was had by all—Salem & Marblehead trips, & one trip by Cook & myself to Haverhill, where we visited an octogenarian friend. Eventually Cole & his wife took me back to Providence in their car—though I stopped at home only one night before embarking on one of the year's most memorable trips to absolutely new soil . . . . the voyage to Nantucket Island.

I dropped you a card from Nantucket—but hades alive! no card could even begin to describe the archaic charm of this surviving fragment of a bygone century! Only 90 miles from this doorstep—& yet I'd never seen it before! Probably the reason for my delay was the formerly expensive steamboat service—plus the fact that I never realised its full charm till Morton described it to me last year. Now that I've seen it, I'll say that Morton didn't exaggerate a bit. What a place! I must get there again if it kills me! Nantucket is the ultimate island outpost of New England, & forms a sort of meeting-place or boundary betwixt the familiar world we know & the mysterious outer realm of unfathomed watery distance. It is 30 miles from the nearest mainland (Cape Cod), & 54 from New Bedford—the ancient port used by Providence voyagers. It makes about a 6-hour trip—1 hour overland to New Bedford & 5 on the water—from here. I had a sunny day, & the ride to New Bedford was delightful.

---

*where I saw the now restored brick cottage where Poe dwelt 1842–44.

The wharves of the old whaling port possessed their accustomed charm, & I almost hated to leave. The ocean trip was pleasant & varied, including stops at Woods' Hole (on Cape Cod) & Martha's Vineyard, as well as a brief period wholly out of sight of land. Finally, after the modern world was wholly cast off, the low line of the ancient island rose ahead. Old Nantucket . . . . famous in legend & history, yet never before seen by my eyes! At last, when the ship rounded the point into the harbour, there loomed up a skyline of venerable wharves & roofs, topped by white spires & hoary belfries, which belongs altogether to the brighter, vanished world of a century or more ago.

I forget just how much information I managed to crowd on my card. Nantucket is about 15×7 miles in extent (see my map), with its principal town (of the same name now, but called *Sherburne* prior to 1795) on the north shore. In some respects this town is the best-preserved fragment of the elder America in existence today—having cobblestoned streets lined with colonial houses; horse-blocks, hitching-posts, & great silver doorplates; picturesque lanes & waterfront; a windmill built in 1746 & still in order; archaic churches with galleries & box pews; whaling & historical museums—everything, in short, that the antiquarian could ask. The town rises from the water's edge, & the tangle of centuried streets climbs several distinct hills. Its numberless gardens & fine old trees are luxuriant, while its aged wooden houses & great Georgian mansions bear suggestions of Salem. Many architectural features are essentially local—particularly the prevalence of the "salt-box" type of house (this—   elsewhere obsolete after the 17th century) & the railed platform or "walk" for marine observation found on most of the roofs. This island metropolis dates back only to about 1720—the first settlement having lain somewhat westward, on a smaller harbour which closed up around 1700. One of the principal features today is the Maria Mitchell Observatory in Vestal St. (formerly Gaol Lane), which adjoins the birthplace of the celebrated female astronomer (professor at Vassar) whose name it bears. The observatory is modern—a memorial to Prof. Mitchell. I had a good chance to observe Saturn through the excellent 5" telescope.

Nantucket was first described by Gosnold in 1602,[18] & first settled by Massachusetts (Essex Co.) families around 1660. It had a fair-sized Indian population, with whom the whites dealt honourably—though it swiftly declined. The last Indian there died a century ago. In 1664 the island was incorporated into the Province of New-York, but in 1692 was transferred to Massachusetts, to which it has ever since belonged. Its great prosperity came from whaling, which began about 1670. Whales were first killed off shore in small boats, but when they grew locally scarce the Nantucketers began to equip larger whaling vessels & scour the high seas. By 1730 they covered the whole Atlantic, & after 1791 they rounded Cape Horn & made the Pacific their own. Though greatly retarded by the revolution & War of 1812, Nantucket whaling reached its apex in 1842, when the island teemed with wealth

& supported a population of about 10,000. Then whales grew scarcer, & the demand for whale-oil fell off through the discovery & introduction of petroleum. Decline set in, & the last Nantucket whaler came back to port in 1870. After the end of whaling Nantucket fell into great poverty, from which the summer-resort industry finally pulled it. It is now mainly a summer colony—with the fine old houses appreciatively maintained by visitors. The permanent population—some 3800—largely descend from the original settlers, & when not in the summer real-estate business conduct a slim & precarious fishing industry. Typical names are Macy, Coffin, Starbuck, Folger, Ray, Wyer, Gardner, & Hussey. Benjamin Franklin's mother was a Nantucket Folger. At one time Quakerism was dominant in Nantucket, but since 1900 has been extinct. The islanders have a sturdy & distinctive character of their own, & use several idioms peculiar to their remote domain. The surface of the island consists mostly of low, rolling moors—almost without stones, & (outside the town) treeless except for some struggling pines planted in 1847. Fresh ponds abound—the vast amount of pure ground water being a puzzle to physiographers. The contour of the coast is frequently altered by the sea, which washes away land in one place, & deposits sand in another. Climatically, Nantucket is like all islands very equable—with cool summers (I nearly froze several times!) & warm winters. This is the only place in New England where the hedges were not killed last winter. It is nearer the Gulf Stream than any other part of the northeastern states. Aside from Nantucket Town the principal settlement is Siasconset (locally pronounced "Sconset") on the southeastern coast—an indescribably quaint quondam fishing village settled in 1690 & wholly a summer resort. Siasconset's rustic, garden-bordered lanes, with the fishers' cottages all restored & occupied, form a sight not easily forgotten. I had 8 days in Nantucket, & saw about all there was to see. I first took an exhaustive "rubberneck wagon" trip all over the island, & then settled down in the cheapest habitable place I could find—an ancient mansion on a crooked hillside lane made over into a hotel. This joint—called "The Overlook" with good reason—soaked me 9 bucks a week for an excellent room with running water & a superb eastward view of the harbour & Brant Point Light. In the days that followed I did—literally—every inch of the town's tangled lanes on foot, & explored all the historic buildings & museums—including the 1746 windmill. Every separate vista was a poem—& I could spend a whole summer just looking around without acquiring ennui. The full charm of the place is something too elusive for words . . . It includes a curious *apartness*—a sense of suspended time & closeness to other ages & other worlds—which no mainland region could possibly duplicate. The curving, cobbled ways of the town make one see around him the actual, unchanged substance of a whaling port of the past; while the mystical impression conveyed by the dreamlike moors & vague marine horizons is something altogether "out of space, out of time".[19] I did Siasconset thoroughly, & absorbed most of the typical island perspectives. One thing was a positive rejuvenation—my first *bicycle ride* in 20 years! In Nantucket wheels are everywhere for rent, & an adult can pedal around without attracting the least notice. Naturally I was quick to take advantage of this—although I had no idea how much of the cyclist's art I remembered. In youth I was a veritable bike-centaur—but two decades is a long time! Well—after all, I hadn't forgotten a thing! I just hopped on my hired steed, & rode off as if I had last dismounted the night before. Nothing was strange or difficult . . . . except the realisation that it was 1934 instead of 1900 or 1903 or 1907 or some other time back in the Golden Age! I've never before or since encountered anything which gave me an equally powerful impression of sloughing off the years & returning into the mist-enshrouded past. I almost felt constrained to hurry home in time for the opening of school . . . . surely the Providence of 1903 with its little open-platformed trolleys & clattering delivery-wagons & smartly groomed horses & victorias & silently whizzing cycles must lie at the other end of my journey! Looking down, I felt just the least bit surprised to find myself in long trousers . . . . it must, then, be after April, 1904 . . . . Bless my old grey head & creaking bones, but what magic resides in the resumption of some aeon-forgotten activity of youth! Actually, I felt no fatigue or soreness afterward. I wish to hades I could get a bike again & circulate around Rhode Island as I used to, but on the mainland an old geezer like me would look like a fool doing such. Well—anyhow—I had my bit of revived youth on the island, & covered all the roads in great style. I'll bet I came close to 25 m. per hour on some stretches when the wind was with me.

I returned home—rather reluctantly—Sept. 3, & lorded it in solitary state for a while, during my aunt's absence in Maine. In mid-October—when the autumn foliage was at the height of its splendour—I visited Cole again in the Boston zone, & was treated to some memorable trips in his car. On one occasion he took me through Lexington & Concord & Groton to a region in north central Massachusetts which I had never before visited—West Townsend, where the vistas of wooded hills, distant valleys, & white-steepled villages are ineffably lovely. It is curious how different the *two* major types of New England scene are . . . . the seaport & marine countryside, with salt winds, slanting willows, & ancient huddles of gambrel roofs; & the inland hill regions with low-pitched cottages, giant elms, triangular commons, & slender white steeples embowered in dense greenery. It was the inland scene that I beheld on this October trip, & I appreciated it to the full. We dined at a 1774 tavern, & penetrated a state reservation of magnificent woods & ravines & waterfalls . . . . all this in the glory of flaming autumn. In the end Cole brought me home, picked up my aunt, & led the Chevrolet expedition into Rhode Island's picturesque South County—the region which Price & I explored in 1933. In the splendour of autumn the landscape (once again, the *seacoast* New England) was exquisite beyond words—the centuried past of Wickford, unchanged since 1800, & the brooding, stone-walled meadows by the Pettaqaumscutt, where still reposes the ancient snuff-mill where Gilbert Stuart was born in 1755. Cole had never before seen the mill, & I was glad to be able to take him over it. Many of the vistas in this region are said to suggest Virginia landscapes—a curious coincidence, since the local life before the revolution was closer to that of Virginia than any other in the north. Alone in New England this Narragansett Country had large estates with many black slaves . . . . my ancestor Robert Hazard leaving 133 negroes in his will. The patriarchal folkways closely parallelled those of the South—though the plantation-houses followed New England gambrel-roofed lines on a larger scale. Most of the planters had town houses across the bay in Newport—of which the greater number are still standing, though only two of the plantation-houses remain. Livestock & dairying were the great economic standby—Narragansett pacers & Narragansett cheeses being known the world over in the early 18th century. The revolution put an end to all this prosperity—though a few of the old families regained affluence by taking up manufacturing. I guess I told you of the trip through the old Robinson house (best surviving specimen) which Price & I made in 1933. And so it goes. In November Cook & I met again in Boston & confabulated with Cole, Lynch, & others of the old group. We also went to Medford & explored the ancient Royall mansion (1737), which Cook had never entered before. December was filled with lectures (Providence conducted an "art week") & Yuletide festivities. I had a Christmas tree for the first time since boyhood—carrying out the rejuvenation which the Nantucket cycling began. On Dec. 31 I went to N Y to visit Belknap for a week—the event becoming rather a convention through the presence of young Barlow & the arrival of both Wandrei boys . . . . Donald after a trip to California during which he saw Clark Ashton Smith, & Howard direct from St. Paul. Jan. 2 the gang held a meeting at Belknap's with 15 present—about as festive a time as we've had in recent years. Later we met at Loveman's & were shewn his collection of almost 400 Klarkash-Ton drawings—recently brought from Cleveland. I had seen them in 1922, but they were new to Long, Barlow, & the Wandreis. Naturally I also did museums, libraries, & bookstalls. Picked up a copy of Lewis's "Monk" for a dollar . . . . & Barlow got Reynolds' "Wagner the Wehr-Wolf" for 15¢! Home Jany. 8, & since then crushed to earth with work. Feeling rotten, too—digestion all shot to hell. This winter isn't as cacodaemoniacally vicious as its predecessor, but it's plenty bad. I don't get out of the house much—& Jan. 23–4 there was a record-breaking snowstorm which paralysed local traffick. Heard some fairly good poetry readings at the college—Archibald MacLeish & Susanna Valentine Mitchell. My most recent acquisition is a couple of dark walnut chests of drawers—acquired cheaply at a fire sale—to take care of the overflowing chaos of my files. By piling one atop the other I get a very neat 10-drawer cabinet—& the conservative, quasi-colonial lines of the outfit harmonise finely with the mellow Georgian atmosphere of my study. A damned useful outfit! Long has a single chest of this type—but with a glossy green enamel finish I wouldn't want.

And so it goes. As for the rest of the gang—the Wandrei boys now have a flat together in Greenwich Village, at 155 W. 10th St., over the rather noisy "Bohemian" restaurant called Julius's. Dwyer—despite his 38 years—has joined the C.C.C. & is winning substantial honours therein. Address— Barrack 5, C.C.C. Camp 25, Peekskill, N.Y. Comte d'Erlette scintillates in accustomed fashion. Price has gone through a veritable Odyssey—leaving New Orleans in April, tarrying a while in Pawhuska, Okla., in an unprofitable garage partnership, visiting Robert E. Howard in Texas, visiting Klarkash-Ton in Auburn, sojourning under the maternal roof at Oakland, Cal., & finally buying a hilltop cottage near Redwood City, in sight of the lower end of San Francisco Bay. Address—Route 2, Box 100-0-5, Redwood City, California. He has wholly left literature to become a high-pressure success in the pulp-fiction field—mostly detective stuff.

Several new weird publications have appeared—all uniformly lousy. I've read none of them. W T is as mediocre as usual, though the Dec. issue was fair, & the Jan. redeemed by Klarkash-Ton's magnificent "Dark Eidolon". Feb. very poor. *Marvel Tales* struggles along—only 3 issues out so far. F F struggles more successfully—as I said, I can let you have copies if you'd like them.

Well—here's wishing you better luck for '35 than you had in '34! And may Yuggoth & allied powers send an early spring!

Yrs for the Black Sign—

E'ch-Pi-El

Notes

1. The proper quotation is: *Forsan et haec olim meminisse juvabit* ("Perhaps it will one day be pleasurable to remember even these things"). Virgil, *Aeneid* 1.203 (referring to Aeneas' memories of his arduous voyage from Troy to Rome).

2. Evidently JVS had attempted a dramatic adaptation of the first part of R. E. Spencer's *The Lady Who Came to Stay*.

3. The proper quotation is: *Parturient montes, nascetur ridiculus mus* ("Mountains will go into labor; an absurd mouse will be born"). Horace, *Ars Poetica* 139.

4. *Cleopatra* (Paramount, 1934), directed by Cecil B. DeMille; starring Claudette Colbert, Warren William, and Henry Wilcoxon. *The Barretts of Wimpole Street* (MGM, 1934), directed by Sidney Franklin; starring Norma Shearer, Fredric March, and Charles Laughton.

5. HPL refers to these films: *The Rise of Catherine the Great* (London Film Productions, 1934), directed by Paul Czinner; starring Douglas Fairbanks, Jr., Elisabeth Bergner (as Catherine the Great), and Flora Robson; *The Scarlet Empress* (Paramount, 1934), directed by Josef von Sternberg; starring Marlene Dietrich (as Catherine the Great), John Lodge, and Sam Jaffe.

6. *The House of Rothschild* (20th Century Pictures), directed by Alfred Werker; starring George Arliss, Boris Karloff, and Loretta Young. *Eskimo* (MGM, 1933), directed by W. S. Van Dyke; starring Edgar Dearing, Peter Freuchen, and Edward Hearn. It was the first film shot in a Native American language (Inupiat).

7. *Double Door* (Paramount, 1934), directed by Charles Vidor; starring Evelyn Venable, Mary Morris, and Anne Revere. Based on the play by Elizabeth McFadden. *What Every Woman Knows* (MGM, 1934), directed by Gregory La Cava; starring Helen Hayes, Brian Aherne, and Madge Evans. Based on the play by J. M. Barrie.

8. *Adventures of Don Quixote* (Nelson Film/Vandor Film, 1933), directed by G. W. Pabst; starring Feodor Chaliapin, George Robey, and Oscar Asche. Based on the novel by Miguel de Cervantes.

9. The article appeared instead in *Fantasy* magazine.

10. HPL refers to works by the Austrian-Bohemian writer Franz Werfel (1890–1945): *Die vierzig Tage des Musa Dagh* (1933; Eng. tr. 1934 as *The Forty Days of Musa Dagh*), a novel about World War I; and *Bockgesang* (1921; Eng. tr. 1926 as *Goat Song*), a domestic drama.

11. Tess Slesinger (1905–1945), "Missis Flinders" (*Story*, December 1932), a story based on the author's experience in having an abortion. It was incorporated as the last chapter of her novel *The Unpossessed* (New York: Simon & Schuster, 1934).

12. HPL refers to the novel by Thomas Wolfe and the story collection by Isak Dinesen.

13. The volume appeared in 1936 as *The Hermaphrodite and Other Poems*.

14. HPL did eventually obtain the first Jorkens collection (*The Travel Tales of Mr. Joseph Jorkens*, 1931). For HPL's reading of the second collection (*Jorkens Remembers Africa*, 1934), see JVS 49. Elsewhere he called the stories "tripe" (*SL* 5.354).

15. Frederick Stuart Greene (1870–1939), ed., *The Grim Thirteen* (New York Dodd, Mead, 1917 [rpt. 1928]), a collection of horror tales that had been rejected by magazines for being too gruesome. John Munday, a member of the Transatlantic Circulator, had mentioned that he had read the book and was not impressed with the contents; HPL had replied: "I must read 'The Grim Thirteen'" ("The Defence Reopens!" [1921]; *CE* 5.49).

16. HPL refers to the *American Mercury* (1924f.), founded by H. L. Mencken and George Jean Nathan. It suffered a decline in quality after Mencken gave up the editorship at the end of 1933.

17. "The Weird Work of William Hope Hodgson," published as a separate article and then incorporated into "Supernatural Horror in Literature."

18. Bartholomew Gosnold (1571–1607) was instrumental in founding Jamestown in colonial America. He led the first recorded European expedition to, and named, Cape Cod.

19. Edgar Allan Poe, "Dream-Land" (1844), l. 8.

[49]   [ANS][1]

[Postmarked Providence, RI,
19 February 1935]

Glad you've seen old St. Paul's, but sorry its neighbourhood is run down. Hope I can explore it with you some day. I'll wager Norfolk is full of quaint byways if one only knows where to look for them. Some time I hope you can

get a glimpse of ancient St. Luke's—which I think is out in the open country. As you doubtless know, a goodly number of the old Virginia parish churches—serving rural regions—were built right in the middle of woods or fields, far from any village . . . the planters attending in coaches or on horseback. That was also the case in Rhode Island's Narragansett country—the part I spoke of as resembling the south. Old St. Paul's (1707) in Kingstown was moved from such a site (called "The Platform") into a neighbouring village (Wickford) in 1800, after the patriarchal plantation life had passed away. The frame was taken down and re-created—the edifice being of wood. Today the ancient site—with neglected churchyard overgrown with weeds—is a spectral place—as is the crumbling parsonage (called "The Glebe") nearby. ¶ Had a letter from Derleth's publishers asking to see some of my MSS. with a view to a possible book publication. Since this is the 5th time I've had this request—with no results so far—I'm not as excited as I might otherwise be.[2] However, I've sent along some junk just to leave no stone unturned. It'll be back soon enough. ¶ Had an unexpected loan of a copy of "Jorkens Remembers Africa" the other day, & read it through. Some of the stories aren't half bad. ¶ Saw a splendid exhibition of Hokusai's prints—with explanatory lecture—at the museum yesterday. ¶ Weather less extreme—50° Saturday, & 51° Friday. ¶ Baldwin has just sent me a copy of Merritt's "Creep Shadow."
Best wishes—
E'ch-Pi-El

Notes

1. *Front:* First Baptist Church, Providence, R. I. [*HPL's note:* built 1775] Founded by Roger Williams in 1638.
2. Loring and Mussey. The four previous prospective book publishers were (*Weird Tales* 1927), Putnam (1931), Vanguard (1932), and Knopf (1933).

[50]   [ALS]

66 College St.,
Providence, R.I.
March 13, 1935.

Dear Jehvish-Êi:—
            Weltering in a turmoil of tasks, I have had no chance to acknowledge yours of Feby. 13—& the subsequent generous *Story* shipment—until now. However, I sent an envelope of F F back numbers which may perhaps form a semi-acknowledgment. Since then I have learned to my regret that the F F has failed—the February issue being the final one. This is really unfortunate, since the modest little magazine filled a distinct place as a forum for the exchange of ideas & suggestions among fantasy-lovers. *Fantasy Magazine* will take over some of the features—including the scheduled biog-

raphy & portrait of me—though its primary devotion to science fiction will prevent it from really supplying the place of the departed. Eheu! It was a good fellow while it lasted! *Marvel Tales* is also having a rocky time. Have you seen any of the issues of this?

Speaking of magazines—let me thank you most particularly for the copies of *Story*, which ought to give me quite a representative insight into current fictional methods. So far, I haven't had a chance to read them (or any thing else)—but I hope to do so soon, & when I do, I'll drop a line discussing the marked items. I am interested in your statement that the barren, skeletonic type of narrative is giving place to something richer. As for the idea that novels tend to repeat needlessly what other novels have presented before—I would analyse that profoundly before accepting it. It is surely true enough that modern novels, *as written*, do indeed possess this defect—but I would hesitate to believe that a reduction to skeleton form constitutes any cure. I would say, rather, that the novels in question err in a far deeper way—that of attempting to be direct psychological documents instead of real novels. Actually, no novel ought to be a conscious illustration of any particular point. It ought to be simply a story—presenting glimpses of life for the sake of the aesthetic pleasure involved in glimpsing, & wholly eschewing the intellectual & philosophical. If this sound course be followed, there will be no need of worrying about the *novelty* of the material. Any experience of life—the old even more than the new—is equally moving when presented for its own sake through the imaginative filtration of a vigorous artistic mind. It is not the *subject-matter*, but the especial *individual perspective*, which needs to be new; & so varied is the imagination of mankind, that there is never any chance of an exhaustion of fresh perspectives. The ordinary experiences of life have been receiving artistic treatment ever since the age of Homer—yet without any diminution in the poignancy of the portrayal. What *does* grow quickly stale—because it never had any firmness of foundation—is the so-called "novel" which is really no more than a laboured intellectual effort to illustrate some special phase of human nature. This kind of thing is simply a psychological essay masquerading under false colours. It tries to present *directly* that which true art presents only *incidentally*. Since it has not the feel of life about it, it naturally becomes boresome except when treating of some unfamiliar corner of man's experience or emotions. But this is only because it is not fully-developed, well-rounded art. It depends upon *intellectual curiosity* alone, whereas true art does not. Art is another matter entirely—reaching an altogether different group of sensations & depending not at all on novelty except in symbolism & perspective. Of course it is easier to gratify curiosity than to create art, hence the beginner has a better chance of getting a quick hearing with "special psychological studies" than with attempts at genuinely artistic, well-rounded echoing of the total substance of life. It all depends on what one is trying to do. The "psychological-document" type of story so popular today is of great historical & scientific importance, but of almost no significance in literature. This is probably one of the blankest ages in literature since the post-Elizabethan petering-out. There will be no real literature until society has re-crystallised sufficiently to allow writers to become interested in *the flux of life as a whole* instead of in special subdivisions of it as overemphasised by transient, chaotic conditions.

Thanks for the compliment regarding my prose style—I wish it were merited! Most of my critics seem to complain of a certain heaviness & involvedness in Grandpa's voluminous periods—though I'm hang'd if I see what can be done about it! My misgivings about my fiction go deeper than the mere linguistic dress, & pertain largely to the marshalling of incidents, selection of significant detail, & establishment of emotional gradations. The length of time I have been attempting fiction forms no real measure of the degree of success attained—or unattained. I finished "The Shadow Out of Time" (second version) Feby. 22, but am too doubtful of its merits to attempt the appalling task of typing its 65-odd pages. I may simply tear it up & begin over again. However, young Derleth has offered to attempt the deciphering of the original pencil scrawl & give a rough opinion (& I'll bet it *will* be rough!) of the yarn—so I've shot the whole business to him. If his report is not too adverse, I shall probably set the thing on the rounds of the gang. No word from Loring & Mussey about the older MSS. as yet.

As to your familiarity with a wide variety of human types & situations—I never supposed it was as extensive as that of the knockabout tramp writers who are nowadays bursting into an ephemeral print. I merely contrasted it with the more limited experience of those whom I personally know. And I don't quite grasp the significance of your distinction regarding generations—since it was with others of your own age that I was comparing you! I have a fair idea of what the boys of the various families I know are doing, & am also in touch with a full score of young fellows through literary correspondence—but have never come across any of the semi-hobo types you mention. Virtually all the boys I know are very restricted in their contacts. They tend—because of the financial stringency of the times—to be very parochial & untravelled; but none has attempted any 'bumming' as yet. They stay at home, go through high-school (general *public* high-schools now) & college, & then manage to work into some business or other (occasionally their father's), or drift into free-lance writing & Greenwich Village stuff (like the Wandrei boys). And I am speaking of *your own* generation—kids under 25. Excepting yourself, I can't think of any boy* who has really talked—on the basis of confidential personal acquaintanceship—with members of the actual working

---

*Robert E. Howard has indeed knocked about a bit—but his 28 years may put him outside your generation. Arthur Leeds (50) has also seen the world from various angles. Morton (64) as well.

class or underworld fringe. They *affect* the proletarian pose now & then, but would hardly know what to do if confronted by some of the types you have described—Ross, &c. &c. Their contacts are very narrow, & they seem to hold rather unreal ideas of the colourful figures of which they learn through books & the stage & cinema. Even when they become sports or Greenwich-Villagish they meet the vague underworld in certain specialised ways. Wandrei thinks he's a regular devil—& so he is, but his associates in the wench-&-gin world are merely other well-born sensation-seekers like himself. He knows nothing of the elemental substances & struggle of life except on paper, & can have no idea of the emotions & tides of action taking form among the seething hordes of waterfront, factory, wheatfield, railway "rods" &c. The average boy has merely read of these seething hordes—& generally in a very superficial way. Well—as you say, your own knowledge of varied types is perhaps not as extensive as that possessed by typical "wild boys of the road", but it certainly exceeds that of any other youth I can think of within my radius of acquaintance. Hence my remark of last month. And it is not all a matter of mere contact, either. The point is that you *notice* the varied type you meet—the ordinary as well as the extraordinary. Others might see people without studying them so closely or singling out their essential & typical qualities . . . . . hence the myriad writers who reflect a wholly unreal world, dissociated from the scenes actually around them. Of persons I know, only Derleth seems to share this trick of observing & exploring character—& of course his range of study is infinitely narrower than yours. ¶ Regarding the element of formal education—it is certainly true that a greater number of untrained or one-sidedly trained persons are writing now, than were writing in the past. Colleges are ceasing to treat the classics as compulsory subjects, & linguistic standards are undoubtedly at a low ebb. Fashion, too, encourages a kind of superficiality involving a disregard of the coördinated facts of human experience & a careless violation of traditions & harmonies whose sources are far deeper than the violators can realise. This general condition combines with the attitude of *enquiry versus artistry* which I previously mentioned (& which may be the direct result of the condition), to render a good deal of current writing wholly ineffective as literature—however valuable it may be as sociological source-material. Fortunately it is not *universal*—especially in Great Britain—so that the torch of literary art may be considered as flickering dangerously rather than as totally extinguished. It ought to be the supreme effort of every well-wisher of civilisation to keep this torch alight—& to avoid any such violent overturn of cultural standards as has occurred in Russia. The Russians have fanatically torn down all the upper stories of their aesthetic temple, & are having to build laboriously over again what they could easily have saved.

Thanks immensely for the glimpse of "Ghost Piece", which seems to me a highly effective adaptation of the first part of Spencer's novel. I'm not enough of a drama critic to complain about the diction & mechanism—

though you might possibly build up something a trifle more casually lifelike through repeated experiments. I enjoyed the play vastly just as it is. Regarding cinematic adaptation—it *would* make an admirable film, though I am told that new writers have virtually no chance to place material with the established corporations. What you say of the exaggerated cautiousness of producers (an attitude probably caused by fake plagiarism-charges) would seem to sustain this latter point. Your idea for a Chaplin musical comedy sounds excellent to a layman. In time Charlie will probably have to talk on the screen—was it you who said that his reluctance is the result of a residual Cockney accent which he can't quite shake off? I should think he ought to have such a thing fairly in hand after all these years!

No—I was never in touch with Fred Lewis Pattee. Amateur journalism's connexion with Penn State (circa 1919–22, if memory serves aright) was established through one of our members—a Mrs. Anne Tillery Renshaw, now head of a school of elocution in Washington—who went there as an associate professor. She organised her classes into a literary club connected with the United Amateur Press Association, hence we of the Association handled a good deal of their work & assisted them to some extent in a critical way. Pattee was there at the time, & Mrs. Renshaw sometimes spoke of him—indeed, she sent me a copy of his weird novel, "The House of the Black Ring."[1] But I can't recall that he ever took any interest in the U.A.P.A. work. I've glanced at his literary history, & agree with you regarding his somewhat anile & Phelpsian perspective.[2]

Thanks for the Dugan cuttings, which I return herewith in case you want them. They certainly are clever in their chosen field—appearing doubly so when one reflects that both wit & drawing come from the same person. That is the kind of thing which is eminently salable—so that I doubt if Dugan will ever be bothered by major financial worries. He certainly must be a brilliant & interesting chap!

Your assorted literary notes are always interesting. I wonder if Bassett Morgan's novel[3] is merely another variant of his single plot? I'd like to read that Wells–Huxley "Science of Life"—indeed, I shall buy it if it ever comes out at a reasonable price. Another thing I want is Wells's later outline—dealing with economics.[4] A friend of mine is highly enthusiastic about the Sheean book—of which some interesting chapters were published in *Harpers*.[5] As for book-of-the-month clubs—they have their naive & absurd side, but they also have their advantageous side. I wish I had the cash to join one—they are just what a lazy guy like me needs. I never have the energy to look up a book at the library, but will read anything delivered at my door. Wish I could see the fantastic items you mention. "New Tales of Horror" contains material wholly unknown to me.[6] Regarding magazines—I shall use your appraisals as a guide in reacquainting myself with the periodical field I have so long neglected . . . . an amusing neglect, since one of my aunt's closest friends is head of the periodical room in the Prov. Pub. Library![7] I haven't seen *The Nation* or *The New Republic* in years. In my day they were too technically political to be interesting—& too intent on their special point of view to be representative. What I want in a magazine is an accurate, disinterested view of recent developments in pure science, the arts, philosophy, history, sociology, government, &c &c., presented in a balanced, straightforward manner within the comprehension of the ordinary civilised layman. To my mind, *Harpers* is just about it. It has no axes to grind, but simply lets the best minds put their own material forward in their own respective ways. I don't see how it can be called "too conservative" unless one bothers to read the editorial pap at the end. Poor Eddie Martin seems obliged to say a few nice, conventional things to placate his elder clientele—but when it comes to *choosing contributions* he certainly takes off the lid![8] Any recent issue of *Harpers* is full of keen, intelligent stuff which literally rips the pants off the smug Hooverites of yesteryear. And the blinder-wearing religionists, too, get it in the neck from articles like Prof. Leuba's survey of American scientific beliefs in the August issue.[9] I'm hanged if I can see how any magazine could be less irrationally conservative than *Harpers*. Remember that a lot of the stuff in the more ostentatiously radical sheets is pure emotional piffle—designed to please the wish-thinking radical element just as the bland, mincing soporifics in Old Lady *Atlantic* are designed to please the octogenarian retired-clergyman element. *Harpers* goes after *the truth*—whatever its political implications may be. And the truth brought out in recent issues is certainly the very last sort of thing Messrs. Mills & Mellon[10] would be likely to relish! As for its *fiction*—that is admittedly insipid. Unfortunately the current fashion is a pallid & effete one, & *Harpers* succumbs because no especial issue of truth versus error is involved. As for the reviews— I'll admit that I haven't followed them very closely . . . . . there are so damned many reviews everywhere! Regarding newspapers & their literary sections—I sometimes see the *Herald-Tribune,* but it strikes me as more superficial & capricious than the *Times.* The reviewers try to be smart & kittenish, & tend to lack thoroughness. The old *Tribune* used to be our hereditary Sunday paper, but it put on so many tawdry affectations & commonnesses in the post-war years that it began to seem like a strange institution. In 1924, when it merged with the *Herald,* I dropped it in favour of the *Times*—which has no silly frills, & usually employs literate reviewers who understand the books they read & the background behind them. The *Sat. Rev. of Lit.* seems pretty fair, but I haven't seen a copy in aeons. About Messrs. Hearst & Brisbane[11]—I can't recall ever reading one of their products through. They were never other than cheap dollar-chasers, & their rabble-catering pap always seemed to me—so far as I stopped to notice it at all—either absurd or vulgarly inflammatory. My family would not have had a Hearst paper in the house. While I haven't seen one of their screeds in 10 or 15 years, I believe they are still playing on the ever-lucrative organ of mass prejudices & wielding the same old weapon of self-profiting propaganda. Exchanges say that they are all for "rugged individualism" of some sort—god knows what sort! So far as the World Court goes—I don't think it matters a damn whether the U.S. joins or keeps out or whether it exists or not.[12] All these pompous international bubbles are 100% meaningless & ineffective—League of Nations &c. &c. They don't do any harm—but they don't do any good either. No glib arrangement of debaters can ever cause any nation to do what it doesn't choose to do. Look at the record since 1919 & draw your own conclusions!

Good luck if you decide to compete for that Doubleday prize! And so Charles Fulton Oursler has tackled the ancient Accomac peninsula? My friend Leeds used to know Oursler well—when the latter was with the Macfadden outfit. He certainly does cover a lot of ground! Yes—I knew he was a magician—Houdini often spoke of him in that connexion.[13] Interesting that your father once knew him. Concerning cinemas—"Don Quixote" still remains the last I've seen. Possibly however, I shall be aroused to further ventures in screen-staring by the establishment in this city of a "Fine Arts Theatre" like some in Boston & N.Y., where unpopular & presumably non-lucrative films will be displayed. I really meant to go the first week, when "Men of Aran"[14] (reputedly splendid) was on, but something came up every day to prevent me. This week the programme is of foreign films—French, Polish, & Swedish. They won't have to run Italian films because we have an enormous Dago colony with 2 or 3 theatres constantly shewing the latest from the old-a countree.

About "War & Peace"—I haven't read it in years, but I don't like Tolstoi anyhow. There is something ineluctably mawkish & incipiently hysterical about he old goof. Some of it, of course, is merely racial or cultural—just the Slav in him—but Dostoievsky & Turgeniev & Chekhov aren't quite so extreme. In some respects Russian fiction was almost unexcelled—its unsparing realism & psychological penetration being marvellous for its period. One wonders whether it will ever develop again when the shattered culture slowly revives & the Marxian fallacy becomes abeyant in aesthetics. Ibsen impressed me greatly in his day—but I haven't read a thing of his for 30 years, & don't know how he would strike me know.

Congratulations on your poetic stirrings! I think you are getting the idea of speaking in symbols & image, & may find this medium very useful for certain forms of self-expression which do not lend themselves readily to fiction. "Life, the Old Bitch" has genuine force—& the "Annie" piece may take form adequately when you decide on the right form & manner. Keep on experimenting!

As usual, I learn of your doings with much interest. Glad the increased size of the bottoms lightens your task a bit—for I assume that the greater ease in catching overbalances the greater difficulty during periods of accumulation. The mill certainly has served to introduce you to some singular & perhaps literarily useful characters! Your notes on the general region—including the city of Norfolk—are highly interesting. I shall read them if I ever get around to the long-postponed (though Derleth-urged) task of pursuing "Look Homeward, Angel." The various Salisbury, Ocean City, & Suffolk character-sketches are certainly raw material for a whole cycle of novels, & I hope you are preserving duplicates in your note books. You may want to draw on them in future. What a curious melange—& yet I dare say one could unearth a comparable assortment anywhere if one knew just how to go about it. But tone must have a keen eye, sharp selective imagination, & retentive memory to capture the essence of some characters.

Regarding political matters—at the moment, it does look as if the rightward pressure were taking dangerous effect on the government; but I fancy it is too early to be dogmatic. The whole problem is to find some course which is not only conceivably feasible, but possible of actual establishment through the existing political machinery. This is harder than it seems, for pressure is brought to bear in multifarious ways. It will have to be a gradual process—with plenty of time for the reactionaries to ponder on the rising rumble of mass demands & modify their obstructions accordingly. Huey Long, Upton Sinclair, & Father Coughlin are salutary irritants—unless the republicans find a way to use them in splitting the liberal vote. The growing response to such appeals is slowly shewing the mossbacks the utter impossibility of restoring a ruthless laissez-faire regime—& therefore preparing them for retreat. Government policies, too, will have to veer again toward courageous experiment in order to meet the demand thus manifested. But it will necessarily be a slow seesawing. Long & kindred extremists could never dominate an election—they could only divide the votes & perhaps let outrageous reactionaries slip in. The safest policy is to stick by the most liberal element *which can actually get its measures into effect*. It will be easier to take this as a first step—a point of departure for further moves—than to attempt to introduce radical changes all at once, when such an attempt is palpably doomed to certain failure. Even if such an attempt could succeed, there is no one plan in existence on which to found a stable regime. Sinclair is for socialism, Long for a curtailed capitalism whose workability is very doubtful, Coughlin for something else again, Townsend for still another panacea . . . . & so on. Fancy the fight which all these factions would have among themselves, with the Marxian Jews leering in the offing & waiting to pounce at the propitious moment! And anybody who can't see the utter impossibility of unity among these elements is blind indeed. Long & Townsend are for something utterly antagonistic to all that Sinclair & Norman Thomas (who themselves differ!) represent. Actually, Sinclair & Thomas are probably right—for it is not likely that private capitalism could stand the strain which "wealth-sharing" would put upon it. Collectivism of some sort is bound to come—it is the only way an entire mechanised nation can be permanently fed & clothed & housed—but he way to get it is to keep pressing on a responsible government capable of a unified (though varied &

experimental) policy & effective action. So for the present I can be set down as still a New-Dealer.

Regarding recent events—possibly I told you of the lecture on Hokusai in connexion with an exhibition of his prints. Great stuff—I've always been a devotee of Sino-Japanese art. Another lecture was on contemporary Russian Soviet art—with lantern slides. Very interesting—& I was astonished to see how relatively well the bolsheviks are doing despite the incubus of the Marxian fallacy of "social purpose". Some of them take their dogma lightly, & produce very passable work in the historic Byzantine tradition. Others, of course, follow the freakish "ideology" of Lenin & produce nothing but cheap political propaganda. Paradoxically, none of this art is as radical in an aesthetic way as the decadent work of western artists—the cubist, surrealist, &c. stuff . . . . "Suicide in Costume" & so on. But even the best of it is merely a fraction as good as what Russia could have had if she had only avoided a violent revolution. Still another interesting lecture was on the recently discovered 9th & 10th century mosaics in the great church of St. Sophia in Constantinople—by Thomas Whittemore,[15] who had charge of the uncovering. Now that the building has been wisely transformed to a museum, the modern trappings are being cleared away—leaving it as it was in its prime. The edifice has always fascinated me— a product of Rome's final decay (A.D. 532–8), yet embodying the majesty of Roman design in one titanic swan-song. It has, of course, the subtle Oriental touches which had begun to develop as a separate Byzantine architecture—& these mosaics, installed 300 to 400 years later, are utterly Byzantine in their technique. The building is one of the best preserved of all the large structures which have come down from the fringe of classical antiquity. When it was erected, Latin was still the tongue of Western Europe & North Africa, & the Roman people has not yet begun to realise that the occidental half of their empire had irrevocably fallen. Justinianus brought the Eastern Empire to its apex of power—even reconquering Italy for the time being. People in that age must have felt somewhat like people today—with impending change in the air—yet nothing really radical happened. It was over 100 yrs. before the Moslem wave swept the Mediterranean littoral; & 400 years before the lowest point of the Dark Ages was reached. Great shifts usually come slowly!

My outing season has begun early this year—precipitated by a visit from an interesting young man (Robert E. Moe, son of an old friend in Milwaukee) March 2–3. This youth, who graduated from U. of Wis. in 1933 with high honours in electrical engineering, at once stepped into an excellent position with the Gen. Electric Co. Lately he was transferred to Bridgeport, Conn., which put him within cruising radius of Providence (130 m) & N.Y. (60 m). I had not seen him since he was a little towhead of eleven—& he certainly has grown to 22 now. He came in "Skippy"—his faithful 1928 Ford—& I shewed him all the colonial sights of Providence & of the quaint little seaports down both sides of Narragansett Bay—Warren & Bristol on the east shore, & East Greenwich & Wickford on the west shore. The weather was very favourable, & I certainly welcomed the sight of the countryside after so long an hibernation. My guest seemed very appreciative, & expects to come again. I'm suggesting that he get in touch with Long & others of the gang in N.Y.—Koenig (an electrical engineer) ought to be especially congenial.

My first *pedestrian* outing occurred March 6, when the temperature rose to *65°*. On this occasion I took a 12-mile walk in the countryside north of Providence, & felt much the better for it. A later excursion—March 9, when a relative took my aunt & me to ride—extended through the terrain east of Providence, just across the line in Massachusetts. We had some excellent vistas of woods & fields & village spires, & could feel on every hand the subtle atmosphere of coming spring.

Social note—the weird-science-fiction-fan population of Providence has just been swelled by a very energetic new electron, as I had impressed upon me last week. I was reading the paper once evening when my aunt entered the library to announce a caller . . . a "Mr. Sterling". Close on her heels the visitor appeared . . . in the person of a little Jew boy about as high as my waist, with unchanged childish treble & swarthy face innocent of the Gillette's passage. He *did* have long trousers—which somehow looked grotesque upon so tender an infant. It appears that he is one of the endless kid fans clustering around the late F F & *Fantasy Magazine,* who had read my stuff & learned my address from someone in the fantasy world. He's a typical New York Yid—but his papa has just been made assistant manager of the local fur emporium, so he's a Providentian now . . . in the Classical High School. And oy, vhat ah shild! Vhat ah shild! If they all come as precocious as this, I don't wonder that Friend Adolf is afraid they'll juggle the shirts off the German people! Damme if the kid didn't talk like a man of 30—correcting all the mistakes in the current science yarns, reeling off facts & figures a mile a minute, & displaying the taste & judgment of a veteran. He has already sold stories to *Wonder* & other pulps, & is bubbling over with ideas. Others in his family have reviewed books for the *Herald-Tribune* & written for various "slicks". And now—being fully weaned from Mellin's Food & encased in long trousers—he is prepared to conquer ancient Providence. He vants he should organise it ah brench of the Science Fiction League here, &c. &c. &c. Vell, vell! I gave him some duplicate F Fs & other items, & he says he's going to call again. Hope he won't become a nuisance—I don't want to discourage him, for he really does seem like an astonishingly promising brat.

Well—let me again thank you for the glimpse of "Ghost Piece", & for the splendid array of *Stories*—of which more anon. Haven't had time to read "Creep, Shadow", or the March W T as yet. Feby. W T very poor. Hope you'll find better industrial conditions as time goes on, & that meanwhile all your literary ventures—novels & other projects—may gradually take shape. ¶

And so it goes. Now to get my programme a bit under control. ¶ Yrs for the black litany of Nug & Yeb—E'ch-Pi-El

P.S. I've just acquired an infinitely useful volume—the new 1-volume Modern Encyclopedia now issued by Grosset & Dunlap for $1.95. Revised to 1935, & full of recent items not to be found elsewhere. I really needed this badly—my latest other encyclopaedia being a 1914 one. I was sorely tempted in 1933, when the original $3.50 edition came out, but now I'm glad I waited. It chronicles some events as recent as last September. Fancy finding neutrons, N.R.A., Nazis, &c. in an encyclopaedia!

Notes

1. Fred Lewis Pattee (1863–1950), a professor of English at Pennsylvania State University (1894–1928). After HPL's death Pattee reviewed *Supernatural Horror in Literature* (New York: Ben Abramson, 1945) in *American Literature* 18, No. 2 (May 1946): 175–77.

2. HPL refers to Pattee's *A History of American Literature Since 1870*.

3. Bassett Morgan (1884–1977), *The Golden Rupee* (London: John Long, 1934). Morgan published numerous stories in *WT* and other pulps.

4. HPL refers to Wells's *The Work, Wealth, and Happiness of Mankind* (Garden City, NY: Doubleday, Doran, 1931). HPL did in fact read the book (*OFF* 379).

5. A reference to Vincent Sheean (1899–1975), *Personal History* (1935), an account of Sheean's journalistic work that won a National Book Award and was filmed as *Foreign Correspondent* (1940). Some chapters had appeared in *Harper's*.

6. *New Tales of Horror* (London: Hutchinson, 1934), an anthology of weird tales anonymously edited by John Gawsworth.

7. Marian F. Bonner (1883–1952).

8. Edward S. Martin (1856–1939), editor of *Harper's* and author of the "Editor's Easy Chair" column at the end of the magazine.

9. James H. Leuba, "Religious Beliefs of American Scientists," *Harper's* 169, No. 2 (August 1934): 291–300.

10. Andrew W. Mellon (1855–1937) and Ogden L. Mills (1884–1937) served successively as U.S. secretary of the treasury under Harding, Coolidge, and Hoover (1921–32 and 1932–33).

11. William Randolph Hearst (1863–1951), publisher of numerous popular magazines and newspapers, and one of his chief editors, Arthur Brisbane (1864–1936).

12. The World Court was the informal name of the Permanent Court of International Justice, established under Article 14 of the League of Nations and functioning from 1921 to 1945. The United States never joined the court, but US judges served on it.

13. Charles Fulton Oursler (1893–1952), American journalist and editor who wrote detective stories under the pseudonym Anthony Abbot. He worked as supervising editor (1921–41) for magazines and newspapers published by Bernarr Macfadden. The Accomack peninsula is on the Eastern Shore of Virginia; presumably Oursler was

speaking there. In the 1920s he worked with Houdini in exposing fake mediums and later wrote the book *Spirit Mediums* (1930).

14. *Men of Aran* (Gainsborough Pictures, 1934), directed by Robert J. Flaherty; starring Coleman "Tiger" King, Maggie Dirrane, and Michael Dirrane. The film, half documentary and half fictional, treats of the difficult life of people who live on the Aran Islands off the west coast of Ireland.

15. Thomas Whittemore (1871–1950), American archaeologist who devoted himself chiefly to Byzantine and Coptic art.

[51]   [ALS]

April 11[, 1935]

Dear Jehvish-Êi:—

Just a brief line to express my renewed appreciation of the *Story* issues—perusal of which I have just completed. They certainly form a splendid glimpse of contemporary life, & a representative sample of the moment's literary methods.

On the whole, they certainly excel the 1933 crop. In art & workmanship, O'Connor's "Michael's Wife" is far & away the best.[1] In actual emotional insight & significance it would be harder to pick a winner. Some of the stories have a high *informative* value—as source-materials of contemporary social history—without being really alive as art. That is, they point out conditions in an accurate illustrative way, though the diagrams often remain obviously such . . . not springing to life & making the reader feel that the characters & scenes have had actual existence. The range of human emotions represented is not as wide as it might be—though such a restriction is perhaps to be expected from a body of authors so young (in the main) that they lack historic perspective. They are so engrossed in the immediate present that they forget civilisation's 10,000-year-old record, which has included many crises more significant than the contemporary one. But naturally, too much cannot be expected of the short story. Its scope is too restricted to allow it to plumb great depths of character & emotion. If it faithfully mirrors certain isolated but reasonably representative bits of life & mood, it can be said to have amply fulfilled its function.

The stories you marked seem largely worthy of that distinction. I haven't yet attempted any thoughtful untangling of the Faulkner allegory, but must say that I don't see much object or value in such an enigmatic form. I agree concerning the essential spuriousness & artificiality of "The Peddler". This is clearly a piece of mechanical dramatic arrangement—with badly motivated emotions & visibly theatrical devices. The dog is a distinctly unreal figure—obeying the laws of melodrama rather than those of nature. This story really falls outside the magazine's tradition. The contributions by assorted Levantines are clever in their way—though this genre of confused reminiscence is getting to be frightfully overdone. I fancy Saroyan is the brightest of the young Asiatics. The Pirandello story is a bit too *philosophical* to be living fiction, & "Acid" is too much of an hypothetical technical report to be fiction at all. It is *illustration* rather than imaginative creation . . . good stuff, but not a story. The same is true of dozens of others—"Fall of Lucifer", "Men Like Gods", "Caballero", "Eine Kleine Nacht", &c. All in all, the one first-rate piece of fiction as fiction is "Michael's Wife". Many of the tales are primarily poetic, symbolic, or allegorical in their appeal—such as "My Father Sits in the Dark", & "With Some Gaiety & Laughter." Next under "Michael's Wife" in order of merit I'd place Alvah C. Bessie's "Night Call." This is hardly a *story*, but it involves some searching analyses of minute mood-variations. For third place I fancy I'd tend to nominate the Saroyan "Resurrection of a Life."[2]

All told, a creditable assortment. If any general tendency is revealed, I imagine it is one of the exploration of odd & obscure corners of life & thought. Backwaters, stunted & undeveloped human types, shabby, furtive emotions & ignominious situations seem to predominate overwhelmingly. The panoramic value of this school is therefore almost as incomplete & misleading as that of the fictional school which deals only with highly-evolved types & major situations. To see man whole, one must study both schools. Another tendency is to substitute scientific documentation & demonstration for creative artistry—to produce sociological & psychological theses instead of imaginative creations which make the reader live the lives of the characters. And of course there is also the disproportionate emphasis on the *present* age— appropriate enough in sociology, but distinctly disappointing in literature. But with all these limitations, I really think that the newer stuff is a decided improvement over the earlier short stories of the Anglo-Saxon tradition. Fiction never was our strong point—we have no Balzacs, Chekhovs, or de Maupassants—& our older stories were so abominably false, artificial, shallow, & visibly mechanical that anything in the line of honest truth—however one-sided or unimaginative it may be—is preferable to the pap of the Quiller-Couch or Stevenson or H. C. Bunner[3] or Kipling or O. Henry age. The break away from artificial unctuousness is a good thing—but now the second step remains to be taken . . . . the restoration of the short story, with its newly acquired virtue of sincerity, to the domain of creative art.

Well—thanks again for the magazines, which certainly gave me a welcome & valuable insight into what is going on. I hope that *Story* may prosper—growing along with the fictional stream itself, & avoiding those pitfalls of fashion & standardisation which have dragged commercial fiction down to a pathetically low level.

Lately read Gustav Meyrink's "The Golem", lent me by young Barlow. The most magnificent weird thing I've struck in aeons! The cinema of the same title[4] which I saw in 1921 was a mere substitute using the empty name—with nothing of the novel in it. What a study in subtle fear, brooding hints of elder magic, & vague driftings to & fro across the borderline betwixt dream & waking! There are no *overt* monsters or miracles—just symbols &

suggestions. As a study in lurking, insidious *regional* horror it has scarcely a peer—doing for the ancient, crumbling Prague ghetto what I have vainly tried to do for certain festering New England backwaters in some of my own laboured efforts. I had never read the novel before, but mentioned it in my article as a result of having seen the cinema. Now I perceive that I ought to have given it an even higher rating than I did. Also read Merritt's "Creep, Shadow"—but this is pretty cheap stuff beside "The Golem." Essentially popular pulp romance—though there are some vivid hints of cosmic *outsideness* & a splendid series of climactic tableaux. Another recent thing I read was Hugh Walpole's "Portrait of a Man With Red Hair"—full of sinister suggestion & sadism, but not essentially weird. Also read Derleth's third detective novel—"Three Who Died". Considerably better than its immediate predecessor—though more of an abstract 'who killed whom?' puzzle than a real story. I guessed the outcome at p. 145—out of 252. The youthful Comte d'Erlette certainly is just about as clever as they make 'em!

The sole cinema I've witnessed since my January N.Y. trip is "Men of Aran"—which played a return engagement at that "Fine Arts" theatre I told you about. Great stuff! Not a drama, but a magnificent transcript of life in a vivid & forbidding setting. Have you seen it? The Aran isles seem to be mere ocean-pounded rocks like that in "Skule Skerry"[5]—& the struggle of the inhabitants with the savage sea & the barren surface are incredible epics of hardship & danger. Potatoes can be grown only in artificial mounds of seaweed & earth (the latter laboriously extracted from rock crevices) laid along the rocky terrain. With this desperate fight for mere physical existence made necessary by conditions, it's a wonder anybody tries to live on the islands—yet they have been continuously inhabited since prehistoric times, as old stone ruins prove. The ancestors of the present islanders were living in much the same way when Caesar landed in Britain & when Sextus Julius Frontinus stationed the Second Legion at Isca Silurum . . . the Hill of Dreams. What the future holds, none can tell . . . but it is significant that the Outer Hebrides are beginning to be abandoned after thousands of years. I have been interested in the Arans ever since reading Synge's magnificent "Riders to the Sea".

Did I mention my *second* step toward getting my files in order? On March 23 I picked up at a bargain sale 6 small 4-drawer cabinets to supplement the two larger ones I got in January. As a result, my papers & cuttings are now in the best order they've been in since around 1910 . . . . though lots of junk still remains in cardboard boxes or on open shelves.

Am attending some excellent lectures on Dr. Franklin & his social-political ideas—by Prof. Verner W. Crane of the U. of Mich.—formerly of Brown.[6] Old Ben was quite a boy—but insufferably tradesman-minded!

I was a bit premature in proclaiming an early spring—some beastly weather has intervened. Damn this subarctic climate!! Travel prospects poor—but I expect to pay Edward H. Cole a brief visit in the Boston zone early in May. Hope all goes as well as possible in Suffolk.

Again thanking you for *Story*—which has really formed a valuable element in my contemporary education—

I remain

Yr most oblig'd & obt Servt

———E'ch-Pi-El

P.S. Yes—the school & collegiate sketches which you selected for mention— "Fratres in Collegio" & "Ad Viros Faciendos"—are really very powerful informative & psychological sketches.

Notes

1. Frank O'Connor, "Michael's Wife," *Story* No. 32 (March 1935): 86–100.
2. HPL refers to the following stories in *Story:* No. 27 (October 1934): Alvah C. Bessie, "A Night Call" (5–21); No. 28 (November 1935): William Faulkner, "Lo!" (5–21); Jerome Weidman, "My Father Sits in the Dark" (22–25); James Van Liew, "The Peddler" (35–50); William Saroyan, "Resurrection of a Life" (71–77); No. 30 (January 1935): Luigi Pirandello, "The Captive" (5–20); William Turner, "Acid" (50–59); No. 31 (February 1935): George F. Meeter, "Men Like Gods" (35–47); Frank K. Kelly, "With Some Gaiety and Laughter" (71–77); No. 32 (March 1935): Amos Godfrey McConkey, "Caballero" (22–30); Peter De Vries, "Eine Kleine Nacht" (68–74); Alfred Grimwood, "Fall of Lucifer" (75–85);
3. Henry Cuyler Bunner (1855–1896), editor of the comic magazine *Puck* and also a popular novelist and poet.
4. *The Golem* (Germany, 1921), directed by Paul Wegener; starring Paul Wegener.
5. A story by John Buchan in *The Runagates Club*.
6. Verner W. Crane (1889–1974), professor of history at Brown (1920–30) and the University of Michigan (1930–59) and author of *Benjamin Franklin, Englishman and American* (1936) and other works.

[52]   [ALS (fragmentary)]

[August 1935?

this might be part of fragmentary letter dated 13 August below]

[Leaf II]

[. . .] Yes, the Hearst anti-red editorial is certainly a gem of absurdity. Propaganda on both sides is about as stupid as anything the war years brought out.

About my stuff—you've read "Cool Air", but I'll lend it to you again when I get home. The others are more recent—but you'll see them in the course of time.

Blackwood's new novel,[1] according to reviews, represents a sort of mild weirdness as seen through the eyes of a small girl—who lives in *part* of an ancient house. The rest of the house has been uninhabited (& untrodden by human feet) for centuries. At the age of about 5 this little girl discovers a long-forgotten door into the uninhabited part of the house, & begins spending long periods in there. She discovers a sort of unreal world amidst this centuries solitude—presumedly a world of the imagination. The whole thing is probably a great deal like "Jimbo"—in which the dream world of a little boy was the central nucleus. I hope to read it in the course of time, but doubt whether it can be classed among the major Blackwoodiana.

Huckleberry Finn? I'd have to read it again in order to give an intelligent opinion. Certainly it didn't impress me profoundly in youth, when I read it. As for Poe—anyone who calls him "dead" is a damn fool. He & Hawthorne share the supremacy in literature on this side of the water. I don't agree with you about the inferiority of his poetry. While his prose comes first, his verse nevertheless remains the best ever written on this continent. Hope O'Neill will write the series you refer to.

Thanks for the specimens of your recent work, which I have read with the keenest interest. The story naturally is a little pulpish—yet displays much cleverness for all that. The other items are all tremendously attractive—& the smoothness of the style seems to augur an early professional landing on your part. You certainly have caught the tempo & atmosphere of the contemporary essay to an astonishing degree. The dramatic analyses are especially acute—& I enjoyed "On Writing in Bed" with its allusion to the handicap involved in typewriter composition. I claim that no serious work can be written on a typewriter. Glad to hear that "The Call" has received favourable mention—even if it didn't win a first prize.

As for the urge to be in motion—to see new things & embark on strange quests—I guess we all have it. Hope you can manage to mix travel & reading in such a way that the disproportion of one will not be too great.

About Col. Lawrence[2]—I think you overrate his love of publicity. He was a complex character, & it seems to me that his seemingly erratic acts & seclusion represent something vaguer & deeper than mere charlatanry. He really accomplished great things—& he felt a sincere bitterness at the way many events turned out.

Hope you aren't in any hurry for "The Science of Life" & "Personal History", since there's no telling when I'll get around to reading them. I suppose they are up at 66 now. Thanks a thousand times for the unsolicited loan!

I have read the curious cinema notes with keen interest—even though my recent cinema attendance (beginning Jan. 1, 1935) has been limited to "Don Quixote", "Men of Aran", "Unfinished Symphony" & "Les Miserables."[3] The principal trouble with the latter, I think, is the novel itself . . . rather than the film or the actors. After all, it is 19th century stuff—with the coincidences, improbabilities, false motivations, sentimentalities, & other stigmata of the period. The character of Javert certainly eclipses that of Valjean—& not wholly because of the superior actor, I think. It is years since I read the novel, but I think the twisted heritage of Javert is in the original. Laughton is really a tremendously clever & versatile performer.

Sorry to hear that your father's recent magical performance wasn't a 100% success, & hope better luck will attend the next one. Hope you can successfully use the carnival in "Posturings." About the title of the latter—I don't see why it needs any change, but you can do as you like about it. Don't worry about this matter till the whole thing is done—& then see what caption seems best to fit whatever you have written. Titling ought to be the very last step in the construction of a tale or novel. [. . .]

[Leaf IV]
[. . .] miser & financier Hetty Green) in S. Dartmouth, where the old whaling barque *Charles W. Morgan* (built 1841) is preserved at a wharf—solidly embedded in concrete as a permanent exhibit. We went all over the vessel—which is tremendously fascinating. On the estate is also an ancient windmill moved from Rhode Island. We then explored a region—where southern Massachusetts adjoins southeastern Rhode Island—which I had never seen before in my life. Splendid unspoiled countryside with idyllic white-steepled villages of the old New England type. Of the latter the two best ones—Adamsville & Little Compton Commons—are both in Rhode Island. In Adamsville may be found the world's only monument to a *hen*—commemorating the Rhode Island Red, a popular breed developed in the village from East Indian & Chinese gallinaceous forbears. At Little Compton Commons can be seen the home & grave of Elizabeth Alden Pabodie—daughter of the celebrated John Alden & Priscilla Mullins of Plymouth, & first white woman born in New England. This region was once the seat of the Sakonnet Indians—whose squaw-sachem Awashanks was persuaded by the noted old warrior Capt. Benjamin Church not to join King Philip's conspiracy in 1675. It was settled from Plymouth about 1673, & (like Barrington, Warren, & Bristol) came into Massachusetts in 1691 & into Rhode Island (when a boundary dispute was settled by George II) in 1747. Capt. Church lies buried not far from Little Compton Commons. Well—at last we turned north through Tiverton, where on our left we had some marvellous vistas of low-lying fields & blue water. Here we passed the home of the navigator Capt. Robert Gray, who in 1792 discovered the Columbia River in the far-off Oregon Country—naming it after his stout Rhode Island barque. Then back home via Fall River (an ugly mill city across the line in Mass.) & ancient Warren. Finally northward to 66—after which I regretfully guided the guest out of town & took a 4-mile walk before returning home. All in all, quite a session! Warm weather, thank gawd, throughout.

The next week-end—May 3–4–5—I visited Cole in the Boston zone, but beastly cold weather seriously hampered our sightseeing. We covered ancient Marblehead, however—which is attractive under any conceivable set of conditions. On May 25th, as related, I had a visit from Charles D. Hornig—editor of *Wonder Stories* & late publisher of the F F. Next came the present major trip.

I set out for the south June 5—my host himself having just returned to De Land after a winter in Washington. Was (& am) so broke that I had to cut out most intermediate stops—pausing merely at ancient Fredericksburg (Va.) & at my beloved CHARLESTON. The moment I hit the hot Carolina low country my health began to perk up—so that I felt (& still feel) really *well* for the first time in 1935. This is the climate for me! I struck De Land June 9 & found the Barlow place much as it was last year—except that Bob's father (Lt. Col. E. D. Barlow, retired) was home, & his elder brother (2nd Lt. Wayne Barlow)—stationed at Ft. Sam Houston, Texas) here on furlough. Of my feline friends of last year, old white Doodlebug has disappeared (alas!), but there are several new residents to atone for his absence—including 2 regal yellow Persians which Bob has brought from Washington. The general routine of things is much like that of 1934—except that a cabin is going up across the lake to house some of Bob's literary & typographical activities. We have been on several trips—the most impressive of which was to Black Water Creek—a winding, slow-moving tropical river perpetually shadowed by the palm-&-cypress jungle. Even more than the river at Silver Springs, which I described in connexion with last year's visit. This curious stream suggests the Congo or Amazon, & all the brooding mysteries connected therewith. Leaning palms—gaunt, moss-hung cypresses, writhing roots twisted at the water's edge, lush creepers & tangles of various vines, sunken logs & grotesque stumps, & pallid, leprous-looking flowers & fungi which can never have seen the fullest light of day. We rowed along in a small boat, & every bend of the tortuous stream a new world of exotic marvel & luxuriance seemed to unfold. Snakes stirred along the black earth of the twilit forest aisles, & now & then the presence of an alligator was manifest. There were three of us in the boat—Bob & Wayne & myself—while others lingered on the shore at the picturesque river-bend forming the main avenue of approach to the outside world. While you have probably never seen so *tropical* a jungle, I fancy that you've had roughly parallel effects in the famous Dismal Swamp in your own present locality. I seem to recall your mentioning this celebrated region at one time.

Well—just how long I'll be down here, I can't say. My super-cordial hosts insist on my making the visit a long-tern one, but I trust I shall not impose on them. Also uncertain about my financial ability to make stops on my northbound route—though I'll include St. Augustine & Charleston if it kills me! ¶ All good wishes—

Your obt Servt Ech-Pi-El

Notes

1. *The Fruit Stoners* (1934), a work for children.

2. T. E. Lawrence (1888–19 May 1935), British Army officer who went by the name Lawrence of Arabia.

3. *Unfinished Symphony* (Gaumont British Picture Corp., 1934), directed by Anthony Asquith and Will Forst; starring Mártha Eggerth, Helen Chandler, and Hans Jaray (a film about Franz Schubert). *Les Misérables* (20th Century Pictures, 1935), directed by Richard Boleslawski; starring Fredric March, Charles Laughton, and Cedric Hardwicke. Based on the novel by Victor Hugo.

[53]   [AHT]

[13 August 1935]

Richard III was my favourite part in youth—I loved to rant heavy and villainous tragedy.

[54]   [ANS][1]

[Postmarked St. Augustine, FL,
23 August 1935]

Well—your timely natal greeting strikes the old man in a town appropriate to his advanced years—no less remarkable a place than historic San Agustin . . . from which point, I believe, you first heard from the patriarch in question in '31. After 2 m & 9 d. of rustic modernity, it surely is good to be back amidst centuried gables & facades & balconies & garden walls—hearing the tinkle of ancient fountains at twilight, & the music of cathedral chimes cast in 1682. Here is a town which was 42 years old when Jamestown was founded, & which still contains houses which had 60 years behind them when the oldest surviving Anglo-American structure (St. Luke's Church, 1632, in your part of the country) was erected. I surely am revelling in the past—absorbing ancient vistas & writing on the old fort. The Barlows have gone to Daytona for a fortnight, & Bob came up for a day's visit yesterday—to bid grandpa a second adieu. ¶ Savannah Monday morning—Charleston in the afternoon. Shall stop at the Charleston Y—but slender finances will prevent a long sojourn. After that only brief stops—though Wandrei may put me up for a week in N.Y. It surely has been a great trip! Shall probably arrive home in mid-September with only a dime in my pocket. My next point for receiving mail—after the Charleston Y—will be % F. B. Long, 230 W. 47th St., New York City. Hope all is prospering in Suffolk. If you send those things to Barlow before Aug. 31, you can catch him at 128 S. Wild Olive Ave., Daytona Beach, Fla. Regards from the aged—
E'ch-Pi-El

[P.S.] Am at the Rio Vista, as before—& eating on 25¢ a day.

Notes

1. *Front:* Charlotte Street, St. Augustine, Florida.

[55]   [ALS]

> 66 College St.,
> Providence, R.I.
> Dec. 5, 1935.

Dear Shavius Vernonicus:—

I read yours of Sept. 2 et seq. with the keenest interest, & enjoyed all the accompanying sketches. I return the latter herewith, since I assume they are meant for such a disposition. Thanks, too, for the pictorial strip—which I rather hope is meant as a permanent contribution to my portrait-gallery, though I'll promptly return it if such was your wish. You have every reason to be satisfied with your appearance if this strip speaks truly— both my aunt & I thought the Shavian visage an extremely likeable one. As a very inadequate reciprocation, here is a shot of the old man which you probably haven't seen. Barlow took it a year ago last June—but it remains the latest, & I hardly fancy it has yet become badly unrepresentative. It is really a very good likeness, gawd help me!

Well, as I said, I read the stories with great interest & not a little admiration. "My Sister Will not Speak" displays a command of the so-called "American Vulgate" which the late Ring Lardner or John V. A. Weaver might well envy.[1] You surely have a rare sensitiveness for speech nuances—a quality which will serve you well as a realist. The story itself seems very well conceived—though some might wonder just how realistic the girl's *extreme* mood is, & just what psychological foundation underlies the symptoms. "The Reveller" is really powerful in its way—leaving a vivid picture. I assume you've looked up the point about incipient leprosy. Usually, I understand, leprous patches are *white*—& the first symptom (about which a rather clever story has been written recently) is an *absence of sensation* in the affected part. Also, I assume you realise that leprosy is not contagious except through very direct contact with an affected area. "The Feast" may seem a bit skeletonic & unsubtle to many—as to the editors of *Esquire* & *New Masses*—but it has its own kind of power none the less. There is a grim irony which lasts, even if it is extremely simple & vigorously emphasised rather than hinted. All these things indicate that you are very much on the right track toward expressing what you have to say, despite the number of rejections encountered. The same holds good for the poetic fragments. All this experimenting strengthens your command of words & images, & teaches you by experience those modes of utterance best suited to your temperament & tastes. Sooner or later the rejections will begin to soften into acceptances. As you see, many of them are even now coupled with genuine encouragement. That incident of Mr. Porter & the Kreisler metaphor is surely curious. Usually one is sceptical about the traditional charges of piracy under such conditions, but the present case certainly strains coincidence to its limits. Incidentally, your verses shew a remarkably clever command of popular contemporary images—names on the lips of the casual newspaper-glancers. I wonder that Porter didn't steal something more individual & distinctive than the fairly obvious Kreislerian comparison . . . . . something, for example, like the crack about bookkeeping & red ink. Well— the seizure (or case of parallelism) surely proves that you are working most emphatically in the accepted popular idiom of the day!

I believe I dropped you a card upon my return home, telling of the safe arrival of the Sheean & Wells–Huxley books. So hopelessly engulfed was I with piled-up responsibilities, that I did not get around to either of them till last week. I have now finished "Personal History", which is surely a phenomenally absorbing document—revealing not only the sensitive & highly individual personality of the writer, but much of the colour & shifting standards of his whole unsettled age as well. The changing scene is fascinating— Chicago, Morocco, China, Russia, Palestine—& the light on various culture-elements helps me to make further progress in the partial interpretation of a chaotic period really beyond all complete interpretation. But the big item is "The Science of Life." Ædepol, what a book! It is by all odds the greatest single exposition of biological knowledge which I have ever seen—a titanic vital panorama of a scope, clearness, accuracy, simplicity, coherence, proportioning, & impartiality exceeding the best of previous efforts in the same line. No question but that good old H G is the master *outliner* of all time. I own his Outline of History, & hope later on to get hold of his similar effort in the economic field. Meanwhile I am now digesting "The Science of Life" in small & careful doses—getting perspectives on modern biology and zoölogy which I never had before. It is certainly the most important book I have read in years. Hope there's no hurry about its return, for I want to take it in slowly & thoroughly. I'm only 250 or so pages into it at present. If you like, I'll return "Personal History" now, so as to release it for further circulation. Let me know. And again—most abundant thanks for the dual loan. Later on, when my present feverish rush is over, I may take you up on some of those latter loans which you so generously suggest. Thanks in advance!

Well—I digested your literary & cinematic reviews with usual interest, & shall use them as a guide in choosing any items I may have time to consider. Some day I must try to go through a typical assortment of contemporary books just to see what the present generation is doing or trying to do. In the cinematic field I'll keep my eyes open for "The Informer." The only films I have seen since last spring are "She" (a few good scenic effects—little of Haggard left), "The Wandering Jew" (not bad), "The Last Days of Pompeii" (architecture splendid—story childish & anachronistic—costuming inaccurate), & "Clive of India"—this last a splendid evocation of the 18ᵗʰ century & of Britannia's power despite some historical compressions & a touch of softness in one or two places. I enjoyed it most of any film since "Berkeley Square", & it formed the occasion of a singularly vivid dream.[2]

Your book reviews beat many of the *Times's* for clearness & close analysis. Next best thing to reading the books themselves! Once in a while I think I take issue with your standards, as when you attack a certain 'placidity' in the style of novelists. I, for one, like a realistic writer to be perfectly detached from his subject matter—treating the whole show as a problem in biochemistry & sociology. What other sound perspective is there? Values are local & transient—one age's burning causes are the next age's jokes—emotions are simply fortuitous reflexes determined by the harmonic discharges of endocrine glands into the blood stream . . . .

I must see something by the bird Caldwell—whom my friend Loveman has met.[3] "The Enormous Room" was widely discussed in '22 or thereabouts, but I never read it.[4] Hemingway's list of classics is a curious one—but perhaps typical of a disjointed transitional age. I ought to read "Dubliners" some time.[5] Aldous Huxley is quite a favourite of Long's, & I must admit that I've seen some pretty good essays of his. Never read "Point Counter Point"—& like you, I distrust all attempts at applying to one art the terms & technique of a wholly different art. Your tentative anthology has an interesting table of contents—though as you say, there would have to be changes in a final version. I'd cut out the flop called H. P. Lovecraft, for one thing.

Comte d'Erlette gave me a copy of "Sign of Fear", & I thought it not half bad as such things go. It stands up well beside his other detective attempts. But of course this stuff is all mere pot-boiling. His serious novel, "Place of Hawks", was very well received—& on the strength of it he has almost landed a contract with Scribners. "Evening in Spring" & "People" remain unpublished—& perhaps in the end young August-Guillaume will regard them as mere foundations or experiments. At present he is delving intensively into the history & antiquities of his native town—exploring attics, studying old letters, newspapers, diaries, & town records, &c.—preparatory to beginning a long series of historical novels perpetuating the life of his community from 1830 onward. This he will regard as his major work. Yuggoth, but the youngster surely is getting ahead!

Yes—little Bobby Bloch has killed Grandpa off for the second time![6] (You may recall that Belknap disposed of the old gentleman a decade ago, in "The Space-Eaters") He is surely developing, & will get somewhere if the pulp formula doesn't get him first. I saw the "Shambler" in MS., but did virtually nothing to the text. The Latin phrase ought to be mine, but somebody (whether Bloch or the compositor) misprinted BUFONIFORMIS as BUFΛNIFORMIS—thus destroying the meaning. I've now written a new story in which I leave Bloch as a staring corpse![7] W T has been generally lousy of late, though the Nov. issue—with 3 passable stories—is a pleasing exception. That thing of Stern's leads the issue—damn good stuff![8] I never heard of the author before, but he'll certainly be worth watching. He knows what atmosphere is—& knows hot to make a sequence of events portentous even when the reader realises perfectly well what's coming.

A new fan magazine—*The Phantagraph* (pub. by Wilson Shepherd of Oakman, Ala. & Donald Wollheim of 801 West End Ave. N Y C)—is trying to take the place of the late F F, & shews considerable promise. *Fantasy Magazine* is delayed—Sept. issue not yet out. Hill-Billy Crawford still stumbles along with his variously named heterogeneities—a *Marvel Tales* out last summer, & an *Unusual Tales* (with really good yarns by Bloch, Petaja, & Dilbeck) just off the press.[9] Belknap & the two Wandrei boys are getting a marvellous foothold in the cheap pulp field—being almost assured financially, though they have sacrificed all their artistic sincerity in the process. Price is flourishing as a popular fiction merchant—he is just back from a trip to Mexico, where he drank in Aztec temples & pyramids, dodged a landslide, & otherwise enjoyed himself. En route he stopped at Cross Plains to see Two-Gun Bob. Klarkash-Ton's mother died on Sept. 9, & he has suffered considerably from the shock & strain. I think I told you of his new accomplishment—grotesque sculpture in the friable stone of his region. Sorrow has also touched Belknap's family—his only aunt[10] having been killed instantly on Oct. 20 in a motor accident near Miami. About the same time Barlow surprised him with a bound copy of his recent poems—a collection called "The Goblin Tower", which Bob & I printed last summer. Long hadn't the least inkling of what was being done—but a fortnight ago opened a package & found a complete book with his own name as author! It was all printed last August, but binding was held up for lack of proper apparatus. Barlow's bindery is now complete, & we may see several interesting items from him in the months to come. He has hopes of issuing Klarkash-Ton's next collection of poems—"Incantations".[11] In the meantime I trust that Bob has sent you his amateur paper, *The Dragon-Fly*, containing your essay "On Writing in Bed." This is a very neat little sheet considering Barlow's typographical inexperience, & it ought to help greatly in fostering the qualitative renaissance of the National Amateur Press Association. By the way—can you be induced to join the National? I enclose a descriptive circular & application blank. I think you'd enjoy this chance to circulate your work, receive a helpful diversity of critical comments, acquire a larger circle of epistolary discussion & debate, & in general reap the encouragement which a limited non-professional publicity provides.

I've just had quite a bit of unexpected good luck—both my "Mountains of Madness" & the new "Shadow Out of Time" having been accepted by *Astounding Stories*. This astonishes me considerably, since none of my stuff is in the pulp vein favoured by this popular enterprise. The $595. derived from the two sales is a veritable life-saver, for I was never closer to the bread-line than this year. The incident encourages me to attempt further writing—although I realise that acceptances can't keep coming. This dual placing is essentially a luck-shot. My new tale—"The Haunter of the Dark"—is now circulating in carbon form, & will reach you in course of time.

Glad you're having some leisure for intensive reading & composition—assuming that the financial consequences of your forced vacation are not disastrous. Wish you could secure a better job—though any job at all means a good deal these days.

The autumn has been almost record-breakingly warm hereabouts, so that my season of hibernation suffered a singular postponement. Despite my all-summer absence among palmettos & live-oaks, I have had such a long outdoor period amidst my own landscape that I hardly feel as if I'd been away at all! I fancy I sent you cards at various stages of my northward journey—St. Augustine & Charleston. I certainly hated to leave the far south, & damn near froze in Richmond—where, however, I had a delightful time amidst Poe sites & in picturesque Maymont Park. In Washington (i.e., ancient Georgetown) all day Aug. 31, & the next morning I struck Philadelphia in the grey dawn. Great time there—I visited the botanic garden of old John Bartram for the first time since 1924, & saw the quaint stone house which the great naturalist built with his own hands in 1731. The place is now a public park maintained in pristine glory—a typical colonial country-seat on the banks of the Schuylkill. It is, however, entirely encompassed by ugly terrain—gas house, cheap suburban villas, & wretched factories across the river. Reached N.Y. the same night, & was a guest of Donald Wandrei for nearly a fortnight. He was then living at 155 E. 10th St., in Greenwich Village, on a flat he had taken with his brother. The latter, however, was absent in St. Paul, so that I occupied his vacant room. (Howard is now married & living at 42 Perry St., while Donald has gone back to 88 Horatio St.) I took my meals up at Belknap's, & saw most of the weird tale & amateur journalism gang old & new—Morton, Talman, Kleiner, Loveman, Koenig, Sterling, Kirk, Leeds, &c. &c. By coincidence, Loveman's proofs from the Caxton Printers (of his coming book of poems) arrived during my visit, so that I helped him give them a searchingly thorough reading. I also met the son of that teeming hack & super-agent Otis Adelbert Kline—who is acting as his father's Manhattan agent. Oh, yes—& I called on young Hornig at the *Wonder Stories* office, though I didn't see Hugo the Rat. Well—on Sept. 14 I reached home, & was damn glad to be back among my books & family possessions. But Yaddith, what a pile of accumulated stuff I had to dispose of! Three months of old newspapers & periodicals to read up—correspondence & jobs which had escaped forwarding . . . . Mehercule, it's a wonder I survived! But even so, my travels were not ended. Sept. 20–23 I visited my friend Cole near Boston, & we had a great series of rural outings in his well-heated Chevrolet—taking in rocky Nahant, ancient

Marblehead, the spectral hills of brooding "Dunwich" [Wilbraham, Mass., in the Connecticut Valley], the sandy, willow fringed reaches of Cape Cod, & so on. A delightful reintroduction to New England scenery!

Oct. 8 my aunt & I had a trip to New Haven in a friend's car—which gave me 7½ hrs for exploration (I'd never been off a moving vehicle in the town before) while my aunt did some visiting. The day was ideally sunny (tho' I could have wished it warmer), & the ride through autumnal Conn. scenery (100 m = 2½ hrs) delightful. New Haven is not as rich in colonial antiquities as Providence, but has a peculiar charm of its own. Streets are broad & well-kept, & in the residential sections (some of which involve hills & fine views) there are endless stately mansions a century old, with generous grounds & gardens, & an almost continuous overarching canopy of great elms. I visited ancient Connecticut Hall (1752—the oldest Yale College building, where Nathan Hale of the class of 1773 roomed), old Centre Church (1812—with an interesting crypt containing the grave of Benedict Arnold's first wife), the Pierpont house (1767—now Yale Faculty Club), the historical, art, & natural history museums, the Farnam & Marsh botanic gardens, & various other points of interest—crowding as much as possible into the limited time available.

Most impressive of all the sights, perhaps, were the great *new* quadrangles of Yale University—each an absolutely faithful reproduction of old-time architecture & atmosphere, & forming a self-contained little world in itself. The Gothic courtyards transport one in fancy to mediaeval Oxford or Cambridge—spires, oriels, pointed arches, mullioned windows, arcades with groined roofs, climbing ivy, sundials, lawns, gardens, vine-clad walls & flag-stoned walks—everything to give the young occupants that massed impression of their accumulated cultural heritage which they might obtain in Old England itself. To stroll through these quadrangles in the golden light of late afternoon, at dusk, when the candles behind the diamond-paned casements flicker up one by one; or in the beams of a mellow Hunter's Moon; is to walk bodily into an enchanted region of dream. It is the past & the ancient mother land brought magically to the present time & place. The choicest of these Gothic quadrangles is Calhoun College—named for the great Carolinian (whose grave in St. Philip's churchyard, Charleston, I had visited less than 2 months before), who was a graduate of Yale. Nor are the Georgian quadrangles less glamourous—each being a magical summoning up of the world of two centuries ago. Many distinct styles of Georgian architecture are represented, & the buildings & landscaping alike reflect the finest taste which European civilisation has yet evolved or is ever likely to evolve. Lucky is the youth whose formative years are spent amid such scenes! I wandered for hours through this limitless labyrinth of unexpected elder microcosms, & mourned the lack of further time. Certainly, I must visit New Haven again, since many of its treasures would require weeks for proper inspection & appreciation.

But even this trip didn't quite end my 1935 travels. Oct. 16 at 6 a.m. Samuel Loveman blew into town on the N.Y. boat, & after a session at 66 we both started out for Boston to absorb bookstalls, museums, & general antiquities. We stayed 2 nights—at Technology Chambers in Irvington St.—& managed to take in quite a few sights. Most of our time was spent in the Egyptian & Greek sections of the Museum of Fine Arts. Back to Providence on the 18th, & did all the local bookstalls. Discovered one so good that Loveman may be back in a month or so to patronise it. Had fine warm weather throughout the trip. On the evening of the 18th Loveman left for N.Y. on the boat. This really ended the travel season, though Cole for a while talked of a trip in his car over the Mohawk Trail & up a bit into Vermont. Vermont in *November!* Iä! Shub-Niggurath! The Goat With a Thousand Young!

Well—besides the sizeable trips I often went out to the local woods & fields until November—taking along my work in the inevitable black bag as I do in summer. There is a peculiar fascination about the New England autumnal landscape when the thermometer stays high enough to let one enjoy it.

Recently my aunt & I attended several lectures on art & allied subjects at Brown University—only a stone's throw from our door. One of them—on "Art, Economics, & the American Future"—was by Prof. Overstreet of N.Y., author of several interesting works on philosophy & psychology;[12] & during the question period the speaker got into a spirited & almost acrimonious debate with the Governor of Rhode Island, Theodore Francis Green, who sat in the seat directly behind me. Green argued that the highest art must be international & non-racial (he himself is a famous collector of Sino-Japanese prints & ceramic art); but Overstreet shewed clearly that every artist, in order to rise to truly universal & international heights, must work through the medium of his own cultural inheritance.

As I write, an especial friend of mine in the depths of a neighbouring easy-chair stirs in his slumbers & emits a few drowsy purrs. He is a huge black person, yet has never seen any year but 1935—having been born on the 14th of last February. Possibly I described him to you last spring as a tiny handful of black fur—but bless me, how the rascal has grown! Little Johnny Perkins! He belongs at the boarding-house across the back garden, but spends a good deal of his time over here. He knows who gives him catnip to chew & roll in—so he's a great friend of Grandpa's! He remembered me perfectly after my 3-month absence.

Well—all good wishes!—Yr obt Servt E'ch-Pi-El.

P.S. As a drama shark, you'll be interested to hear that I witnessed a performance of the Le Gallienne company not long ago—in two short Spanish comedies by the brothers Quintero—"A Sunny Morning" & "The Women have their way". Very clever. First time I ever saw Miss Le Gallienne. A friend invited me—drama being too expensive for Grandpa's lean purse.[13]

Notes

1. John Van Alstyne Weaver (1893–1938), American novelist and poet who published several books of poetry adapting American vernacular into iambic pentameter verse.

2. *The Informer* (RKO Radio Pictures, 1935), directed by John Ford; starring Victor McLaglen, Heather Angel, and Preston Foster. Adapted from a story by Liam O'Flaherty and dealing with the Irish Civil War (1918–22). *She* (RKO Radio Pictures, 1935), directed by Irving Pichel and Lansing C. Holden; starring Helen Gahagan, Randolph Scott, and Helen Mack. Based on the novel by H. Rider Haggard. *The Wandering Jew* (Julius Hagen Productions, 1933; released in the US in 1935), directed by Maurice Elvey; starring Conrad Veidt, Marie Ney, and Basil Gill. *The Last Days of Pompeii* (RKO Radio Pictures, 1935), directed by Ernest B. Schoedsack and Merian C. Cooper (uncredited); starring Preston Foster, Alan Hale, and Basil Rathbone. Based on the novel by Edward Bulwer-Lytton. *Clive of India* (20th Century Pictures/United Artists, 1935), directed by Richard Boleslawski; starring Ronald Coleman, Loretta Young, and Colin Clive.

3. Presumably a reference to Erskine Caldwell (1903–1987), American novelist best known for *Tobacco Road* (1932) and *God's Little Acre* (1933).

4. A novel by e. e. cummings.

5. A short story collection by James Joyce.

6. In "The Shambler from the Stars" (*WT,* September 1935). The first time HPL was "killed" was by Frank Belknap Long in his story, "The Space-Eaters" (*WT,* July 1928).

7. "The Haunter of the Dark" (written 5–9 November 1935).

8. Paul Frederick Stern, "The Way Home" (*WT,* November 1935). HPL later realized that Stern was a pseudonym (by way of an anagram) of Paul [Frederick] Ernst (1899–1985). The other two stories of note were "The Hand of Wrath" by E. Hoffmann Price and "Shadows in Zamboula" by Robert E. Howard.

9. HPL refers to *Unusual Stories* 1, No. 2 (Winter 1935), containing Robert Bloch's "The Black Lotus," Lionel Dilbeck's "The River Dwellers," and Emil Petaja's "The Two Doors" (under the pseudoym "Theodore Pine").

10. Cassie Doty Symmes. HPL ghost-wrote, for Long, the preface to her book *Old World Footprints* (1928).

11. No book titled *Incantations* was ever published, but the poems intended for it are contained in the subsection "Incantations" in Smith's *Selected Poems* (1971).

12. H[arry] A[llen] Overstreet (1875–1970), chairman of the department of philosophy and psychology at City College of New York (1911–36) and author of *The Enduring Quest: A Search for a Philosophy of Life* (1931) and other works.

13. HPL refers to the British actress Eva Le Gallienne (1899–1991), who acted in *A Sunny Morning* (1935) and *The Women Have Their Way* (1930) by Serafín Álvarez Quintero (1871–1938) and Joaquin Alvarez Quintero (1873–1944).

1936

[56]   [ALS]

66 College St.,
Providence, R.I.
Feby. 14, 1936.

Dear Shavius Veronicus:—

This time I'm the epistolary delayer—but Yug-
goth knows I have plenty of cause! Last month I seemed to be the focus of a
cosmically malign flood of obligations—revisory, critical, compositional, &
what the hell—so that all semblance of order & controllableness was knocked
out of my programme. I had to refuse many tasks & transfer many others—
nor have I been able to progress a page further in the stack of borrowed
books (including "The Science of Life") which towers toward the ceiling.
Then, to top everything off, I had a touch of grippe or some damn thing of
the sort—in bed & eating nothing a week, & still shaky & given to a curious
ocular fatigue. Some month! So if the present epistle be a very inadequate reply to yours of Dec. 30, I fancy you can excuse the deficiencies!

I enjoyed your letter & its enclosures very much—the black house picture & Thibetan scenes being highly fascinating. My aunt saw the film of
"Midsummer Night's Dream" mentioned in the cutting, but I was unable to
go.[1] She thought it very good. I enjoyed your story—"The Judge's Hunting
Hounds"—extremely, & believe you speak too disparagingly of it. It has both
atmosphere & punch—& I think it ought to land somewhere sooner or later.
I return it herewith—with many thanks for the glimpse.

Interested to know you are in touch with the author of "I Live in Virginia"—which I've seen favourably reviewed in many places.[2] I have passed
through Danville many times on the 'bus, & it struck me as a rather attractive
town. Sorry I didn't stop to call on Mr. Goldman![3] The other Virginia touches must be of much timely interest. Sorry he thinks unfavourably of the
V.M.I, which has great traditions behind it. I have yet to see the University—
& Monticello.

Haven't succeeded so far in locating the numbers of *The Illustrated London
News* which you recommend, but may later come across them in library files.
They all sound alluring—especially the weird Christmas one. Here's hoping
"Cold in the Night" gets reprinted in an anthology.[4] I'd certainly like to see
Poe illustrations by Segrelles—some of whose weird designs have impressed
me greatly.[5] Weirdness certainly gets a better break in Great Britain than it
does on this side of the ocean. Fancy an issue like that in America!

Regarding the cinema—permit me to say that I *have* seen both "The Informer" & "Ah, Wilderness." Both impressed me vastly, each in its separate way. I am not sure but that "The Informer" is the greatest film I have ever beheld. It is virtually *perfect*—mood, atmosphere, unity, motivations, details, &c. The mists & shadows of ancient Dublin seemed to live in a heightened reality, & the shadows of menace & tightening coils of doom moved with a veritably classic relentlessness. Great stuff! Whether anyone *could* be as naively witless as Gype Nolan seemed doubtful at first—but many have assured me that kindred types do manage to survive in the underworld. At any rate, there is no question of the cinema's having attained the level of first-rate art in this memorable production. The regular stage couldn't go beyond it! "Ah, Wilderness" formed a delightful recapture of the manners & visible moods of a generation ago, & awaked nostalgic memories at every turn. Appropriately enough, I saw it in a theatre which I used to frequent in 1906, & which has changed very little in the interim. I want to see "Mutiny on the Bounty", but have missed it so far. Also "Mad Love"—which not less than 12 or 15 persons have independently recommended to me.[6]

Interested to hear of the proposed weird anthology of Philip Berkeley. Thanks for the compliment of mentioning me to him—he hasn't yet written. I have Onions's "Ghosts By [*sic*] Daylight", but it doesn't contain the story you mention. Would you care to see this book? I didn't care much for the various tales.

Yes—keep that Barlow picture of me if you like. I think it's a fairish resemblance. No—I doubt if the position of the lips comes from any hypertrophy of conscience. Natural contours & badly placed teeth form a likelier explanation! I don't take much stock in the details of physiognomy—most of which are mere literary conventions. For example—as you yourself point out, I am far from mournful in temperament—& yet, when in repose, my countenance suggests a cross between cosmic grief & brooding ferocity. I recall one time when I attended a dinner of the Hub Club back in 1920, & was seated opposite a gentleman (Charles A. A. Parker), now editor of the poetry magazine *L'Alouette*) who prided himself on his bluff, rough-&-ready playfulness. I was enjoying the occasion—the baked beans—tremendously, yet all of a sudden Parker leaned forward & enquired with mock-solicitude, "Why so pensive"? I replied—"Oh, these are just *lachrymae rerum*"[7] . . . but that shews what a woebegone sort of cuss I seem to be! I am my saddest when delivering a comic after-dinner speech[8]—myself moved to sighs; my victims to yawns. Be it said in self-defence that I never make a public address except under the most inescapable compulsion. It hurts me even more than it hurts the crowd.

I'll send you an issue—yea, *two* whole issues!—of *Marvel Tales* . . . but don't expect much. The editor—Crawford—is a curious sort of Hill-Billy with a deadly aversion toward literature. He is going to publish my "Shadow Over Innsmouth" as a booklet soon—& is trying to get illustrations from

Utpatel—the chap who has drawn so many designs for Derleth. "The Shadow Out of Time" will appear in *Astounding Stories*. "The Haunter of the Dark" is in circulation & headed your way. I now send "The Colour Out of Space" & "Cool Air" as per request. These are to be returned (though in no hurry), but you can keep the issue of M T. My stories in this magazine are hideously misprinted—some of the errors giving a tricky impression of illiteracy—but I haven't time to search out the various slips.

Hope you'll join the N.A.P.A. It has its crude spots, but the redeeming features are many. I'll send along a copy of the latest official organ. This year we're trying to make a comeback. Watch for Edkins' paper *Causerie!* Barlow also plans a second *Dragon-Fly*. Your essay was very favourably received, & the association would enable you to get many such things before an appreciative—even if numerically limited—audience.

I am very partial toward novels in a series—whether regional, family, or social. I think a semi-rural region, where conditions are less heterogeneous & chaotic, is better than a large city as the scene of such a series—at least in America, where the cities have so little stability of population or institutions. Derleth will go slowly in his design, & may not complete any of the novels for a long while.

Curious that "My Sister Will Not Speak" has a basis in fact—but then, I suppose the human mind is full of twists & phobias inexplicable without a key. I surely hope the victim will recover in time—& wish her father would take your advice & call in some specialist more appropriate than a chiropractor.

Your reading continues to sound bewilderingly extensive to one now become virtually a non-reader. Many of the volumes you name are familiar—as titles—through reviews. Evidently "The Stars Look Down" is quite a novel.[9] Some time, if I ever get a chance, I'm going to try to cover the high spots of the long period since I stopped keeping pace with new novels. I'll ask some modern reader—like you or Comte d'Erlette—to pick me out the 10 or 15 most important novels published since 1925; & through these I may be able to get some idea of recent tendencies & moods.

Glad you've had some vacational breathing-spells in which to catch up on your reading & writing—& hope they haven't involved too much financial strain. I shiver sympathetically at the temperatures you mention—which almost equal any we have up here. Our lowest for the winter so far has been +4.8°—which is itself unusual for Providence. The special kind of bitterness we've had this winter is not so much a matter of spectacularly low temperatures as of a deadly absence of high temperatures. It always seems to be around +20°. I've been out only once—& that merely to a lecture at the college half a block away—since Jan. 13. Snow has been abundant—& you've probably seen quite a bit yourself. I shall certainly look forward to the coming of the vernal equinox a month & 6 days hence—even though that transition be merely a technical one.

Last two W Ts mediocre—though each has an excellent Moore story. Derleth's "Satin Mask" could be worse, & "Norn" & "The Visitor from far Away" have their possibilities.[10] Reprinting of both "Dagon" & "The Temple" gives me a classically posthumous feeling. In the Feb. *Astounding* Long's "Cones" has a remarkable amount of convincing other-planetary atmosphere, & some splendid suggestions of non-human, utterly alien life, but is ruined by its admixture of cheap, hackneyed romance.

Glad you had a pleasant Christmas. We did also—having a tree once more, as we did last year. Around New Year's I visited Long for a week in N.Y.—seeing most of the gang, old & new, & meeting a few weird fictioneers & fans whom I had never encountered in person before—Arthur J. Burks, Otto Binder of the "Eando" team, Donald A. Wollheim (editor of the new "fan" magazine *The Phantagraph*), & others. At a dinner of the American Fiction Guild I saw good old Seabury Quinn for the first time since 1931. We had several gatherings, during the course of which I had glimpses of Long, Loveman, Morton, Kleiner, Leeds, Kirk, Talman, Sterling, the two Wandrei boys, young Kline, &c. &c. Loveman's book of poems (proofs of which I read last September) was out, & presented an extremely prepossessing appearance. He gave me a lot of circulars of it, which I am distributing among my innumerable correspondents in an effort to boost the sales. I hope it will get good treatment from the reviewers. I will enclose one of these circulars in one of the accompanying envelopes. On two occasions I visited the new Hayden Planetarium of the American Museum of Natural History, & found it a highly impressive device. It consists of a round, domed building of 2 storeys, joined at one point to the museum edifice. On the lower floor is a circular hall whose ceiling is a gigantic orrery—shewing the planets revolving around the sun at their proper relative speeds. Above it is another circular hall whose roof is the great dome, & whose edge is made to represent the horizon of N.Y. City as seen from Central Park. In the middle of this upper hall is a projector (that looks like a fictional "space ship" or like one of the armoured Martians in "The War of the Worlds")[11] which casts on the whitened concave surface of the dome a perfect image of the sky—capable of duplicating the natural apparent motions of the celestial vault, & of depicting the heavens as seen at any hour, in any season, from any latitude, & at any period of history. Other parts of the projector can cast suitably movable images of the sun, moon, & planets, & diagrammatic arrows & circles for explanatory purposes. The effect is infinitely lifelike—as if one were outdoors beneath the sky. Lectures—different each month (I heard both Dec. & Jan. ones)—are given in connexion with this apparatus. In the annular corridors on each floor are niches containing typical astronomical instruments of all ages—telescopes, transits, celestial globes, armillary spheres, &c.—& cases to display books, meteorites, & other miscellany. Astronomical pictures line the walls, & at the desk may be obtained useful pamphlets, books, planispheres, &c. An excellent small planisphere is sold for a quarter—the cheapest I ever saw—& I got one apiece for Belknap and Donald Wandrei . . . in the hope that they'll hereafter make fewer mistakes about the constellations in their stories. The institution holds classes in elementary astronomy, & sponsors clubs of amateur observers. Altogether, it forms the most complete & active popular astronomical centre imaginable. It seems to be crowded at all hours, attesting a public interest in astronomy which did not exist when I was young.

Returning home Jany. 7, I was confronted by the paralysing plethora of work before mentioned. One of the innumerable things I've been asked to do (but am not sure I can find the time & strength to do) is to contribute an article on horror literature to a new magazine called *Nuggets,* edited by B. C. Black, Box 53, Upland, Indiana. This is a new venture, & might not be a bad destination for some of your own work. No pay—except a subscription to the magazine.[12]

Derleth recently sent me a free copy of "Place of Hawks", plus a new British anthology of nightmare stories containing something by Blackwood.[13] Both are at your disposal if you'd care to borrow them. Clark Ashton Smith is going in heavily for statuette-carving, & has even found a moderate professional demand for his products. It would be amusing if he were to end up primarily as a sculptor! Did I tell you of the hauntingly grotesque head of "The Outsider" which he sent me last autumn? One of his designs is to carve an image of Cthulhu which shall be a precise duplicate in size, contours & colour of the archaean statuette described in the story.

Well—good luck with all your ventures, & congratulations on your really good story. Thanks for permission to retain the strip of pictures. Hope that Colour &c. won't bore you on re-reading. ¶ Yrs by the Elder Sign—E'ch-Pi-El

Notes

1. *A Midsummer Night's Dream* (Warner Bros., 1935), directed by William Dieterle and Max Reinhardt; starring Dick Powell, Ross Alexander, and Olivia de Havilland. Based on the play by William Shakespeare.

2. See JVS 23 n.2.

3. Danville is a city in south-central Virginia, on the border with North Carolina, cited in *I Live in Virginia.* Also in that book, Meade discusses a character he names Mr. Goldeman, a "retired gentleman of leisure" who has written a book entitled *The Eternal Sovereign and Divine Lord Absolute of the Universe.*

4. "Cold in the Night" (*Illustrated London News,* 20 November 1935) by Marguerite Steen (1894–1975). It was not reprinted until it appeared in Charles Birkin's *The Tandem Book of Ghost Stories* (1965).

5. Some of the illustrations of Poe's tales by Spanish painter José Segrelles Albert (1885–1969) appeared in the *Illustrated London News* (Christmas 1935); they were never published in any book of Poe's stories.

6. *Mutiny on the Bounty* (MGM, 1935), directed by Frank Lloyd; starring Charles Laughton, Clark Gable, and Franchot Tone. Based on the novel by Charles Nordhoff and James Norman Hall. *Mad Love* (MGM, 1935), directed by Karl Freund; starring Peter Lorre, Frances Drake, and Colin Clive. Based on the novel *The Hands of Orlac* by Maurice Renard.

7. "The tears of things" (i.e., the sadness of life), a celebrated phrase in Virgil's *Aeneid* 1.642.

8. "Within the Gates" (*CE* 1.293–95) was just such a speech, delivered on 4 July 1921 at the NAPA convention in Boston.

9. A novel about English mining life by Scottish writer A. J. Cronin.

10. HPL refers to stories in the January and February 1936 issues of *WT*: C. L. Moore, "The Dark Land" (January) and "Yvala" (February); August W. Derleth, "The Satin Mask" (January); Lireve Monet [i.e., Everil Worrell], "Norn" (February); Loretta Burrough, "A Visitor from Far Away" (February).

11. The novel by H. G. Wells.

12. HPL never wrote the article.

13. See Bibliography under *50 Years of Ghost Stories*.

[57]   [ALS]

66 College St.,

Providence, R.I.,

May 19, 1936

Dear Shavius Veronicus:—

Yours of Feby. 23 & May 3 duly received. I would have acknowledged the former, & sent the books mentioned in it, but for the singular chain of disasters which has transformed 1936 into a nightmare of confusion & helplessness for me. I have not yet read that British anthology, & have only just now gone through the issue of *Story*. Was that, by the way, to be retained? Very shortly I shall send a bundle containing "Ghosts in Daylight", "Place of Hawks", "My Grimmest Nightmare",[1] & your Sheean book. With your permission I'll keep the Wells book a little longer—till I can have a chance to get at it. It goes without saying that I apologise profusely for any delay.

Now as to the linked calamities—in the first place, tasks & letters piled up in January so rapidly that I could not possibly cope with them. Next, I came down with grippe & was flat for a week. And *then*—just as I was able to stagger around again—the *real* trouble began! My aunt was seized with a grippe attack vastly worse than mine,[2] & from mid-February on I was enslaved as a sort of combined nurse, butler, secretary, market-man, & errand-boy. All my own affairs went absolutely to hell—letters unanswered, borrowed books piled up unread, N.A.P.A. duties shifted to others, revision jobs returned unperformed, fiction-writing a thing of the past . . . .

"With ruin upon ruin, rout on rout—
Confusion worse confounded."[3]

But it was a damn sight worse on my aunt than on me! Complications developed, & in mid-March she had to go to the hospital. This changed—without materially lessening—my responsibilities. The patient improved slowly, & on April 7 migrated to a convalescent home—finally returning to #66 April 21. She is now up & about—taking walks each good day—though requiring considerable coöperation in household tasks.

My own programme is totally shot to pieces, & I am about on the edge of a nervous breakdown. I have so little power of concentration that it takes me about an hour to do what I can ordinarily do in five minutes—& my eyesight is acting like the devil. But warmer weather & outdoor activities will be giving me a little more energy later on.

Weather in itself was enough to leave me limp. After a little deceptive warmth in March—followed by the floods which so spectacularly submerged your erstwhile habitat—there came a chilly April which about wore me out. Not till the 28th was there a really warm day. Since then I have been able to take my work out to Prospect Terrace several times—& on April 30 my aunt & I were treated to a delightful motor ride through the awakening countryside to Westport Point, Mass. The landscape is now a captivating spectacle with its fresh verdure & abundant blossoms, & I hope to find time for some rural walks ere long. Barlow has invited me down to De Land again, but I greatly doubt my ability to accept. This, I fear, will be no travel year for Grandpa!

I've heard some pretty good lectures during recent months—at the college a block over the hill & at the School of Design a block down the hill. Subjects pleasantly varied—Plato's Republic, modern painting, Chinese contributions to western culture, Gilbert Stuart, R.I. silversmiths, archaic Greek art influences, early classical sculpture, philosophy & poetry, Mayan ruins, & the Michelson-Morley experiment. Never too aged to pick up new information!

On May 4th the Rhode Island Tercentenary observances began with a parade in colonial costume which started at the college gate—just a stone's throw from here. Later there was a mock-session of the rebel legislature of May 4, 1776—held in costume in the selfsame room of the ancient colony house (built 1761) where the original session was held. In this, each old-time deputy was represented by a lineal descendant—Gov. Green representing his ancestor Col. Arnold, who offered the original set of treasonable resolutions severing Rhode Island from the lawful authority of the Crown. The acting & costumes were so excellent that one might easily have found the bygone period returned—with the intervening 160 years merely a bad dream. I was one of the relatively few spectators lucky enough to get into the colony-house & witness the proceedings. In the afternoon—in a ceremony at the State House which I did not attend—Governor Curley of Mass. presented to Gov. Green a copy of the recently adopted resolution of the Massachusetts General Court, rescinding the banishment imposed on Roger Williams in Oct. 1635.

After 300½ years, Mr. Williams no doubt highly appreciates this delicate mark of consideration.

March & April W T seemed to me not quite as bad as usual. In March, C A S, the Binders, Hamilton (mirabile dictu!), & the newcomer Kuttner (with whom I'm now in touch) presented material worth reading, while in April (as you point out) Jacobi & Bloch had excellent offerings.[4] Bloch is certainly coming along fast—& will be importantly heard from if the mood & technique of pulp fiction don't swamp him. As for Klarkash-Ton's translations of Baudelaire—I have long thought them superior to any others I have ever seen—not excluding the very disappointing version by Arthur Symons.[5] I haven't seen the Millay–Dillon translation, nor do I think C A S has. Later we may get a look & compare notes. Smith has a startling aesthetic kinship to Baudelaire—manifest both in translations & in original poems. I haven't had time to read the May W T, so can't say how disappointing "The Faceless God"[6] is. Yesterday I got around to *Story*, & enjoyed very much the cleverly gruesome shocker by Dunsany.[7] As you remark, the coming horror is pretty clearly foreseen for some time—beginning with the emphasis on the murderer's *vegetarianism*. This does not, however, impair the interest of the tale—& the exact purpose of that woodcutting *did* remain as a surprise . . . at least to my dull old wits. Thanks for the portrait of Robertoff S. Kharovitch[8]—who certainly seems to have become thoroughly assimilated by his Moscovite environment. Hope his surviving literary interest will eventually expand from appreciation to performance! No—I know nothing about "The Ghost Story Omnibus".[9] I'm all behind the times on everything!

Regarding your novel—I trust that you won't let obstacles discourage you. Actually, I fancy the task of composition is giving you the very best of practice. It is certainly well not to be too self-conscious about style. Clear expression is the primary thing—& the best style is that which develops unconsciously as an author strives to convey as simply & directly as possible the moods or ideas which demand utterance. Concerning the sample passage from your book—in general I think it is excellent & vivid. It catches the essence of a mood, & suggests very graphically the emotional effects of certain characteristic scenes. It is, moreover, very well phrased—with apt & vivid words, & with a commendable amount of euphony & rhythm. To attempt any flaw-picking with such material would really be no more than useless cavilling, & I see no reason for not letting it stand as is. If I were to say how *I* would write it, that would mean nothing; for I probably have a basically different theory of expression in prose. *I* would doubtless cut down the "vivid" expressions so beloved by modern authors ("sun fried whitely", the incident of the patch of sun, &c.), & attempt to convey the subject's mood in a more objectively analytical way. I would hesitate about having the subject 'stretch out his arms in transport', unless the novel definitely implied that he were the sort of hyperaesthetic sap who *would* make such a gesture. But hell—what has *another* guy's method to do with *yours?* There isn't anything in the passage which doesn't belong there—which does not, apparently, promote the story's main task of expression—so if you take an old man's advice you'll let it alone! Some day you *may* get a novel out of the basket factory, but I fancy all material has to be viewed *in retrospect* in order to be literarily available one can seldom construct valuable art from experience in which one is still immersed. *Perspective* is what the novelist needs. Sorry "The Judge's Hunting Dogs" hasn't yet found a home in print. Send it to *Donald A. Wollheim, 801 West End Ave., N.Y. City* for inclusion in *Fanciful Tales*—the semi-pro magazine (on the order of *Marvel*) which he is trying to establish in partnership with Wilson Shepherd of Oakman, Ala. These are the youths at present publishing *The Phantagraph*. I still adhere to my original favourable opinion of the tale. It has a certain *atmosphere*—& that's what virtually none of the pulp junk has.

Glad you joined the N.A.P.A. A second *Causerie*—& a second *Dragon-Fly*—ought to be out before long. Don't get discouraged by the lousy papers you receive from various quarters. I warned you that amateurdom has its trivial side, & that the present period is an era of decadence from which we are seeking to emerge. The current year is rather disappointing because of a triangular political feud (Babcock hates Bradofsky & E. H. Smith hates Babcock) which has consumed valuable time & energy, & hampered the plans of the administration. Next year I look for better things.

I read all your book notes with extreme interest—indeed, after one of your letters I could (if I chose) parade quite an impressive smattering of second-hand current erudition! "The Last Puritan"[10] is in this house at the moment—lent to my aunt by a friend. I really want to read this volume, but don't know whether I'll get a chance, since my aunt can't keep it for ever. I have always had the most extreme respect for Santayana.

It is years since I read "Wuthering Heights", but the dark spell of its mood is still upon me. With all its faults I still think it has an elusive, genius-born power (depending upon an instinctive recognition of the obscure symbols which touch off profound & latent emotional reflexes) which amply justifies its revived fame. Today Emily Bronte has quite eclipsed her once-preferred sister Charlotte.

A loan-exhibit of Klarkash-Ton's sculpture is now circulating—Loveman to E'ch-Pi-El, E'ch-Pi-El to Ar-E'ch-Bei, Ar-E'ch-Bei to Klarkash-Ton. I haven't yet seen it, but have high expectations. There are over a dozen statuettes in it—mostly grotesque *heads*. While with Loveman, it will be seen by all the gang in N.Y. C A S is having a hard time—with an ailing father & the care of the whole place on his hands. It's a wonder he can accomplish anything amidst his profusion of handicaps!

Concerning the cinema—did I tell you that I saw "Ah, Wilderness"? I found it very good, despite the incongruous clowning of Mr. Beery. The vague, elusive *atmosphere* of 1906 was all there, & gave me a profoundly nostalgic twinge. Eheu, fugaces! We have lost as much as we have gained—perhaps more—since '06! I hope to see some of the films you mention—though I haven't been to a cinema since Jany. 13. I was greatly interested in your remarks concerning "The Informer". The objections you cite all seem valid—but for all that the net result survives as an atmospheric triumph. And so the recent Chaplin product is a disappointment?[11] Alas for the idols of yesteryear! I haven't seen it—but may some day for old times' sake. In the old days I saw virtually every one of Charlie's productions.

Hope the Pittsburgh prospect materialises—although I, personally, would probably like Suffolk better than the Smoky Metropolis. About the Bread-Loaf Conference—my friend M. W. Moe (the amateur journalist—a H.S. teacher in Milwaukee) is going there next August, & expects to have a very pleasant time. You'd probably like it yourself. As for me—I haven't any use for "arty" atmospheres, & distrust every influence which makes anybody think of himself as "a writer" instead of as simply *a balanced individual member of society*. My ideal is *the gentleman of broad interests*—philosophic, scientific, historical, civic, literary, aesthetic, recreational, &c.—*in his own hereditary setting;* with the practice of the arts as a mere spontaneous & non-self-conscious adjunct to the general processes of living. "Bohemianism", Greenwich-Village-ism, art-colony-ism, &c. &c. give me a formidable cervical pain! However—the Bread-Loaf business is probably far removed from the Greenwich-Village stuff. It really has a very high standing—though if anybody gave me the cash to go there I'd probably spend it on a trip to Charleston or St. Augustine! No—I've never attended such a conference.

Stumbled on an interesting genealogical discovery recently—when I learned for the first time that I am a great-great-great-great-great-great-great-great-great[-]grandson of the Elizabethan *astronomer* who introduced the Copernican theory into England! For one who has always been a keen amateur astronomer, this was quite a find. Ordinarily I'm not much at genealogy, being content to take what preëxisting charts tell me & let it go at that. The other day I ran into some callers of my aunt's—three venerable sisters related to us in the Wilcox & Field lines—& one of them mentioned how proud I ought to be of our common ancestor, *the astronomer John Field*. That had me quite floored, since our set of charts carried the Field line back only as far as the original Providence settler John Field, who died in 1686, & I knew *he* was no star-gazer! Well—it soon turned out that the ancestry of this settler has been known for ages among genealogists, though I never had the least inkling of it. The Elizabethan astronomer (whose ephemeris, published in 1557, contained the first English account of the Copernican system, & who has been called "The Proto-Copernican of England") was the Prov. colonist's *own grandfather*—hence *my* nine-times-great-grandfather. It certainly gave me a kick to get a real man of science in my pedigree—which as a general thing is lousy with clergymen* but short on straight thinkers. Later I looked up the standard Field genealogy (by F. C. Pierce, 1901) & found out all about the line. It comes from Sir Hubertus de la Feld, a follower of William the Conqueror who took lands in Lancashire in 1069; the Prov. stock springing from the Yorkshire branch centreing around Sowerby, Ardsley, & Thurnscoe. I've copied a lot of notes & now have my Field lineage straight back—in exactly 20 generations—to Roger de la Feld of Sowerby, born in 1240. But it's the *astronomer* who interests me. I have more than an average amount of Field blood, being descended from *three* of the Providence settler's grandchildren. ¶ Well—now to struggle with some more letters. Will send books as soon as possible . . . & give me a calldown if I'm keeping "The Science of Life" too long! ¶ Patriarchal benedictions—E'ch-Pi-El

Notes

1. An anthology of weird tales edited by Cynthia Asquith.

2. In fact, Annie Gamwell was hospitalized to undergo a mastectomy.

3. John Milton, *Paradise Lost,* 2.995–96.

4. *WT,* March 1936: CAS, "The Black Abbot of Puthuum"; Eando Binder, "The Crystal Curse"; Edmond Hamilton, "In the World's Dusk"; Henry Kuttner, "The Graveyard Rats"; *WT,* April 1936: Carl Jacobi, "The Face in the Wind"; Robert Bloch, "The Druidic Doom."

5. CAS's translations of Baudelaire—many of them existing only in literal prose versions—were not published in their entirety until they appeared in Smith's *Complete Poetry and Translations,* ed. S. T. Joshi and David E. Schultz (New York: Hippocampus Press, 2007–08), Vol. 3.

6. By Robert Bloch.

7. "The Two Bottles of Relish," *Story* No. 43 (February 1936): 50–62 (as "Two Bottles of Relish"), first published in *Time and Tide* for 12 and 19 November 1932. It is a sardonic detective tale of cannibalism and one of the most frequently anthologized tales in modern literature.

8. I.e., Robert Spencer Carr; see letter 45, n.12.

9. Joseph Lewis French, ed., *The Ghost Story Omnibus* (1933), a combining of French's anthologies *Great Ghost Stories* (1918) and *Ghosts, Grim and Gentle* (1926).

10. A novel by George Santayana. See HPL's discussion in a letter to R. H. Barlow, 30 September 1936 (*OFF* 364–67).

11. *Modern Times* (Charles Chaplin Productions, 1936), directed by Charlie Chaplin; starring Charlie Chaplin, Paulette Goddard, and Henry Bergman. It is generally considered one of Chaplin's greatest films.

---

*& damn me if this new discovery hasn't added *one more* divine to the bunch—for it seems that the Providence colonist's maternal grandfather was the Rev. John Sotwell, vicar of Peniston, Yorkshire.

[58]   [AHT]

[18 June 1936]

[. . .]

I don't agree with the criticism of Loveman's attitude, since attitude has nothing to do with merit. Excellence in expressing any sort of attitude is what makes a poet good.

[. . .]

As for the expression "fascistic socialism"[1]—there is nothing in the least contradictory about it. Fascism is *a method of government*—which may be applied to a state with many different kinds of economic organisation. Socialism is *a mode of economic organisation*—which may exist within many kinds of states including democracies, monarchies, and fascistic dictatorships. A fascist government is one in which functions are centralised in a small group of competent executives (who may be appointed or elected in any fashion) at liberty to act without cumbrous and confusing obstacles and hostile legislative or judicial bodies. When such a government administers a state in which basic industries are publicly owned and operated for the common good, the result is "fascistic socialism". In my present opinion, that is the least irrational sort of government conceivable.

[. . .]

As for "proletarian literature"—I doubt if it can ever be of much importance because of its ulterior motivation. The purpose of fiction is not to teach, but to *express*. What is wanted is a glimpse of life itself—with the permanent essentials of character and vital drift *embodied* but not annotated with diagrams and sermons giving conscious expositions of philosophical, ethical, and political principles. A real artist in fiction, whatever his political sentiments *as a citizen,* is neither "rightward" nor "leftward" *as a story-writer.* He tells what he sees or imagines, and leaves philosophical inference to his readers. The whole idea of "socially motivated literature" is sheer bunk. While of course a strong emotion regarding some political or economic system—as regarding any other issue or standard or institution or person or event or fact—may well colour and animate a depiction of life, it is only a source of weakness when a writer deliberately selects events & human traits in order to illustrate some preconceived thesis. Illustration or proof of the theories and principles belongs to the essay or the treatise—not to the story. If a story is so vivid and so true to life that it does indeed illustrate a social principle, well and good. But such illustration cannot well be more than a by-product. The moment it becomes an end in itself the vitality of the story is lost. Events and traits manipulated for didactic purposes are just as hollow and unreal and unconvincing as events and traits manipulated—as in commercial fiction—for cheaply dramatic and bourgeois-tickling purposes. In either case the discriminating reader feels that he is not seeing an actual fragment of life, but that he is merely witnessing an indifferently-managed puppet-show. The fictionalist's only purpose should be to draw life and character in their natural proportions and with their natural shadings—irrespective of what they illustrate. Only in that way will he ever create anything of genuine vitality and importance.

[. . .]

[. . .]

What I object to is the injection of the *author's* emotions as a visible element into the text of a piece of fiction. I hold that it is the author's business only to exhibit his characters and events—not to gush in his own person over them. Let the dramatic personae tell their own story. It is *they*, not the author, who must arouse in the reader the image or emotion designed to be aroused. De Maupassant, above all others, knew how to do this. Dickens, on the other hand, continually slops over.

[. . .]

As for the reputation of Ford Madox Ford—I guess association with the great explains most of it.

[. . .]

Regarding the difficulty of grasping poetry as compared with prose—I fancy it's because poetry is a special mode of communication in which *statement* is excluded in favour of *suggestion, depiction, symbolisation,* and *description in terms of parallel objects and occurrences.* The two fields meet only occasionally.

[. . .]

As for the kinship of religious feeling with a love of weird fiction—I have frequently said that both emotions (or the main essence of both) spring from a similar or identical human reaction—the resentment and rebellion of the individual at his imprisonment within the narrow and tyrannous sway of time, space, and natural law. The always out-reaching ego cannot bear insignificance, limitation, and impermanence—hence if naive and ignorant, kids itself into the belief that "outside" realms and avenues and powers and linkages exist; and if disillusioned and informed, demands an artistic escape which shall momentarily create the emotional impression (without the intellectual belief) of a cosmos in which the chains of time, space, and natural law can be occasionally thrown off. As to the reason why *macabre* themes are so often turned to—I fancy it is largely because these (for a variety of reasons—largely depending upon the predominance of suffering and fear in real life) seem more convincing examples of supernaturalism than any bright theme could. *Rites,* I think, are favoured through *tradition*—because they form the long-recognised approach to the beings and gateways of the outer dark. The deep influence and basicity of *fear* in human life makes its artificial simulation somehow fascinating.

[. . .]

Notes

1. Shea may have noted its use in HPL's "The Shadow out of Time," in reference to the political organization of the Great Race (see *CF* 3.404).

[59]   [AHT]

February 5, 1937

[. . .]

Now that you come to mention it, it *is* rather curious how fantaisistes peter out. perhaps it is because all their raison d'etre and driving force comes from the desire to portray a single mood rather than from a curiosity about general events and psychological phenomena. An isolated wish can dwindle—or become discouraged—pore readily than can a general curiosity or interest; since it depends more upon delicate emotional adjustments which age and ennui and discouragement can disarrange. I am, incidentally, amused by the definition of fantasy which you quote from Hemingway. The trouble with our literary toreador is, of course, that he tries to draw a parallel betwixt two utterly different and irreconcilable types of aesthetic emotion, each with an antipodal set of goals and origins. Fantaisistes and realists resemble each other only in the accidental circumstance that both usually employ paper and ink. Aside from that, they have no aims or wishes in common. The realist is a person of essentially scientific type, curious about the normal reactions and habits of *homo sapiens* and anxious to record such. The fantaisiste is a person of essentially imaginative type, impressed by the poignancy of man's sense of the unknown and of man's revolt against the galling limitations of time, space, and natural law, and anxious to give that sort of feeling a concrete embodiment. No two artists could have a greater divergence of objects. In real fact, the fantaisiste (who either may or may not *know* how human beings react) is simply one *who doesn't give a goddam how human being beings* [*sic*] *react.* He is not a realist gone astray, he is, instead, one who could never under any circumstances have been a realist or have wished to be a realist. Comparing the two is like comparing a musician with a historian. There is no reason on earth why either human characterisation or general "human feeling" should enter into a fantasy—any more than why dates and events should enter into a musical melody.

[. . .]

Am rather feeble these days—with a combination of intestinal grippe and winter-swollen feet. Blessings—H. P. L.

[60]   [AHT]

[undated fragments]

Glad you found my epistles interesting—but I can assure you they will never be of value. Being an inveterate and voluminous correspondent, I have reeled off so many thousand letters in the last twenty years that—even allowing for the natural discarding of the majority—there must be enough in the hands of my friends to flood the market in the event of any miraculous and unmerited fame! *

There is no room for characterisation in a tale written from the cosmic point of view, in which human figures are only impersonal incidents in a stream of unhumanly motivated events. Characterisation is an attribute of an entirely different species of fiction—albeit a greater species, as I freely admit. It consists of depicting the acts of the various human figures in such a way as to make each one a consistent & individualised entity according to the actual laws of human nature—and does *not* mean merely making certain figures conspicuous, "sympathetic", or likely to linger in memory. . . . I don't think it is well to have too much sympathy with any character in a horror-tale. That leads toward the inane conventionalities of the Seabury Quinn school. The really bizarre author should be wholly objective and impersonal—never taking the part of his human characters against his non-human or anti-human forces. To exult in the triumph of mankind over the powers of night is to take a provincial and stereotyped attitude. A truly original writer is just as likely to side with the powers of night against man, as to take the reverse attitude. . . . Unless they are careful, they will be giving their gaseous spatial entities a suspiciously manlike set of thoughts, values, and emotions. . . . just as cheap interplanetary writers give their non-terrestrial characters names obviously suggested by common Aryan and Semitic linguistic roots. The fact is, that damn few weird stories escape flatness, inconsistency, or absurdity at one point or another. You can see the cheap superficiality of most of this truck in a thousand ways—such as the commonplace tendency to use young and romantically attractive characters, to drag in stock "human interest" motivations and situations, &c. &c. &c. I try as best I can to avoid all this—making each character just the sort (on a realistic & unromantic basis) that would be likely to be in the indicated situation, and emphasising every-day qualities instead of concocting picturesque and out-of-place eccentricities. Thus I scorn a trick puppet like Jules de Grandin, and try to have my various shadowy figures (Wilmarth, Akeley, Armitage, &c) as normal and undistinguished as the average passive agents in a weird happening would be likely to be. Nor do I make them all young and prepossessing. On the other hand, I seek to have them of varying ages and types, just as any assortment of people culled at random would be likely to be.†

Shea's note: Ibid; I believe this belongs among the late July or early August, 1931 letters.
†*Shea's note:* From a fragment of a letter, unfortunately incomplete and undated, that obviously belongs to the 1931 crop.

Carl Ferdinand Strauch

(Courtesy Special Collections, Lehigh University Libraries, Bethlehem, Pennsylvania)

Letters to Carl Ferdinand Strauch

[1]   [ALS]

10 Barnes St.,

Providence, R.I.,

Septr 20, 1931

My dear Mr. Strauch:—

I was glad to receive yours of the 16th, since I had heard of you & your work very favourably from our friend Brobst. I hope to see a copy of your book when it is out[1]—for I appreciate poetry despite the mediocrity of my own attempts in that medium.

I am glad that you have found some of my efforts worth reading—especially "The Strange High House", which I wrote five years ago, when strongly under the influence of Dunsany. Other things of mine in that semi-poetic medium have been more mawkish & unsatisfactory—for in the long run I think a style of greater objective simplicity is my really natural mode of expression.

I heartily agree with you regarding the lame inadequacy of nearly everything that passes for weird fiction in the popular magazines—to say nothing of more pretentious specimens. Poe had an inherent convincingness & brooding menace of style & atmosphere which no one has been able to duplicate, though many living writers have surpassed him in width of cosmic outlook & originality of bizarre invention. Of later weird material I would tend to say that Algernon Blackwood, (despite a wretched style) Arthur Machen, Lord Dunsany, & Montague Rhodes James furnish the greatest abundance of really fine examples. Robert W. Chambers' early "King in Yellow" has a certain sombre convincingness, as have several things—notably "Seaton's Aunt"—by Walter de la Mare. I do not care much for May Sinclair or Fletcher,[2] & believe that Doyle's flat style spoils many tales which would otherwise be extremely powerful. A few years ago I wrote a longish article on the history of the weird tale, which appeared in a magazine (a venture called *The Recluse,* which did not survive its first issue) privately printed by a friend. If I can resurrect a copy, & if it would interest you to see it, I will give you a look at that sketch. If I had more energy I might revise & expand it, & try to get it published as a small book.

Weird fiction is necessarily a minor field of art, since it confines itself to one narrow side of the human personality—the subjective image-building tendency which speculates beyond the realm of the visible & creates a natural rebellion against the inexorable limitations of time, space, & cosmic law. But at the same time it is silly to deny that it is art at all; for the instinct on which it is based is a genuine one, & there is art in any well-presented & sincere manifestation of a genuine human impulse. Like you, I regard the current depreciation of weird writing as a lamentable & conspicuous example of academic pedantry based on artificial standards; & believe that an artist of the right skill & endowments might readily create work of the highest aesthetic quality in the medium. Of modern authors, Blackwood is the only one who treats the unreal with suitable seriousness—& he unfortunately has a crude style & lack of self-criticism (as witness the endless volumes of namby-pamby inanity which he grinds out in addition to masterpieces like "The Willows") which will always prevent him from attaining the heights. The supreme weird writer has yet to appear—& meanwhile Poe still holds first place.

With best wishes, & hoping that I may some day get around to see you & your interesting group (of whose discussions Brobst has sometimes written), I am

Yrs most cordially & sincerely,

H. P. Lovecraft

Notes

1. *Twenty-nine Poems* (Boston: Bruce Humphries, [1932]).

2. Perhaps J. S. Fletcher (1863–1935), primarily a detective writer but author of a few weird novels at the turn of the century.

[2] [ALS]

10 Barnes St.,
Providence, R.I.,
Octr 10, 1931.

My dear Strauch:—

Your letter of the 4th proved exceedingly interesting to me, & I was delighted with all the poems—especially the autumn piece. Of your poetic gifts there can be no question, & I am sure that Allentown must be a notable abode of the Muses if it can produce many genuine rivals! You have the true poet's sense of symbols & images, & a highly enviable command of the right words & rhythms for their aptest conveyance. I have often tried to express in verse the various moods evoked in me by various phases of beauty, but never get very far in that direction. Enclosed is a typical bit of my metrical tripe—a rhymed protest against the wanton destruction of a splendid row of ancient brick warehouses along the Providence waterfront a couple of years ago.[1] Unfortunately the protest did not succeed in its object— which was a pity, because the old buildings formed a priceless link with early maritime days, & gave the central square of Providence a rich quaintness unique among cities of equal size. I possibly mentioned in my former letter that I am an inveterate antiquarian, whose greatest delight is in recapturing the past through contemplation of its architectural vestiges. This is reflected in the bookplate I had designed a few years ago[2]—a typical old Providence doorway—a specimen of which I will enclose.

I trust you have been able to take all the rural rambles you promised yourself—surely the genial weather of last week was favourable enough to such a design! Yes—Brobst has often confirmed my long-standing impression of the beauty of your region, so that I am quite anxious to see it for myself. Rural landscapes exert a very potent charm upon me—being on a parity with colonial architecture in this respect. Fortunately my own section is very beautiful scenically, & I have always been within walking distance of the woods & fields. Indeed, my birthplace[3] was so close to what was then the edge of Providence's settled residence district, that in boyhood I was as much a ruralite as an urbanite. I have always felt very close to the ancient cycle of New England agricultural life with its various seasonal manifestations; so that today I am acutely conscious of belonging to the vanishing rural-minded civilisation rather than to the coming age of machinery and urbanisation. Every sunny day in summer I take my work out to the open fields & woods in a black enamel-cloth bag, & see just as little as possible of paved streets & modern houses. Last week I had a splendid taste of autumn scenery by virtue of a dual trip to neighbouring parts of New England. First I went to Massachusetts on a pleasure jaunt—taking in the unspoiled region south of Boston, (ancient Hingham with its "Old Ship Church" built in 1681 &c) & the exquisite Merrimack Valley (containing the ancient city of Newburyport) to the north. Then, upon returning home, I found a telegram summoning me to Hartford, Conn. to confer about a book revision job I am performing for the Stephen Daye Press of Brattleboro, Vt.[4] I had, curiously enough, never been to central Connecticut before; close though it is to my own doorstep—hence was eager to sample the scenery along the route. It proved surprisingly fine, & an ideal day shewed it at its best. On the return trip I chose—for variety's sake—an indirect route passing through Norwich & Plainfield, & found the scenery even lovelier than on the direct route. Bold hills & valleys—gleaming lakes—breath-taking panoramas—everything to enchant the imagination. The old town of Norwich, where I stopped for a thorough exploration, is ineffably quaint—being built on the steep terraces that rise above a bend in the river Thames.

About that anthology—it has only *one* of my stories, albeit one that is quite a favourite of mine. There are other pieces of much greater merit by other writers, so that the book is most distinctly worth buying. It is called "Creeps by Night", is edited by Dashiell Hammett, & published at $2.50 by the John Day Co. I haven't seen a copy yet—am waiting to see if the publisher gives me one free. There is no published collection of my stuff, though various things of mine are included in anthologies. My "Call of Cthulhu" is in "Beware After Dark", edited by T. Everett Harré & published by the Macaulay Co., & the British "Not at Night" collections (published annually) usually include me among their contents.

I have seen reviews of the work of Egon Friedell,[5] & am inclined to agree that his is one of the profoundest philosophic minds of this generation. I must certainly get hold of his "European Culture" sooner or later. Spengler is already a standby of mine—whom I hailed upon his first appearance as a scholarly confirmer of ideas I had long held in my fumbling & unscholarly way. You are right, I think, in emphasising the indispensably encyclopaedic quality of German scholarship. Indeed, I fancy that history & philosophy would still be painfully primitive but for the contributions made by the relentlessly thorough Germanic mind.

I am aware that your part of Pennsylvania is rich in folklore & superstitions—but was surprised when Brobst told me of the prevalence of weird beliefs in the cities as well as the rural districts. Such superstition as New England still retains is confined wholly to the remotest backwoods—even the ordinarily populous farming districts being to a great extent rational & disillusioned in their dominant attitude. Most certainly, Pennsylvania folklore ought to be better represented in literature than it so far has been—though a few books have centred to some extent around it. In the 18th century Charles Brockden Brown touched this region in what was virtually the first American novel—"Wieland; or, The Transformation"—& in the present generation there has been a rather mediocre book by Prof. Fred Lewis Pattee—"The House of the Black Ring"—covering the same ground.[6] I realise, though, that these things have scarcely scratched the surface. As for the distinction between Pennsylvania "Dutch" & other Germanic elements—the only one I know is that the former have been settled in the Pennsylvania countryside for over two centuries, developing localisms in dialect & folkways, whereas other U.S. Germans date from 1848 & later, & have not formed such a differentiated nucleus—keeping closer to the European German type until absorbed into the Anglo-Saxon cultural stream. I believe, also, that the old Pennsylvania Germans came chiefly from the Palatinate & South Germany—thus being perhaps of a more specialised type than later-comers who hailed in more equal proportions from all parts of the Germanic world. The principal differentiation, I take it, is due to the long isolation of the Pennsylvanians in a remote region where ancestral superstitions were nurtured & magnified rather than weakened by time. This isolation would perhaps account for the element of cruelty or the sinister which you remark—but which I never heard of before. It is paralleled by certain characteristics of back-country people everywhere. The "hex" anecdote you cite is certainly unique—& all the more impressive because of its un-theatrical homeliness. Certainly, the minds of the people are open to all sorts of suggestions; so that every opportunity is offered for the practice of delusive phenomena according to ancient & half-submerged patterns.

This kind of thing ought to be studied soon, I imagine, if it is to be encountered in its pristine purity; for a generation or two of modern standardised life with radios, cinemas, tabloids, & cheap magazines will leave very little of the ancient folk-heritage.

With best wishes, & again expressing my appreciation of the poems sent, I remain

Yrs most cordially & sincerely,
H. P. Lovecraft

Notes

1. "The East India Brick Row."
2. By Wilfred B. Talman c. 1929.
3. 194 (later 454) Angell Street.
4. Leon Burr Richardson, *History of Dartmouth College* (Hanover, NH, 1932; 2 vols.). The Stephen Daye Press was managed by HPL's friend Vrest Orton.
5. Egon Friedell (1878–1938), German historian and philosopher. HPL evidently refers to Friedell's *Kulturgeschichte der Neuzeit* (1927–31; 3 vols.), the only one of his works to be translated into English, as *A Cultural History of the Modern Age: The Crisis of the European Soul from the Black Death to the World War* (New York: Knopf, 1930–32; 3 vols.).
6. See JVS 50 n.1.

[3]   [ALS]

Guy Fawkes' Day
[5 November 1931]

My dear Strauch:—

Very glad to hear from you, & sorry your eyes have been bothering. It pays to rest one's vision all one can, for a tremendous amount depends on that one delicate sense. I had some severe eye strain last winter, but my long spring & summer trip in the South set things right again.

You have my sympathy regarding the tutoring—but it helps, at least, if the subjects are willing & earnest. I don't think I'd make a good tutor in any subject, for I haven't the concise expository faculty which I notice in many.

Good luck with the novel—which, with your general talent, ought to be successful if you stick close to nature for your material. Hawthorne's general type of atmosphere ought to be as effective today as in his own time, though I imagine that a Dickensian treatment of character would need many modifications. I never could abide Dickens—finding him a peculiarly wearisome mixture of hollow sentimentality & grotesque exaggeration. None of his characters ever impressed me as in the least like a human being. But then, I seem to find all Victorian literature alien. I like either the present or the 18th century—anything except the artificiality of the 19th. I see no reason why you should not fulfil your literary ambitions, & expect to hear of you in the course of time as a recognised poet—& perhaps novelist. With such a start at your age, everything is in your favour.

About "Creeps"—amusingly enough, Benét's contribution is unqualifiedly & indisputably the worst thing in the book! It is an attempt to be comic—& succeeds about as well as Poe's similar attempts. To my mind, the best thing is Ewers' "Spider".[1] Most of the stuff, unfortunately, lacks real atmospheric weirdness—but belongs more to the genre of the mere *conte cruel*. There is too much artificial cleverness—I found it easy to predict the outcome of most of the tales at a relatively early point in their structure.

Herbert Asbury edited the pirated American "Not at Night" anthology (containing my "Horror at Red Hook") which Macy-Masius withdrew from the market rather than pay royalty or damages to *Weird Tales*. I don't recall whether or not he ever contributed to the magazine. He is rather clever, & his "Gangs of New York" has become almost a folklore classic. I make no attempt to keep up with contemporary books—for how much of every year's output is really worth reading? A retrospective glance at the best sellers of 1926 or 1921 is sardonically illuminating—how many have really survived?

Glad the material I enclosed proved of interest, & that the verses did not seem too irredeemably flat. Here are a couple of cards reflecting my antiquarian wanderings of last week—my final excursion of the season, since temperature conditions now begin to preclude comfortable travel. I visited four of my favourite ancient towns—Portsmouth, N.H., & Newburyport, Salem, & Marblehead, Mass.[2] Portsmouth & Newburyport are almost solidly archaic, but Salem has a brisk modern life besides its antiquities. Marblehead—now that the herd of summer visitors has dispersed—is like a deserted museum. There is nothing else like it in the U.S. You can see by the enclosed view that it is absolutely an unchanged & miraculously preserved seaport of the 18th century—a tangible bit of the past which makes no demands on the imagination.

With best wishes—

Yrs most cordially & sincerely,

H. P. Lovecraft

[Enclosures: Two postcards ("A quaint old street in Marblehead, Mass." and "Old Witch House, After 1780, Salem, Mass.").]

Notes

1. Stephen Vincent Benét (1898–1943), "The King of the Cats"; Hans Heinz Ewers (1872–1943), "The Spider." The Ewers story clearly influenced HPL's "The Haunter of the Dark."

2. This trip influenced the composition of "The Shadow over Innsmouth" in the weeks following.

[4]   [ALS]

10 Barnes St.,
Providence, R.I.,
Novr 17, 1931.

My dear Strauch:—

Glad you found the postcards interesting. I think I told you that I am something of an amateur antiquarian whose chief delight is to visit ancient towns. If you'd like, I can send you views of other old places, both in New England & the South. Trout Hall must be a very interesting place, & I am glad Allentown has preserved at least that much linkage with the past. As for material comforts & cleanliness—I probably agree largely with you that their citation as a criterion of civilisation is distinctly childish & absurd. Yet on the other hand I think they are so eminently desirable that I wouldn't encourage any attack on them in the manner of G. K. Chesterton— who backs up his ostentatious mediaevalism to the extent of lecturing in visibly soiled linen. (Recalling, no doubt, Dr. Johnson's dictum—"As for clean linen, why, Sir, I have no passion for it!"[1]) Every advance in the standard of neatness & immaculateness is an aesthetic asset, & is intrinsically good. The only silly thing is to magnify these background details into major objects & criteria. They ought, rather, to be understood & taken for granted—for when they are overstressed we have a suspicion that they are rather recent & not quite assimilated acquisitions. When a man talks too much about taking a bath each day, we are inclined to suspect that he did not always do so! But all the same, I'd rather he would take it & talk about it than *not* take it. Ah, me— what a complex fabric is life! New England has much of Pennsylvania's emphasis on cleanliness, though I don't think it wholly displaces an interest in the intellectual & aesthetic. It seems to be an ingrained instinct of the Nordic race—as comparison with our Mediterranean, Slavic, & Semitic newcomers vividly demonstrates. One finds it equally developed among the Dutch families (real Holland Dutch) of the New-Netherland region—New York & New Jersey—of whom more remain than is commonly supposed.

I envy you your sight of Quakertown with its quaint tombstones. My familiarity with the Pennsylvania-German culture is limited to Germantown— the suburb of Philadelphia—but that delightful place has nothing as quaint as what you describe. Germantown, indeed, was never truly rustic—being only 4 miles from the colonial metropolis. Its houses—even back in the 1690's— were solidly & tastefully built, & the gravestones (in Dunkard, Quaker, & Moravian churchyards) quite devoid of the autobiographical & anticipatory features you cite. It was in Germantown, by the way, that the Bible was first printed in the present area of the U.S.—by Christopher Sauer, in 1740- something or other, in the German language. Germantown (as you may perhaps know from first-hand observation) is still one of the most picturesque & unspoiled places in America, with a vast number of the old stone houses (late

XVII & XVIII cent.) still standing in & near the long main street. Wyck—a fine old manor-house of 1690 or so—is in splendid condition & frequently photographed for books on architecture, & several homesteads of the celebrated Wistar or Wister family remain in excellent shape. A good number of the present inhabitants are descended from the old families, & their Site & Relic Society (housed in a fine old 18th century mansion in a small park) has done much to keep the traditions of the past alive. I never visit Phila. without taking a stroll through Germantown. By the way—there is a fine set of rooms from a typical Pennsylvania-German farmhouse (unaffected by British influence) in the new Philadelphia Art Museum—furnished with appropriate material. Also—in Fairmount Park there is a reconstructed stone farmhouse of the 18th century (moved from Frankford) illustrating the transition period when German families near Philadelphia began to speak English & adopt Georgian motifs to some extent in interior architecture.

Oh, yes—we have the usual community chests hereabouts, & I don't doubt but that they are necessary during the present bewildering period when actual industrial & social conditions are out of touch with the available political & economic machinery. Owing to the mechanisation of industry, a vast number of persons are now hopelessly unemployable—& there seems to be nothing to do but to feed them until somebody thinks up some sort of industrial adjustment which can reabsorb a good proportion of them. It is not within the capacity of fumbling, groping human nature to keep basic institutions in step with the rapidly changing conditions of the present. People reared in a simpler age cannot think in terms of this—hence the acute strain for a full generation or two. No perfect social balance, of course, ever has been or ever will be possible; but in time the danger of an unfed mass will probably be recognised enough to bring about a modified set of conditions—employment of large numbers at shorter hours & with sufficient remuneration to remove violent suffering & discontent. Whether such changes will come voluntarily from large industrialists, or whether they will be imposed politically by a more or less fascistic government, still remains to be seen. But I think the solid sense of the Nordic race can be depended on to make the transition of Western Europe & North America less violent & destructive than that of upheaved Russia. In the case of that hapless region the remedy seems worse, from the point of view of a liberal & individualistic civilisation, than the original disease. Meanwhile—in the absence of other machinery for quick equilibration—charity is an absolute necessity as a palliative. This year the chest business in Rhode Island seems fairly well devoid of absurd frills, & the primary relief objects are not so much the scouts, Y, &c., as the actually homeless & foodless. This state is also about to assess special taxes for the aid of the unemployed.

I think I can agree with you on the merit of Hawthorne's style—but somehow I lack the ability of Machen & others to find anything really solid or magical in Dickens.[2] The "immense gusto for living" which many praise in novels of the Dickens type seems to me a sort of insincere & artificial excrescence—something essentially tawdry & detracting from the really impartial & artistic delineation of human life. I recognise the merit of Fielding & other 18th century English writers, yet on mature reflection cannot help thinking that the French novel tradition is at bottom rather sounder than ours. There is more honest objectivity, less irrelevant digression, less meaningless sentimentality, & less traditional hokum disguised as profundity. Less humour, too—a good thing, since much of our overrated humour is at bottom a mere superficiality depending on false, artificial standards & limited insight. Of course the French miss certain atmospheric overtones which only the poetic sense of a northern race could supply—yet even so, I think their assets outweigh their liabilities. But of course, this applies only to serious fiction. In *poetry,* the Northern races hopelessly outclass the precise, logical Gaul from the very start. The same also goes for *weird fiction,* which is in essence a branch of poetry in disguise. Yes—I like Jane Austen, though for personal enjoyment I prefer my homely realism & gentle irony in moderately small doses. Good luck, by the way, with your own novel. Brobst has outlined some of his ideas to me, & I have thought them all excellent. He ought to write a few out in story form—either alone or in collaboration. W.T. once discussed a book of my stuff, but gave up the idea in the end. They prefer to feature popular writers like Otis Adelbert Kline.

> Best wishes—
>> Yrs sincerely,
>>> H. P. Lovecraft

Notes

1. James Boswell quotes Johnson as saying: "[Christopher Smart] did not love clean linen; and I have no passion for it." *Life of Johnson* (1791), 24 May 1763.

2. Arthur Machen (1863–1947) wrote extensively on Dickens, including the essay "The Art of Dickens" (1908), rpt. in *The Shining Pyramid* (1923), and the introduction to *A Handy Dickens* (1941). Dickens is also discussed in Machen's *Hieroglyphics: A Note upon Ecstasy in Literature* (1902; *LL* 571).

[5]   [ALS]

> 10 Barnes St.,
>> Providence, R.I.,
>>> Decr. 8, 1931

My dear Strauch:—

> Yes, indeed—G K C is an odd case, & very amusing if one does not accept him seriously as an explainer of the universe. A match between him & Darrow is really a farcical thing to consider;[1] since the well-meaning Clarence is so relatively naive & primitive in his emotions & attitude toward life. A far better opponent would have been H. L. Mencken or Ber-

trand Russell or George Santayana. The modern civilised man accepts a purposeless & impersonal cosmos of electrical energy as a matter of course, & does not bother to proclaim & preach his doctrines. Religion will die a natural death among the intelligent in time, while the herd will always believe in some sort of supernatural machinery. Propaganda is singularly futile one way or the other—for it doesn't make the least bit of difference whether the majority believe in gods & devils or not. Human actions, in the main, are very largely what glandular physiology & environmental accident make them. People don't mould their actions according to their beliefs, but concoct their beliefs to justify or explain their actions. The one way to head off a theistic believer is to ask him what shred of evidence there is, in the universe as now understood, to justify the invention of any such gratuitous & unmotivated improbabilities as a cosmic consciousness & purpose, a condition of "spiritual" entity, a personal immortality, & so on. Today these assumptions are grotesque & puerile—& all the more so because psychology & anthropology can now account for the religious "intuitions" formerly cited as theistic evidence. We can see that religion was an inevitable phenomenon among primitive men—but must also perceive that every apparent evidence which once suggested it is now destroyed. Only blind tradition causes anyone today to be predisposed toward such a superseded concept. In the universe around us, as now interpreted, there is nothing at all to indicate the existence of the beings & values & purposes postulated by the obsolescent mythologies. When one pulls this truth on a theist, he is forced into defences so absurd & far-fetched that his case suffers before an impartial judge.

Glad you've seen the Philadelphia Museum—whose extension, by the way, as seen atop its Acropolis down the length of the Parkway, is to my mind the most fascinating modern urban vista in America. I am intensely fond of Old Philadelphia anyway. You must see Germantown some time—it is an ineffably quaint & attractive place, with a surprising proportion of the old stone houses still in excellent preservation. Just south of it is the superlatively exquisite wooded gorge of the Wissahickon Creek, (of which Poe wrote an appreciation)[2] in one of whose tributary ravines is the old stone mill where the eminent astronomer & mintmaster David Rittenhouse was born two centuries ago. These snatches of Pennsylvania countryside which I have seen around Philadelphia make me anxious to see wider & less suburban stretches. I don't think I've seen more impressive scenery than the Wissahickon gorge.

I'd be very grateful for postcards of the Pennsylvania landscape with its characteristic architecture, & will send you some of New England when I can get hold of some good rural specimens. No—our barns have no embellishment, since in the last two centuries Yankees have taken their traditional superstitions very lightly indeed. Our houses & farm buildings are almost always of wood, & tend to be low & spreading, in harmony with the gently rolling landscape. They are very simple—with a simplicity that makes for beauty—&

blend admirably with the surrounding orchards, rambling stone walls, & glimpses of distant village steeples. If climatic-physiological reasons ever force me to move southward, I shall be more homesick for this exquisite type of pastoral landscape than for anything else. I am very fond of the country, & seek out a rural spot every sunny afternoon in summer, carrying reading & writing materials in a bag. Those "hex" circles on your barns are intensely interesting—& I had never heard of them before. I certainly must see this region some day. Incidentally—that anecdote of the sheriff is remarkable in the highest degree.[3] Probably the wizard repeated ancient formulae which the sheriff knew of old, & in which he believed, so that the result was equivalent to actual hypnosis. Primitive groups have many seemingly magical practices of this sort; which appear quite effective, & which depend on the perfect credulity of the victim. Africa, the West Indies, & Polynesia supply analogues.

I wish the editor of W.T. shared your point of view regarding a book of my stuff, but unfortunately he seems to have given up the idea. Possibly the indifferent success of other books published by the firm was a deciding factor. However, I don't let the matter worry me.

I trust you managed to secure a good rest during the vacation season. I am a nocturnal bird myself—but I normally make up the sleeping time the next day, since my programme is of my own dictating nowadays. I can concentrate for thinking & writing much better in the dead of night when all the objective world is effaced in darkness & silence. Unmotivated speed & meaningless activity are as irritating to me as to you—leading me often to recall the query of your friend Emerson's—"Why so hot, little man?"[4] Loafing surely is the finest of all arts—the art of being, as opposed to the meaningless treadmill of doing. I love to idle through scenes of quaintness & beauty, letting the atmosphere of accumulated ages filter into me unforcedly & unsystematically. ¶ Best wishes—

Yrs most cordially & sincerely—
H P Lovecraft

Notes

1. In January 1931, during his second trip to America, G. K. Chesterton debated Clarence Darrow at New York City's Mecca Temple on the topic "Will the World Return to Religion?" Chesterton was recognized as the clear victor.

2. "Morning on the Wissahiccon," also known as "The Elk."

3. Cf. HPL to A. W. Derleth, 10 December 1931: "I find that there is still a whole region in the U.S. where witchcraft is believed as uniformly & implicitly as in the Salem of 1692. It is the Lehigh Valley region of Pennsylvania, where the 'hex' murders attracted attention a few years ago. I thought those a rather isolated vestigial case, but I now have two bright young correspondents in Allentown who (themselves as sceptical as I) indicate a widespread surviving belief. 'Hex' doctors have a strong hold on the imaginations of the people; & only last week one of them kept at a distance, by

some quasi-hypnotic psychological menace, a sheriff who wanted to search his garage. The country folk paint on their barn gables great circles filled with labyrinthine lines—to entrap any 'hexes' who may have designs on their livestock & grain" (*ES* 1.428).

4. The quotation has been variously given as "Why so hot, my little man?" or "Why so hot, little sir?" It cannot be definitively found in Emerson's writings and may have been uttered in conversation.

[6]   [ALS]

10 Barnes St.,

Providence, R.I.,

Dec. 23, 1931.

My dear Strauch:—

I am certainly learning a vast amount of contemporary folklore these days! As I recently wrote Brobst, I had no idea that so much literal witch-belief survived on the surface of American life today. New England affords no parallel for things like cowbelled Fords, hieroglyphed barns, barrier-raising wizards, & the like—all our real superstition being in the past, & surviving only in legend & balladry. Pennsylvania's unique cases of survival must be due to special local causes, (isolation, &c) since I don't think German settlements elsewhere have anything approaching them. Wisconsin, with its almost solid German rustic population of the 1848 migration, presents no such baffling anachronism. I must ask my correspondents in that region (especially August W. Derleth, whose work in W.T. you probably know) whether there is much superstition under the surface.

Thanks exceedingly for that Molly Maguire cutting. I do indeed know of the institution referred to, though I had no idea its echoes lasted so long. The *original* Molly Maguires, so named because of the custom of the cutthroats to disguise in women's clothes, came into being in Ireland around 1843. Their object was to injure & intimidate rent collectors—it being a part of the same Irish resistance to landlordism which later appeared in the lawless Sinn Fein & cognate organisations. The outbreak in Pennsylvania in 1875 was engineered wholly by Irishmen familiar with the tactics of the Mollies in the "Ould Counthry". I'm not very certain about the precise cause of the local trouble, but I think it was both industrial & agrarian—hinging on the relation of Irish coal-miners to the companies that employed them & owned their homes. The victims—corresponding to the landlords & rent collectors in Ireland—were mine-owners & overseers. Probably the primary motive in all the murders was intimidation. Many modern strikes produce phenomena roughly comparable to the activities of the Mollies. The attempted suppression of their history is surely a phenomenon of vast interest—& I suppose the active factors are their descendants—or rabid Irish "patriots". Your family is surely lucky in having a copy. There is a vast fascination in the idea of some episode of history so horrible that it is expunged from the books & records of a nation. I have used it in fiction myself.[1] The legend of the hand print is an added feature of interest.

I have heard, though not in detail, of the beauty of Mauch Chunk,[2] & have meant to include it in some future trip when I feel like sparing enough time from the antiquarian to include the purely scenic. I did not know of the Switchback, but hope I may eventually take a ride over it. I am really a tremendous enthusiast for fine scenery, though my extreme antiquarianism & sadly slender purse combine to steer most of my trips to regions where architectural reliques are exceptionally thick. I shall most certainly appreciate any views you may send.

Brobst tells me you have been proofreading your coming book lately—a trying process, though eminently worth enduring in view of results. Typographical errors exasperate me, & I am willing to do anything to forestall them. I hope to see the book when it is out—let me know its price & where to get it. Just now I am on a job worse than proofreading—the revision of crude verse.[3] The only thing worse than this is doctoring up a rotten piece of fiction.

With best holiday wishes, & thanking you again for the cutting, I remain

Yrs most cordially & sincerely—

H P L

Notes

1. In "The Rats in the Walls" (1923) and *The Case of Charles Dexter Ward* (1927). Cf. "The Haunter of the Dark" (1935): "The Pharaoh Nephren-Ka . . . did that which caused his name to be stricken from all monuments and records" (*CF* 3.467).

2. Mauch Chunk, now called Jim Thorpe, is a resort area in the Blue Mountains northwest of Allentown.

3. Possibly Eugene B. Kuntz's *Thoughts and Pictures* (Haverhill, MA: Cooperatively published by H. P. Lovecraft and C. W. Smith, January 1932). Kuntz was an old-time amateur journalist.

[7]   [ALS]

Feby. 16, 1932

My dear Strauch:—

Very glad to hear from you! I expect Brobst over here tomorrow evening, & will tell him how much he is missed at home. Last Saturday afternoon—which fortunately was a fine warm day—I took great pleasure in shewing him over the quaint & ancient parts of Providence; largely the picturesque hill which forms the keynote of local topography. We saw the place where Roger Williams landed in 1636, (now being made into a public park)[1] the old colony house built in 1761,[2] the 1775 church,[3] the 1773 market house,[4] the 1770 college edifice,[5] the hidden hillside churchyard of St. John's,[6] the "haunted" Halsey Mansion[7] & other fine Georgian residences, the home of Mrs. Whitman where Poe used to call,[8] the old Golden Ball Inn[9] where Washington stopped in 1790, the Sign of Shakespeare's Head where the old Providence Gazette was printed in 1762 & onward,[10] & the historic Athenaeum,[11] where Poe & Mrs. Whitman used to ramble through the book alcoves. At this latter place I had an attendant shew Brobst the pencil signature which Poe affixed at Mrs. W's request to the anonymous text of "Ulalume" in the American Whig Review.[12] Mrs. Whitman, ignorant of the authorship, had been praising the poem—when Poe very proudly announced that it was his. Mrs. W. then declared that he ought to sign the copy in the library, which he did casually on the spot. This anecdote floated about orally in Providence folklore for 60 years, though no one had even bothered to verify it. Then—in 1909, at the time of the Poe centenary—Dr. H. L. Koopman, head of the John Hay Library of Brown University, determined to track it down. Going through the old Athenaeum files, he found the issue of the review containing "Ulalume"— & there, surely enough, was the faint pencil signature "Edgar A. Poe" beneath the printed verses. Ever since then many visitors have asked to see the signature. I suppose you know that the last stanza of this early version was subsequently removed—at the excellent critical suggestion of Mrs. Whitman.

I think Brobst will like his new work very much. He is in a ward of very high-grade patients—largely A.M.'s & Ph.D.'s—including my own old high-school principal.[13] The medical staff is of very high repute—the superintendent, Dr. Ruggles, having a wide reputation as a psychological authority. The place & landscape setting are very pleasant.

I am glad you found my descriptive letter of interest. It was written in haste, & probably doesn't amount to much as to form; but the facts are probably reasonably accurate. Hope you can get around yourself during the coming summer, as Brobst said you might manage to do. Brobst's advent is a highly pleasant circumstance—for I find him as brilliant & delightful in person as his letters led me to expect. In time I think he will turn to writing—a field in which he ought to make considerable success.

Glad Derleth sent you *The Midland.* I rather liked "Old Ladies",[14] which is part of a loosely-strung Proustian reminiscence or quasi-novel to be called "Evening in Spring." I have read the other parts, & think the massed effect is really remarkable. Derleth has had no novel published as yet, but I believe he will make great progress in the future. He has all the solid groundwork of real literary substance & poignancy—though he is only 23.

Thanks very much for the Bechtel cuttings. Tragedies of this sort—with cabalistic wounds—are like fragments of fiction out of Machen or Blackwood. It really seems incredible that such dark phantasy can persist till the present day!

Yes—an old & not especially notable tale of mine—"In the Vault"—will appear in the next W.T. My best recent stuff has been rejected.[15]

It turned cold here Sunday, but I hope for early abatement.

With best wishes—
     Yrs most sincerely,
           H P L

P.S. Brobst & I are going to try to find some decently representative post-cards of Providence to send you. It is provokingly hard to get anything really satisfactory.

Notes

1. The Roger Williams National Memorial Park at 150 North Main Street.

2. The Old State House (1762), 150 Benefit Street. Rhode Island declared its independence from England in the Providence Colony House two months before the Declaration of Independence.

3. The First Baptist Meeting House, 75 North Main Street.

4. On Market Square.

5. University Hall, "The College Edifice"—the original, and for fifty years the only, building at Brown University.

6. St. John's Episcopal Church (1810), 275 North Main Street. The churchyard is mentioned in "The Shunned House" (1924) and "The Messenger" (1929). It was there HPL wrote his Poe acrostic, "In a Sequester'd Providence Churchyard Where Once Poe Walked" (1936).

7. The Thomas Lloyd Halsey House (c. 1800, c. 1825), 140 Prospect Street; the home of Charles Dexter Ward in HPL's *The Case of Charles Dexter Ward.* See HPL to A. W. Derleth (10 December 1931): "In the 1850's this fine old brick house was actually feared by the ignorant" (*ES* 1.422n).

8. The John Reynolds House (c. 1785) at 88 Benefit Street. Sarah Helen Whitman (1803–1878) lived at the house when it was owned by Samuel Hamlin, a Providence pewterer. HPL mentions Poe's romance with Mrs. Whitman in "The Shunned House."

9. Only the Golden Ball Inn Ell (1784 et seq.) stands today at 17–23 South Court Street. In HPL's time, the four-story Golden Ball Inn stood across from the State House (150 Benefit Street) and stable (160 Benefit Street). The main portion of the house was demolished in 1941.

10. The John Carter House (1772), 21 Meeting Street. William Goddard published the *Providence Gazette and Country-Journal* (est. 1762) in a shop marked by the sign of Shakespeare's Head on North Main Street. John Carter joined the paper in 1767 and by 1768 was sole proprietor. He and his wife moved the business into the house they built on Meeting Street.

11. 251 Benefit Street.

12. The journal was in fact the *American Review* for December 1847. On this matter see *Collected Works of Edgar Allan Poe,* ed. Thomas Ollive Mabbott (Cambridge, MA: Harvard University Press, 1969), 1.413, 423. Cf. Will Murray's interview of Harry K. Brobst, *Lovecraft Studies* Nos. 22/23 (Fall 1990): 40–41.

13. Charles E. Dennis, Jr., principal of Hope Street High School.

14. Derelth's story "Old Ladies" was rewritten and incorporated into *Evening in Spring* in the section "Take Arms!"

15. The story had been rejected in October 1925, but was accepted upon later submittal by August Derleth.

[8]   [ALS]

Feby. 25, 1932

My dear Strauch:—

Glad to see that your book is out, & many thanks for the notice. I shall try to invest in a copy before long, when I can see a little more financial daylight. Hope it will have a good sale & receive some favourable reviews in important quarters. I suppose the publishers attend to the distribution of review copies.

By all means try to get around this way in the summer—for both the Providence & the Boston zones cannot fail to contain much of genuine interest to you. Possibly Brobst has told you of the quaint & spectral hidden churchyard down the hill not so very far from this house—a picturesque backwater which seems to have especially captivated his own imagination.[1] Unfortunately we could not get the postcards I spoke of—both places I had in mind having given up their sale. Rhode Island is very imperfectly covered by pictorial & guide material—a contrast to the well-exploited historic towns of Massachusetts.

Hope you can get to Baltimore to pay your respects at the tomb of Poe. I have seen it once,[2] & have been meaning to stop off & revisit it some time. It is now well marked & cared for in a corner of the yard of Westminster Presbyterian Church, though unfortunately the neighbourhood is now a slum. Providence is rich in Poe memories—the hidden churchyard mentioned above being a favourite haunt of the bard during his local sojourns.

Your southward travels must have been delightful, & I hope I can some day get a look at the regions involved. I have not seen much of Virginia west of the tidewater region & the main route south, though I once took an excursion from Washington to the Endless Caverns[3] near New Market, which gave me a brief glimpse of the Blue Ridge & Shenandoah Valley. I am anxious to see Charlottesville & the U. of Va. where Poe studied in 1828. I also wish to see your own state—both the weird & historic Lehigh Valley, & the wilder central portions you refer to. Incidentally—Rhode Island, small as it is, is so highly urbanised that much of the back country is left in total isolation. There are places where one might wander indefinitely without sight of a human habitation, & it is a mathematical fact that the state has the greatest proportion of woodland of any of the 48 commonwealths. Deer are increasingly numerous.

Sorry to hear that another witch-cult murder has occurred in Pennsylvania. That is certainly a high price to pay for the picturesque backwater traditionalism which makes such things possible! Probably a few more generations of compulsory education, radios, & the like will eradicate the more extreme phases of this phenomenon—though superstitions are certainly very persistent whenever a population remains rural. Even among urban populations such things are tenacious enough, as witness the almost incredible survival of occultism, astrology, & similar delusions in the most surprisingly informed & prosperous circles. Indeed, the very native credulity which keeps any sort of religion alive guarantees a certain amount of life to less orthodox & disciplined aspects of supernatural belief.

Cold days have been increasingly present of late—though at worst, spring is not far off now. Thanks again for the book list—& renewed congratulations on the appearance of your volume. With best wishes—

Yrs most sincerely,

H P Lovecraft

Notes

1. St. John's Churchyard.
2. In July 1928; cf. "Observations on Several Parts of America" (1928; *CE* 4.28–29).
3. See "A Descent to Avernus," *Bacon's Essays* (Summer 1929; *CE* 4.287–88), and *SL* 2.246.

[9]   [ALS]

[New Orleans]
June 7, 1932

My dear Strauch:—

Yrs. of 19th ult. was duly forwarded to me in the course of my annual travel outbreak, & I greatly appreciated hearing from you. I left home May 18th, & stopped a week in New York visiting Frank B. Long & seeing other members of the local crowd. Then—on the 25th—I hopped off for the journey proper. For the first time in my life I traversed the entire length of the Shenandoah Valley—Winchester—Staunton—Lexington—Roanoke—& was utterly enthralled by the beauty of the Blue Ridge landscape. Then came Knoxville, Tenn., & a ride across country to Chattanooga. Here once more I was reduced to breathless admiration; for the beauty of the Cumberlands—& of the river-bluff environs of Chattanooga in particular—surpassed every possible expectation. I ascended Lookout Mountain & revelled in the marvellous view of the outspread river, town, countryside, & hills—& also descended into the mountain's vast chain of caverns, including the great vaulted chamber (discovered 1930) wherein a 145-foot waterfall roars ceaselessly amidst eternal night. The ride from Chattanooga to Memphis (this whole trip is by 'bus) took me through a continuation of this mountainous wonderland—along what is locally known as the "Grand Cañon of the Tennessee." At Memphis I saw the lordly Mississippi for the first time, &

was duly impressed. Then "down de ribber" through the flat delta cotton country, & finally up the bluffs of picturesque & historic Vicksburg. Between there & Natchez I began to encounter signs of the real far South—gnarled live-oaks with tangles of Spanish moss, & similar forms of luxuriant vegetation. In general, I think the Natchez country has the finest subtropical scenery I have ever beheld. It reminds one of the landscapes delineated in the "Atala" of Chateaubriand—who, indeed, once visited in Natchez.[1] The roads, owing to the soft & friable nature of the local yellow clay, are all deeply sunken below the level of the surrounding terrain; & present a weirdly impressive appearance with their high vertical walls overrun with vines & the roots of ancient oaks & cypresses. These great trees, arching overhead & draped with grotesque festoons of Spanish moss, keep the scene shrouded in a perpetual green twilight.

Natchez itself is a stately old town where the past still lives—a quiet backwater with but little physical change since the early 19th century. Few places can be more fascinating to the historically-minded. The settlement was founded by the French in 1716, as the military & trading post of Fort Rosalie. Ruins of the fort still exist on the high bluff. In 1729 the Natchez Indians massacred all the garrison, but the post was regarrisoned & maintained. In 1763, by the treaty of Paris, the whole region passed to Great Britain as part of the new Province of West-Florida, & Natchez became Fort Panmure. In 1779 the Spaniards then controlling Louisiana invaded the territory & held it till 1798, when it was ceded to the U.S. Many houses of Spanish design attest the solid nature of this occupation. When the Americans came, the great days of Natchez began. It was a logical port for the abundant cotton of the newly-developed delta country, & the rising Mississippi traffic made it a predestined commercial centre. It became, likewise, a town centre for the wealthy Louisiana planters across the river. From about 1810 onward Natchez filled up with stately mansion-houses of the pillared classic-revival type—most of which remain to this day in every stage of preservation from perfect maintenance to utter ruination. The town proper lies atop the great bluff, while on the narrow shore strip at the foot of the 200-foot precipice are the wharves—not quite deserted yet, since steamboats can still carry cotton more cheaply than railways can. Around the wharves cluster the ancient brick houses of what is called "Natchez-under-the-Hill"—once a roaring haunt of roystering seamen, but now a squalid abode of niggers, occasional mills, & desolation. I spent two full days in Natchez, thoroughly absorbing its atmosphere & hating to leave it when the time came. Finally, however, I had to continue "down de ribber." Louisiana is flatter than the Mississippi bluff country, & the soil is grey instead of yellow. I did not pause at Baton Rouge, for this town—the La. state capital—has been disconcertingly modernised. South of there the ground falls to river level & below—giving me my first glimpse of the vast levee system. The great artificial bank slopes very gradually upward from the

land level for a long distance, & then drops much less gradually to the river—
or to some frequently inundated alluvial flat bordering on the river. It is all
these titan embankments can do to control the caprices of Father Mississippi,
& they frequently have to be relocated by means of giant steam shovels. The
older ones are overgrown with grass & form an occasional pasturage for cattle. At one point there is a monstrous spillway under construction—to relieve
pressure during extreme flood conditions like those in 1927.

At length New Orleans was reached—& after settling down at a modest
hostelry I proceeded to explore the town & its environs. N.O. was founded in
1718 by the French-Canadian officer Jean-Baptiste Le Moyne, Sieur de Bienville, & was first peopled rather heterogeneously by the dupes of John Law's
famous real-estate racket—the Mississippi Bubble.[2] In 1763 it was passed to
Spain, though still remaining French in language & institutions. The great fire
of 1788 destroyed nearly all of the old French town, but the area was at once
rebuilt—very solidly, & in a predominantly Spanish style—with the aid of
government engineers. It is this really Spanish town of arcaded, galleried brick
houses with inner courtyards or patios which survives to this day, almost unchanged physically, as the "Vieux Carré" or "old French quarter." This quarter represents the original extent of the town as laid out by Bienville—& as
fortified by Carondelet in 1794. It is now, of course, only a tiny speck in the
spreading expanse of modern New Orleans—clinging tenaciously to its place
at a bend in the river. In 1803 the city & province passed to the U.S., & the
new American town grew up outside the walls of the older Latin city. Prosperity came, & little by little the Creoles & Americans fused; but still certain
essential distinctions remained. French is still spoken in parts of New Orleans, & the modern Creoles build houses with curious affinities to certain of
the ancient Creole types. Outside the Vieux Carré, the American city was very
ambitiously laid out. Draining of the low land was accomplished by means of
open canals in the middle of certain inordinately broad streets—& in later
years these canals were roofed over one by one to form great boulevards with
car tracks in the centre. Of these, the main business artery Canal St. is the
most famous. Only one or two of the open canals still remain to hint at the
original aspect of the American city. Commerce & prosperity tended, from
the very first, to centre in the new town outside the ancient area, so that the
latter—a parallelogram bounded on the north by Esplanade Ave., on the west
by Rampart St., on the south by Canal St., & on the east by the river—had
little reason to replace the bulk of its old Spanish buildings with their arches,
patios, sidewalk arcades, & wrought-iron galleries. There they stand today as a
living reminder of old times, together with a few still earlier buildings (such as
the Ursuline Convent of 1734) which escaped the Great Fire. The cathedral
of 1794, the old Spanish Cabildo or Government House of 1795, & other
quaint edifices still look down on the sleepy old Place d'Armes—now called
Jackson Square & boasting an equestrian statue of the intrepid old warrior.

The whole "Vieux Carré" or ancient section is a perfectly preserved 18th or early 19th century city, vying for architectural honours with Charleston & Quebec. In its day it has been a slum, & it is now slightly touched with the Greenwich-Village atmosphere—studios & antique shops. For this reason it has not quite the utter charm of quaint Charleston & Quebec, which are still leading their simple old lives in unbroken organic continuity with the past. But for all that it's a great old place, & I'm certainly having the time of my life drinking in its archaic colour & getting set on my feet by its life-giving tropic warmth. My hotel is outside the Vieux Carré, but I spend each day in that centuried backwater—wandering through the narrow old streets with no modern impressions intruding upon me, & doing my reading & writing on a bench in old Jackson Square . . . . where the silver chimes of the old cathedral float on the air each quarter-hour. Of late years much tasteful restoration has taken place within the Vieux Carré, so that today even the old small lamp-posts have been put back—albeit with electric lights inside. The fantastic old *cemeteries* of N.O. deserve a word for themselves. On account of the shallow soil all burials are above ground. The wealthy lie in fantastic tombs, while less opulent citizens are enclosed in oven-like vaults along the ten-foot-thick brick walls of the necropolis. Of all these grotesque ossuaries, the old St. Louis cemetery outside the Vieux Carré is undoubtedly the most interesting.

I'm here for over a week, & have seen the modern as well as the ancient city. I have also looked up such old plantation-houses as are near to (or over-taken by & imbedded in) the growing city. Of these country houses there are two general types—the older Creole sort with steep slant roof & dormers, & the early 19th century American type, massive in proportions & of pillared classic-revival architecture. Both of these types can also be found in & around Natchez. From here I shall go to Mobile, Ala., & after that my plans will depend upon finances. I have a *very faint* hope of getting to Charleston, which is still my favourite among towns. New Orleans is quite subtropical in vegetation, being well below the 30th parallel of latitude. The change from Natchez is noticeable; for whereas that town has only a few tiny scrub palmettos carefully nurtured in gardens, New Orleans is crowded with tall Washington Palms & opulent Brazilian date-palms.

But I can see from your epistle that spring in the North also has its idyllic aspects! I can well appreciate such days as you describe, & am always to be found outdoors upon them. The only trouble is that they are so few—& so interspersed with days of chill & raw wind. And our northern nights are always so shivery except in the very middle of summer. I have no real comfort in the north except from about the middle of June to the middle of August. It is tragic to waste so much of each year—but when one is attached to the landscape & architecture of his native region it is hard to break away permanently.

Yes—the love of green Nature—field & hedge, brook & wood—is certainly one of the typical attributes of the British race & its literature. I feel the ancestral impulse strongly, & am never under a roof in summer except when I have to be.

The "hex" story you mention sounds very interesting indeed, & I hope to be able to get hold of a copy sooner or later. It is easy to understand the difficulty in reproducing a regional dialect, when so much depends on inflection & intonation, but one can at least try to capture the grammatical idiom. I'd like to see that sinister "Hexenkopf" some day. Haunted mountains are right in my line! No—I have never heard of the equivalent of an "Hexenbanner" in New England. Our systematic belief in witchcraft hardly survived the 17th century, & there was very little consistency or main-stream traditionalism in such furtive, feeble whispers as survived among the illiterates of the back country. The great Salem upheaval of 1692 more or less purged the atmosphere of witchcraft-belief so far as we were concerned. Moreover—Rhode Island in particular never had any witchcraft beliefs except among the Indians & the negro slaves on the King's County plantations. (We had the only northern equivalent of the Southern plantation system, but the Revolution ruined it) Our colony was, indeed, a sort of protest or reaction against the macabre puritanism which (in common with superstitious popery) inclines the mind to such credences of the supernatural. It is for this reason that I can never feel anything really sinister in Rhode Island's past, but am forced to go across the line into Massachusetts to find a site for any morbidly brooding fictional communities of Arkham, Kingsport, Innsmouth, & so on.

Derleth is right in thinking that many of Brobst's ideas would go splendidly in fictional form, & I surely wish that B. would work up some of them as stories. As you are aware, however, he is reluctant to try his hand at an art for which he has had no special preparation. I agree that the "Hexenbanner" would form a fine & unhackneyed subject for weird tales. Probably you'll get around to this sort of thing in the course of time—for after all, you know the country & its rich folklore, & to an objective artist it doesn't matter very much whether or not he feels personally identified with the background he depicts. The main thing is to *know* it well. So far as that goes, I really feel very little personal kinship with the sombre Massachusetts types I depict. My paternal line is close to *Old* England by way of New York State, & does not include the New England tradition at all. But I know the country, & am perhaps all the more fascinated by it because a good part of me is able to look upon it with an outsider's dispassionate eye. Yes—I think Brobst's excursion into the outside world will prove a good thing for his perspective, & I am very glad to note that he feels himself very congenially placed in Providence & amidst his new & arduous duties. If he ever wants to write, he surely has all the equipment—the question now is to convince him that he wants to!

Glad you enjoyed your New York week-end. I suppose Allentown must wear sometimes on its own inhabitants—though a newcomer might like it very well. No—I've never read von Masoch's "Venus in Furs"—which has done so much to enlarge the vocabulary of psychology. Neither have I perused the equally famous & nomenclaturally potent—though psychologically opposite—works of the late Marquis de Sade.[3]

Your woodland verses are very clever, & form quite a testimonial to your versatility & mastery of light forms. Hope the book is going over well. Here is a card describing the magazine I spoke of.[4] As you see, Derleth is among the contributors. I also enclose a poem by Loveman—one of the editors—which ought to appeal to you.

Best wishes—

Yrs most sincerely—

H P L

Notes

1. François-René de Chateaubriand (1768–1848), *Atala* (1801), a romance based in large part upon a visit that Chateaubriand had taken to wild and uninhabited regions of the American continent. Chateaubriand made use of the bluffs of Natchez, MS, in his novel (see *SL* 4.41).

2. The Mississippi Bubble refers to the disastrous attempt by the Scotsman John Law to exploit the resources of French Canada. He established a trading company at New Biloxi, MS, in 1719, and aggressively promoted the company's stock, leading to wild speculation. The stock collapsed in December 1720, and many of the colonists of New Biloxi died.

3. E.g. *Justine; ou, Les Malheurs de la vertu* (1791) by Donatien Alphonse François, marquis de Sade (1740–1814); first Eng. tr. as *Justine; or, The Misfortunes of Virtue* (1889). Cf. *SL* 3.106.

4. I.e., *Trend.*

[10]   [ALS]

10 Barnes St.,

Providence, R.I.,

Aug. 13, 1932

My dear Strauch:—

Your recent outing along the dry river-bed sounds highly idyllic, & I am sure the attendant antics were no more absurd than any of mankind's accustomed releases for surplus energy. You are fortunate in having such a pleasant countryside within reach—& in having the taste to enjoy it.

I don't wonder that "Vathek" impressed you—or that you found the dark & sanguinary character more likeable than otherwise. Beckford certainly was a singular character—with his fantastic "Fonthill", his travels, his books, & his sundry eccentricities—& it is not the least of his caprices that he composed "Vathek" entirely in French—the existing version being a translation by the Rev. Samuel Henley. As you are probably aware, Henley published the translation prematurely, causing Beckford to hurry out the original French text at once, omitting the extra episodes he had designed for insertion. These episodes, coming to light only in modern times, are to me well-nigh as fascinating as the book itself. Many members of our group have thought of preparing an ending for the unfinished third episode—& I really think that Clark Ashton Smith could do it justice.[1]

I did indeed enjoy your poems—as did my recent guest James F. Morton, (about whom Brobst will tell you) who read some of them here. In time I trust you will assemble another collection. You have the genuine vision of the poet, & I am sure that time will bring you a more than local recognition.

The other day I felt rather pleased at receiving a letter from a Los Angeles composer—Harold Farnese, Asst. Director of the Inst of Musical Art & graduate of the Paris Conservatory (whose 1911 prize for composition he won)—asking permission to set two of my weird sonnets (which appeared in *Weird Tales*) to music.[2] Naturally, I promptly accorded the desired permission—& am now rather curious to see what he will do with my bizarre images. Another moderately pleasing occurrence is the appearance of an article in the July *American Author*—"What Makes a Story Click", by J. Randle Luten—in which the work of Clark Ashton Smith & myself is favourably cited & quoted in connexion with certain problems of narration.[3]

I have been to Newport several times on account of the reduced boat fares—& may go again today. At the end of the month I hope to get north of Boston (though not necessarily in the Maine belt of maximum duration) to see the total eclipse, & afterward I hope to take a cheap rail excursion to Montreal & Quebec. I have never seen Montreal, though Quebec is one of my favourite cities—without doubt the most beautiful city I have ever seen or ever will see unless I get across to Europe.

Brobst has been over twice since his return, & I was surely glad to see him again. He thinks he will be able to get an entire day off before long—on which occasion I'll be able to shew him some scenic & antiquarian high spots he has not seen before. Hope you'll be able to get around this way before the summer is over. I can assure you that the region won't disappoint you.

With every good wish—

Yrs most cordially & sincerely—

H P L

Notes

1. Smith in fact completed "The Third Episode of Vathek" (16 September 1932). It was first published in *Leaves* No. 1 (Summer 1937): 1–24.

2. HPL gave Farnese permission to set "Mirage" and "The Elder Pharos" (*WT*, February/March 1931) to music. HPL never saw or heard the completed scores for the poems. They are now printed in *Fungi from Yuggoth: An Annotated Edition* (2016). A CD of *Fungi from Yuggoth* (Fedogan & Bremer, 2015) includes renditions of the pieces for the first time (piano solo and piano and voice).

3. J. Randle Luten, "What Makes a Story Click?" *American Author* 4, No. 4 (July 1932): 11–13; rpt. in *A Weird Writer in Our Midst: Early Criticism of H. P. Lovecraft*, ed. S. T. Joshi (New York: Hippocampus Press, 2011), 51–54.

[11]   [ALS]

Aug. 22[, 1932]

My dear Strauch:—

    I'll *certainly* be back from my trip by Septr. 10, hence urge you to come to Providence if you possibly can. Brobst & I will be delighted to see you, & there are amply enough sights to keep you busy. Keep me posted on when to expect you. Wish I could offer hospitality, but as a mere congested roomer can do no better than steer you to modest lodgings. The Crown Hotel in Weybosset Street is good—& reasonable—& I'll also see if the landlady at my own joint has any space for an orderly & prepossessing transient. Will send a later bulletin on that point.

    My own trip will begin a week from tomorrow, when I go to Boston to meet my friend W. Paul Cook. The ensuing day he & I will go to Newburyport or Portsmouth to see the total eclipse—probably stopping in Haverhill to add an 80-year-old friend to the party.[1] On Friday Septr. 2 I hope to entrain for Montreal—going thence to Quebec & being back in Boston on the 6th. Thus I'll be in Providence again well before the 10th.

    Glad indeed that one of Muhlenburg's serious & devout youths[2] found pleasure in my frivolous tale of Cthulhu, as well as in other products of my less than pious pen! Glad also that you found the effort acceptable. Cthulhu isn't one of my worst stories, though it doesn't come up to my "Colour Out of Space" or "Erich Zann." By the way—the Hammett anthology containing the latter has just been re-published in England. It goes in for older & more standard work as a general thing, & has some exceedingly powerful items. Benson's "Negotium Perambulans" is great. By the way—if you liked "The White Powder" you ought to read all of Machen's "Three Impostors", of which this episode forms a part. I can lend it to you if local bibliothecae have it not.

    Glad you've had a good outdoor week. I've been keeping in the air pretty well myself—am there now, in fact, writing these lines on my favourite wooded river-bluff. Saturday I went to Newport again—to celebrate my 42nd birthday—& took the *entire* walk along the famous cliffs for the first time in my life. The remoter sections are really much more picturesque than the better-known stretches—offering magnificent vistas of seaward rocks & reefs. You ought to devote a day to Newport when you visit R.I. The sail down the bay alone is worth the price of the trip—& coming back there are delightful sunset vistas. Brobst hasn't taken this trip yet. I hope the boats won't have stopped running by the second week in September.

Well—I'll have to close, for golden sunset has turned to purple twilight. Today has been delightfully hot—weather after my own heart.

With best wishes, & hoping to see you in about three weeks, I remain

Most cordially & sincerely yrs
—H P L

[On envelope:] P.S. Donald Wandrei is now in N.Y. & will get around to Providence some time in September. ¶ I must get hold of the translation of that Perutz novel[3]—many have praised it to me.

Notes

1. Charles W. Smith (1852–1948), editor of the *Tryout.*
2. Muhlenberg College was associated with the Lutheran Church in America, Southeastern Pennsylvania, Slovak Zion, and Northeastern Pennsylvania Synods.
3. *The Master of the Day of Judgment,* a translation of *Der Meister des jüngsten Tages* (1923).

[12]   [ALS]

August 28[, 1932]

My dear Strauch:—

Good news! The landlady *can* give you a room at 10 Barnes, so come right up here when you strike town. If by any chance I'm not there when you arrive, just tell the landlady or servant that you're a friend of mine— & the room will be forthcoming. But I hope I *can* be at home—& I will be if you can let me know about what time to expect you. You can reach me until Thursday ℅ *W. Paul Cook, 7 Hancock St., Boston, Mass.* if there's any eleventh-hour information to be delivered. But in any case I expect to be home again around the 8th. ¶ Now as to the way to get up here—in case you can't supply information which will enable me to reach your vehicle, be it train or motor-coach. You'll land either at the railway station or at one of the nearby 'bus terminals. Ask to have *Dorrance St.* (which in any case will be near at hand) pointed out to you, & walk along that (from the large square called EX-CHANGE PLACE where it begins) toward the south. The first intersecting street (ask, if there's any doubt) is *Westminster St.*—the city's principal business thoroughfare. This is the corner where you wait for your car, which will come up Westminster from the east—or left hand side as you strike Westminster from Dorrance. Wait on the northeast corner—in front of Pierce's Shoe Store or Gibson's soda & candy place. Take any car with an oval or circular sign on the front marked ⓣ ~ [TUNNEL]   —the regular sign will say Hope St., Elmgrove Ave., Butler Ave., Rumford, or Phillipsdale. Ride through the tunnel under the great hill, & get off at the first stop on the other side—Thayer St. Pay as you leave the car—fare 8¢, or 7¢ if you have 5 metal tokens for 35¢. Better buy the tokens, for you'll probably have use for them during your visit. Ask, as you pay, for a transfer to a *Brown St.* bus—which will be free, although other city transfers cost 2¢. Wait for the 'bus where you get off the car—in front of the Abbott Hall Coffee Shop. When you get the 'bus, ask the driver to let you off at *Barnes St.* From this corner—Barnes & Brown—walk along Barnes to the left (reckoned from the direction in which you have been riding). #10 is the farther side of a large brown double house—a fussy wooden affair in the worst taste of the 1880's—about ¾ of a block from Brown, on the right hand side of Barnes St. Keep this sheet of directions for reference—for all this is too complicated to memorise. I'll certainly be delighted to see you when you blow in! By the way—the house telephone is DExter 9617—in the name of the landlady—Miss Reynolds.[1]

If for any reason you want to hunt up Brobst first, proceed to the corner of Dorrance & Westminster as hereinbefore indicated, & take a *Butler Ave.* car. In this case, you won't need to change to any 'bus—just ride straight on beyond the tunnel for a considerable distance, asking the operator to let you off at Butler Hospital—which as you know is in Blackstone Boulevard. You'll recognise the great brick gate when you alight. The hospital buildings are quite a distance within—in the midst of extensive & beautiful grounds. Probably Brobst has told you what building to inquire at—I don't know the right one. N.B. Of course, you're not obliged to choose #10 as a stopping-place. If you'd prefer to be downtown near restaurants, the Crown is an excellent place.

I fancy you'll find enough hereabouts to keep all your available days filled—& I wish you could spare a longer time. I greatly enjoy shewing off the scenic & antiquarian high spots of the town & its vicinity, so you needn't feel that you're imposing on my time-schedule in any way. Glad of the chance to air my accomplishments as a guide! Hope you won't find my modest array of books disappointing. I don't go in for rarities or first editions at all—contents alone determining my purchase of a book. It will be a pleasure to hear some of your new poems—though I'm afraid you'd find my newer tales (I've only written two in the last year) rather a poor recompense because of their great length & slow movement. By the way—if you like my article on Supernatural Horror in Literature I believe I can spare you a copy for permanent retention. I hope we can get down to Newport, & there are other quaint old Rhode Island towns that I wish you could see. It would be doubly pleasant if Donald Wandrei's visit could coincide with yours—but he can't be sure of dates as yet. I assume you have seen his work in Weird Tales.

Your recent reading programme is surely formidable enough. I read an excellent thing of Werfel's a few years ago—the play called "Goat-Song", which was full of macabre tragedy. I thought you'd like the "Episodes of Vathek". The unfinished state of the third & final one is rather a tantalisation,

& I am urging Clark Ashton Smith to use his great ingenuity & command of Oriental exoticism in preparing an appropriate ending. He could do it better than anyone else I know. Powys is undoubtedly an author of real importance, though I don't care much for him as a critic.[2] In Santayana I feel convinced that we have not only the *greatest* living philosopher, but perhaps the *only* living philosopher of the very first rank. He cuts through fallacies which deceive & obscure almost everyone else.

By the way—I must give directions for the Crown Hotel in case you prefer to stop downtown near the restaurants. Go through Dorrance—or any parallel street such as Eddy, Union, or Mathewson—toward Westminster, & keep on *beyond* Westminster (past Middle St.) to *Weybosset Street.* The Crown is on the south (farther) side of Weybosset more than 2 blocks west of Dorrance—between Union & Mathewson. The following sketch of the downtown district may prove useful:

Well—now I'm off for Boston, the eclipse zone, Montreal, & Quebec! Send any last-moment news care of Cook, as previously stated. Hope to see you next week, & am sure that you, Brobst, & I will have some enjoyable sessions.

Best wishes—

Most cordially & sincerely—
H P L

Notes

1. Florence F. Reynolds.

2. John Cowper Powys (1872–1963), author of *Wolf Solent* (1929), a complex social novel set in Dorset. HPL owned his *One Hundred Best Books* (Haldeman-Julius, 1923).

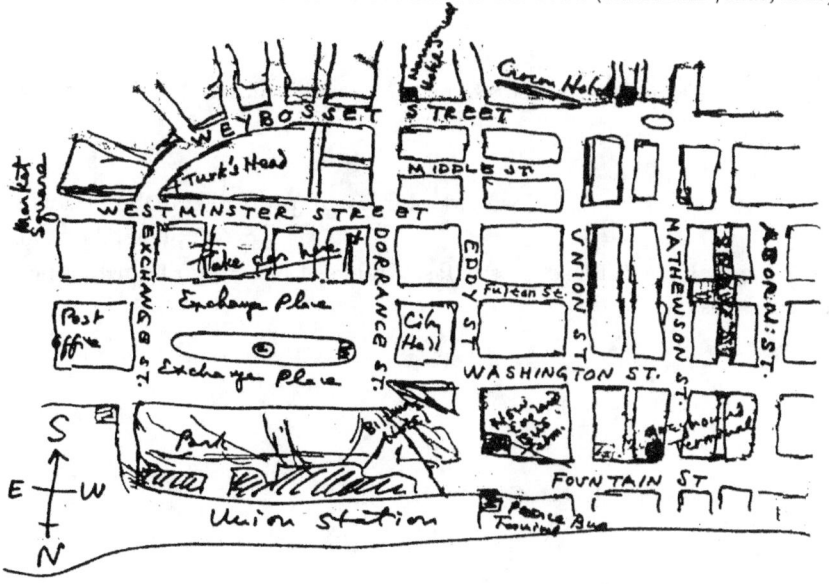

[13]   [ANS][1]

[Postmarked Boston, MA,
1 September 1932]

Had a fine view of the total eclipse from Newburyport. We chose a high rural spot with a view, & saw the countryside bathed in spectral light. Then came darkness, the flaming corona, & the pale stars—& after an interval a weird, sinister dawning. Now for Montreal & Quebec—& home Septr. 7. Hope to see you on the 8th, & trust you received my letter of directions concerning Providence. Regards & best wishes

H P L

I suppose you saw the eclipse as partial.

Notes

1. *Front:* Dr. Peter Toppan House, built 1697, Newburyport, Mass..

[14]   [ANS][1]

[Postmarked Montreal, Canada,
5 September 1932]

Greetings! Montreal is fascinating, though not as full of antiquarian material as Quebec. I start for Quebec tonight—& home Wednesday night. Hope to see you Thursday.

Regards

—H P L

Notes

1. *Front:* Notre-Dame de Bonsecours Church, Montreal, Canada.

[15] [ANS][1]

[Postmark obliterated (probably Quebec, Canada),
c. 6–7 September 1932]

Here's the high spot at last! Utterly fascinating—I hate to go home! Hope to see you Thursday.

Regards—

H P L

Notes

1. *Front:* St. Louis Gate, Quebec, Canada.

[16]   [ANS][1]

Saturday [17 September 1932]

My dear Strauch:—

Welcome home to Allentown! No doubt you received the joint card from Wandrei & me, in which my distinguished guest expressed regret at not meeting you. I've just been shewing him the Harris Collection—where we dug up the work of two forgotten or semi-forgotten poets—Frederick Tuckerman (1813–71) & Park Barnitz[2]—the latter a vivid decadent of the fin de siècle period who modelled his verse on Baudelaire & killed himself soon after graduation from Harvard. Incidentally—here's a poetry critique of mine,[3] issued by the Natl. Amateur Press Assn., which may amuse you for a second. Keep it—I have many copies. Brobst was to have been over last night, but didn't come. He was slightly under the weather Thursday—a feverish touch—but I hope he's better now. I've told him on a card of your impending letter—sorry your finger is out of commission! ¶ Glad your Boston stay was so enjoyable, but sorry you couldn't be in Providence longer. You must get up this way again! ¶ We had a veritable flood here yesterday—they are still pumping out the inundated cellars down town.

Best wishes—

H P L

Notes

1. *Front:* University Hall and Manning Hall, Brown University. The postcard was neither stamped nor addressed, and thus must have been mailed with the booklet mentioned below.

2. Park Barnitz (1878–1901), author of *The Book of Jade* (New York: Doxey's, At the Sign of the Lark [1901]). HPL had visited the Harris Collection with Strauch during Strauch's visit in September, where "perusal of *Mr. Muling* and *Suppose*" by HPL's revision client David Van Bush "convuls'd both young Strauch and the librarian" (*SL* 4.69).

3. *Further Criticism of Poetry.*

[17]   [ALS]

10 Barnes St.,
Providence, R.I.,
Novr. 3, 1932

My dear Strauch:—

I learn with the keenest interest of your progress on the novel, & surely hope that the finished result may amply satisfy your artistic sense. Deciding on the right proportioning must be a gruelling task—but as you say, it helps to train your instinct in such matters, so that each new effort will be at least slightly less exacting than the preceding one. In course of time

I hope to see your novel—& I surely hope it may eventually land with a publisher, though this is indubitably the worst publishing period in recent history.

Enclosed is Smith's "Vathek" ending—together with the comment made by our friend Brobst upon it. I am inclined to think Brobst is right in saying that Smith has not quite caught Beckford's sweep of cosmic shadow—though the style & colouring are certainly reproduced with admirable fidelity. I hope that W.T. may accept this item—for printing, of course, in conjunction with the earlier & Beckfordian part of the episode. So far Wright has not issued any decision. Read this at your leisure—& don't keep it to yourself if you know of anyone else who would enjoy it. Smith likes an appreciative audience, & often sends his MSS. on quite extensive rounds. He would, incidentally, enjoy hearing from you if you like the fragment. Address Box 385, Auburn, California.

Under separate cover I am sending—or will as soon as I can get to the P.O.—a copy of *The Recluse* containing my article on Supernatural Horror in Literature. I have finally dug up three duplicates, & if you find the thing of enduring interest I'd be pleased to have you retain it for your personal library with my compliments. The magazine was an amateur venture launched by W. Paul Cook—whom you didn't get to see in Boston—& it never reached a second issue. You'll find other items in it of interest—including verse & prose by Wandrei, verse by Smith, &c. &c. My article was written 6 years ago, & today I see the need of revision in several respects. In several minor matters I would be inclined to reproportion my opinions, & the style in general strikes me as excessively florid. Moreover, there are many weird things published since 1926 which I would like to include.[1] As a treatise it doesn't amount to much, but it at least forms a rudimentary catalogue of the high spots of weird writing. In preparing it I did more steady reading than I have ever done before or since!

As for current W.T.—I haven't seen the new issue myself, nor have I read the preceding two. Pressure of revisory work has completely disorganised my programme this autumn. Also unread is the new Strange Tales—the final issue,[2] since the house of Clayton has decreed its discontinuance.

I'll remind Brobst of his epistolary delinquencies the next time I'm in touch with him, but I imagine he is desperately busy. He hasn't been over here for a month—& as you see, returned the "Vathek" ending by mail in the greatest of haste. Hope they're not overworking him, & that he'll have more leisure as the season advances. He had quite a touch of feverishness just after your visit—resulting from neglect of the athlete's foot trouble of which he then complained—but a little treatment & time off his feet cleared that up quite effectively in a very little while.

There has been a great deal of rain hereabouts, though sunny days have not been lacking. From what I have seen, the autumn foliage would appear to have been below par; but owing to my heavy work programme my opportunities for observation have been limited. Just now it is too cold for me to enjoy the outdoors—I merely dart from place to place when I have to. That trip to Salem & Marblehead which I think I wrote you about—Octr. 9—remains my last rural outing of the season. I even get down to the Waldorf less frequently than of yore—depending a good deal on cans & their contents for nourishment.

The other day I copied your sketches of anti-hex designs for barn gables in a letter to my friend Talman of Spring Valley, N.Y., who is conducting quite a little research regarding some vaguely similar practices of his own Holland Dutch ancestors of the Hudson River region. In that region the so-called "witch ball" (also known in England & New England) was extensively used—this device being (as perhaps you know) a glass globe filled with vari-coloured threads & hung in the window. A witch, attempting to enter the house, would always pause & try to count the threads—& upon failing would grow discouraged & retreat. Or else she would be detained till dawn, in which case she would have to vanish anyhow. None of this superstition now survives, however.

Well—here's wishing you success with the novel. And I hope the long-awaited weird fiction article won't prove disappointing to you. Get around here when you can, & see if you can better your ice-cream record at Maxfield's![3]

Yr most obt & hble Servt—

H P L

Notes

1. HPL kept a list entitled "Books to mention in new edition of weird article" in the notebook he called his commonplace book. Many items on the list were incorporated into HPL's revision of "Supernatural Horror in Literature" for the *Fantasy Fan.*

2. January 1933. HPL owned all seven issues (*LL* 852).

3. Site (in Warren, RI) of HPL's famous ice-cream eating bout with James F. Morton and Donald Wandrei in July 1927 (*SL* 2.157), where presumably HPL took Strauch (probably with Harry Brobst) when Strauch visited in September Brobst recalls going there "several times" (*Lovecraft Studies* Nos. 22/23 [Fall 1990]: 25).

[18]   [ALS]

Tenbarnes—
Yuletide [25 December 1932].

My dear Strauch:—

Congratulations on the completion of the novel! I can imagine the feeling of pride & relief which must attend the sight of the typed pages. 288 sheets ought to mean a rather ample book, & I surely hope it may find a publisher without too many futile submissions. But of course this is the worst possible season for marketing anything, so you must not feel discouraged if the process proves long & difficult.

I have been too rushed to read any number of W.T. since August, but I did glance through "Alfred Kramer"[1] because Wandrei told me it represented a drastic revision of the MS. version I had previously seen. I thought it excellent—the climax is certainly devastating enough—though perhaps not as good as Wandrei's cosmic stories, such as "The Red Brain." Do you mean to say you haven't read the latter? Ædepol! That is a defect in your education which must be remedied! It is in the Dashiell Hammett anthology—"Creeps by Night"—which your local bibliotheca publica, even if not the bibliotheca universitatis, ought surely to contain. No—Wandrei isn't up to Derleth as a writer, although I think his best tales (so far all weird) excel A W's *weird* work. He is working very hard, however, & has lately experimented in non-weird prose—though I haven't yet seen the results of this experimentation. So far Derleth has a startling lead on all the other members of "the gang". He has a genuine & communicable understanding of life as a whole which most of us seem to lack, & is building up a real standing in the world of midwestern letters. Last week a Chicago speaker conducting a radio broadcast on the younger authors of the midwest singled him out as the salient representative of prose, as George Dillon[2]—a Pulitzer Prize winner—is of poetry.

I haven't seen Summers' "Supernatural Omnibus", though various correspondents have—all pronouncing it very mediocre. I must try to see a copy, if only for the sake of the introduction. Summers surely is a queer old cuss—a tremendously profound scholar in his way, but as naive & superstitious as any of your local "hex" believers. He believes literally in witches, ghosts, vampires, & the like, & is even subject to hallucinations in this direction—having flatly stated that he has *seen* a priest levitate himself several inches from the floor whilst performing some obscure sacerdotal rite. I'd like to get a set of his original works—studies in witchcraft, vampirism, &c. They would form marvellous source-books.

Glad you enjoyed Klarkash-Ton's continuation of "Vathek". I can see what you mean by the occasional let-downs, although I fancy these were not so much unconscious slips as unsuccessful attempts to capture a certain prosy hardness—a Gallic touch—inherent in Beckford's original French. He has read the original Histoire du Caliph Vathek—although he never saw the Episodes till I lent him my copy. As for the plot—as you say, one can't tell just what Beckford would have done with the story. One perhaps misses a sort of supernal terror which Beckford was usually able to infuse into his grotesque terrors—but at any rate the thing is better than any similar attempt of my own could possibly have been. Smith has certainly caught the essential psychological keynote of the suave 18th century eastern tale.

Trust you'll duly enjoy the holidays. Roman literature is surely a diversion worth following—& I'm confident that your choice of a graduate course is very well-advised. I myself have always been utterly fascinated by the civilisation of Rome—indeed, when I survey the ancient world, it is always from the standpoint of a Roman, as if the Imperium of the Tiber were naturally my country before the formation of a settled Anglo-Saxon world. In all historic events I have a sort of involuntary Roman patriotism—being emotionally on the side of Rome, right or wrong, & having an actual anger when people attack or belittle the land of Lucretius, Cicero, & Vergilius. I like to imagine, as a matter of fictitious genealogy, that I am descended through some obscure strain from the Roman invaders of Britain—some legatus in the army of C. Suetonius Paullinus or of Cn. Julius Agricola, or some civil functionary of later years at Eboracum, Isca Silurum, or Aquae Solis. If you choose to send some epistles in the ancient tongue I shall do my best to revive my earlier acquaintance with it—though you must not blame me if the forgetfulness of declining years gives to my replies a less than Ciceronian purity & idiomatic grace!

Sorry you found the last Friedell volume disappointing—but all authors tend to be one-sided. Writers of every different nation survey the field of human achievement from their own particular angle, & formulate lists of salient persons & events which seem grotesquely misproportioned except in the land of the writer himself. Thus in a Frenchman's list of the world's great men, books, & deeds we find dozens of entries which we scarcely recognise, & miss dozens of others whose right to a place we take for granted. And a Frenchman feels the same bewilderment when reading one of our lists. Actually, one is probably about as correct as the other. Only an historian of the year 3932—if there are any historians then, & if any trace of early human civilisations has survived—could have a perspective sufficiently detached to give a perfectly just appraisal of the subdivided fabric of Western civilisation . . . . . . & even he might have his biasses, as I have in favour of Rome.

Some good public lectures at Brown Univ. this month. Heard J. B. S. Haldane on "Biology & Politics", & Walter G. Everett on Spinoza. This latter lecture was one of a monthly philosophic series like that which I attended last winter. Around these courses a new "R.I. Philos. Society" has grown up—which I may possibly join. ¶ With best wishes for the holidays & for 1933—

Yr most obt & hble Servt—

H P L

[On envelope:] Your yuletide card was greatly appreciated! ¶ And now, just as I mail this epistle, comes a quite unexpected hop to the decadent jungles of Manhattan! The parents of my friend Long have invited me down to surprise him with a week's sojourn—& since the 'bus fare is down to $2.00 again, I'm accepting. Thus I'll have two Christmas dinners—one with my aunt today, & another at the Longs' tomorrow—since they've chosen the Monday holiday for Yuletide festivities. If by any chance you should be able to get around to Manhattan during the coming week, look me up % Long, 230 W. 97th St.

Notes

1. "The Lives of Alfred Kramer" (*WT*, December 1932).

2. George Dillon (1906–1968), author of *Boy in the Wind* (1927) and *The Flowering Stone* (1931), the latter of which won the Pulitzer Prize for poetry. Dillon translated Baudelaire's *Fleurs du mal* with Edna St. Vincent Millay (1936).

[19]   [ALS]

230 W. 97th St.,

New York, N.Y.,

Dec. 31, 1932

My dear Strauch:—

Delighted to hear from you! If by any chance I do stay over another week here, I'll certainly keep you posted & arrange to meet you—but I don't wish to presume on the hospitality of my hosts. It seems damnably tantalising to miss you by less than a week—& I'm missing James F. Morton (now out of town) by a *single day* unless I do decide to depart from my schedule. Whenever I am in the metropolis again I'll certainly let you know, & hope that such a season may coincide with some suitable excursion from Allentown. The coach fare from Providence to N.Y., by the way, is down to $2.00. Toward spring I hope you may be able to get to New England again—& I surely wish I did have the influence to secure you a joint headship of the Germanic & Latin departments at Brown! Sorry, by the way, that your last week-end was so gloomy as to call out all your reserves of Catonic & Senecan stoicism!

I mourn the mortality in your congenial piscine circle, & trust that all your suspicions against the squib may prove to be unfounded. It is perhaps well to remove the haunted castle, since such foci of Gothic mystery contain dark influences disquietingly beyond our computation.

About that musical business—there were two sonnets set to melody by Farnese; "Mirage" & "The Elder Pharos". Both appeared in Weird Tales, but if you didn't see them I'll be glad to supply the text as soon as I'm back home. Farnese hasn't sent me the music yet—but I couldn't get it suitably played just now even if I had it.

Your own new sonnet is delightful, & I hope it may obtain publication in some medium worthy of it. Good luck with the "Epistle to the World". Heroics used to be my favourite measure, since I have always been a devotee of the 18th century. Congratulations on the bookplate—which certainly does sound interesting. If you have the main design you want, I'm sure my artistic friend (*Wilfred B. Talman, Scotland Post Road, Spring Valley, N.Y.*—the chap who knows the old Dutch legends I spoke of) could fix you up. Why not write him? I saw him yesterday in his office (Texas Co.) on the 18th floor of the Chrysler Bldg. Why don't you write him? It would surely do you no harm!

Have been making the rounds of the museums with Long & Wandrei—the latter of whom is still in town finishing his novel.[1] You ought to see him on your next visit—his address is 84 Horatio St., Apt. 4-B, in the northwest part of Greenwich Village not far from the Hudson waterfront. You ought to look up Long also—whether or not I'm still here.

The newly acquired Greek Apollo in the Metropolitan Museum is highly impressive. Today I intend to see Whistler's famous painting of his mother, now at the Museum of Modern Art. Weather so far has favoured me—temperatures being unusually high for this time of year. I shall see the old year out (good riddance to a depressing twelvemonth) at the home of my friend Samuel Loveman, whose long prose-poem "The Sphinx" is about to be published as a small book.[2] I think I shewed you his volume—"The Hermaphrodite"—when you were in Providence.

Well—I hope some miracle *will* detain me in N.Y. till your visit! I'll tell you if it does.

Best wishes—

      Yr most obt Servt

      H P L

Notes

1. See JVS 34 n.4.

2. *The Sphinx:: A Conversation* was not published until 1944.

[20]   [ALS]

                                                             Jany. 28, 1933.

My dear Strauch:—

      The visit was surely enjoyable, though I was sorry it could not coincide with your own brief Manhattan appearance. I've forgotten how much of it had occurred when I wrote you—but may mention that I saw a fair number of the gang (though Morton was out of town), did the museums, & indulged in the usual endless arguments. Wandrei is still there, & I saw a good deal of him. On Dec. 30 the group met at Belknap's, & I saw the old year out at Samuel Loveman's new flat in Brooklyn—where for the first time his museum treasures are adequately displayed. Loveman gave me a prehistoric stone image from Mexico & a primitive African flint implement with engraved ivory handle for my own modest collection. Regarding the museums—I saw among other new things the archaic Greek Apollo at the Metropolitan, the two Dutch rooms (Holland—circa 1650) at the Brooklyn, the modernistic horrors & shrieking attic frescoes at the Whitney, & the American primitives (many of Penn. German origin) & Whistler portrait of his mother (lent by the Louvre) at the now adequately housed Museum of Modern Art in W. 53d St. Also—not to neglect the phenomena of the mechanised present—I took my first ride (for exploration—not because it was the best route to my destination!) on the new 8th Ave. subway—which is the finest of the city's systems, though ill-patronised because of its lack of a really central route downtown. I returned to Providence by night 'bus—as I came—thus having 8 full days in the metropolis. Since my return Long has had a sharp attack of influenza, & Talman (the Dutch antiquity enthusiast) has had a son & heir.

As for weather—this, like last, is certainly my kind of winter! No snow hereabouts, & one day this week the mercury was up to 60°! I fear it's too good to last—but meanwhile my complete hibernation continues to be postponed.

Glad you've had an interesting fight with Derleth, whose touch of ego makes him quite a piquant controversialist. His tastes are somewhat capricious, but seem in the main sound. I suppose he pitched into some of your 19th century predilections with his usual gusto. He has just sent me the carbon of his newly revised "Evening in Spring", which promises to be a remarkable piece of work before he is through with it.

As for Rascoe's "Titans of Literature"—I haven't read it as yet, but have heard several opinions in both directions. Nobody seems to love Milton any more—but just the same, I'm not taking down the ancient bust of him which dominates the skyline of my room.[1] The majesty of some of his lines & images, & the sheer beauty of most of his shorter & lighter things, can scarcely be wiped out by an occasional adverse dictum. As for Dante—he is indubitably tedious as a whole, but there are imaginative conceptions & pictures in his stuff which can hardly be duplicated elsewhere. Of course, it is against these old fellows that they were saturated in conceptions & values now obsolete—but for all that they have enough poetic substance to float them irrespective of background.

It's hard to realise that Brobst's first hospital year is almost up. I believe that Boston will be his next post—the N.Y. arrangement having been abandoned by the arrangers of such matters.

I shall be interested to hear what you say concerning the dialect MS.—a highly valuable accession for your library, it would seem to me. My own modest library has had a few accessions lately—notably a 3-volume copy of the famous "Melmoth, the Wanderer", given me by W. Paul Cook. I have wanted this book for ages, but had quite despaired of acquiring it. It is the reprint of 1892—since which (though it is long out of print) I believe no new edition has appeared. Another accession is the delectable phantasy "The

Worm Ouroboros", by E. R. Eddison, which I picked up as a remainder for 79¢. Derleth has just swelled my catalogue by forwarding six weird anthologies just discarded from his library.²

There have been several interesting lectures & poetry readings hereabouts of late. Last Wednesday I heard Schopenhauer expatiated upon, & tomorrow I shall hear Robert Hillyer read from his own poetry.

With best wishes—

Yrs most cordially & sincerely—

H P L

Notes

1. Mentioned in "The Whisperer in Darkness" and seen in the photograph of HPL's study at 66 College Street in *Marginalia* (facing p. 214).

2. See *SL* 4.146–47, where only one—Bohun Lynch's *Best Ghost Stories* (1924; *LL* 558)—is mentioned.

[21]   [ALS]

10 Barnes St.,
Providence, R.I.,
Feby. 11, 1933

My dear Strauch:—

Although I generally see very few modern products, I did happen to read "The Fountain"¹ a couple of months ago. I liked it exceedingly, I believe it has the substance necessary for survival. In some ways it is perhaps heavy & overweighted with pure philosophy—& its whole underlying attitude is one which exaggerates the importance of human emotions—but despite all objections it has a sound vitality & abiding beauty which make it memorable. Derleth does not like it, but other correspondents of mine are almost incoherent with enthusiasm over it. Reviews—including comment by the local literary columnist—seem uniformly favourable. I have not read "People Around the Corner."² As for your novel—you know best how much revision it needs. It would, indeed, be highly unusual if a first novel did not require some further polishing after the completion of the original draught. Long passages of poetic prose probably would be out of place—although of course prose-poetry is sometimes an asset when it contributes something essential to the central theme.

As for the Victorian period—I never could abide anything in it except its zeal for natural science. Faraday, Darwin, Huxley, Haeckel, Tyndall, Lubbock, Kelvin, Clerk Maxwell, Tylor, &c. &c.—those are its real ornaments. In architecture it was an insane nightmare. In painting it was tawdry & unimaginative. In poetry it was shallow & affected. In music—except for Wagner—it was saccharine & insipid. In fiction it was insincere, rambling, unlifelike, & unconvincing. In politics & sociology it was superficial & dependent upon false premises. Scientific progress is what redeems it. And yet I think the present age has many follies & shallownesses of its own, which to posterity will appear as absurd as those of the Victorian age do to us. I like the 18th century—in which I am more at home than in any other period. Like you, I detest the *attitude of revolt,* which seems to me to be antagonistic to the spirit of artistic creation. A civilisation may well eliminate, by gradual steps, elements which are either obviously untrue or obviously anti-social; but to discard or repudiate whole backgrounds of inherited moods & habits is culturally suicidal—for these backgrounds are all that give people the illusions of significance & direction in the cosmos, & all that make life worth plodding through for individuals of highly evolved mind & sensitiveness. To my mind there is nothing but destructiveness in the shrill, whining attitude of discontent held by aesthetes of the e. e. cummings, Waldo Frank, & John Dos Passos school—a school, alas, toward which more than one of my younger friends (including Long, whom I visited last month) seem to be inclined.

What you say of Charles More is interesting in the extreme—& the fact that he is still living adds zest to the matter. You really ought to look him up, for you might be instrumental in gaining for him a belated recognition both local & national. There is certainly a growing regard for regional folklore & literature in the United States—an 11th hour reaction against standardisation—& amidst such a movement the absolutely unique culture of the Pennsylvania German area ought to fare very well indeed.

I read "The Golden Bough" years ago, & marvelled at the erudition of the venerable author.[3] He is a good example of the encyclopaedic & indefatigable scientific man of the Victorian age. This work seems destined to remain as a permanent anthropological landmark.

Your recent 'bus trip was undoubtedly more picturesque than restful. Odd company is one of the penalties of cheap 'bus or excursion travel—but if one lacks cash & wants to get from place to place, there is nothing to do but put up with it. My worst travel experience—bar none—was the return trip of a cheap Quebec excursion in Sept. 1930. Most of the humble fellow-passengers had evidently sought the quaint old French fortress town for reasons less antiquarian & more alcoholic than my own—& their plebeian revelry & bottle-passing from Charny to the U.S. line was a memorable study in coarseness. Thank heaven, most of the swine fell into a drunken sleep in the stretches south of Newport, Vt. And yet, the sight of Quebec was worth the penalty—so much so that I took an equally cheap Montreal–Quebec excursion last summer, despite my full expectation of a similar ordeal. Miraculously, I was spared such an ordeal—for the denizens of the return train were comparatively well-behaved. The clown of the journey (for every cheap excursion seems to have its self-appointed buffoon)—a comical little Jew in an American Legion uniform—was actually sober! ¶ Frightful cold spell last week, but it broke Saturday. On the whole, the winter has averaged very decent!

Best wishes—

Yr obt hble Servt—

H P L

Notes

1. A novel by Charles Morgan.
2. A collection of short stories by Thyra Samter Winslow.
3. A celebrated anthropological treatise by Sir James George Frazer.

[22]   [ALS]

10 Barnes St.,

Providence, R.I.,

Feby. 24, 1933.

My dear Strauch:—

Thanks tremendously for the Muhlenburg views. The old Alma Mater surely does shew up prepossessingly—& the scene of your bibliothecal labours stands out like a fragment of Dunsanian dream. I feel sure that the reality can't be *very* ugly! The landscaping seems to be extremely judicious—& I can well imagine the beauty of the grounds twenty years hence.

What you have added concerning Charles More interests me greatly, & I surely hope you may be able to bring him some of the recognition—both local & national—which he so amply deserves. I hope your library can arrange to get the hand-written MSS. typed before long, so that they may be ready for publication when some opportunity presents itself. Glad your article for the library journal[1] was accepted, & hope you can later plan something of the sort in one of the general magazines.

I read with extreme interest your remarks on the Victorian age, & certainly agree that your generation is more likely to view it with historical impartiality than that which was born during its own declining existence. At the same time I really don't think that my estimate is the product of hate & reaction; since I am not very prone to indignations, & am not at all animated by the hysterical anti-Puritan complex of the Dreisers, Andersons, & Waldo Franks. I think that in many ways the code of the 19th century involved more honour & good breeding than the code—if any—of the 20th. My own objections are quite abstract & impersonal, & based wholly on a love of truth for its own sake. I find the mood & institutions of the 19th century rather absurd & unsatisfying (rather than hateful) because they were so largely based on assumptions contrary to fact. The art of the period seems to me in so many instances curiously *irrelevant*—involving a whole system of values, emotions, &

attributed motivations without any counterparts in the actual working fabric of society, & postulating a purposeful cosmos grotesquely at variance with what the eminent men of science were even then uncovering. There was a singular inability to appreciate the philosophic implications of the expanding conception of the universe & its phenomena. Mankind is just as stupid in one age as in another, but there are times when the discrepancy between its manifestations & reality is especially marked. It was not that the Victorian was *narrower* than the modern, but that the particular direction of his limited vision was (no doubt accidentally) farther from taste & reason than is the direction of the modern's equally limited vision. That is, the modern simply *happens* not to be quite so absurd (although he is in many ways absurd enough).

As for my inclusion of non-English culture-streams in an estimate of the middle 19ᵗʰ century—I cannot help thinking of all Western civilisation as to some extent a unit; though of course sharp local differences do occur, while some nations reach a given identical condition earlier or later than others. But there certainly was a vague homogeneity in the European world of 70 years ago—a common lack of decorative taste, a common background of sententious, romantic, & mediaevally-influenced bombast, & so on. Undeniably, however, the given characteristics appeared most emphatically in the Anglo-Saxon world.

I do not dissent when you point out the 19ᵗʰ century's *historical* importance as part of a modifying culture, or when you find interest in the picturesque figures which its naive individualism produced. I merely state that to me the aesthetic products of the period seem to have disconcertingly little vitality or convincingness. Plato & Emerson do not appeal to me, because I regard their feelings toward the cosmos as hopelessly coloured by conceptions of values & of existence whose whole source lies in myth & error. Matthew Arnold seems to me overrated except in rare poetic fragments like "Dover Beach". For Thackeray—in whom lingered much of the 18ᵗʰ century—I have some respect. Meredith, despite a grotesque moralism, seems at least sincere in his reaching for truth. Pater impresses me as accomplished but insignificant. Swinburne had real poetry at the start, but soon began merely repeating himself in diminishing echoes.

Probably most of the newer writers are inferior as artists to the greater Victorians, but their handicaps are so much lessened (except in the case of the slaves to chaotic theories) that they succeed in producing material much closer to life. They do not cripple their art at the outset by trying to conceal the purposeless, cosmically valueless, impersonal, largely deterministic, & man-dwarfing nature of the blind, automatic universe. Of course I exclude frivolous surface-skimmers like Arlen & van Vechten, & technical experimenters like Joyce & Cummings & Eliot, from the list of actually *producing* artists. Incidentally—I don't think that *any* defence of Victorian architecture, costume, & general decoration can be attempted seriously. The age was simply a lacuna—an hiatus. By the way—I heard a poetry reading by T. S. Eliot this week. Quite a boy—though I disagree with him in nearly all of his artistic theories. ¶ With all good wishes—& asking pardon for opinions which you will no doubt deem superficial—I remain

　　Yr most obt Servt—

H P L

Notes

1. See Appendix.

[23]　　[ALS]

10 Barnes St.,
Providence, R.I.,
March 18, 1933

My dear Strauch:—

　　　　Your reading programme quite overawes me, insomuch as I cannot even begin to compete amidst the turmoil of tasks awaiting my attention. Last week I had to go to Hartford to assist on a job of research which a client was conducting at the library there,[1] & meanwhile the accumulation of material here was appalling. Hartford, though an old city, has lost much of its antiquities; hence is rather uninteresting as a whole—& especially in a raw, drizzling March rain. However, it has two ancient suburbs—Farmington & Wethersfield—which amply atone for its deficiencies. Farmington—where I elected to stop in an ancient inn whose oldest portion dates back to 1638—is situate in a splendid rolling countryside & adorned with magnificent elms. A large proportion of its colonial houses still stand—including a finely preserved 1650 specimen with overhang—& the 1771 steepled church remains in perfect condition. Restrictions on real-estate have made for a great selectness of population & a refreshing preservation of the original quaint atmosphere. Wethersfield is also very quiet, select, & ancient, though of radically different aspect. It lies in level country, & the flat, elm-shaded village common is of singular breadth & spaciousness. The old houses are largely well-preserved 18th century mansions with the distinctive earmarks of Connecticut-Valley architecture, & one of them is duly tableted as the scene of the military conference (May 1781) at which Washington, Rochambeau, Knox, & Trumbull planned the future battle of Yorktown. The church—of brick, erected in 1764—was thought when built to be the finest in New England outside Boston. It has a fine steeple, but the windows have been ruined by Victorian alterations. When the French officers of Rochambeau passed through Wethersfield they remarked upon the magnificent view from the church belfry—a view which even now must be impressive, though I had no time to ascend & sample it. One of the great Wethersfield elms is today said to be the largest east of the Rocky Mountains.

Yes—the youthful Comte d'Erlette is correct in saying that another attempt of mine is to appear in W.T.[2] He, moreover, is wholly responsible for its appearance there. I had given up contributing in disgust, but had lent this tale to M. Auguste-Guillaume for copying purposes. By chance he mentioned it to Editor Wright, & the latter asked to see it. M. le Comte complied, & Satrap Pharnabazus decided that he wished to purchase it. I gave my consent, even though I'm not especially fond of the tale, since the $140 offer looked decidedly alluring to my impoverished purse. It will appear in the July issue—out June 1—& the $140 will probably come hither about a month later. No—there was no violation of confidence on M. d'Erlette's part. Indeed, that amiable & enterprising youth deserves my sincerest thanks for his part in the transaction!

Your prospectus for a magazine sounds highly alluring, & I shall have my prose-poems on the weather (including some of the most thunderous invective ever printed) in readiness as soon as the rest of the text is assembled. I look forward with particular pleasure to Mr. Whitaker's[3] enlightening article, having been delightfully familiar with his poetic perspective in the days when *Peg-ass'-us* (his own pronunciation, as revealed by prosodical employment!) was a member of the National Amateur Press Association. I presume that you will assign to Noah the task of creating new words in emulation of MM. Jolas et Joyce[4]—or possibly you'll divide that fascinating labour. I ought to succeed fairly well at that trade, in view of the scores of synthetic names I have invented for the mythical entities in my horror-tales. Am I not the sponsor of Cthulhu, Yog-Sothoth, Nug, Yeb, & dozens of other daemons? But even so, I run a poor second in that line to Clark Ashton Smith.

How unenterprising of the hexers to let a winter pass without a murder! Well—they still have 2 days in which to make good!

Best wishes—

Yr most ob[t] h[ble] Serv[t]—

H P L

Notes

1. In fact, HPL went to meet his ex-wife Sonia H. Greene for the last time.

2. "The Dreams in the Witch House."

3. Noah F. Whitaker, editor of the amateur journal *Pegasus,* which in 1924 published some of HPL's poems.

4. Eugene Jolas (1894–1952), poet, critic, and editor of the avant-garde magazine *transition,* and James Joyce.

[24]   [ALS]

note well—      66 College St.,

I've got two 6's now!   Providence, R.I.,

May 31, 1933

Dear Strauch:—

Here's just a line to apprise you of my changed address. I think I told you that economic pressure was forcing me to double up with my surviving aunt in a low-rent flat—but I have yet to tell you of the marvellous bargain we found . . . . . a bargain which makes our move *down* look like a move *up,* & which at last—after 40 years—places me for the first time in a *real colonial house.*

You no doubt remember our visit to the marble John Hay Library with its Harris Collection of Poetry. At that time it is just possible that I pointed out to you a yellow colonial house behind the library—at the back of a rather quaint rustic court leading off from the steep slope of College St.—mentioning that a friend of my aunt's lived in the lower half of it.[1] Well—I live in the upper half of it now! My aunt's friend—a high-school teacher of German—had long wanted her to move in above her if ever the flat should be vacant. On May 1st. it *did* become vacant, & my aunt was duly informed. We looked it over, found it would be ideal for both, & at once clinched the bargain. You can imagine how I felt at the prospect of living in a real colonial home! Our respective quarters will be wholly separate except for dining room &c—& yet the general effect will be that of a complete & homogeneous home—my study corresponding to the library & my aunt's living-room to the parlour. She has not yet moved in, although I am wholly settled. The place looks ineffably homelike with my belongings, & since I have 2 rooms of my own I don't have to crowd the furniture as I did at 10 Barnes. Arranging my books & files was a hellish job—I had to get 4 new cases & a cabinet for pamphlets—but it is done at last. Tomorrow my aunt moves in & completes the family circle.

The house is a square wooden edifice of the 1800 period—as you may possibly remember. The fine colonial doorway is like my bookplate come to life, though of a slightly later period with side lights & fan carving instead of a fanlight. In the rear is a pictur-esque, village-like garden at a higher level than the front of the house. The upper flat we have taken contains 5 rooms besides bath & kitchenette nook on the main (2nd) floor, plus 2 attic storerooms—one of which is so attractive that I wish I could have it for an extra den! My quarters—a large study & a small adjoining bedroom—

are on the south side, with my working desk under a west window affording a splendid view of the lower town's outspread roofs & of the mystical sunsets that flame behind them. The interior is as fascinating as the exterior—with colonial fireplaces, mantels, & chimney cupboards, curving Georgian stair-case, wide floor-boards, old-fashioned latches, small-paned windows, six-panel doors, rear wing with floor at a different level (3 steps down), quaint attic stairs, &c.—just like the old houses open as museums. After admiring such all my life, I find something magical & dreamlike in the experience of actually *living in one* . . . . . I keep half-expecting a museum guard to come around & kick me out at 5 o'clock closing time! And yet the whole thing costs only what I've been paying for one room & alcove at 10 Barnes. The house is owned by the university, & steam heat & hot water are piped in from the ad-jacent John Hay Library. Little did I think, when we were there last summer, that from that classic building would come my daily supply of caloric! Since I now have so much space, I have picked up a camp cot to enable me to acco-modate an occasional guest. Thus the next time you're here—which I hope will be during the present summer—you need not worry about hotel bills. What lodging could be more appropriate for you than one next the Harris Col-lection of American Poetry? Brobst has seen the place twice—once before the moving & once since I've been settled. He agrees that it's a pretty homelike dump. Incidentally, he wants to know why he hasn't heard from you lately.

Derleth says that you may be heading for Sauk City before long. Hope you aren't going back on the historic east! A trip to Wisconsin, though, would certainly be delightful—I shall take one myself some day, since I have an un-usual number of friends & correspondents in that state . . . . at least five that I'd want to call on.

Did I tell you that Clark Ashton Smith is issuing six of his unpublished sto-ries as a booklet at the modest price of 25¢? That will be an item worth get-ting—it can be obtained from him at Box 385, Auburn, California. And incidentally, my own "Shunned House" is about to appear at last as a small book. Cook found the unbound edition in good shape, & Walter J. Coates—the *Driftwind* editor—is going to bind & try to market it.[2] I wish him luck! By the way—did I mention in my last that my story "The Dreams in the Witch House" will appear in the *Weird Tales* out July [*sic*] 1st? Hope all goes well with your novel.

I shall not, I fear, be able to take any long Southern trip this year; but may get to New York early in July for the convention of the Natl. Am. Press Association. This moving has kept me from getting out to the country & en-joying the spring weather!

Best wishes—

Yr obᵗ Servᵗ—

H P L

[*On envelope:*] Pardon the envelope. Nobody's dead, but I found some of these in looking over my things & want to get rid of 'em!

Notes

1. The Samuel Mumford House (c. 1825), now standing at 65 Prospect. The downstairs tenant was Alice Sheppard.

2. He never did so.

[25]   [ALS]

Out in the Sunlit Woods—

June 5, 1933.

My dear Strauch:—

Et tu, Brute! Migration seems to be an epidemic, for you are the second person to respond to the news with a report of kindred activities. Congratulations on the quarters into which economy has precipitated you! The place sounds delightful—especially the garden glimpses & the arrangement of your lettered lair—& I trust you can hang on to it as long as possible. I enjoyed your chart very much, & will endeavour to reciprocate with two of my own—Plate A shewing the general plan of the flat, & Plate B illustrating my own individual 2-room layout.

Here is Plate A—the main or second floor. The attic has 2 rooms with low, sloping ceilings & flat windows high up. From each of these rooms little low doors open into a pitch-black, sinister space running around the eaves—just the kind of crypt to hide a nameless body or something of the sort. The small garden around the house is really delightful, & my aunt plans to train ivy up the front facade—she has a slip down from the original ivy of Genl. Washington at Mt. Vernon. The more I see of the place the fonder I become of it. My aunt moved in last Tuesday, & by Saturday night her living-room was fairly settled. In many ways it eclipses my own rooms, since she 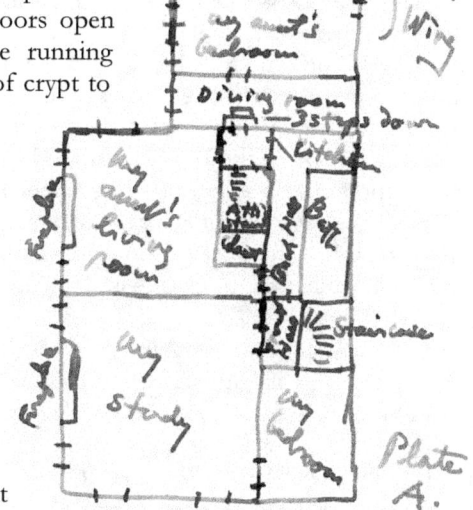 has a more tasteful fireplace, & also many old family possessions (furniture, paintings, statuary) from the old home that excel my reliques. But I don't envy her, since the things I have are the things I need. But here is Plate B,

shewing the arrangement of my personal quarters: (rotten proportioning—I ought to have had the rooms shorter from N. to S.)

I have plenty of old candles, pictures, &c—you know the stuff at 10 Barnes—& they shew to much better advantage at #66. I have had two oil paintings framed, & they fit finely into the scheme. I certainly hope you can get around here next September—or whatever is the best time. Let me know ahead, & I'll be on hand! You'll find the place delectable, I'm sure . . . . even though my collection does not contain any gems comparable to those on your impressive list. The best items I have are a Greek version of the Necronomicon, a copy of the Book of Eibon bound in the tanned skin of an Atlantean emperor, & a copy of the original Düsseldorf edition of von Junzt's hideous *Unaussprechlichen Kulten*—unexpurgated, but with one page missing . . . . probably torn out by some horrified reader.[1] But of course there are many other interesting trifles—& you can also see the collection of my next-door neighbour John Hay!

I am certainly sorry that your job has gone glimmering, & hope that something else will turn up before prospects get desperate. But the enforced leisure really will be a boon for you literarily. Hawthorne owes the unhurried writing of "The Scarlet Letter" to the fact that he lost his job at the Salem Custom House. Glad to hear that the novel is coming along, & hope to see a specimen of it in the course of time. Bring it along when you come hither.

Your local art theatre seems to be a genuine civic asset, & I am glad that it is getting around to the recognition of regional folklore. All over the country—from Vermont to Texas & California—there seems to be a growing interest in local historic backgrounds which gratifies me immensely. Hope your

Charles More article will appear soon, & that it will help in the movement to reëstablish dialect literature.

I wish I could accompany you on your Ephrata explorations. One of the buildings there has always been known to me through descriptions & illustrations in works on colonial architecture, & I can well imagine that a vast amount of bygone atmosphere must remain. The whole Pennsylvania-German scene deserves more popular exploitation than it has yet received. It was an important & distinctive culture, & yet it is not commonly known to any such extent as that to which the New-Netherland Dutch, Louisiana French, & Southwestern Spanish cultures are known. Perhaps a new wave of interest is about to dawn—I noticed last January that Pa. German work figured largely in the folk-art exhibit at the N.Y. Museum of Modern Art.

Glad you've had a poem accepted . . . . & too bad *Wings* is adopting such a flimsy standard. No—Parker hasn't discontinued *L'Alouette,* but its issuance has always been highly irregular. Which reminds me that I must tell P. of my new address—he has an advertisement of my revisory service for his coming issue.[2]

You won't be disappointed in Klarkash-Ton's booklet. I'll later get you a copy of my own "Shunned House", which is likely to be bound & issued at last. Early in July Cook, Parker, & I may all attend the N.Y. convention of the National Amateur Press Association—seeing Long, Loveman, Wandrei, &c. I'll remember you to Brobst when I see him—& trust you'll drop him a line. He will not go to Boston till October.

¶ It's getting a bit cold & windy to write outdoors, so I guess I'll move on & enjoy the scenery . . . . the sun being still goldenly radiant. Fortunately I have a vest in my inevitable black bag. You must see more of the Rhode Island countryside when you get here.

I've just been reading Derleth's two new novelettes "Nine Strands in a Web" & "Place of Hawks".[3] Damn good stuff, although in the last-named he introduces a disconcerting number of *coincidences.* He has a rather chimerical theory about *coincidence* in life & art which is likely to form a substantial literary handicap (though his work is powerful enough to float in spite of it) if he doesn't get rid of it before long.

Fear I can't take any really long trips this year. This is the first spring I have spent in the north since 1928, & I am reminded afresh of the irritating tardiness of the season in these subarctic latitudes.

Well—best wishes, drop a line when you can, & try to get here during the summer.

Yr oblig'd ob^t Servt—

H P L

Notes

1. The *Necronomicon* was, of course, a book of HPL's invention; the *Book of Eibon* was created by CAS and *Unaussprechlichen Kulten* by Robert E. Howard. Here HPL pretends they are real, but in many letters he explained apologetically to inquirers they were not.

2. In the September 1924 issue of *L'Alouette* (ed. Charles A. A. Parker), published a joint ad by HPL and James F. Morton for revisory services; see *CE* 5.283. No doubt the ad referred to here is some amended version of this, as HPL was no longer collaborating with Morton in such services.

3. The novelettes were published in Derleth's *Place of Hawks*.

[26]   [ALS]

66 College St.,

Providence, R.I.,

June 27, 1933

My dear Strauch:—

I envy you your trip through rural Pennsylvania, & hope that I can explore that region some day. While I don't care for fishing, I certainly am an ardent devotee of landscapes & local colour—hence imagine that the Pocono region would prove a rich field for me. Do you find many old-fashioned stone farmhouses? That solitary grave must indeed have been pathetic, & I hope to see your poem on it. No doubt you could unearth whole cycles of spectral folklore if diligent enough in listening to the hearthside grandams.

66 College St. has a chronicle of disaster to record. On June 14 my aunt broke her right ankle while descending the stairs in answer to the doorbell during my absence. Doctor . . . specialist . . . ambulance to R.I. Hospital . . . . X-ray . . . . setting in a plaster cast under ether . . . . room in Ward K . . . . . prospect of confinement to bed for six weeks & crutches for several more . . . . & a financial drain of cataclysmic & ruinous proportions! Naturally I have been kept devastatingly busy—completing the settlement of the house & visiting the hospital each day—& all my plans for travel have perforce been called off. Next week my aunt will probably be brought home—with a trained nurse in constant attendance. It certainly is, so to speak, a hell of a housewarming!

But my spring & summer have not been devoid of modest outings. On warm & pleasant days I have taken some of my typical long walks—among other things exploring a rural region which, despite comparative nearness to town, I had never seen before. It is north of the city & west of my favourite Lincoln Woods region—with atmosphere & scenery of the most fascinating sort. Hills, woods, old stone walls, lakes, farmhouses, & several especially fine vistas. On other days I have walked southward—to Roger Williams Park, to old Fort Independence on the bay (with its striking view up & down the harbour), & to the quaint old fishing village of Pawtuxet. The average distance I cover in any one walk is about 12 miles.

You'll be sorry to hear that good old Mrs. Maxfield—proprietor of the Warren ice-cream emporium—died last month. However, the place is incorporated, & will carry on as usual. This reminds me—I'll bet you couldn't guess what I had for dinner last night! The answer is, an *entire* blueberry pie plus half a pint of ice cream. No more, no less! There is a new cheap pastry shop in a part of the town through which my southward walks take me, & the *10¢* pies in the window have for some time excited my curiosity. Last night I thought I'd try one—so got the ice cream to round the dinner out. Nor was I at all disappointed. Of course the pie was not large, nor did I expect first quality. But it was genuinely palatable, & to all appearances wholesome (no cramps or colic thus far). Good value for the money—I think I'll patronise this joint again. That part of town—seedy & humble—has some good bargains in many lines if one knows where to look for them.

Haven't seen Brobst lately—he must be uncommonly busy. He'll certainly welcome your record-breaking epistle, & before summer is over we must all sample the frigid produce of the Maxfield estate together. I expect W. Paul Cook here Saturday—on his way to the N.Y. convention which I had expected to attend. E. Hoffmann Price (the W.T. author whom I met in New Orleans last year) is also due here soon.

Glad Comte d'Erlette sent you a photograph. Why can't you reciprocate with a good-looking portrait? Nature did her part, & cameras aren't hard to get. Incidentally, I wouldn't mind a shot of you for my private Rogues' Gallery!

Enclosed is a circular of Smith's new brochure—a bargain I can recommend. Great stuff!

Best wishes—

Yr most ob^t hble Servt—

H P L

[27]   [ALS]

66 College St.,

Providence, R.I.,

July 8, 1933

My dear Strauch:—

Knowing of the recent accident, you will be prepared to pardon any laxity on my part as regards promptness, critical comment, & the like. My aunt returned home last Wednesday with a trained nurse, & the arrangement is such as to keep me tied up more than ever. I have to be on duty every afternoon while the nurse is out, & on such occasions can do very little uninterrupted writing. However, the change is an advantageous one, for the patient feels vastly better than at the hospital. She must remain in bed 3 weeks or so more, & then can get about on crutches—complete recovery not being expected till October. Thus you will probably see her during the crutch period.

Hope your N Y trip proved pleasant—though you must have envied the friend so lately revelling beneath classic Grecian skies! As I feared, I couldn't get to the N.A.P.A. convention—but a highly congenial assemblage right here proved ample compensation. E. Hoffmann Price arrived on June 30 in his archaic Ford Juggernaut, & kept things enlivened for the better part of four days. Saturday afternoon W. Paul Cook stopped a few hours on his way to the N Y convention, though I could not persuade him to stay overnight. Brobst was over twice—partaking of the exotic East Indian curry which Price, in his infinite Oriental wisdom, ceremoniously prepared. On one occasion the three of us stayed up all night discussing literature & philosophy—& making a trip to the hidden hillside churchyard (which you doubtless remember) at 3 a.m.[1]

On Sunday Price brought the Juggernaut into the service of antiquarian exploration—taking me to a Rhode-Island region which, despite my lifelong residence less than 30 miles away from it, & my ⅓ ancestral connexion with its ancient families, I had never (through lack of public transportation facilities) seen before. This was the historic "South County" or "Narragansett County" west of the bay, where before the Revolution there existed a system of large plantations & black slaves comparable to that of the South. The scenery of this territory is ineffably beautiful, as I had long known from reading, though some of the finest areas can be glimpsed from the main trunk highways. On this occasion we began with the marvellously unspoiled colonial seaport of Wickford, & worked southward through the magical land of yesterday. We saw the rambling old snuff-mill where Gilbert Stuart was born in 1755, & the vast Rowland Robinson mansion (1705) amidst its gigantic, centuried willows. The lone & deserted Ferry Church on a windswept headland claimed our notice, nor did we ignore the abandoned "Glebe" or rectory of the Revd James MacSpadden (1727), now spectrally overgrown with a lush profusion of vines & briars. We climbed a hill to the well-known "Hannah Robinson's Rock" (around which revolves a pathetic story)[2] & enjoyed what is probably the finest view in Rhode Island, if not in all New England— winding blue river, rich green meadows & woodlands, white headland church in the distance, & the far-off shimmer of the half-glimpsed sea. Great stuff! But the climax was the wholly unspoiled colonial village of Kingston— ancient county-seat of King's County, & virtually unchanged since men in knee-breeches & periwigs congregated there for the assizes. The well-kept, centuried houses, the gigantic shade-trees, the venerable court building, & the quaint 1746 inn all remain as of yore to fascinate the beholder. And to think I had never seen this gem of antiquity before! On our way back Price got a typical R.I. Shore Dinner at the ancient fishing village of Pawtuxet (6 m. S. of

Prov.)—whilst I (whose loathing for sea-food you know) got something fit to eat at a Waldorf when we hit town.[3]

Wright turned down "Feigman's Beard"[4]—the Derleth tale based on Brobst's account. He would! And by the way—if you read any thing in the current W T, be on your guard against 2 bad & misleading misprints— "magical *love*" (should be LORE) on p. 92, & "*human* element" (should be KNOWN) on p. 107.[5]

Now about your story. It arrived during the "near-convention" here, & I brought it up toward the close of a spirited triangular session with both Price & Brobst on hand. Price read the text aloud, & critics were urged to interrupt with comments. I acted as secretary & set down all the opinions expressed. Most of the opinions came from Price himself—as you may see, since I am enclosing my secretarial records with the MS. Hope you can interpret the hastily jotted comment. The session had to break up before we could cover more than 9 or 10 pages (for every point raised brought with it numerous time-consuming side-issues), but in finishing the MS. alone I continued a series of comments which I will append. I hope you won't find the criticisms excessively drastic. Price is quite a carper, & brought up all sorts of minute matters (as you will see) which would never have occurred to me at all. However, I agree with many of his observations. Of course, he realised that this is a *first story*, hence did not mean his pointers to be taken as actual derogation.

As for a general personal estimate of my own—I think that there is damned good stuff in this story, & that with a few changes it ought to have a chance with Wright. The chief fault, perhaps, is a sort of *diffuseness* & excessive length, coupled with a jaunty, 1890-ish style of unmistakable artificiality. I know that this style has been used for weird stuff—Wilde's "Dorian Gray", some of Machen's things, &c.—but really think it is a handicap rather than an asset for this purpose. It does not afford the dark *tenseness* necessary for a macabre theme. If I were you, I would first try to reduce the length of the whole tale by cutting down descriptions, reflections, conversations, whimsical character-touches, & suggestions of scholarship. Abandon the leisurely, conversational, clubroom tone, & let the tempo be feverish, brooding, & rapid. Better take Price's & Brobst's advice & make Hopkins less of a "pretty boy"—that kind of thing savours of Yellow-Book affectation. Also—be less minute in describing the seven old-time philosophers—except, of course, von Hohenloe. Purely as a concession to professional taboos, you'll have to soft-pedal all references to bestiality or anything suggesting abnormal eroticism. Cheap editors draw a rigid deadline against anything of the kind. Also—go over the phraseology closely, & delete anything peculiarly savouring of naiveté. Price & I have pointed out certain passages apparently needing attention. Also—as implied above—kill the touches of "smartness", paradox, & other incongruous elements suggesting the Wilde tradition. Be more *direct* & *simple*.

Analysing more closely—*compression & simplicity* are the things wanted. Make less of Meininglake unless you change the plot & use him as a sort of agent of the long-dead sorcerer. Toward the end be very careful about incidents & climax. The intrusion of Hohenloe's personality & body (oddly enough, a theme I've used in a tale never exhibited or even typed[6]) must be managed with the most extreme care. I wouldn't have actual German over the telephone—be more subtle. When the major climax occurs—the transformation of the newly-shot body—there ought to be a greater impressiveness & intensity of style to register the stark, cataclysmic horror of the spectators—who are witnessing a violation of the basic laws of Nature as they know it.

Cut the post-climactic *explanations* as short as you can, for every word after the main punch tends to have a weakening effect. Try to make everything knit together with the utmost naturalness, closeness, & sense of inevitability. That is, let the motivation of everything seem so plausible as to admit of no question & cause no hesitation or perplexity on the reader's part. As it is, some of the threads seem a little loose or vague at the end. The matter of Meininglake's body & its return somehow carries a faint air of far-fetchedness.

But don't take all this as a "panning." It's a good story—extremely good for a *first* one—& all it needs is a bit of simplification & tightening up. The style shews great power & gracefulness despite the possible inappropriateness of the tone. It is mature, cultivated work, & bespeaks a mastery of your medium which will work to the highest advantage when the problem of tone-choosing is thoroughly worked out. Why not send the text to Derleth (either as it is, or after revision) & let him pull it to pieces? He will probably be as savage in his candour (judging from the way he lit on young J. Vernon Shea's work), but will beyond doubt have many helpful suggestions to offer. You have all the makings of success in the story field if you'll stick to it, exercise care, profit by experience, & refuse to be daunted by the critical observations of competent & unprejudiced readers.

Thanks very much for the privilege of reading the MS. I honestly enjoyed it, & hope that it may achieve ultimate publication—either in its present form or after a suitable course of condensation, simplification, & general strengthening.

Yesterday & today have been delightfully warm—94° yesterday afternoon—but prior to that there was a cold spell which nearly froze me. However, I have got my oil heater repaired, & am now prepared to combat the leering frost-daemon. Work—interrupted by my aunt's illness & by the festivities incidental to Price's visit—is piling up at an alarming rate—but none of it promises any appreciable profit. If I can ever dispose of current obligations I hope to get at some stories of my own—but the date of that disposition seems constantly to recede. Latterly (on warm & pleasant days) I've been doing my writing on Prospect Terrace—that place I shewed you (off Congdon St.) where there is a wide westward view of the lower town & of the bordering hills beyond.

Your bookbuying self-denial is surely commendable. Recently I found a bookshop with certain items priced at *2 for 5¢*. For a single thin dime I procured 2 American histories, a copy of Bulwer-Lytton's "Coming Race", & an edition of Smith's "Student's Gibbon"—all in very fair condition! My new shelves will soon be sadly overtaxed!

Best wishes, & hope you'll find the enclosed critical remarks helpful—

Yr most ob^t h^ble Servt—

H P L

Notes

1. See E. Hoffmann Price, "The Man Who Was Lovecraft," in *Lovecraft Remembered,* ed. Peter Cannon (Sauk City, WI: Arkham House, 1998), 292–93.

2. Hannah Robinson (1746–1773) liked to gaze out at Narragansett Bay from a large boulder at Tower Hill Road in South Kingston, RI. She had eloped with her teacher, Peter Simon, whom her father had forbidden her to see, and they reconciled over the matter only after Hannah had become deathly ill.

3. Ibid., 284.

4. *WT,* November 1934.

5. HPL refers to errors in "The Dreams in the Witch House" (*WT,* July 1934).

6. *The Case of Charles Dexter Ward.*

[28]   [ALS]

66 College St.,

Providence, R.I.,

July 13, 1933

My dear Strauch:—

Glad the returned MS. & critical notes safely reached you—& that the ruthless carping of the Terrible Three did not seem too savage & sadistic after due digestion. I strongly advise you to let Comte d'Erlette see the MS.—although his type of comment may make you see red for a while. As I possibly mentioned—his critical candour seems to have scared off one youth who received a sample of it!

I shall be interested in seeing any later forms which the story may take. The locale is really of rather minor interest—that is, it does not matter much where the setting is, since the real punch is all in the *events* & antique background. However, if you had it in the Pa.-German region you ought to introduce some thread of continuity between the old philosophers & the present scene—some family legend from Germany handed down through successive generations. In later tales, of course, it would be a good idea to use Pa. folklore as a main theme & background. It seems to me that you have made a splendid beginning in fiction, & I have no doubt but that after a few experiments you will produce notable results. In the course of time—after you have applied all the finishing touches of revision that you wish—I hope to see your novel.

Glad the material from Klarkash-Ton duly arrived. "The Willow Landscape" surely is a delightful prose-poem. My own favourites in the brochure seem to be "The Maze of the Enchanter", "A Night in Malneant", & "The Double Shadow." I was interested in your reaction to Smith's very early "Star-Treader"—which coincides with that of many readers. There certainly is a somewhat noticeable emphasis on the rhetorical element, & a devotion to long & bizarre words which mars the directness & simplicity necessary for utmost poignancy. If Smith has any conscious poetic model it is probably George Sterling, whose friend & protege he was. Sterling's "Wine of Wizardry" mood & manner really form the keynote of the poetic Klarkash-Ton. In our group, opinions on C A S's poetry differ amusingly. Wandrei exalts it to an almost amusing degree,[1] & Long is not far behind. Others have almost no use for it. I value it highly, though conceding certain obvious limitations. C A S would be delighted to see any poems of yours—as would I. I shall be awaiting that group including the "Epistle to the World."

No—I haven't seen the Frost magazine,[2] though I have heard many glowingly favourable references to it. I'd certainly be grateful for a glimpse of the July number. These sheets vary greatly in their standards. I don't pretend to keep track of them, but the best I've seen lately is *The Carillon.* I'm sure that Parker couldn't possibly be offended by your comment. He is a rotten correspondent—indeed, I don't think I've heard from him since my visit nearly a year ago! Cook, though, carries news & greetings betwixt us. Parker tries to maintain a fairly decent standard of poetry, though not one of supreme rigorousness. His own taste has improved spectacularly since he first launched the magazine a decade ago.

Brobst was over the other day while I was out—I regretted missing him. I'll give him your greetings when I see him. Last week he was all agog for that record-breaking letter you promised! My aunt sat up yesterday for the first time, & will repeat the process each day. The cast, though, can't come off for a fortnight.

Hope the "Witch-House" won't disappoint you. In the same issue, "The Horror in the Museum"[3] is largely of my workmanship. Glad that others around your way like my stuff. Don't know when I can produce anything more, for my whole programme is shot to hell just now.

Cold weather lately—but my repaired oil stove helps matters. Long & his parents may stop here in a week or so on their way to Onset, Mass. And we shall be looking for you in September.

Regards—

H P L

Notes

1. See Donald Wandrei, "The Emperor of Dreams," *Overland Monthly* (December 1926); rpt. *Klarkash-Ton: The Journal of Smith Studies* No. 1 (1988): 3–8, 25.

2. *American Poetry Journal,* edited by Frances Frost.

3. Ostensibly by Hazel Heald (ghostwritten by HPL).

[29]   [ANS][1]

[Postmarked Providence, R.I.,

15 August 1933]

Glad to hear that all is well in the Lehigh Valley—as, indeed, a recent traveller thither has just reported. Too bad the good old Saint (in whom, I understand, the Great Powers of Muhlenburg implicitly believe) has been dragged into the black void by the emissaries of Tsathoggua! ¶ Glad you liked the W T stuff— has Contemplation been egging you on to the creation of similar material? ¶ Last week I had a letter from the Knopf outfit asking to see some of my stuff with a view to possible book publication. *Possible* is good! I shot along a few items[2]—though previous disillusionments have taught me how little such requests really mean. ¶ Hope to see you around these Plantations before autumn sets in. Have seen Brobst twice since his return. ¶ Blessings of Yog-Sothoth—H P L

Notes

1. *Front:* Betsy Williams Cottage, Roger Williams Park, Providence, R.I.

2. HPL submitted "The Picture in the House," "The Music of Erich Zann," "The Rats in the Walls," "The Strange High House in the Mist," "Pickman's Model," "The Colour out of Space," and "The Dunwich Horror" in his letter to Allan G. Ullman of Knopf dated 3 August 1933. With a subsequent letter (16 August) HPL submitted another eighteen stories.

Graduation Picture of Lee McBride White from the John Herbert Phillips High School, Birmingham, Alabama, 1933

Letters to Lee McBride White

[1]   [Letter non-extant.]

[2]   [ALS]

10 Barnes St.,
Providence, R.I.,
Septr. 12, 1932

Dear Mr. White:—

I found yours of the 3ᵈ awaiting me upon my return from a combined eclipse expedition & antiquarian pilgrimage to points north of here.[1] The eclipse was highly impressive as seen from Newburyport, Mass. (a picturesque & ancient town well within the zone of totality), & I afterward visited Montreal & Quebec[2]—the latter being perhaps the most delightful 18ᵗʰ century survival on this continent with the possible exception of Charleston, S.C. When in the Boston zone I did not fail to visit my favourite seaport village of Marblehead—which remains today much as it was two centuries ago, & which is the prototype of the "Kingsport" mentioned in my tales. I think I told you that I am a confirmed amateur antiquarian whose chief delight is to visit places where reliques of the past survive.

I am glad you agree with me regarding Poe, especially the merit of "Silence—A Fable", which I have long considered notable both as a piece of visual imagery & as a triumph of musical language; Poe has influenced me since early youth—& probably continues to do so more than any other one author. I first came across Dunsany in 1919, & was prodigiously influenced by him—more, really, than I ought to have been; since my own tales became almost imitative of his during the next six or seven years. Now, however, I am trying to be more independent in style.

Baudelaire is certainly a titanic figure, & has greatly influenced Clark Ashton Smith, whose magazine work you doubtless know. Smith has vividly translated Baudelaire, though the translations are still unpublished except for minor items.[3]

Yes—Aristophanes is surely an important figure; & Petronius & Apuleius are permanent enough, though on a somewhat minor level. Among the cheaper modern writers A. Merritt is surely one of the most distinctive—his "Moon Pool" in its original version being almost a landmark of weird magazine fiction. I have never read the famous "Justine" of de Sade, or the equally

353

famous "Venus in Furs" of von Masoch. Both are undoubtedly significant in the history of psychology, though perhaps less so as works of art. Probably they can be obtained at any time from dealers in so-called "curiosa" like the Falstaff Press or Esoterika Biblion of New York. I have read parts of "Maldoror",[4] which is certainly a triumph of impassioned chaos—exceeding even Rimbaud's Bateau Ivre[5] in delirious intensity. I don't know where a copy would be obtainable—indeed, I have forgotten where I saw the extracts I did. "Marpessa" is by the late Stephen Phillips,[6] (author of "Herod") & ought to be obtainable without difficulty at any public library.

I'll send you a copy of "At the Mts. of Madness" very shortly—also any other tales of mine which you may wish to see. Enclosed is a list of my various attempts on which you can check, in pencil, the items that interest you. Some of them, though, are rather crude & poor. I wish you the best of luck in your own literary ventures, & would be interested to see some of your work. Your activities at the camp must have been pleasant & piquant indeed.

Just now I am expecting a visit from Donald Wandrei, whose weird tales & verses you have doubtless seen in various magazines.[7] He has a great deal of unpublished material, including a weird novel—"Dead Titans Waken".

With all good wishes,

Yrs most cordially & sincerely,

H. P. Lovecraft

Notes

1. HPL and W. Paul Cook had gone to Newburyport on 31 August to see the solar eclipse (see *SL* 4.63).

2. HPL visited Quebec on 2–6 September; it was his second trip to Quebec (the first was in 1930), and his first trip to Montreal.

3. Smith translated nearly all the poems in Charles Baudelaire's *Les Fleurs du mal* (most poems remaining only in preliminary literal prose translations), but few of his verse translations appeared in print, most notably in his column in the *Auburn Journal* and in *Sandalwood* (1925). The translations were first published in their entirety in Smith's *Complete Poetry and Translations,* Vol. 3 (New York: Hippocampus Press, 2007).

4. Comte de Lautréamont (1846–1870) [pseud. of Isidore Ducasse], *Les Chants de Maldoror* (1868).

5. Arthur Rimbaud (1854–1891), "Le Bateau ivre" ["The Drunken Boat"]. HPL owned Edgell Rickword's *Rimbaud, the Boy and the Poet* (1924; *LL* 735).

6. Stephen Phillips (1868–1915), *Marpessa* (1900); a poem. The drama *Herod* was also published in 1900.

7. Wandrei visited HPL in mid-September 1932 (see *SL* 4.68–69).

[3]   [ALS]

66 College St.,
Providence, R.I.
May 31, 1935.

Dear Mr. White:—

Very good to hear from you again! Your story is interest-
ing & well-written, & seems to me to indicate marked promise for a fictional
career. You have a vivid way of putting things, & a flow of words bespeaking
competence & assurance. There is, too, a sense of drama & of climax which
augurs well. Later on perhaps you will choose to emphasise modern technique a little less, & to substitute more ordinary phases of life for the extremely dramatic moments here represented—but the best course to follow is
that of natural evolution. You are certainly started splendidly—& perhaps the
newspaper columning will prove a benefit in the end, because of the training
it gives in observation & narrative values. Your extensive reading is all in the
right direction—& I trust that the general college curriculum has not been
quite so barren of benefit as you may at the moment assume.

Your impressions of Shakespeare are not far from those which I have entertained at various times. Ultimately, though, one has to concede the bard's
vast superiority as a whole over any of his contemporaries. He had a breadth
& insight—& a tremendously apt mode of characterisation—which none of
the others could parallel. Of course he was very uneven, so that many dull &
mediocre passages can be found in his works. Some of his plays are undeniably less effective than various single plays of others. But in spite of all this, a
general survey of his achievements will easily demonstrate his superiority. The
idolatry given him during the 19th century was perhaps excessive—but after
all allowances are made, he remains clearly the premier reflector of human
nature so far as our civilisation is concerned.

D. H. Lawrence, on the other hand, is almost certainly overrated at present. He had, of course, great power—but his fame was fortuitously boosted
by the fact that he was a biassed neurotic in an age generally permeated by the
same neurosis.[1]

I have seen reviews—all favourable—of the work of Howell Vines,[2] but
have not yet read any of his books. I surely must repair this omission before
long. Most of the vital writing in America seems to come from the South
nowadays—a condition which I think will increase rather than decrease. A
settled, homogeneous people has much to say & generally says it powerfully.

I think you have Swinburne sized up about right. He tried to make a few
inches go a long way—& really got by largely because of his matchless melody, & because of the fatuous Victorian notions from which he was luckily
free. Henry James was assuredly solid, but I can't bring myself to like him intensely. His care in expressing precise states of mood & meaning often becomes fumbling & old-maidish—& he had an unfortunate habit of confining

his attention to certain very artificial (& basically not very significant) human types. I haven't read much of Aldous Huxley, since literary "smartness" does not appeal to me. That kind of writing seems to involve values & perspectives of very doubtful reality or permanence. However, I'll admit that Aldous is an arresting social thinker when he chooses to be. Accurate thinking runs in the family![3]

I have not read "Ulysses", but believe that the *principle* of the stream-of-consciousness method is a valuable one—destined to influence fiction in the future. However, I doubt its value as an exclusive method of narration.[4] It will probably work best when assimilated to the main stream of fiction—supplementing objective narration in places where thoughts or inner life are at variance with external manifestations. Hope your friend can put his novel across successfully—that kind of thing makes a good beginning even when one grows beyond it or builds upon it.

I liked George Meredith in youth, for he seemed to deal with real people & events—a refreshing contrast to the sentimental caricaturist Dickens, whose work I've always detested. Now I can see how essentially Victorian—how influenced by artificial & erroneous conceptions—Meredith was. But he did try to put serious psychology into fiction. Galsworthy I admire rather than relish. Bennett I don't care for. George Moore doesn't interest me greatly—though perhaps I haven't read his best specimens. Hardy strikes me as overrated—there is an underlying pomposity & sentimentality in him. The fact is, I don't think our race is very successful in fiction. The French are the real masters of that field—Balzac, Gautier, Flaubert, de Maupassant, Stendhal, Proust . . . Nobody can beat them unless it is in the 19th century Russians—Dostoievsky, Chekhov, Turgeniev—& they reflect a racial temper so unlike ours that we really have much difficulty in appraising them. On the whole, I believe that Balzac is the supreme novelist of western Europe. Many try to put Proust ahead of him today, but I believe Proust is too narrow in his field & too specialised—even abnormal—in his psychology to take first rank. Balzac hasn't yet met his match.

The drama certainly fills an important niche. I used to enjoy it vastly, though latterly pure narration seems to captivate me more. Acting is assuredly a major art—as creative in its way as composition. It has not, however, the infinite breadth & depth of composition—since it always involves the interpretation of what someone else has conceived & recorded. That is, unless one acts in one's own plays.

Your assistant editorship has undoubtedly been excellent practice, & I hope you'll remain in college & edit the magazine next year. Editing exercises one's literary judgment as few other things can do.

Clark Ashton Smith's address is *Box 385, Auburn, California*. I'm enclosing a circular of his brochure of fantastic stories—which I advise you very strongly to get if you haven't it already. He is easily the leader of all the writers in W T, & these stories (rejected by Wright) are better than any which have appeared in the magazine.

W T is pretty mediocre lately, though something passable appears now & then. So you saw that "Gates of the Silver Key"? I'll confess I don't think much of it—it doesn't represent any original impulse of mine, & tends to be artificial & mechanical. I simply can't collaborate successfully. Since then I have written two more stories, but have not sent them in for publication.[5] Wright has rejected my best things, & I doubt whether he has much more use for my work. There has been talk of a collection of my stories in book form—Derleth's publishers, Loring & Mussey, having asked to see my stuff[6]—but all this seems to be coming to nothing. By the way—did you see the little magazine devoted to the discussion of weird fiction—*The Fantasy Fan*—during its brief career (Sept. '33 to Feb. '35)? If not, I'll send you one or two issues of which I have duplicates. Another little publication of the same sort—*Fantasy Magazine*—carries my brief autobiography & portrait in its current issue.[7] And have you seen William Crawford's *Marvel Tales?* I can let you have a copy of that.

Hope you'll see New Orleans sooner or later—though as I may have said, I vastly prefer Charleston. Charleston is, in my opinion, the most delightful & fascinating city in the United States. Nowhere else had the mellow beauty of the past so completely survived. Other towns which I prefer to New Orleans are St. Augustine, Savannah, & Natchez. St. Augustine, with buildings going back to the 1570's & 1580's, is something utterly unique.

My trips since last writing you have included one to ancient Quebec in Aug.-Sept. 1933, & one to De Land, Florida (where I visited the young weird tale enthusiast R. H. Barlow for nearly 2 months) in May & June, 1934. On the latter trip I also stopped in Charleston, Savannah, St. Augustine, Richmond, Washington, Fredericksburg, Philadelphia, & N.Y. It is possible that I shall visit Barlow again very shortly, though straitened finances will cut down intermediate stops. In Sept. 1934 I visited the island of Nantucket (only 90 miles from here) for the first time in my life, & found it an infinitely quaint & unspoiled survival of New England whaling days. Around New Year's I visited Long in New York, & met several others of the weird group—including Barlow, who was up from the South. The present spring has been an atrociously late one in the north, & I have had very few outings so far. Just now some real warmth seems to be coming—so that, even if I don't get to Florida, I can probably resume my open-air programme before long.

Well—again let me congratulate you upon your excellent story. Keep it up, & I'm sure you'll be able to do something serious in fiction. I suppose you know that Derleth is really getting into the literary world—making *Scribners* & the *Atlantic*,[8] & being about to have his 4th novel published.[9] Only 26 years old, too.

All good wishes—

Yrs most cordially,

H. P. Lovecraft

Notes

1. "Writers I'd call morbid are D. H. Lawrence & James Joyce, Huysmans & Baude-laire" (*SL* 3.155).

2. Howell Vines (1899–1981) of Alabama, author of *A River Goes with Heaven* (1930) and *This Green Thicket World* (1934).

3. HPL refers to Thomas Henry Huxley (1825–1895), biologist and philosopher, grandfather of Aldous Huxley (1894–1963) and his brother Sir Julian Sorell Huxley (1887–1975), biologist and humanist.

4. James Joyce's *Ulysses* (1922) was banned in the U.S. from its publication until 1933. HPL himself sparingly employed stream-of-consciousness techniques in accordance with this dictum, for example, in the closing paragraphs of "The Haunter of the Dark" (1935).

5. "The Thing on the Doorstep" (August 1933) and "The Shadow out of Time" (November? 1934–March 1935).

6. Cf. *SL* 5.111. The collection was rejected (*SL* 5.317).

7. Actually a biographical sketch by F. Lee Baldwin. The "portrait" is a linoleum cut by Duane W. Rimel.

8. August Derleth, "Crows Fly High," *Scribner's Magazine* 96, No. 6 (December 1934): 358–62; "Now Is the Time for All Good Men," *Scribner's Magazine* 98, No. 5 (November 1935): 295–98. For Derleth's appearance in the *Atlantic Monthly*, see LMW 6, n. 2.

9. *Place of Hawks* (actually a collection of novellas).

[4]   [ALS]

Ancient San Agustin—

August 20, 1935.

My dear White:—

As you may perceive, I am on my way at last! I accompanied the Barlows to Daytona & helped them settle in the flat they are to occupy for a fortnight. Then the diligencia for ancient San Agustin! It surely is good to see centuried gables & facades & balconies & garden walls—& hear the sound of tinkling fountains at twilight, & of cathedral chimes cast in 1682—after 2 months & 9 days of rural modernity! Am revelling in the atmosphere of a 370-year-old city—a city founded when Shakespeare was a year old, & still containing houses which had 40 years behind them when the first settlers landed at Jamestown. I'm staying a week—at my usual hotel, the cheap but cleanly Rio Vista on the bay front—& cutting my food bill down to a minimum. I spend most of my time absorbing ancient vistas & writing atop the

venerable fortress of San Marcos. Moving north at midnight August 25–6—
& will get 5 hours in Savannah before striking my beloved Charleston . . . the
most fascinating town of this continent (north of Mexico, at least) except
Quebec. Am so short of cash that my stay in Charleston will be badly cut
down—& hopes of stopping anywhere north of that grow dimmer & dimmer. However, it surely has been a great trip, all in all! I left home on the 5th
of June—& heaven knows how I'll get all the accumulated papers read up
upon my return!

Now about your story. Bless my soul, but you *are* arriving! Honestly, this
is a tremendous piece of work—with surprising fidelity to human nature, &
tremendous cleverness in manipulating turns of emotion. One of the best
touches is at the very *last*—where you disappoint the anticipations of the mediocre reader, who expects the hero to end it all in the river after his disillusionment. No charge for borrowing my sentiments toward the northern
winter, my preferences in Floridan zones, & my hateful task of revising bum
MSS.![1] The whole thing is natural without being tame, & is full of vividly original illustrative touches. The only change I could possibly suggest is a slight
toning-down of places where the quest for originality tends to torture idiom
into Euphuism, or to dictate obscure words (*geniculate, phantuscular, nemophily,*
&c.) which are really less effective than ordinary words because of their lack
of mellow associations. But these matters are trifles. The point is, that the story
is really powerful & admirable—a conclusive testimony of your writing ability. I
return it as per request—& with a goodly quota of thanks & admiration.

Regarding your "Saddypost" experiments—before you put great
amounts of time & energy into them, I wish you would read Edward J.
O'Brien's "Dance of the Machines", & the introductions to his various year-
books of the short story.[2] For the fact is, that this "slick" sort of story is really
very far from being authentic art—forming, rather, a mere artificial device to
gratify the expectations of an unreflective & un-analytical bourgeois public.
Plot, in the common sense of complex events artificially arranged to produce
certain clashes, interactions, & climaxes, is an utterly meretricious device unworthy of employment by any serious man of letters. It is a distortion—a
concoction of things without a counterpart in actual life. *Action* in the over-
speeded sense is closely akin. *Dialogue can* be an artistic medium of narration—but seldom is as employed by the popular commercial writers. The
trouble with Satevepost junk is that it simply follows an empty formula—
deliberately twisting, obscuring, & misrepresenting human values & motives.
It is clever but meaningless. Certainly, it is hard enough to write—but it is
tragic that so much human energy & intelligence should be wasted on a frivolous & irrelevant object instead of going into actual aesthetic creation. However—don't let me preach!

Yes—I must get a look at "Lust for Life". "Ouroboros" is a favourite of
mine—I must look up Eddison's latest.[3] You size up "Jurgen"[4] pretty well—I

must pass that observation on to Barlow! As for a Bierce–Hearn resemblance—well, I suppose they did have a certain common stylistic element derived from 19ᵗʰ century journalism; but Hearn soon outstripped his contemporary in all the subtleties & musical graces of expression. No—I never heard of a book by Wallace Smith.[5] If he can write as well as he draws, his Mexican tales ought to be worth reading!

Congratulations on discovering a source of old magazines! I'm telling Barlow about it—he has files of *Argosy, Cavalier,* &c. which he might possibly commission you to fill out. Yes—I *do* very much want extra copies of my tales for lending purposes, & will empower you to pick up any that don't cost too much. Just now, however, I'm so broke that I wouldn't dare contract a bill for a quarter! I'm eating on 20¢ to 25¢ per diem—with nickel cans of beans as a basis!

Fine weather so far in St. Augustine. I dread the plunge northward (Salzor[6] has nothing on me!), but shall at least have good furnace heat furnished within a month. Old bones need to be thawed out . . . today is my 45ᵗʰ birthday!

Thanks for permission to retain the cutting. I'm very glad to have a likeness of you for my private Hall of Fame!

All good wishes, & renewed congratulations on the excellence of your story—

      Yrs most sincerely—

        H P L

Notes

1. White had sent HPL another story in his letter of 17 August. He wrote therein, "I regret to say it is not what it was meant to be. I used your feeling for New England winter, and your liking for the central portion of Florida, which I hope you will not mind" (ms., JHL).

2. "Saddypost" refers to the *Saturday Evening Post;* HPL felt that the stories it published were trite and conventional. Edward J. O'Brien (1890–1941), *The Dance of the Machines;* see *SL* 3.32; 4.73, 91. O'Brien edited *The Best Short Stories of the Year* from 1915 to 1941.

3. *Lust for Life* is a fictionalized biography of Vincent van Gogh by Irving Stone. Eddison's "latest" was *Mistress of Mistresses: A Vision of Zimiamvia* (1935).

4. A novel by James Branch Cabell. The book was the subject of an obscenity trial in 1920. Cf. "The Omnipresent Philistine" (1924): "That censors actually do seek to remove . . . legitimate and essential matter, and that they would if given greater power do even greater harm, is plainly shewn by the futile action against *Jurgen,* and the present ban on *Ulysses,* both significant contributions to contemporary art" (*CE* 2.77).

5. Wallace Smith (1888–1937) was primarily an artist, illustrating, among many other things, Ben Hecht's *Fantazius Mallare* (1922). The reference is to Smith's *The Little Tigress: Tales out of the Dust of Mexico* (1923).

6. Possibly a character in the story by White mentioned earlier in this letter.

[5]   [ALS]

66 College St.,
Providence, R.I.,
Octr. 28, 1935

Dear White:—

Well—my total incarceration didn't begin so early as I feared it would, since the autumn has been distinctly above the average in warmth. Possibly I mentioned my visit near Boston Sept. 20–23, when my host & I took many delightful side-trips to places like rocky Nahant, ancient Marblehead, brooding, hilly Wilbraham [the "Dunwich" of my story], & sandy, willow-decked Cape Cod. On Oct. 8 I had a trip to New Haven—a place which I had never thoroughly explored before. Though not as rich in colonial antiquities as Providence, it has a peculiar fascination of its own—& I explored it quite thoroughly, seeing all the old houses, churches, college buildings, &c., & visiting 3 museums & 2 botanic gardens. The most impressive sights of all, perhaps, are the great new quadrangles of Yale University—each an absolutely perfect reproduction of old-time architecture & atmosphere, & forming a self-contained little world in itself. The Gothic courtyards transplant one in fancy to mediaeval Oxford or Cambridge—spires, oriels, pointed arches, mullioned windows, arcades with groined roofs, climbing ivy, sundials, lawns, gardens, vine-clad walls & flagstoned walks—everything to give the young occupants that massed impression of their accumulated cultural heritage which they might obtain in Old England itself. To stroll through these quadrangles in the golden afternoon sunlight; at dusk, when the candles behind the diamond-paned casements flicker up one by one; or in the beams of a mellow Hunter's Moon;[1] is to walk bodily into an enchanted region of dream. It is the past & the ancient mother land brought magically to the present time & place. The choicest of these quadrangles is Calhoun College—named from the illustrious Carolinian[2] (whose grave in St. Philips churchyard, Charleston, I visited only 2 months ago), who was a graduate of Yale. Nor are the Georgian quadrangles less glamorous—each being a magical summoning-up of the world of two centuries ago. I wandered for hours through the limitless labyrinth of unexpected elder microcosms, & mourned the lack of further time. Certainly, I must visit New Haven again. But this was not all. On Oct. 16 my friend Samuel Loveman came on from New York, & we proceeded at once to Boston to absorb books, museums, & antiquities. Stayed 3 days, & had a very enjoyable time. It is just possible that I shall have one trip more—a ride over the Mohawk Trail & just into Vermont in a friend's[3] well-heated Chevrolet—but I'm not counting heavily on that.

Congratulations on your notable record of academic attendance—a record which I hope will not soon be marred! Your studies sound interesting & congenial, & I'd like to see that Gothick tale essay of yours some day. If you have a spare copy, I'll wager young Barlow would be eager to use it in his amateur paper, *The Dragon-Fly*.[4] Have you, by the way, received a copy of this latter? If not, I'll try to induce the editor to send you one. A very high-grade venture despite a trifle of mechanical crudity.

Glad your musical library is growing, & hope the radio will soon be restored to working order. I prefer silence for reading or writing of any kind, but can imagine how some might find a melodic accompaniment agreeable. Glad also that you have had opportunities for choreographic observation. I can't appreciate the dance, but realise that it has a secure place among the arts. Sorry you were disappointed in the cinematic "Anna Karenina"—a production I have not seen.[5] Glad *Marvel Tales* was of some interest. "Sarnath" is an old story—written in 1919—& differs vastly from any of my recent efforts. It shews the Dunsany influence to a marked extent.

Coming to my overcrowded programme, I have read very little this autumn—though a formidable pile of borrowed books still adorns my library table. What I'm going to tackle now—after I wade through Derleth's new detective novel[6] & tell him what I think of it—is the Wells–Huxley "Science of Life"—a really important contribution to the popular understanding of biology, if critics report aright. Your own reading sounds very sensible & solid—& I want to get hold of "The Shape of Things to Come" some day. Sorry H G is trying cheap tricks to attract attention—& he doesn't need to! The place of Wells in pure literature is distinctly problematical. As a *thinker* he is unsurpassed—but most of his works lack a certain imaginative convincingness. They are too didactic—remaining as abstract intellectual problems instead of coming alive. I read "Anthony Adverse" a year or two ago.[7] An excellent panoramic glimpse of the late 18th century, though full of curious drawbacks such as the childish overworking of coincidence, the excessive plastering on of sentimentality & naively obtrusive philosophising, the primitive acceptance of the idea of "fate", & a general slowing-up & letdown during the final third—after the passage of the Alps & entry into France.

Good luck with your stories—& hope the novel will eventually surpass your present expectations. I've never tried a full-length novel, though some of my stuff reaches "novelette" length. The much-rejected "Mountains of Madness" comes to about 38,000 words.[8]

W T is rather lousy of late. In the Sept. issue "Vulthoom" & "Shambler from the Stars" barely save it from being a total loss, while "Cold Grey God" & "Last Guest" perform a similar service for the Oct. number.[9] In one of the Sept. stories the author spoke of New Orleans as a full-fledged city—cathedral & all—in *1720,* whereas of course the site was scarcely cleared at that early date.[10] As for the covers—I never yet saw one that was worth the coloured inks expended on it. Of course the luscious & irrelevant nudes are rabble-catchers & nothing else but—an attempt by Wright to attract two publics instead of one.[11] A similar attempt is represented by the ringing-in of cheap detective junk with a thin, pseudo-weird veneer. What will ever become of the magazine I'm hanged if I know! By the way—have you seen *The Phan-*

tagraph, published by one Wilson Shepherd of Oakman in your own state & edited by Donald A. Wollheim of 801 West End Ave., N.Y.C.? Crudely printed by William Crawford, but not so bad as to contents. It is endeavouring to take the place of the lamented *Fantasy Fan.*

Derleth has another detective novel out—"The Sign of Fear". Price is starting out on a motor trip to Mexico—& will visit Robert E. Howard en route. You'll be sorry to hear that Clark Ashton Smith's mother died Sept. 9—a not unexpected event, yet no less a blow on that account. W. Paul Cook has gone to St. Louis to engage in a neighbourhood newspaper venture.

I'm enclosing a circular & application blank of the National Amateur Press Association—an organisation which sometimes proves very helpful to the literary experimenter, & in which I've been active for 21 years. It is with this society that Barlow's *Dragon-Fly* is affiliated. Despite its occasional crude spots, I think you'd find membership very pleasant and encouraging, hence I hope you'll utilise the blank. I am now a verse critic in the association, & have just prepared my report for the official organ.[12]

All good wishes—

Yrs most cordially & sincerely,

H. P. Lovecraft

P.S. Just had word of the acceptance by *Astounding Stories* of my long novelette "At the Mountains of Madness", previously rejected by Wright. Don't know when it will appear.

Notes

1. The first full moon following the harvest moon, which is the full moon occurring nearest the autumnal equinox.

2. John C. Calhoun (1782–1850).

3. Edward H. Cole.

4. White's essay was not published in the *Dragon-Fly.*

5. *Anna Karenina* (MGM, 1935), directed by Clarence Brown; starring Greta Garbo, Fredric March, and Freddie Bartholomew.

6. *Sign of Fear.*

7. A best-selling novel by Hervey Allen.

8. HPL had submitted *At the Mountains of Madness* (1931) only to *WT.* By "much-rejected" he refers to the generally cold reception of the story by his correspondents.

9. *WT,* September 1935: CAS, "Vulthoom"; Robert Bloch, "The Shambler from the Stars"; *WT,* October 1935: C. L. Moore, "The Cold Gray God"; John Flanders, "The Mystery of the Last Guest."

10. Ethel Helene Coen, "One Chance."

11. Both covers were by Margaret Brundage (1900–1976). Her artwork was featured on virtually all covers of *WT* from mid-1933 through mid-1936.

12. "Some Current Amateur Verse," *National Amateur* 58, No. 2 (December 1935): 14–15.

[6]   [ALS]

66 College St.,
Providence, R.I.,
Dec. 20, 1935.

Dear White:—

Thanks for the congratulations—& you can double 'em if you like, for no sooner had the "Mts. of Madness" incident sunk into my consciousness than I was given a *second* pleasant surprise . . . . in the form of *another* cheque from Street & Smith. It seems that Donald Wandrei, to whom I had lent my newest novelette "The Shadow out of Time", had taken the liberty of submitting the MS. to *Astounding* without my knowledge—& through some inexplicable coincidence the editor was favourable again! This certainly was a life-saving windfall, & it is needless to say that I feel tremendously encouraged by the incident. I know that such "winning streaks" don't keep up—but the impression is pleasant while it lasts. This dual stroke gave me such a psychological boost that I've just written a new tale—a short specimen called "The Haunter of the Dark". From what I hear, the "Mts." will be a 3-part story in the February, March & April *Astounding*. I've no idea when the "Shadow" will appear.[1]

Yes—Derleth certainly is landing big! I must see his *Atlantic* piece.[2] It is very probable that Scribners will henceforward be his publishers, & that he will embark on a series of historical novels dealing with his native Wisconsin background. In preparation for this series he is conducting a course of antiquarian research which puts me to shame. He is going exhaustively over all the old records, newspapers, & diaries he can find in local files, libraries, & attics, & is hiring people to copy headlines & topics from the Milwaukee papers of 50 or 75 years ago. He means to know those times as intimately as if he had lived in them—& the result will be apparent when he comes to write the novels. Of all our group, Derleth is certainly making the greatest progress toward a solid place in literature.

Congratulations on the further *Quill* placements—you'll be giving Derleth a run for his money before long! Don't be discouraged because your present work fails to satisfy you. Every new effort is invaluable practice, & one by one you will overcome the various problems of composition. From what I have seen of your work, I'd tend to say that you are making an unusually good start—& the extent of your reading is also a favourable element.

Commiserations on the loss of your one first-rate professor![3] That surely is a blow—but with the start you have I fancy you'll be able to extract considerable from the course as it is. Meanwhile let me congratulate you upon securing material from Howell Vines. I simply must get hold of something of his—for he seems to be the sort of chap I respect . . . . a man who writes honestly, not "pleasantly", & who will not make himself trivial with the artificial, jack-in-the-box device called *plot!* I can sympathise with his inability to write when worried—& also with his perpetual brokeness! Poverty & anxiety certainly are—as he would say—the goddamdest sons of bitches!

You surely were lucky to get that haul of 16 records for 80¢! I can imagine what a boon the phonograph is to a discriminating music lover. In these latter years I fancy the instrument is acquiring a new dignity and status—becoming a fixture among persons who wish to hear particular selections at particular times, rather than an indiscriminative purveyor of jazz to the herd. The radio has largely absorbed the old-time army of *casual* phonograph-users.

Glad you have some new bookcases. Don't worry about the empty spaces—they'll fill up before you know it, so that a fresh problem of congestion will be on your hands. I keep getting new bookcases, but the volumes pile up & overflow despite all I can do. Nowadays I try to get the sort of cases which take the least space—plain, shallow ones which can be piled atop one another. The effect is that of mere shelving—but of course the cases can be *moved,* whereas shelving can't. I also have ancestral bookcases of a more pretentious sort, some of them with glass doors. One of the latter has its upper shelf reserved for curiosities—an Aztec image, an Egyptian ushabti,[4] a primitive African idol, & so on—a museum in miniature, as it were. I really need more space for this kind of thing, & wish I had a regular display case. Quaint, ancient, & exotic objects exercise a strong fascination upon me.

Your bibliothecal accessions strike me as very sensible on the whole. I seem to have read most of them—though oddly enough, I've never read Rabelais! Incidentally, I lost my copy of "Sartor Resartus"[5] when moving into #66—don't know where it slipped to, but it was the only missing item when the great rearrangement was completed. "Peter Schlemiel"[6] disappointed me when I read it a decade ago. It had been very strongly recommended, but I found it curiously flat. On the other hand, I'm an enthusiastic "Undine"[7] fan. I can understand the fascination exerted upon you by the pictures in historical manuals. They have always charmed me, & I could point to dozens which seem to open gates into a magical world of the past. A couple of years ago I found a marvellous set of 10¢ books at Woolworth's—*all* pictures, but covering British history from neolithic times to the present in considerable detail.[8] Everything illustrated—events, persons, architecture, landscape, costume, articles in common use—a veritable pictorial museum. It would be a marvellous aid if one were composing a story with a bygone setting. It is indeed seldom that we can capture from our youthful fairy-tale reading the same thrill that we derived when 4 or 5 years old—although I'll confess that the Arabian Nights (Andrew Lang's edition)[9] still gives me a kick. What duplicates best the glamour & adventurous expectancy of juvenile reading in my case is *Dunsany*. "A Dreamer's Tales", when I discovered them at the age of 29, gave me precisely the same feeling that Lang's Arabian Nights did when I was 5. Proust is certainly solid & important—the greatest figure, without question, of the early 20th century. I've read "Swann's Way" & "Within a Budding Grove", & mean to go through the whole series some day.[10] It certainly forms a rich & vivid picture of an age—or one angle of an age. You are certainly right in believing that one should know the standard older authors—must have, that is, a sympathetic understanding of the whole literary stream which has moulded our perspective & modes of expression—in order to write intelligently & well. One of the unfortunate things about the present age is its plethora of raw, crude books—things written without background or grace, & with the superficial, fumbling diction of the ignorant & traditionless.

Glad you had an opportunity to see Cornelia Otis Skinner[11]—who is now in Providence, & of whose work my late elder aunt was especially fond. Her father was certainly a great old boy—I recall him in such things as "Kismet". He must be getting toward 80 now, but is still active in many ways. Not long ago I read an article of his—either in *Harpers* or the *Atlantic*.[12] I never saw a performance of Miss Skinner's, since I am curiously unappreciative of dramatic readings. I require a full cast and scenery to get my imagination really working. In late years my interest in drama has greatly waned, & I see very few cinemas. Like you, I deplore the inability of cinema performers to sink themselves in their parts. I agree concerning the merits of Charles Laughton, whom I have seen as Nero, Henry VIII, Dr. Moreau, Edward Moulton-Barrett, & Inspector Javert.[13] His Henry was surely magnificent, & his Nero scarcely less distinctive in its way. Speaking of Nero & books about him—have you read "The Bloody Poet", by Desider Kostolanyi, which was published 7 or 8 years ago? It got at the frustrated artist side of the poor old scab rather well. Further anent the theatre—I heard a pretty good lecture on the recent work of Shaw by the critic Bonamy Dobrée the other night. Also was invited to see the Le Gallienne repertory company last month—in two clever & surprisingly traditional comedies by the brothers Quintero. Smooth but undistinguished. They had "Rosmersholm"[14] the next night, which I'd a damn sight rather have seen. Just my luck to get invited to the wrong show!

Hope the Frentz performance didn't disappoint you. My aunt went to hear Kreisler the other night, but I didn't.

No especial events hereabouts—& winter is obviously at hand. 5-inch snow Nov. 23—earliest in the history of the local weather bureau. I am reading the Wells-Huxley biological outline—"The Science of Life"—& find it a truly monumental piece of popular exposition. ¶ All good wishes—

Merry Christmas & Happy New Year—Yrs most cordially—

H P L

Notes

1. *Astounding* paid HPL a total of $630 for the two stories, $350 (less $35 commission to Julius Schwartz) for *At the Mountains of Madness* and $280 for "The Shadow out of Time" (June 1936).

2. August Derleth, "The Alphabet Begins with AAA," *Atlantic Monthly* 156, No. 6 (December 1935): 734–39.

3. August H. Mason.

4. A gift from Samuel Loveman (see *SL* 4.347).

5. By Thomas Carlyle. An edition was found in HPL's library.

6. Adelbert von Chamisso (1781–1838), *Peter Schlemihls wundersame Geschichte* (1814); tr. as *Peter Schlemihl.* The novel was mentioned in the original version of "Supernatural Horror in Literature" (*Recluse,* 1927), where HPL says of it: "[It] tells of a man who lost his own shadow as the consequence of a misdeed, and of the strange developments that resulted."

7. A weird tale by La Motte-Fouqué.

8. HPL owned six picture books published in 1935 by C. W. Airne by Sankey, Hudson, & Co. of Manchester.

9. The book was given to HPL by his mother on Christmas 1898.

10. HPL never read the final four novels of *A Remembrance of Things Past.*

11. Cornelia Otis Skinner (1901–1979), actress and author of several books of humor.

12. Otis Skinner, "Sneak Music," *Harper's* 171, No. 6 (November 1935): 748–53.

13. HPL refers to several movies starring Charles Laughton (1899–1962): *The Sign of the Cross* (1932), *The Private Life of Henry VIII* (1933), *Island of Lost Souls* (1933), *The Barretts of Wimpole Street* (1934), and *Les Misérables* (1935).

14. Henrik Ibsen (1828–1906), *Rosmersholm* (1885–86; first American production 1904). HPL saw *A Sunny Morning* (one-act play) and *The Women Have Their Way* (two-act play) by Serafin and Joaquin Alvarez Quintero, starring Eva Le Gallienne.

[7]   [ALS]

66 College St.,
Providence, R.I.,
Feby. 10, 1936

Dear White:—

My tardiness in acknowledging yours of Jany. 9 & the interesting issue of *The Quill* springs from an unfortunate combination of circumstances. First I was crowded to the breaking-point with an accumulation of more tasks than I could possibly perform, & then came down with an attack of grippe—which leaves me still rather shaky & easily fatigued. I am surrounded by mountains of unanswered mail, & have had to shelve or transfer many labours which I ought to perform. Therefore besides being late, this epistle may likewise be very disjointed, stupid, & inadequate.

I enjoyed the *Howard Quill*[1] very much—& can scarcely recall seeing a better student publication. The proportion of really vital & well-written material is surprisingly high, & I certainly congratulate all connected with it. The cover, too, is very harmonious in design & colour. I was very glad to get a first glimpse of Howell Vines's work, & enjoyed his closeness to the atmosphere & folklore of his native soil.[2] That is what important novels grow out of. "Leonard Clintstock"[3] also rings true—while "So South the South"[4] very justly points out an especially irritating phase of popular literary hokum. "Michaely"[5] overdoes ultra-modern mannerisms a trifle, but the author shews that he has an ample fund of images for soberer use later on. Your own story[6] is an excellent psychological study—a bit highly coloured, perhaps, but full of the insight which distinguishes the sincere fiction writer. The verse in the magazine includes some splendid stuff—your departing preceptor Mason being especially powerful.[7] As you say, "Shakespeare's Father"[8] is highly unusual—indeed, all the verse seems to reach a gratifyingly high level. Your brief columnar lines are very clever![9] Thanks immensely for this delightful glimpse of contemporary university journalism. Hope you'll do equally well with the future issues—in all of which I wish you the very best of luck.

Your latest bibliothecal additions seem to be as well-chosen as the earlier ones—including several which I lack, & 3 or 4 which I've never read. Before long your walls will consist mostly of shelves! Glad you have read "Seven Pillars of Wisdom"[10]—I must some day. I became acquainted with "The Decline of the West"[11] just a decade ago, & believe it is one of the most important books of the century. There is certainly a great deal of truth behind Spengler's central theses—that agricultural cultures are healthier than industrial-commercial cultures, that cultures have or tend to have a natural rise, summit, & decline, & that our existing civilisation is on the down-grade. Mixed with the truth is a great deal of extravagance—as in the attempt to treat a culture as a typical biological organism—but this is characteristic of all philosophic systems. As you remark, the amount of massed erudition which Spengler puts into his work is almost bewildering. Many an ordinarily well-educated man rises from a perusal of "The Decline of the West" with a feeling of helpless ignorance & scholastic humility!

Your postscript[12] puts me in rather a difficult position, since I am a most emphatic opponent of the critical attitude it embodies. I have, however, tried to comment (on the other sheet) as best I can—at least explaining my own position, which you will probably deem absurd. My notes on—& tentative changes in—your really excellent poem must be regarded only in the light of suggestions—to be put aside, no doubt, as the biassed dodderings of fossilised & unreceptive old age. They at least illustrate a point of view—& may or may not prove vaguely helpful in one way or another.

Speaking of poetry—here's an advertisement listing the collected verse of my friend Samuel Loveman, published last month. You would probably consider the verse reprehensibly traditional & classical, but I regard it as great stuff. Loveman knows—or at least used to know—your fellow-Donnite Allen Tate.

Glad you had a pleasant Yuletide. We had a *tree* here—giving quite a momentary illusion of restored childhood. Around New Year's I visited Long in N.Y.—seeing most of the old group & meeting a number of science-fiction authors (Arthur J. Burks, Otto Binder, &c.) who were new to me. We had several gatherings at various places, & I attended a dinner of the Am. Fiction Guild—where I saw good old Seabury Quinn for the first time since 1931. Long, Morton, Loveman, Talman, Kline, Kleiner, the two Wandrei boys, Leeds, Sterling, Kirk, &c. &c. (some names may be known to you, others not) were on deck, & weird literature received quite a bit of discussion. Fortunately the weather was not as cold as it has since been, & I was not feeling quite as run down.

On two occasions I visited the new Hayden Planetarium of the Am. Museum of Natural History, & found it a highly impressive device. It consists of a round, domed building of 2 storeys, joined at one point to the museum edifice. On the lower floor is a circular hall whose ceiling is a gigantic orrery—shewing the planets revolving around the sun at their proper relative speeds. Above it is another circular hall whose roof is the great dome, & whose edge is made to represent the horizon of N.Y. as seen from Central Park. In the middle of this upper hall is a projector which casts on the concave dome a perfect image of the sky—capable of duplicating the natural apparent motions of the celestial vault, & of depicting the heavens as seen at any hour, in any season, from any latitude, & at any period of history. Other parts of the projector can cast suitably moveable images of the sun, moon, & planets, & diagrammatic arrows & circles for explanatory purposes. The effect is infinitely lifelike—as if one were outdoors beneath the sky. Lectures—different each month (I heard both Dec. & Jan. ones)—are given in connexion with the apparatus. In the annular corridors on each floor are niches containing typical astronomical instruments of all ages—telescopes, transits, celestial globes, armillary spheres, &c.—& cases to display books, meteorites, & other miscellany. Astronomical pictures line the walls, & at the desk may be obtained useful pamphlets, books, planispheres, &c. The institution holds classes in elementary astronomy, & sponsors clubs of amateur observers. Altogether, it is the most complete & active popular astronomical centre imaginable. It seems to be crowded at all hours, attesting a public interest in astronomy which did not exist when I was young.

The latter half of the winter is proving wretchedly cold & snowy hereabouts (I haven't been out of the house since Jany. 13), & believe that even our generally milder region has suffered somewhat from the universal chill. It surely cheers me to realise that the vernal equinox will be reached in a month & ten days!

All good wishes, & thanks again for the *Quill* which speaks so well for your editorship!

Yrs most sincerely—

H P L

[P.S.] As an anti-Donnite I fear I can't be of much real help regarding your verses—but I can at least offer a few concrete suggestions—probably to be rejected at once as the quaint mouthings of an archaic fogy. ¶ In the first place, I think you have rather outdone Donne—or out-Donned Donne!—in deliberate ruggedness. His lines always retained some resemblance to the metres from which they diverged—& I can't recall that he carried his principles into blank verse—which always needs greater regularity. ¶ Secondly, it seems to me you have gone too far in the use of technical & prosaic terms (infra &c.)—a characteristic fault of this age. In trying to offer suggestions for improvement, I have endeavoured not to alter the general atmosphere of the poem—which is really excellent. Because of the blank verse medium, I have felt obliged to make the lines closer to iambic pentameter, & in one or two places I have straightened out diction which seemed to me wilfully & unmotivatedly (& therefore inartistically) obscure or inverted. I may have bungled everything—but here are the suggestions to heed or reject at will.

> Not sweet, this man: more he implacable:
> Unreconciled to sugar of Shakspere,
> Or music of the mighty-lined Marlowe
> Combined of rare components, he remained
> Supple, infrangible, with prism-perception
> Of a vast world and of himself in it.
> Below, above, beyond, this man; his view
> Wide, metasensual; his rugged words
> Dimensioned by mind, soul, body—bound
> By four stern walls of closely coffined space.
> All shining metal, this man's leaping verse—
> The mercury of fluid lyric love
> Silver of resonant God-pointing hymn,
> Rough ore of youthful satire, grating harsh. . . .
> Nor ever sags the bold arc of his flight:
> A force centrifugal keeps tautly strung
> The thin cool wires of subtle intellect.
> Of bright & sudden tangent-thought composed—
> This man, light-winged, eccentric of good things:
> Body of woman, mind of man, God's soul—

> Long time before his fire shall flicker out,
> Yet molder now the canons he defy'd.*

I approach this Donne business with much trepidation, since I am on the other side of the fence. While appreciating the depth, subtlety, & penetration of Dr. Donne, I cannot in any way endorse his manner & medium. He was not primarily a poet—but rather a thinker & minute analyser of human nature. Poetry must be simple, direct, non-intellectual, clothed in symbols & images rather than ideas & statements, & above all limpid & musical—& employing the familiar, traditional words which have had a chance to pick up centuries of half-latent overtones & associations. If it isn't all this—or largely so—it simply isn't poetry. It is prose—psychological analysis, philosophy, or what have you—masquerading as poetry but using the appeal & channels of prose. Wilde knew what he was talking about when he pulled that famous *mot*—"Meredith is a prose Browning, *& so was Browning*."[13] Donne was the typical product of a decadent age—the petering-out of Elisabethanism. He thought that the poets had said everything that could be said about anything—hence began to experiment with minute analyses & intellectual subtleties which are not really poetry at all. He transferred the atmosphere of the Euphuistic conceit to verse—& founded a whole school of rhyming metaphysicians whose cleverness was enormous, but whose products were not poetry. Of course there was poetic *feeling & material* in Donne, but his mode of embodying it & his manner of uttering it detracted enormously from its net force. There was no excuse—no real reason—for his harsh & careless diction. Some of his poems are great *in spite of it*, but none *because of it*. He simply neglected & rejected one of the most valuable adjuncts to poetic expression. Dryden (who admired him) once very sensibly spoke of the need of *translating Donne into English verse.*[14] For remember this always: harshness, obscurity, verbal inversion, far-fetched allusions, thin-spun conceits, &c. *never serve any useful end in themselves*. They are a dead weight to be carried by the poetry unfortunate enough to possess them. Donne was on the wrong track—Shakespeare, Milton, Shelley, & Keats on the right track. Irrespective of temporary fashions cropping up in ages akin to Donne's own in decadence, this is what posterity has confirmed & always will confirm in the long run. You'll live to see the truth reaffirmed—for good taste generally comes back in the end.

I am fully aware of Donne's present wave of popularity—whose beginning 20 years ago interested me greatly.[15] Undoubtedly the restless, unpoetic, over-analytical taste of this jaded & bewildered age—an age upset by the fall of its hereditary illusions through scientific discovery, the reorganisation of its ways of life through mechanical development, & the threat of collapse inherent in its sociological maladjustment—finds a kindred voice in the old meta-

---

*A sentiment with which, in any permanent sense, I basically disagree!

physical poet—but that is the fault of the age rather than the virtue of the bard. This age is too scientific & intellectual to be aesthetic, & all the arts exhibit a pitiful sterility which no amount of radical experimentation & extravagance can conceal. Eliot confesses as much in his "Waste Land". I feel little hesitation in betting that the most recent trends in poetry represent a blind alley—to be rejected in another generation or two in favour of the main line. The wise man, I think, is the one least swayed by fashion. A slave to no one age, but an impartial surveyor of western aesthetics from the beginning.

Notes

1. *The Howard Quill* 8, No. 1 (Winter 1936), edited by Lee White.

2. Howell Vines wrote an article in the issue entitled "In a Novelist's Notebook" (pp. 1–4).

3. A story by Harold R. Dunnam (p. 8).

4. A story by Hugh Frank Smith (pp. 24–25).

5. A story by Morrison Wood (pp. 4–5).

6. "Out of Sorrow" (pp. 26–27).

7. August H. Mason, "Geography Is Good" (p. 21).

8. A poem by LeRoy Mooney (p. 9).

9. White had contributed a brief humorous poem, "Look at Your Thumb," in a section entitled "A Page for Woollcott" (p. 23).

10. By T. E. Lawrence.

11. By Oswald Spengler. HPL read the first volume no later than February 1927 (*SL* 2.103).

12. As a postscript to his letter of 9 January, White attached his untitled poem about John Donne:

> Not sweet, this man: more he implacable:
> Non-reconciled to sugar of Shakspere
> Music of Mighty-lined Marlowe
> Combined of rare component,
> Supple, infrangible, prism-perception
> Of a vast world and of himself in it.
> Infra-ultra, this man metasensual;
> Dimensioned by mind, soul, body
> Bound by four walls of coffins.
> All metal, verse of this man
> Mercury of fluid love lyric
> Silver of God-pointing hymn,
> Rough ore of youthful satire.
> Never sagged the arc of his flight:
> The centrifugal force keeps taut

The thin cool wires of intellect.
Of bright sudden tangent-thought this man
Eccentric of good things:
Body of woman, mind of man, soul of God:
Long time before flash of his fire shall be dying
Yet molders the canon of his defying.

[*In margin, HPL has written:*]
Don't drag in scientific jargon. Simplicity & directness are what make poetry.

See HPL's revised version in the postscript.

13. The statement is in the first section of Wilde's *The Critic as Artist* (1891). HPL quoted this in his "Preface" to John Ravenor Bullen's *White Fire* (Athol, MA: The Recluse Press, 1927), which he edited.

14. "Donne alone, of all our countrymen, had your talent; but was not happy enough to arrive at your versification; and were he translated into numbers, and English, he would yet be wanting in the dignity of expression." *Discourse concerning the Original and Progress of Satire* (1693).

15. The revival of interest in Donne can be traced to Edmund Gosse's *The Life and Letters of John Donne* (1899; 2 vols.).

[8]   [ALS]

66 College St.,
Providence, R.I.,
July 12, 1936

Dear White:—

Glad to hear from you again—though as the fates would have it, the last few months have been such a nightmare of ill health, congested work, & nervous exhaustion that I could hardly have done justice to an earlier letter had I received one. Even now I fear my reply will seem sadly sketchy & inadequate. I believe I was rather down with grippe when I wrote in February. That was only the beginning of 1936's disasters! My aunt soon developed a case infinitely worse than mine, so that I was at once reduced to the state of a combined nurse, secretary, butler, market-man & errand-boy. Later the patient had to go to the hospital—but since April 21 she has been back & is steadily recovering. I myself have been miserable. The cold spring kept my energies at a low ebb, & the hopelessly crowded state of my programme nearly reduced me to a nervous breakdown. My aunt's illness & financial complications made a vacation impossible—so that in general '36 has been a hell of a year so far! I did obtain a time-extension on the heaviest revision job, but am still uncertain about my ability to get it done.

Glad the novel-notes have been progressing well, & hope the magnum opus will be taking shape ere long. Congratulations on the library! One can get some excellent bargains in the second-hand shops if one knows just where to look. Most of the standard works of literature are to be found on 10¢ & 25¢ counters, so that even a very moderate sum will go a long way unless one is fastidious about the physical appearance of the volumes.

Regarding Donne—I trust I didn't do him an injustice in my remarks of last winter. His status is surely secure enough, but I was questioning the wisdom of using him too exclusively as a model & inspiration, as some of the moderns are inclined to do. Poetry, after all, must be essentially emotional & imaginative rather than intellectual; & I believe that some of the modernly despised "romantics" were far truer artists—using their medium in the way it was meant to be used—than any of the thinkers who have tried to write philosophy in verse.

I must read Vardis Fisher[1] & Thomas Wolfe some day—for they seem to be accepted as especially authentic voices of the present. Upholders of the genteel tradition accuse Fisher of "bad taste"—which probably means that he is a serious writer with something to say! By the way—your Communion verses are very clever!

Amidst the prevailing chaos my own reading has been very scant, & even now I am engulfed by tons of unread borrowed books. Recently I've perused two biographies of Roger Williams,[2] plus George Santayana's "Last Puritan"—the latter a splendid study of the moribund culture amidst which I grew up. Not a mere piece of cheap debunking—but a sympathetic study which praises strong points while shewing up weak points. In general, such a work as one would expect from the greatest living philosopher.

I hope you will find it possible to enter Princeton after your graduation. An academic career would, it seems to me, be admirably appropriate for one with your vital & spontaneous devotion to literature.

This has been a bad year for fantasy in general as well as for certain of its devotees—both M. R. James (aet 73) and George Allen England (aet 59) being on its recent necrology roll.[3] Most tragic of all from the standpoint of our little circle is the suicide of Robert E. Howard—who shot himself on June 11 when told that his mother would not recover from her illness. She died the next day without knowing of his act. The blow to his father—a physician—is terrific. His books will be given to his alma mater (Howard Payne College, Brownwood, Texas) as the nucleus of a Robert E. Howard Memorial Collection. Weird fiction's loss is irreparable—for no other popular magazine fantaisiste's work had half the zest & power & spontaneity of his. Poor old Two-Gun Bob!

All good wishes—

Yrs most cordially—

H P L

Notes

1. Vardis Fisher (1895–1968), prolific regional novelist.

2. Emily M. Easton, *Roger Williams, Prophet and Pioneer* (1930); James Ernst, *Roger Williams, New England Firebrand* (1932).

3. James died on 12 June 1936 (one day after Robert E. Howard), England on 26 June 1936.

[9]   [ALS]

Rock Bluff on the Edge of a Woodland
Tarn in the Forest of Quinsnicket, some 6
Miles North of 66 College Street., Prov. R.I.
—Oct. 15, 1936

Dear White:—

One of my last afternoon outings, with work & correspondence along in the inevitable black bag. Autumn closes down early in this subarctic zone, & tropical-constitution'd old gentleman can't enjoy sitting in the open very much after this time of year. Oh, to be in Charleston, now that autumn's here![1]

Glad you have been managing to have a reasonably good time despite minor worries & wearinesses. Don't mind occasional unproductive or even un-studious spells. The best of minds have to lie fallow now & then, & are all the better after their periods of restful idleness. Hope you're rid of asthmatic troubles—which, by the way, always bothered Ambrose Bierce.

Things hereabouts go much as usual. Barlow left for the west Sept. 1st,[2] pausing in N Y to see Long, Howard Wandrei, & others of the weird fiction group, & calling on Miss Moore in Indianapolis.[3] I've had several guests since then—shewing each the usual round of antiquarian sights. Busy as the devil with revision—worked 60 hours without sleep a fortnight ago on a job whose deadline loomed perilously close.[4] My aunt is still improving, & I'm as tolerable as might be expected with cold weather leering threateningly ahead.

And so you are sampling the celebrated Gertrude Stein! I must admit that I've never read any book of hers, since scattered fragments in periodicals discouraged any interest I might otherwise have acquired. I suppose she has been an influence, or something of the sort—otherwise substantial literary figures would not take her so quasi-seriously. But I can't think that she counts very heavily in the long stream of continuous English tradition. As steins go, I think I'll do my betting on Ein!

I wish my camera were of the right size & focussing potentialities to get good views of Klarkash-Ton's grotesque miniature carvings. Donald Wandrei—with a better apparatus—did photograph them, & if I can worm a set of prints out of him I'll be delighted to let you see them. C A S does better in three dimensions than in two, & some of these sculptural horrors are imaginatively provocative indeed.

Glad ideas for tales & novels are not lacking & hope you'll have a chance to develop the best of them. Contact with Howell Vines must be inspiring & beneficial—& I hope Vines will have better literary luck in the future than in the past. The part played by commercialism in writing is infinitely discouraging. Little, Brown, & Co. surely have a curious attitude—willingness to publish but not to push—but that's at least better than unwillingness to publish at all. Hope the new agent will be able to bring about better conditions.

I haven't read "Eyeless in Gaza", but greatly admire Aldous Huxley as an honest & vigorous thinker. He & Julian are certainly nobly upholding the traditions of their grandsire! The picture of Proust surely lacks nothing in force & concrete imagery, & probably does form a cruelly just criticism of Proust's weaker side. It is, however, undoubtedly unjust to Proust on the whole—for the old boy certainly did manage to grind out a tremendously graphic picture of various phases of society & various aspects of human nature. Proust is a veritable idol of sundry friends & correspondents of mine—especially Derleth, Barlow, & J. Vernon Shea. Others—like Long—have no use for him.[5] I take a middle ground (from a very limited acquaintance—only the first two books)—which is none the less favourable enough to place P. at the top of 20th century novelists.

Glad the acrostic[6] sounded passable for a mechanical thing of its kind. That half-hour's churchyard pastime has had an amusing series of echoes—more of which, perhaps, are still to come. Although it would never have occurred to Barlow & me to submit our results for publication, old de Castro *did*—& secured an acceptance from W T! After that, Bob & I did send our results in—but they were turned down because Wright had already taken one. Now that the ball has started rolling, we'll probably let one or another of the "fan" magazines have our specimens. Meanwhile correspondents began to emulate. Young Henry Kuttner devised a splendidly poetic acrostic—best of all because written at leisure. And an old friend M. W. Moe of Milwaukee—a high-school teacher who visited here in July & to whom I shewed the hidden hillside churchyard—prepared a very clever academic variant & is about to incorporate *all* the acrostics into a hectographed booklet for use in his English classes. Nor is that all. Derleth is editing a Wisconsin Poetry Anthology for the publisher Henry Harrison, & having seen Moe's acrostic decided to include it in the volume. All this from little Bobby Barlow's idle notion of writing an acrostic (his original idea was to have each of us contribute parts to a single poem, but this soon proved impracticable) while seated on a tombstone on a summer's afternoon![7]

No—I haven't read "The Circus of Dr. Lao."[8] Thanks abundantly for the proffered loan, of which I trust I may ultimately take advantage. If I borrowed it now, though, I'd have to keep it an indefinite time, since my heaps of unread borrowed books come near to hitting the ceiling. This has been the most feverishly rushed year in my recent annals, & many departments of my activities have perforce lapsed into utter chaos.

By the way—I can understand Vines' preference for the pen over the typewriter. I can't bear the process of typing, & simply couldn't think coherently with a machine in front of me. Well-patterned phrases with me take form only when I can mould them by hand with the traditional equipment of the writer.

The other night I attended a meeting of a local society of amateur astronomers—loosely connected with Brown University—& was astonished by the scope & seriousness of their activities. There was an address on early Rhode Island astronomy, & a reflecting telescope used in 1769 was exhibited. I was half-tempted to join—since astronomy used to be a specialty of mine.

Best wishes—

Yrs most cordially—

H P L

Notes

1. Robert Browning (1812–1889), "Home-Thoughts, from Abroad" (1845), ll. 1–2, but read "England" for "Charleston" and "April" for "autumn."

2. R. H. Barlow visited HPL in Providence from 28 July to 1 September.

3. I.e., Catherine L. Moore.

4. The job was *Well Bred Speech: A Brief, Intensive Aid for English Students* by Anne Tillery Renshaw ([Washington, DC: Standard Press, 1936]; LL 726). Much of HPL's work (including the essay now titled "Suggestions for a Reading Guide") was excised from the final work.

5. HPL gave a copy of *Swann's Way*—"an appropriately sophisticated Christmas present"—to Long in 1928, accompanying it with the poem, "An Epistle to Francis, Ld. Belknap . . ."

6. I.e., "In a Sequester'd Providence Churchyard Where Once Poe Walk'd" (1936).

7. Moe's acrostic was published in August Derleth and Raymond E. F. Larsson, ed., *Poetry out of Wisconsin* (New York: H. Harrison, 1937). All five acrostics appear in David E. Schultz, "In a Sequester'd Churchyard," *Crypt of Cthulhu* No. 57 (St. John's Eve 1988): 26–29.

8. A weird novel by Charles G. Finney.

[10] [ALS]

66 College St.,
Providence, R.I.,
Nov. 30, 1936.

Dear White:—

Congratulations on the first issue of your consolidated magazine enterprise! *Campus*[1] truly presents an admirable blend of good appearance & well-selected contents, & I hope its announced policy[2] may develop with complete success. I read the entire contents, & cannot find any point on which to dissent from the opinions you have expressed. I would say that your own Huxley review[3] & Mason's stream of reflections[4] form the genuine high spots. Both of these seem to me tremendously thoughtful & well-expressed. The news & other items are competent & piquant, while the verse all reflects cleverness & wit. There is a certainly a gratifying absence of crude or conspicuously mediocre spots. I was especially tickled by the column of 'weary words',[5] since one of my recent jobs has involved compiling a set of typical stock phrases.[6] I wish I had had this column before I prepared my list! Glad to note items concerning your dramatic progress,[7] & to see the pleasant-looking snapshot of you in the gallery of celebrities.[8] I appreciate the originality of the consolidation idea, & congratulate you on the honour of launching this innovation as editor-in-chief. It surely must, though, have been a devastating job—considering the complexity & diversity of elements involved!

No very striking events have distinguished the programme hereabouts—though autumn has brought sundry lectures at the college & kindred things to compensate for the waning of outdoor opportunities. The season was not quite as bad & prematurely arctic as I had feared it would be—occasional good days persisting far into October. Oct. 20 & 21 were phenomenally warm, & I went exploring on both days—finding a fascinating forest three miles away *which I had never seen before*. This place—of which I had heard vaguely in the past, but which happens to be between my usual routes of exploration—is called the "Squantum Woods", & lies down the east shore of Narragansett Bay—in the town of East Providence. It is now a state reservation, & was made accessible by the cutting-through of the Barrington Parkway. Ædopol, but what I've missed for almost half a century! Still, I'm almost glad that some new discovery at my very doorstep was held in reserve for my later years. It renews the illusion of youth & of adventurous expectancy to come upon something fresh & unexpected when one had thought all such things were past! Great oaks & birches—steep sloped & rock ledges—& on both occasions a magnificent sunset beyond the trees. Then glimpses of the crescent moon, Venus, & Jupiter—& the lights of far-off Providence from high places along the parkway. Another goal for next year's rural rambles!

Snow fell as early as Nov. 24—unusual even for this subarctic zone—& I fear the winter may be a trying one. Hibernation of greater or less rigidity is my lot from now on.

My "Shadow Over Innsmouth" is now out—but as a first cloth-bound book it doesn't awake any enthusiasm in me. Indeed, it is one of the lousiest jobs I've ever seen—30 misprints, slovenly format, & loose, slipshod binding. The solitary redeeming feature is the set of Utpatel illustrations—one of which, on the dust wrapper, saves the appearance of the thing as it lies on the library table.

With all good wishes, & renewed appreciation of *Campus,*

Yrs most sincerely,

H P L

Notes

1. *Campus: The Newsmagazine of Howard College* 1, No. 1 (October 1936), ed. Lee White and Hugh Frank Smith.

2. The policy was enunciated in an unsigned editorial, "The Beginning: Volume One, Number One": "As it is, this magazine is a combination of *The Crimson,* student weekly newspaper, *The Quill,* literary journal, and *The Alumnus,* alumni quarterly" (p. 1).

3. "For Aldous Huxley" (p. 25) by Lee White, a review of *Eyeless in Gaza.*

4. August H. Mason, "Words on a Sawmill Air" (pp. 17–18).

5. "Weary Words about Campus People" (p. 10), an unsigned humorous article in which various individuals on the campus are described with trite phrases ("John Hollingsworth is building castles in the air").

6. This was a chapter entitled "Bromides Must Go" for Renshaw's *Well Bred Speech* but not published there; it was first published in *Letters to Elizabeth Toldridge and Anne Tillery Renshaw,* ed. David E. Schultz and S. T. Joshi (New York: Hippocampus Press, 2014), 432–37.

7. An unsigned news article, "Masquers' play set for Nov. 13" (p. 7), notes that White will be acting in a production of Oscar Wilde's *The Importance of Being Earnest.*

8. White's photograph appears in a montage on p. 9.

Appendix

J. Vernon Shea, Jr.

On Writing in Bed

With a stronger belief in his illness than his asthma warranted, Marcel Proust sat propped up in bed, writing interminably upon *Remembrance of Things Past.* You wonder if it was not the leisure his bed granted him almost as much as his passion for the truth that made him open those incredibly qualified sentences.

With such an example as Proust before us, should it not be made mandatory for all writers to do their writing in bed? Surely they would welcome the avoidance of the inevitable family squabbles which distract an author. Surely they would appreciate a chance at full repose after a grueling ordeal of creation. And assuredly they would be glad to escape their typewriters.

Has anyone considered the demoniac qualities of the typewriter? It is more nagging than a wife; its constant presence is a reproach to the laggard, and to the industrious it is a slave-driver. Its keys print more rapidly (even when you use all of the two fingers) than you could propel the fastest pen; unlike the pen, which easily takes you to the bottom of the sheet, it seems loath ever to fill a page. It takes a delight in tripping up your spelling and grammar. And when you have finished, its type assumes something of the cold finality of print and defies revision. Is it not the meretricious speed the typewriter grants which is responsible for the hastily spewed books of today?

But when you write in bed the press of time is forgotten. Here you are no longer a slave to your typewriter, but impregnable monarch of your room (keep your wife or cleaning woman out). You lie, awaiting inspiration (and trying not to close your eyelids), and then scribble frenetically. You can permit yourself the luxury of letting inept sheets flutter in a cascade to the floor.

Four Playwrights

Arthur Wing Pinero.

Pinero just died? Remarkable. Next you'll be telling me Barrie is still alive.

Eugene O'Neill.

A writer of moderate talents with an immoderate ambition. The Jules Romains of the theatre. We watch with awed respect, but the trapeze after souring falls to its ordinary swing. After *Mourning Becomes Electra,* his highest upthrust, he descended to the banality of *Ah, Wilderness! Wilderness:* amateurish, a sensitive writer's first play. By O'Neill out of Tarkington, with George M. Cohan. I saw it at a Wednesday matinée in Pittsburgh, prior to its Broadway showing. Had a feeling that O'Neill was in the audience. He was. Had I been able to afford a second balcony seat, I might have sat beside him. So what? The audience seen their duty by O'Neill and done it, laughing with hysterical appreciation. They might have been at a Will Rogers picture.

Noel Coward.

The modern Oscar Wilde. It's easy enough, if you try hard enough, to fashion an epigram. Let's try one: Noel Coward is a clever young man who is appreciated by the young and depreciated by the clover. The clubwoman's idea of A Playwright. *Design For Living* is a Daring Play: the three sexes nicely tucked into bed. With the clubwoman, Coward can weep at the funeral of Victoria.

Maxwell Anderson.

It's difficult to realize the furore *What Price Glory?* caused in the theatre. Read now, it's wholly innocuous. It might be admired by General Mac Arthur. . . . if it were every anything else, *Saturday's Children* has become ordinary and Cinderellaish, a second *First Year*. . . . There remains a suspicion that the loudly attacked *Gods of the Lightning* might better repay reading. . . . Who is going to have the nerve to say that *Elizabeth the Queen, Mary of Scotland* and *Valley Forge,* their worth descending in that order, are beautiful, unhistorical, and dull?

It would take a charge of dynamite to make the partisans of the Dramah admit that Anderson has contributed some of his best work to the despised talkies. *Both Your Houses* was a revision of the movie scenario, *Washington Merry-go-round,* and like most revisions, better. But Anderson has still to equal the scenario he wrote with George Abbott for *All Quiet on the Western Front.*

Carl F. Strauch

The Beauty of Decay

The perfect beauty of a summer day
Is like a water nymph upon the grass
That stains the water's side; she does not play
Her liquid notes like any country lass,
Like blowsy Spring, the girl with rumpled hair.
Ah, no! This maiden plays her reed and stands
Transfixed, eyes shut, the image of Despair.
She drops her instrument, and her pale hands
Trembling she dips into the mossy brook

To lay its water on her pallid brow
And cool it. Death is near. Her lovely throat
Throbs like some pain-impassioned bird. A look
Of mask-like sadness shades her face; and now
Autumnal cornfields hear her wailing note.

The White Fiend Death

When the white fiend Death
    Shall catch hold of me,
Gasping sharp and catching my breath
    And swinging my arms most fiendishly,

Then will he tear my heart from its place
    And fashion it to a chalice grace,
And he and I on the sunny lea
    Shall drink the full heart's blood of me!

A Library Goes Regionalist

Regionalism seems to be the order of the day. In its cruder political manifestations it is reduced to an absurdity: the Poles throw off Russian oppression, and the Ruthenians revolt against the Polish political and racial tyrannies. In the arts, however, it has in the past been responsible for much great work, and it is today a vital creative principle for many writers who feel that they need something closer, something warmer, something more real than a hollow megalopolitanism and an empty universality, which, by forfeiting a county for the world, loses the whole earth. Jean Sibelius, who had been writing music for over a quarter century without much embarrassing acclaim, has within the last two years received favorable notices here and abroad. His work has been identified with his Finnish background even more closely than Stravinsky's and Prokofieff's with their Russian sources. For critics have discovered in the Finn a true regionalist, an idiosyncratic, an artist who feels his land and his people. But Stravinsky and Prokofieff, by the infusion of a modernistic and sophisticated element in their works, have sacrificed the integrity of their music. In literature, regionalism has had its European exponents; Thomas Hardy, René Bazin, Gustav Frennsen, and hundreds of other writers, many of whom will never achieve even national fame, because they so closely identified themselves with their regions by writing in the patois.

In the United States regionalism as a conscious literary movement that possesses national significance has flourished only in the last decade. The Boston and the Concord groups were not regionalists; and whatever sectional literature we have had has either been the creation of isolated writers (Bret Harte in California and James W. Riley in Indiana), or has lacked greatness to make it of national importance. Today, however, young men and women do not flock to New York so eagerly and in such numbers as they did in the lusty dayspring of Eugene O'Neill and Edna Millay; they stay at home and set up literary shop around the corner from the old cracker-barrel or the hitching post. Ernest Hemingway and Glenway Wescott, expatriates, were regionalists in their early work. Elizabeth Madox Roberts and Maristan Chapman are famous regionalists. Caroline Gordon has recently produced a fine regionalist novel, *Penhally;* and the group of Tennessee poets, of whom her husband, Allen Tate, is the most prominent, is a good example of that conscious literary movement we call Regionalism.

All this is by way of introduction to a tale of how one small college library has, by reason of its favorable location, come into a rich store of regional-dialect literature. Obviously, a college library that opens its portals on the clamor and the distraction of a great metropolis will in the first place have no incentive to make such collections and little occasion in the second.

The Pennsylvania-German Dialect

But regionalism is in the air; and Muhlenberg College is situated in a region, one of the really unique sections of these United States. The Pennsylvania-German countries of southeastern Pennsylvania have stubbornly resisted the Anglo-American influences which have elsewhere absorbed less tenacious cultures; and Allentown, the seat of Muhlenberg College, is near the very heart to these rich agricultural countries. Eastward lies Bethlehem, with its Moravian traditions and memories of the almost apocryphal Count Zinzendorf; southward lie Lancaster, York, and the famous cloisters of Ephrata; and southeast, on the main road to Philadelphia, dreams the beautiful suburb of Germantown. These Pennsylvania-German counties have kept the old cultural faiths. They are true to the old superstitions, charms and hexeree, the doctrinal vagaries and quiddities of the sects, Dunkards, Mennonites, Schwenkfelders, the Amish; and to this day Pennsylvania-German dialect holds its own with English in the larger towns and cities, and in the more remote agricultural sections is the preferred speech.

Naturally there has been a vast dialect literature in prose and verse over a whole century; and its historians have had a unique field of research and study. Among these has been Dr. Harry H. Reichard, whose *Pennsylvania-German Dialect Writings and their Writers* is an interesting and valuable study of more than thirty authors, of whom Charles C. More is a distinguished example. Dr. More, who has honored Muhlenberg College Library by making it the permanent depository of twenty-one manuscripts of his dialect writings, is an author whose works are distinguished by a conscious artistic purpose.

Charles C. More

Mr. More was born in Allentown in 1851. At the age of seventeen he went to Europe and studied in Berlin and taught German and French in Switzerland. In 1876 he returned to America, but the same year went back to Germany and was appointed clerk of the American legation at Berlin, then under Bayard Taylor. He remained ten years and became familiar with the dialect writings of Klaus Groth, Hermann Nadler, and Berthold Auerbach, whom he knew. More was inspired to use his own dialect as these authors had theirs; and it was with this inspiration that he returned to Allentown and wrote some remarkable dialect stories and verse. Some of them have been published here, a few in Stuttgart; and Dr. More has been honored for his literary labors by the Munich Academy of Arts and Sciences and received the attention of scholars here and abroad. "More has said," writes Dr. Reichard in a graceful peroration to his story of this dialect writer, "that dialect stories can be written which hold the mirror up to nature, and we need not stoop to vulgarisms to attract attention, for the dialect combines that much vaunted Irish wit with the good old homely German humor; we need only be imbued with an honest pride in our ancestry and their language, and then the dialect will live by its own momentum. More has done more than an ordinary man's share to make it live."

Only three of the twenty-one manuscripts which Dr. More has given to Muhlenberg are typewritten copies. The remaining eighteen are first, second, third, and sometimes fourth drafts and fair copies of his stories. They are all products of his best creative period, the first ten years of the century, altho only three are dated.

Because the Pennsylvania-German dialect is little known and almost never heard outside Pennsylvania I was at first persuaded, against my desire, to omit any specimen of More's dialect-writing. The temptation, however, is too great, for his stories, poems, and aphorisms are worthy of critical attention. Here is a three-stanza poem, which appears on page 176 of the typewritten ms. of "Die Lein Fens," one of his best long stories. It is a good sample of More's work, spontaneous and simple, and of the Pennsylvania-German dialect, which students of German will find an interesting variation:

> Wann die Gnospe widder schpriessen
> Un die Halme widder schiessen,
> Wann die Vejjel widder singe in de Beem,
> Wann die Blume widder bliehen
> Un die Droschel nardwaerts ziehen
> Nort is der Friehling widder do bei uns deheem.
>
> Wie frein sich dann de Leit!
> Deer un Fenschter schpaerre weit,

Zum Willkomm far der Bot' vumm Himmels Zelt.
"Griess Got du Blumme-Ritter!
Mach's gut un komm ball widder!
Uns bischt der liebschte Gascht in daere Welt!"

Doch kommscht, oh Mensch, du haer,
Du finnscht ken uff'ni Deer,
Dir winkt ken freindlich Willkomm vum der Schwell—
Die Sunn geht juscht so nidder—
Du gescht un kommscht net widder,
Oh, heemetloser Wandrer, faerriwell!

The aberrations from the classic German are quite obvious: "Gnospe" for "Knospe," "Vejjel" for "Vögel," "Beem" for "Bäume," "widder" for "wieder," "schpaerre" for "sperren," "liebschte Gascht" for "liebste Gast," and others. The last word in the poem, "faerriwell," is to be regarded as the Pennsylvania-German adoption of the English "farewell" rather than a dialect form of the high German "fahre wohl." One is tempted by the singing quality of the verses to try one's hand at translation; but the special loveliness of this poetry cannot be transmitted from language to language. Its fresh simplicity would become an embarrassing awkwardness and the poem itself seem naked of any beauty.

Of course, none of More's dialect writings has as yet contributed influence or color to our national literature. Like the ballads of the hill country of Kentucky and Tennessee, like the Indian chants of our great Southwest, like the cowboy songs of the vast plains, these writings have been distinguished by their intense preoccupation with the local scene—in this case Lehigh County, its simple and superstitious folk, the humor and the tenderness, the natural poetry.

Our library has in these writings valuable source-material for the writer who wants to saturate himself in the peculiar atmosphere of this Pennsylvania-German region. There are, of course, other such writers and collections of writings; but the Muhlenberg College Library collection of the Dr. Charles More mss. is unique, we believe, and will be of great interest to scholars and creative writers. It is besides the rare beginning of what should with the years become an important collection of the dialect literature of the region in which the college is situated.

Carl F. Strauch, Formerly Assistant Librarian, Muhlenberg College, Allentown, Pa.

Lee McBride White

For Aldous Huxley

To understand Aldous Huxley it is necessary only to have been born too late. To compliment him upon the sternly intellectual quality of his book would be like commenting that Christ's disciples were smart scholars because they wrote in Greek. Aldous Huxley is made up of brain cells. One should not describe him, but define him. "Pure mind—that's all." He hasn't the mind of an Aristotle, a Galileo, a Spinoza, but he could beat them all playing *Categories, Who-sir Me-sir, Twenty Questions*.

In *Eyeless In Gaza* he says that it is remarkable how much an educated man can know today; and verily he is that educated man of whom he speaks. His mind is a Gothic cathedral used by the force of circumstance as a chemical laboratory. He must have read Krafft-Ebing while most boys his age were learning to wave bye-bye.

His critical perception is immense. To play chess with him would be a fatal error to be done at your peril, after prayer and fasting.

In his fifth novel he has recounted, essentially, the history of a professor of sociology whose habit it was from adolescence to stand ill at ease among his futile brother men. Through a series of intuitively well-written stretches is filed into recognizable form the mind of Anthony Beavis. He comes to the belief that the hope of mankind is in pacifism, compassion, love of man for his fellow.

There are strange new words in the vocabulary of this cynic of all beliefs, this fastidious sensualist.

The development of Anthony Beavis, one of the Huxleys in the book, is the central structure of the novel: for it shall be called a novel, although the term must include the work of James Joyce, Wyndham Lewis, Elinor Glyn, Thomas Hardy. There are several splendid essays in this volume, placed so cleverly between melodrama and typical Huxleyan dialogue that the reader is hoodwinked into an occasional intellectual exercise.

Through Gumbril, Quarles, and Fanning, Huxley explores his own being. In the present book, he has been rather more generous of himself, dividing his personality among Beavis, Ledwidge, Mark Staithes, Beppo, and Mary Amberley. It is a triumph of disintegration, if nothing else.

It is typical that he should write in the same book: "To know everything is essential," and "If human beings were shown what they're really like, they'd either kill one another as vermin, or hang themselves."

He does not write with the conscious brilliance of *Antic Hay,* nor does he epitomise a decade as he did in *Point Counter Point,* but he has finally succeeded in reaching a conclusion. The cynic of the twenties (now in his forties) is not so certain of the square root of God. The artificer in words who, in 1927, said "As I grow older, I become more highbrow. It isn't a pose. Softness is the end of everything," has now opened his arms to mankind—to the Common Man, with his sentimentalities, his incompetence, his hopeless stupidity. One might say, since Huxley himself is Hamlet (still hoping to lay the ghost of his grandfather), "Here cracks a noble attitude."

Ten years ago, he was one of England's bright young people, along with the Sitwells, Noel Coward, Beverley Nichols, and G. B. S. (who at the time still considered himself a Bright Young Thing). Noel Coward is still casting his smooth pebbles against the glass houses of his neighbors, Beverley Nichols has written a book about God, and Shaw has written several books about himself: only Huxley, of them all, has progressed mentally. This progression has nothing, basically, to do with his constant readings of the Britannica; he has simply lived, grown older, and in the living gained something no intelligence can comprehend fully before coming of age, which in this instance is 42 years.

Eyeless In Gaza is inordinately comprehensive, the product of a very elaborate and cultured brain. It may be, also, merely a *tour de force* of virtuosity and self-consciousness. The story is told in parallels: an act at the age of thirty is followed by an earlier event that aids in understanding that act. The method achieves the effect of a kind of super-microscope that focuses a portion of the material under observation, then focuses on an inner, more secret portion, and again on an innermost portion There is that uncomfortable effect produced by the picture on the Oysterette cracker box in which a man is holding the box on which is printed the picture of the man holding the box on which is printed the man again . . . and the final picture is never completed.

There are cruel things in this book, and fine things, and sentences that stick in the mind like incredibly sharp splinters, which must be removed carefully, one by one: If Hamlet had known as little as Polonius, he would have been happy . . . Were Freud right, and sex supreme, we should live almost in Eden . . . Hamlet is his own termite and from a tower has eaten himself down to a heap of sawdust . . . Men with strong religious and revolutionary faith, men with well-thought-out plans for improving the lot of their fellows, have been more systematically and cold-bloodedly cruel than any others . . . Dante in the circumstances! Dante, with his steel profile, ploughing forward like a spiritual battleship. . . . How I hate old Proust forever squatting in the tepid bath of his remembered past! . . . Hell is the incapacity to be other than the creature one finds oneself ordinarily behaving as.

Robert Browning himself, smug-seated upon his throne in heaven, will read with greedy eyes the closing sentence of this book, wherein (to the invisible accompaniment of the angels' harps while Pippa passes) Beavis thinks to himself: all will be well.

In each of a fantastic array of books, Huxley has destroyed the earlier personality and risen simultaneously from the ashes, a sound and self-knowing Phoenix. But something went wrong with the apparatus this time, and out of the ashes has arisen the Blue Bird.

Out of Sorrow

She stood high on the thin ledge of a familiar mountain, and held the child in her arms. She was sturdy; one arm held him comfortably. With her strength and her anger, she was sturdy. Her mind was cut off, there was no knowing of anything in her, there was only the consciousness of what she was going to do.

The child she had always disliked. She disliked it because it had made her a mother. She disliked it because it had made Thomas so gentle and considerate. She didn't want gentleness. She wanted only equality with men, to be judged as a man for the things she had done.

Four years of eye- and back- and muscle-wearying labor over microscopes and notebooks and manuscript had been a real labor, an unquestionably worthwhile piece of work. And Thomas had refused to use her name as co-author. The thought made her unable to breathe; if she had him here she would throw him down into the valley with the child. Man, man, man, man, man, the word throttled through her brain. "You've got Junior," he had told her not twenty minutes ago. "I've got to get myself a place in one of the big universities, and this book will do it."

Yes, she had Junior! She had worked five thousand hours or more on that book, and only Lofton's name would appear on it. Even the child had Thomas's name. She would throw it into the valley and free herself of the force that was making her too much a woman.

She was glad Thomas had left her. She hated him so intensely that the thought of him made her quiver. Right here on this ledge they had sat and talked about the book and about the stir it would create. "Evidences of Organic Descent," they had decided to title it. And only his name was to appear as author. What if he had spent seven years at it? She had spent four just as good, just as helpful to the book. . . .

She and Thomas had been sitting here once, making play with the echo that sprang crisp from the thick hair-growth of trees below. "Sit here and call your name enough times," he had told her, "and you will never doubt who you are."

She was Myrtle Wootton. Marriage to Thomas Lofton had never changed that. She worked with him as a contemporary, not a wife. The child had been most bothersome because it kept her from study for so long. Ahh, this child in her arm, this little manthing that was the son of Thomas Lofton, that had Thomas Lofton's name. . . . She raised it in her arms to throw it from her, to rid herself of the woman it made her. She would be willing to do this, in order to gain something soothing and sustaining: it would give her the self-respect it had taken from her.

Man: the thought, the idea of man made her hands clutch the soft limbs of the child harder, hurting him. He began to bawl. She would be glad to rid herself of the crying infant. It was nothing but an experiment that had not worked out; it was nothing but a particular number of bones, organs, plasms, the multiplication of a single cell. It would be easy to get another child, when she would be wanting one.

She would let Thomas know in some way what she had done with his child. She would hurt him intolerably. She would repay him for the thing he had refused to do this morning. She would repay him for the inferiority she felt when he looked at her steadily. When his eyes probed her, she felt translucent, helpless, no more than germ or bacterion surrounded by light, magnified a hundred times through the lens of a microscope.

The little whips of knowledge flicked in her mind. And suddenly she was sorry he was not here to see her do this. It would hurt him more, it would hurt him sharper, if he were here to see her do it. Not because he had left her, not because he did not love her, but because he was a man and jealous of his name. The thought of him made her blood jerk in her arteries with quick beating of heart, and the thought of him pounded in her mind like the sound of a hammer on bronze. He had been glad to leave her! He had been glad to go away! to deracinate their partnership, to divide her as in a process of mitosis.

She held the child of theirs in her arms, and she knew that in a moment she would throw it from her. She was strong, her arms were big with strength and vigor, her body was thick with blood and living plasms and taut tissues. . . .

She looked at the boy: it would be easy. She knew that she would have to close her eyes. It would be easy, but she would have to close her eyes.

She placed the baby on earth, hot with anger. Of course she hadn't done it. She was a woman, she couldn't do it. Not with all her strength could she throw that child of theirs away. It was shameful to do so, it was weak, and motherly. Her nerves were jerking with the quick beat of her heart, and her whole body inside was making her quiver with disgust at herself. Yes, her nerves were quivering like tumblebugs in a bright light. Yes, she, Myrtle Wootton, was quivering over her whole body because she had almost dropped her child into the valley. To think of Thomas at this moment was awful. He would have laughed at her, he would have been amused, when she was going to do it to hurt him, to make him suffer. The whole thing had turned about on her.

She walked in her agitation back and forth, everything pitiable having overtaken her. The book was without her name as collaborator, Thomas had left her, the child was stronger than she. Her whole life slipped away through her fingers like swift sand dropping through an hour glass.

She hurried back to the place where the child lay, for fear he should roll over the ledge and kill himself. She held him in her arms, almost willingly, almost gladly, and suddenly a way became clear for her.

She could wait for this child to grow, and she would teach it things no other child might learn. She would tutor it, give it microscopes, books, the advantage of her knowledge, the things it had taken her thirty years to discover. Her son would begin with a head start on the whole world; he would do things in science no man had yet done. Her son would be doing this, her son!

Thomas was gone, but that didn't matter. He could stay away forever.

She looked up. He was standing there. He'd come up quietly, and the trees had been keeping him covered. She looked at him, and he said, "Couldn't do it, could you?"

He had been watching her the whole time, he had been watching her, smiling at her, laughing at her weakness, despising her for her attempt, condemning her for her weakness. Everything had been contemptible about it, most of all her weakness.

She stood up suddenly and walked to him, leaving the child alone. "Why did you come back? I don't need you." She was angry. Her nerves were beating with her heart again, and she was red and empty and burning inside for the thing he had seen her do. She was glad she had been weak, she was glad she had not thrown the child down, but that another human being should have seen the act was unthinkable, intolerably hurting. With all her hate and her desire to make Thomas suffer, she had failed, so miserably that in the failure he was laughing at her. She became painfully conscious of her large body, her awkward thick arms, her dullgreen eyes. A man had no right to stick the sharp hurting probe of his laughter into a woman's soul. It was sacrilegious, it was intolerably unbearable.

Thomas was still smiling at the ends of his mouth, smiling at her weakness, thinking that he would have gone through with it if he had begun it, knowing his superiority to her. Oh, she would have done it if she could! It had been something intangible, untouchable, that had kept her from it. She looked at him defiantly and said, "Women have souls!"

"How pretty," said Thomas, and smiled again.

She could feel the warm outglow of her blood in her face, the prickling blood at the roots of her hair. She was blushing an awful, unretractable blush. It was saying all the things that had gone on inside her mind. For his presence she hated him, and for her own outburst, she hated him.

"I will be at the house," she heard him say, and she could hear him walking away.

Now, there was only one heart in her body; the thousand beating hearts that had attacked her as she stood with the child had departed, and a solitary, methodical throatbeat was in her, that made her want to take a deep breath, a hard deep breath that would push her lungs down into her body, that would fill her with oxygen and a soothing intangibleness. She walked to the child, that had fallen asleep so quickly, so readily. She picked it up awkwardly, making it to wake up and cry. She began to hum a tune to it, that was a lullabye. The son was waking up, and she was singing him a lullabye. The thought was amusing . . . . She laughed at herself.

Look at Your Thumb

Horizontally extended
Thumb is means of transportation;
Downward thrust signs disapproval;
By its twiddle makes amusement.
Seeking ever lip-sneer symbol
Couched in terms of burleycue,
Man upraises speechless hand,
Is eloquent with thumb to nose!

Glossary of Frequently Mentioned Names

Barlow, R[obert] H[ayward] (1918–1951), author and collector. As a teenager he corresponded with HPL and acted as his host during two long visits in the summers of 1934 and 1935. In the 1930s he wrote several works of weird and fantasy fiction, some in collaboration with HPL. HPL appointed him his literary executor. He assisted August Derleth and Donald Wandrei in preparing the early HPL volumes for Arkham House. In the 1940s he went to Mexico and became a distinguished anthropologist. He died by suicide. HPL's letters to Barlow have been published as *O Fortunate Floridian* (Tampa: University of Tampa Press, 2007).

Bishop, Zealia Brown Reed (1897–1968), revision client of HPL's, for whom he ghostwrote three weird tales ("The Curse of Yig," "The Mound," and "Medusa's Coil") and perhaps other work.

Blackwood, Algernon (1869–1951), prolific British author of weird and fantasy tales whose work HPL greatly admired when he read it in 1924.

Bloch, Robert (1917–1994), author of weird and suspense fiction who came into correspondence with HPL in 1933. HPL tutored him in the craft of writing during their four-year association.

Brobst, Harry K[ern] (1909–2010), late associate of HPL who moved to Providence in 1932 and saw HPL regularly thereafter.

Burks, Arthur J. (1898–1974), frequent contributor to *WT* as well as to other weird and science fiction pulp magazines. HPL particularly appreciated his story "Bells of Oceana" (*WT,* December 1927).

Calverton, V. F. (1900–1940), pen name of American writer and political activist George Goetz. Radical reformer and author, and founder and editor of *Modern Quarterly,* an independent Marxist journal.

Coates, Walter J[ohn] (1880–1941), friend of W. Paul Cook and editor of *Driftwind.*

Cole, Edward H[arold] (1892–1966), longtime amateur associate of HPL, living in the Boston area. Editor of the *Olympian.*

Conover, Willis (1920–1996), weird fiction fan who edited *Science-Fantasy Correspondent* (1936–37) and was a late correspondent of HPL.

Cook, W. Paul (1880–1948), publisher of the *Monadnock Monthly,* the *Vagrant,* and other amateur journals; a longtime amateur journalist, printer, and lifelong friend of HPL. He first visited HPL in 1917, and it was he who urged HPL to resume writing fiction after a hiatus of nine years. In 1927 Cook published the *Recluse,* with HPL's "Supernatural Horror in Literature."

Crane, Hart (1899–1932), eminent American poet who met HPL sporadically in Cleveland (1922) and New York (1924–26, 1930). HPL admired his work, especially *The Bridge* (1930), on which HPL saw him at work in 1924. He died by suicide.

Crawford, William L[evy] (1911–1984), editor of *Marvel Tales* and *Unusual Stories* and publisher of the Visionary Publishing Company, which issued HPL's *The Shadow over Innsmouth* (1936).

de Castro, Adolphe (Danziger) (1859–1959), author, co-translator with Ambrose Bierce of Richard Voss's *The Monk and the Hangman's Daughter,* and correspondent of HPL. HPL revised his "The Last Test" and "The Electric Executioner."

Davis, Robert H[obart] (1869–1942), longtime editor at various Munsey magazines, including *Munsey's* and *Argosy*. Also a columnist with the *New York Sun* (1925–42).

de la Mare, Walter (1873–1956), British writer and poet and author of many subtle weird tales, including the novel *The Return* (1910) and the story collections *The Riddle and Other Stories* (1923) and *The Connoisseur and Other Stories* (1926).

Derleth, August W[illiam] (1909–1971), author of weird tales and also a long series of regional and historical works set in his native Wisconsin. After HPL's death, he and Donald Wandrei founded the publishing firm of Arkham House to preserve HPL's work in book form.

Dunsany, Lord (Edward John Moreton Drax Plunkett, 18th baron Dunsany) (1878–1957), Irish writer of fantasy tales whose work notably influenced HPL after HPL read it in 1919.

Eddy, C[lifford] M[artin] (1896–1967), pulp fiction writer for whom HPL revised several stories in 1923–24 and who also worked with HPL on ghostwriting work for Harry Houdini in 1926.

Edkins, Ernest A[rthur] (1867–1946), amateur journalist associated with the "halcyon days" of the NAPA (1885–95). He came in touch with HPL in 1932.

Gamwell, Annie E[meline] P[hillips] (1866–1941), HPL's younger aunt, living with him at 66 College Street (1933–37). She had been married (1897–1936) to Edward F[rancis] Gamwell (1869–1936).

Hodgson, William Hope (1877–1918), British author of weird fiction whose work had fallen into obscurity until it was rediscovered in the 1930s.

Houdini, Harry (stage name of Ehrich Weiss, 1874–1926), celebrated escape artist and opponent of spiritualism for whom HPL ghostwrote the story "Under the Pyramids" (1924; published as "Imprisoned with the Pharaohs") and for whom he did other revisory work in 1926, just prior to Houdini's death.

Howard, Robert E[rvin] (1906–1936), prolific Texas author of weird and adventure tales for *Weird Tales* and other pulp magazines; creator of the adventure hero Conan of Cimmeria. He and HPL corresponded voluminously from 1930 to 1936. He committed suicide when he heard of his mother's impending death.

James, M[ontague] R[hodes] (1862–1936), celebrated British writer of ghost stories much admired by HPL. His *Collected Ghost Stories* appeared in 1931.

Kirk, George [Willard] (1898–1962), member of the Kalem Club. He published *Twenty-one Letters of Ambrose Bierce* (1922) and ran the Chelsea Bookshop in New York.

Kleiner, Rheinhart (1892–1949), amateur poet and longtime friend of HPL. He visited HPL in Providence in 1918, 1919, and 1920, and met him frequently during the heyday of the Kalem Club (1924–26).

Kline, Otis Adelbert (1891–1946), prolific writer for *Weird Tales* and other pulp magazines; also a literary agent for Robert E. Howard and others.

Koenig, H[erman] C[harles] (1893–1959), late associate of HPL who spearheaded the rediscovery of the work of William Hope Hodgson.

Kuttner, Henry (1915–1958), prolific author of science fiction and horror tales for the pulps and a late correspondent of HPL (1936–37). HPL introduced him to C[atherine] L[ucile] Moore (1911–1987), whom he would later marry.

Leeds, Arthur (1882–1952?), an associate of HPL in New York and member of the Kalem Club. He was the author (with J. Berg Esenwein) of *Writing the Photoplay* (Springfield, MA: The Home Correspondence School, 1913; rev. ed. 1919).

Long, Frank Belknap (1901–1994), fiction writer and poet and one of HPL's closest friends and correspondents. Late in life he wrote the memoir, *Howard Phillips Lovecraft: Dreamer on the Nightside* (1975).

Loveman, Samuel E. (1887–1976), poet and longtime friend of HPL and Hart Crane, and associate of Ambrose Bierce, Hart Crane, George Sterling, and Clark Ashton Smith. He wrote *The Hermaphrodite* (1926) and other works.

Lynch, Joseph Bernard (1879–1952), amateur journalist and member of the Hub Club.

Machen, Arthur (1863–1947), Welsh author of weird fiction whose work influenced HPL significantly after he read it in 1923.

Merritt, A[braham] (1884–1943), writer of fantasy and horror tales for the pulps. His work was much admired by HPL in spite of its concessions to pulp formulae. His late novel, *Dwellers in the Mirage* (1932), may have been influenced by HPL.

Moe, Maurice W[inter] (1882–1940), amateur journalist, English teacher, and longtime friend and correspondent of HPL. He lived successively in Appleton and Milwaukee, WI.

Munn, H[arold] Warner (1903–1981), contributor to the pulp magazines, living near W. Paul Cook in Athol, MA.

Orton, Vrest (1897–1986), a late member of the Kalem Club. He was for a time an editor at the *Saturday Review* and later the founder of the Vermont Country Store. He compiled an early bibliography of Theodore Dreiser, *Dreiserana* (1929).

Parker, Charles A. A. (1880–1965), amateur journalist and editor of the little magazine *L'Alouette,* chiefly devoted to poetry.

Poe, Edgar Allan (1809–1849), pioneering American author of weird and detective fiction.

Price, E[dgar] Hoffmann (1898–1988), prolific pulp writer of weird and adventure tales. HPL met him in New Orleans in 1932 and corresponded extensively with him thereafter.

Quinn, Seabury (1889–1969), prolific author of weird and detective tales to the pulps, notably a series of tales involving the psychic detective Jules de Grandin.

Renshaw, Anne Tillery, prolific amateur journalist and professor. She met HPL during the latter's visit to Washington, D.C., in April 1925. In 1936 she commissioned HPL to revise a textbook of English usage, *Well-Bred Speech* (1936), although much of the work HPL did for it was excised and remains unpublished.

Rimel, Duane W[eldon] (1915–1996), weird fiction fan and late associate of HPL, who revised some of his early tales.

Smith, Clark Ashton (1893–1961), prolific California poet and writer of fantasy tales. He received a "fan" letter from HPL in 1922 and corresponded with him until HPL's death.

Sterling, Kenneth (1920–1995), young science fiction fan who came into contact with HPL in 1934. They collaborated on the science fiction story "In the Walls of Eryx" (1935). Sterling later became a distinguished physician.

Strauch, Carl Ferdinand (1908–1989), friend of Harry Brobst and correspondent of HPL. He later became a distinguished professor and critic.

Talman, Wilfred Blanch (1904–1986), correspondent of HPL and late member of the Kalem Club. HPL assisted Talman on his story "Two Black Bottles" (1926) and wrote "Some Dutch Footprints in New England" for Talman to publish in *De Halve Maen*, the journal of the Holland Society of New York. Late in life he wrote the memoir *The Normal Lovecraft* (1973).

Tucker, Gertrude E., editor of the Reading Lamp, evidently a literary agency. She also edited the *Reading Lamp*, a literary journal for which HPL wrote at least one review (not located).

Utpatel, Frank (1905–1980), artist friend of August Derleth who illustrated some of Derleth's work for *Weird Tales* and later did many jackets and interiors (primarily woodcuts) for Arkham House; late correspondent of HPL.

Wandrei, Donald (1908–1987), poet and author of weird fiction, science fiction, and detective tales. He corresponded with HPL from 1926 to 1937, visited HPL in Providence in 1927 and 1932, and met HPL occasionally in New York during the 1930s. He helped HPL get "The Shadow out of Time" published in *Astounding Stories*. After HPL's death he and August Derleth founded the publishing firm Arkham House to preserve HPL's work. For their joint correspondence, see *Mysteries of Time and Spirit*.

Wandrei, Howard (1909–1956), younger brother of Donald Wandrei, premier weird artist and prolific author of weird fiction, science fiction, and detective stories; correspondent of HPL.

Weiss, Henry George (1898–1946), Canadian-born poet and essayist who wrote weird fiction under the pseudonym "Francis Flagg." He came in touch with HPL in 1930; his communist leanings may have influenced HPL's leftward political shift in the 1930s.

Whitehead, Henry S[t. Clair] (1882–1932), author of weird and adventure tales, many of them set in the Virgin Islands. HPL corresponded with him and visited him in Florida in 1931. HPL wrote a brief eulogy of Whitehead for *Weird Tales*.

Wollheim, Donald A[llen] (1914–1990), editor of the *Phantagraph* and *Fanciful Tales* and prolific author and editor in the science fiction field.

Wright, Farnsworth (1888–1940), editor of *Weird Tales* (1924–40). He rejected some of HPL's best work of the 1930s, only to publish it after HPL's death upon submittal by August Derleth.

Bibliography

I. Works by H. P. Lovecraft

Books

The Ancient Track: Complete Poetical Works. Edited by S. T. Joshi. 2nd ed. New York: Hippocampus Press, 2013.

Collected Fiction: A Variorum Edition. Edited by S. T. Joshi. New York: Hippocampus Press, 2015 (Volumes 1–3), 2016 (Volume 4). [*CF*]

Collected Essays. Edited by S. T. Joshi. New York: Hippocampus Press, 2004–06. 5 vols. [*CE*]

Fungi from Yuggoth: An Annotated Edition. Ed. David E. Schultz. New York: Hippocampus Press, 2016.

H. P. Lovecraft in "The Eyrie." Ed. S. T. Joshi and Marc Michaud. West Warwick, RI: Necronomicon Press, 1979.

The Shadow over Innsmouth. Everett, PA: Visionary Publishing Co., 1936.

Fiction

"The Alchemist." *United Amateur* 16, No. 4 (November 1916): 53–57. In *CF* 1.

At the Mountains of Madness. Astounding Stories 16, No. 6 (February 1936): 8–32; 17, No. 1 (March 1936): 125–55; 17, No. 2 (April 1936): 132–50. In *CF* 3.

"The Beast in the Cave." *Vagrant* No. 7 (June 1918): 113–20. In *CF* 1.

"Beyond the Wall of Sleep." *Pine Cones* 1, No. 6 (October 1919): 2–10. *Fantasy Fan*, 2, No. 2 (October 1934): 25–32. In *CF* 1.

"The Call of Cthulhu." *WT* 11, No. 2 (February 1928): 159–78, 287. In *Beware After Dark! The World's Most Stupendous Tales of Mystery, Horror, Thrills and Terror*, ed. T. Everett Harré. New York: Macaulay, 1929. 223–59. In *CF* 2.

The Case of Charles Dexter Ward. In *CF* 2.

"The Cats of Ulthar." *Tryout* 6, No. 11 (November 1920): [3–9]. *WT* 7, No. 2 (February 1926): 252–54. *WT* 21, No. 2 (February 1933): 259–61. Cassia, FL: Dragon-Fly Press, 1935. In *CF* 1.

"The Colour out of Space." *Amazing Stories* 2, No. 6 (September 1927): 557–67. In *CF* 2.

"Cool Air." *Tales of Magic and Mystery* 1, No. 4 (March 1928): 29–34. In *CF* 2.

"Dagon." *Vagrant* No. 11 (November 1919): 23–29. *WT* 2, No. 3 (October 1923): 23–25. In *CF* 1.

"The Doom That Came to Sarnath." *Scot* No. 44 (June 1920): 90–98. *Marvel Tales of Science and Fantasy* 1, No. 4 (March–April 1935): 157–63. In *CF* 1.

"The Dreams in the Witch House." *WT* 22, No. 1 (July 1933): 86–111. In *CF* 3.

"The Dunwich Horror." *WT* 13, No. 4 (April 1929): 481–508. In *CF* 2.

"The Festival." *WT* 5, No. 1 (January 1925): 169–74. *WT* 22, No. 4 (October 1933): 519–20, 522–28. In *CF* 1.

"The Haunter of the Dark." *WT* 28, No. 5 (December 1936): 538–53. In *CF* 2.

"The Horror at Red Hook." *WT* 9, No. 1 (January 1927): 59–73. In *You'll Need a Night Light,* ed. Christine Campbell Thomson. London: Selwyn & Blount, 1927. 228–54. In *CF* 1.

"In the Vault." *Tryout* 10, No. 6 (November 1925): [3–17]. *WT* 19, No. 4 (April 1932): 459–65. In *CF* 1.

"The Lurking Fear." *Home Brew* 2, No. 6 (January 1923): 4–10; 3, No. 1 (February 1923): 18–23; 3, No. 2 (March 1923): 31–37, 44, 48; 3, No. 3 (April 1923): 35–42. *WT* 11, No. 6 (June 1928): 791–804. In *CF* 1.

"The Music of Erich Zann." *National Amateur* 44, No. 4 (March 1922): 38–40. *WT* 5, No. 5 (May 1925): 219–34. In *Creeps by Night: Chills and Thrills,* ed. Dashiell Hammett. New York: John Day Co., 1931. 347–63. In *Modern Tales of Horror,* ed. Dashiell Hammett. London: Victor Gollancz, 1932. 301–17. *Evening Standard* (London) (24 October 1932): 20–21. *WT* 24, No. 5 (November 1934): 644–48, 655–56. In *CF* 1.

"The Mysterious Ship." Juvenilia. In *CF* 1.

"The Mystery in the Graveyard." Juvenilia. In *CF* 1.

"The Nameless City." *Wolverine* No. 11 (November 1921): 3–15. *Fanciful Tales* 1, No. 1 (Fall 1936): 5–18. In *CF* 1.

"The Noble Eavesdropper." Non-extant.

"The Outsider." *WT* 7, No. 4 (April 1926): 449–53. *WT* 17, No. 4 (June–July 1931): 566–71. In *CF* 1.

"Pickman's Model." *WT* 10, No. 4 (October 1927): 505–14. In *By Daylight Only,* ed. Christine Campbell Thomson. London: Selwyn & Blount, 1929. 37–52. *WT* 28, No. 4 (November 1936): 495–505. In *The "Not at Night" Omnibus,* ed. Christine Campbell Thomson. London: Selwyn & Blount, [1937]. 279–307. In *CF* 2.

"The Picture in the House." *National Amateur* 41, No. 6 (July 1919 [*sic*]): 246–49. *WT* 3, No. 1 (January 1924): 40–42. *WT* 29, No. 3 (March 1937): 370–73. In *CF* 1.

"Polaris." *Philosopher* 1, No. 1 (December 1920): 3–5. *National Amateur* 48, No. 5 (May 1926): 48–49. *Fantasy Fan* 1, No. 6 (February 1934): 83–85. In *CF* 1.

"The Rats in the Walls." *WT* 3, No. 3 (March 1924): 25–31. *WT* 15, No. 6 (June 1930): 841–53. In *Switch On the Light,* ed. Christine Campbell Thomson. London: Selwyn & Blount, 1931. 141–65. In *CF* 1.

"The Shadow out of Time." Astounding Stories 17, No. 4 (June 1936): 110–54. In CF 3.

"The Shadow over Innsmouth." In *CF* 3.

"The Statement of Randolph Carter." *Vagrant* No. 13 (May 1920): 41–48. *WT* 5, No. 2 (February 1925): 149–53. In *CF* 1.

"Strange High House in the Mist." *WT* 18, No. 3 (October 1931): 394–400.

In *CF* 2.

"The Terrible Old Man." *Tryout* 7, No. 4 (July 1921): [10–14]. *WT* 8, No. 2 (August 1926): 191–92. In *CF* 1.

"The Thing on the Doorstep." *WT* 29, No. 1 (January 1937): 52–70. In *CF* 3.

"The Tomb." *Vagrant* No. 14 (March 1922): 50–64. *WT* 7, No. 1 (January 1926): 117–23. In *CF* 1.

"The Whisperer in Darkness." *WT* 18, No. 1 (August 1931): 32–73. In *CF* 2.

"The White Ship." *United Amateur* 19, No. 2 (November 1919): 30–33. *WT* 9, No. 3 (March 1927): 386–89. In *CF* 1.

Nonfiction

"Commonplace Book." In *CE* 5.

Further Criticism of Poetry. Louisville, KY: Press of George G. Fetter Co, 1932. Ms. entitled "Notes on Verse Technique" (18 April 1932). In *CE* 2.

"In Memoriam: Henry St. Clair Whitehead." *WT* 21, No. 3 (March 1933): 391. In *CE* 5.

"Letters to Carl Ferdinand Strauch." *Lovecraft Annual* No. 4 (2010): 46–119.

"Letters to Lee McBride White." *Lovecraft Annual* No. 1 (2007): 31–64.

"[Notes on Weird Fiction]." In *CE* 2.

"Some Dutch Footprints in New England." *De Halve Maen* 9, No. 1 (18 October 1933): 2, 4. In *CE* 4.

"Supernatural Horror in Literature." *Recluse* 1 (1927): 23–59. Rev. ed. (incomplete) in *Fantasy Fan* (October 1933–February 1935). In *CE* 2. In *The Annotated Supernatural Horror in Literature.* Ed. S. T. Joshi. New York: Hippocampus Press, rev. ed. 2012.

"Weird Story Plots." In *CE* 2.

"The Weird Work of William Hope Hodgson." *Phantagraph* 5, No. 5 (February 1937): 5–7. Incorporated into "Supernatural Horror in Literature."

Poetry [all items are in *The Ancient Track*]

"Autumn." *Tryout* 3, No. 12 (November 1917): [3–5]; rpt. [Providence] *Evening News* 51, No. 125 (5 November 1917): 3; *National Enquirer* 9, No. 4 (23 October 1919): 7.

"The East India Brick Row." *Providence Journal* 102, No. 7 (8 Jan. 1930): 13.

Fungi from Yuggoth.

    XXIII. "Mirage." *WT* 17, No. 2 (Feb.–Mar. 1931): 1975.

    XXVII. "The Elder Pharos." *WT* 17, No. 2 (Feb.–Mar. 1931): 175.

    XXXVI. "Continuity." *Causerie* (Feb. 1936): 1.

"In a Sequester'd Providence Churchyard Where Poe Once Walk'd." In *Four Acrostic Sonnets on Edgar Allan Poe* ([Milwaukee, WI: Maurice W. Moe, 1936]); rpt. *Science-Fantasy Correspondent* 1, No. 3 (March–April 1937): 16–17 (as "In a Sequestered Churchyard Where Once Poe Walked"); *HPL*

(Bellville, NJ: Corwin F. Stickney, 1937); *Weird Tales* 31, No. 5 (May 1938): 578 (as "Where Poe Once Walked").

"On an Unspoiled Rural Prospect." *Crypt of Cthulhu* No. 21 [*Saturnalia and Other Poems*] (Eastertide 1984): 36–37.

"Psychopompos: A Tale in Rhyme." *Vagrant* No. 10 (October 1919): 13–22.

Revisions and Collaborations [all items in *CF* 4]

"The Curse of Yig" (with Zealia Bishop). *WT* 14, No. 5 (November 1929): 625–36. In *Switch On the Light,* ed. Christine Campbell Thomson. London: Selwyn & Blount, 1931. 9–31. In *The "Not at Night" Omnibus,* ed. Christine Campbell Thomson. London: Selwyn & Blount, [1937]. 13–29.

"The Electric Executioner" (with Adolphe de Castro). *WT* 16, No. 2 (August 1930): 223–36.

"The Last Test" (with Adolphe de Castro). *WT* 12, No. 5 (November 1928): 625–56.

"Deaf, Dumb, and Blind" (with C. M. Eddy, Jr.). *WT* 5, No. 4 (April 1925): 25–30, 177–79.

"The Loved Dead" (with C. M. Eddy, Jr.). *WT* 4, No. 2 (May–June–July 1924): 54–57.

"The Horror in the Museum" (with Hazel Heald). *WT* 22, No. 1 (July 1933): 49–68. In *Terror by Night,* ed. Christine Campbell Thomson. London: Selwyn & Blount, (1934), pp. 111–41. In. *The "Not at Night" Omnibus,* ed. Christine Campbell Thomson. London: Selwyn & Blount, (1937), pp. 279–307.

"Through the Gates of the Silver Key" (with E. Hoffmann Price). *WT* 24, No. 1 (July 1934): 60–85.

"Two Black Bottles" (with Wilfred Blanch Talman). *WT* 10, No. 2 (August 1927): 251–58.

II. Works by J. Vernon Shea

[Editor] *Strange Desires.* New York: Lion Books, 1954.

[Editor] *Strange Barriers: 17 Stories of Negro and White, Man and Women, Tumult and Passion.* New York: Lion Library Editions, 1955. [188pp.]; as *Strange Barriers: 17 Stories of Tumult and Passion.* New York: Pyramid, 1961.; as *The Black and the White (17 Magnificent Stories of Tension and Passion By America's Greatest Black and White Writers)* New York: Pyramid Books, 1969.

H. P. Lovecraft: The House and the Shadows. West Warwick RI: Necronomicon Press, 1982.

In Search of Lovecraft. West Warwick RI: Necronomicon Press, 1991. *Contains:* Introduction, by Robert Bloch; ESSAYS: The Timeless Lovecraft; The Lovecraftian Saga; "The Outsider"; H. P. Lovecraft vs. Samuel Johnson; H. P. L. and Films; The Fifth World Fantasy Convention; FICTION: The Snouted Thing (with H. P. Lovecraft); Dead Giveaway; POETRY: When Artists Die; Look to the Skies; The Dream-World of H. P. Lovecraft;

"We tire of tyrants . . ."; A Walk in Providence; H. P. L.'s Gravestone; So Little Time Beneath the Stars; Impermanence; Better Days?; What Good Is a Book?; Roses Blooming in November; Here at Swan Point; Tomorrow; Afterword, by Donald Wandrei. [*ISL*]

Short Fiction

"Brother and Sister." Nonextant.

"The Cell." Nonextant

"Dead Giveaway." *Outré* 1. No. 1 (May 1976): 3–17; *ISL* 28–37; *The New Lovecraft Circle*, ed. Robert M. Price. Fedogan & Bremer (1996): 95–111; NY: Del Rey (2004) 110–28.

"The Earth Taint." Nonextant. JVS provided some details on the story in "Icarus Climbs Toward the Sun," p. 5.

"Five-Year Contract." *Magazine of Horror* 1, No. 5 (September 1964): 42–55.

"The Flaw." *Magazine of Horror* 3, No. 3 (Spring 1967): 27–35.

"The Growing Library of Professor Pitts." *Intro* (August 1950): 9–20; *Outré* 1, No. 2 (August 1976): [2]–[13].

"The Haunter of the Graveyard." *Tales of the Cthulhu Mythos*, ed. August Derleth. Sauk City, WI: Arkham House (1969) 259–71; *Tales of the Cthulhu Mythos*. Vol. 1. Ed. August Derleth. New York: Ballantine Books (1971; 1973; 1975) 227–42; St Albans: Panther (1975): 225–54; London: Grafton (1988) 239–53.

"Its Shuddery Embrace." Nonextant.

"The Judge's Hunting Dogs." Nonextant.

"Lost in the Corridors of Time." *Etchings & Odysseys* No. 3 (1983): 93–96.

"The Necronomicon" (ca. 1936). *Dragon et Microchips: Le Seul Fanzine Qui Rêve*.

"The Old Lady's Room." *Over the Edge: New Stories of the Macabre*. Ed. August Derleth. Sauk City, WI: Arkham House (1964): 211–18; London: Victor Gollancz (1964): 211–18; London: Arrow (1976): 182–88.

"Shoe Repairer." Nonextant.

"The Snouted Thing." *Outré* 4, No. 3 (October 1979): 20–24; *ISL* 25–28.

"The Stranger with Blue Spectacles." Nonextant.

"Soon to be Retired." *Etchings & Odysseys* No. 2 (1983): 45–46.

"Ten-Cent Matinee." Nonextant.

"The Tin Roof." Nonextant.

"The Werewolf's Victim." Nonextant.

"When the Communists Took Over Disneyland." *Outré* 4, No. 2 (August 1979): 56–65.

"The Whimpering of a Chile." *Outré* 4, No. 4 (February 1980): 20–25.

"The Wrong Tuesday." *Outré* 4, No. 1 (May 1979): 47–58.

Poetry/Verse

"Alter Ego." *Outré* 1, No. 3 (October 1976): [33].

"Better Days?" *Outré* 2, No. 4 (February 1978); 14. *ISL* 40.

"The Bookworm." *Outré* 3, No. 7 (November 1977): 44.
"A Clerihew." *HPL,* ed. Meade and Penny Frierson. Birmingham, AL (1972): 37.
"The Dream-World of H. P. Lovecraft." *Outré* 2, No. 2 (August 1977): 26. *ISL* 38.
"Dreams Remember Your Face." *Visions of Khroyd'Hon.* Ed. W. H. Pugmire. Seattle: n.p, 1976.
"H.P.L.'s Gravestone." *Outré* 2, No. 3 (November 1977): 44; *ISL* 39.
"Here at Swan Point." *Outré* 5, No. 3 (November 1980): 45; *ISL* 41.
"Impermanence." *Outré* 2, No. 4 (February 1978); 14; *ISL* 40.
"The Innsmouth Shuffle." *Night Gaunts* No. 6 (2 August 1980): 24.
"Look to the Skies." *Outré* 2, No. 1 (May 1977): 11; *ISL* 38.
"Roses Blooming in November." *Outré* 3, No. 4 (February 1979): 72; *ISL* 41.
"Rueful Lines." *Outré* 1, No. 3 (October 1976): [32].
"So Little Time Beneath the Stars." *Outré* 2, No. 4 (February 1978); 14; *ISL* 39–40.
"Surreal Poem." *Outré* 5, No. 4 (February 1981): 33.
"Tomorrow." *Outré* 2, No. 1 (May 1977): 33; *ISL* 42.
"A Walk in Providence." *Outré* 2, No. 3 (November 1977): 44; *ISL* 39.
"We tire of tyrants . . ." *Outré* 2, No. 3 (November 1977): 94; *ISL* 38.
"What Good Is a Book?" *Outré* 2, No. 4 (February 1978); 14; *ISL* 41.
"What Is the Soul?" Nonextant.
"When Artists Die." *Outré* 1, No. 3 (October 1976): [31]; *ISL* 37.

Nonfiction

"The Circle Manqué." *Nyctalops* 11/12 (April 1976): 14–15.; as "The Lovecraft Circle," *Conversations with the Weird Tales Circle.* Ed. John Pelan and Jerad Walters. Lakewood, CO: Centipede Press (2009): 686–89.
"The Creative Musician vs. The Creative Writer." *Abaddon* 1, No. 6 (February 1976): 6–8.
"Did HPL Suffer from Chorea?" *Outré* 2, No. 1 (May 1977): 30–31.
"The Fantastic Cinema: 1975." *Abaddon* 1, No. 6 (February 1976): 8–12.
"Fantasy Writers On Film." *Continuity* 1, No. 3 (May 1976); *Continuity.* New Series No. 2 (May 1999).
"The Fifth World Fantasy Convention." *Outré* 4, No. 4(February 1980): 3–14; *ISL* 17–25.
"Four Playwrights." *Dragon-Fly* No. 2 (15 May 1936): 59–61.
"H. P. Lovecraft and Robert Aickman: Contrast and Comparison." *Outré* 4, No. 4 (August 1979): 6–17.
"H. P. Lovecraft and Samuel Johnson: A Comparison." *Outré* 3, No. 1 (June 1978): 9–10; *ISL* 13–14.
"H. P. Lovecraft: The House and the Shadows." *Magazine of Fantasy and Science Fiction* 30, No. 5 (May 1966): 82–99; *L'Herne.* Cahier No. 12. Ed. François Truchaud. Paris: L'Herne (1969); *Fiction*, No. 183 (March 1969): 134–46.; *Fantasy Empire* (1984): 23–36 (abridged?); as "H. P. Lovecraft: das Haus und die Schatten." *Der Einsiedler von Providence: Lovecrafts ungewöhnliches Leben.*

Ed. Franz Rottensteiner. Frankfurt am Main: Suhrkamp (1992); *Necro-nomicon: De döda nammens bok noveller och texter.* Ed. Sam J. Lundwall. Stockholm: Lundwall Fakta & Fantasi (1995); *Lovecraft Remembered.* Ed. Peter Cannon. Sauk City, WI: Arkham House (1998): 367–69 (abridged).

"H. P. Lovecraft vs. Anton Chekov." *Outré* 3, No. 4 (February 1979): 62–63.

"H. P. Lovecraft vs. Sir Richard Burton." *Outré* 3, No. 4 (February 1979): 46–47.

"Henry Kuttner: A Memoir." In "Recollections of Henry Kuttner by His Friends." *Etchings & Odysseys* No. 4. (1984): 9; *Conversations with the Weird Tales Circle,* ed. John Pelan and Jerad Walters. Lakewood, CO: Centipede Press (2009): 430–31 (excerpted from "A Trip Around the Bloch." *Ibid,* No. 35 [1981]).

"The Homosexual Element In Lovecraft's Fiction." *Gaylactic Gayzette* 5, No. 3 (Winter 1991).

"HPL and Films." *HPL,* ed. Meade and Penny Frierson. Birmingham, AL (1972): 28–30; *ISL* 15–17.

"HPL's New England." *Continuity* 2, No. 2 (February/Candlemas 1976): 8–9.

"'I Am Providence'." *Outré* 5, No. 3 (November 1980): 47.

"Icarus Climbs Toward the Sun: The Aspirations of August Derleth." *Dark Brotherhood Journal* 1, No. 2 (1972): 5–20.

"Iguanacon at Sunstroke City." *Outré* 3, No. 3 (October 1978): 3–9.

"An Introduction to the Cthulhu Mythos." *Fandom Unlimited,* No. 2 (Spring 1977): 18–19; *Fantasy Empire Presents H. P. Lovecraft.* Tampa, FL: New Media Publishing (1984): 4–10.

"Lovecraft's Follies: A Review." *HPL.* Ed. Meade and Penny Frierson. Birmingham, AL (1972): 51.

"The Lovecraftian Who Became A V.I.P." *Miskatonic* No. 13. (February 1976): 20–23; ; *The Miskatonic: Lovecraft Centennary Edition.* Glenview, IL: Moshassuck Press, 1991: 258–61.

"The Lovecraftian Saga" (1976) *ISL* 11–12.

"A Loveman with Little Love." *Crumbling Relicks* No. 10 (October 1976): 3–7.

"Music To Read By." *Abaddon* 1, No. 6 (February 1976): 15–28.

"The Necessity For Adjecivity." *Midnight Fantasies* No. 3 (May 1976).

"The Necessity for Objectivity." *Midnight Fantasies* No. 3 (May 1976): 8.

"A Note on Amateur Letters." *Tryout* 18, No. 7 (June 1937): [9]–[10].

"On Filming 'The Whisperer'." *CineFan,* No. 2. (Summer 1980): 22–23.

"On the Literary Influences Which Shaped Lovecraft's Works." *Outré* 3, No. 4 (February 1979): 3–23; *H. P. Lovecraft: Four Decades of Criticism.* Ed. S. T. Joshi. Athens, OH: Ohio University Press (1980): 113–39.

"On Writing in Bed," *Dragon-Fly* No 1 (15 October 1935): [8]–9.

"The Outsider." *Outré* 4, No. 1 (May 1979): 13; *ISL* 12–13.

"The Professional Writer vs. The Gifted Amateur." *Miskatonic,* No. 11. (August 1975): 3–4; *The Miskatonic: Lovecraft Centennary Edition.* Glenview, IL: Moshassuck Press, 1991: 204–05.

"The Rats in the Walls." *Outré* 4, No. 1 (May 1979): 12.

"R. H. Barlow: Lost Little Boy." (unpublished, intended for Shea's *The Love-craft Circle*.)

"A Rebuttal to Ted White's Column." *Outré* 5, No. 4 (February 1981): 30–31. (White's "My Column" *Thrust: Science Fiction in Review*, No. 16. Ed. D. Douglas Fratz. MD: Thrust Publications [Fall 1980]).

"Revelations Upon a Somber Theme." *Carl Jacobi: An Appreciation*. Ed. Neal R. Blaikie and William H. Pugmire. Pensacola, FL: Stellar Z Productions (1977): 6.

Review. "Kenneth W. Faig's *H. P. Lovecraft: His Life, His Work*." *Lovecraft Studies*, No. 1 (Fall 1979): 30–33.

"A Ride on the Wild Nightmare: The Sixth World Fantasy Con." *Outré* 5, No. 4 (February 1981): 12–21.

"The Secret Member." *Miskatonic*, No. 12. (October 1975): [4]–[5]; *Whispers*, No. 13–14 (October 1979): 119–120; *The Miskatonic: Lovecraft Centenary Edition*. Glenview, IL: Moshassuck Press, 1991: 228–29. (Hoax piece about Lovecraft's illegitimate half-brother Winthrop)

"Some Thoughts about World Fantasy Conventions." *Outré* 5, No. 4 (February 1981): 22–23.

"The Timeless Lovecraft." *Outré* 4, No. 3 (October 1979): 33–6; *ISL* 9–11.

"To the Reader." *Strange Desires*. New York: Lion Books, [February] 1954: 1–8.

"A Trip Around the Bloch." *Ibid* No. 35 (Lammas 1981): 1–19. (Written ca. 1973 for Tom Collins's *IS*).

Letters

WT 8, No. 4 (October 1926. p. 573; *Lovecraft in "The Eyrie"*: 17.

WT 17, No. 2 (February–March 1931): 148.

"'Shrewd,' Yet Somehow Obtuse!" *Astounding Stories* 5, No. 3 (March 1931): 425.

WT 18, No. 2 (September 1931: 148; *Lovecraft in "The Eyrie"*: 35.

WT 18, No. 3 (October 1931): 292; *Lovecraft in "The Eyrie"*: 36.

"Hugh Rankin's Art." *WT* 30, No. 2 (August 1937): 256.

"Give the Nudes a Rest." *WT* 30, No. 5 (November 1937): 638.

"Conte Cruel." *WT* 30, No. 6 (December 1937): 764; *H. P. Lovecraft in "The Eyrie"*: 71.

"Impressive Illustrations." *WT* 31, No. 2 (February 1938): 252.

"Brickbats." *WT* 31, No. 3 (March 1938): 382.

"A Lovecraft Protege." *WT* 31, No. 4 (April 1938): 509; *Lovecraft in "The Eyrie"*: 76.

"An Outre Air." *WT* 34, No. 1 (July 1939): 152.

"Concise Comments." *WT* 35, No. 1 (January 1940): 127.

The HPL Supplement, No. 1. (April–October 1972): [8].

Midfan Supplement. (April 1975).

Letter to Harry O. Morris, Jr., 22 January 1976. *Conversations with the WT Circle*. Ed. John Pelan and Jerad Walters. Lakewood, CO: Centipede Press (2009): 685–.

Under "Pnakotic Manuscripts." *Nyctalops* 2 No. 11/12 (April 1976): 40.

III. Works by Carl Ferdinand Strauch

Twenty-nine Poems. Boston: Bruce Humphries, Inc., 1932. *Contains:* Song: A Drop of Rain Inconsequent; Blackbird, Take the Breeze; [An] Epitaph; Lost Illusion; The Penny; The Sleeper; In Memoriam: Eugene V. Debs; The Beauty of Decay; The White Fiend Death; Things I Shall Not Do When I Am Dead; The Three Graces; A Roman Coxcomb; He To Her; Curse for Kiss; A Legend of Love; Dear, True, and Tender; One Living to One Dead; Song: She Was a Creature Whose Delight; At Evening; Robin Hood; My Tree of Fruits; In His Mango Grove the Buddhist; This Fecund, Gifted Hour; Directions to Make Wine; Too Audacious Curious; Soul Mates; Come Forth, Old Men, into the Sun; Hymn to that Mightiest; Prayer.

"A Library Goes Regionalist." *Wilson Bulletin for Librarians* 8, No. 4 (December 1933): 213–15. *Lovecraft Annual* No. 4 (2010): 119–23.

IV. Works by Lee McBride White

The American Revolution in Notes, Quotes, and Anecdotes: A Sedgewick Archives Book. Fairfax, VA: L. B. Prince Co., 1975.

"For Aldous Huxley." *Campus* 1, No. 1 (October 1936): 25.

"Look at Your Thumb." *Howard Quill* 8, No. 1 (Winter 1936): 23.

"Out of Sorrows." *Howard Quill* 8, No. 1 (Winter 1936): 26–27.

V. Works by Others

Alden, Abner (1758?–1820). *The Reader: Containing the Art of Delivery, Articulation, Accent, Pronunciation, [etc.].* 3d ed. Boston: Printed by J. T. Buckingham for Thomas & Andrews, 1808. (*LL* 16)

Allen, Hervey (1889–1949). *Anthony Adverse.* New York: Farrar & Rinehart, 1933.

The Arabian Nights Entertainments. Selected by Andrew Lang. New York: Longmans, Green, 1898. (*LL* 38)

Armstrong, Martin (1882–1974). "The Pipe-Smoker." *Fortnightly Review* 138, No. 4 (October 1932): 473–81. In *General Buntop's Miracle.* London: Gollancz; New York: Harcourt, Brace & Company, 1934.

Asbury, Herbert (1891–1963). *The Gangs of New York: An Informal History of the Underworld.* New York: Knopf, 1928.

———, ed. *Not at Night!* New York: Macy-Masius (The Vanguard Press), 1928. (*LL* 44)

Asquith, Lady Cynthia (1887–1960) [et al.]. *My Grimmest Nightmare.* [Edited by Cecil Madden.] London: George Allen & Unwin, 1935. (*LL* 45)

Baldwin, F. Lee. "H. P. Lovecraft: A Biographical Sketch." *Fantasy Magazine* 4, No. 5 (April 1935): 108–10, 132.

[Barnitz, Park] (1878–1901). *The Book of Jade.* New York: Doxey's, n.d. [1901]. In *The Book of Jade: A New Critical Edition.* Ed. David E. Schultz and Michael J. Abolafia. New York: Hippocampus Press, 2015.

Barrie, J. M. (1860–1937). *Farewell Miss Julie Logan: A Wintry Tale.* London: Hodder & Stoughton, 1932.

Baudelaire, Charles. *Les Fleurs du mal, Petites Poèmes en prose, Les Paradis artificiels.* Tr. Arthur Symons. London: Casanova Society, 1925.

––––––. *Flowers of Evil.* Tr. George Dillon and Edna St. Vincent Millay. New York: Harper & Brothers, 1936.

Beach, Joseph Warren (1880–1957). *The Twentieth Century Novel: Studies in Technique.* New York: Century Co., 1932.

Beardsley, Aubrey (1872–1898). *The Art of Aubrey Beardsley.* Introduction by Arthur Symons. New York: Boni & Liveright (Modern Library), [1918] *or* New York: Modern Library, [1925]. (*LL* 71)

Beckford, William (1759–1844). *The Episodes of Vathek.* <1912> Tr. Sir Frank T. Marzials. Boston: Small, Maynard & Co., [1922?] or [1924?]. (*LL* 73)

––––––. *The History of the Caliph Vathek.* Printed Verbatim from the First Edition, with the Original Prefaces and Notes by Samuel Henley. <1786> New York W. L. Allinson, [1868? or 188-?]. (*LL* 74)

Benson, E. F. (1867–1940). *Spook Stories.* London: Hutchinson, 1928. [Includes "The Face."]

––––––. *Visible and Invisible.* London: Hutchinson, 1923. New York: Doubleday, Doran, 1923. [Includes "The Horror-Horn" and *"Negotium Perambulans . . .*']

Benson, Stella (1892–1933). *Living Alone.* London: Macmillan, 1920.

Bierce, Ambrose (1842–1914?). *Can Such Things Be?* <1893> New York: Boni & Liveright (Modern Library), 1918. (*LL* 87)

––––––. *In the Midst of Life: Tales of Soldiers and Civilians.* <1891> Introduction by George Sterling. New York: Modern Library, [1927]. (*LL* 88)

Birkhead, Edith (1889–1951). *The Tale of Terror.* New York: E. P. Dutton, 1921. (*LL* 97)

Blackwood, Algernon (1869–1951). *The Education of Uncle Paul.* London, Macmillan, 1909.

––––––. *The Fruit Stoners* (London: Grayson & Grayson, 1934; New York: E. P. Dutton, 1935),

––––––. *Incredible Adventures.* London: Macmillan, 1914. New York: Macmillan, 1914. [Contains: "A Descent into Egypt."]

––––––. *John Silence—Physician Extraordinary.* London: Eveleigh Nash, 1908. (*LL* 96)

––––––. *Julius LeVallon.* London: Cassell, 1916. New York: E. P. Dutton, 1916. (*LL* 98)

––––––. *The Listener and Other Stories.* London: Eveleigh Nash, 1907. New York: Vaughan & Gomme, 1914. New York: Knopf, 1917. [Includes "The Willows."]

––––––. *The Lost Valley and Other Stories.* London: Eveleigh Nagh, 1910. (*LL* 99)

Blair, Hugh (1718–1800). *Lectures on Rhetoric and Belles Lettres, with a Memoir of the Author's Life.* <1783> Philadelphia: J. Kay, Jun., and Brother; Pittsburgh: J. I. Kay & Co., 1829. (*LL* 105)

Bloomfield, Robert (1766–1823). *The Farmer's Boy: A Rural Poem*. Ornamented with Elegant Wood Engravings by A. Anderson. The 5th American, from the 6th London ed. New York: Printed by Hopkins & Seymour, and Sold by G. F. Hopkins, 1803. (*LL* 106)

Bradford, Gamaliel (1863–1932). *The Journal of Gamaliel Bradford, 1883–1932*. Boston: Houghton Mifflin, 1933.

Brontë, Emily (1818–1848). *Wuthering Heights*. London: Newby, 1847. (*LL* 611)

Brown, Charles Brockden (1771–1810). *Wieland*. <1798> Excerpts in *The Lock and Key Library*, ed. Julian Hawthorne. New York: Review of Reviews Co., 1909. (*LL* 400)

Brown, J. Macmillan (1845–1935). *The Riddle of the Pacific*. London: T. Fisher Unwin, 1924.

Buchan, John (1875–1940). *The Runagates Club*. Boston: Houghton Mifflin, 1928. (*LL* 129) [Contains "Skule Skerry," "The Green Wildebeest," and "The Wind in the Portico."]

Bulwer-Lytton, Edward (1803–1873). *The Coming Race; or, The New Utopia*. <1871> (*LL* 132)

———. "The Haunted and the Haunters." In *A Strange Story; The Haunted House* [*sic*]*; Zanoni*. <1862; 1859; 1842> Boston: Desmond Publishing Co., [18—?]. (*LL* 133)

Cabell, James Branch (1879–1958). *Jurgen: A Comedy of Justice*. New York: Robert M. McBride, 1919.

Carlyle, Thomas (1795–1881). *Sartor Resartus*. <1833–34> (*LL* 154)

Carr, Robert Spencer (1909–1994). *The Rampant Age*. Garden City, NY: Doubleday, Doran & Company, 1928.

Casey, Robert J. (1890–1962). *Easter Island: Home of the Scornful Gods*. New York: Blue Ribbon Books, 1931.

Cather, Willa (1873–1947). *Shadows on the Rock*. New York: Knopf, 1931.

Chambers, Robert W. (1865–1933). *In Search of the Unknown*. New York: Harper & Brothers, 1904. (*LL* 166) [First five chapters incorporate the story "The Harbor-Master" (1897).]

———. *The King in Yellow*. Chicago: F. Tennyson Neely, 1895. (*LL* 167)

Chamisso, Adelbert von (1781–1838), *Peter Schlemihls wundersame Geschichte* (1814). As *The Shadowless Man*. Tr. John Bowring. London: Chatto & Windus, 1910.

Coates, Robert M. (1897–1973). *The Eater of Darkness*. New York: Macaulay, 1929.

———. *The Outlaw Years: The History of the Land Pirates of the Natchez Trace*. New York: Macaulay, 1930.

Coblentz, Stanton A. *The Blue Barbarians*. *Amazing Stories Quarterly* (Summer 1931). New York: Avalon, 1958.

Colby, Merle (1902–1969). *All Ye People*. New York: Viking Press, 1931.

Coleridge, Samuel Taylor. *The Rime of the Ancient Mariner*. Illustrated by Gustave Doré. London: Doré Gallery, 1875.

————, [et al.]. *The Poetical Works of Coleridge, Shelley, and Keats.* Complete in One Volume. Philadelphia: Crissy & Markley, 1849. (*LL* 188)

Cram, Ralph Adams (1863–1942). *Black Spirits and White: A Book of Ghost Stories.* Chicago: Stone & Kimball, 1895. [Includes "The Dead Valley."]

Crawford, F. Marion (1854–1909). *Wandering Ghosts.* New York: Macmillan, 1911. London: T. Fisher Unwin, 1911 (as *Uncanny Tales*).

Cronin, A. J. (1896–1981). *The Stars Look Down.* London: Victor Gollancz, 1935. Boston: Little, Brown, 1935.

cummings, e. e. (1894–1962). *The Enormous Room.* New York: Boni & Liveright, 1922.

Damon, S. Foster (1893–1971). *Thomas Holley Chivers, Friend of Poe.* New York: Harper & Brothers, 1930.

Dante Alighieri (1265–1321). *Dante's Inferno.* Tr. Henry Francis Cary <1805–06> . . . and Illustrated with the Designs of M. Gustave Doré. New York: P. F. Collier, 1892. (*LL* 218)

de la Mare, Colin (1906–1983), ed. *They Walk Again: A Collection of Ghost Stories.* New York: E. P. Dutton, 1931.

de la Mare, Walter (1873–1956). *The Connoisseur and Other Stories.* New York: Knopf, 1926. [Includes "All Hallows" and "Mr. Kempe."] (*LL* 228)

————. *On the Edge.* London: Faber & Faber, 1930. New York: Knopf, 1931.

————. *The Riddle and Other Stories.* <1923> New York: Knopf, 1930. [Includes "Out of the Deep," "Seaton's Aunt," and "The Tree."] (*LL* 229)

Derleth, August (1909–1971). "The Case for the Intelligentsia." *Midwestern Conference* (April 1931): 5–6, 40–42 (Part I: "The Cult of Incoherence").

————. "A Day in March." *Frontier and Midland* 13, No. 3 (March 1933): 189–91.

————. *Evening in Spring.* New York: Charles Scribner's Sons, 1941.

————. *The Man on All Fours: A Judge Peck Mystery Story.* New York: Loring & Mussey, 1934. (*LL* 234)

————. "Old Ladies." *Midland* 19, No. 1 (January–February 1932): 5–9.

————. "People." Apparently unpublished or nonextant.

————. *Place of Hawks.* New York: Loring & Mussey, 1935. (*LL* 235)

————. *Sign of Fear: A Judge Peck Mystery.* New York: Loring & Mussey, 1935. (*LL* 236)

————. *Three Who Died: A Judge Peck Mystery.* New York: Loring & Mussey, 1935. (*LL* 237)

Dinesen, Isak (pseud. of Karen Blixen, 1885–1962). *Seven Gothic Tales.* New York: Harrison Smith & Richard Haas, 1934.

Disraeli, Benjamin, earl of Beaconsfield (1804–1881). *Alroy.* <1833> (*LL* 73)

Dunglinson, Robley. *Human Physiology: Illustrated by Numerous Engravings.* Philadelphia: Carey & Lea, 1832.

Dunsany, Edward John Moreton Drax Plunkett, 18th baron (1878–1957). *The Book of Wonder* <1912> [and *Time and the Gods* <1906>]. New York: Boni & Liveright (Modern Library), [1918]. (*LL* 271)

————. *The Chronicles of Rodriguez*. London: G. P. Putnam's Sons, 1922. New York: G. P. Putnam's Sons, 1922 (as *Don Rodriguez: Chronicles of Shadow Valley*). (*LL* 272)

————. *The Curse of the Wise Woman*. London: William Heinemann; New York: Longmans, Green, 1933.

————. *A Dreamer's Tales and Other Stories*. New York: Boni & Liveright [Modern Library], [1917], [1919], or [1921]. (*LL* 273)

————. *The Gods of Pegāna*. London: Elkin Mathews, 1905. (*LL* 276)

————. *The Gods of the Mountain*. In *Five Plays:* <1914> Boston: Little, Brown, 1923. (*LL* 275)

————. *Jorkens Remembers Africa*. New York: Longmans, Green, 1934.

————. *The King of Elfland's Daughter*. London: G. P. Putnam's Sons, 1924. (*LL* 277)

————. *The Last Book of Wonder*. Boston: J. W. Luce, 1916. (*LL* 278)

————. *The Sword of Welleran and Other Stories*. London: George Allen & Sons, 1908. (*LL* 273)

————. *Tales of Three Hemispheres*. <1919>. (*LL* 281)

————. *Time and the Gods*. London: Heinemann, 1906. (*LL* 271)

————. *The Travel Tales of Mr. Joseph Jorkens*. London: G. P. Putnam's Sons, [1931]. (*LL* 280)

Easton, Emily M. *Roger Williams, Prophet and Pioneer*. Boston, New York, Houghton, Mifflin Co., 1930.

Eddison, E. R. (1882–1945). *Mistress of Mistresses: A Vision of Zimiamvia*. New York: E. P. Dutton & Co. 1935.

————. *The Worm Ouroboros: A Romance*. New York: A. & C. Boni, 1926. (*LL* 289)

Eliot, T. S. *The Waste Land*. *Dial* 73, No. 5 (November 1922): 473–85 (*LL* 238). New York: Boni & Liveright, 1922.

England, George Allan (1877–1936). "The Thing from—'Outside.'" *Science and Invention* (April 1923). *Amazing Stories* (April 1926).

Ernst, James. *Roger Williams, New England Firebrand*. New York : Macmillan, 1932.

Faulkner, William. "A Rose for Emily." *Forum* (April 1930). Rpt. in Hammett's *Creeps by Night* (q.v.).

50 Years of Ghost Stories. London: Hutchinson, [1935]. [Contains Algernon Blackwood's "The Woman's Ghost Story."]

Finney, Charles G. (1905–1984). *The Circus of Dr. Lao*. New York: Viking Press, 1935.

Frank, Waldo (1889–1967). *Chalk Face*. New York: Boni & Liveright, 1924.

————. *City Block*. Darien, CT: Waldo Frank, 1922. (*LL* 328)

Frazer, Sir James George (1854–1941). *The Golden Bough: A Study in Comparative Religion*. London: Macmillan, 1890. [Expanded into 12 vols., London: Macmillan, 1911–15.]

French, Joseph Lewis (1858–1936), ed. *The Ghost Story Omnibus*. New York: Tudor Publishing Co., 1926.

————. *Ghosts, Grim and Gentle*. New York: Dodd, Mead, 1926.

Gibbon, Edward. *The Student's Gibbon: The History of the Decline and Fall of the Roman Empire.* Abridged, Incorporating the Researches of Recent Commentators, by William Smith. New York: Harper & Brothers, 1864. (*LL* 352)

Grimm, Jakob Ludwig Karl (1785–1863), and W. K. Grimm (1786–1859). *Fairy Tales.* <1812–15> (*LL* 379)

Gummere, Francis Barton (1855–1919). *A Handbook of Poetics, for Students of English Verse.* Boston: Ginn & Co., 1885.

Hammett, Dashiell (1894–1961), ed. *Creeps by Night: Chills and Thrills.* New York: John Day Co., 1931.

———. *Modern Tales of Horror.* London: Victor Gollancz, 1932. (*LL* 395)

Harré, T. Everett (1884–1948), ed. *Beware After Dark! The World's Most Stupendous Tales of Mystery, Horror, Thrills and Terror.* New York: Macaulay, 1929. (*LL* 397)

Hawthorne, Nathaniel (1804–1864). *The House of the Seven Gables, and The Snow-Image and Other Twice-Told Tales.* <1851; 1852> Boston: Houghton Mifflin, 1886. (*LL* 402)

Hecht, Ben (1894–1964). *Erik Dorn.* New York: G. P. Putnam's Sons, 1921.

Heyward, Du Bose (1885–1940). *The Half Pint Flask.* New York: Farrar & Rinehart, 1929.

———. *Peter Ashley.* New York: Farrar & Rinehart, 1932.

Homer. *The Iliad of Homer.* Done into English Prose by Andrew Lang, Walter Leaf, and Ernest Myers. London: Macmillan, 1883.

———. *The Odyssey of Homer.* Done into English Prose by S. H. Butcher and Andrew Lang. <1881> New York: Modern Library, [1929].

Huxley, Aldous (1894–1963). *Eyeless in Gaza.* New York and London: Harper & Brothers, 1936.

———. *Point Counter Point.* London: Chatto & Windus, 1928. New York: Harper & Brothers, 1928.

Huysmans, Joris-Karl (1848–1907). *Against the Grain [A Rebours].* <1884> Tr. John Howard. New York: A. & C. Boni, 1930. (*LL* 452)

———. *Down There [Là-Bas].* <1891> Tr. Keene Wallis. New York: A. & C. Boni, 1924.

James, M[ontague] R[hodes] (1862–1936). *The Collected Ghost Stories of M. R. James.* London: Edward Arnold, 1931.

———. *A Thin Ghost and Others.* London: Edward Arnold, 1919. (*LL* 470)

Joyce, James. *Anna Livia Plurabelle: Fragment of Work in Progress.* London: Faber & Faber, 1930. [Later incorporated into *Finnegans Wake.*]

———. *Dubliners.* New York, Modern Library, 1926.

———. *Ulysses.* Paris: Shakespeare & Co., 1922.

Kenyon, Theda (1894–1997). *Witches Still Live: A Study of the Black Art To-day.* New York: Ives Washburn, 1929.

Kosztolányi, Dezsö (1885–1936). *A véres költö* (1921). As *The Bloody Poet: A Novel about Nero.* Tr. Clifton Fadiman. New York: Macy-Masius, 1927.

La Motte-Fouqué, Friedrich Heinrich Karl, freiherr de (1777–1843). *Undine.* <1811>

Lawrence, T. E. (1888–1935), *Seven Pillars of Wisdom: A Triumph.* [London], 1926. Garden City, NY: Doubleday, Doran, 1935.

Lewis, Matthew Gregory (1775–1818). *The Monk.* <1796> London: Brentano's, [1924]. 3 vols. in 1. (*LL* 531)

Lloyd, John Uri (1849–1936). *Etidorhpa; or, The End of Earth.* Cincinnati: John Uri Lloyd, 1895.

Long, Frank Belknap (1901–1994). *The Goblin Tower.* Cassia, FL: Dragon-Fly Press, 1935.

Loveman, Samuel. *The Hermaphrodite: A Poem.* Athol, MA: W. Paul Cook, 1926. (*LL* 549)

———. *The Hermaphrodite and Other Poems.* Caldwell, ID: Caxton Printers, 1936.

———.*The Sphinx: A Conversation.* [North Montpelier, VT: W. Paul Cook, 1944.]

Lowell, James Russell (1819–1891). *The Biglow Papers: First Series.* Cambridge, MA: G. Nichols, 1848.

Lynch, John Gilbert Bohun (1884–1928), ed. *The Best Ghost Stories.* Boston: Small, Maynard & Co., [1924]. (*LL* 558)

Machen, Arthur (1863–1947). "The Bowmen." *Evening News* (London) (29 September 1914): 3. In *The Angels of Mons, the Bowmen, and Other Legends of the War.* London: Simpkin, Marshall, Hamilton, Kent, 1915. New York: G. P. Putnam's Sons, 1915. London: Martin Secker, 1923.

———. *The Hill of Dreams.* London: Grant Richards, 1907. (*LL* 572)

———. *The House of Souls.* London: E. Grant Richards, 1906. New York: Knopf, 1922 (abridged). (*LL* 573)

———. *The Terror.* London: Duckworth, 1917. New York: McBride, 1917.

———. *The Three Impostors.* <1895> New York: Knopf, 1930. (*LL* 578)

Matthews, Brander (1852–1929). *A Study of Versification.* Boston: Houghton Mifflin, 1911.

Maturin, Charles Robert (1782?–1824). *Melmoth the Wanderer.* <1820> London: Richard Bentley & Son, 1892. (*LL* 600)

Maugham, W. Somerset (1874–1965). *The Magician.* New York: Duffield, 1908.

———. *Of Human Bondage.* Garden City, NY: Doubleday, 1936.

Maurois, André (1885–1967). "The Weigher of Souls." *Scribner's Magazine* (March 1931). New York: D. Appleton & Co., 1931.

Merritt, A. (1884–1943). *Creep, Shadow. Argosy* (8 September–20 October 1934) (*LL* 40). Garden City, NY: Doubleday, 1934.

———. "The Moon Pool." *All-Story Weekly* (22 June 1918). (*LL* 17)

———. *The Moon Pool.* New York: Putnam, 1919.

———. "The People of the Pit." *All-Story Weekly* (5 January 1918); rpt. *Amazing Stories Annual* (1927).

Meyrink, Gustav (1868–1932). *The Golem.* <1915> Tr. Madge Pemberton. London: Gollancz; Boston: Houghton Mifflin, 1928.

Middleton, Jessie Adelaide (1861–1921). *The White Ghost Book.* London/New York: Cassell, 1916.

Milton, John (1608–1674). *Paradise Lost.* Illustrated by Gustave Doré. London: Cassell, Petter, & Galpin, 1866.

The Modern Encyclopedia: A New Library of World Knowledge. Edited by A. H. McDannald. New York: Grosset & Dunlap, 1935. (*LL* 613)

Morgan, Charles Lanbridge (1894–1958). *The Fountain.* New York: Knopf, 1932.

Norris, Frank (1870–1902). *McTeague: A Story of San Francisco.* <1899> Garden City, NY: Doubleday, Page, 1924.

O'Brien, Edward J. (1890–1941). *The Dance of the Machines: The American Short Story and the Industrial Age.* New York: Macaulay Co, 1929. (*LL* 652)

O'Neill, Eugene (1888–1953). *The Emperor Jones.* New York: Stewart Kidd, 1921.

————. *Mourning Becomes Electra.* New York: Liveright, 1931.

————. *Strange Interlude.* New York: Boni & Liveright, 1928.

Onions, Oliver (1873–1961). *Ghosts in Daylight.* London: Chapman & Hall, 1924. (*LL* 654)

Parker, Richard Green. *Aids to English Composition, Prepared for Students of All Grades.* Boston: R. S. Davis; New York: Robinson, Pratt & Co., 1844. (*LL* 674)

Pattee, Fred Lewis (1863–1950). *A History of American Literature Since 1870.* New York: Century Co., 1921.

————. *The House of the Black Ring.* Harrisburg, PA: Mount Pleasant Press, 1916. (*LL* 679)

Perutz, Leo (1884–1957). *The Master of the Day of Judgment.* Tr. Hedwig Singer. New York: Charles Boni, 1930. (*LL* 688)

Pierce, Frederick Clifton (1855–1904). *Field Genealogy.* Chicago: Hammond Press; W. B. Conkey, 1901.

Pitkin, Walter B. (1878–1953). *A Short Introduction to the History of Human Stupidity.* New York: Simon & Schuster, 1932.

Proust, Marcel (1871–1922). *Cities of the Plain.* Tr. C. K. Scott-Moncrieff. New York: Albert & Charles Boni, 1927.

————. *The Guermantes Way.* Tr. C. K. Scott-Moncrieff. London: Chatto & Windus, 1925.

————. *Swann's Way.* Tr. C. K. Scott-Moncrieff. New York: Holt, 1923.

————. *Within a Budding Grove.* Tr. C. K. Scott-Moncrieff. New York: Thomas Seltzer, 1924.

Quain, Jones (1876–1865). *Elements of Descriptive and Practical Anatomy: For the Use of Students.* London: Printed for W. Simpkin and R. Marshall, 1828.

Railo, Eino (1884–1948). *The Haunted Castle: A Study of the Elements of English Romanticism.* New York: E. P. Dutton, 1927.

Rascoe, Burton (1892–1957). *Titans of Literature from Homer to the Present.* New York: Putnam's, 1932. Also published as *The Story of the World's Great Writers.*

Rawlings, Marjorie Kinnan (1896–1953). *South Moon Under.* New York, London: C. Scribner's Sons, 1933.

Reynolds, George W. M. (1814–1879). *Wagner, the Wehr-Wolf.* London: J. Dicks, 1848, 1857, 1872.

Richardson, Henry Handel (1870–1946). *Maurice Guest.* Melbourne, Australia: William Heinemann, 1908.

Richardson, Leon Burr. *History of Dartmouth College.* Hanover, NH: Dartmouth College, 1932; 2 vols.

Roget, Peter Mark (1779–1869). *Thesaurus of English Words and Phrases.* New ed., enlarged & improved, partly from the author's notes, & with a full index, by John Lewis Roget. New York & Chicago: John R. Anderson & Co., 1882. (*LL* 741) New York: Grosset & Dunlap, 1933.

Sacher-Masoch, Leopold von (1835–1895). *Venus im Pelz.* 1870. First Eng. tr. as *Venus in Furs* (1921).

Sade, Donatien Alphonse François, marquis de (1740–1814). *Justine; ou, Les Malheurs de la vertu.* 1791. First Eng. tr. as *Justine; or, The Misfortunes of Virtue* (1889).

Santayana, George (1863–1952). *The Last Puritan: A Memoir in the Form of a Novel.* London: Constable, 1935. New York: Charles Scribner's Sons, 1936.

Sayers, Dorothy L. (1893–1957) ed. *The Omnibus of Crime.* <1928> Garden City, NY: Garden City Publishing Co., 1931. (*LL* 762)

———, ed. *The Second Omnibus of Crime.* <1931> New York: Coward-McCann, 1932.

Scarborough, Dorothy (1878–1935). *The Supernatural in Modern English Fiction.* New York: G. P. Putnam's Sons, 1917.

Sheean, Vincent (1899–1975). *Personal History.* Garden City, NY: Doubleday, Doran & Company, 1935.

Shiel, M[atthew] P[hipps] (1865–1947). *The Pale Ape and Other Pulses.* London: T. Werner Laurie, 1911.

Sinclair, May (1863–1946). *The Intercessor and Other Stories.* New York: Macmillan, 1932.

Skinner, Conrad Arthur. *Not in Our Stars.* By Michael Maurice [pseud.]. Philadelphia: J. B. Lippincott Co., 1923. (*LL* 809)

Smith, Clark Ashton (1893–1961). *The Double Shadow and Other Fantasies.* Auburn, CA: Auburn Journal Press, 1933). (*LL* 810)

———. *Ebony and Crystal: Poems in Verse and Prose.* Preface by George Sterling. Auburn, CA: [Auburn Journal,] 1922. (*LL* 811)

———. *Odes and Sonnets.* Preface by George Sterling. San Francisco: Book Club of California, 1918. (*LL* 812)

———. *Sandalwood.* Auburn, CA: Auburn Journal, 1925. (*LL* 813)

———. *The Star-Treader and Other Poems.* San Francisco: A. M. Robertson, 1912. (*LL* 814)

Smith, Wallace (1888–1937). *The Little Tigress: Tales out of the Dust of Mexico; with Drawings from a Field Sketch Book.* New York: Putnam, 1923.

Spencer, R. E. *The Incompetents.* New York: Knopf, 1933.

———. *The Lady Who Came to Stay.* New York: Book League of America, 1931. New York: Hippocampus Press, 2009.

Spengler, Oswald (1880–1936). *The Decline of the West.* Tr. Charles Francis Atkinson. New York: Knopf, 1922–26. 2 vols. A translation of *Der Untergang des Abendlandes* (1918–22; 2 vols.).

Stone, Irving (1903–1989). *Lust for Life: The Novel of Vincent van Gogh.* New York; Toronto: Longmans, Green, 1934.

Stormonth, James (1824–1882). *A Dictionary of the English Language.* <1871> The Pronunciation Carefully Revised by the Rev. P. H. Help. New York: Harper & Brothers, 1885. (*LL* 850)

Summers, Montague (1880–1948), ed. *The Supernatural Omnibus.* London: Victor Gollancz, 1931. Garden City, NY: Doubleday, Doran, 1932.

Synge, J[ohn] M[illington] (1871–1909). *Riders to the Sea.* Dublin: Maunsel, 1904.

Thomson, James (1700–1748). *The Seasons; with The Castle of Indolence.* <1730; 1748> New-York: Published by W. B. Gilley, . . . Clayton & Kingsland, Printers, 1819. (*LL* 883)

Wakefield, H[erbert] Russell (1890–1964). *They Return at Evening.* New York: D. Appleton, 1928. (*LL* 913) [Includes "The 17th Hole at Duncaster" and "'He Cometh and Passeth By.'"]

Walpole, Hugh (1884–1941). *All Souls' Night.* London: Macmillan, 1933.

———. *Portrait of a Man with Red Hair.* London: Macmillan, 1925.

Wandrei, Donald. "A Race through Time." *Astounding Stories* 12, No. 2 (October 1933): 18–34.

Warner, Sylvia Townsend (1893–1978). *Lolly Willowes; or, The Loving Huntsman.* London: Chatto & Windus, 1926.

Weigall, Arthur (1880–1934). *Wanderings in Roman Britain.* London: T. Butterworth, [1926]. (*LL* 933)

Wells, H[erbert] G[eorge] (1866–1946). *The Outline of History.* London: Newnes, 1920 (2 vols.). Garden City, NY: Garden City Publishing Co., 1929.

———. *The Shape of Things to Come.* New York: Macmillan, 1933.

———. *Thirty Strange Stories.* New York: Harper & Brothers, 1897.

———. *The War of the Worlds.* London: Heinemann, 1898. New York: Harper & Brothers, 1898.

Wells, H. G. Julian Huxley, and G. P. Wells. *The Science of Life: A Summary of Contemporary Knowledge about Life and Its Possibilities* (1929–30; 3 vols.).

Werfel, Franz (1890–1945). *Goat Song.* Tr. Ruth Langner. Garden City, NY: Doubleday, Page & Co., 1926. A translation of *Bocksgesang* (1921).

Westcott, Edward Noyes (1846–1898). *David Harum: A Story of American Life.* New York: D. Appleton & Co., 1899.

Wilder, Thornton (1897–1975). *The Bridge of San Luis Rey.* New York: Boni, 1927.

Winslow, Thyra Samter (1885?–1961). *People round the Corner,* New York: Knopf, 1927.

Wolfe, Thomas (1900–1938). *Look Homeward, Angel: A Story of the Buried Life.* New York: Charles Scribner's Sons, 1929.

Wright, S. Fowler (1874–1965). *The World Below.* New York: Longmans, Green, 1930. (*LL* 972)

Index